SOCIAL WORK
AND SOCIAL WELFARE

# SOCIAL WORK AND SOCIAL WELFARE

# A HUMAN RIGHTS FOUNDATION

*Katherine van Wormer and Rosemary J. Link*

Oxford University Press is a department of the University of Oxford. It furthers the University's objective of excellence in research, scholarship, and education by publishing worldwide. Oxford is a registered trade mark of Oxford University Press in the UK and certain other countries.

Published in the United States of America by Oxford University Press
198 Madison Avenue, New York, NY 10016, United States of America.



Library of Congress Cataloging-in-Publication Data
Names: Van Wormer, Katherine S., author. | Link, Rosemary J., author.
Title: Social work and social welfare : a human rights foundation / Katherine van Wormer and Rosemary J. Link.
Description: New York : Oxford University Press, [2018] | Includes index. |
Identifiers: LCCN 2017048373 (print) | LCCN 2017051506 (ebook) |
ISBN 9780190612832 (updf) | ISBN 9780190612849 (epub) | ISBN 9780190612825 (alk. paper)
Subjects: LCSH: Social service. | Public welfare. | Child welfare. | Equality. | Human rights.
Classification: LCC HV40 (ebook) | LCC HV40 .V36 2018 (print) | DDC 361—dc23
LC record available at https://lccn.loc.gov/2017048373

1 3 5 7 9 8 6 4 2

Printed by Webcom, Inc., Canada

*This book is dedicated to human rights activists, to those working toward environmental justice and economic and social justice throughout the world.*

# CONTENTS

# DETAILED CONTENTS

# PREFACE

The divisive, callous, and violent climate of our times can be challenging and discouraging for social workers. In the United States, as well as across the world, populist political movements have capitalized on fears of terrorism, job loss to immigrants, and growing inequality by closing the doors to refugees and reducing benefits for the poor. At the same time, globalization of the world marketplace represents the most dramatic global structural change since the Industrial Revolution. Continually expanding international trade is the reality for national economies throughout the world. Major corporations are no longer national but transnational entities. Within this social climate, how does social work act on its commitment to promote "the needs and empowerment of people who are vulnerable, oppressed, and living in poverty" (National Association of Social Workers [NASW], 2017, p. 1)? How does the social work profession continue to promote human rights?

Social work was born in turbulent times at the turn of the last century. When there were attacks on immigrants and the poor, the leaders of the profession offered care; when there was war, social workers protested for peace and reached out to its victims; and when women and minority groups were held back in society, the organizers pushed forward. Then as now, the challenges were many, and the profession has stood firm. Then as now, social workers worked within the system to change the system.

Of course there are differences today. The world has grown ever smaller through information technology and other forms of globalization. Climate change doesn't affect us all equally, but it does affect us all. Communication today is made possible by information technology, the Internet. Thanks to global satellites, we all watch the same news, see the same gratifying or disturbing images. Like the economy, contagious disease, wars, and environmental pollution, we are globally interconnected, and solutions are beyond the scope of any one nation. The call for a sustainable environment will have to be universal.

As we enter this global age then, an age characterized by a massive refugee crisis, ethnic cleansing, suicide bombings, air strikes, and the decline of the welfare state in a global market economy, there is a need for new understandings and new approaches. Many problems that seem endemic to one state or one country can only be understood internationally as common problems with common solutions.

In recognition of our global interconnectedness, the US Council on Social Work Education (CSWE) (2015), which oversees all programs, today urges that students be prepared to recognize the "global influences that affect social work policy" (p. 8). Among the purposes of social work education spelled out in the document are to alleviate poverty, oppression, and other forms of social injustice; promote breadth of knowledge and critical thinking; advocate for policies that advance human rights; and formulate and influence social policies and social services.

New to the accreditation standards is the emphasis on the development of understanding of environmental issues pertaining to social justice and injustice (for example, the placing of polluting factories in low-income, minority neighborhoods). The focus on human rights education was brought forth from the 2008 edition of CSWE accreditation standards.

In line with CSWE standards, *Social Work and Social Welfare: A Human Rights Perspective* is shaped to achieve two often mutually exclusive objectives. The first objective is to critically examine social welfare issues from an international perspective. If social work is going to be a human rights profession, then it is imperative that students of social work acquire a basic understanding of global issues of human rights. We hope this knowledge will better equip students to follow the mission of social work, which is to be agents of social change.

The second objective of this book is to provide a useful and comprehensive study that covers in detail the fundamentals of the history and structure of the US social welfare system. As a general textbook, the content is organized to follow course outlines for basic, introductory, and more advanced courses that examine social welfare programs, policies, and issues. Within a human rights context, *Social Work and Social Welfare* explores the challenges facing specific population groups, both historically and in the present day. The cross-cultural perspective provides a resource for both undergraduate and graduate foundation courses concerned with global problems and development.

This textbook, in short, provides an international lens through which students of social work can view their own country's social work and social policy practices. Although US social work is the primary focus, parallels in social problems and their solutions will be drawn from throughout the world.

## CONTENT AND STRUCTURE

Based on the knowledge provided in this textbook, students who complete the course should be able to critically analyze how values play in to social welfare offerings and social work practice; grasp how a society's social welfare system is dependent upon the financial and human resources available; learn of the structure of the provision of social services during ideological paradigm shifts; be familiar with the social work role in meeting people's needs across the life cycle; and view the social policy issues of the day within the context of the global corporate economy. The emphasis is on those fields of practice in which social workers are most likely to be employed, fields such as child welfare, health and mental health, the care of older adults, and work with persons involved in the criminal justice system. All these areas involve conditions and service activities that relate to human rights.

Divided into two parts, *Social Work and Social Welfare* focuses in Part I on social work as a policy-based profession; US social values within a comparative context; the history of modern social welfare systems; discrimination and oppression against minority groups; human rights principles; and poverty in today's world.

Part II brings the reader into the professional realm. The subject matter centers on arenas in which social workers are actively involved, including child welfare, work with older adults, and health and mental health. The opening chapter concerns environmental justice.

## FULFILLMENT OF COUNCIL ON SOCIAL WORK EDUCATION REQUIREMENTS

The following statement is included in the 2015 CSWE Educational and Policy Accreditation Standards for undergraduate and graduate programming:

> The purpose of the social work profession is to promote human and community well-being. Guided by a person-in-environment framework, a global perspective, respect for human diversity, and knowledge based on scientific inquiry, the purpose of social work is actualized through its quest for social and economic justice, the prevention of conditions that limit human rights, the elimination of poverty, and the enhancement of the quality of life for all persons, locally and globally. (p. 5)

From a human rights perspective, and in accordance with the Council on Social Work Education's (CSWE) competencies, this textbook

- Provides an appreciation of social work as a proud profession inspired by a mission that uniquely focuses on social and environmental justice
- Offers a historical overview of social welfare principles and laws shaped within the cultural context of the age
- Presents the shaping of social welfare policy within the context of North American value dimensions and within the context of universal values as well
- Contains a focus on the impact of economic globalization and discussion of the conflict between corporate interests and welfare policies designed to meet the needs of all the people
- Includes biological content through attention paid to health/mental health care, as well as to human needs pertaining to access to clean air, water, and uncontaminated soil
- Draws parallels between the importance of cultural diversity in human life and biodiversity in plant and animal life
- Analyzes social issues facing impoverished children and families in both industrialized and non-industrialized nations
- Discusses social work values and the social work mission as congruent with principles of the UN Universal Declaration of Human Rights
- Gives attention to the physical environment and the interrelationship between the environment and society, emphasizing the need for a sustainable world
- Focuses on anti-oppressive practices such as harm reduction, trauma-informed care, and restorative justice

- Provides multifaceted content on social welfare subsystems such as child welfare, health care, corrections, and services to older adults (women's and ethnic/racial minority issues are infused throughout the text)
- Emphasizes human rights violations worldwide on the basis of racial, ethnic, sexual orientation, and gender identity with special emphasis on the special circumstances pertaining to women, indigenous populations, and refugees
- Includes dynamic excerpts from international and popular sources revealing the human side of social issues
- Contains a summary and conclusion as well as Thought Questions at the end of each chapter to reinforce emphasis on critical thinking

The countries chosen for a close focus in this textbook are countries in which the authors have also lived and worked: the United Kingdom and Norway. Special sections on Cuba, Chile, and South Korea, provide detailed information on those countries as well. Given its international/human rights themes, this book meets the CSWE requirement that students acquire a global awareness and appreciation for diversity.

Within a global context, *Social Work and Social Welfare* provides a sociological analysis of traditional American values, as well as a comprehensive history of the emergence of US social work and social welfare programming. The advantage to the students and instructor is in being able to appreciate in one course with one textbook the principles and values on which the social work profession is based while never losing sight of the human rights and global context as endorsed by NASW-US and required by CSWE.

## A NOTE TO THE INSTRUCTOR

A comprehensive instructor's manual with essay and multiple-choice exam questions, creative exercises, references to films, and other relevant resources is provided by Oxford University Press. In addition, PowerPoint slides are available for lecture use.

In order to help departments organize course material in the interests of meeting accreditation requirements, a guide to CSWE's (2015) most recent Educational Policy and Accreditation Standards (EPAS) is provided in an opening insert in the book. Each of the nine fundamental competencies is divided into two to five subheadings as defined by CSWE. The purpose of the chart is to indicate at a glance the extent to which a particular educational standard is represented in the book and in which chapter the (for example, on environmental justice) can be found.

As stated in the EPAS, "Social work competence is the ability to integrate and apply social work knowledge, values, and skills to practice situations" (p. 3). A major challenge in constructing the chart was how to link standards to textbook material when the standards are geared to practice outcomes and intervention with clients. Our approach is to provide links to the underlying content, such as, "engaging diversity and difference" (Competency 2) in chapters in which diversity is a key focus, and advancing human rights (Competency 3), which is a central theme in all the chapters. And as for assessment, we do include critical thinking or Thought Questions at the end of each chapter. Human rights principles, as an organizing framework for the book, gels nicely with the spirit of the requirements of the CSWE's (2015) most recent Educational Policy and Accreditation Standards.

## REFERENCES

Council on Social Work Education (CSWE). (2015). *Educational policy and accreditation standards.* Alexandria, VA: CSWE.

National Association of Social Workers (NASW). (2017). *The NASW code of ethics.* Washington, DC: NASW.

# ACKNOWLEDGMENTS

Katherine van Wormer would like to thank her son, Rupert van Wormer, and husband, Robert van Wormer, for their photographic contributions. Additionally, she'd like to recognize her graduate student, Dakota Funk, for his careful proofreading of the text manuscript. Marta Vides Saade, Associate Professor of Law and Society at Ramapo College of New Jersey, deserves our gratitude for providing us with chapters 12 and 13 on health and mental health care for this text. Above all, thanks to Oxford University Press senior editor, Dana Bliss, for making this project possible.

Rosemary J. Link would like to thank Andrew Mitchell Link for his constant love, encouragement, and wisdom through life's losses and gifts. Also to the students in our Slovenian seminar: thank you for grappling with why human rights are fundamental to the social work profession—Ibrahim Sönmez, Tina Kodre, Ana Marija Cimperman, Jožica Magajne, and my colleagues Gabi Čačinovič Vogrinčič and Lea Šugman Bohinc who have co-written, co-created, and celebrated international ideas for so many years.

# PART I

# SOCIAL WELFARE: STRUCTURE AND FUNCTIONS

*Chapter 1 introduces the reader to the uniqueness of social work and the empowerment perspective and lays the foundation for the rest of the book by presenting key theoretical perspectives and definitions. Critical thinking is defined in terms of cultural competence/humility and global awareness. This chapter locates the mission and ethics of social work within the context of social and economic globalization. Chapter 2 broadens the scope to a consideration of American values as the framework within which the structure and policy of social welfare evolved. The Scandinavian institutional approach to social welfare is contrasted with the American residual approach. Values are presented in terms of opposites for the point of discussion, although in reality concepts such as work versus leisure exist along a continuum.*

*Chapters 3 and 4 take a historical view of the emergence of social work as a profession within the backdrop of national paradigm shifts. US history is described through use of the metaphor of the pendulum swinging back and forth from humanistic to more punitive political eras. The origins of the Anglo-American social welfare system are recounted in chapter 3 with attention paid to ideological themes that are extant today. The profession of social work is seen as reflective of the temper of more modern times in chapter 4. Social oppression is the topic of chapter 5. Racial and ethnic discrimination, sectarianism, heterosexism, and oppression against women and children worldwide are among the topics addressed. The task of this chapter was to incorporate the approach recommended in the Council on Social Work Education (CSWE) 2015 Educational Policy and Accreditation Standards to prepare social work students to challenge social forms of oppression.*

*A detailed look at human rights conventions is provided in chapter 6, which also provides an overview of the criminal justice system. The workings of the Anglo-Saxon adversarial system of justice are explained and compared to the burgeoning concept of restorative justice. This more compassionate form of justice, an innovation with ancient roots, has a revolutionary potential in meting out justice to victims and offenders alike.*

*Poverty and Human Rights is the title of chapter 7. Topics covered include the causes and consequences of poverty, increasing economic inequality, and government remedies to prevent poverty and civil unrest. A major focus in the chapter is on work, the meaning of work, and the psychological repercussions of job loss in the new technological age. The final chapter in Part I of the book is devoted to describing government and nongovernment strategies of ending poverty. Attention is to the specifics of social welfare programs—Medicaid, Medicare, Social Security, and so forth. This portion of the book ends with a discussion of welfare rights as human rights.*

CHAPTER 1

# SOCIAL WORK

## *A Human Rights Profession*

> Where, after all, do universal human rights begin? In small places, close to home—so close and so small that they cannot be seen on any maps of the world. Yet they are the world of the individual person.
>
> Eleanor Roosevelt, 1958

You can't talk about social work without talking about context, and social welfare provides the context within which social services are offered. You can't talk about social welfare, likewise, without some sense of the global economy's role in shaping the health and quality of life in all its manifestations. The growing prosperity at one level of society is matched by rising insecurities and impoverishment at another level. This is where social work comes in.

A profession of many faces, social work touches the lives of millions of people every day. The chances are, in your lifetime you will encounter a social worker—whether in a school system, while visiting a loved one in a hospital or nursing home, receiving family counseling, or surviving a natural disaster. Many of the situations that involve a social worker are rooted in flaws in the social structure; others stem from individual difficulty, perhaps related to disease or personal victimization.

Social work practice is shaped by many factors today. These include globalization, an unending war on terrorism, a refugee crisis, advancing technologies, and growing economic inequality. Within this context, the profession of social work is dedicated to the enhancement of the social functioning and health of individuals, families, and communities.

In this chapter, we explore social work in all its uniqueness and social welfare in its transcendent qualities. The basic concerns of social welfare—poverty, disability, disease, and care of the very young and the very old—have been the basic concerns of social work since its inception, and before that, of the faith-based charity work out of which the social work profession sprang over a century ago.

Unlike the other chapters in this volume, chapter 1 is largely theoretical. Its purpose is to lay the building blocks for the more factual material to follow. To this end, this chapter will

- Define social work as a policy-based profession within a human rights context
- Make the case for an international understanding of social policy
- Address how social work relates to other disciplines and describe the basic fields of practice
- Introduce concepts relevant to professional practice—for example, empowerment, strengths perspective
- Introduce concepts relevant to social work theory—for example, ecosystems perspective, functionalist framework, globalization
- Differentiate a worldview from a *world* view or global perspective
- Discuss attributes of the social work imagination

## THE UNIQUENESS OF SOCIAL WORK

Because the field of social work is holistic and encompasses knowledge from a wide range of disciplines—from psychology, sociology, and economics, among others—it is sometimes believed that there is no body of knowledge unique to social work at all. In fact, though, as a glance at a typical social work textbook would indicate, social work can be distinguished from other professions in terms of its social activism and unabashed commitment to the most vulnerable members of the society. Historically, a key characteristic of social work is the dual responsibility of members of the profession to help people in crisis and to engage in advocacy on behalf of social change. As professional helpers, social workers are everywhere there are individuals, families, and communities in need. Social workers are one of the largest providers of mental health services in the country; they are also highly visible in child welfare offices, hospitals, women's shelters, correctional facilities, and schools. Although as counselors and client advocates, their skills may overlap with the skills of other human service workers, what sets this profession apart is the expectation that social workers will work within the system to change the system.

Compared to psychology, sociology, and counseling, social work prepares its students to engage as change agents and social advocates. The titles of some leading textbooks in the field of social work attest to the action focus: *Green Social Work: From Environmental Crises to Environmental Justice* (Dominelli, 2012); *Advocacy and Social Work Practice* (Wilks, 2012); *The Policy-Based Profession: An Introduction to Social Welfare Policy Analysis for Social Workers* (Popple & Leighninger, 2014); *Social Workers Affecting Social Policy* (Gal & Weiss-Gal, 2014); *Social Welfare Policy and Advocacy* (Jansson, 2015); and *Introduction to Social Work: An Advocacy-Based Profession* (Cox, Tice, & Long, 2016).

According to the United States National Association of Social Workers (NASW) (2017), "the constellation of core values reflects what is unique to the social work profession" (p. 1). As spelled out in the NASW Code of Ethics, the mission of social work is rooted in

- Service
- Social justice

- Dignity and worth of person
- Importance of human relationships
- Integrity
- Competence (p. 1)

(A special note concerning NASW's name; we believe that as all other countries refer to their social work professions by their country's name, we should too, for example, CASW stands for the Canadian Association of Social Workers. Because it is cumbersome to continually say United States NASW, this book refers to our national organization by its traditional title with strong reservations. Where practicable, in the book, however, we use the term NASW-US, consistent with our advocacy for cultural humility and global awareness.)

Social work uniquely engages the social context. This fact is manifest most specifically in the Code of Ethic's values of community service, social and economic justice, and human relationships. Social work is the only profession, according to the NASW (2015) policy statement, that is "imbued with social justice as its primary concern" (p. 185).

As social work educators are aware, the social work curriculum is closely scrutinized by the national accrediting body, the Council on Social Work Education (CSWE), for its compliance with national directives for a relatively standardized curriculum. Major content areas to be covered are coursework in human behavior in the social environment, policy, social work practice, community organization, and research, as well as first-hand experience in a field placement. Material on oppression and injustice must be included in the course content at both the bachelor's (BSW) and master's (MSW) levels. Social workers, according to CSWE (2015), "apply their understanding of social, economic, and environmental justice to advocate for human rights at the individual and system levels" (pp. 7–8).

Social work, according to CSWE (2015), is guided by a person in an environment framework. This conceptualization that person and environment are intertwined is a recurring theme that is found in virtually all the social work textbooks. To more accurately reflect the fact that the person and environment are in constant and dynamic interaction, we prefer to use a slash between the words and refer to a person/environment focus. The person shapes the environment and the environment shapes the person. According to the person/environment conceptualization, the social worker, when engaged in individual counseling, must attend to environmental as well as personal factors. The term *environment* until recent times was interpreted by most social work theorists as referring to the social environment, such as one's family and peers. This interpretation has now been reconceptualized to include one's physical or natural environment as well.

A related concept, also unique to social work education and practice, is the joint practice/policy emphasis. This means students of social work are trained in individual counseling skills for individual and group work as well as in community level intervention. This typically involves some sort of advocacy on behalf of marginalized groups. There may be a legislative component—lobbying legislators to introduce or support bills in the interests of social work clients.

The focus on international and human rights education did not take shape until relatively recently in social work education. In recognition of the many ways in which international developments and institutions impinge on US social policy arrangements, CSWE (2003) added to its educational policy and accreditation standards (EPAS) a requirement for the inclusion of international content in the social work curriculum. The decision to "go global" was informed by an awareness that, given the new technologies, the world is growing ever smaller and that common solutions can be found to common social problems if the information is shared. Then in 2008 as in the most recent EPAS, the emphasis on global education and awareness was expanded to incorporate human rights (CSWE, 2015). As stated in competence 3: "Social workers understand the global interconnections of oppression and human rights violations, and are knowledgeable about theories of human need and social justice and strategies to promote social and economic justice and human rights" (p. 7). Altogether in the 2015 EPAS there are 11 references to human rights and, for the first time, students of social work are expected to acquire knowledge of environmental justice.

## WHY A HUMAN RIGHTS PERSPECTIVE IS IMPORTANT FOR SOCIAL WORK

When human beings make social, economic, political, and civil progress in how they organize themselves, the new opportunity, rule, or "right" is soon taken for granted. We forget what it took to achieve, for example, women's right to vote. This has only been the law in most western countries for 100 years, and it is not the law in some countries of the world even in the time of this writing. Human rights are inextricably linked with every aspect of our well-being and therefore to social work. Often the lobbying, committee work, petitions, and awareness campaigns that go into the design of international laws, which we call conventions, are exercises in social and economic justice.

In this book, every chapter draws on human rights language, expectation, and conventions. The concept of human rights evolved over many decades in the 20th century, especially as a result of the terrible human carnage of the World Wars and a questioning of what makes us human.

Human rights are those rights that belong to all of us by virtue of being sentient beings rather than wild creatures; they ensure basic survival, protections from discrimination, and opportunity for participation in society (Reichert, 2011). These include social, economic, political, civil, and cultural rights, including the things we often take for granted and can identify if we think for a moment: the right to a name; the right to be safe from physical violence and abuse; and the right to shelter, to health, to clean water; and the right to be free of racial, age, sexual, and gender discrimination.

Implementing human rights includes professional challenges to social workers related to the constraints of their national institutions, a matter that is further explored in chapter 6. Nevertheless, the reports, conventions, and treaties that have put ideas of human rights for everyone into ink and policy have become useful frameworks and arguments for social workers to plan their action.

Social workers are key actors in ensuring that human rights are respected and fulfilled. However, their path to connecting practice with human rights has varied according to their global location. Although the United States has been slow to relinquish national sovereignty and any legislative power to international institutions, for example, in decisions relating to children held on death row, in recent years there has been a growing respect for the International Court at The Hague. Similarly, some national social work codes of ethics and practice have incorporated human rights more explicitly than others. Britain, for example, includes human rights as a core value. And the European body of the International

Federation of Social Workers (IFSW) has a publication called *Standards in Social Work Practice Meeting Human Rights* that details how social workers should promote and realize human rights (Androff, 2016). Social workers are a leading professional group that both recognizes and implements human rights. Refer to the UN Universal Declaration of Human Rights in Appendix A of this book and chapters 6 and 10 for a full discussion of UN conventions and declarations.

## AN INTERNATIONAL PERSPECTIVE

A human rights perspective takes us across national borders. Consider the following scenarios:

- A woman who has arranged for her child to be adopted tells the social worker that her abusive husband from Scotland is coming to claim the baby.
- A retired couple living on social security payments seeks advice on relocating to a retirement settlement in Mexico where they can afford the medicine they need.
- A social worker helps document the case of the trauma that would be caused to girls if returned to a village in Nigeria where they would risk genital mutilation.
- A military social worker relocates to a base in Germany to counsel American military families in which there is reported spouse abuse.
- A Chinese American social worker working in a veterans administration unit finds that her presence triggers flashbacks in some Vietnam veterans.
- A lesbian couple meets with a social worker in hopes of adopting a child from a foreign country.
- An undocumented migrant worker who doesn't speak English requires inpatient treatment for a substance use disorder.
- Thousands of Burmese refugees have arrived in the local community; they are in need of extensive assistance to get started in a culture far different from the one they left behind.
- An Iraqi American family is subjected to hate crimes, a fact made known to the school social worker when the child falls behind in schoolwork.

The common denominator in every case is the link between the United States and another country; often the link is via the client. For social work practice today, international and intercultural knowledge is essential as is a familiarity with relevant legal and agency resources. A comprehensive understanding of global economic forces that work against a caring social welfare state is essential as well.

*Social Work and Social Welfare: A Human Rights Perspective* is written in the belief that a global/human rights perspective provides the most relevant and comprehensive framework within which to orient students to the social welfare system, which is the context in which social work is practiced. Following Healy (2008), this book is shaped in accordance with the belief that such perspectives are best infused within the curriculum instead of offered as a specialized course elective. Stand-alone international or human rights courses often do just that—stand alone. Specifically, the advantages of the international format are its significance to people everywhere; the gaining of perspective; and the spread of knowledge of innovative solutions to common situations (Midgley, 2017).

## THE SIGNIFICANCE OF GLOBAL EVENTS

At first, it might seem strange to choose illustrations for social policy far removed from everyday life in North America. Yet the teaching/learning dyad is considerably enhanced by material that is emotionally compelling, as well as highlighting common concerns. Such examples drawn far and wide jolt the imagination and prompt us to see parallels closer to home. Witness some recent media headlines and ponder the significance of each:

- Trump's Aid Cuts Risk Pushing African Women into the Dark Ages (York, *The Globe and Mail*, 2017)
- India Ranks 131 on Human Development Index, Norway Number One (Roche, *Live Mint*, 2017)
- A Vision for Floating Cities to Fend Off Rising Seas (Ives, *New York Times*, 2017)
- Europe Fractures as the Migrant Crisis Worsens (John, *Time*, 2016)
- South Sudan Lets Fighters Rape Women as Payments (Abdallah, *Global Post*, 2016)

Consider the human rights issues in these headlines. How about global warming? Which parts of the world will be most affected by the rising seas?

## GAINING PERSPECTIVE THROUGH GLOBAL KNOWLEDGE

People who have lived in another country and have been immersed in its folkways and language have a unique advantage in reviewing the social welfare system of either their home or host country. They can understand the host country's pattern and identify incongruities. They can quickly pinpoint the customs and values of both the country of origin and the adopted country. This same advantage applies to people who have close contact with other cultures within their own environment, and especially to those who are bilingual and bicultural through their families. A view beyond regional borders or cultural boundaries reveals challenges and solutions in a broader light. See Figure 1.1, which shows Puerto Rican children proudly sharing their talents.

Through globalized education, possibilities abound. "Think globally, act locally," the saying of environmentalists, aptly sums up the viewpoint endorsed in these pages. In truth, one does not actually have to leave home to adopt a world view or global perspective. One can get beyond national parochialism through reading and listening and contemplating diverse ways of doing things or at least of viewing things. We all have a *worldview*—this word refers to our own regionalized view of the world and of our world. To adopt a *world view*, on the other hand, is to "see ourselves as others see us," to be able to step back from time to time to recognize our own national uniqueness characteristics—the capitalism, materialism, individual opportunity, whatever the values may be. A global perspective suggests an openness to new ideas and a willingness to work collaboratively toward the mutual benefit of all countries. For creative, well-informed policymaking on the local or global level, a multicultural awareness is paramount. Central to such an awareness and appreciation of difference is an awareness that we are all bound together as by the common human condition, all seeking the same sort of earthly comforts and, at a higher level, searching for a meaning in life.

**FIGURE 1.1.** Puerto Rican children in a cello performance at an outdoor market in Northampton, Massachusetts. Music is the universal language. Photo by Robert van Wormer.

Global interconnectedness is enhanced today by the revolutionary power of the Internet. Government can no longer shut off the news sources, even though countries such as China, South Africa, and Iraq continue to try to do so. Communication across cyberspace helps unmask lies and deceit, as well as human rights violations in individual countries. When the US president visits Europe or the Middle East, for example, one can compare European and Middle Eastern accounts and American accounts of the same visit to gain a multi-dimensional view and see how national overtures and communications are viewed from abroad.

## LEARNING OF INNOVATIVE SOLUTIONS

Common demographic, economic, and technological trends have confronted all the advanced industrialized societies with similar challenges (Kahn & Kamerman, 2009). Prime examples are the aging of the population, the falling birth rates, and the rising rates of labor force participation among women who have young children. Such common problems may have different solutions based on cultural values. Americans can learn from Europeans, as Kahn and Kamerman note, as when they discover that in foreign lands, many workers would be entitled to paid and job-protected leaves following childbirth, one-month paid vacations from work, and subsidized childcare. Two examples of non-material technologies imported from other nations to the United States are the hospice movement from Britain, and family group conferencing from the indigenous population of New Zealand. In substance abuse treatment, researchers, treatment providers, and a few police chiefs and mayors are looking into the harm reduction movement in the Netherlands for its crime-fighting possibilities. Going in the opposite direction, the passage of strict anti-smoking laws to protect people from the health ravages of second-hand smoke has spread from the United States to far corners of the globe. At the macro level, feminist thought has revolutionized women's roles throughout the industrialized world and raised the consciousness of gender inequality practically everywhere.

As we debate policies with skeptics who say, "That will never work; that will be too expensive"—for example, having a government-run health care system—we can show how such systems work in Canada, Japan, and Europe. This situation came up in a recent debate between Democratic opponents running for the nomination of their political parties for the presidency. Bernie Sanders pointed to Scandinavia, and Hillary Clinton later said, "But we are not Denmark" (Tankersley, 2015). Another example might be a debate over improving welfare benefits. The argument, "Providing adequate child care to single mothers (or vocational training or health care) would be nice, but we can't afford it," can be countered with proof that, "We can't afford not to." Models can be found in other countries of those same policies, and they do work.

## KNOWLEDGE FOR INTERNATIONAL SOCIAL WORK

Since social work degrees, especially at the master's level, are recognized internationally, Americans are sometimes recruited to work overseas. (At the time of this writing, widely publicized announcements have appeared in US publications from the United Kingdom and Ireland.) For social work educators, opportunities for exchanges in international teaching engagements are becoming commonplace. Cultural sensitivity and an attitude of thoughtful restraint concerning American accomplishments will go far in enhancing international collegial acceptance.

Social work practice on the home front likely will include work with immigrants and refugees. Taking a global perspective, social workers can anticipate that newcomers will have close, intergenerational family ties and that many aspects of American society (for example, dating customs and sales pitches, such as from "rent-to-own" furniture stores) will be unfamiliar to newcomers.

Each year up until 2017, the United States took in more than 1 million immigrants, including undocumented workers, according to monthly Census Bureau data (Zeigler & Camarota, 2015). Between 2014 and 2015, with a large influx from Mexico, the number surged to 1.7 million. As a consequence, the US population, in fact, has the largest proportion (13.3%) of foreign-born residents at any time since World War I. This influx has been halted significantly, however, under Trump administration policies, including mass deportations and travel bans. Today there are layoffs at refugee centers and social service agencies even while the death toll of war victims mounts (Boyle, 2017).

The refugee crisis is horrendous in the Middle East as millions rush into Europe to escape the turmoil and mass killings. Most of the migrants today are women and children. Around a million have entered Germany alone (Goldman, 2017). Social workers in Europe have much to contend with—finding shelter and distributing food and other supplies, setting up language classes for those given the rights to settle, advocating for the immigrants against violent attacks by native people, and working with a deeply traumatized population. The challenge is to keep the refugees, who sometimes languish in holding centers for months or years, from becoming institutionalized and developing a sense of helplessness given the political constraints placed upon them in many countries (Cox & Pawar, 2013). See Figure 1.2 to appreciate the hardship that many immigrants must endure on the path to freedom.

Students often wonder how they can make a contribution internationally and which kinds of organizations would welcome their skills and values. The Peace Corps offers one such opportunity; recruiters often come to job fairs at the larger universities. Four schools of social work—University of Maryland, University of Michigan (Ann Arbor), Portland State University (Oregon), and New Mexico State University—are now participating in the Michigan program (Blank, 2011). This program combines a master's of social work degree with work in the Peace Corps. Typically, the graduate student spends one or two years in school, then goes overseas for 27 months, and returns to complete graduation. For the most part, those recruited into the program are directed toward specialized skills areas, such as youth work, health, and education. Information is available at the University of Michigan School of Social Work at http://ssw.umich.edu/peacecorps/masters-international.

Although international social work is a competitive field, there are other options not connected to the US government. Among organizations where social workers can volunteer or work in a short-term grant-funded capacity are the International Federation of Red Cross and the Red Crescent Societies that work in disaster relief; advocacy organizations such as Amnesty International and Human Rights Watch, Oxfam International, and the UN High Commission for Refugees that helps provide aid to families displaced by war (Cox & Pawar, 2013; Midgley, 2017).

**FIGURE 1.2.** Syrian war refugees who have survived the trip from Turkey to Greece on an overloaded dinghy. © Shutterstock, photo by Nicolas Economou.

Churches and synagogues sponsor many humanitarian activities in trouble spots around the world, for example, Haiti following the earthquake. A Christian organization that offers a wealth of international assignments, voluntary and paid, is the Mennonite Mission Network. Available assignments are listed at http://mcc.org/get-involved/serve by the Mennonite Central Committee. There are listings for social work in day care, peace advocacy, and other service activities.

This emphasis on international course content and global practice is not unique to the United States. In 2010, the International Association of Social Workers (IASSW) undertook a world census of social work education programs (Barretta-Herman, Leung, Littlechild, Parada, & Wairire, 2014). Results of the survey indicated, first of all that since the previous census, new social work departments are rapidly springing up across the five regions of the world surveyed, and most strikingly in China. Students in Europe, Africa, and Latin America study in other countries more frequently than do students in North America and Asia. Throughout the world, international social work is emphasized in the curriculum, and many programs have a human rights elective. Interestingly, analysis of the data on curriculum content revealed striking similarity in courses offered throughout the five regions.

Social work programs that take a global perspective can prepare students to understand and address how developments in social welfare policies in one nation often reverberate throughout the world and are modeled elsewhere. When such policies are harmful to the masses, for example, welfare retrenchments or privatization of social services, the impact may even go beyond the national level. This is especially true as the more powerful countries often serve as role models for less powerful nations. Knowledge of this fact, that the borrowing of certain social welfare policies can affect the social or environmental security of residents across the globe, obligates citizens to get actively involved in politics and social action in their own country (Healy, 2008). Social workers can hope to have some influence through solidarity with social workers from across the globe. Membership in international organizations opens the door for the exchange of ideas and strategies for effecting social change.

There are today over 200 member nations of the International Federation of Social Workers (IFSW), a formally recognized NGO that reports to the United Nations. Over the past two or three decades, we have seen a revitalized interest by the US social work profession in international affairs, including the promotion of networking with its international counterparts and active involvement in IFSW. In conjunction with the IASSW and International Council on Social Welfare (ICSW), the IFSW undertook the task of developing universal standards for social work education, ethical codes of conduct, and policy positions on issues of international persons. US social work educators played a leading role in bringing these standards to fruition. The final product is the Global Agenda for Social Work and Social Development. The Agenda is committed to "supporting, influencing and enabling structures and systems that allow people to have power over their own lives" (IFSW, 2012, p. 1). Environmental sustainability is listed as one of the major areas of interest.

Nadkarni and Sinha (2014) discuss how social workers can work through health-based nongovernmental organizations (NGOs) to focus on women's health and reproductive well-being. A human rights perspective can inform their advocacy to address human inequalities, including individual case advocacy in clinical and nonclinical settings; policy advocacy, lobbying, and campaigning; and community development. The social-work profession shoulders the responsibility of advocating with and on behalf of women's health for sexual and reproductive rights and access to health care and all related basic amenities, such as food, water, sanitation, education, and development opportunities, on an equitable basis and in an environment that is free from oppression.

## THEORETICAL APPROACHES RELEVANT TO SOCIAL WELFARE

This section looks at some basic perspectives in social work that relate directly or indirectly to social welfare concerns. Several of these theoretical approaches also are closely related to human rights and social justice.

### THEORIES OF HUMAN NEED

Unlike the approach of the psychologist, the sociologist looks at needs subjectively and collectively. Needs are real if people perceive them to be real. Real or imagined, needs may stimulate innovation, social change, and the manufacturing of new products. The marketing of products creates a sense of need where heretofore there was none. Conversely, although living conditions may be quite low, there may be no perception of need.

The concept of human need is an important foundation for social work practice and social policy (Dover, 2015). Children growing up in an impoverished part of the world would define their needs in terms of the basics of survival. In contrast, children from rich countries would include many non-essential products in their list of what they needed. What are people's basic needs? Psychologist Abraham Maslow's (1970) formulation, "the hierarchy of needs" is the most widely known categorization of human needs. According to Maslow's scheme, the basic physical needs of human survival must be met first before higher levels of needs—safety, belongingness and love, esteem, and self-actualization—are realized. Self-actualization refers to a person achieving his or her highest potential as a human being. Because each person in Maslow's conceptualization tries to satisfy these needs in ascending order, high self-esteem is not likely to occur in the absence of love, or self-actualization without a certain degree of financial security. Nor is the stage of self-actualization permanent. Given the uncertainties in life, you could lose your balance at any moment and be reduced to the lower rungs of the ladder, struggling at the level of mere survival.

Maslow's typology is often criticized because of its focus on individual rather than social attributes in achieving self-actualization, with the emphasis on self and therefore on individualism (see Dominelli, 2002). Traditional American Indian culture, for example, was geared toward group and spiritual satisfaction rather than elevation of self. Still, because of its relevance to social welfare, Maslow's conceptualization of human needs is commonly cited in the social work literature. With slight modification (such as linking self-actualization to generativity—giving to others and sharing one's resources), the hierarchy-of-needs construct can offer a holistic guide to personal fulfillment.

The hierarchy of needs offers a paradigm for viewing a society's level of success in meeting its people's needs or one group's needs in society. Take a community with a high crime rate—people may have no trouble getting their physical needs met, and yet there may be serious safety concerns. This does not preclude residents in the community from having a sense of belongingness and love from their families while living in an unsafe neighborhood where gang-related violence may proliferate. Life is of course more complicated than Maslow's paradigm would indicate. Nevertheless, it does have some potential to represent setbacks caused by adulthood socialization and traumatization such as by long-term family violence, the horrors of warfare, or more immediate experiences such as rape.

Michael Dover (2015) has written extensively of human needs theory. In recent years, notes Dover, the explicit use of human needs theory has begun to have a significant influence on the literature in social work. Among social work theorists, he views the work of David Gil as the primary expression of human needs theory. Throughout his writings, Gil has focused on the centrality of addressing human needs for individual and social development. In his most recent book, *Confronting Injustice and Oppression*, Gil (2013) urges that society move toward a politics of common needs within a human rights framework.

From the United Kingdom, Dominelli (2012) discusses the impact of our present-day, market-oriented economy on individual needs. The mass movement of jobs from high-wage to low-wage areas has been devastating for vulnerable people everywhere. Resistance to such changes to the community, however, is possible through the exercise of agency. Similarly, from a community perspective, Mulroy (2013) recommends that social workers use needs assessments that aim to give service users a voice in defining what their needs are themselves. This can be done through focus groups, public meetings, and surveys of diverse constituencies.

There is a close relationship between human needs and a reliance on human rights to claim them, especially in the face of systems of oppression and exploitation. Dean (2013) and Wronka (2008) both stress the relationship of needs to rights and of the importance in identifying needs in order to enforce one's rights in relationship to citizenship.

## THEORIES OF SOCIAL JUSTICE

As a term, social justice is one of the most widely used in social work and the most rarely defined. *The Dictionary of Social Work* (Barker, 2014) defines social justice as

> An ideal condition in which all members of a society have the same basic rights, protections, opportunities, obligations, and social benefits. Implicit in this concept is the notion that historical inequalities should be acknowledged and remediated through specific measures. A key social work value, social justice entails advocacy to confront discrimination, oppression, and institutional inequities. (p. 299)

The concept of legal justice, as discussed earlier, which often refers to punishment for a crime rather than to ideals of fair and principled treatment, is very different from that of social justice. The second of the six core values of social work, as listed in the NASW (2008) Code of Ethics, social justice is emphasized throughout all the social work literature. As members of the profession, social workers have an obligation to promote social justice, or fair treatment of all people. In the *Encyclopedia of Social Work*, Finn and Jacobson (2008) review the social work literature on social justice. "Notions of social justice," they find, "generally embrace values such as the equal worth of all citizens, their equal right to meet their basic needs, the need to spread opportunity and life chances, . . . and when possible eliminate unjustified inequalities" (p. 44). The focus is thus on ending inequality in the society, in sharing the society's resources. This aspect of justice is often termed distributive justice because it relates to the distribution of resources (see Graham, Swift, & Delaney, 2011; Healy, 2008).

Writing in *Inclusion and Democracy,* Iris Young (2002) takes the position we have adopted for this book. Instead of focusing on distribution of resources such as income, she contends, a concept of justice should begin with an understanding of the concepts of domination and oppression. The aim of social justice for Young is to seek institutional remedies for cultural sources of oppression, the manifestations of which are seen in racism, sexism, homophobia, ableism, and so on.

Following Iris Young (2002), who views the aim of social justice as seeking remedies for oppression, Canadian social work theorist Bob Mullaly (2010) favors a structural approach. If advocacy for social justice only is focused on the immediate provision of goods and services, he argues, the social structures, processes, and practices that caused the maldistribution in the first place are ignored.

Linking this concept with human rights, David Androff (2016) suggests that when social workers advocate for social justice, their position is strengthened if they have knowledge of human rights-based approaches. Reliance on principles of human rights elevates the argument to a higher and more objective level. We can illustrate his point with the following example. Making the case that ex-convicts who have been convicted of a felony should be allowed to vote because voting is a basic right in a democratic society might carry more weight than an argument that this is a plot by Republicans to remove likely Democrats from the rolls. By the same token, one can advocate against the death penalty not by an appeal to morals but rather by referring to the Constitutional clause against cruel and unusual treatment.

NASW (2015), in its handbook on social work policy statements, recognizes the power of a human rights focus for social work over the more elusive social justice focus alone. This is because human rights are universal standards, the aim of which is to root out oppression and see that people's basic needs are met. Human rights as a concept encompasses social justice but transcends civil and political customs, according to the policy statement. We will explore the human rights configuration with a focus on United Nations documents in chapter 6.

## STRUCTURAL FUNCTIONALISM

Borrowed originally from biology, the functionalist perspective focused solely on the structure of an organism. However, the functionalist perspective in sociology provided for the viewing of social phenomena in terms of structure and function. In this way, functionalist theory is helpful in discussing social welfare practices and functions.

Functionalist analysis asks the question, how is a given phenomenon functional for society? Or alternatively, how is it dysfunctional? A social scientist, for example, might analyze the functions and dysfunctions of certain welfare benefits such as food stamps. Related concepts are manifest and latent functions of a social phenomenon. *Manifest functions* are the obvious, stated reasons for an activity while the *latent functions* are the secondary, sometimes unintended, often hidden motives behind its existence.

*Functional analysis* is useful technique used in sociology and anthropology to reveal the community value of a cultural trait or institution (such as religious rituals). Viewing a cultural norm (for example, punishing those who shirk responsibility) in terms of manifest and latent functions and dysfunctions leads to new ways of thinking about social phenomena. This approach will be used as a means of explaining a number of concepts (for example, social welfare and poverty) that will be discussed in subsequent chapters of this book.

The terminology of modern functional analysis is derived from the writings of social scientists Piven and Cloward (1993), who used a functional analysis approach in their book, *Regulating the Poor: The Functions of Public Welfare.* The first edition of this classic was published in 1971. The manifest functions of welfare programs, to Piven and Cloward, were to create consensus in the society and to encourage social altruism. The existence of such programs makes people feel good that people in need are being taken care of. But there are latent functions at work that are not so readily recognized. This is where the controversial part comes in. In viewing the social welfare system as a societal device for "regulating the poor," Piven and Cloward were questioning the very goals of capitalism. Their chapter titles say it all: "Enforcing Low Wage Work," "Keeping People off the Rolls," "Socializing the Able Bodied Poor by Degrading Relief Efforts" (p. x).

Piven and Cloward's theoretical insights enhance our critical thinking and help make us aware of the social control function of the social welfare system and of how such control is exercised over the poor and their families. Relevant to human rights, these researchers (and social activists) believed that the availability of welfare benefits for the needy was a basic right of citizenship. Chapter 6, which tackles the foundations of social welfare and poverty, examines the "regulating the poor" thesis in greater depth. Because Piven and Cloward viewed the social welfare system as a reflection of the values of the wider society, their perspective was consistent with the principles of ecosystems theory.

## ECOSYSTEMS THEORY

The view of culture as an integrated whole borrows a concept from the biological sciences in which the organs of the body complement each other in remarkable ways to comprise a functioning system. Like an organism, culture has form and pattern. There is a degree of order and a system that is greater than the sum of its parts. To the anthropologist, the related patterns of the environment, the resources available for exploration within it, the organization of people to use the resources, their beliefs about what they do, and the relationships between the larger group and themselves are all part of the system out of which individuals structure their behaviors (Nanda & Warms, 2015).

Once a sense of culture and its values is acquired, the social scientist can analyze the values in a systematic fashion. Is there internal consistency between ascribed values and practices? Which values are conducive to smooth functioning of the society and which are obstacles to smooth functioning? In Northern Ireland, for instance, the dominant cultural values and beliefs traditionally have favored school segregation for Catholics and Protestants. We might then ask: How is this arrangement conducive to harmony? How might it lead to conflict? What changes might one predict? In many of the countries of Eastern Asia traditional values are being examined in this manner as well.

The term *ecosystem* today is widely used in connection with the concept of environmental sustainability. An ecosystems model views people's welfare and the health of their natural environment as interconnected and looks to the realm of nature for insights. There is much concern with risks to the balance in nature and risks to this balance through overpopulation, overuse of chemicals in industrial agriculture, and the destruction of warfare. Whereas an ecosystems approach for social work is concerned with macro-level forces, the following approach—empowerment—has the attribute of greater flexibility.

## AN EMPOWERMENT APPROACH FOR SOCIAL WORK PRACTICE

Thus far, we have been concerned with macro or societal level theories. These approaches are most relevant to a study of the social welfare system and to human rights. Social work practice most often is with individuals and small groups, however. Empowerment as a central focus of social work cuts across both macro and micro levels of practice in that power is contained in the term and integral to the concept.

As people gain control over their own lives, they become empowered. It is a cliché in social work that social workers don't empower their clients but they help their clients empower themselves to tap into their inner resources. As described by Parsons and East (2013), empowerment takes place through transformation from inside oneself, between oneself and others, and through political liberation.

Influenced by the feminist movement, this model draws upon the connection of the personal and the political and a belief that the personal is political. From an empowerment perspective, individual problems are seen as arising not from personal deficits but from the failure of society to meet the needs of all people. This model, when used in social work practice, encompasses a strengths approach in its focus on helping clients tap into their inner and cultural resources. It goes further, however, in focusing on oppression and power imbalances in society. Empowering practice begins by acknowledging that structural injustices have prevented many individuals and groups from receiving the treatment and resources to which they are entitled. An empowerment approach responds to the individual's and group's experience of oppression (Saleebey, 2013).

At the individual level, empowerment encompasses both a state of mind (as in feeling empowered) and acquiring a sense of power over one's life. The notion of empowerment, when linked with supporting efforts to fight injustice and oppression, can be viewed as transcending individualistic Western values and as applicable cross-culturally.

Empowerment practice is aimed at assisting people who experience systemic forms of discrimination, harassment, and oppression (Robbins, Chatterjee, & Canda, 2012). Of special relevance to victimization is the gaining of a sense of personal power and assuming responsibility for recovery and change, which may entail helping others.

At the macro level, the social work value of empowerment is clearly tied to human rights, as Reichert (2011) suggests. Empowerment requires living conditions conducive to the fulfillment of basic human needs, a social environment in which a person has the opportunity to achieve social security, and access to the essential human resources including a clean environment and access to health care. At its core, human rights approaches are about altering the relations of power in order to equalize the distribution of power (Androff, 2016).

Although often indistinguishable from a strengths perspective, the empowerment framework is more political and apt to be used in a context of work with disadvantaged populations, sometimes at the macro level. The strengths perspective, in contrast, tends to be used in direct practice with individual clients or small groups.

The strengths perspective has been applied to a wide variety of client situations: work with people with mental disorders, child welfare clients, homeless women in emergency rooms, older adults, and African American families. The concept of strength is also part and parcel of the growing literature on empowerment, feminist therapy, narrative therapy, client/person-centered approach, and the ethnic-sensitive model. Pertaining to groups and communities as well as to individuals, the strengths perspective can help reveal the light in the darkness and provide hope in the most dismal of circumstances. As informed by strengths theory, the therapeutic goal is to help people discover their areas of strength so that they can build on them in an ever spiraling movement toward health and control.

### A STRENGTHS PERSPECTIVE

As its name indicates, the strengths approach builds on clients' strengths and resources. Saleebey (2013) calls this a "versatile practice approach, relying heavily on ingenuity and creativity, the courage and common sense of both clients and their social workers"(p. 1). From a strengths perspective, social workers strive to help clients tap into their personal resources and those of their family and community.

The counseling relationship can serve as a powerful tool in helping clients find an alternative course toward fulfillment and beginning to change self-destructive thoughts and behavior. Efforts to build or enhance personal power in people who feel powerless is a basic component of the strengths perspective.

For work in the addictions field, which has traditionally focused on breaking denial and on harsh confrontation, the trend is increasingly geared toward a more positive, empowering, ethnic-sensitive approach (van Wormer & Davis, 2018). Meeting the client where the client is: this is the contemporary focus of substance abuse treatment.

Let us briefly take an excursion from social work theory into a discussion of the field of social work and opportunities in this field.

## CAREERS IN SOCIAL WORK

According to the Bureau of Labor Statistics (2016), employment of social workers is expected to grow by 12% over the next decade, faster than the average for all occupations. Growth will be due to an increase in demand for health care and social services but will vary by specialty. Employment of health care social workers and those in the fields of mental health are expected to grow the most rapidly. One reason for the optimistic projection for the need for social workers is related to the aging of the baby boom generation, many of whom will be in need of counseling and other services in the future at the same time that social workers are retiring in large numbers.

Social workers facilitate change by working with individuals, families, organizations, and politicians such as members of the city council and state legislators. The services they provide as listed in NASW's (Pace, 2012) toolkit illustrates the value of these services. Social workers help

- More than 20% of the adult US population each year living with mental and behavioral disorders to regain social functioning
- Families in crisis cope with stress, which can cause children to be vulnerable to abuse and neglect

- Young people to grow up healthy and productive by coordinating nurturing environments
- Those in the military as they transition back to civilian life
- Citizens in need by bridging the gap between what business and government can provide
- Large groups of people by reducing poverty and major gaps in quality of life
- Patients navigating complex health systems to change behaviors to improve their medical outcomes
- Family caregivers provide the best options for their loved ones (p. 7)

In a light-hearted and uplifting essay comparing the virtues of a social work degree over a law degree, John L. Jackson, Jr. (2016), Dean of Social Work at the University of Pennsylvania, states the following:

> I've had M.S.W. students crying in my campus office because their parents were pressuring them to study something other than social work, usually out of concern about their job prospects. . . . But, ironically, it is the average newly minted lawyer who will probably have the tougher time landing a fulfilling gig in his or her field. In fact, law school applications have been dropping precipitously since about 2010, presumably because fewer people see it as a foolproof way to get the job of their dreams—especially if they don't already know what that dream job looks like.
>
> Social work, by contrast, is increasingly on the forefront of education and employment trends. For one thing, social work teaches marketable skills that cut across traditional disciplines and professions. Students learn how to interpret dense policy briefs and clients' subtle facial cues in equal measure. . . .
>
> Whether it is a San Bernardino or Sandy Hook, the Sept. 11 attacks or urban police shootings, social work is the glue that tries to keep people's lives together when the world seems most intent on ripping those lives apart. (paragraphs 4, 6, and 10; reprinted with permission)

Although the writer focuses on opportunities and salary levels for social workers who have a graduate degree, much of what he says also applies to social workers with a bachelor's degree who also are eligible to obtain professional licenses. Now we provide an overview of the foundational concepts necessary for the understanding of social work and the social welfare system within which it operates.

## TERMS AND CONCEPTS

### SOCIAL WELFARE

Every society grapples with questions of how to distribute its wealth, power, and opportunities. The distributions may be relatively egalitarian as in Scandinavia or there may be huge disparities across the social class continuum. These differences may be modified by societal protections to insulate citizens from the throes of poverty.

The word *welfare* harks back to the Middle English word for well-being. In German the word used for social welfare is *wohlfahrt* and in Norwegian it is *velferd*. The Spanish word is *bienestar*, and in French it's *bien-être*, literally, well to be. All these meanings are highly positive. These words are related to the English word *benefit*, derived from Latin.

*The Social Work Dictionary* (Barker, 2014) gives the following definition of *social welfare*:

- A nation's system of programs, benefits, and services that help people meet those social, economic, educational, and health needs that are fundamental to the maintenance of society.
- The state of collective well-being of a community or society. (p. 402)

Probably because of its association in the United States with the downtrodden of society, social welfare and welfare work have come to assume negative connotations. Persons "on welfare" are stigmatized by the wider society; the welfare system itself and its workers are stigmatized also. The fragmentation of issues encourages the ubiquitous complaint that our social welfare efforts are a hodgepodge of overlapping and conflicting programs that only create waste. Michael Reisch (2014) defines social welfare policy as: "a smaller subset of social policies that regulate benefits to persons defined by society as 'needy' " (p. 7). The policies are shaped to help people meet basic life needs, such as employment, income, food, housing, health care, and personal safety.

## WELFARE STATE

Much more confusing in its usage is the term *welfare state*. This term, which refers to a country with a high level of development, was introduced in Europe in the mid-20th century when government programs to take care of the people—to provide health care, subsidies, and so on—were growing rapidly. Generally we think of a welfare state as a nation that takes care of its population and has well-organized, comprehensive welfare and educational systems. Such countries provide a minimum level of aid for citizens in need; the ideal welfare states are found in Scandinavia. The difficulty with this terminology is determining where to draw the line.

The *Dictionary of Social Work*'s definition (Barker, 2014) of *welfare state* is fairly simple:

> A nation or society that considers itself responsible for meeting the basic educational, health care, economic, and social security needs of its people. (p. 454)

This is the definition that will be used in this text. According to this definition, one could say that the capitalist countries of Japan and the United States have weak forms of the welfare state in contrast to Scandinavian countries.

In the social science literature, the term *welfare state* is used most often to denote a lowering of standards, such as, in a discussion of the dismantling of the welfare state. In fact, we do see a demise of the welfare state today under pressures of global competition and privatization of social services. These trends are seen even in the most advanced welfare countries such as Sweden and the United Kingdom. So far, Norway, which has stayed out of the European Union, has managed to maintain its outstanding welfare system. Unemployment is low and the birth rate is adequate to maintain the growth rate of the population. To what extent the small country of Norway can continue to resist international forces in favor of so-called free market economy remains to be seen.

## SOCIAL WORK

The profession most closely related to the provision of social welfare services is social work. *Social work* as defined by NASW is the professional activity of helping individuals, groups, or communities enhance or restore their capacity for social functioning and creating societal conditions favorable to this goal (Barker, 2014, p. 402). The term *social worker* is restricted to persons who are professionally trained in the skills and ethics of social work practice. Incorrect usage of the term sometimes occurs as, for instance, when the mass media refer to any person who distributes food stamps as a social worker. The worker at a social welfare office may or may not be a member of the profession.

The following definition of global social work was approved by the IFSW General Meeting and the IASSW General Assembly (2014). Compared to the US version, this one is more inclusive and relevant to global concerns. The strong social justice and human rights focus is evident here as well:

> Social work is a practice-based profession and an academic discipline that promotes social change and development, social cohesion, and the empowerment and liberation of people. Principles of social justice, human rights, collective responsibility and respect for diversities are central to social work. Underpinned by theories of social work, social sciences, humanities and indigenous knowledge, social work engages people and structures to address life challenges and enhance wellbeing. (IFSW, 2017; paragraphs 1 and 2; retrieved from http://ifsw.org/get-involved/global-definition-of-social-work)

How does social work differ from other helping professions? A major difference that social work educators can see is that social work is an applied field similar to nursing and teaching as opposed to an academic discipline such as family studies; graduates can get licensed at the bachelor's or master's level for professional practice. *Psychologists* are generally expected to get a Ph.D. in order to be licensed. Many psychologists are purely academic, however, and they conduct research for publication in academic journals. Those in clinical practice rely heavily on psychological testing instruments in assessing their clients. *Marriage/family therapy* requires a master's degree for individuals to be qualified in their field. Graduate degrees in *counseling* are widely available, especially geared toward work in the public schools as school counselors. Some states, such as Iowa, however, have licensing for mental health counselors. The *sociology and criminology majors* prepare one for teaching or research at the doctorate level. *Psychiatrists* are physicians who rely primarily on their medical training for the treatment of mental disorders. Sometimes the term *social worker* is confused with social welfare worker. Welfare workers who work at the departments of human services may or may not have training in social work. See Figure 1.3 of a student standing outside the social work department.

Note that all these occupations except for social work and, perhaps, counseling are specialized. And training is specialized in all those fields except for social workers who are trained in macro-level as well micro-level intervention. Also, rather uniquely, as mentioned earlier, programs must be nationally accredited for their degrees to be accepted for licensing purposes, and all programs must offer education in social welfare policy, as well as skills-based courses.

**FIGURE 1.3.** The choice of a major can be a real turning point in a student's life. Photo by Rupert van Wormer.

## GENERALIST PRACTICE

Because of the versatility required of social workers, social work education provides for the inculcation of an eclectic knowledge base, diversified as opposed to specialized skills (except at the graduate level), and an emphasis on client empowerment. Social workers are generalists, in the sense that they need to be prepared to work with a wide variety of situations and in a wide variety of social milieus. Educational policy 2.0 of the CSWE's (2015) educational standards states that "Generalist practitioners engage diversity in their practice and advocate for human rights and social and economic justice. They recognize, support, and build on the strengths and resiliency of all human beings" (p. 11). Moreover, generalists must be prepared for practice with systems of all sizes—individuals, families, and communities. Like a general practitioner in medicine, the generalist social worker typically coordinates the efforts of specialists by facilitating communication among them (Barker, 2014, p. 174).

Most often, specialization occurs at the master's level, while the bachelor's level social worker typically performs case management, which involves coordination of services for clients. In fields such as substance abuse counseling and hospice work, however, a great deal of versatility is required for working with diverse populations, as is specialized knowledge in the addictions or medical arena. Such knowledge is usually obtained on the job and not through undergraduate programming. Specialization at the graduate level is often in specialized fields such as health, mental health, administration, and child welfare. Hospitals and mental health centers seek out licensed social workers, not only for their expertise, but also because insurance companies increasingly reimburse only for members of this profession for activities related to counseling and therapy. Although many social workers engage in private practice, most are employed by a human service organization such as a school, correctional system, nursing home, or substance abuse treatment center (Morales, Sheafor, & Scott, 2011). Before students choose to major in social work or any related field, they should consult relevant agencies concerning particular qualifications that are desired and particular courses that are recommended (for example, addictions treatment or, increasingly, conversational Spanish).

More details on the social work profession, especially in regard to its growth and theoretical development, are provided in chapter 4. Later chapters describe specialized practice in the criminal justice system, medical social work, child welfare, services for the homeless, and elder care.

## THIRD WORLD, DEVELOPING COUNTRY, GLOBAL SOUTH, AND SO ON

A review of the literature on international social welfare reveals that the most commonly used term to differentiate a society that is less technologically and economically advanced compared to others is *developing country*. The contrast is of the poorer countries of the world with the more industrialized, higher-income countries, sometimes labeled *developed* countries. In their texts on international social welfare, Cox and Pawar (2013), for example, use the term *least developed countries,* as does Midgley (2017). There are two major drawbacks to the use of these terms. First, the differentiation between developing and developed is pejorative. Second, the implication that economic growth necessarily breeds progress for the majority of people is faulty. Quite often progress exists only for the wealthy elite. In contrast to these notions, social development theory includes the meeting of common human needs (Healy, 2008). A newer term, *sustainable development,* refers to the achievement of social progress while preserving available resources for use by future generations.

The difficulty still persists in finding a term to adequately differentiate technologically advanced countries from others. After the 1960s, the terms *First World* (for Westernized nations), *Second World* (for the former Soviet Union nations), and *Third World* (for poor regions of the world) came into use. The term *Third World* implies that those nations are third rate (Healy, 2008). Accordingly, the Third World concept will only be used in this book in quotes and selections from other sources.

The geographical labels such as *North* and *South,* as Healy (2008) suggests, can be confusing, probably due to the location of the advanced nations of Australia and New Zealand south of the equator. Link and Ramanathan (2011) offer the terms *Global South* and *Global North*; these terms clearly describe virtual geopolitical entities; accordingly, we consider them appropriate delineations for today's global era. Midgley occasionally uses these terms in preference to the term *Third World,* which he now sees in agreement with Healy as obsolete. The best choice seems to be to use the more neutral geographical terms, including sometimes *Western society* in conjunction with economically descriptive terms, for example, "technologically advanced regions" or "the non-industrialized world" as a means of highlighting differences in standards of living. Where possible, specific regions of the world will be named as, for example, Latin America, sub-Saharan Africa, and Northern Europe.

## GLOBALIZATION

What is globalization? Is it an opportunity or a curse? Although global interconnectedness was a fact of ancient history, most famously involving the ancient Greeks and Romans, the term *globalization* did not come into general use until the 1990s. The *Oxford Dictionary of Sociology* (Scott, 2014) refers to two common usages—cultural and economic globalization. Cultural aspects include the sharing of fashion, music, sports, knowledge, political movements, and an extension of concepts such as human rights and political systems such as the United Nations. Economic globalization refers to the international power and dominance of world banks and private corporations. In short, globalization involves a new consciousness of the world as a single place. In *That Used to Be Us*, Friedman and Mandelbaum (2012) provide a portrait of a world that has grown amazingly "flat," a world in which the integration of finance markets, nation states, and technologies within a free- market capitalism is on a scale never before experienced.

*Globalization* is defined by Kahn and Kamerman (2009) as "the current buzzword used to describe the growing internationalization of the production of goods and services and the flow of capitalism" (p. 552). Globalization represents the movement over the past two decades from an economy in which national economies participated in a global market to a full blown global economy in which the major corporations and banks transcended national boundaries.

This critical view of corporate business practices echoes that of Marx and Engels (1963/1848), who provided these remarkable insights in *The Communist Manifesto*. The following passage perhaps has more relevance today than when it was written:

> By exploitation of the world market, the bourgeoisie has given a cosmopolitan character to production and consumption in every land. To the despair of the reactionaries, it has deprived industry of its national foundation. Of the old-established national industries, some have already been destroyed and others are day by day undergoing destruction. They are dislodged by new industries, whose introduction is becoming a matter of life and death for all civilized nations: by industries which no longer depend upon the homeland for their raw materials, but draw these from the remotest spots; and by industries whose products are consumed, not only in the country of manufacture, but the wide world over. Instead of the old wants, satisfied by the products of native industry, new wants appear, wants which can only be satisfied by the products of distant lands and unfamiliar climes. . . . It forces all the nations, under pain of extinction, to adopt the capitalist method of production; it constrains them to accept what is called civilization, to become bourgeois themselves. In short, it creates a world after its own image. (p. 30)

The globalization of culture is an obvious aspect of globalization that is not entirely economic. This process is seen in the mass-produced, quasi-American cultural icons in the form of McDonalds, Starbucks, Disney products, Levis, baseball, Coca-Cola, CNN and other TV broadcasts, not to mention the seeping of English words into other languages. As nations are bombarded with foreign images and music, there is concern that native performers will be ignored and indigenous traditions will be lost to the next generations.

Socially, globalization has been happening for centuries due to military occupations, trade, and missionary work. Advances in communication techniques mean that a wealth of information is available at our fingertips. Thanks to the information revolution, there is an equalizing effect in giving small companies advantages they never had before in terms of sending out their messages on the Internet.

Like cultural westernization, the impact of the global economy is mixed. While the global market brings cheaper consumer goods and better jobs for skilled workers (for example, for electronic engineers in Bangalore, India), economies with high wage costs lose jobs to economies with cheaper labor and fewer benefits, so "the race to the bottom" is inevitable. One result is a rising hostility to globalization and a mass movement against the multinational corporations for producing goods at Asian sweatshops or destroying the rain forest for the growth of cash crops.

All of us are heirs to opportunities, knowledge access, and possibilities scarcely imaginable to our grandparents. At the same time, in the name of progress and to spur the global market, rainforests have been leveled, the atmosphere polluted, and people relocated by the millions. In our ever-shrinking universe, our global village, national economies increasingly are interdependent. Decisions that affect all of us are made on Wall Street, by the World Bank, and transnational corporations. The World Bank is an international organization dedicated to providing financing, advice, and research to developing nations to aid their economic advancement.

Across continents, aided by the tools of computer technology, the flow of capital and ideas is happening at the speed of light. As international corporations have grown into transnational corporations whose interests transcend the interests of any one state or enterprise, the national thrust to be commercially competitive becomes all-encompassing. Accordingly, the trends in one country—privatization, industrial automation, downsizing, focus on cost-efficiency—are the trends in every country.

The powerful forces of social, cultural, demographic, and political changes associated with globalization have important implications for the social welfare state and for social work practice. Under the impact of the growth of "free market" economies, existing social welfare institutions are precariously situated between the retrenchment of entitlement programs and the concomitant increase in demands for social services as poverty increases. Social workers thus are compelled to do more with less.

Empowerment can be said to take place when individuals and organizations influence decision making through their representatives and/or by acting independently to effect social change. The goal may actually be to resist the types of changes that have been occurring lately in the social welfare system. In any case, the first step is to organize. Today, networks of grassroots women's groups and indigenous peoples have at their disposal the tools of electronic communications to use as tools of liberation. As social workers unite globally through international organizations and private networking, they can share effective strategies in standing up for worker and client rights.

Workers in the global economy generally are not faring well due to global competition and new technologies. Media reports of the increasing gap between the superrich executives and the average worker have angered many. This residue of anger revealed itself in the 2016 campaign for the US presidency. The large support for the candidacy of business tycoon Donald Trump on the Republican side, with his promises to get the exported jobs back home, and the enthusiastic rallies organized by the campaigns of Bernie Sanders on the Democratic side tell us a lot about the attitudes of many US voters.

While criticized himself for his Palm Beach, Florida, private club's hiring of hundreds of foreign workers, Donald Trump embraced positions on economics and foreign policy anathema to most conservative politicians (Donne, 2016). While speaking out vehemently against free-trade agreements that would move more jobs overseas, and in opposition to members of his own party, Trump seemed at the time to oppose cuts to Social Security and Medicare and to be critical of pharmaceutical companies for their inflated drug prices. His strongest support came from white male and many women voters at the lower end of the socioeconomic scale.

The Democratic candidate, a self- proclaimed Socialist Democrat, was oddly in agreement with Trump on these economic issues. His largest support came from college students and other young adults. Neither of these candidates received financing from the conventional PAC (Political Action Committee) and Super PAC committees that represent the corporations and big banks in funding political campaigns—in other words, from the power structure.

## POWER

Power is a sociological concept of relevance to social welfare as a dimension of stratification, as well as to social legislation and world dominance. In the tradition of Max Weber (1979), power can be defined as the ability to get people to do what you want, even against their will. Perhaps the key issue of interest to social welfare is who in the society has the power to get his or her perceived needs met and who does not. A related issue is who in society can meet these ends—achieving success—without violating the norms of society. For example, who can achieve wealth and status through conventional means and who must use illegitimate means to achieve the same ends?

Control of the media promotes power, and power promotes control of the media. No one has ever described this phenomenon better than George Orwell (1961/1948) in his haunting masterpiece *1984*: "Who controls the past controls the future; who controls the present controls the past" (p. 204). In that book, Orwell also introduced the notion of Thought Police and the personification of the world's scapegoat in the form of a man capable "of wrecking the structure of civilization" (p. 16). Since the election of Donald Trump, *1984* has suddenly risen to the top of the bestseller lists (de Freytac-Tamura, 2017). Plans are currently under way for a new play on Broadway and a remake of the original film.

From another angle, those with power ("the power elite") can shape a society according to the principles they value. In a real sense they control the flow of knowledge as well as the knowledge itself. For instance, corporations and companies advertising in the local newspaper may have an inhibiting effect on news reporting of various sorts because newspapers don't want to lose their funding. Information imparted in a political campaign, similarly, is apt to be influenced by the giant contributors to that campaign. The burgeoning political influence of conservative think tanks on the mass media is described in chapter 4.

At the international level, inequitable distribution of wealth and military might are conditions that shape politics, economic alliances, and relationships. Abuse of this power is seen in industrialized countries, which use sweatshop labor in developing countries to stock their own markets with material goods. In foreign policy, the abuse of political power, as defined in the late Senator Fulbright's (1966) *The Arrogance of Power*, is highly relevant in today's world, where the defense industry has come to assume awesome powers. The weapons industry today generates hundreds of billions of dollars in revenue annually and employs millions of Americans. Political scientist Rebecca Thorpe (2014) shows how America has grown to be a "warfare state" and how members of Congress are powerless to stop it. And the costs of war are now borne overwhelmingly by a minority of soldiers who volunteer to fight, the taxpayers, and foreign populations in whose lands wars often take place.

Connections can be made between the world's military expenditures and a nation's lack of resources to meet individual and family needs (Mary, 2008). A nation engaged in war or a country consumed by the fear of the consequences of war spilling onto its shores—for example, terrorism, mass immigration—is a nation less concerned with improving the living standards of its people. Conversely, in times of peace the social welfare system is strengthened, and progressive ideologies become more acceptable.

## FROM POWER TO EXPLOITATION

Two key elements of exploitation are coercion (to create and enforce inequalities) and ideology (to maintain inequalities and convince the people to accept them). *Exploitation* is defined by Bob Mullaly (2010) as "those social processes whereby the dominant group is able to accumulate and maintain status, power, and assets from the energy and labor expended by subordinate groups" (p. 55). The power invested in global institutions generally promotes free market capitalism at the expense of struggling nations and people who live in abject poverty in those nations. The source of the power is the ability of the institutions (i.e., the world banks) to lend billions of dollars to industrializing nations while imposing stringent requirements upon them. The debtor nations are required, for example, to reduce government spending on social welfare programs, including health care, to privatize public services, and to open their doors to transnational corporations. Such economic stipulations (termed "structural adjustments") have led to an erosion of programs that are the cornerstone of the welfare state. As a result of these measures, the gap between rich and poor is increasing exponentially and the livelihoods of subsistence cultures that have lived off the land have been destroyed.

## BLAMING THE VICTIM

A concept derived from psychologists of the social psychological school, victim blaming refers to a fundamental tendency in American culture (Ryan, 1976; Zastrow, 2014). This tendency occurs when the downtrodden or underdogs of society are held responsible for creating their own distress. Because of the reciprocity involved, the victim tends to internalize the blame attached to his or her condition (the self-talk is "I have failed"), and the negativity may become a self-fulfilling prophecy (the self-talk becomes "I will never amount to anything").

Pervasive in the American psyche, the phenomenon of blaming the victim is a generic process applied to almost every social problem in the United States (Ryan, 1976) As a traditional ideology related to the work ethic, intellectual, scientific, and religious forces have all historically fed the mythology. As noted by Dolgoff and Feldstein (2012), the growth of industrialism and the development of the Protestant ethic and social Darwinism each contributed to an ethos for blaming the victim. When the work ethic is very strong in a society, people who seemingly shirk their responsibilities are looked down on.

A unique phenomenon of the blaming-the-poor rhetoric of the past decades is the success in enlisting the lower-middle classes in the service of the higher-level interests in targeting the poor as society's scapegoats. "Welfare reform," for example, which forced many single mothers off the welfare rolls was a characteristically punitive ploy that received widespread support.

Chapter 7 considers the blaming-the-victim ideology in terms of the social implications relating to poverty.

Much of the popularity of the 2016 candidacy of Donald Trump for the US presidency was associated with his attacks on two vulnerable populations—undocumented workers and Muslim refugees. His call to deport 11 million immigrants who are here illegally, his support for a ban on the entry of Muslims to the United States, his invocation of law-and-order themes and emphatic support for the police, his endorsement of even rougher treatment of terror suspects—all speak to an authoritarian and punitive side of Trump's appeal that clearly resonates with many on the Republican right (Donne, 2016).

What is the opposite of victim blaming? Is it tolerance? Or support? In the helping professions, the opposite of blaming is *empathy*. Empathy is the ability to identify with another person and through a leap of the imagination momentarily to view the world through the other's eyes. The Sioux prayer reveals the difficulty in acquiring this virtue, "Oh Great Spirit keep me from judging a man until I've walked a mile in his moccasins." This sentiment was also expressed in the words of a Kentucky gospel hymn once heard (by van Wormer) in Bowling Green, "Do not accuse, condemn, or abuse, till you've walked in my shoes."

Empathy is one of the most important traits in helping people; empathy is often imparted more through body language and feeling than words. More than empathy is required, however, as many victims tend to blame themselves and lose faith in their ability to find a way out of a seemingly hopeless situation; without help and encouragement, they lose hope. This is where an empowerment/strengths-based approach can be helpful.

## OUR SOCIAL WORK IMAGINATION

A mark of greatness, as Katherine Kendall (1989) suggested, is a breadth of vision. In her portrait of three extraordinary social work leaders of the 1930s—Alice Salomon of Germany, Eileen Younghusband of the United Kingdom, and Edith Abbott of the United States—Kendall explained their deep commitment to international concerns. Every social work graduate at the University of Chicago in Edith Abbott's day, for example, was exposed to a view of the field and the profession that encompassed history and comparative study. Salomon and Younghusband worked with the League of Nations and the United Nations. In their international vision and flexibility, these female pioneers personify what I mean by social work imagination. As Kendall concluded, "In embracing the necessity to join social reform with individual help, they long ago settled the question of whether social work should be equally concerned with therapeutic action and social action" (p. 30).

To paraphrase Kendall, good social work is not therapy *or* social action; it is *both/and*. Both/and as opposed to either/or thinking is the kind of thinking associated with creative thought and also with feminist therapy. (Either/or thinking or black-and-white thinking in addictions treatment is equated with rigidity and a tendency to relapse.)

Because no two clients are alike and no communities are alike, social work is complex, and the key elements are unpredictable. Social work is both an art and a science. (Keep in mind that art and science are intertwined, non-dichotomous components in creation; there is art in empirical truths and science in artistic creations.) That social work is both art and science; this is what continues to make the profession relevant in changing times (Bent-Goodley, 2015). Sometimes social work knowledge is dismissed because of the art aspect; yet good practice requires a tolerance for ambiguity.

In one graduate school (the University of Tennessee, Nashville, where van Wormer attended) students were told that English majors trained in social work made the best therapists due to their ability to empathize with characters in literature. They probably also possessed powers of imagination and an ability to find meaning in a complex situation. Goldstein (2006) corroborates the connection between literacy and human understandings. We need to go beyond reason alone, he suggests, to use our own greater curiosity and imagination. The circumstances we are trying to understand are always in flux and change, full of the kinds of mystery and enigmas that are the essence of great literature.

Like the poet, the therapist must use the medium of language, being forever cognizant of the underlying meanings of words and labels. Saving somebody's life may entail helping the person view his or her life through a different lens, to find meaning in an existence seemingly shattered by alcohol, violence, or physical or mental illness.

Because the family is a system composed of members in constant and dynamic interaction with each other and because each family has developed a pattern—a rhythm that is more than the sum of its parts—family therapy can tax one's creative energies to the maximum, as the therapist acts almost like a stage manager in getting the individuals to change their lines and voice tones to better communicate their needs.

Social workers often need to be intermediaries between people and their worlds, often working to bridge the gap between cultures or even genders. The skilled social worker learns to listen for the "method in the madness" of personal narratives, to recognize the political ramifications of personal despair and to work with troubled persons as collaborators in a mutual quest for truth.

*Our social work imagination*, a term comparable to C. Wright Mills' (1959) concept of the sociological imagination, refers to that combination of empathy, suspension of disbelief, insight, and resourcefulness that makes for exceptional social work practice (van Wormer, 1997). The pronoun *our* is used to provide a more personal touch, a shared enterprise. Social workers need to be intermediaries, to open up the world to another, even as they gain a new or altered perspective from the same source. The energy of mutual discovery feeds on itself, recharges itself. Social work imagination makes it possible to perceive the congruities in the incongruities, to discern the false dualism between the private and the public, to experience the beauty of social work against the bureaucratic assaults, and to see the past in the present. The energy of mental discovery feeds on itself, recharges itself. Such artistry is the foundation for a narrative approach to working with people and their ordeals of living (Goldstein, 2006).

Attend one of the social work regional, national, or international conferences and the wealth of ideas exchanged and the political fervor to challenge injustices makes a sharp contrast to some of the dreary empiricism that dominates the conferences of some of our sister professions (observation based on van Wormer's personal experience) and, if we are not careful, which will seep into our own.

One especially memorable CSWE conference, held in 2010 in Portland, Oregon, had as its theme promoting sustainability in social work. A number of papers were presented on teaching principles of sustainability and environmental justice using innovative assignments and tools. The special plenary ("The New Color of Green") was presented by environmental activist Jerome Ringo (2010), who provided examples of minority populations acting locally in the interests of preserving their natural environment against outside economic forces. Numerous presentations focused on the integration of environmental theory and social work practice.

Zion Barnetz (2015), informed by Mills' (1959) classic *The Sociological Imagination* and van Wormer's earlier adoption of the term for social work, takes the concept into a radical realm. Radical imagination, notes Barnetz, "inspires and helps to enlist people to the struggle, and it enables us to survive the numerous hardships entailed when advocating for social change" (p. 256).

## CRITICAL THINKING

Successful practice depends on solid *theory*. Without a solid theoretical base, the social worker is unable to critically evaluate his or her client's circumstances and thus unable to comprehend human behavior as, in part, a product of structural arrangements and power disparities in the family at the micro level and/or pressures and power disparities in the wider social realm. The key question for the social worker to ask at either the family or societal level is, Who benefits? For example, in discrimination against gays and lesbians in the military, the who-benefits question should help us be aware of any vested interests by individuals or social institutions in punishing non-normative gender behavior. In finding the answers we are brought face to face with intransigent forces in the power structure. Such questioning is at the heart of critical thinking and critical consciousness.

Critical thinking takes people beyond the surface to grasp what is "really going on," not taking as "fact" what you read or hear about at face value, in other words. Kirst-Ashman (2013) delineates two dimensions integral to critical thinking: (1) questioning beliefs, statements, and assumptions and seeking relevant information concerning the veracity of the claim, and (2) formulating an informed opinion or conclusion based on the evidence.

Most relevant to the subject of social welfare is the ability to discern the underlying, latent purpose, in social policy, for example, requiring drug tests for welfare recipients. Critical thinking can help people identify propaganda in the way new government spending policies such as military buildup and changes in the tax law are presented to the public and carried in the mass media. A comparison of national and international news accounts will often reveal alternative perspectives on the same piece of information.

The ability to view contemporary social policy in historical and cultural context (see chapter 3) and to analyze national policy from a global perspective are key aspects of critical analysis. Above all, inasmuch as viewing the world from the perspective of our own cultural beliefs is as inevitable as is thinking in the language we have learned to speak, we need to recognize our own tendency toward ethnocentrism.

See Box 1.1 by social work educator Elisabeth Reichert, who describes how her academic department's study abroad course broadens students' horizons.

*Critical consciousness* involves an understanding of the encompassing social-structural context of human problems. This term has its roots in the form of collective field activities developed in Latin America under the leadership of Paulo Freire. Having lost confidence in the capacity of their official leaders to bring development to their countries, grass-roots organizations formed to work among the poorest and most needy groups of society. Chilean social work education was revolutionized as a result of the pedagogical instruction of Freire, an exiled Brazilian educator living in Chile (Comer, 2013). From 1965 to 1973, after which a military

## BOX 1.1 Study Abroad: A Unique Learning Experience

ELISABETH REICHERT

Since 1996, the School of Social Work at Southern Illinois University at Carbondale has offered a study abroad course in Western Europe, with a focus on Germany. The purpose of the course is to help students learn the connection between human rights and social work within an international and domestic context. Field visits often occur in other countries, including Austria and Switzerland. This course takes place twice each year for eight days, in January and late May.

Participants in the course visit social service agencies in the various countries and learn how those countries address social problems. Specific field visits include trips to an HIV/Aids center, a former concentration camp at Dachau, a migrant and refugee center, a homeless assistance center within the main train station of Munich, Germany, and a harm reduction facility for heroin addiction in St. Gallen, Switzerland. Other field visits cover a range of topics, including domestic violence and child welfare. In addition to field visits, there are lectures to supplement information learned during the visits.

### Purpose of Study Abroad

The primary rationale for a study abroad course in social work is to provide students with the opportunity to obtain knowledge about social welfare policies and practices in other countries not easily obtainable in the classroom. In addition, by directly experiencing social work in other cultures, students can gain insight into universal values held by counterparts. Issues of concern to social workers are becoming increasingly international in scope. Refugees, child abuse and neglect, inadequate health care, lack of water, and drug addiction all present contemporary challenges within a social welfare environment. Learning how other countries address these issues can provide valuable information in confronting the same or similar problems at home.

Today there are many universities offering opportunities for social work students to study abroad. The length of the courses varies, but financial constraints may lead many students to choose a shorter-term course, such as one to two weeks. There are other considerations in choosing a shorter course, such as being away from family and possible culture shock. Usually a shorter course allows the student to better cope with homesickness, cultural differences, and other issues that inevitably arise when traveling abroad. Certainly, though, a longer course can provide a better learning experience and allow the student more time in which to become accustomed to a new environment. There is no "one size fits all" when it comes to study abroad courses.

### Benefits of Study Abroad

A well-structured study abroad course can promote creative thinking and foster intercultural collaboration in education, research, and practice. At a minimum, it can provide knowledge about policies and practices in other countries that would be difficult to obtain in the traditional classroom environment at home. Through this type of educational exchange, students can develop connections to social workers and student counterparts in other countries.

During the last course I taught, one of our focuses was on the assimilation and treatment of refugees in Germany, since Germany had agreed to take up to one million refugees in 2016—an enormous number to absorb, particularly since most of the refugees originated from a culture vastly different from that of Germany. Most could not speak German and needed language training simply to get started. After the course finished, a month later I received an email from one of the students telling me that she was now working in Germany with refugees. The course had provided her with a stepping stone into this full-time work with refugees. While most participants in a study abroad course do not seek work in an international setting, I have found that several of my past students are either working full-time abroad or have at least part-time experiences overseas.

### Student Reactions to Course Experiences

Based on comments from participants in the SIUC social work course in Germany, reactions to practices and policies of other countries can vary dramatically. For example, the field visit to the harm reduction center in St. Gallen never fails to elicit varying impressions. This center dispenses methadone and heroin to people with addictions who meet strict criteria. In conjunction with the visit, students learn about the Swiss policy of publicly dispensing hypodermic needles to prevent the spread of AIDS and other diseases. People with addictions can also purchase needles from machines. Public bathrooms and other areas have receptacles available for hygienic disposal of the needles.

Participants in the course learn that although there is no true legalization of drugs in Switzerland, as is often represented in the United States, the effect of the Swiss policies does allow heroin and methadone to be distributed without legal consequence. Without this visit to the harm reduction center, students might not understand the fine points of how the Swiss try to assist those addicted to heroin.

Another field visit that students often comment on is the trip to Dachau, a former concentration camp in a small city outside Munich. Students learn about the horrors of the Nazi regime during World War II, but also have occasion to reflect on how lessons to be learned can be applied to contemporary society. Resistance against injustices is a necessity if countries are to avoid some of the horrors of Nazi Germany.

### Summary

Over the many years in which SIUC has offered this course, participant responses have clearly indicated benefits from experiencing different concepts of social work policy and practice. Students have emphasized that they felt they obtained knowledge that could not have been adequately conveyed through classroom teaching in their home country. This exposure to a unique cultural and learning experience provides the foundation of all study abroad programs.

---

dictatorship intervened to suppress the program and persecute the social workers who were organizing the countryside, a real participatory democracy characterized social work education. Today, throughout Latin America, schools of social work are training their students in this collectivist form of organization. This development has given Latin American social work its own identity that supplements the elements it shares with social work elsewhere (Healy, 2008). Freire's (1973) description of his emancipatory pedagogy is still valid today: "The critically transitive consciousness is characterized by depth in the interpenetration of problems; by the substitution of causal principles for magical explanations" (p. 17).

Feminist educator bell hooks (1994) articulates Freierian premises in terms of "teaching/learning to transgress," and critical thinking as "the primary element allowing the possibility of change" (p. 202). Within social work, similarly, feminist therapy stresses worker/client collaboration at every stage of the therapy process and the linking of political and personal issues (see Hyde, 2013). A related aspect of critical thinking is, of course, cultural insight, an indispensable ingredient for working in a multicultural diverse and complex environment.

## CULTURE AND CULTURAL COMPETENCE/HUMILITY

The concept of culture is central to anthropology. Culture is social heredity, or a way of thinking, feeling, and believing that sets one group apart from another. Culture is traditional knowledge that is passed down from one generation to the next (Nanda & Warms, 2015). Because of the close relationship between personality and culture, members of one nation or tribe (or sex) appear homogeneous to outsiders. A group member absorbs the essential content of a culture by means of socialization.

Language shapes and is shaped by culture. In Mexico, for example, where there is a complete reliance on the family to provide care, a visiting American social worker had difficulty explaining that her mother-in-law was in a nursing home. In resort areas of Mexico where large numbers of Americans are retiring, however, assisted living and "memory care" centers are springing up to cater to the increasing demand. The cost is around one-fourth that of elder care in the United States, and medicine is relatively cheap (Ifill, 2015). The cultural difference between Mexicans and the foreigners in attitudes toward aging care is pronounced.

*Cultural competence* is the earlier social work term for the knowledge and skills that one needs for effective work with clients from diverse cultural backgrounds. More recently, the thinking is that claims of achieving competence by learning about diverse cultural groups verge on arrogance, or at least overconfidence. CSWE does not use this term any more in its educational standards, but rather speaks of *cultural humility*. We agree with this terminology and will use this term in this book, along with cultural awareness and cultural sensitivity. *Cultural sensitivity* entails more than familiarity with the cultural norms and values of a specific group; it involves an understanding of the uniqueness of one's own cultural beliefs and an openness to other customs, norms, and rituals. The humility aspect requires a willingness to learn and listen nonjudgmentally as we approach persons of a foreign culture or as we travel abroad.

*Cultural humility* entails recognition of the human impulse to have prejudices—ethnocentrism, sexism, classism, heterosexism, and racism—and of our own possession of many of these traits. To fully appreciate cultural differences, self-awareness is a must. Social workers must recognize the influence of their own culture, family, and peers on how they think and act. Cultural awareness requires continuous efforts to gain more knowledge about the client's culture—the norms, vocabulary, symbols, and strengths. The color blind and gender blind notions of many European-American and other Americans are a denial of a person's whole being. Through accepting that significant differences do exist between people of different ethnic backgrounds, professionals are recognizing a person's wholeness and individuality. To tell a lesbian or gay person, "just stay in the closet and you'll be all right," "don't ask, don't tell," is to deny that person an important part of him- or herself. To tell an African American "we're all the same under the skin" sounds like a nice thing to say, as it signifies acceptance, yet the remark may be taken as a denial of the importance of race in the society.

Related to human rights, an attitude of cultural acceptance and humility does not mean that any behavior is acceptable if it is culturally normative. Human rights principles lay down standards to apply universally, such as that everyone has the right to enter into marriage of their own free will and that no one shall be held in slavery. There are also universal proscriptions against certain forms of violence, such as beating one's wife or child. These rights sometimes are in conflict with cultural practices in some societies, yet from a human rights standpoint they should be opposed. In general, though, appreciation of diverse beliefs, lifestyles, and practices becomes more and more critical to effective social work practice as global interdependency increases. Otherwise, instead of cultural sensitivity, ethnocentrism would prevail.

## ETHNOCENTRISM

The paradox of culture is that as we humans learn to accept our own cultural beliefs and values, we unconsciously learn to reject those of other people. Sumner (1906) called the outlook that one's group is superior to other groups *ethnocentrism*, and defined it as "that view of things in which one's own group is the center of everything and all others are scaled and related with reference to it" (p. 13). Anthropologists define ethnocentrism in the same way—judging other cultures from the perspective of our own (Nanda & Warms, 2015). Immigration provides an example of potential conflict as disparate value systems exist side by side. Boundaries between groups can become increasingly thick and exclusionary. Neighborhoods are affected by an influx of immigrants; the workplace is affected also as newcomers flock to accept jobs that locals would find undesirable.

Such a complex set of potential cultural conflicts must be addressed by the social welfare system; a holistic, non-ethnocentric approach to the delivery of services is essential. Awareness of one's own culture's peculiarities is the first place to start. We are like the introspective hero of *Absalom, Absalom*! (Faulkner, 1936, p. 174) who must live up North before he can answer questions regarding the South such as, "What's it like there. What do they do there?"

Margaret Mead, in her autobiography *Blackberry Winter* (1972), provides this approach to unraveling the intricacies of a new culture. The goal is to "understand a myriad of acts, words, glances, and silences as they are integrated into a pattern one had no way of working out as yet, and finally, to 'get' the structure of the whole culture" (p. 275). Speaking of the patterns and structures brings us to a concern about certain structural elements that allow for the consequences of environmental destruction to fall most heavily upon the world's poor.

### ENVIRONMENTAL JUSTICE

The concept of environmental justice gained currency in the public arena during the latter part of the 20th century. The conceptualization of environmental justice sprang out of the public outcry over the dumping of toxic wastes in poor and minority neighborhoods (for example, Anniston, Alabama). As a model, environmental justice embodies social work's person/environment perspective and dedication to people who are vulnerable, oppressed, and poor (Rogge, 2013). It was a breakthrough of sorts when CSWE (2015) included knowledge about environmental justice along with social justice as a required component in social work education.

Much of the writing in the environmental literature concerns environmental injustice. Included under this rubric is discussion of the abuse of our natural resources and resource depletion through overuse. The consequences fall unevenly upon rural and poor communities, as is evident in the water contamination in Flint, Michigan. We pursue this topic in some depth in chapter 5.

Dominelli (2012), in her landmark book, *Green Social Work*, explores social work roles worldwide in pursuit of environmental and human rights. Her book offers a well-documented critique of the contemporary industrialization model that caters to the needs of the few at the expense of poor and marginalized people.

## SUMMARY AND CONCLUSION

The purpose of this introductory chapter has been to provide the vocabulary and theoretical context for viewing social welfare internationally and within a human rights context. Central to our understanding of the American welfare state is a familiarity with some of the basic concepts from social psychology (for example, the nature of victim blaming), sociology (functionalism and power), economics (globalization and the market economy), and anthropology (ecosystems theory). These concepts are just a part of the vast knowledge base relevant to grasping the psychological, political, and social dimensions of social welfare. Social work, the ultimate applied social science, embraces an interdisciplinary knowledge base under the rubric of ecosystems theory. Drawing upon the terminology of the ecosystems perspective, the American welfare state can be viewed both within the context of a seeming jumble of contradictory goals and against the backdrop of a more or less cohesive set of enduring cultural values.

Consistent with social work's focus on the person-in-the-environment, the focus of this book is on the *country-in-the-world*. The country is the United States, the topic is the social welfare system, and the framework is a holistic or ecosystems approach.

The reality of global interdependence extends to everyday social work practice. Increasingly, numbers of undocumented immigrants, refugees, and cross-cultural child welfare cases reflect the growing diversity of the US population. The refugee crisis stemming from wars in the Middle East serves to illustrate many themes of this chapter. Global interconnectedness clearly comes into play as many countries in the Western world start receiving refugees. Globalization is another theme, as the plight of the escaping families is communicated through the mass media worldwide. Cultural clash is a reality as East meets West under situations of dire stress. So the need for cultural acceptance by refugee workers comes into play. Finally, looming over the whole scene is the issue of human rights. The question is, Will people whose human rights have been so cruelly violated in their home countries, often through political or religious persecution, be denied their human rights of resettlement into another country?

Global problems impinge upon the local scene and call for social work's attention. Other problems are both regional and universal. The ubiquity of organized crime, terrorism, drug abuse, and disease epidemics graphically illustrates common ground, as well as the interdependence among nations. Other problems such as high infant mortality, homelessness, and street crime represent the shared failure of nations to meet the needs of all their citizens. In short, for creative, well-informed policymaking on the local or global level, a multicultural worldview is paramount.

In this chapter, the case has been made that to provide empowering social work service, helping professionals will require familiarity with the values and customs of diversified populations. That globalization, or the dictates of the global market, is an ever present force shaping each nation's social policies is a major theme of this chapter, one that will surface again and again throughout the pages of this book as we explore political and human rights issues across the lifespan.

Problems connected to the global economy constitute opportunities for social transformation through united social action. This is where the influence of international social work may come into play. It may seem ambitious and even unrealistic of NASW-US leaders to seek an impact on world policy. And yet if we listen to the words of our leaders and recognize the significant role of the IFSW, an official NGO that reports to the United Nations, we can only wonder what has taken the US social work profession so long to follow this course. In any case, as *NASW News* (Malai, 2015) proclaims, "Social Work Doors Open as U.S. Cuba Relations Evolve," which is just one example of the kinds of global interchanges that are taking place (see also Box 1.1).

Indeed, there is much to learn from social welfare policies and programs in other societies. The Cuban social work team approach to community organizing is instructive. Consistent with the goals of critical thinking, learning about social welfare policies in other lands and of policies related to human rights can help us all comprehend connections between the structure of economic and political systems and their social outcomes. Outcomes, of course, often show a sizable gap between rhetoric and reality.

Highlighted in this chapter was an appreciation of the uniqueness of social work, a profession with a mission. Social work is unique among the helping professions in its policy focus, and it is unique among policymakers in its counseling function. Guiding social work in theory, if not always in practice, is the empowerment framework. The general expectation is that social workers will draw on a strengths approach as both a model and method.

In this age of welfare cutbacks, reliance on privatized services, and focus on accountability and number crunching, sometimes there is little room for the kind of growth that comes from nurturance and the give and take of unplanned dialogue. Effective social work practice requires the best use of what we call our social work imagination to help people find a will and a way to go on in the face of profound difficulty. For the strengths-based therapist, listening is the method—listening to the client's story, not passively and uncreatively, but with full attention to the rhythms and patterns—and then, when the time is right, observing and sharing until, through mutual discovery, events can be seen in terms of some kind of whole. The challenge is to find themes of hope and courage and in so naming, reinforce them.

In the generalist tradition of social work, social workers learn to intervene at any point—at the individual, family, neighborhood, or societal levels. Both as citizens and as professionals, social workers look toward social policy; change efforts directed here have the most potential for improving social services and challenging injustice. We are moving now into the realm of social values, the topic to which we now turn in chapter 2.

## THOUGHT QUESTIONS

1. How does the opening quotation from Eleanor Roosevelt about human rights beginning in our individual worlds relate to the rest of this chapter?
2. Discuss three ways in which social work is a unique profession.
3. What is the mission of social work? How does this relate to ethical values in general?
4. "The world is growing ever smaller." Discuss this statement in light of recent developments.
5. Consider the quotations from Dean Jackson. From your knowledge and research, what is the substance to the writer's recommendation that students might do better to get an MSW than a law school degree? State if you agree or disagree and explain your reasons.
6. Is globalization strictly an economic phenomenon? Discuss positive aspects of international interconnectedness.
7. How can one account for the rise in the 2016 election campaign of the popular following of supporters of Donald Trump and Bernie Sanders?
8. Discuss ways in which the average social worker encounters global problems in everyday work.
9. Review the definition of welfare state. To what extent does the United States qualify as a welfare state?
10. Compare the terms *developing country* and *sustainable development*. What is the effect of globalization on the latter?
11. Discuss contemporary military build-up in terms of manifest and latent functions.
12. Describe the notion of regulating the poor and cite examples from your personal knowledge or media reports.
13. What does Orwell's *1984* have to say about our government today?
14. Marx and Engels' analysis of the world trade performances has more relevance today than in 1848. Discuss the validity of this claim.
15. Why do you think some social work writers are moving away from the term *cultural competence* in preference for the term *cultural humility*?
16. How can "color blind" and "gender blind" notions be a denial of realities?
17. Give some examples of the concepts *ethnocentrism* and *blaming the victim*.
18. Discuss the qualities of a social work imagination.
19. From the perspective of critical thinking, what kinds of questions might one ask about a given social policy?
20. What is the personal/political configuration?

## REFERENCES

Abdallah, M. (2016, March 11). South Sudan fighters rate women as payments. *Global Post*. Public Radio International. Retrieved from www.globalpost.com

Androff, D. (2016). *Practicing rights: Human rights-based approaches to social work practice*. London, England: Routledge.

Barker, R. (2014). *Dictionary of social work*. Washington, DC: NASW Press.

Barnetz, Z. (2015). The role of radical imagination in social work education, practice, and research. *Journal of Teaching in Social Work, 35*, 251–261.

Barretta-Herman, A., Leung, P., Littlechild, B., Parada, H., & Wairire, G. (2016). The changing status and growth of social work education worldwide: Process, findings, and implications of the IASSW 2010 census. *International Social Work, 59* (4), 459–478.

Blank, B. (2011, Summer). Master's international program combines degree with Peace Corps at four schools of social work. *The New Social Worker, 18* (3), 14–17.

Boyle, M. (2017, March 15). Fewer immigrants will cost some nonprofit workers their jobs. *The Denver Channel.* Retrieved from www.thedenverchannel.com

Bureau of Labor Statistics. (2016). Social workers. *Occupational outlook handbook, 2016–17.* Washington, DC: U.S. Department of Labor.

Comer, E. (2013, October). Freire, Paulo. In C. Franklin (Ed.), *Encyclopedia of social work* (20th ed., online publication). New York, NY: Oxford University Press. Available at http://socialwork.oxfordre.com/

Council on Social Work Education (CSWE). (2003). *Educational policies and accreditation standards.* Alexandria, VA: CSWE. Retrieved from https://www.cswe.org

Council on Social Work Education (CSWE). (2015). *Educational policies and accreditation standards.* Alexandria, VA: CSWE. Retrieved from http://www.cswe.org/File.aspx?id=81660

Cox, D., & Pawar, M. (2013). *International social work: Issues, strategies, and programs* (2nd ed.). Thousand Oaks, CA: Sage.

Cox, L. E., Tice, C. J., & Long, D. D. (2016). *Introduction to social work: An advocacy-based profession.* Thousand Oaks, CA: SAGE.

Dean, H. (2013). The translation of needs into rights: Reconceptualising social citizenship as a global phenomenon. *International Journal of Social Welfare, 22,* S32–S49. doi: 10.1111/ijsw.12032

de Freytac-Tamura, K. (2017, January 26). George Orwell's "1984" has seen a sales surge. *New York Times,* p. C4.

Dolgoff, R., & Feldstein, D. (2012). *Understanding social welfare: A search for social justice.* Upper Saddle River, NJ: Pearson.

Dominelli, L. (2002). *Anti-oppressive social work theory and practice.* New York, NY: Palgrave.

Dominelli, L. (2012). *Green social work: From environmental crisis to environmental justice.* Cambridge, England: Polity Press.

Donne, E. J. (2016, February 26). The useful side of Trump. *The Capital Times.* Retrieved from www.host.madison.com

Dover, M. (2015). Human needs: Overview. In C. Franklin (Ed.), *Encyclopedia of social work* (20th ed., online publication). New York, NY: Oxford University Press. Retrieved from http://socialwork.oxfordre.com/view/10.1093/acrefore/9780199975839.001.0001/acrefore-9780199975839-e-554

Faulkner, W. (1936). *Absalom, Absalom!* New York, NY: Random House.

Finn, J. L., & Jacobson, M. (2008). Social justice. In T. Mizrahi & L. E. Davis (Eds.), *Encyclopedia of social work* (20th ed., pp. 44–52). Washington, DC: NASW Press.

Freire, P. (1973). *Education for critical consciousness.* New York, NY: The Seabury Press.

Friedman, T., & Mandelbaum, M. (2012). *That used to be us: How America fell behind in the world it invented and how we can come back.* New York, NY: Farrar, Straus and Giroux.

Fulbright, W. (1966). *The arrogance of power.* New York, NY: Vintage.

Gal, J., & Weiss-Gal, I. (2014). *Social workers affecting social policy: An international perspective.* Bristol, UK: Policy Press.

Gil, D. (2013). *Confronting injustice and oppression: Concepts and strategies for social workers.* New York, NY: Columbia University Press.

Goldman, R. (2017, January 12). *In a shift, Germany turns down more asylum applications.* New York Times, p.A10.

Goldstein, H. (2006). The literary and moral foundations of the strengths perspective. In D. Saleebey (Ed.), *The strengths perspective in social work* (3rd ed., pp. 23–47). Boston, MA: Allyn and Bacon.

Graham, J., Swift, K., & Delaney, R. (2011). *Canadian social policy: An introduction.* (4th ed.). Don Mills, Ontario: Pearson Education Canada.

Healy, L. (2008). *International social work: Professional action in an interdependent world* (2nd ed.). New York, NY: Oxford University Press.

Hyde, C. A. (2013, June). Feminist social practice. In C. Franklin (Ed.), *Encyclopedia of social work* (20th ed., online publication). New York, NY: Oxford University Press.

Ifill, G. (2015, July 6). Why foreign retirees are flocking to Mexico. *Public Broadcasting Company (PBS) News Hour.* Retrieved from www.pbs.org

International Federation of Social Workers (IFSW). (2012, March). *The global agenda for social work and social development: Commitment to action.* Bern, Switzerland: Author.

International Federation of Social Workers (IFSW). (2017). Global definition of social work. Bern, Switzerland. Retrieved from http://ifsw.org/get-involved/global-definition-of-social-work/

Ives, M. (2017, January 27). A vision for floating cities to fend off rising seas. *New York Times*, p. A4.

Jackson, J. L. (2016, February 26). The 21st century JD. *Inside Higher Education.* Retrieved from http://www.insidehighereducation.com

Jansson, B. S. (2015). *Social welfare policy and advocacy: Advancing social justice through 8 policy sectors.* Thousand Oaks, CA: Sage.

John, T. (2016, March 14). Europe fractures as the migrant crisis worsens. *Time*, p. 11.

Kahn, A., & Kamerman, M. (2009). International aspects of social policy. In J. Midgely, M. Tracey, & M. Livermore (Eds.), *The handbook of social policy* (2nd ed., pp. 543–574). Thousand Oaks, CA: Sage.

Kendall, K. (1989). Women at the helm: Three extraordinary leaders. *Affilia, 4*(1), 23–32.

Kirst-Ashman, K. K. (2013). *Introduction to social work and social welfare: Critical thinking perspectives* (4th ed.). Belmont, CA: Cengage.

Link, R. J., & Ramanathan, C. (2011). *Human behavior in a just world: Reaching for common ground.* Lanham, MD: Rowman & Littlefield Publications.

Malai, R. (2015, June). Social work doors open as U.S.-Cuba relations evolve. *NASW News*, p. 5.

Marx, K., & Engels, F. (1963/1848). *The communist manifesto.* New York, NY: Russell and Russell.

Mary, N. (2008). *Social work in a sustainable world.* Chicago, IL: Lyceum.

Maslow, A. (1970). *Motivation and personality.* New York, NY: Harper & Row.

Mead, M. (1972). *Blackberry winter: My earlier years.* New York, NY: William Morrow.

Midgley, J. (2017). *Social welfare for a global era: International perspectives on policy.* Thousand Oaks, CA: Sage.

Morales, A. T., Sheafor, B., & Scott, M. (2011). *Social work: A profession of many faces.* New York: Pearson.

Mullaly, B. (2010). *Challenging oppression and confronting privilege.* New York, NY: Oxford University Press.

Mulroy, E. (2013). Community needs assessment. In C. Franklin (Ed.), *Encyclopedia of social work* (20th ed., online publication). New York, NY: Oxford University Press.

Nadkarni, V., & Sinha, R. (2014). Social work and the United Nations. In C. Franklin (Ed.), *Encyclopedia of social work* (20th ed., online publication). New York, NY: Oxford University Press.

Nanda, S., & Warms, R. (2015). *Culture counts: A concise introduction to cultural anthropology.* Belmont, CA: Cengage.

National Association of Social Workers (NASW). (2015). International policy on human rights. In NASW, *Social work speaks: NASW policy statements 2015–2017* (pp. 182–187). Washington, DC: NASW Press.

National Association of Social Workers. (NASW). (2017). *Code of ethics.* Washington, DC: NASW Press.

Orwell, G. (1961/1948). *1984.* New York, NY: Harcourt, Brace, Jovanovich.

Pace, P. R. (2012, February). Toolkit can help convey importance of social work. *NASW News, 57*(2), 1, 7.

Parsons, R. J., & East, J. (2013). Empowerment practice. In C. Franklin (Ed.), *Encyclopedia of social work* (20th ed., online publication). New York, NY: Oxford University Press.

Piven, F., & Cloward, R. (1993). *Regulating the poor: The functions of public welfare.* New York, NY: Vintage Books.

Popple, P. R., & Leighninger, L. (2014). The policy-based profession: An introduction to social welfare policy analysis for social workers. Upper Saddle River, NJ: Pearson.

Reichert, E. (2011). *Social work and human rights: A foundation for policy and practice.* (2nd ed.).New York, NY: Columbia University Press.

Reisch, M. (2014). U.S. social policy in the new century. In M. Reisch (Ed.), *Social policy and social justice* (pp.5–43). Thousand Oaks, CA: Sage.

Ringo, J. (2010, October 14–17). The new color of green: A collective voice toward change. Keynote presentation at the CSWE Annual Program Meeting, Portland, Oregon.

Robbins, S. P., Chatterjee, P., & Canda, E. R. (2012). *Contemporary human behavior theory: A critical perspective for social work.* Upper Saddle River, NJ: Pearson.

Roche, E. (2017, March 22). India ranks 131 on human development index, Norway number one. Delhi, India: *Live Mint.* Retrieved from www.livemint.com

Rogge, M. E. (2013). Environmental justice. In C. Franklin (Ed.), *Encyclopedia of social work* (20th ed., published online). New York, NY: Oxford University Press.

Roosevelt, E. (1958, March 27). Eleanor Roosevelt, "In our hands." Speech delivered on the 10th anniversary of the Universal Declaration of Human Rights. New York, NY: United Nations.

Ryan, W. (1976). *Blaming the victim.* New York: Vintage Books.

Saleebey, D. (2013). Introduction: Power in the people. In D. Saleebey (Ed.), *The strengths perspective in social work practice* (6th ed., pp. 1–22). Upper Saddle River, NJ: Pearson.

Scott, J. (2014). *Oxford dictionary of sociology.* Oxford, England: Oxford University Press.

Sumner, W. (1940/1906). *Folkways.* Boston, MA: Ginn and Co.

Tankersley, J. (2015, October 13). Why Bernie Sanders loves Denmark but Hillary Clinton doesn't. *Washington Post.* Retrieved from www.washingtonpost.com

Thorpe, R. (2014). *The American warfare state.* Chicago, IL: University of Chicago Press.

van Wormer, K. (1997). *Social welfare: A world view.* Chicago, IL: Nelson Hall.

van Wormer, K., & Davis, D. R. (2018). *Addiction treatment: A strengths perspective* (4th ed.) Belmont, CA: Cengage.

Weber, M. (1979/1922). *Economy and society.* Berkeley, CA: University of California Press.

Wilks, T. (2012). *Advocacy and social work practice.* Berkshire, England: Open University Press.

Wronka, J. (2008). *Human rights and social justice: Action and service for the helping and health professions.* Lanham, MD: Sage Publications.

York, G. (2017, April 6). Trump's aid cuts risk pushing African women into the Dark Ages. *The Globe and Mail.* Retrieved from www.theglobeandmail.com

Young, I. M. (2002). *Inclusion and democracy*. New York, NY: Oxford University Press.

Zastrow, C. (2014). *Introduction to social work and social welfare: Empowering people* (11th ed.). Belmont, CA: Cengage.

Zeigler, K., & Camarota, S. (2015, August). Immigration population hits record 42.1 million in second quarter of 2015. Center for Immigration Studies. Retrieved from www.cis.org

CHAPTER 2

# US SOCIAL VALUES IN INTERNATIONAL CONTEXT

Everyone has the right freely to participate in the cultural life of the community, to enjoy the arts and to share in scientific advancement and its benefits.

United Nations Universal Declaration of Human Rights, 1948, Article 27

Everyone has the right to rest and leisure, including reasonable limitation of working hours and periodic holidays with pay.

United Nations Universal Declaration of Human Rights, 1948, Article 24

Before reviewing the unique history of social work as a profession, the task of the following chapter, a historical and sociological overview of the *context* in which social work has evolved is in order. This focus on context is crucial for both practice and policy considerations. Social work practice exists in a certain time and space; as thoughtful commentators have indicated, it can be neither acultural nor ahistorical (Kreitzer, 2012; Payne, 2014).

In the policy arena, likewise, a clear understanding of the cultural ethos is crucial to effecting social change. Such an understanding can help us to identify stumbling blocks that might impede such change, as well as possibilities that might be exploited in boosting progressive initiatives.

To speak of cultural ethos is to speak of cultural values. Key questions to consider in our professional endeavors, following C. W. Mills (1959) are: What are the values that people cherish? To what extent are these values supported by the growing trends of our era? And to what extent are these values threatened (e.g., by rapid technological or cultural change)? In the latter situation, as Mills informs us, public issues may develop into personal troubles. When this happens on a large scale, personal troubles may become social problems. How society responds to such problems is a product of the social values.

The major purpose of this chapter is to delineate the major, agreed-upon US values and to view each value in international context. Values are viewed not as discrete phenomena but as elements along a continuum, as, for example, individualism versus collectivism, punitiveness versus compassion. A basic assumption of this formulation is that all societies subscribe to relatively the same values (e.g., materialism), but to different degrees. It is a question of priority. This brings us to the second major purpose of discussion which is to reveal how priorities may vary across ethnic and cultural lines. Some Native American tribes may prioritize personal responsibilities over punctuality, for example. The work ethic is clearly prioritized in some Asian countries (for example, Korea and Japan) over family recreation or relaxation.

A third purpose of this chapter is to describe American social work values, values that both reflect and contradict mainstream belief systems. The emphasis will be on the relationship between cultural ethos and the social welfare system. Throughout our discussion, we will be cognizant of both consistencies and dilemmas in each value dimension and of how difficult consensus is to achieve in pluralistic societies such as the United States. The final section of the chapter briefly describes international developments in social work education from various selected regions of the world—Chile, the Caribbean, South Korea, Cuba, and Canada. We will note each country's rank on the United Nations Human Development Index for the most recent year available. The Human Development Index is a composite statistic of life expectancy, education, and income per capita indicators. This index provides some measure of comparison but does not take into account many meaningful social factors. We go beyond the index in describing each social welfare system in terms of cultural values and traditions. Human rights issues are highlighted as well. That the Global North has much to learn from practices of the Global South is one of the lessons of these histories.

## THE STUDY OF CULTURAL VALUES

In working with persons from distinct cultures and backgrounds, knowledge of their group's culture and customs is essential. This includes knowledge of explanations for illness and folk remedies rooted in traditional culture, as well as familiarity with indigenous styles of communication and with leadership roles within the family and community. It also includes knowledge of what they hold dear and their beliefs about the meaning of life.

Given the increasing exposure of social workers to situations involving interracial marriage, international adoption, and cross-cultural foster care arrangements, the task of multicultural social work practice is to consider the cultural milieu when designing treatment approaches. The task is to shape assessments and interventions to be consistent with the beliefs and practices of the community and to acknowledge the multiethnic identities and differing environments of clients. Formal bureaucratic methods (as often required by third-party payers for social services rendered) and a professional frame of reference are often anathema to the treatment mission (see Mullaly, 2010, and his discussion of professionalism, pp. 119–120).

Cultural values are often revealed in the very language that people speak. The words used help shape our preconceptions and viewpoints. The culturally sensitive social worker, in working with people from a different background, will approach language carefully. Hodge and Limb (2010), for example, in their research on Native social work clients, were advised to use the words *ceremonies* and *customs* rather than *rituals*, *Creator* rather than *God*, and *elder* in place of mentor. The best way to find out what members of a particular group call themselves or their practices is to listen closely and adopt the words and phrases they use, or simply, to ask. Some Native groups, for example, prefer to be called Native Americans, others, American Indians, and still others, First Nations People. With reference to gay, lesbian, and transgender clients there is much individual variation in the preferred terms to use. Sometimes a term used by insiders, such as *queer*, is only meant to be used by the insiders, themselves, so sensitivity to client wishes is of the essence.

When people move from one culture to another, they tend to gradually adopt the perspectives of the new culture in which they are immersed. The psychosocial issues associated with the immigration experience, including difficult transitions and a perpetual longing for some of the "old ways" of doing things, the familiar scenery and language, and the favorite food from childhood, are reason enough to justify the development of empathy for people who are newcomers to a particular geographical setting. Elizabeth Torres Herrera (in private correspondence with van Wormer of December, 2015) describes how her mother, now living in Iowa, maintains her cultural heritage (Figure 2.1):

> Learning about our traditional cuisine and observing and helping out my mother cook are Latino family traditions. As I child I enjoyed cooking along with my mother and sisters. Preparing "tamales" at Christmas time and New Year's or any other holiday of festivity is a tradition of most Latino families. Today, I still enjoy going to my mother's house and smelling my mother's cooking. Going to my mother's house is like a step back to Mexico, to eat Mexican food and watch a Mexican show on the television. Most of the decor at my mother's house is Mexican. I am privileged to have my mother, and I still can enjoy her company and cooking.

One can expect, from an ecosystems perspective, that families will experience heightened generational conflict related to differences in the degree of acculturation to the new country, as well as challenges in dealing with discrimination by Native people of the non-natives. González

**FIGURE 2.1.** Elizabeth Torres Herrera proudly holding her flag following the ceremony in which she became a citizen of the United States. Photo with permission of Elizabeth Torres Herrera.

and Acevedo (2013) recommend approaches to clinical practice with Latino families that are attuned to cultural norms that in all likelihood incorporate qualities of *simpatia* (easy-going outlook, avoidance of hostile confrontation); *personalismo* (preference for informal as opposed to bureaucratic relationships), and *familismo* (stress on importance of family ties).

Consider how these characteristics apply in the following example from a social worker who describes his first experience in working with a Latino family:

> My first Latino clients were a 14-year-old couple. The young man was about 100 pounds soaking wet and the young lady looked very physically immature. They came to me because she was pregnant. Thankfully, I was able to consult with a Latino colleague and get insight into possible family dynamics. However, what unfurled next was completely culturally shocking to me. The parents of the teens were notified and came in to meet. They decided that the children would be keeping the baby and that the young lady would move in with the son at his grandmother's. They would be married as soon as possible. The family would be moving both of them to a different school and the young man would be working with relatives to cover the cost of the child. I was dazed as all of this occurred almost immediately upon meeting. Rather than object, the children nodded and accepted it all. I met with them afterwards several times and they seemed to be comfortable with this idea. The young lady was nervous about a new home, but said it was more about who had room and she knew her family would still support her. She was excited about the transition.
>
> This, to me, is the cultural importance of Latino family values and the explanation behind the epidemiological paradox. [Author's note: The *epidemiologic paradox* is the surprisingly low infant mortality rate among Hispanics and their relatively long life expectancy given their low socioeconomic status.] From my perspective, the first conversation would normally be about termination and adoption options. They all instantly dismissed this idea. This was about family and the family stepped up. I never felt disrespected amidst all of this, but I did feel completely out of my cultural depth. (Anonymous contribution shared with K. van Wormer and readers of this book, May 20, 2016)

Keep in mind such cultural characteristics, as well as the challenges facing first generations of immigrants and their families as they confront dominant US cultural values. We explore the dominant US cultural values in a later section in this chapter.

## CULTURAL VALUES AND SOCIAL POLICY

In confronting what Bruce Jansson (2012) termed "the reluctant welfare state" (his book title), our first task is to come to terms with our ideological heritage. The basis of this heritage is found in a people's social values. Values we can define as beliefs about what is good for people and ideals that we cherish. Contradictions come into play in the gap that often exists between the ideal and the real, for example, the ideal of racial equality versus the reality of institutional racism.

Social psychologists posit that through interaction with significant others, we come to see ourselves as others see us: Through internalizing these perceptions, we come to take on the social values of these others (Aronson, Wilson, & Sommers, 2015). This is the process of socialization. Social psychologists have studied social value orientations in small groups (Baron

& Branscombe, 2012). Personal values of cooperation, altruism, competitiveness, and individualism are revealed in problem-solving laboratory situations. Cooperators are more inclined to make prosocial, mutually beneficial choices than are individualists or competitors. Generalizing from the microcosm to society, it can be seen that the socialization of the norms of helpfulness and cooperation is congruent with the dominant value orientations that support the welfare of the group or community. In making prosocial, mutually beneficial choices, cooperators and altruists demonstrate values that are congruent with the guiding principles of the social welfare state.

In this chapter and throughout this book, when we are talking of social welfare we are talking also of social justice and the distribution of resources. How is the wealth in a given country distributed? Which should be given greater weight—equality or freedom? How much poverty and misery is one state or nation willing to tolerate? Why are there such vast sociopolitical differences in the provision of services around the world? The answers can be sought in the predominant social values of a people, that is, the national ethos. The value positions of the majority (elites) in society invariably, according to Gil (2014), will influence the development of policy and will constrain the range of changes of the status quo. Social values and social policies are in constant interaction, social values shaping the political legislation while the legislation promotes and reinforces the values of the society. Consider, for example, how once segregation was ended in the Deep South, the acceptance of the principle of racial integration became the norm, especially strong among the younger generations. (See chapter 4.)

We cannot leave the subject of the interplay between values and policy without recognition of the role of the media in the equation. Media presentations, especially by widely watched television broadcasts, both reflect and promote values. The power of the media to shape public opinion was explored by a British film company ("The War You Don't See") that revealed how evidence was slanted to incite fear in the US public to make them accepting of the buildup to the war in Iraq (Paul, 2011). Then later, the method of "embedding" journalists with the troops (who give them protection) in war zones guaranteed favorable coverage of military operations. According to Goodman (2016), none of the candidates who ran for president in the 2016 campaign had dared to attack military spending or lead a discussion on what the drone strikes are doing to radicalize whole populations in the areas bombed.

Certainly differing mass media portrayals can be expected to reflect and promote social welfare policies as well. Here, again, there is a great divide between American and much more liberal European attitudes concerning the role of the government in providing social benefits. There are, of course, historic and cultural distinctions as well.

The welfare state evolved as a historically purposive phenomenon that differed considerably among individual nations in accordance with predominant religious and cultural strains. Building on de Tocqueville's (1951/1835) and sociologist Robin Williams' (1979) widely cited array of crucial US values (work ethic, equality, individualism, democracy, etc.), we have delineated nine value dimensions of most direct relevance to the US social welfare system. These value dimensions are

- Moralism versus compassion
- Work versus leisure
- Equal opportunity versus equality
- Mobility versus stability
- Competition versus cooperation

- Individualism versus collectivism
- Independence versus interconnectedness
- Materialism versus spirituality
- Nuclear family versus extended family

If you view the set of value dimensions as two columns, the items on the left-hand column are closely interrelated; they represent the essence of US values and, with the possible exception of moralism, the basic qualities of modernization. In any case, this set of continua serves as a framework for the following discussion of American cultural attributes.

## MORALISM VERSUS COMPASSION

Just as work has a strong impact on family roles and patterns of adaptation, so too does work and, that strange bedfellow—the cause of so much good and so much grief—known to students of culture as *moralism*. Were we to describe the essence of the American character in one word, it would be *moralism*. In a sense, moralism transcends the other values such as work and even competition.

Moralism and moralistic rhetoric have figured prominently in the American 2016 election. In an opinion poll conducted by the *Wall Street Journal* and NBC News, Americans were queried about a series of issues prominent in the national conversation and asked which one they found most alarming (Seib, 2015). The answer wasn't terrorism; it wasn't economic inequality. "Decline in moral values" topped the list. Republicans and Independents scored much higher on the item than did Democrats. In Seib's opinion, the earlier Supreme Court decision legalizing same-sex marriage and the rising public acceptance of such is one of the changes in American social values that conservatives are weighing in on. But abortion and the right to carry a gun have come to take center stage in the candidates' debates and be accorded the kind of emotion reserved for beliefs that are held very deeply.

Whereas Seib states that the moralism is strongly evidenced among Republicans but not Democrats in the survey, we could disagree, especially in light of almost religious fervor of the two opposing Democratic candidates on subjects ranging from economic inequality, gun control, and the death penalty.

A carryover from Puritanism, moralism is indeed one of the singular features of American society. Sociologist John Tropman (1989), who wrote the classic, "American Values and Social Welfare," defined moralism as the tendency to be judgmental about affairs and events. So pervasive is this notion to Americans, that poverty becomes a moral issue and money becomes the focus of moral judgment, according to Tropman. Time and again, the issues of responsibility and fault have been major concerns in addressing social problems. These themes generate one of the central social welfare conflicts—punishment versus compassion.

Punitiveness is the negative side of moralism. Punitiveness, as Grimsrud and Zehr (2002) suggest, is an issue having to do with the values by which human beings shape their lives. The paradigm of retributive justice that dominates Western criminal justice is a recipe for alienation. Over the past decade we have seen the construction of new jails and prisons expand exponentially; the war on drugs and the war on welfare have accompanied the prison growth. From a global perspective, almost half of the world's incarcerated people are confined in penal institutions in the United States (Walmsley, 2013). Over two and a quarter million people are incarcerated in US jails and prisons. One million of the total are incarcerated for drug offenses.

Fortunately, as Grimsrud and Zehr further indicate, present-day alternatives to retributive criminal justice are emerging that reflect the general thrust of "biblical" justice. These initiatives, which are at the compassionate end of the continuum and include victim-offender reconciliation programs and healing circles, are discussed in chapter 6.

We have chosen moralism as the primary American value, first because of its historic roots, and second because this theme underpins the other dominant US values—individualism, the work ethic, and equal opportunity (see Hutson, 2012b). Think of the appeal of the "self-made man" on this side of the Atlantic who might be looked down on as *nouveau riche* in other parts of the world. Virtually all the candidates running for nomination by their political parties in the 2016 campaign proudly related their stories of a rise from "rags to riches." Donald Trump's attempt to join the club, however, was lampooned far and wide. "It has not been easy for me. It has not been easy for me. . . . My father gave me a small loan of $1 million" (Trump, 2015). And Jeb Bush's sense of entitlement turned out to be a liability rather than an asset.

In this section, we have placed moralism on one end of the continuum and compassion on the other. Let us now consider compassion, which we might define as sympathy for the underdog. The World Values Survey (2015) is helpful in its finding from a survey of values worldwide. In a summary of the findings, the authors of the survey note that as long as physical survival remains uncertain, the desire for physical and economic security tends to take higher priority than democracy. When basic physiological and safety needs are fulfilled, there is a growing emphasis on self-expression values. The self-expression values are defined as those that "give high priority to environmental protection, growing tolerance of foreigners, gays and lesbians and gender equality, and rising demands for participation in decision-making in economic and political life." Cultural values are also influenced by philosophical, political, and religious ideas, such as those carried over from the French revolution, and can consequently be observed especially in countries with a long history of social democratic or socialistic policy. The World Values Survey lists Sweden, Norway, Japan, Germany, France, Switzerland, Czech Republic, Slovenia, and some English speaking countries as nations that score high on values of self-expression.

Compared to the United States, Swedish respondents to the survey were much more likely to stress the importance of leisure time and to mention self-expression as desirable for children, while Americans much more often stressed the values of religious faith and hard work for children.

## WORK VERSUS LEISURE

The right to work—implying the right to be provided with a job—and the right to leisure are embodied in the UN (1948) Universal Declaration on Human Rights (refer to chapter 5). Neither of these rights is recognized in the US Constitution as a given.

Work, in the sense of the work ethic, is one of the oldest and most enduring (if not endearing) of the American cultural attributes. The notion of the work ethic encompasses the traits that the typical employer desires: punctuality, efficiency, and productivity. Workers deficient in these qualities will be eliminated. This impulse has its roots in the religious beliefs of the early colonists, the Puritans, beliefs later bolstered in the secular sayings of Benjamin Franklin.

The value placed on hard work is closely tied to moralism. Few ideas dominate western political and social discourse as much as the idealized work ethic—the view that all who are able-bodied and of working age have a moral obligation to work and that they are lazy or pathological if they do not (Schram, Soss, & Fording, 2014).

Without launching into a historical thesis, we will briefly set forth the principles described so brilliantly by the German sociologist Max Weber (1958/1905) in his classic, *The Protestant Ethic and the Spirit of Capitalism*. Weber compared work productivity levels in Protestant and Catholic regions of Germany, and elsewhere, as evidence for his theory correlating Protestantism and capitalism. Protestantism emphasized the autonomy of the individual and repudiated dependence on the Church, priesthood, and ritual, according to Weber. The qualities of self-discipline, hard work, and communal service were viewed as a likely sign of salvation. Martin Luther's belief in work as a "calling" gave Protestantism a singularly practical bent. John Calvin, who was Luther's counterpart in France and later Switzerland, provided the first great systematic formulation of the Reformation faith. Taking Luther's argument one step further, Calvin introduced the notion of predestination into the Protestant vocabulary. Predestination is the doctrine of God's election or choice of souls to salvation or damnation. The interpretation of predestination, carried by way of England and Scotland (through the preaching of John Knox) to America, was that those predestined to salvation could be identified in this life through the evidence of their wealth. Although one's fate was sealed, in a sense, Calvinist philosophy posited that indications of this fate could be detected on earth. Using this line of reasoning, the wealthy could justify not only their wealth but also their exploitation of workers to accumulate it (Day, 2012). The belief system also legitimated forcing people to work for their own good. Max Weber described Calvinism as activity that served to increase the glory of God. Waste of time thus was perceived as a deadly sin. And condemnation of the sinner was justified. With its emphasis on individual achievement, frugality, and opportunity, the creed of Calvinism has very much affected the American character, even long after the direct religious connection has been lost. In this vein, the 18th century inventor and atheist Benjamin Franklin espoused the principles of the Protestant work ethic in his often quoted sayings: for example, "early to bed, early to rise makes a man healthy, wealthy, and wise;" "the early bird catches the worm;" "time is money;" "a penny saved is a penny earned."

In locating the roots of the American work ethic, we need to take into account geographical as well as ideological factors. As settlers arrived on the bountiful American landscape, there was no limit to the possibilities for work that needed to be done. So the work ethic was continually rewarded at every turn; in the American colonies, unemployment was unknown. Just how intransigent was the religio-economic ideology is seen in its ability to outlast its religious roots and to influence welfare policy to this very day.

"Americans Are Working So Hard It's Actually Killing People" is the title of an article in *The Nation* (Kaplan, 2014). *Time* magazine recently published a similar story (Dickey, 2015). Observers, according to these articles, have long remarked on the sharp disparity between American and European work habits. According to the Gallup poll, which takes an annual survey of full-time US workers, the average workweek is 47 hours. Salaried workers work more than those paid an hourly wage (Saad, 2014). The survey also showed that a minority of workers (12%) are working two full-time jobs. According to Saad, the length of the work week has steadily risen.

Kaplan (2014) describes in frightening detail conditions in nursing homes in which patients die at night because of the reduction in staff numbers to care for patients on the night shift. The same problem exists in the meatpacking industry where line speed has increased to levels that almost guarantee that life-threatening accidents will occur.

How about time off? By law, every country in the European Union has at least four work weeks of paid vacation (Hess, 2013). Austria, which guarantees workers the most time off, has a legal minimum of 22 paid vacation days and 13 paid holidays each year. Compared to nations in Western Europe, there is no guaranteed vacation time in the United States and the leisure time for US workers is declining. Factors that have led to this development, according to Dickey (2015), are the rise of a service economy full of interchangeable workers; the decline of organized labor; and the fact that vacations are expensive when wages are flat. American workers do typically accrue paid vacations of 10 days after one year on the job. Curiously, many Americans do not use their vacation days. Reasons that workers in a survey give for not taking all their vacation days are that there is too much catch-up work to do when they return and the fact that nobody else can replace them. When they are on vacation, Americans often continue to work on their computers.

Despite the strong work ethic in the United States, most Americans would prefer to have more time for themselves. Forces in the global market combined with the relative weakness of the worker have resulted in the present situation. This is not to say, however, that Americans are the hardest worked people in the world. Work-related stress is so high in China, for example, that people (600,000 a year according to one report) are dying of heart attacks and strokes at relatively young ages (Oster, 2014). Even more shocking, the government praises such workers for their intense loyalty to the country and as models for party members. According to the article, which is in *Business Week*, these attitudes are not a part of Communism but have developed as China has opened the door to capitalistic competition.

In South Korea, according to *The Economist* (2015a), a military-type discipline prevails in businesses, and bosses are treated as father figures. Changing expectations of younger workers who have been educated abroad are forcing some companies, however, to relinquish their corporate demands. Japanese culture, which similarly has a work ethic that would put Americans to shame, is beginning to change as well. The government is making an effort to reduce the death toll from overwork—the term *karoshi* means dying at your desk. Support centers are being set up at work to help reduce the death toll (Oster). And families who could show that their loved ones committed suicide due to extreme conditions at work have been compensated.

Indeed, a focal point of American culture is work and preparation for work. Through one's occupation or profession, an individual gains status and a sense of self importance. Since 1996, when welfare reform was introduced under the Clinton administration, millions of adults and their children were removed from the welfare rolls. The purpose was to get their parents, mostly single mothers, off the welfare rolls and into work. The salient value of the work ethic in American society was also seen in the earned income tax credit which is a blessing to so many, is shown by Schram et al., (2014) to be another way to strengthen work incentives for the poor (see chapter 7). In recent years as well, families eligible to receive Supplemental Nutrition Assistance Programs (SNAP, formerly known as food stamps) must register for work or lose their benefits.

In a professional visit to South Korea in 2003, van Wormer learned about a society with a work ethic so strong that much of the fun of childhood seemed to be absent. The competition for a place at one of the prestigious universities begins early. As teenagers, students are tutored during most waking hours until their education culminates in rigorous university entrance exams. In late adolescence, students return home from crash courses at midnight only to be awakened for school in the wee hours of the next morning. Private schooling is provided for five additional hours after the regular school day to help students prepare for the university entry exams (*The Economist*, 2015b). This cramming starts around age 13 and lasts 5 years. It is hoped, according to *The Economist* (2015a), the shortage of young people in an aging society is leading to better treatment of youth and should lessen the competition among them. Consistent with the traditional Korean work focus is, of course, the situation in a neighboring country, Japan. An English teacher (Butler, 2003) from Texas who lives in Yamogota, Japan observes:

> It's fair to say that Japanese people are unbelievably busy. Working ten hours a day, and often coming in on days off, they rarely take a vacation of more than three or four days. A straight week is a hedonistic luxury. Students have less than a month for summer vacation, and even then they have all kinds of assignments to do (p. 65).

The Norwegian work ethic is very different. Children there are pampered to keep the stress low. Working in Norway, van Wormer observed that Norwegians are an industrious people, but that much of their work is done off hours—building cabins in the woods, training and grooming their dogs, and washing the windows. Many jobs are only six hours per day; little work is done at Easter, Christmas, and July. The right to leisure is a fiercely guarded right. Yet when productivity is calculated per hour, Norwegians are found to be more productive than Americans (Lakey, 2016).

In France, and Australia too, leisure is one of the top values, as indicated in surveys. Schwartz (2012) analyzed results of the World Values Survey, which measured values related to happiness in samples of people worldwide. Respondents in poor countries, in contrast, did not prioritize leisure as of any importance. This is probably because of their preoccupation with matters more directly related to survival. A set of values closely related to attitudes toward work and leisure are equal opportunity and equality of outcomes. Again there are different levels of belief in one focus over the other, and the preferences are best viewed as along a continuum.

## EQUAL OPPORTUNITY VERSUS EQUALITY

In this section we are talking about a belief system that states "America is the land of opportunity." Opportunity means the opportunity to fail as well as to achieve success. Equality is used here in the European sense of equalizing social benefits and living standards "from the cradle to the grave."

Opportunity is the counterpart not of equality but of inequality in the sense that when taxes are low, economic incentives for business are favorable, income disparities are high, and the climate is ripe for some to "be more equal than others."

The American system of mass education that is relatively accessible and affordable is consistent with the belief in equal opportunity. When we're talking about people's beliefs that success is achieved through hard work, we're tapping into the value system that fuels "the American Dream." Samuel (2012), author of *The American Dream: A Cultural History,* notes that the phrase goes back to 1931, but the ideology behind it was with the first settlers on the American continent and extends through the present time. The idea of perpetual progress across the generations is a taken-for-granted notion that encourages people to try to do better than their parents and sets many up for failure.

Consistent with the North American opportunity ethos are minority-targeted early education programs, job training, and higher educational, "opportunity-enhancing" programs to help disadvantaged individuals compete on an equal footing with more privileged youth.

There is undeniably much truth to the "rags to riches" ideology. With ambition, luck, education, and a support system, refugees and other immigrants often do achieve their dreams. We all know the uplifting stories of immigrants, including political refugees, who have arrived with nothing, couldn't speak the language, and now live in nice homes while their children attend college. Unlike the nations in Europe that have policies geared toward temporary asylum for refugees, the United States historically has encouraged assimilation into US culture, and children born in the United States gain citizenship at birth.

An important distinction needs to be made between values of equality of opportunity (the North American value orientation) and equality of living standards (the Nordic model). Often the impetus toward equality means differential treatment of unlike people to equalize the result. As Blakemore and Warwick-Booth (2013) indicate, conservatives tend to put the stress on opportunity and liberals on equal outcomes. Liberal policies will discriminate positively on behalf of people who are at a disadvantage, such as on the basis of race, gender, or economics.

Consider this news story from Finland as reported in *The Atlantic*—"Finland, Home of the $103,000 Speeding Ticket," Pinsker, 2015). Like other Scandinavian countries, according to the article, Finland imposes fines based on income. So it happened that a wealthy man, his income along with his wealth calculated along with the fine on the policeman's computer, was fined $103,000 for driving over the speed limit! The purpose of this approach? To ensure that the penalty will hurt as much whether you are rich or poor. Sweden, Denmark, Germany, Austria, France, and Switzerland also have some sliding-scale fines in place, while in the United States, flat-rate fines are the norm. The different approaches represent a difference in value systems between these European countries and the United States.

Societies that pride themselves on egalitarianism take an *institutional* approach to social welfare provision. At the opposite end of the continuum is the *residual* or "safety-net" approach characteristic of what we have in the United States. These terms were originally coined by Wilensky and Lebeaux (1958) as ideal-typical constructs to contrast the narrow role the government plays in providing social services in those societies with an approach more overtly geared toward the needs of the people.

In the residually oriented society, of which the United States and Japan are prime examples, a stigma is attached to receiving welfare aid. The causes of welfare clients' difficulties are often seen as rooted in their own malfunctioning—the persons themselves are blamed for problems perceived as stemming from their own inadequacies (Zastrow, 2017). Only when unemployment becomes extremely high overall (such as in the Great Depression) do we begin to reduce the stigma and move from a residual position to an institutional one. Under conditions of mass economic crisis, then, the system rather than the individual receives the blame.

In social welfare, residual thinking leads to the kind of programs in which eligibility is based on proving a need—proving the breakdown of the other systems that should be working. In order to investigate eligibility, officials must be thoroughly familiar with the circumstances of their clients' lives, thereby ensuring that only the deserving poor receive assistance. Programs are deemed successful in terms of reducing rather than expanding the numbers who receive help. Getting the able-bodied off welfare and on the work rolls is the rallying cry. Aid, such as it is, is only provided on a short-term basis for individuals in crisis situations. The values that underpin residual thinking are capitalism, independence, and belief in opportunity.

Welfare spending for the poor has been greatly reduced in recent years. "Welfare spending cut in half since reform"—so reads a headline from CNN Money (Luhby, 2012). One of the central points of welfare reform, according to the article, was to reduce poverty by moving more people into work and promoting self-sufficiency. But given the volatile economy, many of the former welfare recipients have been left without jobs or income.

An *institutional* or social insurance approach to public welfare would provide a very different scenario with regard to aid. The institutional approach is preventive rather than curative, universal rather than particularist. Social welfare, according to this perspective is a necessary and desirable part of the social structure. To provide economic security as an alternative to the historic patterns of inadequate, piecemeal relief is the basic purpose of the welfare state. Why allow people to fall into destitution at all when you can offset poverty at its source? An individual's difficulties, according to this conceptualization, are attributed to causes beyond his or her control.

Programs for the poor such as the Temporary Assistance for Needy Dependent Children (TANF) are criticized for their stigmatizing and punitive implications (Midgley, 2010). We can contrast this program with the British National Health Service or Canadian Medicare, which provide a range of tax-funded medical and health services to all citizens without regard for their ability to pay. In the United States, Social Security and public education are two of the nation's few universal social programs. Both these programs are regarded as rights for the many rather than privileges for the few. As a result, they are willingly funded. Poor people's programs, in contrast, can be abolished in the next political campaign.

The metaphor of the safety net, associated with the residual approach, is in fact a better descriptive term for the institutional mode of social welfare. To grasp the meaning of the metaphor, imagine the trapeze artist losing his or her balance and falling down hundreds of feet to be saved by the safety net below. Without universal health care, there is no safety net at all. The universalist social welfare state, in contrast, does provide a real safety net to the troubled citizen, but for the most part it is not needed at all.

Under the economic pressures of globalization, there is a tendency of convergence in regard to social welfare provisions. Drawing on government data on the high numbers of children in the United Kingdom who live in poverty, Mason (2015) cites experts who recommend an increase in the minimum wage to help families in need. In the Scandinavian countries, in contrast, despite a rise in levels of unemployment, income inequality remains relatively low. So much is equality a Nordic and particularly a Norwegian value, as *The Economist* (2015c) indicates, that even up against the pressures of the global economy associated as it is with higher unemployment, the Nordic countries still manage to maintain a high level of equality in the distribution of income.

In summary, one could say that the residually based society offers avenues of success to "those who can" and will, while providing for only a minimum of protection for persons not in a position to seize the opportunity to achieve success.

## MOBILITY VERSUS STABILITY

A value related to work is the desire to "get ahead," to move upward and onward. A significant proportion of Americans are geographically mobile as well, moving their households every five years. Children will often have attended school in several school systems before they are done. The American ideology promotes a belief in progress; workers are expected to climb the corporate ladder and to be willing to relocate if necessary for career advancement; persons receiving government aid are expected to get training and to quickly gain their independence. Because the United States had been a land of unparalleled resources and opportunity, people who are downwardly mobile or who remain at the bottom are often held responsible for their lowly status.

We are using the term *mobility* to describe more than social and geographical mobility to get at the kind of restlessness that often has been said to typify the American character. Thus from the most widely quoted commentator on early American society, Alexis de Tocqueville (1951/1835), we learn

> America is a land of wonders, in which everything is in constant motion and every change seems an improvement. The idea of novelty there is indissolubly connected with the idea of amelioration. (p. 18)

Thom Hartmann's (1997, 2015) hypothesis of genetic traits carried over from hunter and farmer societies gives some credence to the notion that societies that evolved out of an agricultural tradition tend to be more stationary and less adventure-seeking than societies (or tribes) of hunters. Farmers, according to Hartmann, are cautious, not easily bored, and patient. Hunters are more impulsive and multi-focused on the environment. Descendants of hunters as schoolchildren find it hard to concentrate, are easily distracted, highly energetic, and restless. They are liable to be diagnosed as having ADHD (Attention Deficit Hyperactivity Disorder). Significantly, Hartmann's most recent book is entitled *ADHD and the Edison Gene*. Children and adults with this genetic characteristic are inclined to excel in many ways beyond the classroom, especially in sales and other competitive fields. ADHD is prevalent in America but rare in Japan. As Hartmann notes, the ancestors of the Japanese people lived in a purely agricultural society for at least 6,000 years.

Empirical research has validated the behavior styles among hunters and farmers in Kenya. Scientists have shown that an ADHD-associated version of the gene DRD4 is associated with better health in nomadic tribesmen, and yet may cause malnourishment in their settled cousins (BMC Evolutionary Biology, 2008). This gene is likely to be involved in impulsivity, reward anticipation, and addiction. When the men with this gene leave the nomadic situation, their personality traits that made them successful in the wilderness are apparently disadvantages to them when living a more sedentary lifestyle.

Europeans view Americans and Australians as "brash and risk-taking," as Hartmann suggests. Consider the types of people who would have fled the "old world" to take a dangerous journey across the Atlantic. These adventurers, presumably, would have carried with them the genetic material that might have caused their descendants to crave mobility over a more routine lifestyle and competition over cooperation.

## COMPETITION VERSUS COOPERATION

One need not search far in the American popular press for evidence of competition. (Just glance through the advertisements.) Typically there are stories in any given week celebrating personal and team victories in events ranging from sports to spelling bees; the win-or-lose outcomes of courtroom battles; TV reality shows that feature survival exploits or intense dating competitions; and intense pressure among youth to gain entrance into certain elite colleges. In other words, competition is everywhere in a society that prides itself on being the world's superpower (Figure 2.2).

Perhaps we should have labeled this value personal achievement instead of competition. The fact is that competition may be the means rather than the end to the kind of high personal achievement that is so valued in American society. To win, nevertheless, Americans from childhood are taught to compete. Writing on the US system of education, Diane Ravitch (2014), who worked as assistant director of the US Department of Education under President George H. W. Bush, likens the emphasis on student and school competition as a spur to learning to the tenets beliefs of the marketplace economy. She sees the rise of the charter school system as a deliberate effort to replace public education with a privately managed, free-market system of schooling. Proposals for a voucher system of schooling pits charter schools against regular public schools in attracting students. Many services in these new schools are privatized to reduce costs. Free technological equipment may be provided along with programs containing advertising that students then watch in class. As charter schools proliferate, the teachers' unions are effectively smashed.

**FIGURE 2.2.** The value of competition is revealed symbolically in this bike race. Photo by Rupert van Wormer.

Mass testing programs compare individual children, schools, and whole school systems on the basis of standardized measures of achievement. We can compare this approach with one of cooperation such as characterizes education in Finland. Advocates of cooperation favor helping students individually to proceed at their own pace to learn what they need to learn and want to learn. Educators today are looking to Finland, as the students there score the highest in the world in international testing. As Ravitch notes, little testing is actually done in the Finnish system; the highly paid teachers determine the curriculum.

The best way to discover a nation's values is to move into the country; learn the language; work in an indigenous, non-academic setting; use the local services; and above all else, send your children to the local schools. In Norway, one of the authors (van Wormer) did all these things. Although she was more interested in seeing the fjords than in studying values, it was the striking uniqueness in Scandinavian culture that has had the most lasting impact. The theme of the Norwegian and Scandinavian cultural ethos can be summed up in one word, *egalitarianism*. See Figure 2.3 to see how Norwegians celebrate their independence day.

On the competition-to-cooperation continuum, the Norwegians are far over to the co-operation end. This value (*samarbeid*, literally "to work together") is instilled in the family in early childhood and reinforced throughout school life; it permeates every aspect of culture. The school anti-bullying programs originated in Norway; in fact, bullying in Norway is exceedingly rare. One brief note from van Wormer's personal files illustrates the point:

> My twelve year-old son returned from his first day of school. He seemed amazed. "Mom, a boy fell down on the playground," he said. "He was crying and crying; the other children went over to him and comforted him."

**FIGURE 2.3.** On May 19 is National Constitution Day, which is a celebration led by school children who parade with their teachers. © Shutterstock, photo by Paul D Smith.

This comment was of course as much a comment on life on the American school playground as it was on the Norwegian.

The research of Shavitt, Johnson, and Zhang (2011) provides the kind of empirical verification of cross-cultural differences concerning individual achievement that is a rare find in the literature. The comparison is between American and Danish students. Danes, as the authors indicate, share a similar language and culture with Swedes and Norwegians; all three groups look down on conspicuous success and bragging. Denmark and Norway additionally share a ubiquitous, unwritten social modesty code; this code is reflected in interpersonal norms as well as in benevolent social welfare policies toward the least fortunate in society. The American notion of equality is actually equal opportunity. This notion is reflected in the tax system and resource allocation, as the authors further suggest.

In their review of the research findings on values related to achievement, Shavitt et al. (2011) found that in Denmark, achievement goals are not a high priority. In open-ended responses and quantitative ratings, US individuals discussed the importance of achievement more frequently and evaluated achievement values more highly than Danes did. Like Norwegians, Danes do not appreciate displays of wealth or boasting. An earlier study by Nelson and Shavitt (2002) on cultural differences as depicted in local advertisements provided this telling illustration found in beer slogans:

> *Probably* the best beer in town.
>
> —Carlsberg Beer advertising slogan

> Best-selling beer in America
>
> —U.S. beer slogan (p. 439)

## INDIVIDUALISM VERSUS COLLECTIVISM

If you compare mainstream American value orientations with traditional Asian values, the Asians would seem to be more communitarian and Americans more individualistic (Appleby et al., 2010). The United States, in fact, is especially noted for its individualism, in some ways (mainly to do with competition and self-reliance) and for its conformity in others (for example, teens conforming to peer pressure).

Shavitt et al. (2011) draw a distinction between individualistic and collectivistic, or independent and interdependent, cultural attributes. In individualistic cultures, people tend to see themselves as independent or separate from others and to subordinate the goals of their in-groups to their own personal goals. In collectivistic or interdependent cultures, in contrast, people tend to prefer interdependent relationships to others and to subordinate their personal goals to those of their in-groups.

Although Americans tend to conform to their peers (to work rules, for example, submitting to urinalysis and even lie-detector tests for employment), they are noted for "rugged individualism." According to Anthropologist Alvin Wolfe (2001), the American cultural creed extols the virtues of self-reliance and rugged individualism. The belief that each person shapes his or her own destiny, denial of structural causes of poverty, blaming of victims, and acclaim of the wealthy as heroes are all a part of this cultural ethos. This ethos is embodied in American tradition.

In the 1830s, the French social philosopher, Alexis de Tocqueville (1951, orig. 1835) characterized the people on this continent as individualists. The risk to the American character, said de Tocqueville, was that in the future, isolation might prevail. Still, today, the primary value dimension that sums up the cultural climate in the United States is this trait of individualism, this sense of "I" rather than "we." The focus on self at the personal level is matched on the political level by unilateral foreign policy.

On this side of the Atlantic, welfare programs are geared to specific individuals or groups who are functioning poorly. (In Europe the focus is more on the population as a whole). In the United States, social welfare programs that focus on changing the internal person, rather than the external system, have been favored. This is not to say that a collective spirit has not prevailed at various key periods in American history. Reisch (2014) provides careful documentation to show that public opinion in the post-World War I era favored strong government intervention; surveys of that time reveal that a substantial portion of the population thought in collectivist terms. He contrasts the collective spirit of progressive periods in US history such as the mid-1960s with the denial of social responsibility surrounding the continuing attacks on welfare benefits of today. (Chapter 3 will expound on this argument further.)

In his book on group dynamics, Levi (2017) draws a sharp contrast between the American emphasis in business on individual competition and the Japanese emphasis on cooperation through teams. Americans are bent on fostering a competitive spirit in the child and encouraging self-sufficiency from an early age, whereas the Japanese cultivate a sense of group identity and solidarity. Unlike in American society, however, social structure in Japan is hierarchical.

Collectivist ideology accords prime importance to collective forms of association in which people share resources and decision making (Levi, 2017). The custom of mutual aid among African Americans as a carryover from African tribal culture is an example of this tradition.

## INDEPENDENCE VERSUS INTERCONNECTEDNESS

Independence is closely related to individualism in the same way as interconnectedness is related to collectivism. Within the family as well as society, Americans strive to be fiercely independent. The word, *codependency*, which signifies a too-close emotional dependence, accordingly, has taken on extremely negative connotations. Parents train their children to be independent and to one day leave the "nest." The myth of independence suggests that each individual is singularly in control of his or her own destiny, according to Tropman (1989). As people age, they fight to hang on to their independence as long as possible. The value of independence has important implications for social welfare. Prolonged dependence on government help is actively discouraged and many Americans refuse to accept benefits because of personal pride. "The Lord helps those who help themselves" is a commonly heard refrain.

The sense of interconnectedness is a staple of traditional indigenous culture. The Native American (and Canadian) Medicine Wheel exemplifies the wholeness of all life. The Medicine Wheel teaches about the cycle of life. Don Coyhis, the director of White Bison, a substance abuse treatment center, incorporates the wisdom of the Medicine Wheel in his treatment programming. In Indian country, the heart of the sobriety movement, as explained by Coyhis and Simonelli (2008), revolves around a return to cultural values and folkways. Among these values are: a strong emphasis on *being* not doing and on cooperation over competition; group emphasis; work only to meet one's needs; nonmaterialism; right brain orientation; and to live in harmony with nature. The theme of these values is social interconnectedness.

## MATERIALISM VERSUS SPIRITUALITY

The United States is clearly a capitalist nation, and status is accorded to those with high earning power or, in upper-upper class settings, to those who have access to inherited wealth. Americans may be accused on occasion of flaunting their wealth. The number of toys that many American children have would be considered in some circles obscene. And at the macro level, American capitalism is a cause of both resentment and emulation in every part of the globe.

Throughout her writings, bell hooks captures the essence of the search for meaning that sadly has caused so many to worship at the throne of money. In *Salvation: Black People and Love*, bell hooks (2001) describes how the focus on material gain has affected the black family: "Like the culture as a whole, masses of Black people now look to material success as the sole measure of value and meaning in life . . . Gaining access to material privilege will never satisfy needs of the spirit. Those hungers persist and haunt us" (p. 15).

Otherworldly, Americans are not. From the traditional Native perspective, Coyhis and Simonelli (2008) define mainstream culture as geared toward the "seen world" (p. 1932):

> Native understanding of the "seen" and the "unseen" world is one expression of spirituality that Native people in recovery often respond to. . . .
>
> An interconnectedness teaching that has guided many Native people in their search for recovery and healing says, "The honor of one is the honor of all, and the pain of one is the pain of all." (pp.1932–1933)

Although most Americans are not otherworldly, the United States as a nation has a strong religious character. In a survey by the Pew Research Center of people from 44 countries, it was found that people in richer nations are less likely than those in poorer nations to say religion plays a very important role in their lives (Gao, 2015). But Americans are more likely than their counterparts in economically advanced nations to deem religion very important. More than half (54%) of Americans said religion was very important in their lives, much higher than the share of people in Canada (24%), Australia (21%), and Germany (21%), the next three wealthiest economies that were surveyed. Another Pew survey found that 53% of Americans say that belief in God is a prerequisite for being moral and having good values, which was far higher than that found in the European countries surveyed yet far below the surveyed populations in the Middle East (Gao, 2015).

Evangelical Christianity has made a strong comeback in recent years as reflected in interests of many of the Republican voters in the 2016 presidential campaign. Social workers often work with clients who are evangelical in their personal beliefs or who are influenced by family members who adhere to a strict religious code. Such values, when shared, can be a major source of strength for the family and comfort in times of loss. But conflict may arise through cultural clash and rigidity as well.

Organized religion is often much more visible in the United States than is spirituality, yet among young people, more and more are identifying themselves as spiritual but not religious. Spirituality as defined by Canda and Furman (2010) "refers to a universal and fundamental human quality involving the search for a sense of meaning, purpose, morality, well-being, and profundity in relationships with ourselves, others, and ultimate reality, however understood" (p. 3).

## NUCLEAR FAMILY VERSUS EXTENDED FAMILY

*The extended family*: such a family conjures up the image of *My Big Fat Greek Wedding* with dozens of cousins talking all at once, the African American three-generation household, and the traditional Irish wake. For the child growing up in such a commonwealth of relatives, what a life! Think of the nuclear family, in contrast, and images of small, isolated family groupings in large spaces flood the mind.

The size of the American family, in fact, is shrinking. Whereas four children used to be the norm back when family-size data was first recorded in 1976, now two-child families are most common. Childlessness (15% in 2014) actually is at its lowest point in a decade, according to census data; this is because more women with graduate degrees are having children, often at older ages than before (Levin, 2015). Key factors in reducing family size are the expense of having children; the longer working hours; career ambitions by many women; and the lack of intergenerational support in raising the kids. In addition, since the last century, the necessity of geographical moves to "where the jobs are" leaves the older generation and aunts and uncles behind. In terms of economic support, the vulnerable members of the family, such as older relatives and people with disabilities, are more likely to be supported through social welfare provisions than by their kinfolk.

Throughout the non-industrialized world, kinship arrangements are very different. Marriage may be viewed as a union between families rather than individuals. Residences may be shared intergenerationally. In India, for example, the social institution that is key to Hindu life is the joint family (Chadda & Deb, 2013; Nimmaggada & Martell, 2008). Within Indian society, social workers who provide counseling or other help to troubled family members, such as to those in a family dealing with mental health issues, may find that there is a sense of fatalism about disease but that they can draw on the family as a strong support system. Although trained in Western models of individualism, Indian social workers routinely adapt these foreign models to the norms of the local culture.

For a compelling description of a Bedouin-Arab social worker's role as conflict mediator in complicated marital situations, some of which involved polygamous relationships, see Al-Krenawi and Graham (2008). The emphasis in the intervention, consistent with Arab cultural norms, was on the good of the family rather than the good of the individual.

The very form that the social work takes comes to reflect the society in which it exists. Kreitzer (2012) notes that the American NASW code of ethics has sometimes been modified to better reflect the values of another country. New Zealanders, for example, wrote their ethical code in order to express the strong family values of their indigenous population, the Maori people. Ghana, in contrast, simply adopted the code without adapting it to their own priorities.

Gillum (2009) recommends that social workers be cognizant of African American cultural perspectives and approach these from a model that focuses on assets rather than deficits, while recognizing the importance of extended support systems in the African American community. Evidence indicates, furthermore, that African American women coping with domestic violence may look to the church, as well as the family, for support. Increasingly, social workers trained in a strengths perspective look to the wider family as a major resource for all families. In child welfare situations, kinship care can be relied on as the traditional, informal arrangement. This arrangement is preferred over adoption by the Association of Black Social Workers for children in need of care (Suppes & Wells, 2012).

Let us now turn from our overview of US cultural values to a look at how these social values are translated into social policy.

## THE SHAPING OF US SOCIAL POLICY

A major goal for internationally oriented social workers is to develop the competence to influence public policy on issues relevant to social and economic development. This development is not the sort of corporate economic growth benefiting only a nation's ruling classes. Rather it is the enhancement of the living conditions for all the nation's people. We can define social policy as "the activities and principles of a society that. . . . includes plans and programs in education, health care, crime and corrections, economic security, and social welfare" (*The Social Work Dictionary*, Barker, 2014, p. 399). When we think of social policies we often think of government-sponsored plans and programs for the school systems, health care, crime and corrections, economic security, and social welfare benefits.

A variety of historical, cultural, and political forces shape social welfare policy. In our delineation of US value constructs, the work ethic emerged as one of the most enduring themes in social welfare history. Relevant to this ethic, programs that require work or are work-related (unemployment benefits and social security) have more political clout than programs that are not work related (aid to families in need). The most vigorously challenged programs involve aid to able-bodied people.

Because mobility and competitiveness are basic tenets in US society, workers are expected to be willing to compete with fellow workers and even relocate to "get ahead." Pay raises based on merit rather than seniority reinforce the sense of competition. Those unwilling to do so are not highly regarded.

The emphasis on personal achievement and independence encourages citizens to strive for success. Those who fall behind may be regarded as losers and treated accordingly. Proposals designed to equalize the distribution of wealth predictably make little headway in a competitive social structure. In the United States, lack of compassion for the poor is compounded by the ethos of moralism. Because poor people are stigmatized and even blamed for their circumstances, there is no strong working class political movement and no labor party with a platform of social benefits.

As the tides of political change come and go, and as the public mood shifts, so do the social policies. Once ingrained, they tend to reinforce the social values that shaped them in the first place. The cycle is complete with values shaping policies, and policies shaping values. One could make the case, for example, that the value of equality of opportunity led to racial integration, while the policy of integration greatly furthered the belief in equality. The value-policy configuration is further impacted by economic forces. Values such as a religious belief that hard work is good for the soul can promote economic investment and growth; economic growth, in turn, can reinforce the Protestant work ethic. At the same time, the religious value of compassion can influence a willingness to donate to charity to help others who have fallen on hard times.

The economic and welfare crises caused by the sudden huge influx of refugees arriving into the nation test the levels of compassion of a nation. Other crises related to global markets similarly had an impact on social welfare programming. *The Economist* (2015c), a conservative British magazine, compares Norway, suffering great losses from the drop in oil prices, with Sweden. Sweden, according to the article, has "reinvigorated its model by shrinking its state, allowing private firms to run its schools, hospitals and surgeries, and reducing its tax burden." In contrast, Norway continues to maintain "its over-ripe welfare state" (p. 69). As the article continues:

> The state is undermining the work ethic as most people enjoy a 37-hour week, and three-day weekends are common. . . . Norwegians have coined a verb, "to nav", meaning to get money from NAV, the state benefits agency. (p. 69)

*The Economist* recommends that Norway learn from Sweden about how to put prosperity ahead of what we might term compassion. We should also explain that since Sweden has joined the EU, its policies have had to change in conformity with EU principles. We also should add that Americans who live in Sweden still see the society as very people-friendly with free college tuition and a housing stipend available for students, mass transit everywhere, and collective goods that boost the middle class (see Heberlein, 2016).

We can see how economic policies and social values intersect in the examples of Norway, where compassion overrides the work ethic, and Sweden, a very liberal nation but one that has compromised based on forces in the global economy.

In the United States, we can see how economic policies and social values intersect in the preference for means-tested welfare programs. Such programs, only available for the poor and minorities, tend to be stigmatized and generate more opposition than support from the rest of the public and the politicians they elect. As Piven and Cloward (1993) correctly observed some years ago, the effects of the stigmatization are far-reaching and dampen support for other welfare state programs. Citizens resent paying taxes for services for which they themselves receive no benefit. Accordingly, fragmented initiatives that reach only narrowly defined groups, such as affirmative action programming, are subject to being underfunded and phased out over time.

## SOCIAL WORK VALUES AND US VALUES

A profession that emerged out of a socio-religious ethos with the goal of helping society's vulnerable people, social work has promoted values that generally reflect a more compassionate stance than that of many other professional groups This is most clearly revealed in the NASW-US Code of Ethics (2017).

So referring back to our list of American value dimensions, the contradictions between social work's altruism and the American creed become more apparent. Competition as opposed to co-operation, materialism versus spirituality—the contradictions abound. Popple and Leighninger

(2014) exemplify such value conflict in the societal reluctance to provide adequate care for poor, especially non-working families. The objective of discouraging adult dependency is addressed, according to these authors, by the values of individualism and work.

In its ideal incarnation the welfare state is most congruent with social work values, beliefs, and principles; social insurance such as social security programs; universal as opposed to residualist benefits; and a collectivist orientation.

Among the core values of social work, the most prominent and perhaps least well understood is the value of social justice. In the toolkit distributed by NASW (2016) for March, which is the National Social Work Month, "Forging Solutions out of Challenges" is the year's theme. Some of the challenges listed on the website that relate to human rights are

> After earthquakes, floods and other disasters social workers are on the front lines, helping survivors get needed services and handle stress and anxiety. In fact, more than 40 percent of mental health volunteers trained by the Red Cross are social workers. Social workers are also active in organizations such as Doctors without Borders that address disasters that occur abroad.
>
> Social workers work with community organizations, legislators, the public and others to ensure equal rights for all, including women, people of different races and cultures and people who are LGBT. (p. 2)

NASW (2015) supports peaceful, nonviolent resolution to conflict and diplomacy instead of war and advocacy for peace by the profession. This position is articulated in the NASW book of policy statements (*Social Work Speaks*). Contained in the chapter, "Peace and Social Justice" is a quotation by Martin Luther King that peace is not merely a long, distant goal but a means by which we arrive at that goal. This position is consistent with policy positions that the social work profession has taken over the years on a number of issues, included among them poverty, the death penalty, use of violence against children, and human rights.

The core social work values and broad ethical principles that serve as guidelines are codified in NASW's (2017) Code of Ethics. The values it sets forth (for example, social service, social justice, integrity, competence, respect for human dignity, the importance of client self-determination) are embodied in the design of our social work curriculum as well (Robbins, Chatterjee, & Canda, 2012). The Code of Ethics is available online at https://www.socialworkers.org/pubs/code/default.asp. Pay special attention to Section 6.04: (c) which states

> Social workers should promote conditions that encourage respect for cultural and social diversity within the United States and globally. Social workers should promote policies and practices that demonstrate respect for difference, support the expansion of cultural knowledge and resources, advocate for programs and institutions that demonstrate cultural competence, and promote policies that safeguard the rights of and confirm equity and social justice for all people.

This statement, although it refers to "rights" instead of human rights, is the most germane to the focus of this book. The international code of ethics of IFSW (2017) is available at www.ifsw.org. You can also find on this website the codes of ethics of membership nations. A scanning of the codes of ethics from the United States, Britain, Scandinavian countries, and Australia reveals that the codes from Denmark and Britain contain the strongest statements on human rights. Characteristically, the Norwegian code expresses concern for children, Sweden's places adherence to human rights ahead of local laws. And we learn from Kreitzer (2012) that India rewrote their code of ethics to include a recognition of respect for the intrinsic worth of all human and non-human life, consistent with Indian cultural beliefs.

In its definition of social work, the IFSW (2017) includes several terms—for example, empowerment, liberation of people, and human rights—that represent fundamental humanitarian values of social work, values that are culturally universal. Social work's dedication to the moral principle of empowerment can function as a unifying concept to transcend the individualistic values found in western textbooks.

Let us now consider how cultural values are played out when aspects of social work practice and social work education are transplanted from one nation to the next. In the following international descriptions, note the ubiquity of far-right policies associated with the global market.

## CHILE: FOCUS ON HISTORICAL DEVELOPMENTS

The country of Chile extends all the way down to the tip of South America. It is ranked as number 38 on the United Nations (2017) Human Development Index, which places it with countries that are at the highest level of human development. The credit for the birth of the social work profession not only in Chile but in the whole of South America goes to Alejandro del Rio, a doctor and leader in the field of public health, and his friend and advisor René Sand, a renowned Belgian physician (Kendall, 1989; Saracostti, Reininger, & Parada, 2012). In 1925, at the invitation of Sand, Alejandro del Rio visited the newly founded school of social work at Brussels, and upon his return to Chile, he set up a comparable two year course, with government help, at Santiago (Healy, 2008). Initially, as Finn and Jacobson (2008) inform us, European influences predominated. However, by the 1940s, with the establishment of a Chilean-US exchange, American texts were translated into Spanish, and a US model of professional social work came to dominate. Social work in Argentina followed the same pattern (Healy, 2008).

All this was to change in the 1960s in conjunction with radical social forces that swept through Latin America, as well as the rest of the world, during this time. In Chile, the urban poor, workers, students, and teachers came together "to claim voice, space, and political power" (Finn, 2002, p. 454). Having lost faith in the capacity of their official leaders to bring development to their countries, grass-roots organizations formed to work among the poorest and most needy groups of this society. Imported models of social work were discarded. Under the pedagogical leadership of Paulo Freire (see chapter 1), Chilean social work education was revolutionized. Freire's influence on social work theory extended far beyond Chile's borders.

Chilean social work thrived under the socialist Allende government. All this was to come to an untimely end, however, when a CIA-backed military coup launched 17 years of dictatorial rule. Concomitant with the dismantling of the progressive Chilean welfare state, social work faculty and students were among those detained and "disappeared." Others suffered as well through elimination of the pension system and the workers' compensation fund, which was initiated to lower the cost of labor (Borzutzky, 2002). This transformation of the administration of social security funds to the private sector was to be widely touted in the United States as a model program.

In the 1980s, the IFSW, with its keen interest in human rights, focused an intensive campaign on Chile with investigations to locate the missing social workers (Healy, 2008). Then in the 1990s, no longer under the control of a brutal military regime, Chile became a freer society, although one ridden with social and economic inequalities and with a weakened sense of solidarity, according to Borutzky. Structural adjustment requirements of the international banking system have had a negative impact on the social welfare system of Chile, as on all debtor nations of the global economy. The term *structural adjustment* refers to the set of adjustments or so-called reforms that are required by international banks as a condition for future loans and for refinancing on payments due on existing loans. Under Chile's market economy, such adjustments have placed particularly heavy burdens on women (Finn, 2002).

According to Amnesty International's (2017), annual human rights report, plans are under way for a new constitution to replace the one from the previous military dictatorship. Some trials have been held convicting former military officers of torture and killing under the old regime but information and documentation gathered by the commission on politically motivated torture and imprisonment during the Pinochet era remained classified as confidential, even from the judiciary, and therefore secret for 50 years and unavailable to those seeking justice for the victims. The annual report on Chile also noted that there were renewed allegations of excessive use of force and arbitrary detention against indigenous populations during police operations. On the positive side, following trends in other countries, same sex marriage was legalized, and there has been some progress toward granting women reproductive rights.

Despite the economic retrogression in Chile, the legacy of Friere's collectivist work that started among the peasants and clergy lives on. His teachings have inspired educators and organizers throughout the world, educators such as bell hooks, who argues so eloquently that learning is teaching and teaching is learning, and activists such as Mary Bricker-Jenkins of the welfare rights movement. Friere's message that social work must be understood in the context of social structure and of the importance of linking theory and action through praxis shaped the mission of social work throughout Latin America.

## THE CARIBBEAN: FOCUS ON SOCIAL WORK PRACTICE

The Caribbean is a multi-ethnic, multilingual group of islands and mainland territories that were once colonies of the Netherlands, England, France, and Spain. Jamaica is ranked 94 out of the 188 countries ranked by the United Nations (2017) Human Development Index. Although Haiti, Puerto Rico, and Cuba are within this region, our focus in this section is on the English-speaking regions, as these regions are members of IFSW and IASSW. Social work educators from these regions are actively involved in international conferences.

At a special presentation on critical issues in Caribbean social work at the CSWE Annual Program Meeting led by Lynne Healy (2003), an interesting discussion ensued during the question-answer stage. The issue had to do with offenders from Jamaica and other Caribbean countries who were deported after serving time in the United States for drug violations. Because the ex-convicts had been criminalized in prison as a result of America's war on drugs, their return has resulted in gang violence and organized crime. One country even tried to refuse to accept them back until the United States put pressure on the government. Jamaica was advised to place these unwelcome ex-convicts in special prisons. The tragedy, as pointed out by the discussants, was that migrants who had gotten caught up in mostly minor violations, then became hardened and far more antisocial after a stint in a US prison. The implications for their social workers involved helping family members deal with family violence and other related problems. The situation shows how a policy based on values in one part of the world can have unanticipated consequences somewhere else.

Human rights violations as reported by Amnesty International (2015c) consist of police killings, domestic violence against women, attacks on gays and lesbians, and mistreatment of children in juvenile institutions. The report confirms a very high homicide rate and influence of gang delinquency in Jamaica.

Related to globalization, the negative impact of structural adjustment programs on social welfare systems of debtor nations is clearly evidenced in Jamaica. Under structural adjustment incentives, cutbacks in public services in health, education, housing, and public assistance are mandated to make loan repayment the priority. In Jamaica, the impact of structural adjustment mandates on social welfare, and therefore on the burgeoning profession of social work, were especially pronounced. Between the late 1970s and 1980s, the percentage of public expenditure on debt payments rose from 17.7% to about 40% while the percentage on education dropped significantly as did spending on all the social services, including health care (Healy, 2008; *The Guardian*, 2013). As the debt level mounted in the 1980s, this gave the IMF and World Bank the leverage to impose large-scale structural adjustment policies. The impact was devastating. During the 1980s, the level of health care declined as the number of registered nurses fell by 60%. Currency devaluation made food costs skyrocket, while the International Monetary Fund (IMF) held down wages. Formal control over economic policy has shifted from Jamaica to the world banking system. Other nations in the Caribbean face similar problems with indebtedness that is beyond their ability to pay.

Professional social work education was introduced in 1961 at the Mona, Jamaica campus of the University of West Indies (Baker & Maxwell, 2012). The field of community development is an area in which the English-speaking Caribbean was an early pioneer. The social work department today is in a consortium with other programs and has a large, impressively qualified faculty and conducts vibrant programming in the area of violence prevention and child welfare. Degrees are offered at the undergraduate and graduate levels. (Read about the department at www.mona.uwi.edu.)

## SOUTH KOREA: FOCUS ON SOCIAL VALUES

Globalization has brought much prosperity to the countries of East Asia, especially to China, where labor is cheap and the workers industrious, but also to Japan and South Korea due to their high-quality exports. At the end of the Korean War, South Korea was poorer than India; by the 1990s it had joined the Organization for Economic Cooperation and Development (OECD), the club of the advanced industrialized nations. Stiglitz and Greenwald (2014) credit the South Korean government with the active steps taken to ensure that the rising tide of growth did, in fact, lift most boats. In the resulting economic environment, business flourished. The bubble did burst in 1997, however, a fact that Stiglitz attributes in part to stringent IMF policies, such as the suggestion that Korea borrow money from foreign bankers. This act increased its vulnerability to world markets and to further pressure from the IMF. Fortunately, in recent years the economy has rebounded. South Korea is ranked 17 on the United Nations (2015) Human Development Index.

Canda and Furman (2009) attribute the Korean philosophical belief in a balanced social order to the traditional worldview of Confucianism. Balanced order can be achieved only when the needs of humanity and nature are in order. Neo-Confucianism emphasizes that everyone is capable of becoming a sage through cultivation of their true nature through diligent study and effort. For social workers who work with East Asians and Asian Americans, Canda and Furman state it is important to understand the influence of this social ethical system. Buddhism, which is the predominant religion in South Korea, emphasizes compassion. Korean social work is built on this principle.

A study of the results of the World Values Survey (2015) gives us clues about the patterns of a culture, although the researchers do not provide any analysis of the results. We can compare differences in the values across the countries surveyed. A comparison between citizens of South Korea and those of the United States revealed that both countries valued hard work for the children as very important at around 65% of the respondents. Yet almost twice as many Koreans as Americans stated that work was very important. For children, religious faith was stressed more by Americans than by the Koreans surveyed. Two items that were stressed far more than Americans as important attributes for children were tolerance and using one's imagination.

Speaking at the same conference, Sung Ja Song (2002) traced the roots of Korean social work to the aftermath of the Korean War in the 1950s. Early programs were for refugees and people in need of public relief. Following the mass unemployment that occurred in 1997, social workers and members of non-governmental organizations have played a key role in distributing aid to people. Today, amazingly, as Song indicates, there are 62 social welfare departments in two-year colleges, 103 departments in four-year colleges, and 82 graduate programs. Each year 9,000 social workers graduate.

> In his presentation, Song was highly critical of the importation of individualistic models from the West that are not suitable for the more family-centered Korean society. In Korea, in contrast to the individualized societies such as the United States and Scandinavia, personal interdependency is encouraged. Accordingly, the treatment focus is not just the children but the whole family (Song, 2002).Korean families are more family relationship-centered systems, have male dominance values, and the families of parents-in-law have more influence in the family decision-making process. These are the aspects which one cannot find in the western literature. Therefore, we need critical thinking about the traits of Korean families and attention to differences in cultures. (p. 11)

During the formalized critique that followed this paper presentation, discussants acknowledged trends related to the global market—the drastic decline in the birthrate, increasing reports of violence, changing roles for women, and unmet need for care of the aged. To meet the changing needs of society, according to discussants, social work needs to adopt macro-level approaches to problems, not base interventions on so-called problem families.

According to Amnesty International (2015c), the situation regarding human rights in South Korea is improving with some recognition of the rights to conscientious objection and some attempts to abolish the death penalty. The National Security Law continues to restrict freedom of expression, and there have been arrests of people, for example, who publicly speak out in praise of North Korea. Amnesty International (2017) reported continued violations of the rights of people to peaceably assemble.

For a study of Korean college culture with its unique hierarchal patterns from the point of view of three Korean academics, read Box 2.1.

## BOX 2.1 Understanding Campus Hakbun Culture in Korea

Ga-Young Choi, Eun Koh, & Sam Choi

If someone says "I am class of 2017," most people in the U.S. will think that this person graduated from his or her university in year 2017. But, can you expect the same in the Republic of Korea (South Korea)?

Well, not really. Although the phrase, "class of 2017," refers to a cohort in college just like in the U.S., this is not a cohort who would graduate in the same year. Rather, it indicates a cohort of students who entered the college in the same year. Therefore, "I am class of 2017" means, 'I started my college education in 2017.' " The class of a year" is translated into Korean word, hakbun. The person who entered college in year 2017 refers him/herself as "17 hakbun." It's a common practice to identify one's hakbun by the last two digit of the college entrance year; for example, one-seven-hakbun.

If a person has spent some time in Korea, he or she will soon realize that hakbun is more complicated than its literal meaning. The person's relationship with other students and others' expectations of that person could change depending on his or her hakbun. In this essay, we'll briefly explore the general meaning of hakbun and how it is immersed in campus culture in Korea, a culture that distinguishes groups of cohorts (donggi in Korean), seniors (sunbae in Korean), and juniors (hoobae in Korean).

Before we explain the meaning of these cohort groups, it will be helpful to examine Korean culture, particularly, the general social expectations for building relationships with others. Influenced by Confucianism, it is a virtue in Korean culture for an older person to become an exemplary person to a younger person, offering guidance, and for the younger person to respectfully treat the older person. In the school setting, the society anticipates that a person who has gone through schooling guides those who are currently going through schooling. Although there are nontraditional students, typically cohorts are distinguished by students' age in Korean colleges. The hierarchy based on the age and college entrance year sets certain behavioral expectations for people's interactions. When the two types of hierarchy do not match, that is, when a younger person has higher hakbun than an older person or vice versa, Koreans often talk about how they would address each other when they first meet. This is because it is considered impolite to call someone by name when this person is older or in higher hakbun than you are. You need to add a title such as sunbae (meaning a senior) or hoobae (a junior) to indicate that one person is in a higher or lower hakbun than the other. Or an older person can be addressed as an older brother or sister (like big brothers and sisters in mentoring programs) to show and respect age hierarchy regardless of one's hakbun. Therefore, Koreans in this intermixed hierarchical relationships try to find the appropriate way of interacting with each other.

A person who has entered college in earlier years is called sunbae in Korean , and is expected to take a leading and/or mentoring role; and the person who has entered college a year or a few years later is referred as hoobae. As expressed in English, a sunbae has higher seniority than hoobae. The social norm for the hoobaes is that they respect their sunbaes and assist them if they need any help.

Hoobaes could learn a great deal from sunbaes, which can help them to succeed in college. Sunbaes help hoobaes in selecting courses and extracurricular activities. They also teach the culture of the given university. Once a close sunbae and hoobae friendship or mentorship is developed, they often become more like older/little brothers or sisters to each other, who would extend their support and help beyond college: for example, they may support each other in job searches or family matters. Similar "alumni" ties exist in the U.S., but it seems like sunbae-hoobae relationships are stronger, particularly during college years. The sunbae-hoobae relationship is also reciprocal.

A group of cohorts who share the same hakbun are called "donggi" in Korean, which means that the group started or entered college in the same year. Usually, there is a strong sense of comradery among donggis. Just like freshmen in the U.S. colleges, being new to college is exciting, but the transition from high school presents challenges for many freshmen in Korea. The sense of "donggi comradery," perhaps, grows based on such shared excitement and challenges that they experience as they go through this new journey together. In addition, going through the college experiences together, donggis can create friendship quite easily, and donggis are in a less or non-hierarchical relationship than sunbae-hobae relationships. For many Koreans, this sense of comradery among donggis lasts beyond college years even when they don't graduate in the same year.

The expectations for collaborative relationships exist in all group dynamics of hakbun including donggi, sunbae, and hoobae. From our own experiences, we recognize that such expectations are likely to have stemmed from the Korean culture's strong cultural emphasis on a community rather than an individual. In other words, collectivism is more valued than individualism in Korean culture, which leads to the general belief that when a community (e.g., a college cohort; or alumni) thrives, individuals also thrive. Almost all social groups in Korea have donggi, sunbae, and hoobae, but the relationships based on hakbun is unique to college settings, which often leads to stronger relationships.

Source: Original essay by Ga-Young Choi, Associate Professor of Social Work at California State University, Los Angeles, Eun Koh, Assistant Professor at the Catholic University of America, National Catholic School of Social Service, and Sam Choi, Assistant Professor of Social Work at Alabama A & M University.

## CUBA: FOCUS ON SOCIAL CHANGE

The Universal Declaration of Human Rights contains two categories of human rights—civil and political rights on the one hand; and economic, social, and cultural rights on the other. As a Communist nation, Cuba does well on human rights standards related to social welfare policies; it often receives recognition for its almost perfect literacy rate and low infant mortality. Cuba has the highest doctor-patient rate per capita in the world, and it provides medical services to many poor countries. But what they have in the way of basic welfare rights (for example, universal health care) is countered by what they lack in the political area. Cubans lack basic freedoms, especially of the political sort, but so long as they do not challenge the government, they enjoy a degree of public safety and social security that is rare in Latin America (Miroff, 2016).

Given their exceptionally low crime rate even in the poorest neighborhoods, rare for a region characterized by gang fighting and drug wars, Cubans have a relatively harmonious and peaceful existence. They even have a special term for this—*tranquilidad social*, which means something like "social peace" as well as law and order (Miroff, 2016).

On the United Nations (2015) Human Development Index, Cuba is ranked number 66. In its annual report, Amnesty International (2013) found Cuba in violation of the rights of freedom of expression and to peaceful assemble. Journalists and others who criticized the government have been subject to arrest.

After 56 years and a long history of economic and political hostility between the two countries, the United States and Cuba resumed ties as a major act under the Obama administration (Malai, 2015). President Obama opened the doors to Cuba in 2014, and now US tourists can visit more freely. As the next president, Donald Trump, moved into the White House, the future for this open-door policy became problematic, however.

Fidel Castro's death at age 90 left many citizens in Havana in mourning and many in Miami holding parties of celebration. Castro's death has forced Cubans to think about what kind of future they want for their island and left many Americans wondering if Castro's crumbling economic model and authoritarian political system can carry on without him (Miroff, 2016).

Even before the death of Fidel Castro, many were wishing to use the opportunity of the reduced trade barriers to get the Cuban government to change. Yet others, such as law professor Marjorie Cohn (2016), believe it is hypocritical for the United States to criticize Cuba for human rights violations while ignoring our own in the economic sphere. "The US government criticizes civil and political rights in Cuba," Cohn notes, "while disregarding Cubans' superior access to universal housing, health care, education, and its guarantee of paid maternity leave and equal pay rates" (p. 1). We have a lot to learn from Cuba, she further states.

Indeed, social workers and other professionals have been visiting Cuba and studying their social system for some time. The delegations were organized by representatives of NASW and CSWE; we can learn much from their reports about social work practice within the Communist nation. David Strug (2015), a former social work educator who has organized some of these tours, fills us in on the history of social work and how the profession is practiced today. The information that follows concerning the history of Cuban social work is from his report.

In the turmoil of its revolution in the 1950s, Cuba closed its school of social work, a school that had been founded at the University of Havana in the 1940s. Like other Communist nations, Cuba did away with social work training in the belief that the profession was unnecessary under a Marxist government. Then under economic pressures after the Soviet Union dissolved and withdrew its financial support, Cuba brought back social work education for practical reasons. Unique to the school was the idea for these youths to help other youths and the integration of social work practice skills with political sociology. Over 50,000 social workers were trained. Then, in 2008, the university programs were closed again, this time due to a belief that the needs had been met. Nevertheless, today, as in another Communist country—China—social work in Cuba is strong.

Hermon, Zlotnik, and Collins (2011) write of their impressions of Cuban social services based on professional exchanges between Cuban and American social workers that were organized by NASW. There are many lessons American social workers can learn from the Cubans according to Hermon, Zlotnik, and Collins (2011). Compared to social services in the United States, the visitors found the social services in Cuba to be highly integrated. Social workers are members of interdisciplinary teams consisting of nurses, doctors, and psychologists; they work in teams. Cuban social workers practice not only in health care settings but also in schools, the criminal justice system, and general social services. Working for the state, they often live and work as community organizers in needy communities.

The visiting social workers were impressed by the strength of Cuban family values and of the care that older adults received and by the intergenerational living arrangements. The government provides free educational activities for the older citizens, including university courses and workshops on topics of interest.

Challenges for social work are discussed by David Strug (2015), a retired social work professor, who previously led groups of students and educators for educational trips to Cuba. Based on his many visits over the years, Strug observed many changes in the country related to economic crisis and social welfare reforms instituted by the government. The stated goal of these reforms is to make the economy more efficient by establishing microcredit, bank accounts, cooperatives, and wholesale markets for the private sector. As an incentive to start the small businesses, such as selling agricultural goods on the streets, workers are being laid off from state jobs. At the same time, reduced spending on food rations and health care is leaving many of the citizens vulnerable. The cutbacks, in combination with the capitalist opportunities and profits from tourism, have generated noticeable social inequalities that were not so obvious before. While the American press applauds these changes (for example, see Malai, 2015), the impact has been a mixed blessing for some of the people who are not young or educated enough to prosper in a new economy. Living on small pensions, many of the older people and those with disabilities do not have enough money to make ends meet. A small percentage, however, live well because of aid sent by relatives in the United States.

## CANADA: FOCUS ON HUMAN RIGHTS

Canada, which is the United States' number 1 trade partner, is ranked at number 8, just below the United States on the United Nations (2015) Human Development Index. Canada is officially a bilingual country with English and French as the official languages. Aboriginal peoples are around 4% of the total population. There are 10 provinces in Canada under a parliamentary system of government. Modeled on the British political system, the prime minister is the elected leader of the majority political party.

The social work profession in the English-speaking provinces has roots in both the United Kingdom and United States with a tradition of charity and settlement house work (Watkins, Jennissen, & Lundy, 2012). In Quebec, the French-speaking region, the early roots of social work are in France, where social services were operated largely by the Roman Catholic Church.

At the beginning of the 21st century, a formal joint relationship was formed between NASW-US and CASW (the Canadian Association of Social Workers). One of the purposes of the alliance is to strengthen the collaboration to act jointly on IFSW issues; these two nations are member countries of the North American region of IFSW (Stoesen, 2003). According to Terry Mizrahi, cited in the article by Stoesen, "We looked at issues of poverty as human rights issues, how to improve child welfare systems, developing standards for international social work practice and dealing with racial, ethnic and cultural diversity" (p. 6). Mizrahi singles out Canadian models of practice, the Canadian health care system, and entitlements as areas about which we have a lot to learn from Canada.

The impact of the global market on Canada is twofold—pressures of NAFTA (North American Free Trade Agreement) and from the wider corporate-controlled economy. In *Canadian Social Policy*, Graham, Swift, and Delaney (2012) argue that, at least in part, because of NAFTA, Canadian politicians have started looking south of the 49th parallel for political precedents. Although social welfare cutbacks have not been as severe as those in the United States and the United Kingdom, retrenchment and workfare are, as Graham et al. (2012)) suggest, policies that are under consideration. In recent years, the qualifying characteristics have become increasingly restrictive for recipients of social welfare benefits, and programs that were formerly universal have become means-tested (Shier & Graham, 2014). In the years since, the Free Trade Agreement was formalized between the United States and Canada, the gap between rich and poor has deepened considerably. Child poverty among the Native population is now a major problem.

A major shift in the Canadian social welfare state that has taken place in recent years, according to Shier and Graham, is the heavy reliance today on community-based organizations (such as domestic violence services, addiction treatment, shelters for the homeless) in responding to local needs. Under this emerging model, service users are encouraged to be active participants in the grassroots organizations. The success of these programs and initiatives is dependent on the level of government support and funding.

A major threat to the provision of services is privatization, one of the standards of the global market's cost-saving policies. Under such policies, worker performance is quantified, caseloads have risen, and agencies are expected to do more with less (Westhues, 2012). Services have been subcontracted out to private firms, which save money by hiring unqualified human services workers. The results are particularly damaging to Aboriginal peoples and recent immigrants. Nevertheless, Canada's schools of social work continue to operate from a structural/ human rights perspective with a strong commitment to social justice and equality for all people (Watkins et al., 2012).

In contrast to the Canadian Conservative party, the Liberal party traditionally draws on an institutional as opposed to a residual model of social welfare. With the election of Prime Minister Justin Trudeau of the Liberal party in 2015, major social policy changes were underway. During the first two years, the Liberal government introduced measures toward the legalization of recreational marijuana, raising taxes on the very rich and lowering them on the middle classes, increasing funding for schools for First Nations People, and boosting parental benefits (Geddes, 2017). The CASW (2016) website described passage of legislation outlawing violence against children (spanking) by teachers and parents alike. The site welcomes proposals in Parliament on the introduction of a guaranteed income as a key piece of poverty reduction strategy. CASW is also pleased about plans to rebuild the social infrastructure of Canada and to further support for the rights of First Nations People. (See CASW, 2016, www.casw-acts.ca.). A later report discusses the problem of child poverty in Canada and strongly endorses a basic income guarantee in the form of a universal, tax-free grant, similar to what is available for seniors. This strategy would shift the notion of social security from that of a social safety net to that of universal equality (CASW, 2017).

Recent criticism has been directed toward the Canadian government for its continuation of neoliberal economics, for example, its attempts to privatize the Canadian infrastructure, such as airports, roads, and bridges (Rochon, 2017). Amnesty International (2017) points to the following issues in need of remedy: the widespread violence against Indigenous women and the failure of the government to protect the lands and environment of First Nations peoples through the building of the Northern Gateway Pipeline. The human rights organization extended credit to Canada for welcoming over 38,000 Syrian refugees to the country.

## SUMMARY AND CONCLUSION

The world over, common societal needs generate similar institutional responses, and national ideologies shape the level of care provided. Despite surface similarities, however, there are vast international differences in the magnitude of the problems encountered and in the nature and pattern of services developed to deal with them. The idea that social welfare is a guarantee of well-being for all citizens is more firmly rooted in some countries (for example, in the northern parts of western Europe) than in others. Countries that value independence, autonomy, and minimal governmental interference, like the United States, are likely to be resistant to sweeping welfare legislation. Countries with strong labor and socialist parties, on the other hand, are more apt to be amenable to the social service provisions.

The study of social welfare systems, therefore, must attend to values within which this system derives. A society that provides universal cradle-to-grave protections to all citizens is apt to include in their numbers many who lack the drive to "get ahead." A society conversely, whose values center on equal opportunity to achieve or fail (but without any cushion to protect those who fail), a society that allows for a huge income and wealth differential among its citizens, is apt to include in their numbers many who live in the throes of poverty.

The purpose of this chapter was to examine US social values from an objective viewpoint (to the extent that is possible) to help us "see ourselves as others see us." Filtered from the literature of international social work and anthropology, nine value dimensions emerged with relevance to social welfare: work versus leisure; equal opportunity versus equality; mobility versus stability; competition versus cooperation; individualism versus collectivism; independence versus interconnectedness; materialism versus spirituality; nuclear family versus extended family; and moralism versus compassion. Comparative analysis showed that except for the family construct that is associated with modern industrialization (where family size is shrinking) the attributes on the left-hand side of the continua (work, equal opportunity, etc.) are characteristically American, while those on the right hand side are representative of advanced welfare states such as are found in the Nordic countries. Moralism is a trait that in American politics and policymaking transcends all the others (except perhaps for materialism and the nuclear family arrangement).

The final sections of this chapter viewed how the values and social policy are intertwined and how social work and US values are not always compatible, sometimes even contradictory. With examples drawn from Chile (whose grassroots efforts have inspired social work the world over); South Korea (representative of a highly vigorous East Asian model); Jamaica (illustrative of a modernizing region); Cuba (illustrative of a Communist nation that is introducing some elements of capitalism); and Canada (representing a progressive nation of the Global North), we have seen how globalization has affected the profession of social work. Looming through all these national reports is the lesson that the model of social work that is used must be culturally relevant to the norms of the region and adapted accordingly. Also revealed in these international portraits is the global interconnectedness among nations' social values. This international thrust is reminiscent of the international contacts between the profession's founding mothers in Europe and the United States in the late 19th century. Today our global interdependence is being strengthened by common forces, common concerns. The problems facing social workers transcend national boundaries. By the same token, whether their method is psychotherapy or community action, and whether they work in Singapore, Ireland, Canada, or the United States, social workers are united by common professional values; such values emphasize altruism and goodwill and transcend the cultural nuances of a particular region.

The next chapter extends this cultural understanding into the historical arena, the focal point of which is the growth and development of social work. Because this profession is the one most closely bound to social welfare, the history of social welfare, in effect, becomes the history of social work.

## THOUGHT QUESTIONS

1. How does the food from our ethnic group that we ate growing up relate to our cultural identity? Cite some examples.
2. Explain the meaning of the title of Jansson's book, *The Reluctant Welfare State*. How does this relate to US values?
3. According to social scientists, how do people come to acquire social values?
4. Discuss how the media both reflect and promote social values. What is the role of the media in wartime?
5. Which of the values listed in the nine value dimensions, in your opinion, best encapsulates the "American way of life"?
6. Trace the historical roots of the work ethic. What was Max Weber's theory? Relate to the teachings of Calvinism and Benjamin Franklin.
7. Today we are a secular nation: To what extent do you think the Protestant work ethic applies or does not apply at this time?
8. Discuss the value put on work in several countries. How do these patterns relate to the quote at the beginning of the chapter on the right to leisure?
9. How can you differentiate equal opportunity from equality?
10. Discuss welfare reform (enacted in 1996) as a residually based program. What were some of the consequences of this act?
11. To destroy a social welfare program, make it means tested. What is the evidence for this statement?
12. Argue that mobility is a key characteristic of US society. Do you know of any personal examples of someone who left home because of a related cultural value?
13. Describe a society in which the social climate is cooperation-based rather than competition-based. What is *samarbeid?*
14. Contrast the concept of the Indian Medicine Wheel with the mainstream US focus on independence.
15. How is individualism a fact of life, even a corrupting force worldwide?
16. "The Incredible Shrinking Family": Is this claim true or false today?
17. Relate the force of moralism to punitiveness in American society. What do the statistics tell us?

18. Discuss a shift in social welfare policy initiatives. How does this shift parallel the shift in society's values?
20. What is unique about social work values, and how do they contrast with mainstream values?

## REFERENCES


Al-Krenawi, A., & Graham, J. R. (2008). *Helping professional practice with indigenous peoples: The Bedouin-Arab case.* Lanham, MD: University Press of America.

Amnesty International. (2013, May 23). *Annual report: Cuba.* Retrieved from Amnesty International (2015a). *Annual report: Canada 2015/2016.* Retrieved from www.amnestyusa.org

Amnesty International. (2015c). *Annual report: Jamaica 2015/2016.* Retrieved from www.amnestyusa.org

Amnesty International. (2015d). *Annual report: South Korea 2015/2016.* Retrieved from www.amnestyusa.org

Amnesty International. (2017, February 22). *Amnesty International report 2016/2017: The state of the world's human rights.* London: Amnesty International, Ltd.

Appleby, G. A., Cohen, E., & Hamilton, J. (2010). *Diversity, oppression, and social functioning: Person-in-environment assessment and intervention.* Upper Saddle River, NJ: Pearson.

Aronson, E., Wilson, T. D., & Sommers, S. (2015). *Social psychology* (9th ed.). New York, NY: Pearson.

Baker, P.-A., & Maxwell, J. (2012). Social work in the Caribbean. In L. M. Healy & R. J. Link (Eds.), *Handbook of international social work: Human rights, development, and the global profession* (pp. 383–387). New York, NY: Oxford University Press.

Barker, R. (2014). *The social work dictionary* (6th ed.) Washington, DC: NASW Press.

Baron, R., & Branscombe, N. (2012). *Social psychology.* Upper Saddle River, NJ: Pearson.

Blakemore, K., & Warwick-Booth, L. (2013). *Social policy: An introduction* (4th ed.). New York, NY: Open University Press.

BMC Evolutionary Biology (2008, June 10). Is ADHD an advantage for nomadic tribesmen? *Science Daily.* Retrieved from www.sciencedaily.com

Borzutzky, S. (2002). Chile's fully funded system. An analysis of its impact on the state and the society. Paper presented at the *International Conference on Social Welfare.* Seoul, Korea, Seoul National University, October 11–12.

Butler, L. (2003, January–February). Living on Tokyo time. *Utne,* p.65

Canadian Association of Social Workers (CASW). (2016). Press releases. Retrieved from http://www.casw-acts.ca/en/news/press-releases

Canadian Association of Social Workers (CASW). (2017, October). *Universal basic income guarantee: The next big thing in Canadian social policy.* CASW. Retrieved from https://casw-acts.ca

Canda, E. R., & Furman, L. D. (2010). *Spiritual diversity in social work practice: The heart of helping.* (2nd ed.). New York, NY: Oxford University Press.

Chadda, R., & Deb, K. S. (2013). Indian family systems, collectivist society, and psychotherapy. *Indian Journal of Psychiatry, 55* (Suppl. 2), S299–S309.

Cohn, M. (2016, March 18). Human rights hypocrisy: U.S. criticizes Cuba. *Common Dreams.* Retrieved from www.commondreams.org

Coyhis, D., & Simonelli, R. (2008). The Native American healing experience. *Substance Use and Misuse, 43,* 1927–1949.

Day, P. (2012). *A new history of social welfare* (7th ed.). Upper Saddle River, NJ: Pearson.

de Tocqueville, A. (1951/1835). *Democracy in America* (Trans. P. Bradley). New York, NY: Alfred A. Knopf.

Dickey, J. (2015, June 1). Save our vacation. *Time*, pp. 44–49.

*The Economist.* (2015a, November 28). Corporate culture in South Korea: Loosening their lives. *The Economist*, pp. 61–62.

*The Economist* (2015b, September 19). The crème de la cram. *The Economist*, p. 38.

*The Economist* (2015c, October 10). Norwegian blues. *The Economist*, p. 69.

Finn, J. L. (2002). Raíces: Gender-conscious community building in Santiago, Chile. *Affilia, 17*(4), 448–470.

Finn, J. L., & Jacobson, M. (2008). *Just practice: A social justice approach to social work.* (2nd ed.). Peosta, IA: Eddie Bowers Publishing Co.

Gao, G. (2015, March 12). How do Americans stand out from the rest of the world? Pew Research Center. Retrieved from www.pewresearch.org

Geddes, J. (2017, June 22). *What Trudeau says his government has achieved in 2017 so far. Maclean's magazine.* Retrieved from www.macleans.ca

Gil, D. (2014). Confronting injustice and oppression: Concepts and strategies for social workers. New York, NY: Columbia University Press.

Gillum, T. (2009). The intersection of spirituality, religion, and intimate partner violence in the African American community. University of Minnesota: Institute on Domestic Violence in the African American Community. Retrieved from www.idvaac.org

Goodman, L. (2016, February). The military-media complex. *In These Times*, p. 16.

González, M., & Acevedo, G. (2013). Clinical practice with Hispanic individuals and families: An ecological perspective. In E. Congress & M. González (Eds.), *Multicultural perspectives in social work practice with families* (3rd ed., pp. 141–156). New York, NY: Springer.

Graham, J., Swift, K., & Delaney, R. (2011). *Canadian social policy: An introduction* (4th ed.). Don Mills, Ontario: Pearson Education Canada.

Grimsrud, T., & Zehr, H. (2002). Rethinking God, justice and treatment of offenders. In T. O'Connor (Ed.), *Religion, the community, and the rehabilitation of criminal offenders* (pp. 259–285). New York, NY: Haworth.

*The Guardian.* (2013, April 16). Jamaica's decades of debt are damaging its future. Retrieved from www.theguardian.com

Hartmann, T. (1997). *Attention deficit disorder: A different perception.* Grass Valley, CA: Under Wood Books.

Hartmann, T. (2015). *ADHD and the Edison gene: A drug-free approach to manage the unique qualities in your child* (3rd ed.). Rochester, VT: Park Street Press.

Healy, L. (2003). Social work values, ethics and standards: International perspectives. Special presentation at the *Council on Social Work Education 49th Annual Program Meeting.* Atlanta, Georgia: February 27–March 2.

Healy, L. (2008). *International social work: Professional action in an interdependent world* (2nd ed.). New York, NY: Oxford University Press.

Heberlein, T. (2016, March 19). Am I crippled by Swedish taxes? No. Appreciate benefits? Yes. Madison, WI: *Capital Times.* Retrieved from www.madison.com

Hermon, C., Zlotnik, J., & Collins, S. (2011). Social services in Cuba. NASW website. Retrieved from https://www.socialworkers.org/nasw/swan/cubaReport.pdf

Hess, A. E. (2013, June 8). On holiday: Countries with the most vacations. *USA Today.* Retrieved from www.usatoday.com

Hodge, D. R., & Limb, G. E. (2010). Conducting spiritual assessments with Native Americans: Enhancing cultural competency in social work practice courses. *Journal of Social Work Education, 46*(2), 265–283.

hooks, b. (2001). *Salvation: Black people and love*. New York, NY: Harper Collins.

Hutson, M. (2012a). Our inner Puritan. *Psychology Today*. Retrieved from www.psychologytoday.com

Hutson, M. (2012b, August 5). Still Puritan after all these years. *New York Times*, p. SR4.

International Federation of Social Workers (IFSW). (2017). Statement of ethical principles. Retrieved from http://ifsw.org/policies/statement-of-ethical-principles/

Jansson, B. (2012). *The reluctant welfare state*. Belmont, CA: Cengage.

Kaplan, E. (2014, November). Americans are working so hard it's actually killing people. *The Nation*. Retrieved from www.thenation.com

Kendall, K. (1989). Women at the helm: Three extraordinary leaders. *Affilia 4*(1), 23–32.

Koretz, G. (June 11, 2001). "Why Americans work so hard." In *Business Week*, p. 34.

Kreitzer, L. (2012). *Social work in Africa: Exploring culturally relevant education and practice in Ghana*. Calgary, Canada: University of Calgary Press.

Lakey, G. (2016). *Viking economics: How the Scandinavians got it right—and how we can too*. Brooklyn, NY: Melville House Printing.

Levi, D. (2017). *Group dynamics for teams*. Thousand Oaks, CA: Sage.

Levin, M. (2015, May 11). Even as American families shrink, more educated women having children. *Houston Chronicle*. Retrieved from www.chron.com

Luhby, T. (2012, August 9). Welfare spending cut in half since reform. Cable News Network (CNN) Money. Retrieved from www.moneycnn.com

Malai, R. (2015, June). Doors open as U.S. Cuba relations evolve. *USA Today*. Retrieved from www. usatoday.com

Mason, R. (2015, June 25). UK "not on track to end child poverty by 2020" as figures remain unchanged. *The Guardian*. Retrieved from www.theguardian.com

Midgley, J. (2010).The theory and practice of developmental social work. In J. Midgley & A. Conley (Eds.), *Social work and social development: Theories and skills for developmental social work* (pp. 3–30). New York, NY: Oxford University Press.

Mills, C. W. (1959). *The sociological imagination*. New York, NY: Oxford University Press.

Miroff, N. (2016, December 2). Fidel Castro is dead, but Cubans want some of his policies to continue. *Washington Post*. Retrieved from www.washingtonpost.com

Mullaly, B. (2010). *Challenging oppression and confronting privilege: A critical social work approach*. Don Mills, Ontario, Canada: Oxford University Press.

National Association of Social Workers (NASW). (2015). Peace and social justice. In *Social work speaks: NASW policy statements 2015–2017* (10th ed.). Washington, DC: NASW Press.

National Association of Social Workers (NASW). (2016). Forging solutions out of Challenges. *NASW social work month toolkit*. Washington, DC: NASW Press.

National Association of Social Workers (NASW). (2017). Code of ethics. Washington, DC: NASW Press.

Nelson, M. R., & Shavitt, S. (2002). Horizontal and vertical individualism and achievement values: A multimethod examination of Denmark and the United States. *Journal of Cross-Cultural Psychology, 33*(5), 439–458.

Nimmagadda, J., & Martell, D.R. (2008). Home-made social work: The two-way transfer of social work practice knowledge between India and the USA. In M. Gray, J. Coates, & M. Yellow Bird (Eds.), *Indigenous social work around the world: Towards cultural relevant education and practice* (pp. 141–152). Aldershot, England: Ashgate.

Oster, S. (2014, July 7). In China, office work can be deadly. *Bloomberg Business Week*, pp. 14–16.

Paul, H. K. (2011, June 24). "The war you don't see": Iraq, Afghanistan, and Israel/Palestine. *Global Policy Forum*. Retrieved from www.globalpolicy.org

Payne, M. (2014). *Modern social work theory* (4th ed.). Chicago, IL: Lyceum.

Pinsker, J. (2015, March 12). Finland, home of the $103,000 speeding ticket. *The Atlantic*. Retrieved from www.theatlantic.com

Piven, F., & Cloward, R. A. (1993). *Poorhouse politics. The Progressive, 59* (2), 22–24.

Popple, P., & Leighninger, L. (2014). *The policy-based profession: An introduction to social welfare policy analysis for social workers* (6th ed.). New York, NY: Pearson.

Ravitch, D. (2014). *Reign of error: The hoax of the privatization movement and the threat to America's public schools*. New York: Vintage Books.

Reisch, M. (2014). *Social policy and social justice*. Thousand Oaks, CA: SAGE.

Robbins, S. P., Chatterjee, P., & Canda, E. R. (2012). *Contemporary human behavior theory: A critical perspective for social work* (3rd ed.). Upper Saddle River, NJ: Pearson.

Rochon, L.-P. (2017, February 5). Opinion: The great Canadian hoodwink. Canadian Broadcast Company (CBC). Retrieved from www.cbc.ca/news

Saad, L. (2014, August). The "40-hour" workweek is actually longer—by 7 hours. Gallup. Retrieved from www.gallup.com

Saracostti, M., Reininger, T., & Parada. H. (2012). Social work in Latin America. In K. Lyons, T. Hokenstad, Pawar, M., Huegler, N., & Hall, N. (Eds.), *Sage handbook of international social work*. London, England: SAGE.

Schram, S. F., Soss, J., & Fording, R. (2014). Welfare and welfare reform in the age of neoliberal paternalism. In M. Reisch (Ed.), *Social policy and social justice: Social work in the new century* (pp. 377–403). Thousand Oaks, CA: Sage.

Seib, G. (2015, June 30). "Decline in moral values" likely to be big topic in 2016 debate. *Wall Street Journal*. Retrieved from www.blogs.wsj.com

Shavitt, S., Johnson, T., & Zhang, J. (2011). Horizontal and vertical cultural differences in the content of advertising appeals. *Journal of International Consumer Marketing, 23*, 297–310.

Shier, M., & Graham, J. R. (2014). Social policy in Canada. In C. Franklin (Ed.), *Encyclopedia of Social Work*. NASW, New York: Oxford University Press.

Song, S. J. (2002). Changes in family and social work practice in Korea. Paper presented at the *International Conference on Social Welfare*, Seoul National University. Seoul, Korea. October 11–12.

Stoesen, J. (2003, January). Canadians/Americans bolster relationship. *NASW News*, p. 6.

Strug, D. (2015, May 4). Cuba and Cuban social work at a time of change. Katherine A. Kendall Institute. Council on Social Work Education. Retrieved from www.cswe.org

Suppes, M. A. and Wells, C. C. (2012). *The social work experience: An introduction to social work and social welfare* (6th ed.). Upper Saddle River, NJ: Pearson.

Tropman, J. (1989). *American values and social welfare: Cultural contradictions in the welfare state*. Englewood Cliffs, NJ: Prentice Hall.

Trump, D. (2015, October 26). Quoted by C. Campbell. "Donald Trump: My father gave me a small loan of a million dollars." *Business Insider*. Retrieved from www.businessinsider.com

United Nations. (2015). *Human development index*. New York, NY: UN Development Programme.

Walmsley, R. (2013). *World prison population list* (10th ed., p. 1). London, England: International Centre for Prison Studies.

Watkins, J., Jennissen, T., & Lundy, C. (2012). Social work in North America. In L. M. Healy & R. J. Link (Eds.), *Handbook of international social work: Human rights, development, and the global profession* (pp.400–407). New York, NY: Oxford University Press.

Weber, M. (1958/1905). *The Protestant ethic and the spirit of capitalism.* New York, NY: Charles Scribner & Sons.

Westhues, A. (2012). Becoming acquainted with social policy. In A. Westhues & B. Wharf (Eds.), *Canadian social policy: Issues and perspectives* (pp. 3–22). Waterloo, Ontario, Canada: Eddie Bowers Publishing Co.

Westhues, A., & Kenny-Scherber, C. (2012). The policy-making process. In A. Westhues & B. Wharf (Eds.), *Canadian social policy: Issues and perspectives* (pp. 23–42). Waterloo, Ontario, Canada: Eddie Bowers Publishing Co.

Wilensky, H., & Lebeaux, C. (1958). *Industrial society and social welfare.* New York, NY: The Free Press.

Williams, R. (1979). Change and stability in values and values systems: A sociological perspective. In M. Rokeach (Ed.), *Understanding human values: Individual and societal.* New York, NY: The Free Press.

Wolfe, A. W. (2001). Welfare reform: Self-sufficiency or what? In A. Podolefsky & P. J. Brown (Eds.) *Applying cultural anthropology: An Introductory reader* (pp. 282–285). Mountain View, CA: Mayfield Publishing.

World Values Survey. (2015). World Values Survey Wave 6: 2010–2014. Stockholm, Sweden. Retrieved from www.worldvaluessurvey.org

Zastrow, C. (2017). *Introduction to social work and social welfare* (12th ed.) Belmont, CA: Cengage.

# CHAPTER 3

# EMERGENCE OF SOCIAL WORK: PART I

> The General Assembly proclaims this Universal Declaration of Human Rights as a common standard of achievement for all peoples and all nations, to the end that every individual and every organ of society, keeping this Declaration constantly in mind, shall strive by teaching and education to promote respect for these rights and freedom.
>
> The Universal Declaration of Human Rights, Preamble, 1948

A true understanding of history comes not from knowing the facts alone but in seeing how the facts are interrelated. And to know the interconnectedness of things, we need to journey backward and forward in time. Knowing the rhythms and patterns of the past (how wars start, how technology alters culture) offers insight into the present and even gives us grounds for predicting the future. History, as they say, repeats itself.

The story of social work begins with the history of social welfare, and the history of social welfare goes back at least to the late Middle Ages. In this chapter, we will lay the groundwork for our story of the emergence of social work. We start by reviewing selected milestones in early social welfare history that had a bearing on the evolution of social work—the technological discoveries, paradigm shifts related to the new technologies, and religious upheavals.

The major portion of this chapter chronicles the history of social work; this history is presented in terms of influential people, events, and turning points. Before presenting the case for an international focus in social work as an imperative for the 21st century, we describe social work as an empowering profession for today's world. As a profession whose roots are planted in the informal and formal responses to human misery in England and North America, and as a profession that was both shaped by historical movements and helped fashion them, social work has managed to survive by blending with the times.

In the previous chapter, we focused on values. This chapter views the values of the age historically and in the form of ideology or belief systems. The values of the profession have evolved in response to forces in the political, economic, and social environment (Berg-Weger, 2016). Reamer (2014) views this evolution in five distinct phases. The moral phase in the late

19th century had social workers focusing on their clients' morals and work ethic. During the second phase, which lasted from the early to mid-20th century, social workers were engrossed in social reform movements and improving the environment for poor people, especially immigrants. The concern of the next two periods was with ethical issues and professional development, while the fifth and present period is a time of wrestling with ethical issues of the digital age.

Our approach is to explore how social work has responded to the ideological ethos of the times by offering interventions—community action during progressive times and individual casework in conservative periods—that were compatible with the popular currents of the day. In our consideration of these trends we have to remember that there was much overlap between the interventions, until one or the other won out, and that countervailing forces were always present simultaneously. Shining through all the periods were vestiges of empowerment. (So it is today, as the leaders of the social work profession relentlessly and forthrightly confront the conservative onslaught on the social welfare state.) This remains no less true now than formerly and no less true in other parts of the world than in the West.

In examining the practice of social work cross-culturally in this chapter, two key themes emerge. The first is that social work as a profession somehow has managed to maintain a shared value base across time and space, even during the most palpable shifts in ideological temperament. The second, and this one seemingly contradicts the first, is that social work necessarily must reflect the cultural ethos of which it is a part.

Chapter 3 provides a study of the foundations of social work from the earliest days of social welfare history through the founding of the profession around the turn of the last century. The more modern history in which modern society underwent rapid change from the 1960s is the topic for chapter 4: The Emergence of Social Work: Part II.

## MILESTONES IN EARLY SOCIAL WELFARE HISTORY

The history of social welfare beginning in Europe and continuing in America over the last several hundred years is a tale of neglect and cruelty. It is also a tale of paternalism (or maternalism) and compassion as well as of attempts at social control punctuated by racism, sexism, and classism. Ideologically, new ideas were superimposed on old ideas; and finally, old ideas were superimposed on the new. Looming over the whole scene was the age-old dilemma of how to balance the care for the weak and needy against the push for strong work incentives. A society too soft may breed laziness and malingering; one too harsh may breed death and isolation. Over the centuries, nation states have leaned one way or another between these warring forces and espoused various doctrines ranging from survival of the fittest ideology to a belief system favoring taxing the rich to provide for the poor.

A perusal of Box 3.1 reveals the key roles of foreign conquest, modern technologies, and political ideology on the system of public welfare. The road from 1066 when the Normans (French speakers of Scandinavian descent) under William the Conqueror brought feudalism to the British Isles to the enclosures that sent the serfs scurrying across the land to the cities to the Protestant Reformation to the Industrial Revolution and, finally, to union organizing and social reform can be viewed in terms of one long progression toward modern capitalism. Except for the religio-economic changes associated with the Protestant revolution, and the Black Death

### BOX 3.1 Milestones in the Development of British Social Welfare

1066: Norman Conquest; feudalism, introduction of French words into English, and unification of the country under law.
1348: The Bubonic plague (The Black Death) kills one-third of the population of Europe; religious minorities and poor women are scapegoated.
1350: Statute of Laborers passed to restrict workers from traveling or organizing to take advantage of the labor shortage resulting from the plague
1517: Martin Luther posts 95 theses on the door of a Catholic Church.
1533: Henry VIII breaks away from Rome and converts himself and therefore the nation to Protestantism.
1536: John Calvin systematizes Protestant thought; his notion of Predestination is to have an indelible effect in Britain and the New World.
1601: Elizabethan Poor Law provides for local poor relief allocations, transfers responsibility for welfare aid from the church to the government.
1750–1850: Industrial Revolution reinvents the meaning of work.
1769: Steam engine invented and hastened population migration to the cities.
1776: Adam Smith publishes *The Wealth of Nations,* which provides a rationale for the cruelties of unfettered capitalism.
1800: London's population reaches one million.
1834: The New Poor Law embodies the principles of survival of the fittest into law with the purpose of making public aid less attractive.
1838: Dickens' *Oliver Twist* gives human misery in the industrial age a human face.
1845–1855: Irish potato famine kills nearly one million while even more emigrate.
1848: Marx and Engel's *Communist Manifesto* published, puts a new face on the notions of capitalism and class struggle.
1859: Darwin's *Origins of Species* published, which shows the advantages to various species of survival of the fittest.
1869: Charity Organization Society established; this development is to help professionalize charity work.
1881: Germ theory of disease is generally accepted.
1883: In newly united Germany, Chancellor Otto von Bismarck establishes a national health insurance system.
1884: Toynbee Hall, the first settlement house, established in London.
1895: The first social worker, called a hospital almoner, Mary Stewart was hired to work in a hospital in London.
1899: First school of social work (a two-year program) founded in Amsterdam, The Netherlands.
1904: Establishment of the first British schools of social work.
1911: National Insurances Act passed, inspired by Bismarck's lead, the Act provided unemployment insurance and became a model for other nations.
1914–1918: World War I; several hundred thousand British troops killed.
1939: Britain declares war on Germany.
1942: Beveridge Report recommends an integrated social security system for Britain.

1945: World War II ends; United Nations established.
1945: New Labour government introduces strong welfare system.
1946: National Health Service established.
1948: Universal Declaration of Human Rights adopted by the UN General Assembly
1979–1990: With Margaret Thatcher as Prime Minister, right-wing free market economic policies transform the British welfare system.
1992: European Union emerges out of previous European common market agreements with the United Kingdom as a member.
2003: The United Kingdom joins the United States in the war on Iraq.
2016: Attacks of terrorism related to wars in the Middle East create a climate of fear throughout Europe and a mass refugee crisis.

of 1348, the other turning points were accompanied by technological advances such as the ox-drawn cart and the invention of the steam engine.

Most prominent among all these events for US social welfare history was the Protestant Reformation of 1517. The religious event was to have repercussions that were to extend far beyond the realm of the church into the realms of capitalism, social welfare, work, education, and the British settlements of the "New World." The United States, as we know it, emerged out of these settlements. And so we will start from there.

## THE PROTESTANT REFORMATION

After he was excommunicated for posting his 95 theses on the door of a Catholic church in Wittenburg (opposing the use of indulgences and other corrupt church practices), Martin Luther founded what later would turn out to be Protestantism. By challenging the notion of papal authority, encouraging church members to read and study the scriptures in their own language, and replacing rituals with sermons, the Protestant church increased the involvement of parishioners in their own religious lives (Jansson, 2014). While Luther's memorable act of defiance weakened the Holy Roman Empire politically and fostered the development of the nation-state, the course of social welfare history was forever changed as well. At the heart of the change was Luther's introduction of the notion of vocation as a calling to do God's work in all things—whether as a member of the clergy or as a teacher, farmer, or laborer (Day & Schiele, 2012). This notion of a calling ultimately revolutionized the social system, in that it gave a meaning to work that went beyond work itself. As Dolgoff and Feldstein, (2012) indicate, Luther's teachings improved the morale of laborers, giving them a sense of duty in an honest day's toil. The reformation would not have been as far-reaching, however, had it not been for the conversion of the king of England.

Seventeen years after Martin Luther posted his 95 theses, Henry VIII, denied by the pope his request to have his marriage to his first wife annulled so he could have a male heir through remarriage, seized control of the English branch of the Catholic Church (Vowell, 2009). His establishment of the Church of England marked the start of the Protestant Reformation in England. The king's conversion to Protestantism brought the entire country with him under force of law. See the portrait of Martin Luther in Figure 3.1.

**FIGURE 3.1.** Monument of Martin Luther in Wittenberg, Germany. It was the first public monument of the religious reformer. © Shutterstock, photo by photolike.

When Martin Luther posted his 95 theses on the door of a German Catholic church, he little could have known the wave of reform he was setting into motion.

Changes in church doctrine that gradually emerged were far-reaching. No longer would the clergy be the interpreters of the Bible, but the Bible would be translated into the languages of the people so that they could read the Holy Book for themselves. This resulted in a great impetus for ordinary people to learn to read. By challenging the notion of papal authority, encouraging church members to read and study the scriptures in their own language, and replacing rituals with sermons, the Protestant church increased the involvement of parishioners in their own religious lives.

The stress on literacy in Protestantism, reading the Bible in one's own language, had quite an impact on the impetus for education (Jansson, 2014). An unintended consequence was the split of Protestantism into various denominations and sects related to interpretations of Christ's teaching. The Puritans and Quakers were among the dissenters from the established Church of England who would eventually set sail for what is now America. Dissident Catholic groups were to follow. To summarize: one defiant act of a disenchanted priest in 16th century Germany had a monumental impact on US history and accordingly, on the world. (Refer back to chapter 2 to read about the Protestant work ethic.)

## THE ELIZABETHAN POOR LAW

A year with special significance for social work history is 1601 (see Box 3.1). With the end of the Catholic Church charities and in the wake of enclosures, population growth, and urbanization, government overseers of the poor administered laws providing for public relief. Local parishes and counties were now required to provide work for the poor and houses of correction for criminals and idlers. For the first time, care for the poor was a secular, not a church, function.

The Elizabethan Poor Law was to remain the major codification of laws for dealing with poor and disadvantaged people for over 200 years (Barker, 2014). It also was destined to become the basis for dealing with poor people in Colonial America. The principal provisions of the Elizabethan Poor Law as described by Berg-Weger (2016) and Jansson (2014) are as follows:

1. Administration of poor relief at the local level.
2. Relative responsibility, which was the doctrine that parents were responsible for the support of their children and grandchildren, and grown children for their dependent parents and grandparents.
3. The taxing of people in each parish to pay for their own poor.
4. The classification of the destitute into three categories: the able-bodied or "sturdy beggars," the impotent poor who could be cared for at the poorhouse ("indoor relief") or be given "outdoor relief" or aid in their homes such as food or fuel, and dependent children who could be given apprenticeships or trained for domestic service.

Conditions at the workhouse were intended to ensure that no one with any conceivable alternative would seek public aid (Jansson, 2014). Compassion and punitiveness were thus skillfully linked in one composite piece of legislation. Separating the poor into "deserving" and "undeserving" made poverty for some a blameworthy condition. This significant development still has an impact on us centuries later throughout the Anglo-Saxon world.

Consistent with their structuralist conception of welfare as a means to regulate the poor, Piven and Cloward (1993) argue that western relief systems arose not out of, but as a desperate response to, mass disturbances that threatened the status quo. When the emergence of the wool industry put a premium on available land, and when the impact on the dispossessed farmers threatened political unrest, the provisions for relief were expanded.

## THE NEW POOR LAW OF 1834

The New Poor Law was an attempt to reform the prior Elizabethan Poor Law in Britain. The underlying emphasis of the new law was on self-reliance. Its vision was deterrence, its methods were repressive, and its purpose was to cure the perceived evil of pauperism (Kendall, 2000). The new, harsh moral view of poverty reflected in this law allowed the destitute to be admitted to the workhouse and to receive the in-kind, as opposed to cash, form of relief only. Public assistance was not considered a right, nor was government seen as responsible for the unemployed. Most memorable, perhaps, the principle of *less eligibility* was established. According to this principle, people who were given aid had to get less than the lowest-paid worker (Barker, 2014). The aim of this poor law, in short, was not to end poverty but to force relief applicants to accept any type of labor available. The reader will not find it hard to see that many of the attitudes of the mid-19th century that were incorporated into the New Poor Laws remain with us today.

As always, even in the mid-19th century there were mitigating factors at work. The brutal working conditions in the new industrial age, which demanded serious reform, were both immortalized and dramatically exposed in the collective works of Charles Dickens. Dickens' popular novels, serialized in journal form and read across all of England, produced an outcry that helped generate an awakening of sorts, a new humanitarianism.

Then there was the influence of Karl Marx. Marx (1818–1883), who was preeminently a theorist of capitalist society, set the stage for revolution and bloodshed when he and Friedrich Engels collaborated to write the *Communist Manifesto* (1848). Exiled from Europe after the Revolutions of 1848, Marx and Engels moved to London. The economic and political philosophy introduced by these writers views the history of society as the history of class struggle. From the Marxist perspective, the relationship between capitalists and workers derives from the control the capitalist has over the means of production and the product. The labor and socialist movements adapted many of their principles from Marxism.

Political organizations such as the Fabian Society, an English Socialist group, were influential in instituting practical reforms such as working hours legislation, housing projects, and mass education. Charity organizations and settlement houses sprang up out of the same impetus toward reform. In the United States, less influenced by a socialist and labor party voice than Britain, the welfare system was modeled on the English poor laws and the ideologies that undergirded them. These practices were carried out in a manner that was more blaming than compassionate (see Jansson, 2014; Piven & Cloward, 1993).

## COLONIAL AMERICA

Just after the passage of the Elizabethan Poor Law in 1601, settlements began to be established by colonists in North America. As dissenters from the Church of England, Puritans were inspired by Calvinist theology (belief in predestination) and favored a strict religious creed.

In an analysis of early town records in 17th-century Massachusetts and Connecticut, Dolgoff and Feldstein (2012) reveal how the "deserving" poor were maintained and supported by the townships. Vagrant and idle persons, on the other hand, were warned to leave town. Vagrants and those who harbored them were subject to prosecution. The Poor Law mentality was alive and well in the so-called New World; provisions were followed scrupulously because they were widely familiar to England's emigrants and they helped maintain order in the new land. Concepts of the worthy and unworthy poor, the favoring of indoor (such as in a workhouse) over outdoor relief, and the principle of less eligibility (the poor must be supported below the level of the lowest paid worker) were implanted early in the Atlantic coast colonies. Because of the absence of unemployment, the work ethic made even more sense here than in the home country. And then, there was the religious factor: the ethos of the Protestant ethic was suffused throughout the whole social system.

European Christians, as Zinn and Konopacki (2008) indicate, long held the belief that their duty was to try to convert the indigenous population to Christianity. The heathens who did not convert could be exploited in various ways. The Americas, of course, were densely populated with indigenous tribes. As the emigrants from Europe grew more and more plentiful, the greed to have access to all forested and other unfarmed land became all-consuming. Native Americans were pushed into signing various treaties under threat of coercion, while intoxicated, or in exchange for gifts including guns. The Native peoples, we must keep in mind, had a different concept of land than did the white settlers. Consistent with their sense of spiritual interconnectedness and reverence for nature, the concept of private ownership of land, water, and plant life was completely alien (Gesino, 2001). The end result of the clash of cultures and interests was that the US government broke the treaties and the Indians were relocated further and further west. See Box 3.2 for a brief timeline of key historical events in US social welfare history.

### BOX 3.2 Milestones in the Development of US Social Welfare: 1776-1956

1776: Declaration of Independence.
1788: Constitution ratified by the states.
1791: Bill of Rights ratified.
1810: The beginning of the Black Trail of Tears in which around one million slaves were moved in chains from the coastal South to the cotton South.
1838–1839: Trail of Tears: Forced march of the Cherokees further West.
1860: Over 27,000 miles of railroad track built through federal funding.
1861–1865: US Civil War.
1863: President Lincoln passes the Emancipation Proclamation freeing all slaves in the Confederate Territories.
1865: Thirteenth Amendment to the Constitution abolishing slavery.
1865–1872: Freedmen's Bureau provides relief for newly freed slaves.
1865–1900: Rapid US industrialization.
1848: Mexican government forced to cede Texas and California.
1852: First compulsory education law passed in Massachusetts.
1854: President Pierce vetoes bill inspired by Dorothea Dix to provide aid for the mentally ill. Most states built public mental hospitals, nevertheless.
1865–1900: Rapid industrialization.
1877: America's first Charity Organization Society.
1880–1914: 21,000,000 immigrants arrive.
1881: Practice of medicine revolutionized through germ theory of disease.
1889: Hull House opened, Chicago.
1898: First US training for social workers established, later becomes Columbia University School of Social Work.
1899: First juvenile court in Chicago.
1918: Compulsory education laws established in all states.
1919–1933: Prohibition leads to much corruption.
1920: Nineteenth Amendment grants suffrage to women.
1929: Great Depression begins with crash of stock market.
1931: Jane Addams is awarded the Nobel Peace Prize.
1933: New Deal proclaimed by Franklin Roosevelt.
1935: US Social Security Act passed; Aid to Dependent Children, Alcoholics Anonymous founded.
1945: World War II ends; UN established.
1948: Universal Declaration of Human Rights passed by nations of UN.
1952: The Council on Social Work Education is founded to accredit schools of social work.
1955: The National Association of Social Workers (NASW) is created through a merger of existing organizations in the United States.
1956: IFSW established as an international social work organization.

In summary, the major social and cultural factors that shaped American social welfare policies in the Colonial era were an emphasis on individualism and limited government; the lack of a large class of landless people; a weak central government; and the subjugation of persons of color. As for themselves, the leaders of the new country elevated the concept of liberty over that of equality.

## INFORMAL AND SEMI-FORMAL HELPING

Most of the help for the poor has come from its own—the poor helping the poor with limited resources. Mutual aid among African Americans was based on a cultural heritage which stressed strong extended family ties and the tradition of adopting nonrelatives into the family network. Individual interests were not placed above the group; cooperation and sense of community prevailed. Before the Civil War, there were half a million free persons of African descent in the United States (and four million slaves); half of the freed slaves were in the South (Day & Schiele, 2012). A great deal of charity work was done by these free blacks; they had churches, relief associations, and societies for mutual aid. Among the slaves, obligations to kin and a general altruistic behavior promoted the collective survival of a people in a cruel and racist society. Today, a whole re-examination of slavery and slave society has been bolstered by a recent broadcast of interviews with older survivors of slavery that were undertaken as a part of the Federal Writers' Project in the 1930s. These audio recordings of former slaves, excerpts of which were aired on Public Radio International, are riveting in their language and personal revelations of another time (van Wormer, Jackson, & Sudduth, 2012).

Farmers of all races and ethnicity historically have maintained their common welfare through offering collective aid in times of need, such as during crop failures, barn burnings, and illness. Men have generally been responsible for the heavy labor while women have bonded together for childbirth, childcare, cooking, and other nurturant activities. Such a sense of communalism is preserved to some extent in rural areas and maintains its pure form among the Amish today.

Since the early colonial period, much help has been provided by the churches. Good works were viewed as an obligation owed to God and as more rewarding to the giver than to the receiver. In the North, as private fortunes accumulated, individuals and private groups supplemented public relief activities or assisted families whom they knew. In the South, private efforts of a large-scale variety were even more sustained (Trattner, 2004). There, according to Trattner, Calvinist principles of hard work were less pressing, while the spirit of *noblesse oblige* and chivalry was engendered in a class of people who were trying to maintain a social system not unlike that of feudalism.

In the United States, in contrast to many European nations, the separation of church and state had a significant bearing on the manner in which aid to the indigent populace was distributed. The flourishing of numerous sects in America led to a near-competitive atmosphere for helping the poor and, it was hoped, of winning converts. Nearly all forms of relief emanated from church groups: Protestants established orphanages, reform schools, mental hospitals, new kinds of prisons (an area of recognized Quaker activity), and institutions for the handicapped. The Quakers, in particular, spent an enormous amount of time, effort, and money aiding the needy (Day & Schiele, 2012; Reisch, 2014). Their work in rescuing slaves and abetting their escape is well known. The Catholic Church gave special attention to the needs of African and Native Americans, and especially to needy children (Day & Schiele, 2012). Formed in the 18th century in New Orleans, the Ursuline Sisters ran a private home for mothers and children left homeless, initially from wars with the Indians. This home became America's first residential institution for orphaned children. See Box 3.3 for the history of the Ursuline Sisters and the photo in Figure 3.2 from the New Orleans archives.

### BOX 3.3 The Ursuline Sisters

Mary Anne O'Neil

The Ursulines, an order of French nuns, were the first female religious presence in the New World. Devoted to the education of women, they established convent schools in French Canada and Louisiana in the 17th and 18th centuries that served girls of all races and economic and social classes. In Louisiana, their ability to bring large numbers of girls from varied populations into their classrooms resulted in the highest female literacy rate among both the descendants of Europeans and women of color in North America during the Colonial Period. Their schools were not only places of instruction but also refuges for poor, orphaned, and mistreated women and children. In their efforts to care for the physical as well as the spiritual and intellectual needs of their students, they performed the dual functions of social workers and teachers.

The Ursulines were founded in 1532 by Angela Merici. A devout woman from Northern Italy with no ties to any religious order, she and her unmarried female companions established a hospital in Brescia to care for the needs of women and children victimized by the Wars of Religion. They called themselves the Company of St. Ursula after a 4th-century medieval virgin martyr. The movement begun by Merici caught on most rapidly in France, and by the end of the 16th century, groups of lay Catholic women throughout the country organized themselves as Companies of St. Ursula, taking as their principal duties the instruction of girls and women in religious doctrine and reading. Often conducting their classes in town squares or outside of churches, these early Ursulines provided the only education available to poor females. In 1612, the Ursulines formally became a religious order. Unlike other nuns of their time, they were semi-cloistered, that is, not completely cut off from society. Like cloistered nuns, they took the traditional vows of poverty, chastity, and obedience and lived in convents. However, they had the right—and obligation—to open their convents to the world and receive girls as boarders and day students.

The French Ursulines were sometimes called the female Jesuits, because, like their male counterparts, they were proselytizers and missionaries. Motivated by the desire to counteract the Protestant Reformation, they taught in order to form Catholic wives and mothers, who would, in turn, create strong Catholic families. By the 17th century, their zeal for conversions caused them to look beyond Europe to Canada and its native populations. In 1639, the Ursulines from Tours received permission to establish convents, schools, and orphanages in Quebec City and along the St. Lawrence River. The first dictionaries in the Algonquin and Iroquois languages were composed by these Ursulines for use in their classrooms. The French Ursulines' willingness to perform a variety of tasks resulted in their assignment by the Company of the East Indies to operate a military hospital in the colony of Louisiana almost a century later. In 1727, 12 Ursulines from Rouen traveled to New Orleans to care for soldiers but also to convert and teach.

From the earliest years of their presence in New Orleans, the Ursulines succeeded in bringing together girls from all strata of colonial society. The daughters of French, but also slave girls, lived in the convent as boarders. Day classes with shortened hours and curricula were created to reach those girls, free and enslaved, obligated to perform farm or domestic work. The nuns took in orphans—black, white, and from native tribes—often without funding from either church or civil authorities. Penniless widows and abused women found temporary shelter and employment in their convent. The social inclusiveness practiced by the Ursulines set an example of female solidarity that was soon imitated by lay Catholic women in New Orleans, who formed confraternities to extend the work of teaching and conversion beyond the convent walls. When Louisiana was sold to the United States in 1803, President Thomas Jefferson recognized the success of the Ursulines. In a letter promising the nuns that they would be allowed to pursue freely their vocation in the United States, he assured them that the Protestant country to which they now belonged was grateful for their "furtherance of the wholesome purposes of society."

*The Règlements des religieuses ursulines* ("Rules of the Ursuline Nuns"), a book of detailed guidelines that were updated and adapted to circumstances by French and American nuns from the 18th through the middle of the 20th century, reveals a teaching method based on the relationship of a loving mother to her children. The health, nutrition, and hygiene of boarding students were to be watched over more closely than their academic success. The hours of instruction for girls in day school were adjusted so they could travel safely in daylight. Classrooms were heated or open to fresh air in accordance with the seasons. Daily class schedules included ample time for recreation and physical activity. The Rules specified that corporal punishment was forbidden and that the nuns must treat their charges with gentleness and moderation. The nuns avoided distinctions of wealth and social status among their students. Paying and charity students dressed alike and were treated alike. Although the curricula for boarders and day students were different in the 18th century—day students were instructed in reading, catechism, and mathematics, while boarders added fine arts, foreign language, and literature to the basic subjects—the Rules instructed teachers to provide additional opportunities to any girl who showed aptitude and enthusiasm for advanced study.

The education provided by the Ursulines was practical, with a strong emphasis on literacy, numeracy, rational thinking, and economics, as well as religion. As they created pious wives and mothers to solidify the reach of Catholicism in North America, the nuns also formed women prepared to manage their households and who were instilled with the desire to serve others. In both French Canada and Louisiana, Ursuline classrooms produced a society of educated women, unusual in both Europe and the New World in the 18th and 19th centuries, who mitigated the harsh conditions of colonial life. In the words of Emily Clark, historian of the Ursulines of New Orleans, these "women made life in this world more bearable, even as they continued working for humanity's salvation in the next" (Clark, 2007, p. 93).

---

Reference: Clark, E. (2007). *Masterless mistresses: The New Orleans Ursulines and the development of a new world society, 1727–1834.* Chapel Hill, NC: University of North Carolina Press.

Source: Mary Anne O'Neil, Professor Emerita of French, Whitman College.

**FIGURE 3.2.** The Ursuline Sisters were a popular teaching order in New Orleans. Here they are in 1958 in their summer habits. Permission by Mary Lee Berner Harris, Ursuline Academy Archives.

## FORMAL AID

Whereas outdoor relief was more common in the South, poorhouses in the North existed as a carryover from the early poor laws. By 1832, practically all of New York's counties had poorhouses run by political appointees whose pay was drawn from the inmates' work. The deserving and undeserving poor alike were confined in places where the rates for malnutrition and disease were quite high. The death rate for children was astronomical. After 1875, laws removed children from these work "dungeons of death" and placed them elsewhere.

When Sunday School teacher Dorothea Dix volunteered to teach at an insane asylum in 1841, she was set to embark on one of the most memorable crusades of the century—an effort to end the barbaric treatment of the indigent mentally ill. To Dix, the only way to rectify the problem lay in federal intervention. Building a network of support from the clergy, the press, and politicians, Dix ultimately got a bill to allocate funds and land for the construction of mental hospitals passed by both houses of Congress. President Pierce's veto of the bill was based on the argument that the states, not the federal government, should provide charity. This single act set a precedent for the next 75 years that the federal government refrain from providing social welfare services. However, as Dolgoff and Feldstein (2012) indicate, federal aid and land were given readily for the building of railroads and to reward soldiers for their service.

Like other major catastrophes, the Civil War created conditions that demanded immediate public aid. Singularly, affirming federal responsibility over states' rights, the Civil War laid the groundwork for the United States to ultimately become a welfare state (Day & Schiele, 2012). First, even before the war was over, the social welfare needs of the soldiers and their families demanded attention. Whether in regard to medical care, housing, or financial support, the needs of the veterans were considered apart from the needs of the civilian population. The veterans' needs were addressed without stigma or vacillation. In fact, from the time of the Revolutionary War, veterans were recipients of aid, universally, in recognition of their personal service and sacrifice. Generous grants to federal lands, pensions, and other types of aid were bestowed upon them.

Although the nation had abolished slavery forever, little thought was given for the welfare of the former slaves or of the society in which they would live. Thousands of ex-slaves took to the roads, wandering aimlessly from county to county. The very fact that they embarked on such a desperate search for their loved ones shows the persistence of the strength of black family ties. But these were terrible times of hunger and dire poverty in the South following the Civil War. Thousands of newly freed men and women died of disease and starvation or were victims of violence. The vast majority became sharecroppers who worked on white people's farms. Meanwhile, in the North, sweeping industrial activity resumed.

Although reluctant to assume a welfare role, the federal government in 1865, during Reconstruction, established the Freedmen's Bureau as part of the War Department. The purpose of this first federal welfare agency was to provide temporary relief, education, and health care for the newly freed slaves (Zinn, 2005; Reisch, 2014). One of the interesting functions of the Bureau was the work it did in reuniting families separated by slavery and the war, solemnizing prior slave unions, and arranging for the adoption of orphans. Despite the fact that it was seriously underfunded and ended its work abruptly, the Freedmen's Bureau established an important precedent in its offering of emergency, comprehensive relief during a serious social upheaval. Foreshadowing the New Deal of the 1930s and the War on Poverty of the 1960s, the history surrounding the Freedmen's Bureau provides backing for Piven and Cloward's (1993) basic premise that, "relief arrangements are initiated or expanded during outbreaks of civil disorder produced by mass unemployment, and are then abolished or contracted when political stability is restored," (p. xv).

## EUROPE: A CONTRAST

While the Protestant ethic still prevailed in "the land of pilgrims' pride" and the British reform movement got under way in earnest, over in Europe, the birthplace of Protestantism, the first general social insurance scheme was introduced. Chancellor Otto von Bismarck's sickness insurance law provided medical care and cash benefits during a period of sickness to employees, in defined types of industry (Barkin, 2015). These benefits were to be financed through contributions by both employers and employees (*Encyclopaedia Britannica*, 2016). In 1884, accident insurance was made compulsory. Several years later, workers' pensions were introduced. Austria followed suit, as did Sweden, and the Netherlands in 1901. In contrast, in Britain and the United States, where the threat of revolution was less potent, self-help through friendly societies and savings banks was provided.

Heclo (2010) offers an interesting contrast between England and Sweden in terms of treatment of the landless poor. Whereas England engaged in a brutal process of forcing the rural poor off the land, Sweden where industrialization arrived later, transferred land to peasant ownership. These historical differences between the two countries remain fundamental to understanding the more positive attitudes of Swedish people to government and the welfare state to the present day.

## INDUSTRIAL GROWTH IN THE UNITED STATES

Within the span of one person's lifetime, industrialization, which came later than in Britain and was first apparent in the North, literally transformed the American landscape. Energy production soared to such an extent that the nation went from being primarily agricultural in 1859 to primarily producing manufactured goods 50 years later. The vast increases in both the population and the physical sizes of the cities presented the country with a set of problems reminiscent of England in earlier days. The streets of American cities were overcrowded, filthy, and rampant with disease (tuberculosis was common) and crime. Factory conditions were abominable—18-hour days were not unheard of; women worked night shifts; and industrial accidents were frequent.

Two countertrends responded to the dehumanizing social conditions of the day: social Darwinism and Christian charity. *The Origin of Species*, written by Charles Darwin (1859), discussed the evolution of plants and animals. A happy union of laissez-faire economics and the doctrine of survival of the fittest, social Darwinism became the prevailing philosophy of the era (Reisch, 2014). As the wounds of the Civil War began to heal and wealth became almost an end in itself, the poor were once again blamed for their condition of poverty.

A severe economic depression of the 1870s threw large numbers of people out of work, and rioting and disorder ensued. Unions, which were just beginning to organize, were blamed by many for the economic crisis of the nation. Churches and private citizens set up soup kitchens and distributed fuel and clothing to the poor. Charity organization societies and settlement houses were established to provide formal but voluntary services to the poor.

## PARADIGM SHIFTS

Social work in Europe and the United States began in the 1890s in response to problems caused by industrialization and its corollary, urbanization. An outgrowth of the charities and corrections movements, social work practice has been greatly influenced by the development of the social welfare system. Whereas technological advances have often outpaced our ethical and political understanding of how to cope with them, social workers and their antecedents have been key mediators between societal forces and the people they serve. Social workers, in other words, have helped those caught in the grip of rapid social change adjust to new circumstances. As society's "great humanizers," social workers alternately have been accused of overidentifying with the poor and of "being co-opted" by the system. This apparent dualism, between individual and society and between inner and outer directedness, in fact, is as old as social policy and, of course, far older than its professional link, social work. This dualism has haunted the profession since well before it even could be considered a profession.

Thomas Kuhn (1962) introduced the world of science to the notion of *paradigm shift*. A paradigm shift is a dramatic change in worldview by society, often representing a revolutionary break with past ways of viewing reality. Such shifts in thinking generally take place as a result of some sort of crisis, whether due to scientific discoveries or economic/military forces. Relevant to social welfare history, our concern is where society places the blame for personal impoverishment—on the individual or on the society. We can term this the social/self dualism. Causal attribution has important treatment and public policy implications.

We can characterize America's social welfare history, accordingly, as one long series of pendulum swings between two opposite poles with the focus of individual attribution at one end and the focus of social reform at the other. Although both currents have run simultaneously throughout the last century, one side or the other typically has tended to dominate at any one time. One generation's certainty may be lost on the next. Or to continue with our metaphor, we might say that gravity invariably pulls the pendulum downward toward the other direction.

A social reform emphasis characterized the Progressive Era before World War I, the 1930s, and the 1960s. Social work leaders rose to prominence in each era. The foremother of social work, Jane Addams, is associated with the urban reform movement of the Progressive Era; social worker Harry Hopkins helped initiate the New Deal and the creation of the modern welfare state; and the idealistic war on poverty offered a bonanza in jobs for community action workers, and social work education expanded enormously during this period.

And then there were the in-between years when individualism triumphed. The private interest of the hedonistic 1920s, the political hysteria and anti-idealism of the 1950s, the attack-the-underdog mentality of the Reagan era, and the war on welfare aid as launched under the Clinton administration were all manifestations of ideological shifts away from the social activism of the previous age.

Reisch and Garvin (2016), in their history of social justice and social work, discuss the emergence of three specific social work methods of practice—social casework, group work, and community organization. The origin of each method is linked, curiously, to the prevailing ideology of a specific political theme in US history. We could almost say, taking a literal meaning of the term, that each dominant practice modality was "politically correct" in its day. Whether society's focus was more on personal troubles, on public issues, or somewhere in-between, the priorities of social work and the methods of treatment have followed.

## THE ORIGINS OF SOCIAL WORK

Social work as we know it today was derived from a merger of the Charity Organization Societies (COS) and the settlement house establishments (McNutt, 2013). Whereas the professional side of social work has its roots in COS altruism, the social justice strain is grounded in the settlement house tradition. Both movements were based largely on English models and tradition. Patronage, piety, poor laws, and philanthropy—these are the four Ps singled out by Specht and Courtney (1994) in their incisive book, *Unfaithful Angels: How Social Work Has Abandoned Its Mission.* The four Ps are different arrangements for dealing with social problems that developed after the breakup of feudal society but that preceded the modern period. Of the four Ps, the values of the *poor laws,* which are reflected in the middle-class morality that regulates the poor and their receipt of government aid, most fully correspond to attitudes that are extant today. Programs for the poor are both means tested and mean spirited, and most are deliberately made unattractive (Specht & Courtney, 1994).

## CHARITIES AND CORRECTIONS MOVEMENT

Claiming that individual failure was the reason for poverty was the underlying rationale of the Charity Organization Society, which was founded in London in 1869. The Victorian reformers saw lack of character as the reason for poverty, not starvation wages, slum housing, lack of education, or poor health care (Kendall, 2000). Gradually, in Britain, it took the influence of the Fabian socialists to prove the fallacy of the belief that the poor were responsible for their own condition, as Kendall points out. This shift in the British focus was later reflected in the form that social work education took in the United Kingdom, with its emphasis on the social sciences. In contrast, social casework was to become the hallmark of US social work education. The social casework–based COS quickly moved to virtually every large city in the country, beginning with Buffalo, New York. In Canada, too, the COS legacy, the reform-the-person approach, was a guiding educational principle (Mullaly, 2006).

The decades from 1877 to World War I were a time of deep economic, social, and political crisis. Consistent with the ethos of the age, a scientific solution was directed to both the protection of the poor from starvation and a validation of the work incentive. Key organizing principles of the operation of the COS were the use of business methods in controlling the flow of allocations, the perpetual focus on the moral status of the clients (Were they deserving of aid?), and the key role of the friendly visitor or caring helper and mentor (Reisch, 2014). As these often upper-class charity workers became immersed in the world of the poor, a curious but predictable thing happened to them—they began to recoil at the paternalism and victim blaming inherent in the social system and to see poverty as a cause as well as a result of certain forms of social behavior (Reisch & Garvin, 2016; Trattner, 2004).

Mary Richmond, later renowned for establishing the principles of social work education, began her career with the COS of Baltimore in 1888. Unlike other founders of the profession, Richmond was not a member of the privileged classes; she was entirely self-educated, in fact. Although she did not intend it, Richmond's individualistic casework focus helped prepare the profession for its later embrace of psychiatry, psychoanalysis, and psychotherapy (Specht & Courtney, 1994). Nevertheless, Richmond's keen attention to the individual as a part of a social unit and her advocacy of understanding the person in the situation is surprisingly consistent with modern multifocused formulations. Richmond's ideas were set forth in *Social Diagnosis* (1917), the first major textbook to be used by practicing social workers. The psychosocial conceptualization of human behavior introduced in this work might have come to fruition in the years that followed, with the usual revision and reformulation of new theoretical paradigms, had it not been for the influence of something even more overwhelming—the voluminous works on the unconscious by Sigmund Freud.

In the meantime, as the COS began to develop a relevant knowledge base and to formalize social casework techniques of social service and delivery, the way was paved for the emergence of a new profession. Emphasizing personal attention and individual work with clients, this well-formulated model gained preeminence in conjunction with social work's transition from a voluntary to a paid enterprise. The inevitable tendency of scientific charity, with its emphasis on the objective and factual, was to make the use of volunteer visitors, untrained and part time, increasingly difficult to justify (Trattner, 2004).

The credit for being the world's first professional social worker goes to Octavia Hill, an English pioneer in housing management who worked to improve the lives of the tenants even as she managed the property. Inspired by Christian socialism, Hill's work in helping the poorest of the poor reorganize their lives has been sadly neglected in the chronicles of social work. Fortunately, Katherine Kendall (2000) has perused her writings and other historical material of 19th-century England to make her contribution now a part of the historic record.

The first salaried social worker was a trained COS worker, Mary Stewart, who was hired in 1894 to interview patients at the Royal Free Hospital in London (Dalrymple & Boylan, 2013). Her major role was to determine whether or not patients qualified for free treatment at the clinic. What she found was that very few were asking for services they didn't need. By the turn of the century, the organized charities were establishing formal training as the first step in professionalization. Volunteers were now being placed under the authority of social workers who shaped policy and covered the field. The professional charity workers, not the volunteers, began to be acknowledged authorities on the needs of disadvantaged and/or deviant people (Day & Schiele, 2012). As mentioned earlier, social work derived from two movements, each with a very different ideological base. Whereas the individualistic casework method had come to prominence later when the emphasis on personality superseded the social action thrust, the community-oriented focus never has been entirely absent from a profession bent on "helping people help themselves." Nor is it entirely absent today.

## THE SETTLEMENT HOUSE MOVEMENT

An outgrowth of the deplorable urban conditions of the time and also modeled on English innovations, the settlement house movement began in the 1880s (Carlton-LaNey, 2013). After visiting Toynbee Hall, a house for the poor in the worst part of London in 1889, Jane Addams returned to Chicago to found with her associate, Ellen Gates Starr, the American equivalent of Toynbee Hall at Hull House. Eventually, Hull House was to become the most famous settlement in the world. Secular from the beginning, settlement houses in the United States had social change as their focus rather than spiritual goals. The individual religious motivation of the founders and volunteers, however, is not to be underestimated.

Settlements sprang up in most large cities over the next 15 years, their number reaching 300 at their peak in 1915. Set up in immigrant neighborhoods, upper and middle class people themselves—unmarried women, college students, teachers, and doctors—moved into slums as residents. The belief that poverty perhaps could be eliminated was a theme of the liberal Progressive Era.

There was in fact, a strong undercurrent of thinking during the decades before World War I that was to offer a source of inspiration to the settlement house workers. The principal sources of such inspiration for early social workers included the secular and religious utopian philosophies of the 19th century, early feminist thinkers like Elizabeth Cady Stanton, radical trade unionism, Social Gospel Movement, and the Socialist and Communist parties (Reisch & Andrews, 2001).

The years from 1900 to the 1920s are characterized as the time of progressivism. In contrast to their friendly visitor counterparts, settlement house workers regarded themselves as social reformers rather than charity workers. With their goal to bridge the gap between the classes and their emphasis on prevention rather than treatment, these workers lived beside their urban neighbors and worked together with them to improve social conditions. Settlement houses were often used as meeting locations for community activists to organize strikes and other public demonstrations. In addition, in actively participating in the life of the neighborhood and of their poor and immigrant clients (in the United States), these upper- and upper-middle-class young men and women (mainly women) sought to raise the cultural, moral, and intellectual level of the community. The settlements provided a day nursery for working mothers, health clinics, and classes in English, dance, drama, art, and sewing.

Gradually, consistent with their intimate knowledge of their charges, the settlement workers became politicized and pursued social reform through legislation and social policy change. We must recognize too, as we learn from Reisch and Andrews (2001), that many of the first generation of social workers, like Florence Kelley or Ellen Gates Starr, were radicals before they became social workers. Addams' seeming radicalism stemmed from her pacifist Quaker upbringing rather than socialism (Jimenez, Pasztor, & Chambers, 2015). These reformers helped bring about changes in child labor laws, in women's labor laws, and in the institutional care of persons with disabilities. The establishment of child welfare services and juvenile courts, likewise, had its inception here. Rather than looking down upon the poor or seeking to impose their way of life upon them, settlement workers placed their focus on reforming society. Out of this heritage came one of social work's primary methods of intervention, a self-help model of community organization (Mullaly, 2006). As Jane Addams stated in her autobiography (1910):

> We early found ourselves spending many hours in efforts to secure support for deserted women, insurance for bewildered widows, damages for injured operators, furniture from the clutches of the installment store. The settlement...constantly acts between various institutions of the city and the people for whose benefit these institutions were erected. (p. 167)

To view an amazing collection of historical documents and images, visit the Hull House website at www.uic.edu/jaddams/hull/urbanexp/ Less well known to Americans but no less interesting is the Heatherbank Museum of Social Work in Glasgow, Scotland, the only museum totally dedicated to social work and welfare in Europe (information at http://www.theglasgowstory.com). The collection of paintings is now housed at Glasgow Caledonian University.

A question not addressed in Jane Addams's autobiography is, How did the settlement movement, which focused on helping immigrants, respond to the needs of black people who were just beginning to migrate into the northern cities during the Progressive Era? Trattner contrasts attitudes of the COS workers, who stressed the individual moral causes of poverty and were largely indifferent to the problems of the destitute blacks, with settlement house workers, who advocated the unpopular cause of equality for all Americans. Long before it was in vogue to do so, at least some settlement house workers helped foster black pride and Afro-American culture, according to Jimenez et al. (2015). To their credit, settlement leaders actively participated in the creation of the National Association for the Advancement of Colored People (NAACP) and the National Urban League. Jane Addams wrote a paper and spoke out against segregationists in the South and other parts of the United States. Yet consistent with the social climate of the day, while they opposed racism, these leaders did not advocate integration. Realists as well as idealists, these women, such as Jane Addams and Mary McDowell, knew that neighborhood prejudices militated against the mixing of blacks and whites in settlement houses. They believed that black culture had been broken by slavery and that, unlike the immigrants, black people were not ready for integration.

After 1900, according to Philpott (1978), settlements for "colored people" never had the capacity to provide black Chicago with adequate, much less equal service. Moreover, the nation's settlement houses were largely segregated, with many in the South created and staffed by African American women and reserved for blacks only. In Chicago, argues Trattner (2004), the Frederick Douglass Center had workshops and clubrooms for boys, and held classes in manual training for boys and domestic service for girls to prepare black youths for the only jobs open to them in that day.

Philpott (1978), however, is less charitable concerning the true purpose of the segregated settlement houses. His documentation, drawn from historical records of the day, suggests that the Douglass Center's true purpose was not to help the poor blacks but to attract the black elite and to insulate them from the less educated blacks who were pouring into "the black belt" in large numbers. The Emmanuel Settlement, founded and directed by Fannie Emmanuel, a dedicated African American, operated under a different philosophy. Fostering neighborhood pride, this center was a place where a person could get relief, both in the monetary and emotional sense of the word. With little or no financial support from whites, however, the settlement closed in less than five years. To learn the history of the little known settlement schools where black and white women together delivered services to the community, see Whitaker (2013).

## PORTRAIT OF JANE ADDAMS

By the turn of the last century, as Specht and Courtney (1994) indicate, Jane Addams was the most famous woman in America. By the culmination of her career in 1931, she was awarded the Nobel Prize for her efforts for peace during World War I. But who was Jane Addams really?

Although recounting some facts from her early life, Addams' autobiography *Twenty Years at Hull House* reveals very little personal detail about the author. The qualities that do shine forth are an abiding concern for the underdog, optimism, perseverance, and feisty leadership. Her fondness for her father, a devout Quaker to whom the book is dedicated, clearly set the stage for Addams' unpopular pacifism during World War I—a position that branded her a subversive and radical for the rest of her life. Jane Addams was to be given the dubious honor of first being made a life member of the Daughters of the American Revolution and then subsequently being expelled. Just as she had been universally acclaimed prior to the war, Addams experienced a fall from grace unparalleled among public figures in US history (Reisch & Andrews, 2001).

Works on Quaker history include Jane Addams and others associated with the settlement movement as Quakers by upbringing. As described in *The Story of Quaker Women in America* (Bacon, 1986, p. 147): "Jane Addams herself was the daughter of self-styled Hicksite John Addams, whom she adored. Although never a member of a Quaker meeting, she maintained close ties with Quakers throughout her life." Addams, in fact, was sent as a representative of the Society of Friends to distribute aid following the human wreckage of World War I.

Feminist and lesbian sources, too, proudly claim Addams as one of their own. A documentary on Jane Addams and her companion presents the couple as gay icons (Loerzel, 2008). Faderman (1991) includes Addams among those whose love for women was at least in part a search for allies to help wage the battle against women's social impoverishment. Changing the lives of the poor, these women themselves were changed by their confrontation with the cruel realities from which they otherwise would have been sheltered. Ellen Starr, the close friend with

**FIGURE 3.3.** Jane Addams, the mother of social work. © Chicago History Museum/Contributor/ Getty images.

whom Addams co-founded the Hull House, was Addams' first serious attachment, according to Faderman. Her devoted companion throughout most of her life, however, was Mary Rozet Smith. Most historians and social work scholars, nevertheless, have preferred to present Addams as one who never knew love. In any case, the pairing off of unmarried women into so-called "Boston marriages" did not raise comment in her day, as it did not have sexual connotations. See the photograph of Jane Addams in Figure 3.3.

## PROFESSIONALIZATION

Less interesting perhaps, but of more significance to the development of the social work profession, was the training furnished to the friendly visitors and resident workers of the COS and settlement houses—the two precursors of social work, respectively. At first, the training consisted mainly of apprenticeship. Then, in addition to teaching on the job, agencies began to use more formal training, which consisted of lectures, reading, and discussion (Jansson, 2014). Participation at the annual National Conference of Charities and Corrections drew together all those concerned with social welfare issues. Although their reform efforts were major and considered radical by the standards of the day (for example, they rallied for a 40-hour work week), the charities and corrections people were ruled by a fierce Victorian morality.

Social work education began in rudimentary form in the training provided by Octavia Hill to the women who wanted to help impoverished people manage their lives and finances. "It all began," notes (Kendall, 2000) "with Octavia Hill, a pioneer in housing management, when she embarked in the late 1870s on the training of her 'fellow workers,' as she called them, in the principles necessary for helping impoverished tenants to help themselves" (p. v). This training occurred not in New York but in London and later expanded in 1890 into a more formally organized program of courses under the auspices of the Women's University Settlement in London.

Earlier, toward the end of the 19th century, Mary Richmond presented a paper titled, "The Need for Training Schools in Applied Philanthropy." The impact of this presentation was considerable because it paved the way for the founding of formal social work education. In 1898, a professional summer course was sponsored by the COS of New York. This led in 1904 to a one year graduate program of what was to become the first American School of Social Work at Columbia University. Parallel developments took place in Germany as well. But the credit for establishing the first clearly defined school of social work goes to a group of social reformers in the Netherlands (Healy, 2008). According to documentation provided by Lorenz (1994) and Kendall (2000), the first school of social work was founded in Amsterdam in 1899 and owed its existence to philanthropy and the international settlement movement.

The term *social work* was used for the first time, according to Lorenz (1994), in Germany (*Sozial Arbeit*) and in the American settlement movement. The use of the term attests to the social nature of the profession and is consistent with the occupation's historical origins. In his historic address to the National Conference of Charities and Correction in 1915, Abraham Flexner, MD, uttered a stinging rebuke to the social work occupation, much to the disappointment of his audience. Social work he declared, unlike law and medicine, could not claim to be a profession. The field lacked a systematic body of knowledge and theory, as well as autonomy, as social workers merely assisted the real professionals as auxiliary staff. Although this historic commentary could have been regarded as a male attacking a female-dominated profession by using criteria of the male model of achievement, the listeners buckled under. They would acquire professional status somehow. The social workers were determined to get the recognition due them.

## THE FREUDIAN INFLUENCE AND GROWTH OF CASEWORK

The lifeline thrown to a fledgling profession came in the form of psychoanalytic theory, the teachings of which began to disseminate among US social work educators after Freud's historic visit to Clark University in 1912. However, according to Lorenz (1994), the wholesale adoption of these theories from another discipline in the United States and Britain still would have failed to satisfy the criteria set forth by Flexner. Ultimately (but not before still another major paradigm shift during the Great Depression), the significance of the adoption of the Freudian paradigm was that it paved the way for social workers to reinvent themselves in the form of psychotherapists.

The liberal political climate disappeared almost overnight when, under the presidency of Woodrow Wilson, the United States entered World War I. This was when settlement house leaders fell out of favor with the public sentiment because of their active opposition to the military buildup and ensuing aggression. Other factors also reinforced the reactionary drift of the country. The victory of bolshevism in Russia, which culminated in the Red Scare of 1919–1920, put a taint on all community-type collective activity. As public suspicion and distrust grew, the settlement houses suffered considerably (Trattner, 2004). Financial support was withdrawn, and people began to look elsewhere to solve social problems. Social reform became now equated with radicalism, and radicalism was considered dangerous.

As the war ended, women also lost much of the independence they had acquired. Identifying women as the weaker sex, Freudian theory provided a rationale to justify a return to the status quo at a time when women, having had a taste of power, might otherwise have been inclined to want to keep it (women were given the right to vote but very little else).

Then there was the matter of racism. As the middle classes and socially mobile immigrants moved out of the central city into the suburbs, new people moved in—Puerto Ricans, Mexicans, and African Americans replaced the Europeans of an earlier day. Less public sympathy was generated toward these darker-skinned residents; assimilation was less an option for them and their children than for their predecessors, in any case.

With the settlement house philosophy demoted in the public eye, Mary Richmond was catapulted to leadership within the profession. In 1922 she "clarified" the social casework method to bring it more in line with the personality focus, which was rapidly gaining currency. The psychosocial view of human behavior was replaced by a more narrow perspective, but one that was as exciting as it was revolutionary. In her autobiography, Bertha Reynolds (1963) uniquely captures the thrill of her own education into the mysteries of the human mind and beyond:

> We learned about the working of the subconscious, and many things in everyday life became clear to us. We saw fears displaced from childhood, jealousy displaced from other persons, hostility disguised as solicitude, desire as fear, and wish as certainty. We watched each other's slips of the tongue with glee and lived in a world where nothing was quite as it seemed and was frequently the opposite. We learned that the normal could best be understood through study of the abnormal, just because, in states of disease, inhibitions are lost and the workings of the mental mechanism can be seen, as are the works of a clock when its back is removed. No wonder we felt that we had been fooled by appearances all our lives and that we now had the key to wisdom in human relations. (pp. 58–59)

## THE GREAT DEPRESSION AND SOCIAL WORK

But alas, no sooner had the discovery of the unconscious rewritten our understanding of human behavior than a national economic calamity struck. A fascination with probing the unconscious gave way to more immediate concerns.

When the Great Depression hit following the stock market crash of 1929, the unemployment rate reached a high of 24% by 1933. President Herbert Hoover's response was to rely on the voluntary social welfare sector. Demonstrations, strikes, and riots occurred nationwide as the financial panic worsened. Images recalled by Olsen (1994) represent the decade: apple sellers, the bread line, the migrant-worker, and the man with his sign stating, "I will work for food." When Franklin Roosevelt assumed the presidency in 1933, the banking system was threatened with collapse, millions of transients roamed the nation, and one of every four farms was foreclosed. The magnitude of mass suffering, in short, was intense; everyone was affected one way or another by the crisis. In the climate of social upheaval, which was fast approaching, the time was right for a startling departure from prior welfare traditions. As Roosevelt promised in his campaign speeches, he worked to regularize production, provide federal public works and unemployment insurance, and get the federal government to assume responsibility for relief. Much of what he accomplished was done in a dazzling 100 days.

As a part of a wave of New Deal legislation, the Civilian Conservation Corps provided jobs immediately in the National Forest. The Public Works Administration, in contrast, was slower to get started but had more impact when it did so. Social worker Harry Hopkins of Iowa was appointed to head the Emergency Relief Act program and after that, the Works Progress Administration. He was one of President Roosevelt's closest advisers. Frances Perkins, also a social worker, was appointed to serve as Secretary of Labor. Perkins thus became the nation's first female Cabinet official and helped draft much of the New Deal legislation in the 1930s and 1940s. Her most notable achievement was her influence in the development of the landmark Social Security Act (Jansson, 2014). Much of the inspiration for the programs instituted under this Act came from progressive European developments; Perkins, in fact, traveled to Europe to study European provisions as a model for the United States.

As the driving force behind the 40-hour work week, the minimum wage, unemployment compensation, worker's compensation, and the abolition of child labor, Perkins did more to improve the conditions of working Americans than any cabinet member in our history (Maloney, 2015). And yet, her great contributions to the social welfare state that we have today are largely unrecognized in the history books.

To all needy, unemployed persons and their dependents, massive relief grants were provided under the auspices of the Federal Emergency Relief Administration. In order to preserve people's self-respect, the president called for a public works program to provide a job for every able-bodied unemployed person; wages were to be below those paid by private employers but higher than relief payments. Piven and Cloward (1993) assess the overall significance:

> Work relief is remembered mainly for these accomplishments—for the dams and roads and schools and hospitals and other public facilities built by so many men in so short a time. . . . By once more enmeshing people in the work role, the cornerstone of social control in any society, it went far toward moderating civil disorder. (p. 97)

Roosevelt's reform of the economic system established safeguards to curb exploitation of workers while obtaining the benefits of regulation of prices, wages, and production for businesses and the nation. Business leaders had to agree to refrain from using child labor, to allow workers to join unions, and to honor specified minimum working conditions (Jansson, 2014).

The greatest legacy, by far, from the wave of measures known collectively as the New Deal was the Social Security Act of 1935. Designed to alleviate financial dependency through two lines of defense—contributory social assurance and public assistance—the Social Security Act included a national old-age insurance system; federal grants to states for maternal and child welfare services, aid to dependent children, medical care and rehabilitation for the handicapped; and a federal-state unemployment system. Opposition from the American Medical Association prevented the adoption of a national health plan (Barusch, 2014). Health insurance for those persons over age 65 (Medicare) and for the very poor (Medicaid) were not added to the Social Security Act until 1965.

The lack of provision for the unemployed, able-bodied worker was a significant deficiency in the Social Security Act. Yet despite its shortcomings, the legislation contained in the Social Security Act in 1935 provided the framework for the United States' social welfare system and was a demonstration of the federal responsibility for meeting the urgent needs of the nation's citizens. Above all, the solution for social problems was sought at this historic time in the system or in the social and economic conditions of the day, not in the individuals themselves.

While the United States moved swiftly to offset social unrest under the leadership of a determined President Roosevelt, north of the border in Canada, men were herded, military style, into relief camps reminiscent of poorhouses (Black, 2014). By the end of the decade, however, Canadians also realized that it was the economy at fault, not the individuals. World War II solved the unemployment problem (as in the United States), but Canadians demanded full economic and social security and, therefore, a comprehensive welfare program was launched. A universal system of family allowances and old age benefits were included in the program. Universal health care, however, had to wait until later.

The Great Depression had a radicalizing effect on the nation's conscience and on the social work profession as well. During a time of disillusionment and despair with the capitalist system, caseworkers grew critical of the narrow Freudian focus. The growing prevalence of poverty made it difficult to lay the blame on individual weakness. Due to the massive programming introduced "to get America moving again," the demand for social workers, especially trained social workers, increased exponentially. Under social legislation enacted under the New Deal, the administrators and planners drew heavily upon the knowledge, assistance, and heritage of social workers, and the profession assumed an unprecedented importance in American life (Trattner, 2004). So, as always, the focus of social work shifted in tandem with the exigencies and ideologies of the day, and caseworkers moved away from one-on-one counseling and probing of the mind to client advocacy and intervention geared toward providing resources.

As new public welfare workers faced taxing working conditions, huge caseloads, crowded workplaces, and little job security, they looked toward social work unions and other activist groups for help (Popple & Leighninger, 2014). Despite the heightened awareness of the effectiveness of collective action during a period of social change, American social workers were torn between their image of professionalism and the desire to better working conditions through collective bargaining. In the Depression era, according to Popple and Leighninger, mainstream social work chose to resolve the dilemma by endorsing the roles of "expert witness" and "consultant" to policy workers, rather than assuming a more adversarial stance. This resolution of a potentially volatile issue has never been seriously challenged. European social workers, in contrast, perceived no inherent conflict between unionization and professionalism and in many countries, in fact, the professional organization is the union.

On both the North American and European continents, the pendulum, which so recently had swung toward social action and government relief efforts, now had predictably gravitated toward the other direction. A growing national backlash against New Deal reforms and union strikes, along with the escalation of war in Europe and Asia, contributed not only to hostility against the labor movement in the early 1940s, but also to social work's renewed interest in the individual treatment aspects of the field (Popple & Leighninger, 2014). So social work was back to shaping the individual to fit the system, instead of adjusting the system to help the individual, back to wrestling with private troubles over public issues. After World War II, group work became professionalized, borrowing a reconceptualization of Freudian thought to relate the basic principles (transference, defense mechanisms such as regression and repression, and so on) to the dynamics of group interaction. Then, as professional training was required, this form of social work practice "came of age."

## AN OVERVIEW OF WOMEN'S LEADERSHIP IN THE PROFESSION, 1910–1955

Unique among the social sciences and most of the professions, the field of social work was created and given its shape and character by women. In the words of Kendall (1989, p. 23):

> There were men in the field—even some good men—but women ran the show. Many if not most, of the great deans of schools of social work in that period were women. Private agencies were run by women, even when they were headed by men . . .

The field of social work, as we have seen, emerged out of the work of charity organization societies and the engagement of the settlement movement in immigrant and working class neighborhoods. Of the top best-selling and most influential books in social work, six of eight were written by women (Chambers, 1986). While men outnumbered women in executive positions, according to Chambers, women dominated in supervisory roles.

The women's influence in Europe was especially strong. Lorenz (1994) recounts the history. As women were regarded by society as the natural and traditional embodiment of charity, most schools of social work founded by churches had a clearly defined mission for women within the organizations. Middle-class and upper-class women entered social work as a means of carving out personally rewarding and socially acceptable occupations for themselves. The energetic pioneer of German social work, Alice Salomon, who had a Ph.D. in economics and was closely linked to the American settlement movement, was convinced that only women could create a culture of caring that would raise welfare services above a preoccupation with material concerns. To preserve women's preeminence in the field, Salomon reserved the schools of social work exclusively for women. Furthermore, the schools effectively resisted being accorded university status to resist absorption by male-dominated institutions. Although by far the largest number of women's schools of social work existed in Germany, a practice that continued until after the Second World War, other European countries also had separate social work schools for women. In Austria, France, Hungary, Italy, Norway, Portugal, Romania, and Switzerland, these women's schools represented the only social work training institutions. The underlying theme of the early female social work schools, according to Lorenz (1994), was the commonly heard motto, "the personal is political." For the pioneers of social work education, the transfer of female nurturing qualities into professional attributes was a means of transforming society to being maternalistic rather than paternalistic or bureaucratic.

Examining the events that led to an eventual male "takeover" of the profession in the United States, Andrews (1990) and Jabour (2012) argue that women not only led the profession in its early years but also continued to shape the course of social work until as late as 1955.

Perhaps for a combination of reasons, including the decline of feminism after 1920, the unique partnership of "strong women and gentle men," which shaped the profession of social work during the formative periods, began to fragment when men emerged largely in command of agencies, graduate school education, public policy, and welfare administration (Chambers, 1986). The rapid and vast expansion of welfare bureaucracies and the emphasis on public accountability, cost effectiveness, and the like tended to favor having men in management positions and women in hands-on positions.

## EUROPEAN INFLUENCE

Rarely in the American literature is the European influence on the US social work profession mentioned. The reader of American textbooks, therefore, is apt to be unfamiliar with the international sweep of knowledge or with the historical precedence of ideas. Yet knowledge, like the economy, reflects the global interconnectedness of human phenomena; ideas and methodologies are enriched cross-culturally.

A notable exception to the ethnocentric histories that characterize the social work literature is Kendall's (2000) *Social Work Education: Its Origins in Europe*. Born in Scotland in 1910, Kendall was keenly aware of the tendency to overlook the voices of the past in recording history. Kendall's work, informed by years of international social work and, in recent years, research at the Washington, DC Library of Congress (where she was provided with her own study room), offers a comprehensive picture of the origins of social work that we hope will broaden our perspective in the years to come.

Another major contributor to the history of social work is German social work educator Walter Lorenz (currently professor of social work at the University of Bolzano, Italy). In his evaluation of the profession's unwitting service as pawns of the Nazi state, surely the grimmest episode in social work history, Lorenz (1994) reveals the repercussions on both sides of the Atlantic. Because of a climate of patriotism, tyranny, and lack of organized resistance to an immoral regime, social work ended up complying with the fascist, exclusionary policies of the Nazi period. An early form of mandatory reporting to the government required social workers to turn in the names of people who had various forms of mental disorders and intellectual impairments as well as those with physical handicaps (Healy, 2008). These people were sterilized or killed. In turn, the inevitable siege against the profession took the form of direct threats to its members and particularly to its educators. The large proportion of social workers who were Jewish or who had Jewish connections were forced to surrender their positions and flee the country, including Alice Salomon, the founder of the first school of social work in Germany (Healy). Many others were attacked and persecuted for their social democratic leanings.

And then there were social work heroes of the age. Two among them were Irena Sendler and Gisela Konopka. The subject of a 2009 Hallmark Hall of Fame TV movie, the rescue feats of social worker Irena Sendler in Warsaw, Poland, are little short of extraordinary. We learn from a *New York Times* story that Sendler who had connections from her work in Warsaw was able to rescue around 2,500 Jewish children by slipping them out of the ghetto where they were trapped with their families and taking them to the homes of the Jewish people outside of the ghetto (Jones, 2008). Her work was done through an organization called Zegota, which was formed and financed by the Polish Government in Exile (in London). She herself was captured by the Nazis, tortured, and amazingly able to escape when a guard was bribed on her behalf. Following the war, she continued her work as a social worker in Poland.

American social work was considerably enriched by the enforced wave of emigration of Jews. Gisela Konopka, who had worked in the German underground and been imprisoned, was one such emigrant whose contribution to social work practice was major. Konopka managed to flee to the United States and then returned to postwar Germany to play a key role in developing West German social work in a humanistic direction. She provided a theoretical grounding for group work practice, which enhanced its prestige and professional image (Carson, Lewis, & Fritz, 2014). Konopka is considered the mother of social group work in Germany. For a biography of Konopka's fascinating life, read Andrews (2002).

German and Scandinavian social work benefited from cross-fertilization as Konopka and many other visiting experts forged the link between European and American traditions. In Europe, as Lorenz indicates, social work had an important part to play in rebuilding societies devastated by war. Through imparting self-help skills and replacing fascist authoritarianism (and countering the communist variety) with egalitarian practices, American social work methods had high priority within foreign aid programs of the United States and the United Nations. The availability of American social work literature translated into several European languages enhanced the assimilation of American methods in social work education on the wider European horizon.

The famous Beveridge Report set up the British social welfare system, as we know it today, with its National Health Service and the attempt to end poverty through enhanced social policies (Dalrymple & Boylan, 2013). The Marsh report in Canada echoed the British report. Both were blueprints for a comprehensive and largely universal welfare state; the publication of these reports represented a shift from residual to institutionally based ideology (Graham, Swift, & Delaney, 2012). A universal Family Allowances program came into being in 1944; regardless of family income, *all* Canadian mothers of children under the age of 16 received a monthly allowance. In 1951 the Old Age Security Program was converted from a selective to a universal program as well; everyone over age 70 became qualified to receive a pension. Universal health care was achieved in 1966.

## PROFESSIONAL VULNERABILITY AND THE MCCARTHY ERA

Social work, as we have seen throughout this chapter, cannot be understood apart from the dynamics of the larger society. To know the temper of the age is to know social work. As Bertha Reynolds (1963) observed from personal bitter experience, "Adaptation to the climate of community opinion was, of course, as old as social work itself" (p. 261). Between the reality and the ideal, and the politics and values, the tension at times can be overpowering. Inasmuch as social workers tend to work for the state either directly or indirectly (through funding), they have to answer to the state. Therefore, their helping roles may be circumscribed at times. Under Hitler, as we have seen, social work's vulnerability to political misuse was especially pronounced. Social work assessments, in fact, were used to separate out the unworthy and non-productive elements from society; this use of professionals trained in scientific methods helped justify the ultimate annihilation of large segments of the population. Social workers, in effect, were rendered accomplices to murder. First, the state came for their clients; welfare workers failed to protest; and, in the end, the state came for them—the workers.

Social work's vulnerability to serving the interests of the state is evident in the extreme of Nazi Germany. In Khomeini's Iran, similarly, social workers and students of social work found it impossible to uphold their professional values under the severe duress of a reactionary social revolution (Healy, 2008; van Wormer & Link, 2016). To learn the remarkable story of Sattareh Farman Farmaian, who founded the first school of social work in pre-revolutionary Iran, then had to flee the country, see Saleh (2008).

Under repressive regimes in Chile and South Africa, the vendetta against social workers once included political imprisonment. Although the magnitude of comparable events in the United States pales beside the horrors inflicted elsewhere, the ethical dilemma—how to maintain one's personal and professional integrity in an unfree society—is the same. We are talking here of that ultraconservative and almost paranoid period during the late 1940s and early 1950s when free speech was stymied under the banner of anticommunism and the social work profession was effectively quashed.

The emphasis on security in a repressive and war-ready society perpetuated a climate of suspicion of all behavior outside of the mainstream. This hysterical climate was personified by Senator Joseph McCarthy, who stood in the national limelight to ferret out Communists and "fellow travelers." In the melee that followed, thousands of teachers, social workers, journalists, movie directors, and government workers lost their jobs for supporting unions or other liberal causes (Kemp & Brandwein, 2010). The age—the 1950s—has since been characterized as the McCarthy era.

In the United States and Canada (where anticommunist campaigns were somewhat less public and extensive than in the United States), homosexuality became viewed as a national, social, and sexual danger. In right-wing conservative and even liberal discourse, gays and lesbians were associated with communism and spying for the Soviet Union due to their supposed targeting for blackmail (Johnson, 2009). Homosexual vulnerability to compromise with Soviet agents was taken for granted even in the absence of evidence to back it up. Mass firing and transfers were carried out in the US military and among the Canadian police, national defense units, and civil servants. The criminalization of homosexual behavior made the task in both countries much easier than it would have been otherwise.

In the southern United States, the uncertainty and budding paranoia on the part of the power structure pertained to the issue of integration. Change was in the air and many southern whites feared that their society would be turned upside down as "separate but equal" was ruled to be unequal. Many white southerners claimed that states' rights was the real issue and they suddenly became concerned with the issue of voter literacy. White and black integrationists were branded as red, since the emergent movement for civil rights was labeled as communist-inspired, an accusation that stuck well into the next decade.

Out of the political darkness and enforced silence of the McCarthy era, women were also suppressed. Freudian teachings about proper roles for women, which had been played down during the duration of the war when women were needed for industrial work, now resurfaced to send white women home and African American women back to their menial labor (Kemp & Brandwein, 2010). Ambitious women "did not know their place," as it was said then, and they were not considered appropriately feminine. Female social workers, likewise, had to step aside for the sake of men, who now became the majority of those who held doctorates in social work. Tracked into dead-end casework positions, women watched while men were groomed for agency administration and policy leadership.

Mass persecutions, witch-hunts, fallout shelters, air raids, the mandate for conformity in word, deed, and dress styles—all attributes of the 1950s—raise the difficult question of why these phenomena occurred at this time. One possible explanation is that in the aftermath of war, despite the sense of prosperity and optimism, there was also a sense insecurity. The buildup of defense industry, labeled by President Eisenhower as "the military-industrial complex," was a related factor in the growth of a repressive mentality. Then the propaganda machine, launched to perpetuate the war industry in the absence of a major war, helped stimulate a national hysteria. Whatever the reasons for the climate of intolerance that shook the nation in the 1950s, the important point is that everywhere critics of the government and of "the American way of life" were branded as public enemies and were socially and professionally ostracized.

Even during this time of severe repression, there were internal challenges urging the social work profession to take a stand. These challenges, however, fell on deaf ears until the emergence of a completely new political experience in the turbulent but exciting 1960s. In the 1950s, in light of the political nature of their profession, social workers found themselves especially vulnerable. Refusing to stand together, they were "bumped off" one by one for signing petitions for peace, attending a radical meeting, or merely from being so accused. Although most social workers suffered from the fallout of the climate of fear, the profession did little or nothing to protect them. Dean of Social Work at Smith College Bertha Reynolds strongly opposed McCarthyism, was a pro-union activist, and, as a consequence, lost her job. Her (1963) memoir, *An Uncharted Journey*, provides an excellent resource for grasping the essence of a bygone era, a time that is often forgotten but of no small consequence.

Attacks were directed toward not only individual social workers such as Bertha Reynolds, but also against social work in general as a profession suspected of having "socialist" (i.e., Communist) leanings (Murdach, 2016). And yet, like the rest of the media reports in the 1950s, the social work literature of the day does not mention the kinds of ideological pressures people in public service were under. So while group work was evolving into group psychotherapy, social workers were playing it safe politically, and, sadly, a mood of quiescence prevailed. Many good people were sacrificed and had their high profiles suppressed, never to be regained.

The weeding out of progressive individuals from public life was paralleled by attacks on public assistance in the press and on people "on welfare." And the way was prepared for new stern "economic" measures against the sick, aged, and needy children across the states. Thus the intolerance in one area of life was matched by equal intolerance in another area—against the least advantaged segment of the population.

Looking back from the vantage point of today, we can see some early signs that the national consciousness would shift once again. One of the most significant developments for human rights came with the appointment of Eleanor Roosevelt by President Truman to serve as US Ambassador to the United Nations. In her role as head of the United Nations Human Rights Commission, she played a key role in drafting the UN's Universal Declaration of Human Rights. See chapter 6 for the remarkable story of the passage by the United Nations of this landmark document in 1948. Another development that was little noted at the time was the birth of a new generation, born at the end of World War II, who were destined to shape not only shape their own futures, but to also open the possibilities of a more just world for the generations to follow.

## SUMMARY AND CONCLUSION

The history of social welfare is as old as humankind. The roots can be traced back, at least in part, to the mutual aid of an agrarian community, the medieval church, and the paternalism associated with feudalism.

In understanding how the social welfare system grew and changed, it is important to note not only the milestones (such as the codification of laws), but also the impact of religious belief systems, social values, and the spread of new technologies. Then there were the upheavals—the kinds of unpredictable cataclysmic events that threw the whole social system out of balance. An overview of the course of human history shows how the impact on one part of the system evokes compensatory change in other parts of the system as well. This chapter chronicled such changes brought about by the forces of new technologies, wars, and plague.

As serfdom in England gave way to a system of wage labor built on factory work, a complex class and gender stratification system developed. Help to the poor was provided by the church. Then the Protestant reformation, which led to the demise of the monasteries and convents, removed this source of charity and a new way to provide for the destitute had to be found. New laws were passed in England, and by the 1600s provisions for the "deserving poor" came to be distributed according to a standardized set of criteria. The same devotion to determining eligibility for services was seen much later across the ocean in the 1880s. The founding of the Charity Organization Societies and the much more radical settlement house movement had the effect of ushering in a new profession—social work—to provide for qualified workers to help people, such as poor immigrants and their families, assimilate into the society.

The early social workers were social activists, bent on social change. The predominant model was altered drastically, however, when America entered World War I, which had a dampening effect, as do all major wars, on progressive social thought. Dr. Flexner's stunning rebuke of social work for its lack of autonomy as well as a lack of a unique body of knowledge plunged the field in a new direction. These dual influences, in conjunction with growing anti-immigrant and racist sentiment in the United States, created a situation ripe for a wholehearted endorsement of the psychoanalytical approach. With its relatively coherent theory of personality, psychoanalysis provided a rationale for diagnosis and treatment that had been lacking.

When the Great Depression hit, social workers thrived under the New Deal as society set out to rebuild itself. Canada experienced a comparable shift from attention to personal attributes (or lack thereof) to putting the "social" back in social work.

Going from action to counteraction or counterreaction, a new war fever built up and a conservative mood followed. In the aftermath of World War II, group-work based on psychodynamic principles was introduced as a new trend, the teaching of which rapidly spread to Europe. Minimal attention was paid to social concerns until the 1960s, another period of rejuvenation for the community approach.

To summarize the themes of this chapter, the history of social work is a proud history, the story of strong-willed, idealistic women and good men who worked for social reform or to help individuals in distress. There were, of course, some low moments—conformity under Hitler's Germany and under McCarthyism in the United States, and the dominance of psychoanalytical theory in the 1920s and 1950s.

That social work has come a long way since the 1950s, heavily influenced in the late 20th early 21st centuries by progressive social forces, including civil rights and women's activism, will be seen in the following chapter.

## THOUGHT QUESTIONS

1. How did Martin Luther's split with his church's practices come to have such an impact in England?
2. Relate Luther's teachings to the American work ethic. How do you think these teachings have an influence today?
3. List the principal provisions of the Elizabethan Poor Law. How did it come about? What is the historical significance?
4. Compare the New Poor Law with its predecessor. What is the principle of less eligibility? Is that principle still with us today?
5. What were some of the major social and cultural factors that shaped American social welfare in the Colonial era?
6. Describe the culture brought by the early European settlers to the so-called New World. How were the Puritans unique?
7. How were the "deserving" and the "non-deserving poor" treated in colonial America?
8. Describe the form that mutual aid took among African Americans in the South.
9. What was the role of the churches in providing informal care?
10. What contributions did the Freedman's Bureau make to social welfare?
11. Recount how industrialization transformed the American landscape. How did the shift affect workers' and their families' lives?
12. Discuss the evolution of social work in light of political shifts of the pendulum. Can the personal and the political be truly separated?
13. During which period was a community action emphasis apparent? When did individualism triumph?
14. Trace the history of the COS. How did the philosophy and work of the COS and settlement home workers differ?
15. How did the settlement house leaders respond to the needs of African Americans? What was the contribution of the Emanuel Settlement?
16. Give the personal history of Jane Addams. How did she fall out of public favor?
17. Discuss the growth of formal training for social workers. How did the new profession get a name?
18. What are Mary Richmond's contributions to social work? How was the interpretation of her theoretical formulation reshaped by psychoanalytical thought?
19. What was the impact of Flexner's stinging rebuke to social work in 1915? How did the profession strive to remedy the situation?
20. Describe the excitement generated by the new Freudian view of human behavior. What was the impact on social work practice?
21. How would you describe the economic and social situation that existed in 1933 when Franklin Roosevelt assumed the presidency?
22. What were the highlights of the New Deal legislation? What is the significance of the Social Security Act of 1935? What were the deficiencies?
23. How did the Great Depression change things? How did the New Deal impact social workers?
24. Discuss the backlash against the New Deal reforms that followed World War II. How does being at war affect national belief systems?

25. Recall the pioneering work of Gisela Konopka. How did she combine theory with method in a unique way?
26. Discuss the role of the anticommunist hysteria. How did homosexuality enter the picture? What happened to social work?
27. What were some factors in the rise of McCarthyism? Relate to the life of Bertha Reynolds. What was the view of persons receiving social welfare benefits? Discuss parallels between the 1950s and today.

## REFERENCES


Addams, J. (1910). *Twenty years at Hull House*. Norwood, MA: Norwood Press.

Andrews, J. (1990). Female social workers in the second generation. *Affilia* 5(2), 46–59.

Andrews, J. (2002, fall). Reflections on writing a biography of a living hero: Gisela Konopka. *Reflections, 8* (4),11–22.

Bacon, M. (1986). *The story of Quaker women in America*. San Francisco, CA: Harper and Row.

Barker, R. (2014). *The social work dictionary* (6th ed.). Washington, DC: NASW Press.

Barkin, K. (2015, July 22). Otto von Bismarck. *Encyclopaedia Britannica*. Retrieved from http://www.britannica.com/biography/Otto-von-Bismarck.

Barusch, A. (2017). *Foundations of social policy: Social justice in perspective (6th ed.)*. Boston: Cengage Learning.

Berg-Weger, M. (2016). *Social work and social welfare: An invitation*. New York, NY: Routledge.

Black, C. (2014). *Rise to greatness: The history of Canada from the Vikings to the present*. Toronto: McClelland and Stewart.

Carlton-LaNey, I. (2013). Social policy: History. In C. Franklin (Ed.), *Encyclopedia of social work*. New York, NY: Oxford University Press. Retrieved from www.socialwork.oxfordre.com

Carson, C., Lewis, E., & Fritz, A. (2014). *Growth and development through group work*. New York, NY: Routledge.

Chambers, C. (1986). Women in the creation of the profession of social work. *Social Service Review 60*(1), 1–26.

Clark, E. (2007). *Masterless mistresses: The New Orleans Ursulines and the development of a new world society, 1727–1834*. Chapel Hill, NC: University of North Carolina Press.

Dalrymple, J., & Boylan, J. (2013). *Effective advocacy in social work*. London, England: Sage.

Darwin, C. (1859). *The origin of species*. London, England: Murray.

Day, P., & Schiele, J. (2012). *A new history of social welfare* (7th ed.). Boston, MA: Pearson.

Dolgoff, R., & Feldstein (2012). *Understanding social welfare* (9th ed.). Boston, MA: Pearson.

Encyclopeadia Britannica. (2016). Social welfare program. Retrieved from http://www.britannica.com/topic/social-welfare-program

Faderman, L. (1991). *Odd girls and twilight lovers: A history of lesbian life in twentieth-century America*. New York, NY: Columbia University Press.

Gesino, J. P. (2001). Native Americans: Oppression and social work practice. In G. Appleby, E. Colon, & J. Hamilton (Eds.), *Diversity, oppression, and social functioning: Person-in-environment assessment and intervention* (pp.109–130). Boston, MA: Allyn & Bacon.

Graham, J. R., Swift, K. J., & Delaney, R. (2012). *Canadian social policy: An introduction*. (4th ed.). Don Mills, Ontario: Pearson Education Canada.

Healy, L. (2008). *International social work: Professional action in an interdependent world* (2nd ed.).New York, NY: Oxford University Press.

Heclo, H. (2010). *Modern social politics in Britain and Sweden: From relief to income maintenance (2nd ed.).* Colchester, UK: European Consortium for Political Research (ECPR) Press.

Jabour, A. (2012). Relationship and leadership: Sophonisba Breckinridge and women in social work. *Affilia, 27*(1), 22–37.

Jansson, B. (2014). *The reluctant welfare state: Engaging history to advance social work practice in contemporary society* (8th ed.). Belmont, CA: Cengage.

Jimenez, J., Pasztor, E., & Chambers, R. M. (2015). *Social policy and social change: Toward the creation of social and economic justice.* Thousand Oaks, CA: Sage.

Johnson, D. K. (2009). *The lavender scare: The cold war persecution of gays and lesbians in the federal government.* Chicago, IL: University of Chicago Press.

Jones, M. (2008, December 28). The smuggler: Irena. *New York Times Magazine*, p. MM46.

Kemp, S. P., & Brandwein, R. (2010). Feminisms and social work in the United States: An intertwined history. *Affilia, 25*(4), 341–364.

Kendall, K. (1989). Women at the helm: Three extraordinary leaders. *Affilia, 4*(1), 23–32.

Kendall, K. (2000). *Social work education: Its origins in Europe*. Alexandria, VA: Council on Social Work Education.

Kuhn, T. (1962). *The structure of scientific revolutions.* Chicago, IL: University of Chicago Press.

Loerzel, R. (2008). Friends—with benefits? *Chicago Magazine.* Retrieved from www.chicagomag.com

Lorenz, W. (1994). *Social work in a changing Europe*. Abingdon-on-Thames, UK: Routledge.

Maloney, C.B. (2015, August 18). Frances Perkins, unsung heroine of social security. *The Observer.* Retrieved from www.observer.com

Marx, K., & Engels, F. (1963/1848). *Communist manifesto.* New York, NY: Russell and Russell.

McNutt, J. C. (2013). Social work practice: History and evolution. In C. Franklin (Ed.), *Encyclopedia of Social Work.* New York: Oxford University Press. Online publication. Retrieved from www.socialwork.oxfordre.com

Mullaly, B. (2006). *The new structural social work: Ideology, theory, practice (3rd ed.).* New York: Oxford University Press.

Murdach, A. (2016, February 17). What's in a word? *NASW California News.* Retrieved from www.naswcanews.org

Olsen, T. (1994, January 3). The thirties: A vision of fear and hope. *Newsweek, 26–27.*

Philpott, T. (1978). *The slum and the ghetto.* New York: Oxford University Press.

Piven, F., & Cloward, R. A. (1993). *Regulating the poor: The function of public welfare* (updated ed.). New York, NY: Vintage.

Popple, P., & Leighninger, L. (2014). *Social work, social welfare, and American society* (6th ed.). Boston, MA: Pearson.

Reamer, F. G. (2014). The evolution of social work ethics: Bearing witness. *Advances in Social Work, 15*(1), 163–181.

Reisch, M. (2014). U.S. social policy and social welfare: A historical overview. In M. Reisch (Ed.), *Social policy and social justice* (pp.43–100). Thousand Oaks, CA: Sage.

Reisch, M., & Andrews, J. (2001). *The road not taken: A history of radical social work in the United States.* Philadelphia, PA: Brunner-Routledge.

Reisch, M., & Garvin, C. (2016). *Social work and social justice: Concepts, challenges, and strategies.* New York, NY: Oxford University Press.

Reynolds, B. (1963). *An uncharted journey.* New York, NY: Citadel Press.

Richmond, M. (1917). *Social diagnosis.* New York, NY: Russell Sage Foundation.

Saleh, M. (2008). Sattareh Farman Farmaian: Iranian social work pioneer. *Affilia, 23*(4), 397–402.

Specht, H., & Courtney, M. (1994). *Unfaithful angels: How social work has abandoned its mission.* New York: Free Press.

Trattner, W. (2004). *From poor law to welfare state: A history of social welfare in America* (6th ed.). New York, NY: The Free Press.

van Wormer, K., Jackson, D. W. III, & Sudduth, C. (2012). *The maid narratives: Black domestics and white families in the Jim Crow South.* Baton Rouge, LA: Louisiana State University Press.

van Wormer, K., & Link, R. J. (2016). *Social welfare policy for a sustainable future: The U.S. in global context.* Thousand Oaks, CA: SAGE.

Vowell, S. (2009). *The wordy shipmates.* New York, NY: Penguin.

Whitaker, M. C. (2013). *Peace be still: Modern black America from World War II to Barack Obama.* Lincoln, NB: University of Nebraska Press.

Zinn, H. (2005). *A people's history of the United States.* New York, NY: Harper Collins.

Zinn, H., & Konopacki, M. (2008). *A people's history of the American empire.* New York, NY: Metropolitan Books.

CHAPTER 4

# EMERGENCE OF SOCIAL WORK: PART II

> Whereas the peoples of the United Nations have in the Charter reaffirmed their faith in fundamental human rights, in the dignity and worth of the human person and in the equal rights of men and women and have determined to promote social progress and better standards of life in larger freedom . . . .
>
> Proclaims this Universal Declaration of Human Rights as a common standard of achievement for all peoples and all nations . . . .
>
> United Nations, 1948, Universal Declaration of Human Rights Preamble

Chapter 4 continues with where Chapter 3 left off. We hope that the reader will find that the historic period covered in this chapter is every bit as dynamic and interesting as the ones before. Many of the events described in the following pages will be familiar to the reader—the well-intended but failed war on poverty, the rise of mass movements to effect social change, the passage of meaningful civil rights legislation and sweeping welfare policies, and the legacy of the war in Vietnam. Less familiar, perhaps, are events of the subsequent years rooted in neoliberal economics, developing power of global markets, and corporate control of politics. But social workers and others are well aware of federal and state policies that have become ever more restrictive in providing aid for vulnerable populations and that favor privatization and cost reductions in social services (see Box 4.1).

This chapter begins with the transformative but often misunderstood era of the 1960s. We will see how emerging progressive ideas helped define the teachings and values of social work, values that did not waver as the climate of opinion hardened. That social work has not lost its mission, as several notable social work scholars have claimed, is a major argument of this chapter.

## THE 1960S: SOCIAL FORCES OF THE ERA

If we could travel back in time to the year 1960, we would be astonished by the traditionalism and ultra-conformity of the era. We would first note that women in the United States and Europe

### BOX 4.1 Milestones in the Development of US Social Welfare: 1964–2016

1964: Great Society programs, food stamp program, Civil Rights Act.

1965: Medicare and Medicaid are added to the Social Security Act.

1969: Stonewall Inn riot initiates gay rights movement.

1972: Supplemental Security Income program enacted as a social insurance program for workers who had paid into the system. The Clean Water Act passed to set water quality standards.

1975: Passage of the Education for All Handicapped Children Act now known as Individuals with Disabilities Education Act provides for appropriate, often mainstreamed education for children with disabilities.

1978: Passage of the Indian Child Welfare Act to prevent the removal of Native American children from the Native American community.

1980: President Ronald Reagan ushers in a return to free market economics and lowering of percentage paid in taxes paid by high-income earners.

1990: The Americans with Disabilities Act protects persons with disabilites from work discrimination. The UN Convention on the Rights of the Child takes effect.

1996: President Bill Clinton signs into law The Personal Responsibility and Work Opportunity Reconciliation Act with the goal of ending "welfare as we know it." The Temporary Assistance for Needy Families (TANF) replaces AFDC.

2000: The election of George W. Bush, who cuts the taxes, further downsizes the social welfare system, and invades Iraq; the toll taken by the war on US troops reinforces the social work profession's work with trauma as war-wounded soldiers return.

2001: September 11 becomes a day etched in the world's memory as the airplane bombings of New York's Twin Towers leads to a war on terrorism and much additional loss of life in Afghanistan and Iraq.

2003: Medicare drug bill is signed into law by President George W. Bush, providing some coverage for prescription medication and a windfall for pharmaceutical companies and private health care organizations.

2007–2009: The Great Recession with the collapse in the housing market increased the level of poverty, unemployment, and housing foreclosures.

2008: Election of first African American president, Barack Obama, who is elected to two terms; during the first term, he signs into law the health care reform bill, the Affordable Care Act, and repeals the military's discriminatory "Don't ask, don't tell law."

2010: Citizens United: Supreme Court case strikes down limits on campaign spending for political elections.

2011: The Occupy Wall Street movement took off nationwide, inspiring young people and others to set up tents in public parks and publicize the fact that 1% of the population had accumulated a huge, disproportionate amount of the wealth.

2015: The Supreme Court rules that same-sex marriage is a right that must be recognized by the states.

2016: The U.S. Treasury Department announces that an image of Harriet Tubman, abolitionist and activist in the women's suffrage movement, will replace that of Andrew Jackson.

2016: After the most volatile election campaign in modern history, Republican Donald Trump is elected president of the United States.

dressed for college and work in skirts and stockings and the men in the United States had close-cropped hair. Checking the news reports, we would read of the Communist menace that was considered a threat to America, and we might find rare references to the social unrest among "Negroes" in the South. During the 1960s the US Congress was under the control of southern white Democrats, most of whom favored the status quo, which was segregation. If there was any hint of the noteworthy shift in social behavior from the 1950s, of the social revolution that was to come, it was in two major developments. The first was in technology, and the second was in the political ethos. See Figure 4.1 to grasp how the placement of television sets in living rooms set the stage for a revolution in family life.

The influence of TV on family life and politics was incalculable; the news broadcasts provided a national and even global perspective that would have an educational impact only to be realized much later. A second factor at work that is probably given too little recognition has to do with child-rearing. The youth of the 1960s was raised from infancy in a way that was different than all previous generations. The 1950s was a child-centered period; consider all the Walt Disney films, records, books, and toys that came out during this time. And even more fundamentally there was the influence of Dr. Spock—Benjamin Spock, the baby doctor. We have this baby doctor to thank for a drastic shift in child-rearing practices. His *Common Sense Book of Baby and Child Care* hit the bestselling list in 1946 and remained there in the years following. This book called into question the emphasis on strict schedules for infant

**FIGURE 4.1.** By the early 1950s, millions of Americans had TV sets in their homes. © Getty Images, Francis Miller.

feeding, physical discipline for children, and enforcement of rigid gender differences in behavior and dress. It promoted spontaneous displays of affection, which had been discouraged before. Parents were encouraged to provide a more natural, indulgent upbringing for the child.

Half a million copies were sold, almost instantly; and in the following years 50 million copies were sold in over 40 languages. This was a book that "changed the world," according to an article in *The Chicago Tribune* (Stevens, 2012, 3rd paragraph). Even following the death of the author, the book, which has been updated, is still widely read today (Spock & Needleman, 2013). It should be mentioned that the TV families also displayed an appreciation for children and for their feelings and wishes. The significance of this revolutionary shift in child-rearing practices from an authoritarian to a more democratic approach helped pave the way for a generation of youth who would later feel free to question authority and be less conformist in thinking, tastes in music, and dress styles.

Keep in mind, however, that paradigm shifts, as we saw in chapter 3, are rarely discernible at the time and usually are realized only in hindsight. So despite the dual influences of a modern, more democratic approach to child care and thought-provoking TV broadcasts, noticeable societal change did not really take place until almost a decade later. The 1950s were a remarkably conservative time, a legacy that was carried over for some years to follow.

## POLITICAL DEVELOPMENTS IN THE 1960S: CIVIL RIGHTS MOVEMENTS

From his leadership in the Montgomery, Alabama bus boycott of the late 1950s, Martin Luther King's oratory powers, self-sacrifice, and Gandhi-like willingness to die for a cause galvanized the nation. The mass movement for the rights of African Americans, which culminated in the historic passage of the Civil Rights Act of 1964, set the stage for political mobilization of a host of oppressed groups. Throughout the 1960s, the nation was growing increasingly fractured; one generation was continually shocked and appalled at another. By 1969, the universities were the scene of rebellion; radical groups within the institutions, which were seen as representatives of the establishment, looked to take over the reins of power (Kirkpatrick, 2009). The mood of the country was such that history would forever divide the period and the one before into a "before" and an "after." Young people were split from each other, college students from working class youth, and parents from their children. The mood of the era was reflected in its psychedelic music, drugs, peace protests, and black activism. "Never trust anyone over 30"—this was a common refrain.

Central to an understanding of the ethos of the age (an ethos that was not even apparent until the decade was over) is a recognition of the transformation of young people that occurred through the hope and optimism generated by the Civil Rights movement. As a result of mass mobilization, public martyrdom, and a sympathetic press, justice prevailed. People said, "We shall overcome," and in truth, they did overcome. This brilliantly successful movement set the pattern for others to demand their and others' rights—Mexican farm laborers under the charismatic leadership of Cesar Chavez; women; gays and lesbians; Native Americans; and older people. Catholics in Northern Ireland similarly sang Civil Rights songs and held sit-ins and mass rallies to protest discrimination against Roman Catholics. In the United States and Europe, mobilized protests against the war in Vietnam helped bring that conflict to a close even in the absence of military victory. After he helped push the Civil Rights Act through Congress, perhaps sensing the mood of the nation, President Lyndon Johnson declared a war on poverty, and a major expansion of social welfare programs followed. The optimism of the era is captured in the term, the Great Society, to refer to the war on poverty and what it represented. The phrase sounds grandiose today; then it did not. Under the umbrella of the Office of Economic Opportunity, many programs were introduced, including Volunteers in Service to America (VISTA); Upward Bound, a program to help poor and ghetto children enter college; Operation Head Start to prepare lower-income children for school; Legal Services; and Job Corps. Part of the impetus for these programs sprang out of massive urban riots in poor black communities during the mid-1960s.

Social workers were actively involved in protesting against segregation and picketing places that were segregated. In fact, members of the profession had played important roles throughout the 1940s and 1950s, and during the 1960s, social workers were involved both professionally and personally in the fight for civil rights (Nguyen, 2013). (Read Box 5.1 on Dorothy Height's leadership in Chapter 5.)

When the war in Vietnam broke out, public sentiment was enthusiastic about the stand against Communism. The peace movement against the war got off to a slow start, and, in fact, during all the years that the war was waged (1964–1973), protesters were commonly attacked and beaten up by bystanders. People who spoke out for peace were accused of breaking the morale of the soldiers and aiding the enemy. Males who were drafted (in the early years students were exempted) had no choice but to be shipped out, go to prison, or escape to Canada. As in all wars, the men who refused to fight were considered cowards. (In the early years, students were exempted from the draft.) It wasn't until the end of the decade, when the futility of fighting an unwinnable war became evident that the tide began to turn. TV broadcasts brought the fierceness of the battles right into the living rooms. Popular radio stations stopped playing the song, "The Green Beret," in favor of peace songs by Bob Dylan and John Lennon. Mass protests took place on virtually all the college campuses, which now involved the mainstream of students. Instead of attending class, students attended teach-ins given by faculty who knew the history of Vietnam and returning soldiers who were disillusioned by what they had seen. The year 1970 is etched in the memory of many former peace protesters, as that is when President Nixon, who had been elected on a campaign to bring the war to an end, ordered bombing of another country—Cambodia. The rage escalated into violence against campus buildings associated with the war effort in some places and into the occupation of buildings on the college campuses all across the nation. Four students were killed by the National Guard at Kent State University, and two were killed by city and state police at Jackson State University. To stop the protests, college administrators simply shut down these and many other colleges for the remainder of the academic year. Figure 4.2 depicts a major slogan of the antiwar protests, which was to bring our soldiers home.

Although social work students and social workers engaged in the anti-war protests and otherwise opposed the war in large numbers, the profession of social work was curiously silent about the ravages of the war all during this time. This was even more surprising considering that many social workers were employed by the VA (then called the Veterans Administration) and familiar with the psychological problems that many of the returning soldiers had. A literature search of the academic writings in the major social work journals from 1965 to 1975 provides evidence of this neglect (Chandler, 2004). Not only did the journals fail to editorialize against

**FIGURE 4.2.** This antiwar protest in New York City's Central Park is typical of what was going on in cities all across the United States in the early 1970s. © Getty Images, David Fenton.

the war itself, but they even failed to discuss the toll that the war was taking on families who had lost loved ones and the skills that would be required to treat the returning soldiers, many of whom needed treatment for physical and psychological trauma. Chandler (2004) conducted an analysis of the leading journals of social work 1965–1975 and found this absence of attention to a war that ultimately resulted in the loss of 58,000 Americans and over one million Vietnamese disturbing. The focus of the profession, no doubt, was not to engage in controversy at this time. Cowger (2013) addresses the issue as well of NASW's reticence to speak out against the unpopular war. (However, the NASW, as Cowger indicates, did oppose the war in Iraq.)

With the advent of the 1960s, the Neo-Freudian formulations and emphasis on human development gave way to community organization and direct action strategies. There was a great deal of criticism of social casework, some from outside the profession. Most notably, Saul Alinsky (1971) urged against helping people adjust to the system; his aim was to radically change the system. Many social workers, and schools of social work, stressed community organizing based on the teachings of Saul Alinsky.

Strongly influenced by the Civil Rights movement and the Great Society program in 1964, the social work profession began to shift its focus from casework to social policy. The new goals of the eradication of poverty and racism fired up a new generation of social workers. The shift in the profession's emphasis became apparent in the editorial content of social work's leading journals. This progressivism, in fact, is still evident today as editors of the mainstream journals continue to focus on the crises in social welfare, human rights issues, and the need for social and political action. The social work code of ethics (see Appendix 1) reflects an expanded interest in social policy and in the ramifications of such policy for the poor and vulnerable populations.

## THE NEW CONSERVATISM

In the final analysis, who can say why the pendulum swings the way it does throughout history? Piven and Cloward (1993) offer at least a partial answer: We should never underestimate, they note, the power of the well-organized social action by the masses or the threat of such action in compelling the administration to embark on a change of course. Fear of a major challenge to the established order, indeed, may be a key motivating factor in gaining concessions for workers and others in need. Conversely, mass apathy and lack of organization by the working and lower class can be their undoing. Whatever the reasons, for the first time since the 1920s, under the leadership of newly elected President Ronald Reagan, the radical right boldly attempted to re-form American society. In the absence of viable opposition, laissez-faire capitalism resumed its hold on the nation. This ideology cast high taxes, regulation, and welfare assistance to the poor as the major impediments to economic growth and prosperity (Jimenez, Pasztor, & Chambers, 2015). The decade brought us a tax cut, particularly for the highest income group, large cuts in domestic spending, and the largest peacetime military buildup in American history. This paradigm shift, which edged up slowly on the nation, was reinforced in externally funded academic writings and in the corporate controlled mass media. The idea that government programs (such as Aid to Families with Dependent Children and food stamps) represented a giant drain on tax dollars went virtually unchallenged by political leaders. In the political rhetoric of the time, only those governmental programs and services that were intended to help the poor and the powerless were seen as a problem.

In 1988, drawing on negative stereotypes of poor women, advocates of welfare reform justified the need for a mandatory work program designed to channel welfare recipients into the low-wage labor market (Haas & Springer, 2014). The Family Support Act transformed welfare aid from an income-maintenance program to what Haas and Springer refer to as a punitive government work program. The focus seemingly was more directed to monitoring the morality of welfare clients than to providing them with sufficient financial aid. "Democrats and Republicans alike," as Piven (1995) astutely observed, "have hit upon welfare bashing as a way to appease an anxious and increasingly angry electorate" (pp. 22–23).

When President Bill Clinton gave his first inaugural address, the wave of joy and optimism at the prospect of a Democratic administration was palpable. The mood was eloquently captured in the words of the inaugural poet, Maya Angelou (1993), who shared them on this proud occasion:

> Lift up your eyes upon
> This day breaking for you
> Give birth again
> To the dream. (verse 10)

But, alas, with a conservative mood sweeping the nation and an eventual Republican controlled Congress, the promise of change (for example, the open acceptance of gays and lesbians in the military; health care reform) did not occur (Karger & Stoesz, 2013). To many progressives, the Bill Clinton administration was a disappointment. This brings us to the 1996 Personal Responsibility and Work Opportunity Reconciliation Act, popularly known as "welfare reform." With the passage of this Act, at the end of President Clinton's first term, the 60-year entitlement to family assistance essentially was over.

To appreciate how the significance of the passage of welfare reform was grasped at the time of its passage, we can review a newspaper clipping from *The New York Times* (Pear, 1996). The front page headline entitled "Millions Affected" stated:

> It is expected to save $55 billion over six years as it dismantles a welfare program created by Democrats in the New Deal...With today's action, Mr. Clinton fortifies his credentials as a "new Democrat" and strengthens his position going into this fall's Presidential election. But he disappointed many Democratic party loyalists, and civil rights advocates, labor union leaders, and religious organizations. (p. 1A)

The bill that Clinton signed effectively supplanted the Aid to Families of Dependent Children (AFDC) with Temporary Assistance for Needy Families (TANF). As the name implies, TANF was time-limited: two years for welfare recipients to enter the workforce; five years as a lifetime limit to receive the temporary help. Funding was provided to the states in the form of block grants; these grants placed food stamps, child care, and school meals in the hands of the states. As a result, there is a great variation among TANF programs in the various states.

Restrictions were placed upon the states as they administered the federal block grants (Karger & Stoesz, 2013). One provision barred any recent immigrants from receiving federally funded welfare benefits for 5 years. Another denied cash assistance and Food Stamp benefits to people convicted of felony drug use or possession.

Historian Michael Katz (2008) fills us in on the often overlooked role of the governors of the states, foremost among them, Tommy Thompson, of Wisconsin in leading the campaign to devolve public assistance to the states. A new consensus among conservative governors rested on a dislike of welfare, hostility to its recipients, and faith in mandatory work as the key to reform. In seizing the initiative, as Katz points out, state governments had precipitated a historic transformation of American welfare.

Over the decades that followed, large numbers of welfare recipients were moved off the rolls. An economic boom during the Clinton years led to the creation of sufficient low-wage jobs in the service industry to make leaving welfare possible. Major obstacles to future success of the program were the rise in unemployment; lack of access to health care benefits for many of the working poor—such access was provided AFDC recipients; the fact that many of the poor people lived in ghettos or rural areas where job opportunities are few; the low pay of minimum wage jobs; and the lack of affordable child care for many.

All these policies were brought back into the public eye during the 2016 election through the candidacy of Hillary Clinton, who had publicly supported many of them in her role of First Lady. The author of *The New Jim Crow*, Michelle Alexander (2016), was among the most critical:

> From the crime bill to welfare reform, policies Bill Clinton enacted—and Hillary Clinton supported—decimated black America. . . . Bill Clinton presided over the largest increase in federal and state prison inmates of any president in American history. Clinton did not declare the War on Crime or the War on Drugs—those wars were declared before Reagan was elected and long before crack hit the streets—but he escalated it beyond what many conservatives had imagined possible. (www.thenation.com)

President Clinton deserved praise for balancing the budget and helping many former recipients of welfare benefits become self-sufficient. Great strides were made in providing health care for children whose parents could not have afforded it. But keep in mind the words of William Faulkner (1948), "Tomorrow night is nothing but one long sleepless wrestle with yesterday's omissions and regrets" (p. 431). Faulkner, through his fiction, probably had in mind the trauma of slavery and the Civil War that followed. Today, we can think of the turmoil that has engulfed much of the world following the wars in the Middle East, the responsibility of the next administration.

## THE GEORGE W. BUSH AND OBAMA ADMINISTRATIONS

The closely contested 2000 election of Republican George W. Bush ushered in decreased public spending for social welfare programs and a focus on privatized and faith-based initiatives (Berg-Weger, 2016). Bush, who was the son of President George H. W. Bush, served as the governor of Texas before he became president. Bush led the United States' response to the 9/11 terrorist airplane attacks on the New York Towers building, the Pentagon, and the crashing of United Flight 93, through an international coalition to destroy Al Qaeda and other terrorist organizations in Afghanistan. Bush's interest was more in declaring war on Iraq, however, and finishing what was perceived as his father's unfinished war in that country. The trillions of dollars spent on fighting two foreign wars, in conjunction with huge tax cuts on the rich, depleted the budget surplus left by the Clinton administration as the Bush administration drew to a close.

Liberals were overjoyed at the election of President Obama in 2008. There were great expectations at the start of this administration by America's first African American president. Unfortunately, Obama inherited the worst financial crisis, which was centered on a collapse of the housing market, since the Great Depression. Yet in the midst of the Recession of 2007 to 2009, and solid Republican opposition, Obama was able to get the Affordable Care Act passed. Under this Act, millions of Americans were added to the health care rolls. Moreover, during his first term, Obama succeeded in expanding opportunities for women to sue over pay discrimination and in seating two women as justices to the Supreme Court, including the first Hispanic justice. And he oversaw the end of the discriminatory "Don't Ask, Don't Tell" policy, which banned openly gay and lesbian Americans from serving in the military. Although Obama withdrew troops from Iraq and most from Afghanistan, there were serious setbacks in restoring peace to this part of the world and the repercussions were global. At the end of his administration, Obama opened the doors to Cuba and achieved a nuclear deal with Iran in hopes of preventing Iran from manufacturing nuclear weapons. (See Figure 4.3.) A significant disappointment to liberals was Congress's refusal to allow the president to select a Supreme Court justice during the last year of his presidency. This decision by Congress was to have repercussions long into the nation's future.

Already controlled by conservatives in 2010, the Supreme Court issued a ruling of enormous consequence for future elections in Citizens United vs. the Federal Elections Commission. Based on the 14th amendment to the Constitution which provided former slaves and other persons the rights to protection under the law, the Supreme Court ruled that the corporation also has such rights. This decision considerably expanded the rights of protection to campaign lobbyists in their financing of politicians running for office. In an interesting side note, some environmental activists have seized the occasion to argue that if the corporation is considered a legal person,

**FIGURE 4.3.** President Obama, his wife, Michelle, and daughters upon their historic arrival in Cuba. © Getty Images, Anadolu Agency.

why not natural elements, such as mountains and rivers? (Ludwig, 2017). The United States can look to other countries, in fact, such as Bolivia and Ecuador, which have passed similar laws affirming the legal rights of nature.

The liberal voice directed criticism not only at the Supreme Court but also at the Obama administration itself. One major source of concern was in the area of foreign policy. The heavy use of drone attacks against enemies and their leaders in the Middle East and the support of regime change in a number of nations seemed to only have increased hostility toward the United States and furthered the destabilization of the whole region. For liberals, however, more setbacks lay ahead.

Democrats were heavily divided during the election of 2016 between Vermont Senator Bernie Sanders, who had a large following among the young generation of liberals and radicalized baby boomers, and Hillary Clinton, who seemed destined to follow Obama's legacy and had an enthusiastic feminist following. Clinton drew much mainstream and media support, excelled in debates, and won the nomination. On the Republican side, numerous candidates competed; the debates became downright combative as Donald Trump flung personal accusations against Marco Rubio, Ben Carson, Jeb Bush, and Ted Cruz and received insults back.

When Donald Trump received the Republican nomination, which the polls showed he had little chance of achieving, the Republican establishment was appalled. Trump's bombastic remarks against Mexican migrants and his reported history of sexual harassment of women were a national embarrassment.

On the night of the election, huge rallies of Clinton's supporters and women all across the nation prepared for the celebration of the first female president in American history. But there was to be no celebration that night, and as the TV results rolled in and Trump captured the electoral votes in state after state, the reality sank in, many of the women at Hillary's headquarters could be seen to be crying.

It is worth noting that the majority of the people voted for Hillary Clinton, a Democrat with a relatively progressive platform. Although Clinton received over two million more votes than Donald Trump, Trump won the presidency through gaining the needed votes through the electoral college. (This unique method of choosing a president was designed historically to strengthen the influence of the less populated areas.)

The surprising results of the 2016 election, which brought right-wing conservatives into power at every level of government, meant that many of the United States' cherished social welfare programs were suddenly at risk. Given the atmosphere of political uncertainty following the election's outcome, the National Association of Social Workers (NASW-US) issued the following statement:

> The Association is deeply concerned by statements Mr. Trump has made regarding women, people of color, and immigrants. At the same time, we acknowledge we must work with the new administration to address pressing issues of the day, including justice reforms, racial and gender inequality, access to health care for all, and helping more Americans achieve economic self-sufficiency and stability.
>
> The NASW Code of Ethics makes clear the importance of social justice. We cannot support any efforts to marginalize or oppress any group of people, and will always work to assure that human rights extend to everyone. Social workers continue to strongly advocate for our country's most vulnerable populations. (2016, 2nd and 3rd paragraphs).

## IMPACT OF HISTORICAL TRENDS ON SOCIAL WORK

Social work practice is created within a political, social, cultural, and economic matrix that shapes the assumptions of practice, the problems that practice must deal with, and the preferred outcomes of practice (McNutt, 2013).

The question for social workers who cherish the social action model of Jane Addams and Bertha Reynolds and programs to end poverty is, How will they manage to serve clients in a conservative America? In the following section of this chapter, we will ask the question, so relevant under present circumstances, Will social work abandon its mission?

The means available to help clients are increasingly limited. Even before the switch from a Democratic to a Republican regime, the near obsessive emphasis on accountability for every dollar spent and cost-effectiveness translates into mounds of paperwork and fundraising efforts by progressively harried staff has become the norm. Most social workers who remain in stressful positions conform to the dictates of the system. Some others move into areas of greater political influence; still others leave the profession altogether.

Some social workers, perhaps reluctantly, flee agency work into private practice. As they explored the issue in *Unfaithful Angels: How Social Work Has Abandoned its Mission,* Specht and Courtney (1994) were less than empathetic toward members of the profession who established careers in psychotherapy. Their work is widely cited today, and social work authors such as Hardcastle (2011) agree that community practice today is in decline and that social work has abandoned service to the poor. Jimenez et al. (2014) praise *Unfaithful Angels* for its articulation of the silence of the social work profession at times when the government has passed draconian measures against poor people. According to Ambrosino, Heffernan, Shuttlesworth, and Ambrosino (2015), Specht and Courtney's message continues to resonate worldwide.

Well-written and refreshingly iconoclastic, *Unfaithful Angels* is a highly useful resource for viewing today's variety of social work practitioners in a historical context. Specht and Courtney (1994) correctly take the psychotherapeutic field to task for having fallen captive in many instances to popular therapies such as "codependency work," excessive individualism, and the like. They also take the social work field to task for bestowing professionalism, prestige, and respect singularly to clinicians. Many of their points are well taken.

Another critical analysis of the social work profession is Stoesz, Karger, and Carrillo's (2010) provocative *A Dream Deferred: How Social Work Education Lost Its Way and What Can Be Done.* In the authors' words, "In refutation of its Progressive Era legacy, social work finds itself sitting on the curb, watching events go by as opposed to driving them" (p. 197). In contrast to Specht and Courtney, Stoesz et al. (2010) argue for more educational rigor and selectivity of students admitted to graduate study; they decry "the profession's emphasis on values while demoting research" (p.197).

From our perspective, we most respectfully disagree with the essence of the criticisms. Our pride as contributors to the social work profession relates to its principles and values and to the continued activism of many of its members. Social work journal literature, moreover, is replete with empirically based research, research that enriches the field by providing data geared toward client needs. In the following section, we take issue with the criticism and argue instead that social work is alive and well, and so is its mission. Having taught over the years on different campuses, we find that students majoring in social work are as idealistic and socially active as ever.

## HAS SOCIAL WORK ABANDONED ITS MISSION?

In discovering principles that were later to become the standards of the burgeoning profession of social work, the founding mothers were clearly individuals of vision and courage. The original twin missions of social work are those of enhancing the functioning of individuals and their families and of building a more just and human order. These intertwined missions continue to command the allegiance of members of the empowerment tradition. NASW (2017) echoes these sentiments in the Preamble to the Social Work Code of Ethics in its focus on enhancing the empowerment of marginalized people.

Unlike related fields in the social and behavioral sciences and counseling education, social work is highly self-critical, culturally aware, and therefore introspective. Every accredited social work program stresses policy as well as counseling issues. The fact that academics of the caliber of the late Harry Specht and his associate Mark Courtney have chastised the field for its parochialism, paradoxically, may actually be one of the many encouraging developments in social work today. Specht and Courtney's book offers a kind of soul-searching that is the attribute of a truly altruistic profession. Other positives in this enduring field are the outpouring of politically relevant articles, editorials, and policy statements in *Social Work* and *NASW News*, the leading professional journals in the field promoting social justice and peace; the continuing idealism of social work students; and the strident, multicultural emphasis, reinforced by progressive mandates by the Council on Social Work Education.

So evident is the progressive ethos of social work, that even researchers such as Jimenez et al. (2015), who agree with the basic message of Specht and Courtney that social work has abandoned its mission, also give credit to the profession for its progressivism. Although the opportunities for social workers to engage in paid social reform and political action are limited, they state, "social work education continues to be a center of progressive thought" (p. 87). Unique among the professions, social work, as these writers claim, has a singular professional commitment to social justice.

To bolster our arguments against the Specht and Courtney thesis, we draw on the focus of the literature of the profession, studies of our social work students, and consider professional mandates for multicultural social work education, feminist social work, and outreach to the global community.

### PROFESSIONAL WRITINGS AND POLICIES

NASW is a politically viable and dynamic organization with a membership of around 130,000 (keep in mind that only approximately one-fourth of social workers are official members; Stuart, 2013). With membership, subscription to *Social Work, NASW News* and a chapter newsletter are automatic. A survey of *NASW News* headlines from across the past two decades concern such issues as: pressing governors on child welfare; lobbying for mental health parity; curtailing the ill effects of welfare reform; transgender rights, and the prevention of school bullying. These headlines say a lot about social work's continued social action on behalf of the poor and oppressed.

Among journals in the field devoted specifically to human rights and poverty issues are *Affilia: Journal of Women and Social Work, Journal of Gay/Lesbian Social Services, Multicultural*

*Social Work*, and *Journal of Progressive Social Work* and the newly launched *Journal of Human Rights and Social Work*. Each year during March, Social Work Month, NASW-US distributes booklets to its members containing the annual theme.

Does this sound like a profession that has lost its soul?

## THE IDEALISM OF SOCIAL WORK STUDENTS

What brings students to major in social work? Why do people choose social work as a career today? Has their motivation shifted over the years? Critics point to trends of MSW graduates aiming to work in private practice as evidence that the former idealism of social work students is dead. But the fact that some students, at the MSW level, might seek out work in the private sector does not mean they will be in violation of the code of ethics (Barsky, 2014). Barsky reveals how such social workers typically give back to the community in various ways. For example, many have a sliding fee scale, and social workers in all fields engage in legislative advocacy for improved social services, and at agencies, they supervise students from departments of social work. Most MSW students, in any case, do not choose private practice as their area of concentration.

We can look also at the CSWE (2016) survey of graduates of social work programs. The results show that for those with Ph.D. degrees, only 7.1% are working in clinical/private practice. Employment outcomes for other graduates is not given in the report. Regarding primary practice areas, around one in six of majors and well over one-third of graduate students were placed in health/mental health agencies. Child welfare and school social work were other popular areas.

One major advantage of licensing laws for MSW practitioners is the opportunity to be self-employed and to provide counseling for individuals in need of psychotherapy. Sliding fee scales make such counseling more affordable than treatment by other mental health professionals. Another interesting fact about social workers is the high representation of minorities around half of whom receive graduate social work degrees and the high percentage of women (81.7%) of those receiving master's degrees; CSWE, 2016).

Theoretical trends in social work education and the literature provide further testimony to the vitality of the field. Keep this in mind as you read the following sections of this chapter, which cover multicultural education, feminist theory, the empowerment perspective, and the renewed global awareness.

## MULTICULTURAL SOCIAL WORK EDUCATION

People of color and other diverse groups constitute a large proportion of the clients social workers serve. In recognition of the need for multicultural competence, the CSWE mandate is for the social work course curriculum to include content on populations at risk such as ethnic minorities, women, and sexual orientation, ideally infused throughout the entire curriculum. The emphasis of the Educational Policy and Accreditation Standards (CSWE, 2015) as stated in Competence 2 is that social workers understand the forms and mechanisms of oppression and discrimination. (See www.cswe.org to read the requirements in their entirety.)

The basic idea of multiculturalism in social work education, according to Alvarez (2013), is that social work students need to learn to work effectively with people from many different cultures. Self-awareness and an awareness of one's own cultural heritage is a logical starting point (Gutiérrez & Lewis, 2012). There is general agreement in the social work literature that familiarity with cultural differences is helpful and will have a positive impact on social work practice and on outcomes for those with whom social workers work.

The popularity of books such as *Culturally Competent Practice* (Lum, 2011), *Multicultural Perspectives in Social Work Practice with Families* (Congress & Gonzalez, 2012), and *Diversity, Oppression, and Social Functioning* (Appleby, Colon, & Hamilton, 2010) speaks volumes. And announcements of more recent publications, such as *Multicultural Social Work Practice* (Sue, Rasheed, & Rasheed, 2016) and *Social Work with Muslim Communities* (Al-Krenawi, Graham, & Habibov, Eds., 2016) portend well for the future of the profession.

The Canadian professional social work associations, similar to their US counterparts, are pursuing initiatives to promulgate multiculturalism through cross-cultural immersion activities (Graham et al., 2012). The CASWE (Canadian Association for Social Work Education) requires educational content to prepare students for a multicultural practice. On its website, CASWE (2016) states as its vision in accreditation: "Achieving such a vision calls for critical analyses of power relations, the dismantling of inequitable social structures, and solidarity with populations that experience poverty, oppression, and exploitation." At Carleton University in Ottawa, Canada, as described on its website, for example, students are prepared to address personal and social problems from a structural perspective with an emphasis on ameliorating structural inequalities (http://carleton.ca/socialwork/about).

## THE FEMINIST AND OTHER EMPOWERMENT INFLUENCES

Just as the African American and gay/lesbian lobbies within social work have been well-organized and effective in shaping CSWE and NASW-US policies, feminism has also been a major influence in the field.

Founded as a field of strong women (many of whom remained unmarried by choice) and supportive men who stood alongside them, social work stands uniquely among the professions as woman-centered. The fact that writers of the feminist school today decry the underrepresentation of females in top administrative positions, and the fact that they make their voices heard on related issues of concern to women, shows that the feminist voice in social work is alive and well (see Dominelli, 2012; Payne, 2014; Valentich, 2011).

Feminist social work, the aim of which is to remove oppression due to sexism, has its roots in the women's movement of the 1970s. In its concern for social justice and commitment to initiating change as a collaborative effort, social work shares a number of features with feminism (Dominelli, 2012). Parallels between feminist thought and social work are found in their mutual belief that the personal is political and vice versa; the problems lie in the structures of society rather than in the fault of the disadvantaged; the perpetuation of poverty in women is systemic; and violence inflicted against women and children is an instrument of power (Valentich, 2011).

A proliferation of workshops, papers, and conference sessions focused on women's issues and gender sensitivity gives credence to the female voice and experience within social work. In fact, there is published today the *Journal of Feminist Family Therapy*. According to the website at www.tandfonline.com, the journal is "an important resource for scholars and practitioners, the journal critiques family therapy concepts from a feminist perspective while paying careful attention to cultural and contextual differences such as race, class, religion, age, and sexual orientation." In light of developments since the mid-1980s, Mary Valentich (2011) fully expects that feminist perspectives will become even more influential for all social work practitioners and their clients. Significantly, within the field of corrections, gender-specific counseling with female offenders has recently made tangible inroads, especially for juveniles (van Wormer, 2014).

Social work practice with women has developed from a concern about sexism and woman's issues to an emerging model of practice grounded in feminist theory, scholarship, and social action (Dominelli, 2012). So, far from arguing that social work today has abandoned its mission, one could much more accurately conclude that social work, on the contrary, has expanded its horizons, moving into new directions without losing sight of the old. Whether social work will be able to maintain its historic position as advocates for the poor and marginalized depends on the force of the present-day right-wing backlash against all victims of society in conjunction with the economic dictates of managed care. In a society driven by high economic competition, a barrage of criticism against the entire social work field and a reduction in client benefits can be anticipated.

Related to feminist social work, and in fact an outgrowth of the feminist movement, is the empowerment framework and its correlate, the strengths perspective. Within the social work practice literature, a focus on client strengths has received increasing attention in recent years, as noted in chapter 1. The strengths perspective, as Saleebey (2012) notes, assumes that power resides in people and their communities and that we should do our best to promote power by refusing to label clients and trusting them to make the appropriate decisions. Effective social work practice, to Saleebey, is both an art and a science. The linking thread between them is the creativity and breadth of vision we can call our social work imagination. The term *social work imagination* refers to a drawing on one's inner resources to help advance the cause of social welfare at the macro level and to help individuals cope, at the micro level. Such imagination challenges all our creative resources to discover, in collaboration with the client, what countless others may have overlooked, some obvious solution to a problem, perhaps, or some new way around a difficulty (see chapter 1).

## THE IMPETUS FOR A GLOBAL AWARENESS

As we saw in chapter 1, the social work profession is today returning to its roots in recognition that it has a global role to play. The social work profession the world over is concerned with the devastating effects of poverty, hunger, illness, homelessness, inequality, injustice, and violence. The globalization of the economy and society affects social work practice in every nation. Just as the nations of the Global North have dominated free market economics and the diffusion of technologies, social work practice knowledge has pursued a similar course with knowledge flowing in one direction—from north to south. From the global perspective, a fact that has so often been overlooked is that social workers in industrialized nations, where there increasingly are problems of poverty and homelessness, have much to learn from social workers in countries that have been facing myriad human and social ills for some time. Much has already been learned, such as of grass-roots organizing from Latin America, as we will see in chapter 5 on economic and social oppression.

## CURRENT TRENDS

Although the literature consistently articulates the importance of a stress on clients' strengths and competencies, we must all be cognizant of the reality of standard clinical practice built on a treatment problem/deficit orientation, a reality shaped by agency accountability and the dictates of managed care. Third party payment schemes mandate a diagnosis based on relatively serious disturbances in a person's functioning (e.g., organic depression or suicide attempts) and a short-term therapy to correct the presenting problem. Furthermore, the legal and political mandates of many agencies, the elements of social control embodied in both the institution and ethos of the agency, may strike a further blow to the possibility of partnership and collaboration between client and helper (Saleebey, 2012). In the United States, as in every nation, pressures from the global market economy impact social welfare policies in terms of retrenchment in treatment offerings. The decline in social welfare standards, of course, presents a major obstacle to strengths-based practice in combination with budget cuts for "talking forms of treatment" and reductions in resources available.

### FOCUS ON SUSTAINABILITY

In recent years, the perspective of social work had broadened to challenge widely held assumptions of industrial society, assumptions equating unsustainable economic growth with progress. The sustainable development model is a central theme of such books as *Social Work in a Sustainable World* (Mary, 2008); *Environmental Social Work* (Gray, Coates, & Hetherington, 2013); *Green Social Work* (Dominelli, 2012); and *Social Welfare for a Sustainable Future* (van Wormer & Link, 2016). What is needed now, argue Hoff and McNutt (2009), is nothing less than a complete rethinking of our relationship to the natural world. An understanding of the interplay between poverty and environmental degradation is central to the social development model. The imminent threat of global environmental collapse compels the social work profession to adopt a truly comprehensive ecological framework and to take a pro-active stance toward the depletion of resources and the promotion of policies toward sustainable social development (see chapter 7).

Yet American social workers are just at the crossroads of assuming a worldwide and environmental focus and of grasping the fact that social problems are becoming more interconnected and nations more interdependent in a global economy. We urge the infusion of international content in social work education as a means of sharpening critical thinking skills, and for providing exposure to comparative options and innovations for addressing economic and social issues.

### GLOBAL PERSPECTIVE AND HUMAN RIGHTS

In Africa, Latin America, and Asia, social work as a profession is rapidly gaining in respect, and programs of formal education are being developed rapidly to meet the need. Although much of the curriculum is generally borrowed from the West, the forms of social work have been molded to the contours of the local landscape. Knowledge imparted from the outside, in this context, develops a life of its own. Frameworks employed that are irrelevant can be discarded and modified or exchanged for those that are a good fit. At the same time, social work educators in the West are seeking new forms of intervention and looking globally for workable ideas. The days of unilateral exchange of knowledge from West to East or North to South may be over. And maybe, in the future, people the world over will look beyond their individual cultures to universal values, such as those set forth in the Universal Declaration of Human Rights.

Inasmuch as human rights are universal, a human rights model for social work necessarily uses a global lens. For example, when we look at the mistreatment of Indigenous people in North America in terms of violations against their rights, we are using standards of self-determination that also apply to Aboriginal people in Australia, the Sami in Nordic countries, and the Maori in New Zealand. And when social workers work with immigrants who have fled their countries because of persecution, they are dealing with the survivors of human rights abuses as well as dealing with global issues.

Using a human rights lens, our worldview becomes more of a world view (see chapter 1). Mapp (2014) gives the example of how we would view the recipient of welfare benefits from this perspective. Instead of seeing the person as receiving a charitable handout, we would be focusing on one's entitlement to the right to a basic standard of living. The historic division of deserving and undeserving poor would no longer apply. Social workers would still advocate, as they have from the beginning of the profession, for people's rights to have adequate food, income, education, shelter, and health care. And they would be referring to all people.

Informed by human rights principles, as Androff (2016) suggests, social workers will be well equipped in pursuit of social justice and prepared to challenge forces in the society that perpetuate inequality, oppression, and disempowerment. Ideally, social welfare programs will become more preventive of crises, rather than being put into practice after the crisis has occurred. This is the classic public health approach (Wronka, 2016).

An important recent trend is the CSWE requirement, initiated in 2008, to include course content on human rights in the social work curriculum. Until the late 20th century, there were virtually no social work textbooks with a human rights focus. Joseph Wronka (1998, 2016), was a pioneer in the field of social work in showing the linkage between the US Constitution and the Universal Declaration of Human Rights in his first book, and later how human rights can be considered the cornerstone of social justice (*Human Rights and Social Justice*, 2nd edition). Australian social work educator Jim Ife (2001, 2013), author of *Human Rights and Social Work*, deserves special credit for getting social work recognized as a human rights profession. He played a prominent role through his leadership in the International Federation of Social Workers (IFSW). Well known for her several volumes of writings on current issues relevant to both human rights and social work, Elisabeth Reichert (2003; 2006; 2011) has authored boxed readings for chapters 1 and 6 in this book. You will see also citations in this book from the major contributions by Susan Mapp (2014) who takes a global perspective and David Androff (2016) who focuses on key practice areas of social work practice from a human rights framework. In conclusion, human rights is gaining prominence within the social work profession today.

Now we turn to some final thoughts based on our time line of key events related to social welfare and social work. Our focus is on the way policies that are intended to have one outcome often end up having quite another. It takes a long view to of course and follow-up research to discover which policies work and which ones do not.

## UNINTENDED CONSEQUENCES OF PUBLIC POLICIES

The history of social policy development is replete with examples of policies that were put into practice with the best of intentions, even those based on appropriate research, that backfired entirely and later became an embarrassment to its designers (Aspalter, 2017). Unintended consequences are not to be confused with latent or hidden functions. Latent functions, as described in chapter 1, often appear to be unintended but actually may not be. The concept of latent functions is most famously described by Piven and Cloward (1993) in their conceptualization of "regulating the poor." Their thesis was that public welfare system are designed for social control functions as well as to provide needed aid to the poor. Prevention of civil unrest by unruly elements in the society is an underlying purpose of providing relief.

Unintended consequences of providing relief are different. These might include over dependency on the system or the breakup of families so that single mothers could qualify for help or the reluctance of individuals to seek work because of threatened loss of child care or health benefits if they were removed from the welfare rolls. We now look at examples from a variety of fields relevant to social welfare.

### LESSONS RELATED TO WAR

World history is full of "the plans of mice and men gone awry" to paraphrase Robert Burns (1786/1979). Virtually all wars are in this category. One thinks of World War I, the war to end all wars, and the war on drugs that has increased the price of drugs and therefore the profits in their sale.

Following the teachings of Martin Luther King who bemoaned the fact that war spending (for the war in Vietnam) had destroyed the chances for a war on poverty, Smiley and West (2012) considered the economic toll of the wars in Iraq and Afghanistan. At a cost of over one trillion dollars, the wars created a huge national deficit. The Bush-era tax credits for the rich further exacerbated the situation and "pushed the country into the Great Recession" in 2008 (p. 105). Although the spending priorities were intentional, the economic crisis that followed was surely not a part of the grand capitalist plan. This is a good illustration of blowback. *Blowback* by Johnson (2004) is a landmark book about the consequences of American foreign policy. The title *Blowback* refers to a CIA term for the unintended consequences of American intervention abroad. Another good example of blowback to consider is that when the United States armed the Taliban to aid them in their war against Russian occupation of Afghanistan (see Hussain, 2015). The rest is history.

### LESSONS FROM HEALTH CARE

In medical terminology, *iatrogenic* refers to the phenomenon where the treatment itself is the cause of the problem. The widespread use of antibiotics by doctors has caused many to develop resistance to the drugs. And the ready use of opioids has led to a drug addiction crisis now considered to be an epidemic.

As in medicine, the use of new technologies elsewhere that carry short-term benefits are sometimes the cause of problems over time. Prime examples come from industrial agriculture and the release of wastes that pollute the water and atmosphere (Zimmer, 2012). As a related example, take farming, where the use of pesticides led to a more virulent breed of insect that, in turn, has led to the demand for ever more powerful pesticides. Today the bee population, necessary to pollinate plants, is suffering an unanticipated decline; the culprit is said to be the widespread use of pesticides and herbicides (Zimmer, 2012; see chapter 7). And due to the widespread antibiotic use in farm animals, antibiotic-resistant bacteria are moving from the farm to the hospitals.

In mental health, the deinstitutionalization of mentally ill persons in the interest of human rights closed the mental wards; jails and prisons then became the new mental hospitals.

### LESSONS FROM THE CRIMINAL JUSTICE SYSTEM

One of the most absurd instances of legal reform "gone awry" was associated with the women's movement for equality. When women correctional officers won the right to perform the same duties as men, a victory in terms of women's career advancement in correctional work, men were given comparable rights to perform strip searches of residents of women's institutions. Soon nearly every state was plagued with lawsuits against correctional officers (see Amnesty International, 1999; van Wormer & Bartollas, 2014). Sadly, the outcome could have been easily predicted through a study of the history of women's prisons when the prisons were male-run and the scandals commonplace.

Karger and Stoesz (2012) add the policy of drug interdiction and enforcement, "the war on drugs," to the list of unintended consequences of government policy. After a half a century of huge expenditures aimed to eradicate the supply of drugs, we have an explosion in incarceration rates, the creation of international drug cartels, and a dramatic increase in killings related to drug wars. Meanwhile, the supply of drugs is as available as ever.

The key lesson that we can learn from a review of the unanticipated negative impacts of social policies is a recognition that, although there are no easy solutions to systemic problems, carefully developed, multidimensional policy analysis is essential to the creation of effective policies that endure. Sometimes a knowledge of history is all it takes to convince us that a policy that did not work before (for example, Prohibition) probably will fail once again under similar circumstances. Informed planning is therefore crucial; central to informed planning is critical thinking about historical themes.

From the vantage point of history, one can predict unintended consequences will follow from many of the proposed policies of the Trump administration—from the anti-immigration laws, privatization of public schools and federal prisons, withdrawal of funding for family planning, and removal of regulations to control toxic emissions. To the extent that there are cutbacks in social welfare and health care programs, we can logically predict that the profession of social work will be adversely affected. But only time will reveal the actual outcomes of current developments.

## SUMMARY AND CONCLUSION

The history of the development of the social work profession and of its educational institutions reveals that its evolution has often been stymied by the ideological rhythms of the wider society.

Historically, the ideology has alternated between two seemingly opposing foci—one, the personal, and the other, the political. This chapter has focused on developments in modern US history with a brief description of legislation that was passed during key administrations, whether Democratic or Republican, that had a bearing on social welfare and human rights. Emphasis was placed on the rather extraordinary paradigm shift that took place following the conformist 1950s when people who were oppressed and their allies began to mobilize to obtain their rights. Television coverage of the civil rights protests and of brutal attacks on the protesters went far to shape public opinion in the direction of change. The movement started with one group of Americans who were deprived of their rights, and their success in mobilizing public opinion spread across the country and world to other groups to mobilize in turn. Eventually there was momentum for women's rights, gay/lesbian rights, and rights based on age. There would be no going back from that point on; the world had changed. Bob Dylan was prescient. His song—"The Times They Are A' Changing"—written as early as 1964. can be considered a theme song for his and future generations.

Social work, as a profession for the people, was energized at this time. Its interventions, which were hardly new—community action, social casework, group therapy—were compatible with the popular currents of the day and the idealism of its workers (McNutt, 2013).

As Europe opened its borders intellectually with free exchanges through the European Union, and the cross-fertilization of ideas and approaches from faculty and students enhances the growth of knowledge, social workers share a global mission. The social ills confronting the profession—inflation, national indebtedness, the influx of political and economic refugees, underemployment, homelessness, and disease pandemics—differ in degree but not in kind. Every country's economy today is affected by a global market and intense competition to market products. In the past, models of practice were superimposed into various educational structures by representatives from the Euro-American world: visiting instructors were British or American; the textbooks were in English and emphasized individualized models; and therefore the transfer of knowledge was largely unilateral.

The challenge to social work today, as previously shown, is the strain on local social services related to the current conservative climate and public resentment of welfare benefits and of the people who receive them. At the national level, the pervasive neoliberal or free market economics favors tax cuts for the rich and the growth of global corporations over social welfare programming. Privatization of public services is a related worldwide trend affecting social work conditions of employment, unionization, and the availability of mental health services. While some nations, such as those in Scandinavia, continue to look to the government for solutions to social ills, in other parts of the world the increasing chasm between rich and poor and the conservative onslaught on the social welfare state have created difficulties for the social work profession. A deliberate targeted attack on Britain's social workers has been especially forthright, for example (see Dominelli, 2010, 2012). Nevertheless, as this history of social work shows, the profession has survived in tough times before, and, in the United Kingdom as in the United States, the spirit of the foremothers of social work lives among us now, critical and irrepressible.

## THOUGHT QUESTIONS

1. Consider key factors that helped set the stage for the social revolution that took place in the late 1960s. What was the influence of a certain baby book?

2. Discuss the impact of the Civil Rights movement on social work. What was the paradigm shift that occurred?
3. Describe the climate of social change that took place in the mid- and late 1960s. What was the Great Society and what were the results?
4. Discuss the changes in attitudes and policies toward social welfare as a result of the new conservatism of the 1980s. What was the economic legacy of Ronald Reagan?
5. Discuss unique aspects of the 2016 election campaign. What are key factors in the surprise Trump victory?
6. What is the basic thesis of *Unfaithful Angels: How Social Work Has Abandoned Its Mission?* Argue in favor or against the position taken by Specht and Courtney.
7. Describe NASW-US and its political activity. What is special about the ideology and make-up of the profession, including students' attitudes?
8. What are the parallels between feminist thought and social work?
9. What is the strengths perspective and how is it applied in social work practice?
10. List some examples of unintended consequences related to war. From your own perspective, what are some social policy developments that have backfired in other situations?

## REFERENCES

Alexander, M. (2016, February 10). Why Hillary Clinton doesn't deserve the black vote. *The Nation*. Retrieved from www.thenation.com

Al-Krenawi, A., Graham, J., & Habibov, N. (Eds.). (2016). *Diversity and social work in Canada*. New York, NY: Oxford University Press.

Alinsky, S. (1971). *Rules for radicals: A practical primer for realistic radicals*. New York, NY: Random House.

Alvarez, A. R. (2013). Social work education and multiculturalism. In C. Franklin (Ed.), *Encyclopedia of social work* (20th ed.). New York, NY: Oxford University Press. Retrieved from www.socialwork.oxfordre.com

Ambrosino, R., Heffernan, J., Shuttlesworth, G., & Ambrosino, R. (2015). *Social work and social welfare: An introduction*. Belmont, CA: Cengage.

Amnesty International. (1999). *Not a part of my sentence: Violations of the human rights of women in custody*. New York, NY: Author.

Angelou, M. (1993, January, 20). *On the pulse of the morning*. Poem read to the nation at President Clinton's Inauguration Ceremony.

Appleby, G. A., Colon, E., & Hamilton, J. (2010). *Diversity, oppression, and social functioning: Person-in-Environment assessment and intervention*. Boston, MA: Pearson.

Androff, D. (2016). *Practicing rights: Human rights-based approaches to social work practice*. New York, NY: Routledge.

Aspalter, C. (2017). Preface. In C. Aspalter (Ed.), *The Routledge international handbook to welfare state systems* (pp. xxix–xxxi). London, England: Routledge.

Barsky, A. (2014, winter). Ethics in private practice. *The New Social Worker*. Retrieved from www.socialworker.com

Berg-Weger, M. (2016). *Social work and social welfare: An invitation*. New York, NY: Routledge.

Burns, R. (1786/1979). "To a louse," Line 8. In A. Partington (Ed.), *Oxford dictionary of quotations* (3rd ed., p. 115). Oxford, England: Oxford University Press.

Canadian Association for Social Work Education (CASWE). (2016). Vision, mission, principles, and activities. Retrieved from www.caswe-acfts.ca/about/mission

Chandler, S. (2004) "Curiously uninvolved": Social work and protest against the war in Vietnam. *The Journal of Sociology & Social Welfare, 31*(4), 3–20.

Congress, E., & Gonzalez, M. (2012). *Multicultural perspectives in social work practice with families.* New York, NY: Springer Publishing Co.

Council on Social Work Education (CSWE). (2015). *Educational policies and accreditation standards.* Alexandria, VA: CSWE.

Council on Social Work Education (CSWE). (2016). *2015 annual statistics in social work education in the United States.* Alexandria, VA: Council of Social Work Education.

Cowger, C. D. (2013, February 25). Peace. In C. Franklin (Ed.), *Encyclopedia of social work.* New York, NY: Oxford University Press.

Dominelli, L. (2010). *Social work in a globalizing world.* Cambridge, UK: Polity Press.

Dominelli, L. (2012). *Green social work: From environmental crises to environmental justice.* Cambridge, England: Polity Press.

Faulkner, W. (1948/1994). *Intruder in the dust.* New York, NY: Library of America.

Graham, J. R., Swift, K. J., & Delaney, R. (2012). *Canadian social policy: An introduction.* (4th ed.). Don Mills, Ontario: Pearson Education Canada.

Gray, M., Coates, J., & Hetherington, T. (Eds.) (2013). *Environmental social work.* New York, NY: Routledge.

Gutiérrez, L., & Lewis, E. A. (2012). Education, participation, and capacity building in community organizing with women of color. In M. Minkler (Ed.), *Community organizing and community building for health and welfare* (pp. 215–228). New Brunswick, NJ: Rutgers University Press.

Haas, P., & Springer, J. F. (2014). *Applied policy research: Concepts and cases.* New York, NY: Routledge.

Hardcastle, D. (2011). *Community practice: Theories and skills for social workers.* New York, NY: Oxford University Press.

Hoff, M., & McNutt, J. (2009). *Social policy and the physical environment.* In J. O. Midgley and M. Livermore (Eds.), *The handbook of social policy* (pp. 295–312). Thousand Oaks, CA: Sage.

Hussain, D. (2015, March 23). ISIS: The "unintended consequences" of the U.S.-led war on Iraq. *Foreign Policy Journal.* Retrieved from www.foreignpolicyjournal.com

Ife, J. (2013). *Human rights and social work: Towards rights-based practice.* Cambridge, England: Cambridge University Press.

Jimenez, J., Pasztor, E., & Chambers, R. M. (2015). *Social policy and social change: Toward the creation of social and economic justice.* Thousand Oaks, CA: Sage.

Johnson, C. (2004). *Blowback: Costs and consequences of American empire.* New York, NY: Henry Holt.

Karger, H. J., & Stoesz, D. (2013). *American social welfare policy: A pluralist approach* (7th ed.). New York, NY: Pearson.

Katz, M. B. (2008). *The price of citizenship: Redefining the American welfare state.* (updated ed.). Philadelphia, PA: University of Pennsylvania Press.

Kirkpatrick, R. (2009). *1969: The year everything changed.* New York, NY: Skyhouse Publishing.

Ludwig, M. (2017, November 10). *Nature Has Rights: Activists Call for a Legal Transformation.* Truthout. Retrieved from www.truth-out.org

Lum, D. (2011). *Social work practice and people of color: A process-stage approach* (5th ed.). Belmont, CA: Brooks/Cole.

Mapp, S. C. (2014). *Human rights and social justice in a global perspective: An introduction to international social work* (2nd ed.). New York, NY: Oxford University Press.

Mary, N. (2008). *Social work in a sustainable world.* Chicago, IL: Lyceum.

McNutt, J. C. (2013). Social work practice: History and evolution. In C. Franklin (Ed.), *Encyclopedia of social work.* New York, NY: Oxford University Press. Online publication.

National Association of Social Workers (NASW). (2016). NASW statement on Donald J. Trump election as 45th U.S. President. Washington, D.C.: NASW. Retrieved from www.socialworkers.org

National Association of Social Workers (NASW). (2017). *Code of ethics.* Washington, DC: NASW.

Nguyen, A. (2013, February 25). Civil rights and social work. *Social Work License Map.* Retrieved from www.socialworklicensemap.com

Payne, M. (2014). *Modern social work theory* (4th ed.). Chicago, IL: Lyceum Books.

Pear, R. (1996, August 1). Millions affected: After *hearing* president, more in party back measure in house. *New York Times,* p.1A.

Piven, F. (1995). Poorhouse politics. *The Progressive 59*(2), 22–24.

Piven, F., & Cloward, R. A. (1993). *Regulating the poor: The function of public welfare,* updated edition. New York, NY: Vintage.

Reichert, E. (2003). *Social work and human rights: A foundation for policy and practice.* New York, NY: Columbia University Press.

Reichert, E. (2006). *Understanding human rights: An exercise book.* Thousand Oaks, CA: Sage.

Reichert, E. (2011). *Social work and human rights: A foundation for policy and practice* (2nd ed.). New York, NY: Columbia University Press.

Saleebey, D. (2012). Introduction: Power in the people. In D. Saleebey (Ed.), *The strengths perspective in social work practice* (6th ed., pp. 1–22). Boston, MA: Pearson.

Smiley, T., & West, C. (2012). *The rich and the rest of us: A poverty manifesto.* New York, NY: Smiley Books.

Specht, H., & Courtney, M. (1994). *Unfaithful angels: How social work has abandoned its mission.* New York, NY: The Free Press.

Spock, B., & Needleman, R. (2013). *Dr. Spock's baby and child care* (9th ed.). New York, NY: Simon and Schuster.

Stevens, H. (2012, January 6). Dr. Spock's baby and child care empowered, encouraged parents. *Chicago Tribune.* Retrieved from www.chicagotribune.com

Stoesz, D., Karger, H. J., & Carrilio, T. (2010). *A dream deferred: How social work education lost its way and what can be done.* New Brunswick, NJ: Aldine Transaction.

Stuart, P. (2013). Social work profession: History. In In C. Franklin (Ed.), *Encyclopedia of Social Work.* New York, NY: Oxford University Press. Online publication.

Sue, D. W., Rasheed, M., & Rasheed, J. (2016). *Multicultural social work practice: A competency-based approach to diversity and social justice* (2nd ed.). Hoboken, NJ: Wiley.

United Nations (1948). *Universal Declaration of Human Rights.* New York, NY: United Nations.

Valentich, M. (2011). Feminist theory and social work practice. In F. Turner (Ed.), *Social work treatment: Interlocking theoretical approaches* (pp. 2015–2223). New York, NY: Oxford.

van Wormer, K. (2014). *Women and the criminal justice system.* New York, NY: Pearson.

van Wormer, K., & R. J. Link (2016). *Social welfare policy for a sustainable future: The U.S. in global perspective.* Thousand Oaks, CA: Sage.

Wronka, J. (1998). *Human rights and social policy in the 21st century: A history of the idea of human rights and comparison of the United Nations Declaration of Human Rights with United States federal and state constitutions* (rev. ed.). Lantham, MD: University Press of America.

Wronka, J. (2016). *Human rights and social justice: Social action and service for the helping and health professions* (2nd ed.). Thousand Oaks, CA: Sage.

Zimmer, C. (2012, March 30). Two studies point to common pesticide as a culprit in declining bee colonies. *New York Times*, p. A20.

CHAPTER 5

# SOCIAL FORMS OF OPPRESSION

> Everyone is entitled to all the rights and freedoms set forth in this Declaration, without distinction of any kind, such as race, colour, sex, language, religion, political or other opinion, national or social origin, property, birth or other status.
>
> UN Universal Declaration of Human Rights, 1948, Article 2

> Everyone has the right to seek and to enjoy in other countries asylum from persecution.
>
> Article 14.1.

*Oppression* is a term, as Iris Young (2011) argues, that is favored by social activists, a central term of political discourse. We use the term *oppression* in the sense of social oppression, to refer to the personal forces in keeping people from achieving their potential.

Oppression, as defined by the *Social Work Dictionary* is

> The social act of placing severe restrictions on an individual, group, or institution. Typically, a government or political organization that is in power places these restrictions formally or covertly on oppressed groups so that they may be exploited and less able to compete with other social groups. The oppressed individual or group is devalued, exploited, and deprived of privileges by the individual or group who has more power. (Barker, 2014, p. 303)

Some of the words used in this definition—*power, exploited, deprived, privileges*—are key variables related to oppression. In each form of social oppression—racial, ethnic, religious, sexual—there is a dominant group that receives the unearned advantage or privilege, and a targeted group that is denied the advantage. Each form of oppression creates a unique injustice and an inequitable power structure (Reichert, 2011). Such inequalities are kept in place inasmuch as the powers that be are able to maintain their position through ideology or force. Violence or the threat of violence may also come into play in suppressing rebellion.

Think back to the Deep South under segregation. The ideology of paternalism was highly effective in alleviating the guilt of a caste of people who prided themselves on taking care of members of an "inferior race." According to the ideology of the day, "colored" people needed to be taken care of; servants were emotionally seen as like family members while financially they were more or less in bondage (see Dollard, 1998/1957, *Class and Caste in a Southern Town*).

Mullaly (2010), citing Foucault (1977), brings our attention to the more usual and subtle forms of oppression. His suggestion is that we go beyond viewing oppression as the inherent or even conscious acts of one group against another and consider the institutionally based forms that flow from the social structure itself. Oppression is ingrained, according to Mullaly, in our systems of education, criminal justice, the delivery of health and social services, and the like. Dominelli (2002), similarly, talks of the tyranny of the workplace as one of the structural elements of power that is located in the institutional and cultural domains. Because oppressive dynamics are embedded in ordinary social activities, they do not consciously have to be thought about either by oppressor or the oppressed and are easily denied by most.

## SOCIAL EXCLUSION

Closely related to the concept of oppression is the European term, social exclusion. This formulation originated in France in the 1970s and is useful to denote the relational aspect of oppression. Social exclusion is defined in *The Social Work Dictionary* as the "marginalization of people or areas and the imposition of barriers that restrict them from access to opportunities to fully integrate with the larger society" (Barker, 2014, p. 397). Social exclusion applies both to countries that lose out in global competition and to classes of people within nations in the grip of poverty or living with mental or physical disability.

A prime example of social exclusion is the historical treatment of American Indians. As a result of deliberate policies of exclusion and extermination, not to mention illnesses, firearms, and alcohol, the Indian population in the Americas went from an estimated 30 million to 5 million in the first 50 years after contact with the Europeans and fell to one million by 1890 (Johnson & Yellow Bird, 2012). The passage of the Chinese Exclusion Act and the herding of 100,000 innocent Japanese Americans into internment camps are often-overlooked racist policies involving Asian American and Asian people (Levin & Nolan, 2011). Such measures were adopted in both the United States and Canada. Razack (2012) traces the history of racial minority groups that have been marginalized and excluded from Canadian society, including the mistreatment of the aboriginal people and the marginalization of people who are Arab in appearance today.

Social exclusion is often used to refer to immigrant groups, persons who are usually unemployed and live in poverty and who are shut off from opportunities available in the wider society (Healy, 2008). The concept of exclusion gained currency in Britain under Conservative administrations and also under New Labour (Lyons & Huegler, 2012). This term also is commonly applied to the long-term unemployed, ex-offenders, and persons with mental or physical disabilities. The European Commission (2015) formally adopted an action plan for combating poverty and social exclusion. The plan calls for better understanding of exclusion and national action of the member states of the European Union and will remain active until 2020. The literature on social exclusion broadens the focus from disadvantage on purely economic grounds to include marginalization through the denial of civil, political, and social rights of citizenship. The European Union has been especially concerned with the institutionalized discrimination against the Roma people (formerly referred to as "gypsies"), the most despised and persecuted minority group in Europe, especially in Eastern Europe (Council of Europe).

Similarly, sociologist Lori Peek (2011) uses the concept of exclusion in her documentation of personal attacks on people identified as Muslim. In *Behind the Backlash: Muslim Americans after 9/11*, Peek explores how disasters and other crisis events impact the most marginalized members of society. Civil rights organizations recorded thousands of anti-Arab harassment and hate crimes that took place following the airplane attacks on the New York twin towers. Her interviews with 140 ordinary Muslim Americans showed how these citizens were verbally harassed at this time. Such attacks are not surprising, given that surveys today show few Americans understand the Islam religion and that 53% have a negative view of this minority group.

And then again in 2015, a surge in hate crimes against US Muslims took place. An investigation based on official police reports in 20 states found that there were about 260 hate crimes—the highest number since the 481 such crimes in 2001. Speculation is that the attacks were driven by "political vitriol from candidates like Donald J. Trump, who has called for a ban on immigration by Muslims and a national registry of Muslims in the United States" (Lichtblau, 2016).

These examples of hate attacks on minority groups are clearly instances of human rights violations. Article 2 of the Universal Declaration of Human Rights, as quoted at the start of this chapter, states that people cannot be deprived of their basic rights through discrimination such as on the basis of race, color, sex, language, religion, political or other opinion, national or social origin, property, birth, or other status. We can extend the categories to include gender identity and sexual orientation issues as well, since these are other statuses that set people apart.

## A HUMAN RIGHTS APPROACH

Special categories of people who need special attention globally are women who are apt to live in poverty and to be vulnerable to domestic violence, racial, ethnic, and religious minorities, immigrants, and sexual minorities. In a human rights context, as Reichert (2011) asserts, the stress on equality does not necessarily mean treating everyone the same; it might mean that different treatment must be applied in order that women (and other minority groups) can enjoy the same rights as the dominant group.

Social workers, according to the CSWE, 2015 standards, should "understand the global interconnections of oppression in human rights violations" (competency 3, p. 7) and be prepared to engage in "diversity and difference" (p. 7).

Oppression and social exclusion, as discussed earlier, are general terms. In order to be more specific, the focus of this chapter is on the isms—classism, racism, sexism, heterosexism, sectarianism, and ethnocentrism. One item to keep in mind as you read about each of these isms, concerns the interesting but often overlooked fact of causation. These phenomena—classism and racism, for example—are inclined to be self-sustaining and cyclical. The way this works is this: the society may discriminate due to prejudice; then the disadvantaged group may fail to achieve what others achieve, and then they may be called ignorant or lazy. A related truth from social psychology is our tendency to externalize—if we exploit or otherwise mistreat an individual or group, we will come to blame these people for their disadvantaged state. Class, racial, and gender divisions are reinforced thereby.

Another concept that is closely related to social exclusion and widely used in the social science literature is privilege. On US college campuses workshops on privilege are commonly conducted in which students are directed to list which categories of privilege they have membership in. Examples are white, college student, heterosexual, male, Christian, US citizen, and middle class or upper class privilege. In some situations, a minority status such as Cherokee tribal member or Latter Day Saint (Mormon) membership bestows privilege, while in other situations, such membership may be a disadvantage. As far as social class is concerned, the higher the class, the greater the privileges attached to it.

Before reading this chapter, it is important to note that these isms—racism, sexism, and so on—all overlap to varying degrees as particular individuals occupy more than one category at once. Moreover, the effects of membership in dual or multiple categories are more synergistic than additive. A woman who is poor and uneducated, for example, might suffer from sexism far more than might her middle or upper class counterpart. So keep these facts in mind as you contemplate the dynamics of classism, racism, sexism, and so on. In actuality there are no clear-cut divisions between and among these categories; these phenomena are discussed separately here for the sake of simplification. Classism, the first topic of this chapter, extends our discussion of economic oppression from previous chapters into the realm of interpersonal dynamics.

## CLASSISM

Class, or a person's socioeconomic status in the community, is a key determinant of one's life chances, one's access to health, educational opportunities, and marital/partner prospects. Renowned educator bell hooks (2000) addressed this issue as follows:

> Class matters. Race and gender can be used as screens to deflect attention away from the harsh realities class politics exposes. Clearly, just when we should all be paying attention to class, using race and gender to understand and explain its new dimensions, society, even our government, says let's talk meaningfully about ending racism without talking about class. (p. 313)

### IMPORTANCE OF SOCIAL CLASS IN AMERICA

*Classism* refers to the social exclusion of people on the basis of social stratification; it is oppression of people thought to be socially inferior—whether on the basis of poor living standards, or lack of education or grammatical speech. Classism is probably the most fundamental and neglected of the isms in the social work and political literature. In fact, the spelling check of the Word program only just recognized the term as valid in the last several years.

Classism can occur at all levels of society. Its existence is singularly pronounced at the higher echelons by the upper-uppers against the class just beneath them, the "nouveau riche" who are thought to lack taste and refinement. The nouveau riche, in turn, resent the upper-uppers, who mostly inherited their wealth and did not earn it on their own merits. But the kind of classism that we are concerned with in this book is more closely related to deprivation than snobbery, the deprivation of the lower, including working, classes by the social, political, and economic institutions of society. We can call this *institutional classism*, a term that parallels the concept of institutional racism, to refer to the sort of routine practices built into the system that restrict people's life chances on the basis of socioeconomic status, unintentionally or not. Examples might be a school's scheduling of parent-teacher conferences at times when working-class parents cannot attend, or a social agency's refusal to have a sliding fee for therapy services, or paying workers below a living wage and then expecting them to maintain a certain standard of living. The funding of public schools in the United States, done in a large part by property taxes, means that children in poor neighborhoods will have poorly funded schools. A recent investigation by National Public Radio (NPR) found a tremendous discrepancy in educational spending across school districts with results that are unfair and inequitable (Turner, 2016).

Any number of novels and autobiographies—most famously, *The Grapes of Wrath, Angela's Ashes,* and *Bastard out of Carolina*—depict the cruelties in life at the bottom and the tremendous resilience of each book's hero in overcoming his or her conditions of oppression. What we can learn from such works is the extent to which socioeconomic exploitation is realized through the structural relationship between the haves and the have-nots. Classism extends beyond the mere distribution of material resources into the area of social status.

Today, under the kind of free-market conditions—pro-corporations, anti-union—stratification by class becomes ever more pronounced. Under free-market conditions, the rich grow richer and the poor, poorer. Equalization of wealth and privilege is not a priority of transnational corporations or the political structures which they, to a large degree, control. Whether between countries or individuals, socioeconomic inequality generates more inequality as the comfortable come to disavow the needy. The dominant group reinforces its position, as Mullaly (2010) suggests, by measuring all groups according to the dominant norms. A form of blaming the victim and holding the individual responsible for his or her failure to overcome adversity prevails. It is easy to imagine that defects of character or differences of culture explain economic difficulties.

Most people in the United States identify with the middle class and are as oblivious to class privilege as they are to the notion of class itself. Class identity, as Mantsios (2009) suggests, has been stripped from popular culture. Yet if we turn to research, we learn that the class position of one's family, rather than hard work or even intelligence, is probably the single most significant determination of future success. The differences start before birth and relate to matters of maternal health and nutrition, prenatal care, and infant mortality. The quality of child care and school education, for example, closely parallel one's position in the social strata. Since 45% of school funding comes from local sources such as property taxes, the per-pupil spending in poor school districts is far below that in prosperous suburbs (Pinkerton, 2003). Curiously, the right to education is not included as a basic right in the US Constitution.

African Americans' educational backgrounds may be weak due to the low quality of many public schools in predominantly minority neighborhoods, thus making it harder for them to obtain professional training and to compete for jobs on any level. The decline in high-paying, blue-collar jobs will decrease the opportunities through which parents without much education themselves have been able to earn enough to help their children go to college. More and more, African Americans are laid off from manufacturing jobs, overrepresented in the service industries, and underrepresented in the professions. The clamping-down on affirmative action programs which has taken place under the Trump administration leaves African Americans and Latinos especially vulnerable to shifts in the economic winds (Savage, 2017). As quickly as blacks moved ahead in the 1990s, they have now fallen backward. The black unemployment rate now stands higher than that of the Hispanic rate and double the rate for whites (Pew Research Center, 2014).

## SOCIAL MOBILITY

Traditionally, the United States has prided itself on being a land of high social mobility and opportunity, where hard workers can achieve "the American dream." This fact is brought stunningly to life in the 1950s award-winning portrait of black Chicago family life, *A Raisin in the Sun* (Hansberry, 1994), as Mama remembers: "Big Walter used to say . . . 'Seem like God didn't see fit to give the black man nothing but dreams—but he did give us children to make them dreams seem worthwhile'" (pp.45–46). Mama is a maid, her son a chauffeur, but her daughter plans to be a doctor and as the son says to a white racist in the play's dramatic climax, "We are proud of her." And this play was written before the Civil Rights Act was passed. A great deal of social mobility has taken place since that time. We should not become complacent, however.

Young people—those of the so-called Millennial Generation—are far more aware than are their elders of the economic aspects of the class system and of global inequalities in America. This fact was reflected in the recent Bernie Sanders campaign and the widespread support it drew from young people of diverse racial and social class backgrounds. In fact, as the first of a series of polls conducted by the AP-NORC Center for Public Affairs Research and the Black Youth Project, both of the University of Chicago, found that black Millennials favored Bernie Sanders to Hillary Clinton 53 to 39% (Johnson, 2016). Their support reflected concerns about the need for a living wage, affordable college, the outsourcing of jobs, and higher taxes on the rich in the interests of economic equality. The Sanders campaign galvanized young people for social change and had a strong influence on shaping the Democratic platform for the 2016 election.

Class status makes a big difference in the opportunities that minority groups have, even their desirability as immigrants to certain countries, for example, immigrants from Hong Kong to Canada with the resources to open businesses received a warm welcome. In the United States, inner city blacks generally have a much harder time of "achieving the American dreams" than do African Americans of a professional class who own their own homes and send their children to the best schools. See chapter 6, which is devoted to an in-depth analysis of the impact of poverty on people and their families.

## INTERSECTIONALITY

Intersectionality takes place when minority members are in two or more oppressed categories at once. *Intersectionality* is the term used in oppression theory to address the experiences of people who are subjected to multiple forms of oppression and domination. The term was first coined by African American lawyer Kimberlé Crenshaw in a legal article published in 1989 (Moe, 2014). She was referring to the difficult of a lawsuit that involved discrimination against black women but not white women or black men. The concept therefore grew out of black women's experience and has since been expanded to refer to all types of multiple identities.

In their recent book, *Intersectionality*, Patricia Hill Collins and Sirma Bilge (2016) explain how through this multidimensional lens we can understand how membership in one minority group, such as female gender, combines with other key social characteristics and statuses related to oppression, such as race or ethnicity, to produce a synergistic or multiplying effect. When an African American woman, for example, is a member of a black activist group and also the women's movement, her specific issues remain subordinated within each movement because the entire discrimination that she faces is not addressed. This effect is stronger than even the sum of the separate categories of difference. National origin, culture, religion, caste or class, age, gender identity and sexual expression, (dis)ability, and/or having the status of ex-convict are other categories that in combination can subject people to heightened levels of discrimination.

It is rare to find experimental research to gauge the degree of discrimination inflicted upon individuals who occupy two categories of difference simultaneously. One exception is the research of sociologist Devah Pager. Pager (2003) tested the concept of intersectionality in labor market research. She sent out pairs of white applicants (100) and otherwise identical black applicants (250), where one member of each matched pair had a criminal record (see also Pager, Western, & Bonikowski, 2009). Pager and her colleagues found that employers strongly discriminated against the black applicants and especially against those with supposed criminal records. They were even more likely to make job offers to whites with criminal records than to African Americans with clean records. This research provides evidence that the effect of race can be magnified by additional factors such as criminal history.

The tragedy of the poisoned water in Flint, Michigan is an excellent example of the systemic neglect of a whole city that was mostly black and over 40% living below the poverty line. The water became contaminated with lead; the children who were tested had extremely high levels of lead in their blood, and 10 people have died. The water contamination was the result of a decision made by the governor's office to save money by hooking the city's water supply to the polluted Flint River instead of Lake Huron (Moore, 2016). According to Michael Moore, a native of Flint:

> This is racial crime. . . . Everyone knows this would not have happened in predominantly white Michigan cities like West Bloomfield or Grosse Point, or Ann Arbor (p. 39).

The National Association of Colored People (NAACP) president drew a direct connection between Flint's socioeconomic factors and the toxic drinking water (Martinez, 2016). As well as an example of intersectionality regarding race and class, the Flint water crisis is an example of environmental justice as will be discussed in chapter 7.

Tim Wise (2010) refutes the liberal dogma that we can separate the forces of racism from the forces of classism. He also debunks the claim that color-blind policies will overcome racial inequality through treating everyone the same. Moreover, by not considering the intersections of our multiple roles and identities, we can easily fall into arguments of comparison about which form of oppression is worse—for example, is it racism or is classism?

In *Under the Affluence*, Tim Wise (2015) discusses the uniqueness of the class system in the United States and how it evolved. Historically, race and class were intersected and black people relegated to work in the fields from childhood and prevented from obtaining the education or skills that would have enabled them to rise. Progressive government programs during the 1960s and well-paying job opportunities during an economic boom, did help many to pursue the so-called American dream, but, as Wise suggests, many of those jobs have now disappeared, and a "culture of cruelty" or a contempt for the nation's poor prevails (p.21).

Thinking back to the racial oppression in yesterday's world in the hills of Kentucky, bell hooks (2009) reflects on the dualism of race and class:

> I was a little girl in a segregated world when I first learned that there were white people who saw black people as less than animals. Sitting on the porch, my siblings and I would watch white folks bring home their servants, the maids and cooks who toiled to make their lives comfortable. These black servants were always relegated to the back seat. Next to the white drivers in the front would be the dog and in the back seat the black worker. Just seeing this taught me much about the interconnectedness of race and class. (pp. 148–149)

Now we move from a focus on instances of discrimination to a consideration of one of the insidious forms of oppression—racism.

## RACISM

Racial discrimination, which may involve social exclusion, exploitation, enslavement, and environmental injustice, is clearly contrary to the principles of human rights. Racism and classism, as mentioned earlier, are closely intertwined. In this section, our goal is to examine the economic factor in racism and to show how racial antagonisms have been used by powerful interest groups to maintain support for its self-serving policies. (An example of the success of this strategy is evidenced in rural Kentucky, where poor farmers vote Republican in clear violation of any personal interests.)

Racial identity is not always clear cut. It was only in 2000 that the US Census Bureau included categories of mixed race. This is what we learned from the 2010 Census report on people identifying as being of mixed race. Four groups were the largest multiple-race combinations, each exceeding 1 million people in size: white and black (1.8 million), white and "some other race" (1.7 million), white and Asian (1.6 million), and white and American Indian and Alaska Native (1.4 million; US Census Bureau, 2011). President Obama (2004) is the most famous representative of a mixed race category with a white mother and African father. Although raised by white people, his identity is African American.

*Racism* can be defined as a form of racial oppression based on the color of one's skin or other distinctive or imagined physical features. Racial oppression, like sexual oppression, is reflected in both individual and institutional acts, decisions, and policies that neglect, overlook, or subjugate the individual or the group (Appleby, Colon, & Hamilton, 2011).

At the personal level, the impact of verbal attacks based on prejudice can be severe, especially for children. Kelsey Ulrich, a Native American student of social work, (in private correspondence with van Wormer of September 23, 2013) completed a consciousness-raising exercise based on feeling responses to a situation of discrimination or mistreatment. Here is her response which exemplifies resilience following an experience of oppression:

> The situation was when I was younger and in elementary school. I am Native American, so when I was younger I was a very tan little kid. In school the white kids didn't want to play with me because they didn't know what I was. I wasn't as dark as the other black kid but I wasn't white either.

> *I heard* daily from other kids "what are you?" "what's wrong with your skin?" "why are you so dark?"
> *I saw* many other kids just being mean and being able to play together but I was excluded.
> *I smelled* grass and outside. The only times this happened was when we were all on recess and all the other kids played on the main playground while I was left with the very small and outdated playground, which was also rusty.
> *I tasted* at times, tears. I was so upset and hurt and didn't understand why these kids were so mean to me over something I couldn't control.
> *I felt* at times unbelievable sadness and I didn't understand. Yet this was the time I decided to ask my family why I was the way I was and where we came from. Learning and knowing about my past and about the culture of my ancestors instilled a point of pride for who I was and our family story. *This to me was* my life changing moment. If those kids weren't mean to me I am not sure I would have pressed my family so hard to know where I came from. Without knowing where I came from, looking back I feel that I would be missing a whole entire part of me.

That racism is a worldwide phenomenon was evidenced in the United Nations Conference against Racial Discrimination, Xenophobia, and Related Intolerance held in 2001 in Durban, South Africa, and followed up twice with Durban II and Durban III (United Nations, 2011). At Durban III the United Nations General Assembly held a one-day high-level meeting in New York to commemorate the 10th anniversary of the adoption of the Durban Declaration and Programme of Action. This document, which is the international community's blueprint for action to fight racism, was adopted by consensus at the 2001 UN Durban World Conference. When the Palestinians threatened to dominate the discussions, however, Israel and its ally, the United States, pulled out. The success of this conference was in its addressed issues of race hatred against minority groups ranging from the Roma (pejoratively called Gypsies) of Europe to the slaves in Sudan to the Dalits ("untouchables") of India to the indigenous peoples of Australia.

No one with any self-respect and no politician seeking a following would claim to be a racist. It is not difficult, however, to practice racism under the guise of something else—for example, welfare reform, promoting equal opportunity, and the like. When welfare assistance began to be seen as income support for unmarried mothers, a large portion of whom were black, the program no longer seemed like insurance. It began to look like a handout to the undeserving poor. Racialized assumptions about the poor, then as now, kept working-class whites from supporting strong social welfare programs (Wise, 2015).

## IN THE CRIMINAL JUSTICE SYSTEM

In *The New Jim Crow: Mass Incarceration in the Age of Color,* Michelle Alexander (2012) reveals how the war on crime became a war on black people and was linked to a racial agenda on welfare. Today, as she famously states, there are more African American adults under correctional control than there were slaves in 1850. And more black men are disenfranchised today (who can't vote because of their drug-related felonies) than in 1870.

Police shootings and killing of unarmed young black men, many caught on cell phone cameras, have ignited protests across the United States. In Ferguson, Missouri, after an officer shot Michael

Brown, several nights of riots and weeks of protests began. An investigation conducted by the *New York Post* found that although black men make up only 6% of the population, they account for 40% of the unarmed men shot to death by police in 2015 (Kindy, Fisher, Tate, & Jenkins, 2015). An unprecedented number of officers have been indicted in shooting cases in the most recent year, but most of them have had the charges dropped or been acquitted following a trial. One positive development is that police departments are ordering body cameras for the officers, which will be used to show the actual sequence of events. And the FBI has decided to replace its current program with a more accurate database. Perhaps the most memorable outcome of the national furor over the shootings was the birth of the Black Lives Matter movement.

In response to the acquittal of off-duty security guard George Zimmerman in the shooting death of Trayvon Martin, the phrase "black lives matter" went viral on the social media (Cobb, 2016). Following a succession of high-profile police shootings, the Black Lives Matter movement galvanized protestors everywhere. Although the movement initially addressed the killing of unarmed young black men, black women are equally committed to the rights of working people and to gender and sexual equality. The impact has been especially strong in the 2016 election campaign, as candidates for president have been called upon to give their support to the saving of black lives.

## THE TRUTH ABOUT WELFARE REFORM

According to Michelle Alexander's (2012) thesis, the crackdown on welfare recipients was part of a new racialized social control that affected poor people of all races. The new Democratic politics exploited the vulnerabilities and racial resentments of poor and working-class whites. In this way, powerless people were doing the bidding of powerful interest groups.

Welfare reform, passed by the Clinton administration in 1996, was billed to the public as a workfare scheme, a way to help single mothers become self-sufficient. From there it was an easy step to establish time limits for the mothers still receiving aid. Racism entered the picture in that large numbers of the children whose mothers have been forced off the welfare rolls are children of color (and so perceived by the public). The attack against welfare, as Wise (2015) suggests, is preeminently a racial attack. The same racial agenda is behind both welfare cutbacks and attacks on affirmative action, often coded in language of "no special rights," as if people of color were currently equal and asking for privileged treatment. Seccombe (2014), who conducted extensive interviews with welfare recipients for her book, *So You Think I Drive a Cadillac*? concurs. The racist view that welfare is a program primarily for the African American community was acknowledged by interviewees of both races to be a widely held attitude by the general public.

Statistics reveal the results of welfare reform for black families: One in two black children lives below the official poverty level (Children's Defense Fund, 2016). The United States, with its high level of relative poverty, ranks 34th worldwide, right before the poor country of Romania. The recession of 2007–2009 hit African American families the hardest of all racial/ethnic groups due to extensive loss of housing. During the recession, home values went down and foreclosure rates went up, resulting in black households losing more wealth than white households. The wealth of white households was eight times the median wealth of black households in 2010. The wealth gap actually increased during the recovery period with the median wealth gap between the races now significantly larger than even before, according to Pew Research (2014). Tabron (2016), the CEO of the Stanford Social Innovation Review, recommends closing the wealth gap for families of color through providing economic incentives in housing and jobs. Factors holding African Americans back according to researchers are the lack of technical skills, shortage of jobs in the inner city area, inner city crime, high arrest rate, and the legacy of slavery (Billingsley & Morrison-Rodriguez, 1998; Schiele, 2013).

Nevertheless, to overemphasize historical abuse and community problems as the cause of poverty may be to fail to acknowledge the very real structural influences stemming from intense global competition and technological change. The economic downturn has been especially hard on workers without a college degree—the segment of the population that is disproportionately composed of blacks. The loss of well-paid manufacturing jobs for black males has had a ripple effect on the stability of the black family.

Writing of the outpouring of support for both Donald Trump and Bernie Sanders in the 2016 election campaign, Jim Hightower (2016) effectively captures what he terms "the real story" behind this support (p. 70). It is not just about walling off Mexico or banning Muslim refugees, he suggests, but it is about "waves of ordinary people" who are responding to their leaders who have turned their backs on American manufacturing and the struggling families who count on those jobs. Instead of comprehending the public's rage, as Hightower further suggests, the establishment and liberal media have simply dismissed Trump's supporters as racists. And yet, many of them were people who resented the attempts by liberals to promote the interests of minorities ahead of their own interests as working-class whites.

European American cultural oppression in which "the other" is vilified has led to internalized racism and placed many African American youths at risk of self-destructive behavior (Schiele, 2013). The lack of hope that they and other poor young people have today for future success is related at least in part to the exportation to foreign countries of the kind of jobs that would have made the reality of stable employment possible. Resentment and alienation are the predictable consequences by those affected by the developments.

## RESILIENCE IN THE FACE OF RACISM

Resilience is not the cheerful disregard of one's difficult and traumatic life experiences or of one's personal pain; rather, it is the ability to bear up in spite of these ordeals. Resilience is a process, the continuing growth of "capacity, knowledge, insight, and virtues derived through meeting the demands and challenges of one's world, however chastening" (Saleebey, 2012, pp. 13–14). From an Afrocentric perspective, Robert Hill (2007) directs our attention to cultural traits that have helped people of color survive in the context of societal oppression and social exclusion.

Resilience, like oppression, is both a psychological and sociological phenomenon for an individual growing up in a racially hostile environment. Ethnically and racially diverse families and communities can help children cope with discrimination by teaching them means of resisting the oppression and by helping them to avoid internalizing the message.

Born in 1925, Annie Victoria Johnson, had the least education of the interviewees; yet, in many ways she was the best storyteller and provided the most details about her upbringing in Ripley, Mississippi. In her words,

> We would wash and iron for white people. They would give us canned fruit, clothes that their kids outgrew, and shoes. When the time came to plant gardens, we all worked together. ...There were no rules in the white woman's kitchen. We would go in and do just like we did at home. And they would help. During the winter they would have quilting parties. And maybe today we would go to one of the white women's houses. They would have food and they would quilt all day. And maybe next week we would go to my mother's house. (p.90)

Mrs. Johnson described the harshness and mistreatment of black people in the Delta which she attributes to the legacy of slavery. In contrast, she describes the hilly northern region where she came from as having a different history. As she tells the story:

> Where I came from, the whites were more Christian. ...The blacks maybe had something to do with them becoming Christians. Because just about everyone, even the sheriffs, the doctors, most of the law enforcement believed in God. There used to be a white man who came to our house, all the time with a Bible. Him and my daddy would sit and read the Bible together. My daddy could read. I don't know how he learned to read, but there is always a way for anything!...And he used to read us Bible stories. (van Wormer et al., 2012, p. 99)

Her strong religious faith is a major strength that shines through. Mrs. Johnson's outlook on life was positive and even forgiving of the poverty and discrimination she had endured under Jim Crow laws and work in domestic service and sharecropping. When asked what was the attitude of the white people toward the black people, she said, surprisingly, "It was good." To prove the point, she gave an example of how, during Prohibition, the sheriff allowed her daddy to keep making his home brew as long as he didn't make more than 5 gallons.

In *The Maid Narratives: Black Domestics and White Families in the Jim Crow South* (van Wormer, Jackson, & Sudduth, 2012), resilience emerged as a major theme. The narratives are drawn from a collection of 40 interviews of African American women of the Great Migration. The women once worked as sharecroppers and domestic servants in the South.

In their stories of growing up under conditions of gross economic exploitation and disempowerment, these women demonstrated a remarkable degree of resilience. Their later success in rearing a family and in participating in church and community life in an integrated Midwestern city further attests to their ability to prevail over their personal hardship. Several of the major themes of resilience commonly found among older African Americans were evidenced in the interviews—respect for family and elders, valuing education, strong religious faith, and a belief in the meaning of life.

Figure 5.1 shows a photo of Charletta Sudduth with her mother. As Mrs. Stevenson (the mother of the book's co-author, Charletta Sudduth) tells us:

> I know I always wanted to go to college. Always. At that time I really wanted to enroll in Ole Miss, which we couldn't because of the color of our skin. Only whites could go there. So I turned my mind to Jackson State. I never wanted to just do that kind of work (domestic service) all my life. I wanted a better job so I could provide for my family like the couple I worked for who were going to college to better themselves. (pp. 133–134)

As she looks back on her experiences today, Mrs. Stevenson, a highly religious person, is reflective:

> I wouldn't trade anything for the experience. I learned how to treat people. It was a learning experience, and by the way, I don't hold any animosity. I often wonder why not. It just made me the person I am today. Like that incident with the floor (she learned to tell the truth after she falsely claimed to mop the floor and was caught). I love everyone. Some of the things we went through—if there ever was a time to have hate in your heart that was it. But we didn't. Because that was the way of life and we adapted to it. (p. 137)

**FIGURE 5.1.** Charletta Sudduth and her mother, Annie Pearl Stevenson, who shared her personal narrative for *The Maid Narratives*. Sudduth was a co-author. Permission by Charletta Sudduth and Annie Pearl Stevenson. Photo by Toril Sudduth.

Resilience is also evidenced in organized resistance to the status quo, what Gandhi famously called "soul force." One of the most compelling examples took place in 1955, in Montgomery, Alabama, when women who worked as maids, cooks, and washerwomen in the white part of town collectively organized to force the bus company to integrate the buses. Forced to walk miles to and from the white homes in which they worked, the protesters brought the bus company to the brink of bankruptcy in a little over a year. As individuals working in white homes, they were powerless, but pooling their resources, they found their power and used it. And when they won, and the buses were integrated, these poor but proud African American women had accomplished something that was to be much bigger than anything they or others could have imagined. For this was the beginning of the Civil Rights movement; this was where the young Martin Luther King got his start as a national leader of civil rights. (For a fictional portrayal that uniquely focuses on the role of the servants and the response of the white families they served, see the 1990 film *The Long Walk Home*.)

African Americans can take great pride in their history and what they have overcome. The new Smithsonian National Museum of African American Culture records this history from the days of slavery to the Black Lives Matter movement. Pride and resilience are themes that also permeate the biography of Dorothy Height, a social worker and major organizer of the Civil Rights movement. See Box 5.1.

**BOX 5.1 The Contributions of Dorothy Height (1910–2012)**

In 2010, Dorothy Height was awarded the NASW Lifetime Achievement Award for her extraordinary contributions to civil rights and social justice for nearly half a century (NASW, 2010). Height was a renowned civil rights leader who had been a vital force in the struggle for human rights and equality. According to her obituary in the *New York Times*, Height was "one of the last living links to the social activism of the New Deal era. Ms. Height had a career in civil rights that spanned nearly 80 years, from anti-lynching protests in the early 1930s to the inauguration of President Obama in 2009" (Fox, p. A25). She worked alongside Martin Luther King, Andrew Young, and the other national leaders, and was seated near King when he gave his "I have a dream" speech. As a woman, however, she was relegated to a background role so her leadership went unrecognized for many years.

Following the passage of the Civil Rights Act, Height continued organizing her people. She helped set up Freedom Schools and voter registration drives in the South. The focus of much of her advocacy was for the rights of women of color.

Dorothy Height attended the New York School of Social Work and began her career as a caseworker in the New York Welfare Department. Later, as the assistant executive director of the Harlem Young Women's Christian Association (YWCA) in the late 1930s, she was in a key position to work with politicians to speak out against oppression, for example, the exploitation of black women who worked as day labor. Through her work with the YWCA, she was in a position to lead efforts toward racial justice resulting in the integration of YWCA facilities nationwide (NASW, 2010).

In 1952, Height served as visiting professor at the Delhi School of Social Work in India. The school was founded by the YWCAs of India, Burma, and Ceylon. She became known in India and other parts of the world for her internationalism and humanitarianism, as she conducted international studies and travel to expand the work of the YWCA (The National Council of Negro Women, 2016).

Throughout her life, Height received many awards from US presidents for her humanitarian work. She also received dozens of honorary degrees from colleges. But the one that held a very special meaning for her was the honorary degree she received from Barnard College. As a young student with an outstanding academic record she had been accepted only to be turned away by the dean. She could not enroll, he said, because they had already met their quota for black students for that year—two (Fox, 2010). This is how she ended up at New York University instead.

In common with the other women whose portraits were included in chapter 2, Height never did retire. In later years, she worked to reinforce traditional family ties and established the Black Family Reunion Celebration. When she died at age 98, President Obama gave the eulogy at her funeral. She was, he said, "a drum major for freedom" (Cooper, p. A16). He ordered the American flags to be flown half-mast in her honor.

REFERENCES

Cooper, H. (2010, April 30). Civil rights leader is eulogized by Obama. *New York Times*, p. A16.

Fox, M. (2010, April 21). Dorothy Height, largely unsung giant of the civil rights era, dies at 98. *New York Times*, p. A25.

National Association of Social Workers (NASW). (2010, March 3). Dr. Dorothy I. Height receives NASW Lifetime Award. NASW Press Release. Retrieved from www.naswdc.org

National Council of Negro Women. (2016). *Dr. Dorothy I. Height*. National Council of Negro Women website. Retrieved from www.ncnw.org

Angela Davis, a controversial activist and well-known fugitive from justice due to her affiliation with the Black Panther Party, is today a former professor and popular campus speaker on human rights. See Figure 5.2 for a recent photo of her giving a speech. In a lecture given at the University of Northern Iowa on social change and human rights, Davis (2013) referred to the Montgomery bus boycott. "Who refused to get on the bus?" she asked. "Black women." This was the beginning of revolutionary change that was to last until the mid-1970s. The long 1960s, according to Davis, was the period that encompassed the publication of *The Feminist Mystique* and the women's liberation that followed, the "ban the bomb" movement, Black Power, the peace movement against the war in Vietnam, the national students' strike, Native American occupation of Alcatraz, and the campaign for her freedom when she was incarcerated for a lengthy time while awaiting trial for her affiliation with a Black Panther group. The collective consciousness that characterized this period of history is no more, according to Davis. Still, as she conceded, despite the birth of the gay liberation, she never dreamed that in her lifetime she would see marriage rights for gays and lesbians come to fruition. Nor could she have imagined the election of a black man as president.

In the pre–civil rights South in which Angela Davis grew up, there were many other forms of resistance by ordinary people to the injustices of the day. *The Maid Narratives*, as described in a previous section, contains the personal stories of women of the Great Migration who used various forms of resistance, including packing their bags and getting on a north-bound train for Iowa. One former maid rose to prominence in the Mississippi Civil Rights movement, survived an attack by the Ku Klux Klan, and was invited to the White House as a consultant to President Kennedy over the situation in Mississippi.

All these instances of horror in the backgrounds of minority groups leave a residue of fear, often that is passed down the generations. The next section explores the psychological ramifications of systemic racial, Native, and economic abuse and exploitation.

## HISTORICAL TRAUMA

We often hear of the trauma of the tens of thousands of West Africans who were uprooted from their families to arrive in New Orleans on the transatlantic slave trade before it was ended in the early 1800s. But we rarely hear of the forced migration of African-Americans to the region

**FIGURE 5.2.** Angela Davis describes for student audiences how she went from being on the FBI's Most Wanted list to being a successful college professor. © Getty Images, Paras Griffin.

on the 'Slave Trail of Tears' which brought 25 times the number of black people to be auctioned off to cotton planters or to be resettled. Altogether during the 50 years before the Civil War as many as one million people were marched in chains and handcuffed in pairs in the long journey from the tobacco regions of the East to the cotton- and sugar-growing lands of the Deep South. Narratives from the historical archives and personal documents are provided in Edward Ball's (2015) groundbreaking article, "Slavery's Trail of Tears". The article tells in almost unbearable detail the story of human bondage and family break-up. Social scientists today are looking at the historical trauma associated with this often overlooked mass deportation of people.

And the horrors inflicted upon black people did not end with slavery. During the years 1882 to 1930, more than 1,200 blacks were lynched in the South, according to official records (Stovel, 2001). The fear experienced by African Americans in segregation-era rural Mississippi was so intense that it would remain alive for years in those who experienced it. This is what Kim Rogers (2006) discovered in her interviews with civil rights workers from the area. Under a system of injustice that these workers dared not confront, their sense of powerlessness had been absolute. Black men in the Jim Crow South could not defend their women folk from unwanted attention by white men. They also knew to stay away from white women at the risk of their lives.

Regular exposure to a hostile and dehumanizing environment is unhealthy and can bring out the worst in people in the absence of strong insulating or protective compensatory factors. Moreover, maltreatment of a population across generations can result in what some researchers call historical trauma. *Historical trauma* is defined by Brave Heart (2007) as the "cumulative emotional and psychological wounding, over the life span and across generations, emanating from massive group trauma experiences" (p. 177). Historical trauma is considered to be a major factor in the high Native American mortality rates from alcohol-related conditions, including suicide and homicide, and in the fatalism evidenced in some of the most impoverished regions of Appalachia (van Wormer & Besthorn, 2017).

The historic oppression of African Americans by whites, for example, has understandably left a residue of distrust and suspicion. The effect works its cancer in ways that crush the spirit of many young people. The phenomenon of *internalized oppression*, or aggression turned inward, is common among all oppressed groups throughout the world. Repeated exposure to maltreatment, whether on the basis of race, class, gender, nationality, or sexual orientation, may lead members of the oppressed group to internalize the negative self-images projected by the external oppressor (Shulman, 2009).

## IN APPALACHIA

In *Belonging: A Culture of Place*, hooks (2009) discusses the effect of racism on its victims. Self-segregation is often the dysfunctional result, she argues. After describing the social context of racial oppression in our society, she states that what she calls "racialized post-traumatic stress disorder" (p. 84) often leads individual black people to experience tension, anxiety, and fear in the presence of white people, even those who are well meaning. Stereotyping all white folks as a potential threat is as dehumanizing as judging all Black people from a racist bias, she writes. Although we recognize that the initial causes of racial segregation and even those of today are largely structural, hooks uniquely suggests that even when the barriers to integration are lowered, the fear of being targeted lingers and keeps black folks confined to certain neighborhoods and social relations. This fear, which is often expressed against poor whites and "rednecks," often holds people back, according to hooks, leading them to feel safer even in a violent inner city than in the mountains of Kentucky. This attitude, which hooks views as a form of psychological trauma that is passed on cross-generationally, can be regarded as the legacy of white supremacy, unrelenting exploitation, and oppression.

The similar but not unique history of Appalachia reveals how external exploitation can leave a land and its people broken and bruised and how the normative adaptations to the crises of unemployment and grinding poverty have become ingrained in the culture today. On the subject of Appalachia, sociologists such as Cattell-Gordon (1990) and popular authors such as bell hooks, speak of the cultural traits of the people of this region as bearing a residue of past wrongs and exploitation. Introducing the concept of culturally transmitted traumatic stress syndrome, Cattell-Gordon refers to the traumatic effects of the loss and absence of work over generations in southern Appalachia. Today, the closing of the coal mines is a big political issue in this region. Social worker Ed Miner (quoted in van Wormer &d Besthorn, 2017) echoes these sentiments from the vantage point of having worked with impoverished Appalachian and African American populations in Columbus, Ohio:

> People who have been oppressed can develop a sense of resignation, deep depression, and other symptoms that lead to dysfunction. I witness the evidence of this every day. I work with many families who, during their mental health history, tell about legal, economic, and psychological

> struggles that go back generations. Most of them have families who were coal miners. They relate stories of death from black-lung disease, companies that did not care for employee health, and acceptance of disasters such as mine accidents. I see the sense of resignation in an interesting phenomenon in one mostly Appalachian neighborhood called "the Bottoms." (pp. 190–191)

J. D. Vance (2016) writes in his best-selling memoir, Hillbilly Elegy:

> It would be years before I learned that no single book, or expert, or field could fully explain the problems of hillbillies in modern America. Our elegy is a sociological one, yes, but it is also about psychology and community and culture and faith. (pp. 144–145)

This is a region today that is plagued with an opioid addiction crisis. The escape into drug use stems from a loss of hope that can be seen in economic numbers, like declining wages, or the number of factories and coal mines closed. West Virginia, for example, has a death rate of drug overdoses that is twice the national average (Associated Press, 2016).

## AMONG NATIVE AMERICANS

Similarly, Johnson and Yellowbird (2012) and Blue and Blue (2001) speak of the legacy of cultural oppression of North American First Nations People brought about by the European invasion. The existence of these traumas must be taken into account when evaluating First Nations people in the Canadian penitentiary system, as Blue and Blue suggest. And from Australia, we learn from research summarized at Australians Together (2015) of the impact of centuries of maltreatment of the Aboriginal people. Cultural genocide was expressed in the form of child removal, leading this minority group to fear state social services to the present time. The high rates of poor physical health, mental health problems, addiction, incarceration, domestic violence, self-harm, and suicide in Indigenous communities are linked to experiences of trauma. These issues are both results of historical trauma and causes of new instances of trauma which together can lead to a vicious cycle in Indigenous communities. In fact, alcoholism, combined with poverty, has been a serious problem for indigenous groups across the globe (van Wormer & Davis, 2018).

The impact of social and structural oppression is nowhere better expressed than in the treatment of sexual minority groups. Laura Kaplan (2007) addresses insidious traumas faced by lesbian, gay, and transgender people on a daily basis. They face multiple types of oppression in the mental health system. The effects of coming to terms with one's own identity, relationships with families, discrimination that is legal, religious struggles, and so on are stressors with a direct impact on mental health. This fact often results in diagnosis and treatment for mental health problems that are actually structural in nature.

In her presentation at the 15th Annual Cedar Valley Conference on Human Rights, Erica Littlewolf (2013) describes her Montana Native tribe's experience with past and present trauma and how cultural changes emerged through colonization of the Indians by Europeans and European Americans. She works for the Mennonite Central Committee with the Indigenous Visions Center, where she is committed to the work of decolonization and healing. In her words:

> In our Northern Cheyenne tribe, women were sacred. But in 1884, patriarchy was imposed upon us by the federal government and everyone was forced to take men's last names in the family. The children were given English first names. . . .

> I am a survivor of a parent who was raised in a boarding school. Sending all Indian children ages 5–18 away to school was the government's policy to destroy the culture. The children were only allowed to go home in the summer and were seriously punished for speaking their own language at school. There was sexual abuse and other forms of abuse inflicted upon the children in these schools. This later led to substance abuse problems in the survivors. The effects of the historical trauma are with us still. Joy De Gruy (2016) describes this process in her book, *Post Traumatic Slave Syndrome.*
>
> There are movements today to promote healing. In Canada, I attended the Canadian Truth and Reconciliation Commission to promote healing from the legacy of abuse and exploitation. To work through my issues of trauma and to help others, I have attended trauma training. This included sweat lodges and ceremonies to help survivors get at the root causes of their pain and call the spirit that was wounded, invite the lost spirit back.

Because of the significant impact of personal trauma in the backgrounds of youth who come into the juvenile justice system, and because of our awareness, at the adult level, of the psychological problems associated with military service in war zones, the government has placed much emphasis on the provision of trauma-informed treatment approaches. Basically, this is a recognition by correctional and treatment organizations of the risks of re-traumatizing at-risk populations through harsh and confining treatment (as for example, the use of bodily restraints, placement in a noisy or unsafe environment, and the use of seclusion cells for confinement (see Bloom &Farragher, 2013). To date, there has been little emphasis, however, in the treatment literature on the impact of historical trauma on individuals receiving mental health and related services and on meeting the needs of these clients. Trainings in cultural sensitivity for treatment providers would do well to prepare practitioners to work with people who may have significant trust issues with authority figures due to a legacy of cultural exploitation by dominant groups. The hiring of staff members persons from similar racial and ethnic backgrounds as the population served can be extremely helpful in establishing such trust although self-destructive behavioral patterns may still be evident when institutional rules do not allow for flexibility. The Council on Social Work Education (CSWE, 2013) has issued guidelines for graduate programs of social work that have a trauma-informed concentration. Social work educators are urged to take into account disproportionate exposure to trauma on the basis of culture, race, and national origin, and to "incorporate an understanding of the influence of historical trauma on various cultures into assessment activities" (p. 15).

## SEXISM AND THE FEMINIZATION OF POVERTY

The Universal Declaration of Human Rights does not mention women specifically except in the preamble, and as was true in all publications of the time, it is male-oriented and uses the traditional masculine pronouns "he" and "him" to refer to both genders. The movement to promote women's rights did not start until later. In 1980, the United Nations passed the Convention on the Elimination of All Forms of Discrimination against Women. The majority of the world's nations have approved this document. President Jimmy Carter signed the document for the United States in the first year, but it has yet to be ratified by the Senate. Objections pertain to reproductive rights for women. The NASW (2015b) urges in its policy statement on women's issues that the United States ratify the document and that international programs address women's rights as human rights.

## FEMINIZATION OF POVERTY: UNITED STATES

The human rights aspect of sexual oppression is one of the subjects of chapter 6 to follow. Here we will emphasize the economic and occupational realities of female oppression. The fact that of families in the United States headed by single women, 37.1% are below the poverty line has led some scholars to coin the term *feminization of poverty*. The combined effects of the dual labor market, occupational segregation, and sex and race discrimination have resulted in a median income for single women with children of $36,151 and for single men with children of $53,684 (US Census Bureau, 2015). When the ratio of women's full-time income reached 79.3% in 2003, it was an all-time high (US Bureau of Labor Statistics, 2003). It is the same ratio today. The increase is a reflection, however, not of a rise in women's income as much as a decline in men's income during this period. Nevertheless, men still earn substantially higher wages than women, even when they are working in traditionally "female" occupations such as nursing and social work.

The causes of female poverty are complex. The high divorce rate coupled with the infrequency of mothers receiving child support from the fathers forces many women to find jobs immediately or go on welfare. Low-paying service jobs—such as waiting tables in fast-food restaurants and motel housekeeping work—drive many women to welfare dependency as a means to escape from such daily drudgery, lack of essential work benefits, and childcare concerns. Programs designed to compensate for the absence of a male breadwinner in the family are means-tested and highly punitive. When men are absent, women's prescribed role as family caretaker is ignored and devalued by the system—a fact which reinforces women's marginality in society and ensures women and their children's high representation among the destitute. Until the importance of nurturing and shaping young lives through domestic caretaking is regarded as primary work, the feminization of poverty will continue.

Many older women struggle to make ends meet. Qualifying far less frequently than men for adequate pension plans and lower social security payments, more than twice as many women (nearly 2.9 million) as men (over 1.3 million) live in poverty. Poverty rates are particularly high, at about one in five, for black (20%), Hispanic (23%), and Native American (21%) women 65 and older. Poverty rates are lower at 9% for white, non-Hispanic women 65 and older, and 13% for Asian American women 65 and older (National Women's Law Center, 2015).

## GLOBAL WAR AGAINST WOMEN

How are women doing worldwide? According to a report from the United Nations (2015) on the state of the world's women:

- Worldwide, 35% of women have experienced physical and/or sexual violence by an intimate partner or sexual violence by a non-partner at some point in their lives.
- In the majority of countries, fewer than 40% of the women who experience violence seek help of any sort.

- Acceptance of wife-beating is generally higher in Africa, Asia, and Oceania and lower in Latin America and the Caribbean and nations of the Global North. However, attitudes are starting to change.
- At least 125 million girls and women alive today have been subjected to female genital mutilation. This has happened more frequently to older than to younger women.
- Child marriage is still common; almost half of the girls in southern Asia and sub-Sahara Africa are married when under age 18.
- An estimated 781 million people aged 15 and over remain illiterate. Nearly two- thirds of them are women, a proportion that has remained unchanged for two decades.
- In the Global South, statutory and customary laws continue to restrict women's access to land and other assets and inheritance.
- Women remain at the lower end of a segregated labor market and continue to be concentrated in a few occupations, to hold positions of little or no authority and receive less pay than men. (www.unstats.un.org)

India is witnessing growing violence against women including horrific rapes even in major metropolitan areas that have attracted considerable media attention. Verma, Qureshi, and Kim (2016) write that the insecurity and physical threat to women is real and a major concern in that country. Although times are changing, and there is a highly educated female workforce in India, the country ranks 143rd of 145 countries for its female-to-male sex ratio (World Economic Forum, 2015). What this means is that Indians continue to prioritize male children, often aborting female ones repeatedly.

Concerning the world's abuse of women, perhaps there is no more blatant a violation of human rights as the genital mutilation or cutting of girls. The process involves the primitive practice of partial or totally removing girls' external genitalia (UN News Centre, 2016). The more education a woman gets, the less likely she is to subject her daughter to this trauma. Recently, two African countries—Gambia and Nigeria—have criminalized the practice.

The UN Human Development Report (UNDP, 2015) focuses on gender equality and women's empowerment as a human rights issue. In the UN report a gender empowerment measure based on reproductive health, empowerment, and the labor market is used to compare countries. The Scandinavian countries, not surprisingly, earn the top rankings for female empowerment. The United States is number 8. Generally, countries in the Global South such as Niger and the Central African Republic are at the bottom, while the more economically prosperous nations are at the top.

Foreign-born women make up 15% of employed women over age 16 in the United States (American Immigrant Council, 2014). One-third of immigrant women work in service occupations and others in sales, office, and professional fields. Women immigrants earn far less than foreign-born men, and less than native-born men or women. Mexico is the single largest country of origin for female immigrants, and Mexican women are the least educated of the top foreign groups, including India, China, the Philippines and other Latin American countries.

The mistreatment of women globally (for example, in Afghanistan) tends to be expressed in the guise of an attack on modernization which includes exposure of their daughters and wives to new ideas (Hyde, 2013; van Wormer, Kaplan, & Juby, 2012). Organized physical attacks against women are common in parts of the Middle East. We can consider this a part of the anti-feminist backlash that is seen in the United States as well with the striking growth in the women's incarceration rate as well as in the fathers' rights to child custody movement. In the United States, attacks on women's rights have taken the form of attacks on reproductive health, including attacks on services offered by Planned Parenthood (Steinhauer, 2017).

## HETEROSEXISM

Related to sexism and to the rigid codes of gender conformity is the societal oppression of gays, lesbians, and bisexuals. This form of discrimination, although not inevitable is worldwide. Cultural attitudes play a significant role in all matters related to sex and sexuality. Discrimination against persons perceived as sexually deviant can be horrendous.

As defined by Barker (2014), *heterosexism* is: "the institutionalized assumption that heterosexuality is the norm and, therefore, preferable or superior to homosexuality or bisexuality" (193). The term *homophobia*, in contrast, implies a stronger feeling involving feelings of "irrational fear or hatred" (p. 197). From a Freudian perspective, homophobia derives from unconscious anxiety in the identified heterosexual that he or she might have homosexual tendencies. In fact, there is some experimental validation of this assumption.

Gays and lesbians are one group that can be attacked generically even as they are standing there because their presence is so often not realized. This is a part of heterosexism, the tendency to assume that the people you know and work with are heterosexual. Sex education in school, for example, generally pertains only to heterosexual practices in their safe-sex campaigns. Yet at the same time, as a recent Gallup (2015) poll confirmed, members of the general public estimate that a large percentage of the population—around one in four—are gay or lesbian. The actual figure found in the Gallup poll of gay, lesbian, bisexual, and transgender (LGBT) people was only 3.8%. In a national school survey of over 15,000 students, which is a first government survey of its kind to ask about sexual identity along with important health issues, the Centers for Disease Control and Prevention (CDC) found that 2% of the girls identified themselves as lesbian as did 2% of the boys. More identified themselves as bisexual—9.8% of the girls and 2.4% of the boys.

### HOMOPHOBIA

Homophobia goes beyond heterosexism; it entails a phobic or fear response to homosexuality accompanied by heightened attention to the doings of gays and lesbians and sometimes scapegoating of persons who are seemingly of a different sexual orientation. Of all the forms of oppression, the oppression of gender non-conformity is perhaps the most virulent. Unlike most victims of acts of prejudice and discrimination, sexual minorities are taunted on the basis of behavioral characteristics and inclinations that are thought to be freely chosen. There is an element of teaching persons so disposed to non-conformity a lesson, often a very public lesson. School children in middle school, given their own sexual identity issues and hormone changes in their bodies, are probably the worst perpetrators of heterosexual teasing and bullying. The CDC (2016) survey of GLBT youth found that around a fourth of males and over a third of females reported that they had been victimized by taunts and other forms of abuse. Many were afraid for their safety at school; more than one in 10 said they'd missed school because of safety concerns. A related finding was that nearly one in five of the sexual minority youth said they'd been raped at some point in their lives, compared to one in 20 heterosexual students.

Unlike members of other minority groups, moreover, the very groups they might use for support—their families, their church—may be the first to turn against them. Parents of gender non-conforming children perhaps put the pressure on their kids to the greatest extent of all. Pressure comes in the forms of attacks on one's dress and hair styles, the way one carries oneself, and the types of peer group the teenager chooses to hang around with. The psychological toll of being attacked on all fronts can be enormous.

Sometimes society's hatred is turned within. More than 40% of sexual minority students reported that they had seriously considered suicide, and 29% had made attempts to do so in the year before they took the survey (CDC, 2016). The rate was higher for lesbian and female bisexuals than for gay or bisexual males. Sometimes youth like people of all ages seek escape though use of addictive substances. The CDC survey found that the percentage of school youth who used illegal drugs was many times greater than their heterosexual peers. While 1.3% of straight students said they had used heroin, for example, 6% of the gay, lesbian and bisexual students reported having done so. The use of methamphetamines among gay male youth is significantly higher than that for any other group.

More worrisome is the figure for trans or gender non-conforming people surveyed—41% of whom have attempted suicide (Malone, 2015). (Transgender youth were not specifically surveyed in the CDC report.) The suicide attempt and suicide rate is the highest among male gay youth who lack a support system. School programs such as a Gay-Straight Alliance (GSA) and community programs which work with their parents such as Parents Families and Friends of Lesbians and Gays (PFLAG) can do much to save the lives of these children. Social workers should refer families dealing with these issues to these groups.

Legislation does matter as laws and government policies reflect public attitudes and breed a sense of acceptance or rejection to the parties involved. Moreover, public attitudes are apt to change when the restrictive laws change (for example, Jim Crow laws in the South and discriminatory anti-Catholic policies in Northern Ireland). So we can expect that LGBT youth will experience a higher acceptance rate now that discrimination against LGBT people has been outlawed in many contexts. When the US Supreme Court issued its ruling that same-sex couples had constitutional right to marry, this was a breakthrough in social legislation. And when President Obama repealed the "don't ask, don't tell" policy for the military, service men and women could now serve freely in all branches of the military. According to a survey from the Pew Research Center (Fingerhut, 2016), 55% of Americans now favor same-sex marriage, a huge increase over the previous decade. Younger, more highly educated, and less religious people are the most apt to support same sex marriage.

## HATE CRIMES

Hate crimes at the societal level against gays and lesbians, especially by young males are commonplace. These crimes came into the spotlight in 2009 when Congress passed the Matthew Shepard Act, which added gender identity to the list of possible motivations for hate crimes (Federal Bureau of Investigation [FBI], 2016). (Matthew Shephard was a gay student at the University of Wyoming who was cruelly tortured and murdered in 1999.) Despite the large numbers of hate crimes inflicted upon gays and lesbians (over 1,250 cases of victimization were reported to the FBI in 2015), few are reported to the police or they might be reported as simply ordinary crime.

Hate crimes can result from early childhood indoctrination. See Figure 5.3 for a hate-filled demonstration.

**FIGURE 5.3.** After a gay man was tortured and killed in Waterloo, Iowa, followers of Fred Phelps from Topeka, Kansas arrived to protest the memorial service that was held. Photo by Robert van Wormer.

In Orlando, Florida, in 2016 terrorism and homophobia were linked as Omar Mateen shot and killed 49 attenders at a gay nightclub. This is said to be the deadliest mass shooting in American history. Most of the victims were Latino and gay (Alvarez, Pérez-Peña, & Hauser, 2016). Mateen's father said that his son hated gays but he himself believed it was up to God to punish homosexuals. Mateen, who talked shortly before the shootings, said he was acting out in allegiance to the militant group Islamic State, as a message to halt US bombing in Iraq and Syria. Several survivors claimed they had seen him at the nightclub on earlier occasions or to have been contacted by him on gay websites, a claim that the FBI couldn't confirm (Hennessy-Fiske, 2016).

In 2017, there were 25 recorded homicides of transgender people, an increase over previous years. Federal statistics are now kept on such crimes since 2009 when Congress passed the Matthew Shepard Act, which added gender identity to the list of possible motivations for hate. Many of the trans people who were murdered in 2017 were victims of hate crimes; the majority were perpetrated against trans women of color (Human Rights Campaign, 2017).

In addition to crimes of violence, trans women of color (black or Hispanic) are around eight times as likely as the general population to live in conditions of extreme poverty. Employment is a serious problem for members of this group. Homelessness was a common experience as well. Some trans people turn to sex work and/or drug dealing for a means of support.

### LEGAL DEVELOPMENTS

A big issue for transgender children in the school system (as for trans adults) is bathroom access. Transgender women, groomed as women, would find the men's room off-limits and a blow to their identity and use of the female restroom possibly uncomfortable, as well, if the women thought a man was in their restroom. In 2016, it became a big public issue as some states passed laws forbidding transgender people from using restrooms that matched their transitional state. Then the Obama administration issued another important ruling on LGBT rights concerning the right of trans students to use the bathroom consistent with their gender identity (Davis, 2016). Just weeks after President Donald Trump took office, however, the White House rescinded guidance from his predecessor that instructed schools to let transgender students choose their bathrooms (Glum, 2017).

The rejection of gays and lesbians by such major social institutions deprives a sizeable segment of the population of the help and support they need. Alienation from the traditional church's teachings, lack of awareness of counseling services, and abuse inflicted by peers and family members all combine to close the avenues to much needed social support. Discrimination in employment is still allowed in many states and will continue to be so until sexual minorities are included in the Civil Rights Act. The results of such deprivation of legal protection is a loss not only to gays and lesbians but also to the society generally, which is deprived of gay and lesbian talents and contributions.

To enhance critical thinking in the classroom, teachers and faculty sometimes have their students engage in a self-awareness exercise. The Heterosexual Questionnaire devised by Rochlin (2000) that begins, "What do you think caused your heterosexuality?" is widely used.

Earlier, we discussed one's estrangement from the church as a possible outcome of one's coming out to oneself as gay or lesbian. It is paradoxical that religion, a source of strength to so many, can also be a force of destruction when an individual's very being is condemned. We turn now to a discussion of oppression that is built on traditional, doctrinal beliefs in the form of religion.

## SECTARIANISM

The Oxford English Dictionary (2007), defines *sectarianism* as "bigoted or narrow-minded in following the doctrines of one's sect; a bigot." Our definition of *sectarianism* is that it is a form of political and/or personal oppression in the name of religion. When one of the authors (van Wormer) lived in Northern Ireland, for example, she was told the differences between Protestant and Catholic were not about religion but about politics. She was also told it was a question of class or economic rivalry. Only one woman, a teacher, wanted to talk about the religious aspect. She said the religious differences in Northern Ireland made more sense than the racial differences in America because it pertained to "things of the mind." As in most situations, it was not a case of either/or but of both/and: Politics and religion were combined.

Similarly, with Islamism, politics including beliefs about gender roles, are both fused and confused with the religious message. Here, and we underscore this point, we are referring not to Islam proper but to the fundamentalist branch of Islam, the revival of which has marked a tremendous setback for Muslim women throughout the world. Muhammad, the prophet and founder of Islam preached kindness toward women and showed great tenderness and respect for his wife. So when women are forced to cover their entire bodies in the burqa to protect them from arousing lust in men, is this the driving force religion or is it sexism? And in its expression as terrorism, is Islamism an attack on the infidel, a "holy war"—*Jihad*—against Jews and capitalism or is it an expression of political brotherhood?

Suffice it to say, religious fundamentalism is behind much of the extremist politics today. And religious hatred is as virulent as any other kind; fanaticism of any sort is dangerous. From mass bloodshed in the Bible and the slaughter of the Crusades to today's terrorist attacks in Europe and suicide bombings and Zionist retaliatory strikes in the Middle East, violence in the name of religion has a long history.

Religious oppression at its most extreme took place in Afghanistan, which fell under the control of Taliban zealots. Theologian Karen Armstrong (2001) puts this kind of religious fanaticism in context:

> During the 20th century, the militant form of piety often known as fundamentalism erupted in every major religion as a rebellion against modernity. . . . Fighting, as they imagine, a battle for survival, fundamentalists often feel justified in ignoring the more compassionate principles of their faith (p. 48).

The World Trade Center, of course, was the prime symbol of capitalism and the global economy. Although the American response to the mass destruction on New York City was far more nationalistic than sectarian in character, the anti-Muslim backlash by the American people took on a character that could be construed as sectarian.

A social psychological phenomenon that surfaces in times of national crisis that is related to mass insecurity and even hysteria is the phenomenon of *displaced aggression* as described in Allport's (1954) classic, *The Nature of Prejudice*. This natural tendency to redirect one's personal discomfort on to a vulnerable source can readily be exploited by a nation's rulers. Through skillful use of propaganda, a people's righteous anger can be redirected away from criticism of the government onto a vulnerable target such as criminals or immigrants or terrorists. Clearly the master of such redirection of anger of all time was Hitler. How could Hitler happen? Students of human behavior have been trying to answer that for over half a century and probably never will. Certainly part of the answer lies in the severe economic crisis that Germany faced following the horrendous defeat of World War I. And part of it is likely familial—related to the rigid norms of obedience to authority, militarism, and denial of feelings characteristic of the German family during that period in history. Sectarianism came into play here as well in that Jews were religiously and ethnically different and economically successful in times of hardship; they easily could be targeted as scapegoats, accordingly. In the concentration camps of their confinement, Jews joined others designated as different—known homosexuals, Roma people, conscientious objectors, Jehovah Witnesses, persons with mental disabilities, and common criminals. The suffering of such individuals is now immortalized in their personal histories, pieces of clothing, photographs, and recordings as displayed at the US Holocaust Memorial Museum in Washington, D.C. Box 5.2 provides a descriptive tour of this museum. The tour guide is social worker Tammy Wanger, who, with her 17-year-old son, embarked on a journey into the darkest corridors of modern human history.

### BOX 5.2 A Visit to the US Holocaust Memorial Museum

by Tammy Wanger, MSW, of Rochester, Minnesota

Not only will a visit to the US Holocaust Memorial Museum clear up any misinformation you may have about the Holocaust but it will also engage you in a way that is everlasting. The time spent there will never leave you and will commit you to being a witness, bound to the responsibility that comes with it, to share what you have seen and learned with others. The experience will not only teach you about the means of the extermination but also about the victims behind the raw numbers. Because you will leave the museum as a witness, it is important to experience it all. To visit the Holocaust Museum is to be a witness to "man's inhumanity to man" but also to the strength of the human spirit, to resilience.

Although this visit was several years in the planning, now that I was there, I stood staring at the front door and asking myself, "Why did I ever want to do this?" I was there to do research, I told myself, and because I care deeply about this horrible violation of humanity. The research role provided a way for me to distance myself, a top layer of protection for my emotional defenses. Attached to that was the duty to teach my 17-year-old son.

Placed among the other stately buildings in Washington, D.C., the museum building is stylish and modern, the sidewalks teeming with tourists. Yet because this was no ordinary museum, the sight of people, teens among them, casually exiting the building seemed suddenly incongruous. Was the teen's laughter a mask for their pain, the ultimate denial?

Almost immediately, on entering the museum, my son became engaged. This was mostly due to the personal qualities of the woman conducting the orientation. The museum's objective, as the guide explained, was not to teach us about 900 years of Jewish or European history; it was to concentrate on the cataclysmic events from 1933 to 1945, events that were executed in a "systematic" process. This knowledge is critical to an understanding of how the forces for genocide can build.

The museum uses a process to systematically engage visitors. By physically walking among the photos and artifacts, listening to the audio accounts and viewing the videos, one becomes personally engaged in mind and body. Exposed steel beams and brick walls provide an eerie quality to the experience. The exhibits begin on the fourth floor and wind down to the first, step by step, following the sequence of events, of the systematic extermination.

A basket held identification cards. We each chose one, a booklet that tells the story of a real person who lived during the Holocaust. It looks like a passport, and on the front one reads, "For the dead and the living we must bear witness," written over the United States crest. The identification card I would carry was #5395, Alida Nathans Wijnberg. On the first page was a small square photo of her, some vital statistics of her birth in Vries, Netherlands, on April 10, 1887. She was the oldest of eight children and born to religious Jewish parents. Her family owned a textile business, and it was her job to carry goods to the farmers in a suitcase that was attached to the handlebars of her bicycle. She married Samuel Wijnberg, and they had three sons and a daughter.

I walked on to read and learn how the system gained its energy. It began on February 27, 1933, when the Reichstag (German Parliament) was burned. Hitler blamed the Communists and President von Hindenburg invoked Article 48, at Hitler's insistence. Emergency orders thus went into effect; all individual and civil liberties, including freedom of speech, press, and assembly were suspended. Other decrees issued at the same time instituted the death sentence. It was these emergency decrees that became the legal excuse for the concentration camps, camps that held not only Jews but homosexuals, Roma people, mentally ill and physically handicapped persons.

The exhibit of the "burning of the books" in Berlin on May 10, 1933 welded me to that spot. There is a picture of a mountain of books, engulfed in tall flames while a crowd of jeering onlookers cheered wildly. Next to the picture of the burning books is a quote from Jewish poet, Heinrich Heine, written a hundred years earlier that reads, "Where one burns books, one will, in the end, burn people." A sad prophecy was unfolding.

I looked at Alida's identification card and turned to her next page. It read that Alida's husband had died and she and her children continued to run their hotel until the Germans confiscated the property. The Wijnbergs were relocated to a shack with no running water, her son went into hiding, as did her daughter.

The Evian Conference of July 1938, as we learned, left no hope and no haven. By 1938 as many as 150,000 Jews had successfully fled Germany but then the annexation of Austria in 1938 brought an additional 183,000 back into the Nazi orbit. There would be no escape for most Jews. The refugee segment displayed the ship's photo and told of the voyage of the *St. Louis*. This sickened and shamed me, as I have seen the same shoreline area of Miami as did the passengers of the *St. Louis*. They of course sailed the return voyage to their deaths after being turned away from Havana, Cuba and other ports in North America.

Following the system, our journey took us next to the T-4 program. That was a program involving virtually all of the German psychiatric community. The fact that the doctors involved did not immediately become killers is yet more evidence of the deliberateness used in designing and implementing a system that led to genocide. They soon adopted the philosophy of "life unworthy of life" which led them to murder the handicapped and mentally ill patients in their care. Gas chambers were first developed at the handicapped killing centers where incurably sick children were seen as a burden on the Volk (the German people).

The mobile killing squads single handedly killed about one fourth of all Jews in the Holocaust. We saw pictures of mass graves, one containing over 7,000 people. Past the life-sized photos and captions, we arrived at a real freight car. This was an authentic, 15-ton Deutsches Reichbahn freight car. It is positioned in the path of the exhibition route, as a bridge to the next segment exhibits. My son and I stood together in there for a long while. We talked softly of Elie Wiesel's (1982) ordeal that he described in his book, *Night*. The reality gave me chills. Again everything, the people and their suffering, had to be multiplied as each train car would carry as many as 80 to 100 people and each train could carry one to two thousand people.

I was now on the last page of Alida Wijnberg's life. The Gestapo caught Alida during her attempt to go into hiding and on October 12, 1942, she arrived in

Auschwitz, where she soon perished. I felt myself looking for her in the next display. This exhibit was "Crematorium II," one of four. The figures are of people and the process used to kill them, based on documents and the trial testimonies of SS guards.

A significant portion of the museum is designated for exhibiting information pertaining to rescues. And over this section are the words, "Whoever [shall] save a single life, saves an eternal world," from *The Talmud*. Short stories, many photos and clips were bound together in an arrangement. There were articles describing the saving of the Jews of Denmark, and telegrams from the War Refugee Board that appeared to offer too little too late. Other displays were of people who were caught and killed for trying to help.

The last phase of the Holocaust Museum experience is for reflection, grief, and even mourning. After the intense journey through the exhibits, it provides a place to respect and acknowledge the cloud of witnesses above us. In this last room burns an eternal flame and a stone ledge on which to sit down and rest. Since the time of my witness I have experienced a multitude of feelings and I know that I am not alone. I don't believe that we will ever be able to understand *why* the Holocaust happened. But I do believe that one visit to the Holocaust Memorial Museum will provide those who care with a structure for learning and understanding *how* it happened.

Our visit to the past ended, ironically, via modern technology, when back at the hotel my son and I sent an e-mail, to a dear friend. My son wanted to ask our friend who is Jewish if he had lost anyone in the Holocaust and to tell him that he looked for their family name on the wall of remembrance during our visit. He wanted to ask our friend if he spoke Hebrew, but mostly, he said, he just wanted to tell our friend, he was sorry.

---

Printed with permission from Tammy Wanger.

Note: For details of the Holocaust Memorial Museum, including haunting photographic displays, see www.ushmm.org.

## ETHNOCENTRISM

*Ethnocentrism*, briefly defined, is the taken-for-granted assumption that your way is the only way or at least the best way. Because inevitably we view the world through the lens of our own culture, we are all ethnocentric to some extent. So we cannot say we will be free of cultural bias any more than we can say we will part with the tastes we have acquired or the language.

Ethnocentrism relates to differences in values and perceptions in values. Consider this statement, for example: "The Vietnamese don't value human life"—during the war in Vietnam, this is what the American people were told about the slaughter of Viet Cong and civilians. Ethnocentrism plays into a natural distaste for the unfamiliar and foreign. It also plays into the fact that when one's class or country mistreats another class or country, the natural tendency to hate the victims as a way to justify their mistreatment.

In a nation at war, the social climate relevant to foreigners is apt to change, to harden. The public in wartime, wracked by insecurity, is susceptible to scapegoating outsiders, especially those of the ethnic group of the designated enemy. Some may be citizens who just look like the enemy. Since the start of America's war on terror, for example, many countries have become wary of foreigners, including refugees.

Much of human migration from poor to rich countries is linked to economics—need of industry for cheap labor and need of migrants for self-sustaining work. Since Mexico borders directly on the United States, there is a constant flow of traffic northward. Families in Mexico depend on their relatives to send checks to help in their support. In recent years, a surge in people fleeing Central America includes potential refugees, not just economic migrants (Lakhani, 2016). These are asylum seekers entitled to a hearing. All such migrants are desperate for one reason or another to come north of the border. As a result, smuggling operations have become a multibillion-dollar industry. Incidents of deaths of would-be migrant workers abandoned in locked semi-trailers and rail cars reveal the desperation of Mexicans to find work (Randall, 2015).

Before September 11, plans were under way to negotiate immigration agreements including an amnesty offer to Mexican residents to give them legal status as workers. After that fatal date, however, when "immigrant" became almost synonymous with terrorist in the minds of fearful Americans, all immigration talks ceased (Randall, 2015). Today would-be migrants are turned away at the border, and plans are under way to build a 30-foot wall to keep them out. Refugees who do manage to meet with an asylum officer may now face a tougher screening than they would have in the recent past (Gordon, 2017).

An ABC News report exposes the role of the private prison lobbies in influencing government policy to turn over the operation of detention centers to private companies such as the Corrections Corporation of America and to guarantee substantial numbers of federal inmates in its facilities, through increased funding. The system has become one in which more deportations and longer detentions mean increased profits, giving companies a financial incentive to lobby for stricter immigration laws (Hesson, 2012).

Ethnic-sensitive practice raises social workers' awareness of racism in a wider society, and of how social conditions related to powerlessness are integral to the experiences of persons of color. To be effective, social workers must be aware of their own prejudices and fears before they can help their clients achieve self-awareness. By identifying and building upon existing strengths, the worker empowers the client to get involved in mutual aid groups for social support as a first step in the change process.

## LATINOS: DEMOGRAPHIC FACTS

According to the US Census (US Census Bureau, 2015), Hispanic Americans reached approximately 17.4% of the population which makes them the largest minority group in the United States and African Americans, now the second largest minority. (Note: The word *Hispanic* is that used by the government in the collection of data such as census data and therefore used in this book in a statistical context only. This term is not wholly representative, however, as it technically refers to persons of Spanish descent; yet many Latin Americans are of Portuguese or other ancestry.) According to US Census data, about three-quarters of Hispanics reported as Mexican (63%), Puerto Rican (9%), or Cuban origin (4%); 3% of Hispanics are people from El Salvador. Since 2000, the numbers of Hispanics have grown in every region of the United States.

On the whole, Latinos/Latinas are the least educated of all ethnocultural groups in the United States, with high dropout rates. And yet educational attainment among US Latinos has been changing rapidly in recent years, reflecting the group's growth in the nation's public schools and colleges. Over the past decade, the Hispanic high school dropout rate has declined and college enrollment has increased (Pew Research Center, 2015a). Economic factors keep the rate of college enrollment low; 66% of Hispanics who got a job or entered the military directly after high school cited the need to help support their family as a reason for *not* enrolling in college.

Latinos participate in the labor force in large numbers, mostly in laboring and service occupations except for Cuban Americans. Large numbers of Mexican Americans and US residents from Mexico have joined the military, this, despite the fact that the Mexican government actively opposed the war against Iraq. Some enlisted because there is less discrimination against them in the military than elsewhere, others to get a boost in their applications for citizenship. Those with lower family income are more likely to join the military than those with higher family income, and a large percentage of Latinos who have served in the armed forces are children of immigrants (Sanchez, 2013).

## LATINOS: CULTURAL FACTORS

Traditional views of family and roles can be protective factors against the experience of poverty; at the same time, they make it more difficult to seek help. Protective factors identified in a study of 60 young, low-income, predominantly Mexican American women include a cohesive family of origin, adequate rule-setting by parents, and a strong social support system.

Latino/Latina traditions sharply differentiate the roles of males and females (Gonzalez & Acevedo, 2013). Women are expected to be the moral authority of the family and provide family connection and care for children, while men are expected to be the provider for the family as well as the disciplinarian and decision maker in financial matters. Women in traditional families are highly discouraged from using alcohol or drugs because of their critical role in child-rearing. Although there is great individual variance, many males relate strongly to the value of "machismo," that is, being brave, strong, a good provider, and dominant. Identification with these qualities may make it difficult to handle loss of employment (van Wormer & Davis, 2018).

Poverty is still a major risk factor. Hispanic families have a high poverty rate, ranging from 26.3% for Dominicans to 25% for Puerto Ricans and Mexican Americans to 16.2% for Cuban Americans (US Census Bureau, 2015). As in any culture of poverty, this condition provides few opportunities to buffer the hardships of life, few resources to avoid harmful social and health-related consequences of drinking and using drugs, and greater vulnerability to social sanctions such as jail, prison, and discrimination.

Kinship (*familismo*) is highly valued, as mentioned in chapter 2, and extended family members commonly participate in child-rearing and other activities that support the family. Although few have health insurance, and Mexican Americans have a high teen birthrate, the infant mortality rate is relatively low, comparable to that among Anglo-Americans. This is probably due to the close family ties and nurturance provided to the pregnant women. Still, the stress of immigration, poverty, discrimination, isolation from extended family, and acculturation can cause dramatic effects and strain on the traditional Latino/Latina support system. These hardships may contribute to an attitude of fatalism, or the belief that life's problems are inevitable and must be accepted (Moreno, 2013).

A major problem for Latinos in accessing social services is the language barrier. Even among the documented workers in the United States (those included in census data), many who were not raised in the United States do not speak English well. About six in 10 US adult Hispanics (62%) speak English or are bilingual (Pew Research Center, 2015b). Hispanics in the United States break down into three groups when it comes to their use of language: 36% are bilingual, 25% mainly use English, and 38% mainly use Spanish. Among those who speak English, 59% are bilingual.

A commonly reported situation is that of Spanish-speaking clients talking to mental health professionals while their highly personal stories were being interpreted by their children or by maintenance personnel. To meet the need and prevent this circumstance, intensive recruitment of bilingual students to major in social work is under way. All across the United States, agencies and policymakers are taking steps to increase their capacity to serve Spanish-speaking clients.

A unique tool, developed by social work educators Elaine Congress and Winnie Kung (2013), is the culturagram. The culturagram is a family assessment device that social workers can use when working with people from other cultures, the purpose of which is to prevent stereotyping of the ethnic groups; for example, of confusing issues relevant to undocumented Mexican immigrants with Puerto Ricans who have lived in the country for a long time. The culturagram finds out first-hand from the clients' information about their unique values, including beliefs about health care, experiences of oppression, and family values. Using such a tool, social workers can appreciate the role that a person's ethnic identity plays in his or her life.

Sarah Reeves (2012), a social work student, shares her identity resolution as she grew up with one foot in one culture and one in another:

> My grandparents were never too thrilled that my dad had married a Mexican woman, not to mention one who didn't speak English. . . . Micro-aggressions were very common throughout my mom's relationship with my grandparents. In college I decided that I wanted to become a bilingual educator. By this time my dad had passed away, and I chose this path as a legacy to him and my *familia mexicana* in celebration of our Mexican culture. I only hoped that I could use my passion and experience as a bicultural person to make a difference in the lives of others. Today being Latina defines me to my core. Although judgment of others is an everyday occurrence, *mis raices* (my roots) in the Mexican culture are what remind me, "This is who I am." (p. 67)

## ANTI-IMMIGRANT SENTIMENT

Since September 11, the most blatant discrimination in the workplace has been against Arabs and others of Middle Eastern descent. Even over a decade and a half later, South Asian, Arab, Muslim, and Sikh communities in America record their ongoing experiences with hate, violence, discrimination, government surveillance, and profiling (Iyer, 2015). A notably horrible example took place in Chapel Hill, North Carolina with murders of a young couple and the woman's sister by a neighbor who had argued with them over car parking rights. All across the United States are reports of spray-paint graffiti, other acts of vandalism, and crude remarks directed at Muslims.

## ANTI-MUSLIM PROTESTS IN THE UNITED STATES AND EUROPE

After every act of terrorism it seems that a new surge of anti-Muslim protests and acts of violence take place. *The Huffington Post* is keeping a count of such attacks based on mass media accounts (Mathias, 2015). There have been near-daily reports of violence, harassment, intimidation, and bigotry against Muslims in the United States and Canada since the self-described Islamic State claimed responsibility for the November 13, 2015 terrorist attacks that killed 130 people in Paris. Dozens of reports of anti-Muslim events are described in the article, including burnings of Mosques and a threatened public burning of the Koran; physical attacks on individual male and female Muslims; airport and airplane removal of people who spoke Arabic; disturbing YouTube videos; and insulting train graffiti.

Ethnic cleansing, which has not been seen on this scale since the break-up of Yugoslavia in the 1990s, has erupted in Myanmar (Burma) where over 300,000 Rohingya Muslims were forced to flee their homes (Bruce, 2017). With support from government officials, the perpetrators inflicted house burnings, killings, mass rape, and other atrocities on this minority group who were labelled as foreigners who belonged in Bangladesh.

The situation in Europe involves refugees fleeing wars in the Middle East. As of March 2017, more than 5 million Syrians have fled the country and 6.3 million people were displaced internally; hundreds of thousands have been killed, most of them civilians (Cable News Network, CNN, 2017). The surrounding countries are in turmoil as well. More than a million migrants and refugees crossed into Europe since 2015, sparking a crisis as countries struggled to cope with the influx, and creating division in the EU over how best to deal with resettling people (Dillon, 2016). Thousands have died at sea on the journey westward. Some of the European countries, such as Germany, the United Kingdom, and Sweden, initially volunteered to take large numbers, while other nations absolutely refused to do so.

Racist attacks on the unwelcome arrivals have become increasingly common throughout Europe. At least in part because a majority of people in the United Kingdom did not want to cooperate with the European Union in accepting their share of refugees, the British people voted in a referendum that had been planned earlier to leave the EU (British Exit, known as Brexit; Wheeler & Hunt, 2016).

## BACKLASH AGAINST LATINO MIGRANTS

Much of the popularity of the Donald Trump campaign is owed to the anti-immigrant rhetoric. Trump, as the leading Republican candidate for the presidency, stated that he would not let Muslims enter the United States, and that he would build a wall to keep Mexicans out, Mexicans he branded as rapists and drug dealers (Martin, 2016).

In its report on 20 years of immigrant abuses, Human Rights Watch (2016) documents how the 1996 Clinton provisions on mandatory detention and fast-track deportations contributed to much harm and heart-break for families. The report describes the cases of: people who lived in the United States. for decades but were deported because of old drug violations; a gay man whose life was threatened in Honduras which caused him to escape to the United States only to be put in detention; a woman who escaped death threats from gang members in El Salvador, only to be sent back. Human Rights Watch calls for such unjust detention and deportation to end in the name of humanity and international human rights. Since the Trump administration has attempted to stop emigration from six Muslim nations in the Middle East and moved to restrict the number of foreigners arriving on visas, many families in desperate circumstances have found the doors slammed shut (Ordonez, 2017).

According to the Migration Information Service, the US immigrant population in 2016 stood at more than 42.4 million, or 13.3%, of the total US population (Zong & Batalova, 2016). In 2014, almost 70,000 kids from El Salvador, Guatemala and Honduras arrived at the US-Mexico border (Wiltz, 2015). Throughout Central America huge numbers of children are escaping situations of horror, sometimes with their parents, sometimes alone. They are on the run from gangs. In El Salvador, Honduras, and Guatemala, boys are threatened that they will be killed if they don't join; girls are at risk of being sold into sexual slavery. Those who have fled to the United States endured unimaginable obstacles on the dangerous flight. Many of these children are still in the United States today; some have been reunited with their parents; most remain in a state of legal limbo, especially now that the Trump administration is embarking on mass deportations (Santiago, 2017). Fear has spread throughout the immigrant groups as residents without proper documentation, including people who have grown up in the United States are subject to being detained.

## POLICY ISSUES CONCERNING REFUGEES

Refugees who have been accepted by the authorities are in a much better position regarding social services than are people who have crossed the borders illegally. Still, in the United States refugees have on average just 90 days of case management and must learn the language and customs as well as get a job during this time (Jackson, 2016). Not surprisingly, given all they have been through, many in this group have diagnosable mental health disorders, such as post-traumatic stress disorder, panic attacks, depression, and anxiety. And the hostile social and political climate is a major setback to the comprehensive services that social workers wish to provide.

A key political issue affecting non-refugees is immigration status, whether the new arrivals or older residents have entered the country legally or whether they are "undocumented"—lack the proper documentation to apply for jobs. Young people who have grown up in the United States but who never could be naturalized citizens because their parents did not have legal status do not qualify for in-state tuition at state universities in many states and are treated as foreigners even though they grew up in the United States.

Sum total, hundreds of thousands of immigrants, most from Latin America, have been removed each year for the past eight years, according to official records (US Immigration and Customs Enforcement [ICE], 2017). In the most recent year, around 58% of the number were removed due to conviction of a crime, and most of the rest because of illegal entry. The escalation in deportations in recent years means that high levels of anxiety are being experienced, and many former immigrants have become depressed and withdrawn. Over time, according to Psychiatrist James Gordon (2017), such chronic stress, unrelieved, will make them far more vulnerable to heart disease, asthma, diabetes, and post-traumatic stress disorder. As he further states:

> Trump's threats and promises have reawakened fears and physical symptoms that patients of mine, long-ago refugees from tyrannical regimes, thought they'd left behind. Like the Salvadoran youth studying for his GED, memories of the danger and dictatorships they fled are intruding on their

> thoughts and agitating their bodies. During the past week, many of my and my colleagues' patients have been panicked by stories of people with green cards prevented from returning to the United States. (eighth paragraph)

## SOCIAL WORK IMPLICATIONS

Standard 6.04 of the NASW (2017) Code of Ethics states: "Social workers should act to prevent and eliminate domination of, exploitation of, and discrimination against any person, group, or class on the basis of race, ethnicity, national origin, color, sex, sexual orientation, gender identity or expression, age, marital status, political belief, religion, immigration status, or mental or physical disability" (last page).). The seeds are sown for an ethical conflict when undocumented immigrants are prevented under state law from receiving certain social services that are provided by an agency where social workers are employed.

Furman et al. (2012) discuss the ethical dilemmas facing social workers in a climate of xenophobia and ethnocentrism, when government policies enforce "the criminalization of immigration" (p. 170). Do they send families in need of services away? Do they violate agency policy? Or do they discriminate? Each social worker, like other members of the helping professions, will have to decide for himself or herself the path to follow.

These widespread ethical challenges force social workers to consider the values of the profession they represent. If they turn to a reading of the NASW-US Code of Ethics, they will note that the profession, true to its historical roots, urges social workers to become agents of reform, to align their actions with their values (NASW, 2017).

The hostile attitude that is prevalent today against foreign newcomers to the country shows a lack of appreciation for the economic and social gifts that these people bring. Given the rapid aging of the population associated with a drastic need for younger workers, not only to do the work but also to pay into the system, the continuing influx of foreign laborers is in the economic interests of this country. The immigration of workers with advanced technical and scientific talent is a major bonus. Big business and labor leaders alike, welcome the arrivals and have spoken out in support of amnesty for undocumented workers, most of whom are Mexican.

## TRAUMA-INFORMED SERVICES

The social work profession is positioned to play a critical role in redefining policies surrounding historically marginalized immigrants in the United States. Regarding refugees, the NASW (2015a) policy statement supports policies that "ensure fair treatment and due process in accordance with international human rights for all asylum seekers" (p. 179). In addition, the statement supports policies that "provide resettlement programs to include trauma and mental health counseling" (p. 180).

The children of escaping refugees are apt to have nightmares, fear, anxiety, and depression. In teens, fear responses may be expressed through acting-out behavior and aggression (Clervil, Guarino, DeCandia, & Beach, 2013). Their sense of trust has been violated. Children need to understand the impact of the situation on their parents so, if the parents become noncommunicative in some way, the children can recognize it is not their fault or not that the parents no longer love them. Counseling from a social worker as an outsider who is aware of their situation can be extremely helpful under these circumstances.

For immigrants and refugees of all ages, a constant need to be vigilant for danger makes it difficult for survivors to ask for help when they need it. Bureaucratic requirements for settlement, including extensive questioning and paperwork, may act as triggers for a trauma response. Agency rules and regulations may be perceived as disrespectful, and not dissimilar to prior acts of victimization (Clervil et al., 2013).

Recommendations from the National Center on Family Homelessness, based on their intensive, two-year pilot project designed to offer trauma-informed services to recently displaced families and children, are relevant for social workers responding to the needs of refugees (Clervil et al., 2013). Using a trauma-informed approach, the agency is composed of engaged staff at every level trained to meet the psychological needs of survivors. This means understanding that rough treatment of survivors can trigger memories of horror and that building trust may take a long time. This means designing environments that instill a sense of safety, are welcoming, flexible, and responsive to individual needs, including those of culturally and linguistically diverse populations.

Healing from mental health-related issues begins when the survivors are trustful enough to share their stories of trauma and to describe their current issues related to the trauma such as having nightmares, flashbacks, or general feelings of despondency. To build a sense of trust, social workers need to use reflective listening skills, ask open-ended questions (such as how did you survive?), and respect the social work value of self-determination with regard to what the client wishes to share or not to share (Jackson, 2016). It is important, in addition, to recognize the resilience in newcomers and the strength that they have to adapt and thrive.

## SUMMARY AND CONCLUSION

This was the chapter of isms—classism, racism, sexism, heterosexism, sectarianism, and ethnocentrism. All these forms of oppression are human rights issues in that they involve discrimination against vulnerable populations. Three obvious omissions—adultism (discrimination against children), ageism, and ableism are subjects of other chapters. Classism in the United States was discussed in terms of the ever expanding gap between the rich and the poor, non-stigmatized welfare programs for the rich, the war against the poor which is occurring simultaneously on two fronts: (1) in the work place and (2) through welfare reform geared to force the poor to take the jobs nobody wants, often at less than a living wage.

Racism, closely aligned to classism was explored as a reality of conservative politics. Indeed racism can be regarded in the service of conservative politics as its presence effectively obviates working-class solidarity. Racism clearly figures in the war on crime that has become a war on minorities; its presence is evidenced as well in the war on welfare that has become a war on single non-working mothers. In recent times, use of a racial profile of another sort is applied in the war on terror. The statistics presented in this chapter and some that we will entertain in the next reveal the omnipresence of racial and class oppression in American life.

Ethnocentrism is evidenced in a nation's treatment of foreigners. The foreigner is often seen as less human (as well as humane) than native citizens. In recent years, there has been a resurgence of an "us" versus "them" mentality with regard to immigrants. And the concern with national security has been extended to ethnic groups that pose no threat of terrorism or of harming the economy.

Poverty in America, a major theme of chapter 6, was also a consideration in this chapter as we entered the world of work and the worker in the global economy. The focus here was on the uneven distribution of resources, locally and globally. For man, woman, and child to live in poverty in the midst of plenty is one of the cruelest forms of oppression. Coupled with the high unemployment rate for unskilled workers, the dreams of many American families must be put on hold. For the best expression of the human condition, we can turn to poetry, calling up the widely cited lines, of famed African American poet, Langston Hughes (1951/1967)who asked what happens to a dream deferred, does it sag like a heavy load or does it explode? His words apply equally at the individual or collective level.

Institutionalized sexism is a reality the world over, including North America as widely publicized in the #MeToo movement. Sexual oppression is revealed in comparative data from international non-governmental organizations and United Nations reports. Such reports chart the progress (and non-progress) of women in various parts of the world in achieving social and economic equality. For economic development to become social development, women must be adequately represented at the policy and family decision-making level. Only in this way will domestic and international economic policies be instituted so as to protect the welfare of women and children.

Heterosexism, sectarianism, and ethnocentrism were other forms of social oppression that were discussed in this chapter. The extremes of heterosexism and homophobia were seen in hate crimes inflicted upon persons viewed to be sexually different. Ethnocentrism, in its extreme form, was seen to be expressed as anti-immigrant harassment following September 11. The example of sectarianism that is the most memorable is found in Box 5.2 concerning the historic persecution of European Jews and other minority groups. This chapter, like the one before, it is written in the spirit of CSWE's (2015) standard to prepare students "to be knowledgeable about theories of human need and social justice and strategies to promote social and economic justice and human rights" (p. 7). Related to ethnocentrism is anti-immigrant sentiment. Social exclusion of immigrants is evidenced today in stringent policies threatening their lives and livelihood.

In light of the consequences of the global market imperatives, social work's ethical emphasis on social and economic justice assumes a rare importance. Social work is unique among the professions in its commitment to advocacy on behalf of the poor and dispossessed. Increasingly, a human rights focus is a part of this mission. It is this focus to which we next turn our attention.

## THOUGHT QUESTIONS

1. Make a list of privileged categories. Which ones are you a member of? Don't forget citizenship.
2. How are racism and classism intertwined? Sexism and racism? Sexism and heterosexism?
3. Explain how classism can occur at all levels of society. How are class differences apparent within a racial or ethnic category?
4. How does intersectionality work? Give two examples.
5. Review the consciousness-raising exercise—I heard, I saw, and so forth. How can you make this exercise apply to yourself?

6. According to Alexander (2012), how did the war on crime become a war on black people?
7. Read the story of Dorothy Height. Why do you think her role in the Civil Rights movement has been overlooked until now?
8. What role did domestic servants play in the Civil Rights movement? Relate to the narratives in *The Maid Narratives.*
9. Who is Angela Davis? How did she become an icon in the 1970s?
10. What is historical trauma? Relate this concept to Appalachian history and culture.
11. What is the Native American experience relative to historical trauma?
12. Describe the concept of the feminization of poverty. Does it apply in the United States as well as worldwide? If so, how?
13. Compare working conditions in the United States with those in other countries, more progressive and less progressive. How could having an American labor party affect workers' rights and benefits?
14. Discuss the notion of the war against the poor. Refer to *Nickel and Dimed.* What are some of the reasons for male/female pay inequities?
15. Why do Scandinavian countries score better on gender equality measures in United Nations reports than does the United States?
16. Compare heterosexism and homophobia as concepts. How are they manifest in the US social structure?
17. Define sectarianism. How does it relate to religious fundamentalism?
18. What is the purpose of the US Holocaust Museum? Relate this historical exhibition to the concept of displaced aggression.
19. Argue whether or not ethnocentrism is, to some extent, inevitable. Can we avoid being ethnocentric as we visit foreign lands?
20. What are the basic facts related to Latinos? Discuss aspects of Latino culture.
21. What form has anti-immigrant harassment taken after September 11?
22. Account for the popularity of Donald Trump in certain circles. What do surveys outside of this text show are some of the fears and hopes of his followers?
23. Discuss some of the difficulties that Mexican-Americans face in achieving "the American dream." Consult Langston Hughes' poem on a dream deferred?
24. Consider the situation facing undocumented residents from Latin America. How are national policies affecting the mental health of many?
25. What should social workers know about trauma-informed care?

## REFERENCES

Alexander, M. (2012). *The new Jim Crow: Mass incarceration in an age of color blindness.* New York, NY: The New Press.

Allport, G. (1954). *The nature of prejudice.* Reading, MA: Addison-Wesley.

Alvarez, L., Pérez-Peña, R., & Hauser, C. (2016, June 13). Orlando gunman was "cool and calm" after massacre, police say. *New York Times.* Retrieved from www.nytimes.com

American Immigrant Council. (2014, September 10). Immigrant women in the United States: A portrait of demographic diversity. Retrieved from www.immigrationpolicy.org

Appleby, G. A., Colon, E., & Hamilton, J. (2011). *Diversity, oppression, and social functioning: Person-in-environment assessment and social functioning* (3rd ed.). Boston, MA: Pearson Allyn & Bacon.

Armstrong, K. (2001, October 1). The true, peaceful face of Islam. *Time*, 48.

Associated Press. (2016, June 29). Agriculture secretary to talk opioid abuse in Appalachia. *Modern Health Care*. Retrieved from www.modernhealthcare.com

Australians Together. (2015). "Just get over it": Understanding intergenerational trauma. Retrieved from www.australianstogether.org.au

Ball, E. (2015, November). Slavery's trail of tears. *The Smithsonian, 46*(7), 58–82.

Barker, R. (2014) *The social work dictionary* (6th ed.). Washington, DC: NASW Press.

Billingsley, A., & Morrison-Rodriguez, B. (1998). The black family in the 21st century and the church as an action system: A macro perspective. In L. See (Ed.), *Human behavior in the social environment from an African perspective* (pp. 31–47.) New York, NY: The Haworth Press.

Blue, A. W., & Blue, M. A. R. (2001). The case for aboriginal justice and healing: The self perceived through a broken mirror. In M. Hadley (Ed.), *The spiritual roots of restorative justice* (pp. 57–80). Albany, NY: State University of New York Press.

Bloom, S. L., & Farragher, B. (2013). *Restoring sanctuary: A new operating system for trauma-informed systems of care*. New York: Oxford University Press.

Brave Heart, M. Y. (2007). The impact of historical trauma: The example of the Native community. In M. Bussey & J. B. Wise (Eds.), *Trauma transformed: An empowerment response* (pp. 176–193). New York, NY: Columbia University Press.

Bruce, N. (2017, September 12). Crisis called ethnic cleansing. New York Times, p. A9.

Cable News Network (CNN). (2017, April 9). Civil war fast facts. Cable News Network (CNN) library. Retrieved from www.cnn.com

Cattell-Gordon, D. (1990). The Appalachian inheritance: A culturally transmitted traumatic stress syndrome. *Journal of Progressive Human Services, 1*(1), 41–57.

Centers for Disease Control and Prevention (CDC). (2016, August 12). Sexual identity, sex of sexual contacts, and health-related behaviors among students in grades 9–12. *Morbidity and Mortality Weekly Report, 65* (9). Retrieved from www.cdc.gov

Children's Defense Fund. (2016). Ending child poverty now. Washington, DC: Children's Defense Fund. Retrieved from www.childrensdefense.org

Clervil, R., Guarino, K., DeCandia, C. J., & Beach, C. A. (2013). *Trauma informed care for displaced populations: A guide for community-based service providers*. Waltham, MA: The National Center on Family Homelessness, a practice area of American Institutes for Research.

Cobb, J. (2016, March 14). The matter of black lives. *The New Yorker*. Retrieved from www.newyorker.com

Collins, P. H. & Bilge, S.(2016). *Intersectionality*. Cambridge, England: Polity Press.

Congress, E., & Kung, W. (2013). Using the culturagram to assess and empower culturally diverse families. In E. Congress & M. Gonzalez (Eds.), *Multicultural perspectives in social work practice* (pp. 1–20). New York, NY: Springer.

Council on Social Work Education (CSWE). (2013). *Guidelines for advanced social work practice in trauma*. Alexandria, VA: CSWE.

Council on Social Work Education (CSWE). (2015). *Educational policy and accreditation standards*. Alexandria, VA: CSWE.

Davis, A. (2013, November 8). Organizing for social change and human rights. Keynote presentation at the *15th Annual Cedar Valley Conference on Human Rights*. Cedar Falls, IA: University of Northern Iowa.

Davis, J. H. (2016, May 13). U.S. directs public schools to allow transgender access to restrooms. *New York Times*, p. A1.

De Gruy, J. (2016). *Post-traumatic slave syndrome.* Portland, OR: De Gruy Publishers.

Dillon, P. (2016, July 28). Opening the door: Nonprofit rallies support for Syrian refugees. *Isthmus, 41*(30), 3.

Dollard, J. (1988/1957). *Caste and class in a southern town.* New York, NY: Routledge.

Dominelli, L. (2002). *Anti-oppressive social work theory and practice.* New York, NY: Palgrave MacMillan.

European Commission (2015). *Smarter, greener, more inclusive? Indicators to support the Europe 2020 strategy.* Luxembourg: Publications Office of the European Union.

Federal Bureau of Investigation (FBI). (2016). *2015 hate crime statistics. Uniform Crime Reports.* Washington, D.C.: US Department of Justice.

Fingerhut, H. (2016, May 12). Support steady for same-sex marriage and acceptance of homosexuality. Pew Research Center. Retrieved from www.pewresearch.org

Foucault, M. (1977). *Discipline and punish.* New York, NY: Pantheon.

Furman, R., Ackerman, A., Loya, M., Jones, S., & Negi, N. (2012). The criminalization of immigration: Value conflicts for the social work profession. *Journal of Sociology and Social Welfare, 39*(1), 169–185.

Gallup (2015, May 21). Americans greatly overestimate percent gay, lesbian in U.S. Retrieved from www.gallup.com.

Glum, J. (2017, April 12). Transgender students avoid school bathrooms despite health consequences. *Newsweek.* Retrieved from www.newsweek.com

Gonzalez, M., & Acevedo, G. (2013). Practice with Hispanic individuals and families: An ecological perspective. In E. P. Congress and M. J. Gonzalez (Eds.), *Multicultural Perspectives in Social Work Practice with Families* (3rd ed., pp. 141–156). New York, NY: Springer.

Gordon, J. (2017, February 10). Living in fear of deportation is terrible for your health. *Washington Post.* Retrieved from www.washingtonpost.com

Hansberry, L. (1958/1994). *A raisin in the sun.* New York, NY: Vintage Books.

Healy, L. (2008). *International social work: Professional action in an interdependent world* (2nd ed.). New York, NY: Oxford University Press.

Hennessy-Fiske, M. (2016, June 23). FBI investigators say they have found no evidence that Orlando shooter had gay lovers. *Los Angeles Times.* Retrieved from www.latimes.com

Hesson, T. (2012, September 11). Five ways immigration system changed after 9/11. American Broadcasting Company (ABC) News. Retrieved from www.abcnews.com

Hightower, J. (2016, July/August). The uprising of the outsiders. *The Progressive*, p. 70.

Hill, R. B. (2007). Enhancing the resilience of African American families. In L. A. See (Ed.), *Human behavior in the social environment from an African American perspective* (2nd ed., pp.75–90). New York, NY: Haworth.

hooks, b. (2000). *Where we stand: Class matters.* New York, NY: Routledge.

hooks, b. (2009). *Belonging: A culture of place.* New York, NY: Routledge.

Hughes, L. (1951/1967). A dream deferred. In L. Hughes (Ed.), *The panther and the lash: Poems of our times* (p. 14). New York, NY: Knopf.

Human Rights Campaign (2017). Violence against the transgender community in 2017. https://www.hrc.org/resources/violence-against-the-transgender-community-in-2017

Human Rights Watch (2016, April 25). 20 years of immigrant abuses. Retrieved from www.hrw.org

Hyde, C. (2013). Feminist social work practice. In C. Franklin (Ed.), *Encyclopedia of social work.* NASW. New York, NY: Oxford University Press. Retrieved from http://socialwork.oxfordre.com/.

Iyer, P. (2015, September 11). The stories Americans tell about 9/11 leave out discrimination against Muslims. *The Guardian*. Retrieved from www.theguardian.com

Jackson, K. (2016, July/August). Treating trauma in America's refugees. *Social Work Today, 16*(4), pp.10–13.

Johnson, J. (2016, July 18). The millennial revolt against neoliberalism. *Common Dreams*. Retrieved from www.commondreams.org

Johnson, J. T., & Yellow Bird, M. (2012). Indigenous peoples and cultural survival. In L. Healy & R. Link (Eds.), *Handbook of international social work: Human rights, development, and the global profession* (pp. 208–213). New York, NY: Oxford University Press.

Kaplan, L. E. (2007). Insidious trauma and the sexual minority client. In M. Bussey & J. B. Wise (Eds.), *Trauma transformed: An empowerment response* (pp. 176–193). New York, NY: Columbia University Press.

Kindy, K., Fisher, M., Tate, J., & Jenkins, J. (2015, December 26). A year of reckoning: Police fatally shoot nearly 1,000. *The Washington Post*. Retrieved from www.washingtonpost.com

Lakhani, N. (2016, July 27). US and Mexico fueled humanitarian crisis, report. *The Guardian*. Retrieved from www.theguardian.com

Levin, J., & Nolan, J. (2011). *The violence of hate: Confronting racism, anti-Semitism, and other forms of bigotry* (3rd ed.). Boston, MA: Allyn & Bacon.

Lichtblau, E. (2016, September 18). Hate crimes against American Muslims most since post-9/11 era. *New York Times*, p. A13.

Littlewolf, E. (2013, November 8). Indigenous women's issues. Keynote presentation at the *15th Annual Cedar Valley Conference on Human Rights*. Cedar Falls, IA: University of Northern Iowa.

Lyons, K., & Huegler, N. (2012). Social exclusion and inclusion. In L. M. Healy and R. J. Link (Eds.), Handbook of international social work: Human rights, development, and the global profession (pp. 37–43). New York, NY: Oxford University Press.

Malone, L. (2015, July 15). Transgender suicide rates are staggering. *Vocativ*. Retrieved from www.vocativ.com

Mantsios, G. (2009). Class in America: Myths and realities. In P. S. Rothenberg (Ed.), *Race, class, and gender in the U.S.* (pp. 177–190). New York, NY: Worth

Martin, P. (2016, January 5). Trump pushes racist attack on immigrants, Muslims. *World Socialist Web Site*. Retrieved from www.wsws.org

Martinez, M. (2016, January 28). Flint, Michigan: Did race and poverty factor into water crisis? *Cable News Network* (CNN). Retrieved from www.cnn.com

Mathias, C. (2015, December 16). A running list of shameful Islamophobic acts since the Paris attacks. *Huffington Post*. Retrieved from www.huffingtonpost.com

Moe, K. (2014, April 9). Intersectional! Or, why your movement can't go it alone. *Yes! Magazine*. Retrieved from www.yesmagazine.org

Moore, M. (2016, February 1). This is a racial crime. *Time, 187*(3), 39.

Moreno, C. L. (2013). Latino families affected by HIV/AIDS: Some practical practice considerations. In E. P. Congress and M. J. Gonzalez (Eds.), *Multicultural Perspectives in Social Work Practice with Families* (3rd ed., pp. 297–310). New York, NY: Springer.

Mullaly, R. (2010). *Challenging oppression and confronting privilege*. (2nd ed.). New York, NY: Oxford University Press.

National Association of Social Workers (NASW). (2015a). *Immigrants and refugees. Social work speaks: Policy statements* (10th ed., pp.176–181). Washington, DC: NASW Press.

National Association of Social Workers (NASW). (2015b). Women's issues. *Social work speaks: NASW policy statements, 2015–2017* (10th ed., pp.332–341). Washington, DC: NASW Press.

National Association of Social Workers (NASW). (2017). Code of ethics. Washington, DC: NASW Press.

National Women's Law Center. (2015, February 23). Women and social security. Retrieved from www.nwlc.org

Obama, B. (2004). *Dreams from my father: A story of race and inheritance.* New York, NY: Broadway Books.

Ordonez, F. (April 11, 2017). Officials defend Trump's travel ban on Syria as unrelated to chemical weapons. *Miami Herald.* Retrieved from www.miamiherald.com

*The Oxford Modern English Dictionary* (6th ed.). (2007). New York, NY: Oxford University Press.

Pager, D. (2003). The mark of a criminal record. *American Journal of Sociology, 108*(5), 937–975.

Pager, D., Western, B., & Bonikowski, B. (2009). Discrimination in a low-wage labor market: A field experiment. *American Sociological Review, 74,* 777–799.

Peek, L. (2011). *Behind the backlash's Muslim Americans after 9/11.* Philadelphia, PA: Temple University Press.

Pew Research Center. (2014). America's wealth gap between middle-income and upper-income families is widest on record. Washington, DC: Pew Research Center. Retrieved from www.pewresearch.org

Pew Research Center. (2015a, May 26). Five facts about Latinos and education. Washington, DC: Pew Research Center. Retrieved from www.pewresearch.org

Pew Research Center. (2015b, March 24). A majority of English-speaking Hispanics in the U.S. are bilingual. Washington, D.C.: Pew Research Center. Retrieved from www.pewresearch.org

Pinkerton, J. (2003, January-February). A grand compromise. *The Atlantic Monthly,* 115–116.

Randall, L. (2015). *Changing structure of Mexico: Political, social and economic prospects.* New York, NY: Routledge.

Razack, N. (2012). Racism and antiracist strategies. In L. Healy & R. Link (Eds.), *Handbook of international social work: Human rights, development, and the global profession* (pp. 237–242). New York, NY: Oxford University Press.

Reeves, S. (2012). Quotation taken from Box 2.3, How I resolved my ethnic identity crisis. In K. van Wormer, L. Kaplan, & C. Juby, *Confronting oppression, restoring justice: From policy analysis to social action* (2nd ed., pp. 66–68). Alexandria, VA: CSWE Press.

Reichert, E. (2011). *Social work and human rights: A foundation for policy and practice* (2nd ed.). New York, NY: Columbia University Press.

Rochlin, M. (2000). Heterosexual questionnaire. In K. van Wormer, J. Wells, & M. Boes, *Social work with lesbians, gays, and bisexuals: A strengths perspective* (p. 50). Boston, MA: Allyn & Bacon.

Rogers, K.L. (2006). *Life and death in the Delta: African American narratives of violence, resilience, and social change.* New York, NY: Palgrave/Macmillan.

Saleebey, D. (2012). Power to the people. In D. Saleebey (Ed.), *The strengths perspective in social work practice* (6th ed., pp. 1–23). Boston, MA: Pearson.

Sanchez, E. (2013, January 1). U.S. military, a growing Latino army. NBC Latino. Retrieved from www.nbclatino.com

Santiago, F. (2017, March 28). Trump policy of separating children from immigrant parents is plain evil. *Miami Herald.* Retrieved from www.miamiherald.com

Schiele, J. (2013). *Human services and the Afrocentric paradigm.* New York, NY: Routledge.

Seccombe, K. (2014). *So you think I drive a Cadillac? Welfare recipients' perspectives on the system and its reform* (3rd ed.). Boston, MA: Pearson.

Savage, C. (2017, August 2). US rights unit shifts to study anti-white bias. New York Times, p.A1.

Shulman, L. (2009). *The skills of helping individuals, families, groups, and communities* (6th ed.). Belmont, CA: Brooks/Cole.

Steinhauer, J. (2017, March 31). Targeting Planned Parenthood clears Senate. *New York Times*, p. A11.

Stovel, K. (2001). Local sequential patterns: The structure of lynching in the Deep South, 1882–1930. *Social Forces 79*(3), 843–880.

Tabron, L. J. (2016). Closing the wealth gap for families of color. *Stanford Social Innovation Review*. Retrieved from ssir.org

Turner, C. (2016, April 18). Why America's schools have a money problem. *National Public Radio*. Retrieved from www.npr.org

United Nations. (1948). *Universal Declaration of Human Rights*. New York, NY: United Nations.

United Nations. (2011). *10th anniversary of the Durban Declaration and Programme of Action*. New York, NY: United Nations. Retrieved from www.un.org

United Nations. (2015). *The world's women 2015*. UN statistics division. New York, NY: United Nations.

United Nations Development Programme (UNDP). (2015). Gender inequality index. *Human Development Reports*. Retrieved from www.hdr.undp.org

United Nations News Centre (2016). Majority oppose female genital mutilation in countries where practice persists – UN agency. Retrieved from www.un.org

US. Bureau of Labor Statistics, (2003). Usual weekly earnings summary. United States Department of Labor. Retrieved from www.bls.gov

US Census Bureau. (2011). *Overview of race and Hispanic origin: 2010*. Washington, DC: US Government Printing Office.

US Census Bureau. (2015). *Income and poverty in the United States: 2014*. Washington, DC: US Government Printing Office.

US Immigration and Customs Enforcement (ICE). (2017, February 10). FY 2016 ICE immigration removals. Department of Homeland Security. Retrieved from https://www.ice.gov/removal-statistics/2016

van Wormer, K., & Besthorn, F. (2017). *Human behavior and the social environment, macro level* (3rd ed.) New York, NY: Oxford University Press.

van Wormer, K., & Davis, D. R. (2018, 4th ed.) *Addiction treatment: A strengths perspective*. Belmont, CA: Brooks/Cole.

van Wormer, K., Jackson, D. W., & Sudduth, C. (2012). *The maid narratives: Black domestics and White families in the Jim Crow South*. Baton Rouge, LA: Louisiana State University Press.

van Wormer, K., Kaplan, L., & Juby, C. (2012). *Confronting oppression, restoring justice: From policy analysis to social action*. (2nd ed.). Alexandria, VA: Council on Social Work Education.

Vance, J. D. (2016). *Hillbilly elegy: A memoir of a family and culture in crisis*. New York, NY: HarperCollins.

Verma, A., Qureshi, H., & Kim, J. Y. (2016). Exploring the trend of violence against women in India. *International Journal of Comparative and Applied Criminal Justice, 41 (1–2)*. http://dx.doi.org/10.1080/01924036.2016.1211021

Wheeler, B., & Hunt, A. (2016, July 21). Brexit: All you need to know about the UK leaving the EU. British Broadcast Company (BBC) News. Retrieved from www.bbc.com

Wiesel, E. (1982). *Night*. New York, NY: Bantam Books.

Wiltz, T. (2015, August 24). Unaccompanied children from Central America, one year later. Huffington Post. Retrieved from www.huffingtonpost.com

Wise, T. (2010). *Color-blind: The rise of post racial politics and the retreat of racial equity*. San Francisco, CA: City Lights Books.

Wise, T. (2015). *Under the affluence: Shaming the poor, praising the rich and sacrificing the future of America*. San Francisco: City Lights Books.

World Economic Forum. (2015). Economies: India; Gender gap index 2015. Retrieved from www.reports.weforum.org

Young, I. M. (2011). *Justice and the politics of difference* (2011 edition). Princeton, NJ: Princeton University Press.

Zong, J., & Batalova, J. (2016, April 14). Migration information source. Retrieved from www.migrationpolicy.org

# CHAPTER 6

# HUMAN RIGHTS AND RESTORATIVE JUSTICE

> All human beings are born free and equal in dignity and rights. They are endowed with reason and conscience and should act towards one another in a spirit of brotherhood.
>
> United Nations Universal Declaration of Human Rights, 1948, Article 1

> No one shall be subject to torture or to cruel, inhuman or degrading treatment or punishment.
>
> United Nations Universal Declaration of Human Rights, 1948, Article 5

A key theme for this book is that human rights belong to everyone. They permeate our actions every day and support civilized life. When the principles of the right to vote, to be peaceful, to denounce torture, to value children and their work not their labor, to honor the sanctity of the human body and abolish rape were written down and put into laws and conventions, each time this was accomplished human beings took a step toward well-being and civilized society. As famously stated by Eleanor Roosevelt (1958), human rights "begin in small places, close to home—so close and so small that they cannot be seen on any map of the world. Yet they are the world of the individual person." They are the world of social work as well, and social workers benefit from this collective work of human kind. We are all human—right?

As explained briefly in the introduction to this book, when human beings make social, economic, political and civil progress in how they organize themselves, the new opportunity, rule or "right" is soon taken for granted. Our grandmothers and great grandmothers struggled, some of them went on hunger strikes and handcuffed themselves to railings, but today we forget what it took to achieve a woman's right to vote. Although this right has only been the law in most western countries for one hundred years it is still not the law in some countries of the world even in 2018. It bears repeating that human rights are inextricably linked with every aspect of our well-being and therefore of social work. The committee work and awareness campaigns that go into the design of international laws are exercises in social and economic justice.

The reader now sees that every chapter of this book draws on human rights language. International laws are called "conventions" by the United Nations (UN), and they are generated by the UN under their Charter's commitment: "to promote higher standards of living, full employment, and conditions of economic and social progress and development" (United Nations Department of Public Information (UNDPI), 2008, p. 149). The inspiration for the early debates about human rights came in the form of concern for the rights of prisoners of war, refugees and the right not to be tortured or most recently the depressing debate about water-boarding. Added to these major concerns is increasing awareness of the impact of industry and mining, including fracking, de-stabilization of the earth's crust and pollution of the air, plus degradation of the environment with the inevitable impact on human health. This is particularly evident in the currently debated right to have access to clean water.

The concept of human rights evolved over many decades in the 20th century, especially as a result of the terrible human carnage of world wars and a questioning of what makes us human and civilized. Human rights are those rights that belong to all of us by virtue of being sentient beings rather than wild creatures; they ensure basic survival, protections from discrimination and opportunity for participation in society (Reichert, 2011). These include social, economic, political, civil and cultural rights including the things we often take for granted and can identify if we pause for a moment: the right to a name, the right to be safe from physical violence and abuse; the right to shelter, to a sense of home, to health, to clean water, to be free of racial, age, sexual and gender discrimination.

Although human rights have been evolving slowly, there are some clear dates that mark progress: the foundations of the United Nations began with the Red Cross/Red Crescent organization that was established in 1863 by representatives of 16 countries. The organizers' goal was to address the treatment of prisoners and victims of war, plus express concern about the impact of new weapons on humans. Conversations began, including at the Hague in 1864, on ways to settle disputes without war and the horrible aftermath. Then after the terrible losses in the First World War, with thousands of young men (age 17–24 years) dying in single battles such as the Somme, the League of Nations was established in 1920, directly building on the work of the Red Cross and the Red Crescent. The work of establishing human rights through the League took decades, followed by the more global United Nations, established in 1946 (see Box 6.1 for a brief history of the United Nations).

The UN was a ground-breaking institution and is today a center of advocacy and research in Geneva, New York, Delhi, and The Hague that many of us cannot imagine being without. With the current (2018) wars and bombing in countries such as Syria and Iraq, this quest for a more peaceful way to work with one another and to truly respect human rights to be safe from violence, environmental destruction and poverty is a challenging journey. Often social workers are caught in the midst of human need, for example to protection or shelter and the resources needed to provide such protection.

In discussion with a group of students from a variety of cultures and backgrounds it is clear that human rights are a hope for the future, students see the value of working across countries and continents to share their initiatives and innovation and feel a sense of solidarity when progress is slow (IASSW Interns, United Nations, Newsletter February 2017). Increasingly the human rights conventions drafted and approved in the 20th century become the templates for action in the 21st century. This is the century that will see human rights become more real and part of our lives, or in Wronka's words, "dragged into our awareness and everyday existence"(2012, p.440). In Jamaica, for example, the education system has adopted the Convention on the Rights of the Child (CRC) as school policy, and a small book with pictures and explanations of the CRC has been published for children. In the United Kingdom, the

European Convention on Human Rights, built upon the United Nations Declaration, was incorporated into UK law in 1998. More recently there has been concern about the lack of coordination amongst agencies that has resulted in the death of children at the hands of their "caregivers." To encourage this coordination by the health, education, housing, criminal justice, and social service professionals, Broadhurst, Glover, & Jamieson (2009) report: "A single unified instrument sets forth the basic underpinning principles and defines the essential responsibilities of all entrusted with the care of children . . . and a preferable alternative (to domestic law) is the incorporation of the United Nations Convention on the Rights of the Child (CRC) into domestic legislation" (p. 41).

Social workers are central to implementing human rights and some countries have made more progress than others, in part due to their history of participation or isolation—for example, Geneva is set in a small country that collaborates with those on its borders, while the United States has a history which is repeating itself under a nationalist president since 2017 of isolationism.

Most countries now adhere to and respect the role of the International Criminal Court in the Hague. Also, the European body of the International Federation of Social Workers (IFSW), "has a publication called Standards in Social Work Practice Meeting Human Rights 2010 which extensively discusses how social workers should promote and realize human rights."(Androff, 2016, p. 3).

In the Child Welfare chapter 10 of this book (under the section: physical punishment of children), the connection between the goals of child protection, for example, and social work practice utilizing the UN CRC is emphasized and illustrated with current examples. No individual social worker can think up all the elements of child development and social roles that are covered in the CRC and its 54 Articles and sub sections. The CRC is a ready-made resource and in its clearest form, a checklist for action. The idea of what is a "child" must be defined—of course we know, a child is someone under 18, then we ask, is that worldwide? According to the UN, this is the world's definition now. Every child should be safe from physical punishment—not such an easy one to agree on but part of global agreement (see chapter 10 for a full discussion). Every child needs a name—we take it for granted, of course. In the 1990s in the United Kingdom, it was still practice to give a child with multiple disabilities a letter—Baby M—for example, while in process for adoption. Now the world is faced with rapidly changing laws concerning surrogate parents and the infants in question, born to surrogates often for example in Mexico, to biological parent(s) in the United States and caught between new legislation in several states in Mexico (New York Times, Sunday March, 2017).

Human rights conventions cover all aspects of life including the most broad to the most specific:

The Universal Declaration of Human Rights (1948)

The Convention against Torture and Other Cruel, Inhuman, or Degrading Treatment or Punishment (1984)

The International Covenant on Economic, Social and Cultural Rights(1966)

The Convention on the Elimination of All forms of Racial Discrimination

The Convention on the Rights of the Child (1989)

The Convention on the Elimination of All Forms of Discrimination against Women (1979)

These documents can at first seem daunting. It is important for social work students to know that these templates for action exist and they can easily access them, for example through the

### BOX 6.1 Ten Reasons to Learn about Human Rights

Reasons for social work students and practitioners to study, reflect on, and implement human rights:

- Human rights represent the work of more than 300 years of human activity to come to together on earth to establish basic agreements on humans' treatment of one another as sentient beings who can respect one another.
- Human rights propel us to examine our current practices that are cruel or unusual, such as perpetrating torture; incarcerating children with adults or placing them on death row; executing prisoners of war; using chemical weapons. Leaders responsible for war crimes can now be brought to trial at the International Court in the Hague. In 2005 the Supreme Court of the United States abolished the death penalty for people under 18, recognizing the United Nations Convention on the Rights of the Child.
- Human rights encourage us to work on the tension between "my" culture and beliefs and our collective norms, for example discussing physical punishment of children versus non-violent discipline; domestic violence as private to the marriage or public concern and criminal abuse; fair and exploitive labor; respect for people who are transgender, respect for people with physical challenges and people who are nomadic versus with fixed address.
- Human rights focus attention on the whole world, not just the nation state or region and place that we live, and focus attention and lead to a recognition of our interdependence—economically, socially, culturally, and politically.
- Human rights become the voice for those who cannot speak or are powerless to be heard.
- Human rights become an instrument of advocacy for emerging issues, such as the right to clean water.
- Human rights conventions become a template that countries can incorporate into their own legislation and policy, rather than "inventing the wheel."
- Human rights declarations and actions promote education and awareness.
- Human rights provide a sense of solidarity and hope for refugees and migrants.
- Human rights set an expectation that we focus on the sustainable future of the planet for future generations to be able to meet their own needs for food, clean water, shelter, survival, and, we hope, the well-being of all our descendants.

---

List generated in conversation with the International Social Work seminar at the University of Ljubljana, Slovenia, April 2017, with Professors Lea Sugman Bohinc and Rosemary June Link and students (names included with permission) Tina Kodre, Ibrahim Sönmez, Ana Marija Cimperman, and Jožica Magajne.

websites of the UN or the United Nations International Children's Emergency Fund (UNICEF) or the International Labor Organization (ILO). Currently thousands of social workers and human rights specialists across the world are working with the UN and the IFSW and IASSW to contribute to the development of these policies and conventions, plus their amendments, called Optional Protocols (see chapter 10 on child welfare for the list of these protocols for the Convention on the Rights of the Child).

The important learning for students is that social workers learn how to access and use the resources and information they need according to the client community and environment they are working in. These resources give a template for action that need not be re-invented; the international community has generated a vast amount of ideas and research that assist social workers in co-creating solutions with their client and service user communities.

Thus, human rights belong to everyone, and while we all benefit from the work of our great-grandmothers and grandfathers, they would be shocked at the slow pace of change. Women, despite having the vote in the majority of countries, still in many places are excluded or undermined in their efforts to impact the political leadership process (it is startling that the United States for example, has yet to elect a woman as President) and from leading the worlds' Fortune 500 companies, which remain a men's club with just a few women breaking through. Recently, Iceland approved legislation to require employers to address the gender gap in pay, and yet Iceland is ranked first in the world in women's employment and representation in Parliament (*The Economist*, 2017).

There is a crisis in violence across the world and the Human Rights Watch staff members have been ensuring that hard won steps toward civilized behavior, such as the right of a prisoner not to be tortured, and the right of a woman not to be assaulted are maintained. Human rights are what all of us have created as sentient human beings, and in the hopes for more peaceful futures for our children and their descendants. In their international social work seminar in the spring of 2017, students from the University of Ljubljana, Slovenia, discussed the value of human rights and came up with at least ten reasons social workers study, analyze and practice human rights as fundamental to the profession, see Box 6.1.

In this chapter we cover the following topics, and, as a refresher, we provide the United Nations Universal Declaration of Human Rights in Appendix A:

1. Brief history of the early days of human rights, establishing of the United Nations and the Universal Declaration
2. Overview of the definitions, categories, and current organization of the United Nations and the Commission for Human Rights, identifying connections to the social work profession
3. Human rights and conventions in action; for example the Convention on the Elimination of All Forms of Racial Discrimination (CERD), the Convention on the Elimination of All Forms of Discrimination against Women (CEDAW), including human rights and war crimes
4. Criminal and restorative justice as a form of human rights
5. Restorative justice

## BRIEF HISTORY OF HUMAN RIGHTS

The template for human rights is the United Nations Universal Declaration. The rights spelled out in that document are multidimensional: they relate to social and economic security, rights before the courts of law, political rights and cultural protections for minority populations.

That economic rights are even included along with political and civil rights under the rubric of human rights may come as a surprise to many Americans (Wronka, 2012). Part of the reason may be because, as Gil (2013) informs us, the Bill of Rights of the US Constitution guarantees civil and political rights only. The United Nations Universal Declaration of Human Rights, in contrast, provides for civil and political rights supplemental to comprehensive economic rights.

The key aspects of civil rights and criminal justice—the crime, courts, and corrections—are part of the fabric of Western society, indeed, of virtually any society and build upon the standards set by human rights covenants. In a court of law in the US for example, (unlike in Europe where the death penalty was abandoned decades ago) the "ultimate sanction," the death penalty, will be examined against a human rights backdrop. Infused with ideology and emotion, the US criminal justice labyrinth does not offer a pretty picture, but rather one marred by the public's seemingly insatiable appetite for vengeance rather than reconciliation and rehabilitation. In his recent documentary, Michael Moore (2015) examines the Norwegian criminal justice system and finds an approach where inmates have civil rights protected, for example, they are allowed to vote; where they have dignified living quarters and community goals and expectations of one another in order to practice a better way of living on release.

Drawing on the Universal Declaration of Human Rights as a framework, such issues as capital punishment, war and peace, terrorism, war crimes, and violence of the most brutal sort resulting in maiming and death and systematically practiced in many parts of the globe are constantly connected to social work practice and response (for example, working with refugees). Also closely connected to human rights and social work professional's responsibilities is the US criminal justice system. Later in this chapter is an examination of crime rates, mass incarceration, the war on drugs as a war on minorities and the death penalty, state-sanctioned violence against the person In our discussion of human rights violations taking place in US prisons, we will rely on facts and figures from investigations by Amnesty International and other nongovernmental organizations such as Human Rights Watch in exposing human rights violations throughout the world.

Many of the solutions to problems related to personal and international conflict the world faces today can be found in the centuries-old principles of restoring peace and justice. In the 20th century, most social workers, if asked to summarize the value base of their practice, would probably have used the term social justice rather than human rights (Ife, 2001) but now and into the 2020s, social workers are embracing the frameworks and usefulness of a human rights framework (Wronka, 2012). While the 1900s were the century of design, awareness building and collective action through the United Nations and international organizations such as the World Health Organization (WHO), the 2000s is the century of action, for example, banning children (people under 18) from death row (Waldmeir, 2006). To learn of milestones in the history of human rights, see Box 6.2.

Just in the first decades of the 21st century, it has become a natural part of the social work profession to draw upon the policies and knowledge embodied in human rights laws. Human rights are included in the International Federation of Social Workers (IFSW, 2004) Code of Ethics, Section 2, definition of social work practice, Section 3, International Conventions and Section 4.1, Human Rights and Human Dignity. The majority of the nation members of IFSW (for example, Australia, Britain, Denmark, France, and Turkey) include a reference to human rights. The United States has not yet done so but as an active member of IFSW can be expected to do so in the future. (See www.ifsw.org to compare the various Codes and to read the IFSW Code of Ethics.)

While human rights as a framework and resource for social work practice has gained ground, research and publications have also increased to inform practitioners. Human rights

**BOX 6.2 Human Rights: From Early Days to 2020**

- 1863: Red Cross, 16 countries came together following concern at human impact of new weapons
- 1864: International Peace Conference at The Hague adopted "A Convention for Peaceful Settlement of International Disputes"
- 1918: WWI Treaty of Versailles
- 1920: League of Nations but the United States did not join
- 1921: League brokered disputes successfully

Birth of the United Nations

- 1942: 26 nations met in New York to draft first declaration of UN
- 1945: San Francisco 50 nations signed the UN Charter; ratified by 5 permanent members of the Security Council (United States, United Kingdom, China, France, Russia)
- 1948: The Universal Declaration of Human Rights was approved and passed by the General Assembly
- 1950s–1990: Cold War undermined the UN, but view of success depends which country you ask
- 1951: The Geneva Convention on the Status of Refugees was created, including articles defining prisoners of war and their treatment
- 1995: The International Association of Schools of Social Work issued its resolution on the Human Rights of Women at the UN World Conference of Women in Beijing, China

UN Organization

- Security Council: 5 permanent members plus 10 temporary seats in New York
- General Assembly: 191 countries in New York
- General Assembly Human Rights: in Geneva
- International Court of Justice: The Hague (settles disputes Iceland and Canada, Nicaragua and the United States) 15 judges, nine-year terms
- International Criminal Court: tries individuals for crimes against humanity

Secretariat

- Headed by Secretary-General, appointed by General Assembly
- 2016 was Ban Ki-Moon's second term, since January 2017 António Guterres
- 5-year renewable term
- Extensive staff (6,900+) in New York, The Hague, Nairobi, Kenya, Geneva

Supporting Programs and Funds

- UNICEF, focus on children and poverty, State of the World's Children reports
- UNDP, focus initially (1980s) was on economic development, now on sustainable social and economic development
- UNHCR, (Recently new High Commission for Human Rights in Afghanistan)

Specialized/Cooperating Agencies

- International Labour Organization (ILO)
- Educational, Scientific, and Cultural Organization (UNESCO)
- World Health Organization
- World Bank
- International Monetary Fund

was indexed in the introductory texts by van Wormer (1997), Jansson, (2001), DiNitto (2003), included in the *International Handbook* by Healy & Link (2012), and most recently in books on social work and human rights by Reichert (2011) and Abramoff (2015). Also the Council on Social Work Education (CSWE) requires that social and economic justice content be grounded in an understanding of human and civil rights and the global interconnections of oppression. NASW's policy statement endorses a human rights focus; NASW's alliance with Canada as joint members of IFSW; and the increasing globalization of the social work profession all incorporate human rights.

## CONNECTIONS OF HUMAN RIGHTS TO SOCIAL WORK: DEFINITIONS AND CURRENT ORGANIZATIONS

A milestone in social work recognition of the significant of human rights occurred in the adoption of human rights language by the International Federation of Social Workers and the International Association of Schools of Social Work, plus publications such as *Social Work and Human Rights: A Foundation for Policy and Practice* by Elisabeth Reichert (2003, 2011). This book helps us connect the dots between values set forth in the NASW-US Code of Ethics and human rights documents. For the occasion of writing of the present book, we invited Reichert to share with us her understanding of human rights, the definitions, covenants and of social work as a human rights profession. Reichert generously shares her expertise to provide an overview of human rights in Box 6.3 which is the second section of this chapter.

In "A World Made New: Eleanor Roosevelt and the Universal Declaration of Human Rights," Mary Ann Glendon (2001) takes us step by step into the political history that culminated in one of the greatest global documents of all times. Clearly ahead of its time, this document which has been called "a Magna Carta for all humanity" had as its basic assumption, according to Glendon, the belief that the causes of atrocities and armed conflict are rooted in poverty and discrimination. It is, in fact, an international human rights document that recognizes that civil and political rights cannot be assured in the absence of economic rights (Gil, 2013).

To ensure that the horrors of the Holocaust would never happen again and in the aftermath of the Nuremberg war crimes trials which prosecuted leading Nazis under the novel charge of crimes against humanity, the framers of the United Nations Declaration set to work. President Truman appointed Eleanor Roosevelt as US delegate to the United Nations. No person could be better qualified to bring the late President Franklin Roosevelt's Four Freedoms—freedom of speech and expression, freedom to worship, freedom from want, and freedom from fear of aggression—as outlined in his 1941 State of the Union address—than was his wife, Eleanor. This reserved but courageous woman chaired the Human Rights Commission during its first crucial years, building upon the work of the League of Nations. From that vantage point she focused her attention and lobbying efforts on the creation of international law for the promotion of human rights. The resulting document, which forged an uneasy path of compromise between the warring doctrines of capitalism and Communism and between East and West, was largely Roosevelt and her team's gift to the world. In 1948, marking a milestone in human relations, the General Assembly of the United Nations unanimously adopted the Universal Declaration of Human Rights. View the photo of Eleanor Roosevelt in Figure 6.1.

## BOX 6.3 On Human Rights

Elisabeth Reichert, MSSW, Ph.D.

> Human rights have gone global not because it serves the interests of the powerful but primarily because it has advanced the interest of the powerless.
>
> Ignatieff, (2001, p. 7)

### WHAT ARE HUMAN RIGHTS?

The concept of human rights has occupied social workers, educators, philosophers, lawyers, and politicians for ages. The proposition that all individuals who inhabit the planet Earth share inherent privileges and rights has great attraction. This commonality among all who reside on the planet, regardless of country or nationality, aims to bring individuals closer together than might otherwise be the case. After all, if someone residing in the United States acknowledges that someone residing in Russia or China has the same right to a safe, non-violent environment, this link can lead to better cooperation in resolving key issues affecting the human existence.

Of course, human rights cover domestic, as well as international, circumstances. Unless individuals, communities, corporations, governments, and other groups recognize human rights at home, promotion of human rights on a broader level appears meaningless or, at best, superficial. The most appropriate place to begin the study and application of human rights lies within a person's own environment. Only after the individual, entity or group thoroughly understands human rights in a local sense can human rights be expanded to a broader spectrum of circumstances.

### DEFINITION OF HUMAN RIGHTS

While no single definition could possibly cover the entire gamut of what human rights involve, the idea of human rights can generally be defined as "those rights, which are inherent in our nature and without which we cannot live as human beings. Human rights and fundamental freedoms allow us to fully develop and use our human qualities, our intelligence, our talents and our conscience and to satisfy our spiritual and other needs. They are based on mankind's increasing demand for a life in which the inherent dignity and worth of each human being will receive respect and protection." United Nations (1987). People from different backgrounds readily endorse the concept of human rights, which refer to those rights that every human being possesses and is entitled to enjoy simply by virtue of being human (Ife, 2001).

### UNIVERSAL DECLARATION OF HUMAN RIGHTS

The starting point in understanding human rights lies within the Universal Declaration of Human Rights. Most nations, including the United States, have approved this 1948 document, which lists specific human rights. The declaration is not legally binding on any country that approves the declaration. Yet at a minimum, approval of the declaration by a country indicates a commitment to satisfying the specified rights.

The Universal Declaration contains three distinct sets or generations of human rights. The first set or generation lists political and individual freedoms that are similar to what Americans view as human rights. The right to a fair trial, freedom of speech and religion, freedom of movement and assembly, and guarantees against discrimination, slavery, and torture fall within these political and civil human rights (United Nations, 1948, Articles 2–15).

While much of the Universal Declaration addresses political and individual freedoms similar to those contained in the US Constitution and its Bill of Rights, the Universal Declaration goes further. Reading beyond the initial set of human rights in the declaration reveals another set of human rights that address economic and social welfare concepts. This set of rights attempts to ensure each resident of a country an adequate standard of living based on the resources of that country. Under this second set of human rights, everyone "has the right to a standard of living adequate for the health and well-being of himself and of his family, including food, clothing, housing and medical care and necessary social services." In addition, "motherhood and childhood are entitled to special care and assistance" and everyone has the right to a free education at the elementary level (United Nations, 1948, Articles 16–27).

While Americans applaud themselves for their strong commitment to the first set of human rights enumerated in the Universal Declaration, it is within the second group of human rights that Americans frequently come up short. Compared to many other countries, the United States fails to fulfill its obligation to promote economic and social human rights (Reichert & McCormick, 1997; Reichert, 2011). The infant mortality rate, meaning the death of children in the first year of their lives, was higher in the United States than in any other industrialized country (National Vital Statistics Reports, 2014). With the passage of the Affordable Care Act legislation, however, this rate is expected to decline. Within the United States itself, disparity in infant mortality rates exists among racial groups, with African-American infants suffering a mortality rate more than twice that of non-Hispanic whites (Center for Disease Control and Prevention, 2015).

A third and final set of human rights involves collective rights among nations. This set of rights is the least developed among the three types of human rights. Under the 1948 declaration, everyone "is entitled to a social and international order in which the rights and freedoms" listed in the document can be fully realized (United Nations, 1948, Articles 28–30). Essentially, promotion of collective human rights requires intergovernmental cooperation on world issues, like environmental conditions to another group when these conditions would inhibit the growth or prosperity of the other group. Industrialized countries should not take advantage of less economically developed countries by exploiting resources.

Clearly, as defined by the Universal Declaration, human rights cover much more than political rights. Social welfare benefits are as important a human right as the right to live without discrimination. The Declaration also provides that "everyone" is entitled to all the rights and freedoms listed in the Declaration without distinction.

## UNIVERSALITY AND INDIVISIBILITY

The concept of universality underpins human rights. Every individual has a claim to enjoyment of human rights, wherever the individual resides. For example, human rights include adequate health care and nutrition for everyone. Perhaps a country's resources are insufficient to provide universal health care and food, and therefore, not everyone receives adequate care and nutrition. However, because health care and food are integral to human rights, governments have an obligation to provide a framework for ensuring the delivery of these rights.

Not all human rights are so clear-cut as the preceding examples, which can result in reluctance to promote a particular human right. The notion of universality may clash with particular cultures, laws, policies, morals, and other regimes that fail to recognize a particular human right in question. In some countries, employment or other discrimination against gays and lesbians is allowed because cultural or religious norms permit this type of discrimination. Such discrimination violates human rights principles even though human rights require sensitivity to culture and religion. This clash between human rights and cultural or religious norms raises a basic question: Which should prevail, the cultural or religious norm or the human right? If human rights apply to everyone, then the human right must prevail. Of course, the issue is not so concrete. Who defines a human right? Who benefits from the definition? Who loses from the definition? Whose voices are being heard in enforcing human rights? Who defines culture and cultural norms? Does one government have the right to tell another government that its policies violate a human right? In the case of disagreement over interpretation of a human right, who decides? The infusion of human rights into a society often requires great consideration.

In addition to universality, the other concept important to human rights is that of indivisibility. The concept of indivisibility refers to the necessity that government and individuals recognize each human right and not to selectively promote some rights over others. As noted previously, the United States tends to recognize political and civil human rights over social welfare rights. For instance, the United States is still working on guaranteeing health care to all its citizens (currently costs are only partially covered by Medicare for seniors) but guarantees (at least on paper) due process in criminal trials. Can the right to due process then be more important than the right to adequate health care, especially where the individual has never been arrested for any crime? Ironically, individuals detained in jail or prisons in the United States are guaranteed health care, something other individuals are not.

After the Universal Declaration, numerous other documents addressing specific areas of human rights have come into existence, including the International Covenant on Civil and Political Rights; International Covenant on Economic, Social, and Cultural Rights; Convention on the Rights of the Child; and Convention on the Elimination of all Forms of Discrimination against Women. However, the starting point for any contemporary human rights discussion remains the Universal Declaration.

## HUMAN RIGHTS AND SOCIAL WORK

While social workers must have knowledge of human rights to apply human rights principles to their practice, knowledge alone may not provide a sufficient basis with which to connect human rights to social work practice. Social workers may be familiar with the Universal Declaration but have not yet made the connection to their practice. If social workers are tempted to view human rights as too theoretical or legalistic, they will miss out on key resources and will have difficulties in connecting human rights to their practice

However, a relatively straightforward way exists by which social workers in the United States can readily see the connection between human rights and their profession. The NASW Code of Ethics, 2017, under which most US social workers practice contains numerous references to human rights. Provisions of the code essentially require adherence to human rights principles, without actually stating the term human rights. By identifying the code as a human rights document, social workers can better understand why their profession is a human rights profession and apply human rights to practice.

The importance of human rights to the social work profession cannot be overstated. In confronting social issues, human rights provide an important link between the individual and the broader spectrum of society. As an example, human rights do not view women battering as a problem of a particular individual. Instead, human rights define women battering as a structural and political problem. A woman has a human right not to be battered, regardless of cultural norms or other accepted practices allowing or justifying the battering (Bunch, 1991). This classification of domestic violence into a human rights issue communicates to victims of domestic violence that they are human beings entitled to protection and not simply "sick" and in need of treatment (Witkin, 1998). Reframing a social problem like domestic violence into a human rights issue also creates an international context in which to combat domestic violence. International pressure may induce governments to actively try to prevent domestic violence, knowing that to do otherwise can result in allegations of violating human rights.

Human rights issues, such as freedom from physical abuse and a right to medical care and housing, clearly fall within the ethical responsibilities of social workers. By emphasizing the human rights aspect of social work, social workers can enhance their own fulfillment of ethical responsibilities. Social workers who connect human rights issues with ethical principles can also better identify issues that go beyond individual circumstances. For instance, from a human rights perspective, a social worker would not view domestic violence as simply an issue involving the dynamics of the individual or couple, but also as an issue that operates on a national or international scale. If it is a human right to be safe and secure, then this right would apply to everyone at any place anytime, irrespective of circumstances.

Individuals alone may not always be capable of overcoming oppression, especially when obstacles arise from broader structural difficulties. Adopting a human rights perspective can help social workers more readily identify structural difficulties in planning appropriate interventions.

Human rights are continually evolving, especially at the grassroots level. Tensions caused by differing viewpoints on human rights will always exist. Issues of culture, religion, and power will always be part of the struggle for human rights. Unquestionably, social workers everywhere have a unique role to play in promoting further development of human rights into every society.

## REFERENCES

Bunch, C. (1991). Women's rights as human rights: Toward a revision of human rights. In C. Bunch & R. Carrillo (Eds.), *Gender violence: A development and human rights issue* (pp. 3–18). New Brunswick, NJ: Center for Women's Global Leadership.

Centers for Disease Control and Prevention, (2015) Infant mortality statistics from the 2013 period linked birth/infant death data set. National Vital Statistics Reports, Table A. Retrieved from www.cdc.gov/nchs/data/nvvsr6409.pdf

Ife, J. (2001). *Human rights and social work: Towards rights based practice.* Cambridge, England: Cambridge University Press.

Ignatieff, M. (2001). *Human rights as politics and idolatry*. Princeton, NJ: Princeton University Press.

National Association of Social Workers. 2008. Code of ethics. Retrieved from www.socialworkers.org on August 9, 2016.

National Vital Statistics Reports, 2014, September 24 Volume 63, No.5. Retrieved from www.nvsr6305.pdf on August 9, 2016.

Reichert E., & McCormick, R. (1997). Different approaches to child welfare: United States and Germany. *Journal of Law and Social Work, 6*(2), 17–33.

United Nations. (1948). *Universal declaration of human rights*. New York, NY: Author.

United Nations Development Programme (2003). United Nations human development report. Online at http://hdr.undp.org

Witkin, S. (1998). Editorial: Human rights and social work. *Social Work, 43*, 197–201.

---

Elisabeth Reichert is professor of social work, Southern Illinois University at Carbondale. This boxed reading is adapted from Reichert, E. (2011). *Social work and human rights: A foundation for policy and practice* (2nd ed.) New York, NY: Columbia University Press.

Read the complete Declaration in Appendix A of this text. As you read through the 30 articles, keep in mind the fact that collectively they are about the ways in which a state treats its citizens. The standards provided in the Declaration relate not to the violation of individuals in personal crime but to violations sanctioned by the state such as in police torture of suspects. Non-governmental organizations (NGOs) such as Amnesty International and Human Rights Watch conduct research on such violations and report their findings to the United Nations.

Although originally non-binding, the principles immortalized in the Declaration increasingly have acquired legal force, mainly through their incorporation into the laws of individual nations. Today, in the United States, the principles laid down in this document compose what is called, in legal jargon, customary international law. Following a federal decision in 1980

**FIGURE 6.1.** Eleanor Roosevelt proudly holds up a copy ofThe Universal Declaration of Human Rights. © Getty Images, Fotosearch/Stringer.

which ruled against a torturer in Paraguay, governments are beholden to universal principles (Wronka, 2012).

One serious flaw in obtaining justice in the United States under the auspices of the UN Declaration is the fact that the United States has ratified only that portion of the document that is consistent with the US Constitution, in other words, the recognition of political and civil rights.

In 1977, then US President Jimmy Carter, hoping to correct this omission, signed the UN International Covenant on Economic, Social, and Cultural Rights. Nevertheless this document, which has been signed by 145 nations, still awaits US Senate ratification (Food First, 2002). The wait may be a long one.

As a global profession, social work is concerned with economic and social rights as well as with civil rights. (When people are hungry, in fact, their concern with personal liberties is apt to be slight.) As a global profession, social work can be expected increasingly to look to human rights documents such as the Universal Declaration as a blueprint for policy practice. The standard is there. Consider Article 25, for example:

1. Everyone has the right to a standard of living adequate for the health and well-being of himself and of his family, including food, clothing, housing and medical care and necessary social services, and the right to security in the event of unemployment, sickness,

disability, widowhood, old age or other lack of livelihood in circumstances beyond his control.

2. Motherhood and childhood are entitled to special care and assistance. All children, whether born in or out of wedlock, shall enjoy the same social protections.

Three broad categories of rights are provided in the Declaration: (1) economic and cultural rights; (2) protection against discrimination based on race, color, sex, language, religion, and political opinion; and (3) civil and political rights against the arbitrary powers of the state. Those articles of the Declaration concerned with economic, social, and cultural rights range from the less urgent rights of "rest, leisure, and reasonable limitation of working hours and periodic holidays with pay" (Article 24) to the more fundamental rights of food, housing, health care, work, and social security (Article 25). The fact that these rights are not included in the US Constitution (but in many European constitutions) has hindered the American people in their claims to basic social and economic benefits.

Alisa Watkinson (2001), writing from a Canadian perspective, argues that the inclusion of human rights documents and legal decisions arising from them are an essential part of social work education. Human rights laws, as Watkinson indicates, "provide a valuable theoretical and practical base for assisting in social change" (p. 271). Because Canada was a signatory (unlike the United States) to the Covenant on Economic, Social, and Political Rights, social workers in that country can use the document as a touchstone by which to examine social policy and to hold the government accountable. All the provinces in Canada as well as the federal government, in fact, have human rights legislation that is administered by a Human Rights Commission. For Canadian social workers, as Watkinson argues, human rights laws can be a valuable tool for advocacy for social and economic justice within the era of globalization.

The NASW (2015) strongly promotes US ratification of the Universal Declaration in its entirety and critical UN treaties such as the Covenant on Economic, Social and Cultural Rights, and the Convention on the Rights of the Child. NASW also urges passage of the Convention on the Elimination of All Forces of Discrimination against Women (CEDAW) which President Jimmy Carter signed but which the Senate never has ratified.

The IFSW established a Human Rights Commission to ensure that the organization maintains a human rights orientation in all their activities. The Commission advocates for the release of social workers who are incarcerated because of their work and others at risk of torture or death throughout the world. The Commission works closely with the United Nations Commission on Human Rights (www.ifsw.org). The IFSW commission also has an official liaison to Amnesty International.

## UNITED NATIONS CONVENTIONS IN ACTION

In this section, we discuss International Convention on the Elimination of All Forms of Racial Discrimination (CERD), and CEDAW, as well as human rights and war crimes.

The writer and researcher Louise Erdrich has recommended using a human rights lens to address newly recognized social problems such as violence against women (2012). Rather than viewing such violence as a relationship or psychological issue, social workers can reframe the anti-woman attacks from a human rights perspective. Such reframing brings the force of international law to bear on governments that allow for such violence and encourages the development of resources such as shelters for abuse victims. In "The Round House" Erdrich narrates a fictional story about the devastating impact on an American Indian family of the rape of the mother. Erdrich adds a section on her actual research before writing the fictional story, research into the disproportionate number of rapes of American Indian women and girls, and the shockingly high rate of European American (white) perpetrators. In her afterword she states the following:

> The tangle of laws that hinder prosecution of rape cases on many reservations still exists. "Maze of Injustice," a 2009 report by Amnesty International, included the following statistics: 1 in 3 Native women will be raped in her lifetime (and that figure is certainly higher as Native women often do not report rape); 86% of rapes and sexual assaults upon Native women are perpetrated by non-Native men; few are prosecuted. In 2010, then North Dakota senator Byron Dorgan sponsored the Tribal Law and Order Act. In signing the act into law, President Barack Obama called the situation "an assault on our national conscience." (p. 319)

Finally, in 2015, despite extensive opposition by Republicans, an update was added to The Violence Against Women Act to protect Native women. Now, for the first time, tribal law enforcement will have the ability to intervene in cases of physical and sexual assault and prosecute outsiders who commit crimes on the reservation (Bendery, 2015).

The rights contained in the Declaration and the two covenants were further elaborated in such legal documents as the CERD, adopted by the UN General Assembly in 1969, which declares dissemination of ideas based on racial superiority or hatred as being punishable by law; the CEDAW, adopted by the General Assembly in 1979, covering measures to be taken for eliminating discrimination against women in political and public life, education, employment, health, marriage and family; and the Convention on the Rights of the Child, adopted by the General Assembly in 1989, which lays down guarantees in terms of the child's human rights. Of these important initiatives, the United States has ratified only the Elimination of All Forms of Racial Discrimination.

In 2002 and 2016 however, major milestones were reached. In 2002, at a ceremony at the United Nations the last two of the 60 nations needed to formally ratify the treaty, the International Criminal Court became a reality. The creation of this new war-crimes tribunal, the world's first permanent such tribunal is hailed by human rights activists but strongly opposed by the United States (Lederer, 2002). The US objection is based on the fear that American citizens would be subject to politically motivated prosecutions. Then in 2016, the first successful trial for a member of ISIS who led the destruction of monuments in Mali is of cultural significance not just in the region but to the world. The trial led to the definition of cultural destruction as a war crime.

America's reluctance to be judged in accordance with international law cannot shield it from the scrutiny of non-governmental organizations (NGOs) such as Amnesty International (AI) and Human Rights Watch (Amnesty International, Maze of Injustice, 2009). A significant development in recent years is the fact that Amnesty International and Human Rights Watch investigations are given much more media attention than in the past in their documentation of human rights abuses. AI today devotes much attention to prison conditions, the "cruel, inhuman or degrading treatment or punishment" mentioned in Article 5 of the United Nations Universal Declaration of Human Rights (Refer to Appendix A).

Each year AI presents its findings on the countries of the world in terms of violations of citizens by the state. More than any other human rights monitoring organizations, AI (like Human Rights Watch) can make a reasonable claim to being politically non-partisan. Accordingly, their relentless research findings give meaning to the concept of universal standards of humanitarianism. A disturbing new report by Amnesty International (2017) exposes the Syrian government's calculated campaign of extrajudicial executions by mass hangings at Saydnaya Prison. Over 13,000 political prisoners are thought to have been killed at this prison.

The dangerous complexity of the situation in Syria has been identified by the global economics writer, George Friedman (2016) as the "pivot" of tensions between Europe, Russia, the United States, and Iran. The human rights violations in Syria such as bombing humanitarian aid trucks and gassing non-combatants, including children, occurs at a time when the so called leader of the government, Bashar-al-Assad, seems impervious to criticism of his brutal regime which blatantly violates human rights.

The seven-year conflict in the state of Borno on the Nigerian border has lost headlines to Syria and the ravages of war crimes committed by Bashar-al-Assad's government. In 2014 nearly 300 school girls were abducted, raped and forced to marry. Only recently have survivors been able to tell their story. In his chilling essay, "The World Is a Thriving Slaughter-House," Roger Rosenblatt (2016) records the experiences and testimony of people surviving ethnic cleansing in Bosnia and Rwanda, abduction by Boko Haram in Borno, Hiroshima nuclear bombing, killing on the Palestine/Israeli border, death in Brussels, and massacre in San Bernardino, California and Southern France.

Rosenblatt (2016) recognizes terrorism as a new and more intensely personal form of war, and one that has brought new levels of slaughter (such as the deaths of thousands of Tutsi children in Rwanda). In this new form of intensely personal combat we have inadequate concepts to explain the surprise attacks. Rosenblatt asks, How is it that suicide bombers can kill innocents checking in at an airport, or sipping coffee in a neighborhood café? He goes on:

> My sifting of news proceeds, and news arrives of the explosions at the Brussels airport, a wave of bombings in Baghdad, an attack in Bangladesh. Could anybody have seen all this coming back then (when war was declared with boundaries)? I doubt it. Generals aren't the only ones who fight the last war. Students and observers of world conflicts have been accustomed to conceiving of wars, no matter how deadly, as contained, with international powers fighting, even during a world war, in discrete theaters. But the world war we are in now—and it is that—is informal and seems uncontainable. (p. 95)

Governments are not entitled to respond to terror with terror. They are obliged at all times to act within the framework of international human rights and humanitarian law. The people who organize and perpetrate bombings of airports and bus stations in Brussels or Tel Aviv or Bali, who ambush and kill civilians in Burundi and Aleppo, or who take hostages in Paris must be brought to justice in accordance with standards of fair trial. So too must the Israeli soldiers who carry out unlawful killings in the Occupied Territories, the Indonesian police who torture in Aceh and Papua, the Russian security forces who rape villagers in Chechnya. The United States is under critical scrutiny for its stand not to participate in the International Criminal Court.

Social work and the peace movement have a longstanding connection in relation to laws that transcend borders and peace-making. Jane Addams, the founding mother of social work was a pacifist who saw herself as a citizen of the world. Addams believed that violence was used because people lacked knowledge of other ways to fight injustice (Farrell, 1967). Social work has continued to have a strong peace movement within its ranks. According to the NASW (2016) statement on peace and social justice on its website, "The reliance by many nations on military force as a prime instrument of foreign policy has jeopardized the entire world. In the United States, the preoccupation with national defense so permeates the structure of society that livelihoods, civil liberties, and values have become inextricably entwined with military preparedness" (2nd paragraph). Social workers have a moral responsibility to work toward redirections in federal spending with its emphasis on military buildup and toward spending to build a more equitable and just society.

Under the US Patriot Act of 2001, passed in response to September 11, the Attorney General of the United States was given unprecedented powers to detain non-citizens on national security grounds. Under this act non-citizens suspected of terrorist acts could be held in custody indefinitely (Human Rights Watch, 2002a). New orders by the president permitted military jurisdiction over non-citizens and military commissions to hear cases that were not subject to the rules governing due process safeguards required at regular military courts-martial. Such safeguards as presumption of innocence, protection against forced confessions, and the right of appeal would no longer apply. Over time, as new technologies were introduced, the law led to roving wiretaps and the much-criticized collection and storage of US citizens' phone and Internet data and mandates for communications companies to hand over that data (Ali & Abdullah, 2016). Sharp criticism has been mounted by civil liberties groups against the human rights violations being practiced under this act.

Civil liberties do not count for much in a warfare state; the rights of people who look like the enemies count for little as well. Just as peace and social justice are interdependent, so the impact of war is brutalizing on all those who are caught in its web. Not only the tragic loss of life and traumatized lives, but the enormous drain on the world's dwindling natural resources are antithetical to global social welfare and security as well as to the central purpose of the social work profession (George Friedman, 2016). Even in the face of overt terrorist attacks on the United States, it is vital to work through international organizations to reduce violence against innocent civilians (Healy & Link, 2012). Following September 11, a war mentality has ensued and continued in a widening arc of references to both national and international acts of violence as "terrorism." In an article entitled "The Troubling New Face of America," Nobel Prize recipient, Jimmy Carter (2002), expressed his concern:

> Fundamental changes are taking place in the historical policies of the United States with regard to human rights, our role in the community of nations and the Middle East peace process—largely without definitive debates (except at times within the administration). (A 31)

In fact, however, wars and terrorism invariably have a dramatic effect on the systems of law and justice. In the American Civil War, President Lincoln curtailed many of the citizens' constitutional rights, an act for which he was greatly criticized. Restrictions on freedom of the press have characterized more recent anti-terrorist operations. In the national interest, many of the traditional civil liberties are suspended. Britain, for example, responded to the Irish Republican Army's (IRA) bombing attacks with repressive measures that resulted in claims of human rights violations (Fairchild, 1993). Imprisonment of suspected terrorists without trial, searches and seizures without warrants, and suspension of the right to remain silent under questioning ensued. Amnesty International published a report on political killings of IRA suspects by government officials in Northern Ireland. The US Patriot Act passed in 2001 thus takes its place in a long line of actions associated with fear of internal strife. In the United States, efforts to tighten Homeland Security paralleled mobilization for a "pre-emptive strike" on an enemy nation and assassination of national leaders who posed a threat, and these policies continue into the second decade of the 21st century.

During wartime, the standards of ordinary conduct concerning respect for human life, personal dignity, and personal property give way. Under the exigencies of war, horrible crimes against humanity are sometimes tolerated in the interests of defeat of the enemy or in wreaking revenge for atrocities inflicted by the other side. In wartime, the enemy is demonized; soldiers are trained to kill, and normal inhibitions against violence are loosened, including genocide. From their outset, according to the encyclopedia, war crime trials were dismissed by critics as "victor's justice" because only individuals from defeated countries were prosecuted.

What constitutes a war crime; how can it be differentiated from ordinary combat? War crimes are acts of war determined to be characterized as atrocities by international oversight bodies. According to the entry, "War Crime" in the Encyclopedia Britannica (2015), the term war crime has been used in a very imprecise fashion; modern definitions are more expansive than earlier, criminalizing atrocities by civilians as well as by military personnel. Included under the rubric of war crimes are crimes against humanity or political, racial, and religious persecution of civilians. Genocide, or the attempt to wipe out an entire population or ethnic group, as took place in Nazi Germany, Nigeria, Cambodia, Rwanda, and Yugoslavia, is the most obvious form of crimes against humanity.

Throughout history, most nations have "turned a blind eye" to genocidal campaigns, only becoming involved as refugees migrated across borders. Despite the UN Genocide Convention in 1948, the West, until recently, had remained as reluctant to respond to genocidal campaigns as it was initially regarding the situation of Turkish Armenians and the Nazi-led Holocaust. The reluctance in a nation that has long been sensitive to issues of human rights and genocide, given their own history, apparently was due to fears of upsetting Turkey and the 3.5 million Germans of Turkish origin living in Germany today (Kessler, 2015). Now, in a major reversal in Turkey's top trading partner in the European Union, Germany has joined other nations and institutions including France, the European parliament, and Pope Francis in using the term. Sometimes nations that were involved in persecutions of their people (such as Saddam Hussein's massacre of Iraqi Kurds) continued to receive military and other assistance, as Power suggests.

Since World War II, war crime trials were conducted by an international tribunal in Nuremburg, Tokyo, and more recently at The Hague regarding Rwanda and former Yugoslavia. In none of these trials were individuals relieved of criminal liability for war crimes committed under orders from authorities ("War Crime," 2015). The general procedure set by the Nuremburg trials is the hearing of cases against the smaller number of principals responsible for the atrocities. The advantage of an international tribunal is in sending a message worldwide that such violence is widely condemned and in the image of impartiality. The "power of shame" can play a role both as an enforcement tool and in helping to impart justice to the victim population.

The International Criminal Court, has jurisdiction over crimes against humanity for those countries signing the treaty (Human Rights Watch, 2015), and as of 2015, 90 countries have ratified this treaty. Unfortunately, the United States under the Obama administration expressed opposition to the existence of the world court due to special concerns about the liability of US soldiers at war. This concern has still to be addressed. Moreover, special arrangements were made with the United Nations to protect US "peacekeepers" from accountability to the international body for human rights violations. Despite this US opposition, however, the establishment of such a world court of justice, a dream ever since the United Nations was established, is a major victory for world peace and human rights.

Amnesty International has played an important role in lobbying for the ICC. To learn of the human rights violations in any particular country, simply go to Amnesty International's annual report, contained in most academic libraries, or on the *Internet* to www.amnesty.org and, under search, type in the name of the country. Type in Turkey, for example, and you get: "Turkey: End Sexual Torture against Women in Custody!" The report describes the plight of Kurdish women in police custody, among other abuses. Check out the USA and you will find among the violations, the detention without charge of foreign nationals captured in Afghanistan and still held at Guantanamo Bay, Cuba. Other topics covered include detentions of Muslim men of Arab descent in the United States, conditions in super-maximum prisons, and the death penalty. Under violations by the Canadian government, you will find a description of police violence against Native Canadians and denial of rights to asylum seekers, and readers of the Amnesty website will see these violations in detail.

Another recent development of consequence is the recognition of rape of the enemy's women—a common occurrence during and after a war—as a war crime. The International War Crimes Tribunal in The Hague took a revolutionary step when three Bosnian soldiers were convicted of rape and sexual enslavement as crimes against humanity. Women's rights activists participated in every major United Nations preparatory meeting on the ICC (Human Rights Watch, 2014). Rape of the enemy's women is a complete violation of human rights and a terrible part of war. Its aftermath under conditions of military occupation—for example the African terrorists fighting under Boko Haram, abducting school girls in 2014—persist through the birth of children and the deadening of the spirit. The rape that accompanies war involves both an act of aggression and humiliation against a conquered people.

Law professor Adrien Wing (2013), herself a descendant of Confederate General Beauregard and one of his slave-mistresses, uses the term "spirit injury" to refer to a psychological phenomenon characteristic of women who are subjected to sexual violation through slavery or as captives of war. In an earlier publication, Wing and Merchan (1993) drew a gripping parallel between the ethnic cleansing and forced impregnation in Bosnia or Rwanda and the history of rape and miscegenation in the American South. On six key attributes related to spirit injury, which Wing (2013) defines as "the slow death of the psyche, of the soul, and of the identity of the individual" and of the group, Bosnia and Rwanda share a common ground with the pre-Civil War American South (p. 186). These traits are rape as defilement not only of the individual woman but of a whole culture; rape as silence as the women internalize their experience of oppression, rendering them more vulnerable to males within their own group; rape as sexuality with raped women seen as promiscuous and impure; rape as emasculation of men due to their sense of helplessness to protect their wives and daughters; rape as trespass on the "property" rights of men, most pronounced under slavery where the women were the property of their white masters, as were the racially mixed offspring as well; and rape as pollution of the victim and of her children born as a result of nonconsensual sex.

In the name of victory and the power of the gun, war provides men with a tacit license to rape as reported by Dionne Searcey (2016) in "Boko Haram Rages in Nigeria, but the World's Eyes Are Elsewhere":

> The crisis spawned by Boko Haram has drawn hundreds of thousands of people to a relatively little-known city in Nigeria that has finally become safe enough for them to wait out an end to the awful, deadly war.
>
> With villagers from the countryside pouring in, it is almost as though the entire city, Maiduguri, has become a sprawling refugee camp.
>
> Tented government encampments dot the exurbs where people wait for bags of food to arrive. Once-quaint neighborhoods overflow with cardboard hovels filled with young children who are lucky to eat three meals a day. Squatters live in old university buildings or crammed inside homes with relatives or kind strangers. Old men sit along busy streets asking for money. At the massive Monday Market, women sell handfuls of fruit or jewelry, hoping to earn enough to pay for a meal. (Dionne Searcey, September 22, 2016. Retrieved from: www.nytimes.com/2016/09/23/world/aftrica/boko-haram-terrorism)

That the ICC has come into force today as a potentially powerful instrument for protecting women's rights is a testament to the mass networking and courage of women's rights activists throughout the world (Human Rights Watch, 2012). The injury to women and their families in war time can be seen as well in uprootedness; mental trauma; lack of food, potable water, and electricity; health problems stemming from exposure to chemicals such as uranium, violence, and sexual assault in refugee camps; and the numbers resorting to sex work to feed their children. Since women are so often the victims of war, it is essential that their voices be heard (UN Women, 2016). Work with the children of refugees is important too in resettlement to help them realize they are now safe. See Figure 6.2, which shows such children listening to a story at a refugee center in Kentucky.

We can credit the United Nations for its expression of political commitment to women's special needs in war-torn societies. With 80% of the refugees now women and children, it is time for women to be at the forefront of peacemaking following war and of humanitarian relief efforts during war. This is according to global affairs expert Izabella Watts (2016), who has worked with UN Women. According to Watts, the resources allocated to the relief efforts are entirely inadequate to meet the needs of women, given their high rate of victimization. Reports from the Democratic Republic of the Congo, for example, estimate that up to 40% of women and girls have been victims of war-related sexual violence. Such conflict, as Watts indicates, victimizes women in three ways—first by the offense; second, after the crime with no access to justice or health and psychological assistance; and third, by segregation within the local community and shame for families and a loss of dignity. This is especially true of victims of sexual assault, since often their families refuse to take them back.

One model program that helps such rape victims find their way back to their families or to a safe place to live is operated by the International Rescue Committee (IRC). Highly rated by charity experts, the IRC has worked all over the world in war zones. Its workers most recently have set up a reception center on the Greek island of Lesbos, where many Syrians seeking refuge in Europe land after traversing the dangerous route at sea from Turkey (Bernard, 2015).

Save the Children is another highly respected organization which focuses on the needs of children in war zones. The organization supports 55 schools in northern Syria as well as health care facilities and provides emergency care for pregnant women inside Syria (Bernard, 2015). It also runs child-friendly spaces for children affected by the conflict as well, which provide a sense of normalcy.

**FIGURE 6.2.** Flora Templeton Stuart, a Bowling Green lawyer, volunteers her time to read stories to children of refugees at the International Center in Bowling Green, Kentucky. Photo by Crystal Akers. Permission of Albert Mbanfu.

Often the subject of news reports, Doctors Without Borders is run by courageous doctors who provide medical services in war zones. This organization operates in Syria, where some staff members have been killed in bombings, and in Lebanon, Jordan, and Iraq, providing vaccinations, maternity care, burn treatment, and emergency care for wounds (Bernard, 2015). The medics even have operated search-and-rescue ships in the Mediterranean, which, to date, have rescued more than 18,000 people attempting the voyage to Europe.

To grasp the extent of global human rights crises, ponder the following headlines:

"Australia's Hidden Refugees Embrace Art to Reveal Their Plight" (Smyth, 2017, *Financial Times*)

"Boko Haram Rages in Nigeria, but the World's Eyes Are Elsewhere" (Searcey, 2016, *New York Times*)

"India Records Huge Spike in 'Honor Killings' in 2015" (Associated Press, 2016)

"More Female Inmates Allege Sexual Assault at Lackawanna County Prison" (Morgan-Besecker & Singleton, 2016, *The Times-Tribune*)

"Women Travel Migrant Trail with Risk" (Bennhold, *New York Times*, 2016)

"Female Genital Cutting: Not Just an African Problem" (Belluck & Cochrane, *New York Times*, 2016)

"Christians of Egypt Hit by ISIS in Palm Sunday Bombings" (Malsin, *Time*, 2017)

Even though evidence of research and concern for women's rights is building, the United States stands alone among Western nations in its reluctance to ratify CEDAW. President Jimmy Carter signed it, but the US Senate has never ratified it. Conservatives, as Goodman (2002) suggests, worry about the destruction of the family. If the United States would join other nations in endorsing this treaty, it would provide a tool for women fighting for their lives across the world. "Women from Columbia to Rwanda have used the treaty as a standard to rewrite laws on inheritance and domestic abuse, to change the patterns of education and employment," as Goodman indicates (p. 15A).

The Beijing Fourth World Conference in 1995 marked a milestone in women's rights history as women of the world let go of their cultural differences and stood united against anti-woman violence, whether in the home or community. Still the horror stories persist—the infanticides in China of unwanted girls, the public stoning of rape victims in Pakistan (Dobiesz, 2017; Stewart, 2014). There is a saying in Russia, "If he beats you, it means he loves you" (Litvinova, 2016). Russian men who beat or rape their wives or partners are unlikely to face prosecution. With a population nearly half the size of the United States, Russian women are murdered by family members at ten times the American rate. But the highest suicide rate for women in the world occurs in China. World Bank researchers found that young, rural Chinese women are killing themselves at an alarming rate of 500 per day (Ren, 2016). Arranged marriages are still common there, and the young brides are expected to wait on their mothers-in-law as servants.

Domestic violence is the leading cause of female injury in almost every country in the world and is typically defined by the state as a private matter or simply ignored. According to WHO (2016), based on extensive surveys of women from 80 countries from around the world, around one in three (35%) of women report having been physically and/or sexually assaulted by a partner. The prevalence estimates range from 23.2% in high-income countries (including the United States) and 24.6% in the Western Pacific region to 37% in the Eastern Mediterranean region, and 37.7% in the South-East Asia region. Such violence is now regarded by the United Nations as a worldwide public health problem.

In the past, violence against women in the home was viewed as a private matter; today the international community has recognized such violence against women as a human rights issue and holds the state responsible to take steps to protect women (Amnesty International, 2015). In Amnesty International's 2015 Annual Report, Salil Shetty states, "Your rights are in jeopardy: they are being treated with utter contempt by many governments around the world" (www.ai.org). The report states that more than 60 million people were displaced from their homes by war in 2015.

Such collective support and attention, including by social workers around the world, also sees some positive outcomes. For example, in 2015, after years of pressure from Amnesty International and its supporters, Shell's Nigerian subsidiary announced a $75 million settlement to 15,600 farmers and fishermen in Bodo, Nigeria (Rebmann, 2015). Their lives had been devastated by two large Shell oil spills in 2008 and 2009. The quiet actions of women activists in Ogborodo, Nigeria, against Chevron Texaco's terminal also produced agreements in terms of access to clean water and employment a few years earlier. (In the United States, victims of violence sometimes turn to the criminal justice system for assistance, and it's this system to which we now turn).

## CRIMINAL JUSTICE IN THE UNITED STATES

Although the United States human rights tradition is weak in terms of providing economic rights and security to its citizens, its provisions of individual rights and freedoms over the arbitrary abuse of power by the state is an area in which most Americans are justifiably proud. The concepts of human rights, liberty, and equality are deeply engrained in American history; their roots go back to the founding of the American Republic. Out of the revolt against the British colonizers came various documents expounding on "the rights of man," including the Declaration of Independence, that held life, liberty, and the pursuit of happiness as self-evident, and later, the US Constitution (Reichert, 2011). The first ten amendments, the Bill of Rights, specify certain civil and political rights such as the basic freedoms of religion, speech, and the press and the right to counsel in all criminal cases, and provide guarantees against unreasonable search and seizure, against violations of due process in criminal proceedings, speedy, fair trial, impartial jury, and prohibits cruel and unusual punishment.

In the United States, there are two strains of thought and tradition that in some ways are at war with each other but in other ways are juxtaposed or blended. We are referring to respect for individual rights and dignity, as previously discussed, on the one hand, and the punitive tradition, on the other.

*Moralism* is one of the cardinal American values so difficult for US citizens to explain to outsiders (see chapter 2). The death penalty, harsh mandatory sentencing laws for drug users and dealers, the exposure of inmates to violence within the prison—these are just a few examples that come to mind. The absence of prevention measures, such as strict gun control laws, censorship of violence in video games and mass media portrayals, and affordable substance abuse treatment also sets the United States apart from other industrialized nations. By any standard, but especially within European eyes, the United States is considered a highly punitive nation (Lacey, 2016). Although the crime rate has been dropping palpably for years, media-generated horror stories have instilled fear and anger in the American public and led to a prison-industrial complex such as the world has never known.

During the 1960s, rehabilitation was the primary goal of corrections. Programs in counseling, education, and training were set up for the purpose of "correcting" inmates' behavior to help them lead law-abiding lives upon their return to society (Phelps, 2011). The enthusiasm, however, was short-lived. Research findings that seemed to point to the ineffectiveness of treatment were used by conservatives to disparage the belief that criminals could be rehabilitated, and over the next two decades punishment was back in full force. Gradually, ideals were forgotten, and the reformatories and custodial prisons were merged into the medium-security design that we have today. These dramatic increases in the correctional population were largely the product of a series of sentencing and policy changes at the federal and state levels. Key among these changes was the move to determinant sentencing with sentencing guidelines and rubrics, mandatory minimum sentencing laws that mandated tough sentences for drug offenses, habitual offender laws, and the abolition of parole in the federal system.

Human rights concerns enter the picture when the severity of the punishment is out of proportion to the offense and when there is inequity in how the laws are made and enforced. In the United States, both of these conditions apply. First, mandatory minimum sentencing laws, introduced in the 1980s, removed judicial discretion and created a system in which drug offenders, in many cases, are serving more time in prison than are violent offenders. Second, human rights abuses occur on a regular basis within the US prison system; the erosion of offenders' constitutional rights is unceasing.

The public today is aware of these injustices. That is the good news; attitudes are changing, reinforced by a rehabilitation focus, relaxing of mandatory minimum sentencing requirements, and mass commuting of sentences for nonviolent drug offenses under the Obama administration. National surveys show that two-thirds of the public favor treatment, not jail, for people in trouble due to heroin or cocaine use (Pew Research Center, 2014). Just 26% think the government's focus should be on prosecuting users of such hard drugs. And most states are acting to revise drug laws. Between 2009 and 2013, 40 states took some action to ease their drug laws according to a separate analysis of data by the Pew Research Center. Compared to previous years, the more recent survey shows a significant liberalization in attitudes. See Box 6.4 for the facts at a glance, information from the Bureau of Justice Statistics.

Box 6.4 reveals some very interesting trends and has some important political implications. The fact that crime rates are down, significantly down, while the incarceration rate continues to rise is reflective of the carryover of punitiveness related to the war on drugs. Note the decline in the numbers of men murdered by partner violence is not matched by a comparable decline in the homicides of female intimates (see van Wormer & Bartollis, 2014). The theory that makes the most sense is that women's shelters are giving battered women an alternative to resorting to violence, a chance to escape. Many do not escape, however, as the statistics on female intimate homicide tragically bear out.

### BOX 6.4 US Criminal Justice Statistics

OVERVIEW OF CRIME RATES

- The violent crime rate today is only half what it was in 1995; it has decreased for all races.
- Guns were used in 71.5% of homicides in 2015; 9,616 people were murdered by firearms, which was 40% of the total killed. Most firearm victims died by suicide.
- Persons 12 to 24 years of age sustained the most violent victimization.
- In 2015, most (78.8%) of the 10,608 murder victims for whom supplemental data were received were male. Most male victims were victimized by strangers; most females by intimates or friends.
- Of the murder victims for whom race was known, 52.3% were black, 43.5% were white, and 2.7% were of other races.
- The FBI's hate crime statistics show that around half of the victims were targeted on the basis of race, around 9% for ethnicity, 18% on the grounds of sexual orientation, around 20% on the basis of religion (most were Jewish; 21.9% were Muslim), and 1.6% were targeted because of their gender identity.

INTIMATE PARTNER VIOLENCE (HOMOSEXUAL RELATIONSHIPS ARE INCLUDED)

- 1,005 women and 265 men were killed by an intimate partner in 2015 (FBI, table 10).
- The rate of intimate violence against both men and women fell significantly since 2000.
- Between 1976 and 2015, the number of males killed by an intimate partner declined from 1,357 to 265; the number of female murder victims declined only from 1,600 to 1,005.

CORRECTIONS

- There were 2.1 million people incarcerated in jails and prisons in 2015; the numbers declined in the federal prisons due to a release of drug offenders who were given excessively long sentences.
- Fifty percent of federal inmates and 16% of state prisoners were convicted drug offenders.
- The rate of incarceration in the United States is the highest in the world.
- An estimated 3% of all black males in the population were in prison or jail, compared to 1% of Hispanics and under 1% of whites in 2015.
- Among Hispanics, 57.7% of federal inmates were convicted drug offenders, and 26% were sentenced for immigration offenses.
- Women are only 7% of the prison population but the percentage increase in women inmates continues to surpass that of male inmates. Fifty percent of the female prison population were white and 21% were black.
- Black females were around 2 times more likely to be imprisoned than white females across all age groups. Among females in state prisons, one in four were convicted drug offenders.
- Twenty people were executed in 2016, a significant decline since a high point in 1998; still there are almost 3,000 people on death row of whom 44% are white, 43% black, and 10% Hispanic (Death Penalty Information Center, 2016).

Sources: Unless otherwise indicated the sources for these statistics are the Federal Bureau of Investigation (FBI, 2016, fall), Uniform Crime Reports, *Crimes in the United States 2015*, Washington, DC: US Department of Justice; FBI (2016), *Hate Crime Statistics 2015*; Bureau of Justice Statistics (BJS, 2016, December). *Prisoners in 2015*, Washington, DC: US Department of Justice.

## THE JUVENILE JUSTICE SYSTEM

Over the years, following the reforms inherent in the founding of the first juvenile court in 1899 to provide non-punitive treatment of children in trouble with the law and victims of child abuse and neglect, the philosophy of the juvenile court has moved in the direction of greater legalization. Although the providing of civil rights protections to juveniles was a progressive and much needed development, from the 1980s up to the early 21st century the impetus toward treatment and diversion gave way in most states to legislation allowing for reduction in the age of criminal responsibility for serious crimes. Juvenile cases were often transferred to adult criminal courts. Although fewer youths under the age of 18 are being tried as adults than formerly, thousands are still being prosecuted as if they were fully grown, according to The Sentencing Project (2015), an advocacy group for criminal justice reform. Although generally juveniles convicted in adult courts serve their time in juvenile institutions until they reach the age of 18, when they are moved to adult prisons, over 5,000 youths today are confined in adult jails and prisons.

There has been much improvement in the juvenile justice system since 2000 with a renewed emphasis on treatment, on gender-specific approaches for females, and in avoidance of institutionalization when it is not necessary. Research has shown, according to the Sentencing Project (2015), that incarceration of youths increases their chance of reoffending. Nevertheless, in many states placement in juvenile facilities is the norm and regularly used for youths who are confined for simple assault, property offenses, drug offenses, public order offenses, status offenses, and technical violations. African American youth are 4.3 times as likely as white youth to be committed. Latino youth are 1.6 times as likely, and Native youth are 3.7 times as likely to be committed as are whites.

In light of the underfunding, understaffing, and racism evident in current juvenile justice policies, the NASW (2015b) has issued a policy statement recommendation that the processing and treatment of children and youths who enter the juvenile justice system be differentiated from the treatment of adults through every phase of contact. Further recommendations are for oversight to ensure non-discrimination of minority and indigent youth, the provision for family services, and a reliance on restorative justice practices including restitution and community service. (See the section on restorative justice later in this chapter.) Many of the youths have backgrounds of abuse and neglect in their families; research shows, according to NASW, that such children are 11 times more likely to be arrested for violence and criminal behavior than are those from more stable homes. Concern is also expressed that the school system has become criminalized with high suspension rates for students, especially for African Americans, and that they and Latino youths are incarcerated at a much higher rate proportionately than are whites.

As indicated in chapter 10, the United States, one of two nations to refuse to sign the Convention on the Rights of the Child (United Nations, 1989), is in clear violation of a number of its principles. Article 3, for example, states that in all actions concerning the child, including in courts of law, the best interest of the child shall be a primary consideration. And Article 37 states that no child shall be subjected to cruel, inhuman, or degrading treatment or punishment.

## ADULT CORRECTIONS

Private corporations compete with state governments for lucrative prison contracts. Major correctional corporations are large political lobbying groups; profits are tied in to the incarceration boom. Their representatives lobby for keeping the prisons full such as through abolishing parole, legislation restrictions on lawsuits, and maximum minimum sentencing. When private companies run prisons, hiring is of minimum wage workers to reduce costs. Their economic incentive is to keep the beds full by any means. The prison industrial complex is expanding in Europe, especially in the United Kingdom. One major advantage for the government in privately owned and operated prisons is that it exempts the state from lawsuits in the cases of maltreatment and wrongful death (see Volokh, 2014).

The United States ratified the Convention against the Torture and Other Cruel, Inhuman, or Degrading Treatment or Punishment in 1994. The US government only signed this treaty with the stipulation that individuals would be given no more rights than those provided by the US Constitution. This restriction has important implications for prisoners who are mistreated in the custody of state. While women in prison have been subjected to gross violations at the hands of correctional officers (especially males), incarcerated men have often found themselves in grave danger from fellow inmates.

The prison industry too, especially in its privatized dimension, has been a significant force in blocking criminal justice reform. The more private prisons are built, the more lobbying of politicians will take place to keep the prison construction going and to keep the beds full. "Build it and they will come," goes the popular slogan. The prisons today have become warehouses for the poor and unemployed, and jails have become the new mental asylums. In 2016, however, the most prominent private prison operation, Corrections Corporation of America, in expectation of a shrinking prison population in the federal system and in response to a decision by the government to phase out reliance on private prisons in the federal system, was moving community corrections instead (Barrett, 2016). Under the Trump administration, no such move is necessary.

## Detention of Refugees and Immigrants

We start with Australia, where asylum seekers arriving in boats from all over the world have been denied entrance to the country and detained in appalling conditions on Manus Island near New Guinea. Several refugees have died in the holding camps where over 900 men live in cramped compounds with inadequate medical care (Smyth, 2017). To aid their psychological survival the detainees are embracing the arts: writing articles and books, drawing cartoons, and even making a full-length film shot on smuggled equipment.

The United States relies on detention centers where asylum seekers are held until they come before a judge to present their case. Corrections Corporation of America (now renamed CoreCivic) operated under a $1 billion contract with the Obama administration (for Immigration and Customs Enforcement) to build a massive detention facility for women and children seeking asylum (Harlan, 2016). The contract was signed out of a sense of urgency as Central American asylum seekers, mostly from El Salvador, Guatemala, and Honduras escaping the gang and drug-related violence that have grown so rampant that their murder rates are now three of the world's five highest, according to UN data. The four-year contract was a boon for the private company, which gets the money regardless of how many people are detained at the facility. By 2016, over 33,000 people were confined in these facilities (Reuters, 2016).

Immigrant rights advocates have long criticized private detention facilities for the inhumane conditions provided and restrictions on the detainees' access to lawyers. Reports of abuse have been rampant. Female immigrants, including refugees in detention, are a group of women who have suffered serious human rights violations. Even before the war on terrorism was declared, brutal treatment of detained political refugees was the norm.

Following a series of scandals with these prisons, plans had been made under the Obama administration to end the contracting with these private prison corporations. But all of this changed following the election of 2016. Now CoreCivic, a generous contributor to President

Trump's campaign, is in a position to expand rather than shrink its immigrant detention centers (Schuppe, 2017). Construction of prisons to hold citizens who violate the nation's drug laws is expected to boom as well.

## Impact of the War on Drugs

First declared by President Ronald Reagan as a public relations strategy to rally middle America against inner city crime, America's war on drugs has been fought with greater and greater zeal (and economic support) by each successive administration (van Wormer & Davis, 2018). Today's zero tolerance of certain drugs has culminated in a war on drugs of vast proportions: A military crusade in drug-supplying countries is matched on the home front by the incarceration of over one million people for drug-related crimes. Meanwhile, the sale of illegal drugs has become an underground enterprise entailing high risks, violence, corruption, and unconscionable profits.

That the national anti-drug policy has not been a success is a generally acknowledged fact. Consider the following: Afghanistan resumed its opium poppy trade since the overthrow of the Taliban regime and US occupation; the percentage of American teens who have used marijuana is about three times that of teens in the EU; and there is no decline in the supply of heroin from Latin America and other drugs that continue to flow north of the border (van Wormer & Davis, 2018).

Even though drug use is spread fairly evenly across the population, three-fourths of those locked up are minorities. Black people comprise 31% of those arrested for drug law violations and nearly 40% of those incarcerated in state or federal prison for drug law violations (Drug Policy Alliance, 2016). Similarly, Latinos comprise 17% of those arrested for drug law violations and comprise 20% of those in state prisons for drug offenses and 37% of those in federal prisons for drug offenses. Families are greatly affected by the extremely high incarceration rate for drug offenders, especially families of color. Two-thirds of these parents are incarcerated for nonviolent offenses, including a substantial proportion who are incarcerated for drug law violations. One in nine black children has an incarcerated parent, compared to one in 28 Latino children and one in 57 white children. Latino families, if they are not US citizens, risk loss of members convicted of drug use to deportation.

The war on drugs has increased the surveillance by police. With virtually everyone a suspect, all citizens must be observed, checked, screened, and tested. Law enforcement has become increasingly militarized, and SWAT teams that perform drug raids sometimes attack innocent people by mistake. Today, officials have the power to canine sniff and search almost at will.

Civil liberties also suffer in terms of mandatory sentencing laws enacted in 1986 which take sentencing discretion away from judges and in the hands of prosecutors. Only by providing the prosecutor with information to prosecute other offenders may defendants get their sentences reduced. Wives and girlfriends of drug dealers, accordingly, are often sentenced as conspirators. Because they typically lack information about the drug trafficking operation that the prosecutors seek, the traffickers' partners may wind up with longer sentences than the men who implicated them.

Steps toward serious criminal justice reform were well under way by 2016 with a focus on community corrections for drug users and the release of hundreds of prisoners who were serving extremely long sentences for nonviolent drug offenses (Wheeler, 2016). This more humane treatment was consistent with public opinion poll results showing that most Americans now favored treatment over incarceration for illicit drug users (Pew Research Center, 2014). The pendulum now, however, by most indications, has swung back the other way (Smith, 2017). At the same time, the concern for people addicted to prescription pain killers, opioids, even as they have been caught in possession of heroin, has led to incentives to look toward harm reduction approaches at least to save the lives of people having an overdose from opioids.

## Harm Reduction Initiatives

The National Association of Social Workers (NASW; 2015c), in its policy statement handbook, endorses a comprehensive public health approach for the prevention of alcohol, tobacco, and other drug problems. It also endorses "harm reduction approaches and alternatives to incarceration" for persons affected by such problems. And the recent publication by NASW Press of *Harm Reduction for High-Risk Adolescent Substance Abusers* by Maurice Fisher (2014) is evidence of NASW-US's endorsement of strengths-based harm reduction models.

The focus of the harm reduction approach is on saving lives through monitoring rather than forbidding drug use. In Europe, it took the AIDS epidemic of the 1980s to catapult harm reduction strategies into prominence. Drug use was defined as a public health rather than criminal justice problem and the behavior of the drug user closely monitored at methadone and other clinics where a safe supply was provided under medical supervision. Several US cities, including Baltimore and Seattle, use such progressive policies, at least with regard to needle exchange and methadone maintenance programs (See van Wormer & Davis, 2018).

European programming has been especially successful in reaching the hard-core addicts like no other program can. Pharmaceutical heroin is administered to such addicts in a clinic in Berne, Switzerland according to a belief in harm reduction, or aiding drug addicts to reduce the harm to themselves, even by taking small steps. Heroin maintenance is practiced in the United Kingdom, Canada, and the Netherlands, as well (Tufft, 2014).

As many social workers are aware, the harm to society from the war on drugs is often greater than the harm of the drugs themselves. And treatment offerings are highly inadequate, even for clients with strong insurance policies. The US Justice Department seems bent, under Attorney General Sessions, to reverse the decarceration efforts of the previous administration and to return the United States to harsh anti-drug sentencing laws once again (Smith, 2017). Social workers and social work educators are thus advised if they wish to advocate for sentencing reform to provide their legislators with Fact Sheets providing the latest data concerning treatment effectiveness studies and sentencing reform. (To present evidence of drug court versus imprisonment cost savings, check out the drug policy alliance at www.drugpolicy.org).

# HUMAN RIGHTS VIOLATIONS OF PRISONERS

> With prison labor, there is no union organizing, no health benefits, and no need to worry about strikes or paying at or above the minimum wage. From the inmate point of view, the opportunity to work at a real job is of course a plus. Labor exploitation, however, is clearly an area of human rights concerns. (Benns, 2015)

The laws pertaining to prison labor go back to the freeing of the slaves following the Civil War when farm owners and companies could lease convicts from the state. Convict leasing was cheaper than slavery, since those who leased them did not have to worry at all about the health of their workers. Then in 1979, to ensure a cheap labor pool, Congress began a process of deregulation that allowed private corporations to exploit the captive labor market for profit.

Modern day prison labor bears a frightening resemblance to slavery that few people acknowledge. At Angola Prison in Louisiana, for example, inmates who are in good health can be forced to work under threat of punishment as severe as solitary confinement. Legally, this labor may be unpaid, but usually inmates are paid as little as two cents an hour for their full-time work in the fields, manufacturing warehouses, or kitchens. Such prison labor practices still today bear a striking resemblance to slavery that is more than coincidental. In fact, involuntary servitude as punishment for crime is *legal* under the US Constitution (13th Amendment), but not under the Universal Declaration of Human Rights (1948, article 4), which, as a more comprehensive document, outlaws slavery in all forms.

As we review conditions in the US prison system, we need to bear in mind Article 5 of the UN Universal Declaration of Human rights on cruel, inhuman, or degrading punishment. This standard, which seems identical to that of the US Bill of Rights, is in fact a higher standard due to the word *or.* The application of the Eighth Amendment's "cruel *and* unusual punishment, according to an article in *The Harvard Environmental Law Review* (Geer, 2000), requires that both elements apply at once—cruel *and* unusual. According to at least one Supreme Court ruling, the majority determined that if the cruelty is usual, then it is constitutional!

Under international guidelines, conditions in prison easily qualify as "cruel and inhuman." Consider that around half of prison inmates have a serious mental health problem. In jails and prison, these inmates rarely receive treatment. A recent report by the Urban Institute examines the costs to society by incarcerating persons who break the law because of their mental health problems (Kim, Becker-Cohen, & Serakos, 2015). Once behind bars, many fail to follow the rules, get involved in fights, and end up in solitary confinement cells as troublemakers. In the absence of receiving treatment, their recidivism rates upon release are high. The authors of the report are encouraged by the introduction of mental health courts across the United States to meet the special needs of persons with mental illness who get into trouble with the law. These courts provide close supervision by mental health professionals and other staff who help them locate suitable housing and see that their use of medication is carefully monitored.

## Men in Prison

Prisons are brutalizing institutions. In all-male places of confinement, men are subject to constant power games; the premium is on toughness. Within the walls of prison, violence and the threat of violence is a constant, much of it racially motivated. Few law-abiding citizens are aware of the brutalities that routinely take place behind the barbed wire fences, especially to inmates who are not "street wise."

Government-collected statistics show that prisons are unsafe places for the people confined there, and that the staff are often the perpetrators of sexual attacks (Bruenig, 2015). Estimates are that nearly 200,000 people were sexually violated in American detention facilities in 2011. The report indicates that inmates with mental health problems and inmates who identified as gay, lesbian or bisexual are at higher risk for sexual abuse than the general population. Minors contained in juvenile detention facilities were even reported to be at much higher risk than adults contained in adult facilities. In light of much publicized scandals within the men's prisons,

Congress in 2003 passed the federal Prison Rape Elimination Act (PREA). According to Fellner (2013), the passage of this act was a breakthrough because it gave recognition to the fact that rape in prison was a human rights violation that must be stopped. Under this act all states are required to submit statistics on the occurrence of sexual assaults in the states' correctional institutions and report the steps that were taken to end the violence. Enforcement of this act has yet to be fully implemented, however, and rape of inmates is still commonplace (Bruenig).

## Women in Prison

The UN standards for prison treatment carry less legal weight than treaties, but nevertheless they carry moral power. Relevant to female inmates is the UN Standard Minimum Rules for the Treatment of Prisoners. Rule 53 (3) provides that women should be attended and supervised only by women officers. In the United States, however, nondiscrimination guidelines (to promote gender equality in employment) have removed most restrictions on women working in men's prisons or men working in women's prisons. Accordingly, more often than not, women incarcerated in the United States are guarded by men; uniquely in this country, men are sometimes placed in contact positions over female inmates (van Wormer & Bartollas, 2014). In Canadian prisons, in contrast, practically all of the officers are women.

Violations in the form of sexual harassment have been reported in virtually every state. The New Jersey Department of Corrections, for example, has referred over a dozen cases of sexual assault against female inmates by male officers to prosecutors (Sullivan, 2017). The worst violations have come from privatized prisons; these prisons are staffed by poorly trained and poorly paid correctional officers. The stories of rape, revenge deprivations, forced nudity in lockup, pregnancies in a closed system where only males were the guards, forced abortions, and solitary confinement of complainants and witnesses to the abuses barely received notice until seven or eight years ago. It was thanks to the facts revealed in a string of lawsuits that organizations such as Human Rights Watch were able to run investigations of their own. According to Human Rights Watch at least 15% of incarcerated females have been the victims of prison sexual assault. These assaults occur at the hands of prison staff and other inmates (Piecora, 2014).

A major setback to the civil rights of inmates came in the form of the passage of the Prison Litigation Reform Act in 1995. This act limited judicial supervision of prisons and thereby reduces the civil rights of inmates. The difficulty of litigation notwithstanding, substantial settlements have been awarded in a number of high profile cases.

Behind bars, flagrant violations of international law take the shape of the sexual abuse of female inmates by male correctional officers and male rape by other inmates in US prisons. But the greatest human rights violation of all comes with the state-sanctioned homicide.

## The Death Penalty

One of the most extreme forms of brutality is represented by state assisted murder, better known as the death penalty. Most major democracies and dozens of other countries have abolished the death penalty. The traditional support by American public and politicians of this form of punishment is one of a kind with the harsh welfare cutbacks and "the race to incarcerate."

Capital punishment has been abolished by all the major democracies except the United States, Japan, and India. For large parts of the world, around half of the countries, capital punishment is now regarded as barbaric and unnecessary. As we learn from a recent Amnesty International (2015) report on capital punishment, countries use various methods to kill: hanging, shooting, lethal injection, beheading. In 2015, the number of executions worldwide has significantly increased. Nearly 90% of all these killings happened in just three countries: Iran, Pakistan and Saudi Arabia. Iran executed at least 977 people, mainly for drug-related crimes. These figures exclude China, a country that is thought to be the world's top executioner.

Despite the large numbers of executions in 2015, Amnesty International is optimistic that the forces for abolition are winning out. In the United States, so far 18 states, including most recently Pennsylvania, have abolished the death penalty for all crimes.

NASW (2015a), in its handbook in policy statements, takes a strong position against the practice of capital punishment. Because the death penalty violates the US profession's broad ethical principle that social workers respect the inherent dignity and worth of each person, the organization prohibits support of the death penalty. Imposing the death penalty further violates the ethical principle that applies to efforts by social workers to enhance clients' capacity and opportunity for change. Arguments against the death penalty cited in this entry are that the expense is extremely high, money that could be used for social welfare programming; the fact that the states that execute the most people have the highest murder rates; inequities in the system (90% can't afford their own attorney); and the fact that 75% of the cases involve a white victim.

Public opinion has shifted on the death penalty, and it is used far less today than formerly (Death Penalty Information Center, 2016). Part of the reason for the shift is the widespread knowledge, thanks to media reports, of people who were on death row proven to be innocent of homicide and exonerated. Others who had been sentenced to death row had their sentences commuted thanks to Supreme Court decisions stating it was unconstitutional to execute persons with mental and intellectual disabilities.

Sister Helen Prejean, spiritual leader and social activist and the author of *Dead Man Walking* (Prejean, 1994), spearheaded the national campaign for a moratorium on the death penalty (check out www.MoratoriumCampaign.org). Prejean continues her speaking engagements counseling both families of the person on death row as well as the families of the victims, and is an active spokesperson of Ministry against the Death Penalty. Recently she provided these statistics on executions in her home state of Louisiana:

Of the 241 people that Louisiana has sentenced to death in the past 30 years,

- 28 have been executed
- 127 have had their sentences reversed due to serious errors
- 9 have been exonerated (Prejean, 2016)

In common with social work values is belief by members of the moratorium campaign that it is wrong to take human life, but beyond that is the belief in human redemption. The prime example of a life totally turned around was that of Karla Faye Tucker who was executed in 1998 in Texas. Few doubted that her repentance was real, least of all her pastor who married her in prison. Many anti-death penalty activists such as Sister Helen Prejean, as well as conservative religious leaders, took up her cause. In the end, however, then Governor George W. Bush refused to stay her execution.

Tucker's death may or may not have provided a sense of closure to the victims' families. This element of capital punishment has been played up extensively in the media to the extent that the public believes the killing of the murderer of their child or relative somehow helps the family recover from the loss. Members of the organization, Murder Victims' Families for Reconciliation (2016), feel otherwise, however. The organization, conducts a national speaking tour of people who have lost loved ones to murder but oppose the death penalty. The supposed cathartic power of watching their loved one's murderer die is a myth, they say. You have to let go; hate can literally destroy you. "You become what you hate," is their slogan. The teachings of these groups generally are ignored by prosecutors and the media, however, who have other agendas. Victims' needs, accordingly, tend to be narrowly defined in terms of retribution and "closure" from state-sponsored vengeance. According to spokespersons of Murder Victims' Families for Reconciliation (nd), the mainstream philosophy complicates grieving and impedes healing.

For a gripping account of an African American teenager who was sentenced to death row, a sentence that was later commuted to life, and who took college courses in prison, eventually becoming a professor of social work at Ohio State University, see *To Ascend into the Shining World Again* by Rudolph Alexander, Jr. (2001). Alexander strongly endorses principles of restorative justice.

## RESTORATIVE JUSTICE

In an aboriginal peacekeeping circle, members of the community open the session with a prayer and reminder that the circle has been convened to discuss the behavior of a young man who assaulted his sister in a drunken rage; an eagle feather is passed around the circle, held by each speaker as he or she expresses feelings about the harmful behavior. This process is about reconciliation and the healing of wounds. It is about restoring the balance or the sense of justice that was lost.

Social workers in the field of corrections certainly should want to know about restorative justice. In Canada, perhaps due to the influence of First Nations Peoples, restorative justice principles are well known. In the United States, restorative justice practices have begun to make inroads within the criminal justice field (an August 2016 search of *Criminal Justice Abstracts* reveals hundreds of relevant articles, while *Social Work Abstracts* has 36). For social work, this represents a substantial increase; one decade ago, there were only four listings for social work.

Compared to New Zealand, the United Kingdom, and Canada, the US profession of social work has been slow to incorporate principles of restorative justice in social work research or in the social work curriculum. Turning to relevant sources from social work literature, restorative justice got its start within the field of US social work through the work of Mark Umbreit, the Director of the Center for Restorative Justice and Peacemaking and Professor of Social Work at the University of Minnesota. Mark Umbeit's 2013 film, *Being with the Energy of Forgiveness,* effectively shows the power of restorative justice in interviews with people who have been through the process (available to watch at http://www.youtube.com). Promising developments in the United States are taking place today in the states of Minnesota (in juvenile justice and adult corrections), Vermont (in juvenile justice), and Hawaii (in reentry from prison programs). Social work students at Bluffton College, a Mennonite college in Ohio, all take a course in restorative justice theory.

So what is restorative justice? As defined by the *Encyclopedia of Social Work*:

> Restorative justice is an umbrella term for a method of handling disputes with its roots in the rituals of indigenous populations and traditional religious practices. A three-pronged system of justice, restorative justice is a non-adversarial approach usually monitored by a trained professional who seeks to offer justice to the individual victim, the offender, and the community, all of whom have been harmed by a crime or other form of wrongdoing. (van Wormer, 2013, p. 1)

In communities across North America, an unusual coalition of idealistic lawyers, religious leaders, and even conservative victims' advocates are at the helm of this restorative policy movement. Both an ideal principle—providing justice to the offender, victim, and community—and a method of dispensing justice when a violation has been committed, this form of justice can be considered a form of social justice because of its fairness to all parties. Restorative justice is highly relevant to social work in terms of its: focus on healing, emphasis on face-to-face communication, spiritual qualities in allowing for expiation for guilt, and underlying assumption that if you seek the good in people, you will more likely find it.

On the international stage, the thrust for a restorative vision has been embraced through the role of the United Nations. In consultation with nongovernmental organizations, the United Nations (2006) provided standards for countries to use in restorative justice programming. A growing international movement, restorative justice neatly achieves the NASW ethical standard (NASW Code of Ethics, 2017, 6.04c), which states that "social workers should promote conditions that encourage respect for cultural and social diversity within the United States and globally." More specifically, CSWE (2015; Competency 3) urges that social workers "apply their understanding of social, economic, and environmental justice to advocate for human rights at the individual and system levels" (p. 8). The United Nations, in fact, has taken notice of alternative forms of justice, such as offender/victim conferencing and informal means of dealing with certain crimes as a development consistent with human rights initiatives.

The four basic kinds of restorative justice are victim-offender conferencing, family group conferencing, circle sentencing, and reparations (truth and reconciliation commissions.) We describe family group conferencing and circle sentencing briefly in this section, and then focus on victim-offender conferencing and reparative justice. Reparative justice is the form of justice most closely linking to human rights. Whereas victim-offender conferencing operates most generally at the micro level, reparations can extend to what sociologists might call the macro-macro level.

Family group counseling was introduced by the Maori people in New Zealand as a form of protecting children in need of protection, usually related to family abuse and neglect. This process is characterized by a reliance on extended family members to reach a decision to support the parents and protect the child. In New Zealand, family group conferencing has totally changed the way social workers approach families with issues of child protection. And other countries have learned from New Zealand the importance of drawing on the resources from the child's relatives for solutions to caregiving problems. (For details, see http://www.cyf.govt.nz/about-us/who-we-are-what-we-do/index.html.)

Circle sentencing is a manner of meting out justice in cases of crime; this process takes place outside of the formal court system. Sentencing circles have been developed most extensively in Saskatchewan, Manitoba, and the Yukon to serve First Nations people. The tradition, in fact, is rooted in tribal customs of justice. Typically, members of the community provide a healing circle for the victim, a healing circle for the offender, and a sentencing circle to develop consensus on the elements of a sentencing plan; and follow-up circles to monitor the progress of the offender. (Information is available at the Canadian website http://www.courts.ca.gov/documents/SentencingCircles.pdf.)

## VICTIM-OFFENDER CONFERENCING

Fania Davis, who had once been supportive of the Black Panthers, like her sister, Angela Davis, underwent "a life-changing epiphany, one that 'integrated the warrior and the healer in me'" upon learning of the power of restorative justice to change lives (Duxbury, 2013). With the help of judges, lawyers, social workers, and a member of the city council, she founded Restorative Justice for Oakland Youth. The results of her work have been extraordinary in terms of changes brought to the school system in Oakland, California, and to the students in interrupting the school-to-prison pipeline (Davis, 2015). Today restorative justice strategies have been incorporated into programming in almost 30 schools in Oakland, a city infested with gang activity and drugs. And in 2015, the school district announced it would allocate over $2 million to further expand the program. School social workers have much to learn about the use of these healing circles for schools in high crime areas.

The variety of initiatives that fall under this rubric have their roots in ceremonies of indigenous populations from across the globe but most especially from Canada and New Zealand. (Canadian Mennonite probation officers played an important role as well.)

Restorative justice has as its purpose the repairing of the harm that has been done to the victim, community, and offender himself or herself. Note that the starting point is always the *victim*. From the offender's standpoint, restorative justice condemns the criminal act but not the actor and holds the offenders accountable to the community (Umbreit & Armour, 2011). The restorative process can take place either in addition to or instead of standard judicial proceedings. This three-pronged approach—to the needs of victim, offender, community—gives individuals and families most directly affected by wrongdoing the opportunity to be involved in the resolution process. Providing a possible antidote to punitive politics, restorative theory can apply to a wide variety of contexts ranging from the most extraordinary forms of injustice considered by national courts to the meeting-room of a neighborhood school.

In many states, representatives of the victims' rights movement have been instrumental in setting up programs in which victims/survivors may confront their violators. For both victim and offender, restorative justice protects individual rights by providing options that no mere legalistic resolution could offer; participation is strictly voluntary. With regard to the matter of reparations for violations of human rights to whole classes of people, the restorative process is the method of choice for addressing the wrongs that have been done, both by individuals and by the state.

The standard variety of justice goes as follows: For the offender charged with a crime, the goal is to "beat the rap." The process of adjudication typically involves "copping a plea" to a lesser charge through a deal between prosecutor and defense attorney or participation in the adversarial arena, the modern equivalent of trial by combat. Consistent with its origin in trial-by-combat, the adversary system is built on dueling as opposed to negotiation and compromise. In civil cases, the plaintiff's lawyers, paid on a contingency basis, share up to 40% of the winnings.

In both civil and criminal cases, one party wins; the other party loses. The dominant form of justice in most of the Western and non-Western world is retributive justice. The ultimate form of retribution is of course found in the death penalty.

In contrast, the campaign for restorative justice advocates alternative methods to satisfying the victim's needs other than through harsh punishment. Accountability to the victim, however, is indispensable here, as is accountability to the community. Restitution is often involved in situations of property offenses, for example. But restitution can go far beyond mere monetary compensation.

Social workers in Hawaii have been quietly incorporating Native Hawaiian, culturally based tradition into their human service interventions. The impetus for introducing the culturally specific programming came in the 1970s when it was noted that Native children were not responding to the standard forms of psychotherapy provided. Following in the ancient Hawaiian tradition of conflict resolution, Lorenn Walker facilitates *hulkahl* restorative circles for prison reentry in Hawaii. In Hawaiian *hui* means "group" and *kahl* means "individual,: so the term perfectly describes the inmate's conferencing with his or her family members. With a focus on family healing and reconciliation with loved ones, the program is open to all inmates to prepare them for a return to the community; around 30% agree to participate (Walker & Greening, 2013). The reasoning behind the conferencing among prisoners who are about to be released and their family members is to clear up sources of difficulty and misunderstandings that typically arise when people who have been locked up for years come face to face with long-standing family resentments and blaming. Children may express anger toward their parents for the feelings of abandonment they experienced earlier; relatives may doubt former drug users will be able to remain clean. There is much to work out in these healing circles. Extensive state-sponsored research has been conducted on the reentry circles. Results indicate strong satisfaction with the ritual for bringing family members together to form a covenant and giving voice to the loved ones of prison inmates. Moreover, the recidivism rates of the former inmate are significantly reduced.

Lorenn Walker also conducts victim-offender conferencing within prison walls as well. She travels the globe to conduct workshops and facilitate conferencing. Her personal story is interesting. A lawyer who recognized that the adversarial system in family court was tearing families apart with its winner-take all manner of settling conflict, Walker left her legal practice and has devoted her life to teaching and practicing the principles of restorative justice. (See a meeting of murder victim families with the murderer at Walla Walla prison, facilitated by Lorenn Walker, Oprah Winfrey Network, available at: https://vimeo.com/45818900.)

Most cases of victim-offender work do not involve serious crime; many involve property offenses such as vandalism. What do victim-satisfaction evaluations show? The most extensive and comprehensive studies of the impact of restorative justice interventions to date have been conducted at the Center for Restorative Justice and Peacemaking in Minnesota under the leadership of Mark Umbreit. His research shows that for victims, the possibility of receiving restitution appeared to initially motivate them to enter the dialoguing process. After meeting the offender and being able to talk about what happened, the session turned out to be more satisfying than receiving restitution. Even in cases of extreme violence, victims and offenders often highlight their participation in mediated dialogue as a powerful and transformative experience that helped them express personal pain, let go of their hatred, and, finally, heal (see Umbreit & Armour, 2011).

## HEALING THROUGH REPARATIONS

Truth and Reconciliation Commissions are temporary bodies that investigate past human rights abuses. Healing for the woundedness of whole populations of people is the ultimate goal of reparative justice. Whereas the other methods of restoring justice generally relate to wrongdoing within a personal or criminal justice context, *reparative justice* as the term is used here refers to reparations for violations of human rights where the state is the culprit. Reparations may be in the form of cash or territorial payments as material compensation for historical wrongs done. Reparation with or without an apology is an admission of past wrongdoing and a recognition by perpetrators or their descendants of the need to amend for past wrongdoing. The global trend of providing restitution for historical injustices is a trend based on the belief that nations as moral beings must acknowledge their past wrongdoing if we are ever to get beyond them.

In the United States, in 1988, long after the wrongs inflicted upon Japanese Americans who were herded into concentration camps during World War II, President Ronald Reagan, on behalf of the US government, acknowledged the wrongs and issued an apology to each person affected by the human rights violation (Takahashi, 2013). The Civil Liberties Act of 1988, which was passed by Congress, authorized the establishment of community funds to educate the public and to help honor Japanese Americans collectively. The US government eventually disbursed more than $1.6 billion in reparations to over 80,000 Japanese Americans. This reparations settlement, along with the formal apology for wrongs committed by the US government, set a precedent for other mistreated groups to seek compensatory measures. Among them are the Native American claims for treaties broken and brutal practices forcing assimilation. Australian aboriginal peoples are currently organizing to get their government to provide reparations for their "stolen childhoods." The reference is to the forced removal of mixed race children from aboriginal mothers into orphanages or white homes. In Japan in 2000, a tribunal held in Tokyo, Japan was convened by various women's rights groups to hear testimony from survivors from Japan and Korea, women who were forced to be sexual slaves or "comfort women" of the World War II Imperial Army (Kingston, 2016). Although the Japanese government has offered a large settlement as part of an accord with South Korean government, their refusal to fully accept responsibility for the crimes committed against the victims has led to world condemnation. The United Nations has issued a yellow card to Tokyo on the accord, with CEDAW stating that it "did not fully adopt a victim-centered approach" and was evasive on responsibility for the human rights violations endured.

Well before the United States was considering compensation for Japanese Americans, the West German government offered reparations to survivors of the Holocaust and to the state of Israel. Although there was strong resistance by many Israelis to allow the country that had so wronged them to appease their collective conscience in the form of money, eventually Israel agreed to accept monetary compensation. From 1953 to 1963, West Germany paid Israel more than $7 billion in today's dollars (Coates, 2014). Individual reparations claims followed—for psychological trauma, for offense to Jewish honor, for halting law careers, for life insurance, for time spent in concentration camps.

Reparations alone, however, are not sufficient to bring peace among the people who have been divided under a repressive regime. Full commissions—Truth and Reconciliation Commissions—are needed to incorporate restorative justice principles by responding to victims' needs and attending to the social harm and fractured relationships caused by violence (Androff, 2013). On a global scale, the most astonishing example of public truth-telling and catharsis for crime took place in South Africa before the Truth and Reconciliation Commission. The core purpose of the national inquiry was to promote national unity through public disclosure of the nature and extent of the human rights violations under apartheid. Victims of the old regime under apartheid testified, and former officials who had committed unspeakable crimes under the former government were forced to own up to these crimes. In exchange for taking responsibility for the wrongs inflicted on black and mixed race people, the former officials were offered amnesty. The world has learned much from the way reconciliation took place between members of the former government who had so wronged the people and the new government that sought a way to end the hatred. "Unearthing the previously silenced voices of victims in a supportive environment can contribute to the narrative healing of victims from trauma by satisfying the desire to tell their stories and providing a measure of emotional relief or catharsis" (Androff, 2013, p. 207).

Less widely known are events that took shape in Rwanda, riven by a genocide in 1994 that claimed an estimated half a million lives. Internationally, the United Nations established the International Tribunal for Rwanda. Because women were seen by many as better at forgiveness and reconciliation, women were guaranteed a minimum of 30% of government seats of power. What was not done was to award significant compensation to the survivors. Mugiraneza (2014) argues that now, 20 years later, is the time for financial reparations, not only from the government but from the United Nations itself for its failure to intervene when the genocide was taking place. (To learn more about the work of such tribunals worldwide and other contemporary forms of restorative justice, check out www.restorativejustice.org.)

The African American movement for reparations incurred by the ancestors of persons brought to America and sold as slaves has been widely publicized. Writing in *The Atlantic*, Ta-Nehisi (2014) stirred up much controversy in his presentation of the case for reparations for descendants of the former slaves. As he indicates, there was even a precedent for this when, in the 18th century, Quakers decided as a religious body to free their slaves, they were also directed to provide compensation for their labor and many of them did so in the form of land. This cause has been taken up more recently by the Black Lives Matter movement (see https://policy.m4bl.org/reparations/). And in the US Congress, Representative John Conyers, Jr. introduces a bill each year to set up a committee to study the legacy of slavery and recommendations for appropriate remedies. The bill, however, is never allowed to come to the floor of the House.

## SUMMARY AND CONCLUSION

Human rights, harm reduction, and restorative justice are the three key models that were explained in depth in this chapter. A notion of human rights is the cornerstone for both the other two models—harm reduction and restorative justice, as we have seen in this chapter. Harm reduction is an antidote to the war on drugs, a way of protecting drug users from the law and themselves until they can find healthier ways of coping with life. Restorative justice approaches provide alternatives to prison in some cases and help convicts repair the harm in others. At the societal level, reparations are sought by minority and indigenous populations for past wrongs done to their people through war crimes such as genocide, slavery, removal of their children, and other extreme human rights violations.

One theme that emerged in the writing of this chapter is how much US policy makers (whether politicians or social workers) can learn from international sources including non-governmental organizations such as Human Rights Watch and Amnesty International. The very concept of human rights is a global concept based on universal principles of justice and security. Seen from a human rights perspective, the United States is strong in the area of political and civil rights but remiss in providing economic rights including health care and housing. The importance of a human rights perspective for the social work profession was stressed in Box 6.3, a contribution written by Elisabeth Reichert.

This chapter is informed by the Universal Declaration of Human Rights, the body of which is included in Appendix A. This remarkable document from which so many other remarkable documents and treaties have sprung can serve as a template against which to measure the level of civilization of a given country. With this framework we considered the treatment of women globally and the treatment of various minority groups. That war, in its preparation and glorification has a dampening effect on citizens' human rights is of course an understatement. Civil liberties do not count for much in a nation at war or in a warfare state.

In our overview of the US criminal justice system, the negatives in the ruthless war on drugs and pervasive racism were pointed out. Positives were the introduction of the harm reduction model and restorative justice strategies.

The theme of gender emerged once again in this volume in the discussion of women in crime and women in confinement and of female victimization under conditions of war. Unlike incarcerated men engaged in endless power struggles, women in prison seem more interested in reproducing family-type ties for their emotional survival. The section on war and rape described specific human rights violations suffered by women universally in war-torn areas.

Viewed as a whole, chapter 10 has demonstrated how the work of the United Nations has provided a set of international policy instruments to address human rights violations, during ordinary day-to-day political and civil rights, to economic, social cultural and rights during war not to be tortured or raped. The United Nations provides a forum whereby the world can identify, witness and act for human rights as a path to peace. The policies and covenants generated and ratified by the United Nations also provide a framework for social work policy and practice. Implications for the profession are further discussed in relation to the well-being of children and the Convention on the Rights of the Child in chapter 10 of this book.

## THOUGHT QUESTIONS

1. Define human rights as a concept that goes beyond social justice.
2. Discuss the relevance of a human rights perspective to the social work profession.
3. Study the Universal Declaration of Human Rights in Appendix A. Mark the basic divisions or generations of human rights.
4. What is the significance of the International Criminal Court? Discuss possible reasons for United States' refusal to join.
5. What is the role of Amnesty International in regard to human rights?
6. What is a war crime? How is a war crime legally different from ordinary combat? What is a war crime tribunal? Give examples.

7. Discuss the phenomenon of rape in war. What is "spirit injury" as defined by Adrien Wing?
8. Discuss the special suffering of women in wartime.
9. Study the newspaper headlines listed in the section "Violations of Women Domestically" and discuss their ramifications.
10. Differentiate the US Bill of Rights from the Universal Declaration.
11. What is controversial about the US Patriot Act that followed September 11?
12. Analyze the meaning of the statistics provided in Box 6.4.
13. Debate America's concept of and operation of a war on drugs. Draw on global comparisons. What is harm reduction?
14. How is incarceration big business in the United States?
15. Compare issues of men in prison with those of women in prison.
16. Debate pros and cons of the death penalty.
17. Define restorative justice. What are the basic types? What is the relevance of social work?
18. What is the relevance of reparations to crimes against humanity?

## REFERENCES

Alexander, R. (2001). *To ascend into the shining world again*. Richmond, TX: TheroE Enterprises.

Ali, S. S., & Abdullah, H. (2016, September 8). Did the Patriot Act change US attitudes on surveillance? National Broadcast Company (NBC) News. Retrieved from www.nbcnews.com

Amnesty International. (2009). Maze of injustice. Retrieved from http://www.amnesty.org.

Amnesty International. (2015). Highest number of executions in 25 years. Retrieved from http://www.amnesty.org

Amnesty International. (2017, February 7). Syria: Secret campaign of mass hangings and extermination at Saydnaya Prison. Retrieved from http://www.amnesty.org

Androff, D. (2013). Treatment and reconciliation communities and transitional justice in a restorative justice context. In K. van Wormer & L. Walker (Eds.), *Restorative justice today: Practical applications* (pp. 205–214). Thousand Oaks, CA: Sage.

Androff, D. (2016). *Practicing rights human rights-based approaches to social work practice*. New York, NY: Routledge.

Associated Press. (2016, December 7). India records huge spike in "honor killings" in 2015. *New York Times*. Retrieved from www.nytimes.com

Barrett, P. M. (2016, September 12). Incarceration is falling so private prisons try new businesses. *Bloomberg Business Week*, pp. 23–24.

Belluck, P., & Cochrane, J. (2016, February 5). Female genital cutting: Not just an African problem. *New York Times*, p. A6.

Bendery, J. (2015, March 6). At last, Violence Against Women Act lets tribes prosecute non-Native domestic abusers. *Huffington Post*. Retrieved from www.huffingtonpost.com

Bennhold, K. (2016, January 3). Women travel migrant trail with risk. *New York Times*, p. A1.

Benns, W. (2015, September 21). American slavery reinvented. *The Atlantic*. Retrieved from www.theatlantic.com

Bernard, T. (2015, December 26). How to help in a global refugee crisis. *New York Times*, p. B1.

Broadhurst, K., Glover, C., & Jamieson, J. (2009). *Critical perspectives on safeguarding children*. Chichester, England: Wiley-Blackwell.

Bruenig, E. (2015, March 2). Why Americans don't care about prison rape. *The Nation*. Retrieved from www.thenation.com

Bureau of Justice Statistics (BJS). (2016, December). *Prisoners in 2015*. Washington, DC: U.S. Department of Justice.

Coates, T.-N. (2014, June). The case for reparation. *The Atlantic*. Retreived from http://www.theatlantic.com

Council on Social Work Education (CSWE). (2015). *Educational policy and accreditation standards*. Alexandria, VA: Author.

Davis, F. (2015, October 5). Interrupting the school to prison pipeline through restorative justice. *Huffington Post*. Retrieved from www.huffingtonpost.com

Death Penalty Information Center. (2016, August 30). Facts about the death penalty. Washington, D.C. Retrieved from www.deathpenaltyinfo.org

DiNitto, D. (2003). *Social welfare politics and public policy* (5th ed.). Boston, MA: Allyn & Bacon.

Dobiesz, V. (2017, October 25). It's not just O'Reilly and Weinstein: Sexual violence is a "global pandemic". *Scientific American*. Retrieved from http://www.scientificamerican.com

Drug Policy Alliance. (2016, February 10). The drug war, mass incarceration and race. New York. Retrieved from www.drugpolicy.org

Duxbury, M. (2013). Box 5: Circles of change: Bringing a more compassionate justice system to troubled youth in Oakland. In K. van Wormer & L. Walker (Eds.), *Restorative justice today: Practical applications* (p. 107). Thousand Oaks, CA: Sage.

The Economist. (2017, March 8). Daily chart: The best and worst places to be a working woman. Retrieved from www.economist.com

Erdrich, L. (2012). *The round house*. New York, NY: Harper Perennial, p. 319.

Farrell, J. (1967). *Beloved lady: A history of Jane Addams' ideas on reform and peace*. Baltimore, MD: John Hopkins University Press.

Federal Bureau of Investigation (FBI). (2016). *Crimes in the United States 2015*. Washington, DC: U.S. Department of Justice.

Fellner, J. (2013, September 4). Stop prison rape now. *The Daily Beast* (*Newsweek*). Retrieved from www.dailybeast.com

Fisher, M. (2014). *Harm reduction for high-risk adolescent substance abusers*. Washington, DC: NASW Press.

Friedman, G. (2016). Why Syria matters to you: Geopolitics investment newsletter. Retrieved from: www.mauldineconomics.com/this-week-in-geopolitics

Geer, N. (2000). Human rights and wrongs in our own backyard—A case study of women in US prisons. *Harvard Human Rights Journal, 13*, 71–133.

Gil, D. (2013). *Confronting injustice and oppression: Concepts and strategies for social workers* (updated ed.). New York, NY: Columbia University Press.

Goodman, E. (2002, July 2). Signing treaty is least US can do for women. Topeka, KS: *Topeka Capital Journal*, p.15A.

Harlan, C. (2016, August 14). Inside the administrations $1 billion deal to detain Central American asylum seekers. *Washington Post*. Retrieved from http://www.washingtonpost.com

Healy, L. M., & Link, R. J. (2012). *Handbook of international social work, human rights, development & the global profession*. New York, NY: Oxford University Press.

Ife, J. (2001). *Human rights and social work: Towards rights-based practice*. Cambridge, England: Cambridge University Press.

Kessler, V. (2015, April 20). Germany to declare Turkey's 1915 war crimes against Armenians a genocide. *Newsweek*. Retrieved from www.newsweek.com

Kim, K., Beckler-Cohen, M., & Serakos, M. (2015, March). *The processing and treatment of mentally ill persons in the criminal justice system.* Washington, DC: The Urban Institute.

Kingston, J. (2017, November 26). The Japan lobby and public diplomacy. *The Asia-Pacific Journal, 14*(9), 1–26.

Lacey, G. (2016). *Viking economics: How Scandinavians got it right—And how we can too.* Brooklyn, NY: Melville House Press.

Lederer, E. (2002, April 12). U.N. creates new war-crimes tribunal. Associated Press. Printed in *The Daily Iowan*, Iowa City, Iowa.

Litvininova, D. (2016, August 5). "If he beats you, it means he loves you." *The Moscow Times.* Retrieved from https://the moscowtimes.com

Malsin, J. (2017, April 24). Christians of Egypt bit by ISIS in Palm Sunday Bombings, *Time*, p. 15.

Moore, M. (2015). *Where to invade next.* Documentary film. Produced by Anchor Bay.

Morgan-Besecker, T., & Singleton, D. (2016, December 9). More female inmates allege sexual assault at Lackawanna County prison. Scranton, PA: *The Times-Tribune.* Retrieved from www.thetimes-tribune.com

Murder Victims' Families for Reconciliation (2016). Why we oppose capital punishment. Retrieved from www.mvfr.org

National Association of Social Workers (NASW). (2017). *Code of ethics.* Washington, DC: NASW Press.

National Association of Social Workers (NASW). (2015a). Capital punishment and the death penalty. *Social work speaks: NASW policy statements 2015–2017* (10th ed., pp. 26–31). Washington, DC: NASW.

National Association of Social Workers (NASW). (2015b). Juvenile justice and delinquency prevention. *Social work speaks: NASW policy statements 2015–2017* (10th ed., pp. 188–193). Washington, DC: NASW.

National Association of Social Workers (NASW). (2015c). Substance use disorder treatment. *Social work speaks: NASW policy statements 2015–017* (10th ed., pp. 296–297). Washington, DC: NASW Press.

National Association of Social Workers (NASW). (2016). Peace and social justice. NASW website. Retrieved from http://www.socialworkers.org/pressroom/events/911/peace.asp

Pew Research Center. (2014, April 2). America's new drug policy landscape. Washington, DC: Pew Research Center. Retrieved from www.people-press.org.

Phelps, M. S. (2011). Rehabilitation in the punitive era: The gap between rhetoric and reality in U.S. prison programs. *Law & Society Review, 45*(1), 33–68.

Piecora, C. (2014, September 15). Female inmates and sexual assault. *Jurist Twenty.* Retrieved from http://www.jurist.org/dateline/2014/09/christina-piecora-female-inmates.php

Prejean, Sister H. (1994). *Dead man walking.* New York, NY: Vintage Books.

Prejean, Sister H. (2016, April/May). Death penalty discourse. Ministry against the death penalty. Retrieved from http://us7.campaign-archive1.com.

Rebmann, R. (2015). Annual Report. Retrieved September 2016: www.AI/annualreport/2015

Ren, Y. (2016, October 20). Young Chinese women are committing suicide at a terrifying rate—here's why. UK: Telegraph. Retrieved from www.telegraph.com.uk

Reichert, E. (2011). *Social work and human rights: A foundation for policy and practice* (2nd ed.) New York: Columbia University Press.

Reuters (2016, September 9). Closing private detention centers for migrants could raise more problems. *Fortune.* Retrieved from www.fortune.com

Rosenblatt, R. (2016, October). The world is a thriving slaughterhouse. *The Atlantic*, p. 95.

Schuppe, J. (2017, February 26). Private prisons: Here's why Sessions' memo matters. National Broadcast Company (NBC) News. Retrieved from www.nbc.com

Searcey, D. (2016, September 22). Boko Haram rages in Nigeria, but the world's eyes are elsewhere. *New York Times*. Retrieved from www.nytimes.com/2016/world/africa/boko-haram-terrorism.

The Sentencing Project. (2015, December 11). Declines in youth commitments and facilities in the 21st century. Washington, D.C. Retrieved from www.sentencingproject.org

Smith, C. (2017, March 11). Is AG Jeff Sessions quietly waging a second 'war on drugs'? *Justice Policy Institute*. Retrieved from http://www.justicepolicy.org/news/11280

Smyth, J. (2017, April 20). Australia's hidden refugees embrace art to reveal their plight. *Financial Times*. Retrieved from www.ft.com

Sullivan, S. R. (2017, March 22). N.J. corrections officer accused of sex abuse at women's prison to pay inmates $75K. Retrieved from New Jersey.com: True Jersey. Retrieved from www.nj.com

Takahashi, R. (2013). Restorative justice almost 50 years later: Japanese American redress for exclusion, restitution, and incarceration. In K. van Wormer & L. Walker (Eds.), *Restorative justice today: Practical applications* (pp. 225–232). Thousand Oaks, CA: Sage.

Tufft, B. (2014, November 23). Heroin to be prescribed to Canadian addicts by doctors. *The Independent*. Retrieved from www.independent.co.uk

Umbreit, M., & Armour, M. (2011). *Restorative justice dialogue: An essential guide for research and practice*. New York, NY: Springer Publishing Company.

UN Women. (2016, October 20). Women between war and peace. Retrieved from www.unwomen.org

United Nations. (1989). *Convention on the rights of the child*. Geneva, Switzerland: Office of the High Commission. Retrieved from http://www.ohchr.org/en/professionalinterest/pages/crc.aspx

van Wormer, K. (1997). *Social welfare: A world view*. Chicago, IL: Nelson Hall.

van Wormer, K. (2013). Restorative justice. In C. Franklin (Ed.), *NASW encyclopedia of social work* (20th ed., online publication). New York, NY: Oxford University Press. Retrieved from www.socialwork.oxfordre.com

van Wormer, K., & Bartollas, C. (2014). *Women and the criminal justice system* (4th ed.). New York, NY: Pearson.

van Wormer, K., & Davis, D. R. (2018). *Addiction treatment: A strengths perspective* (4th ed.). Belmont, CA: Cengage.

Volokh, S. (2014, February 19). The surprising truth about suing private prisons. *Washington Post*. Retrieved from www.washingtonpost.com

Walker, L., & Greening, R. (2013). Hulkahl restorative circles: A public health approach for reentry planner. In K. van Wormer & L. Walker (Eds.), *Restorative justice today: Practical applications* (pp. 173–184). Thousand Oaks, CA: Sage.

"War Crime." (2015). *Encyclopaedia Britannica*. Retrieved from https://www.britannica.com/topic/war-crime

Watkinson, A. M. (2001). Human rights laws: Advocacy tools for a global civil society. *Canadian Social Work Review, 18*(2), 267–286.

Watts, I. P. (2016, March 19). WWP: Women, war and peace. E-international information. Retrieved from www.e-ir,info

Wheeler, L. (2016, September 3). President Obama's aggressive use of clemency power is stirring controversy. Washington, DC: The Hill. Retrieved from www.thehill.com

Wing, A. (2013). Brief reflections toward a multiplicative theory and praxis of being. *Berkeley Journal of Gender, Law and Justice, 6*(1), 181–201.

Wing, A., & Merchan, S. (1993). Rape, ethnicity, and culture: Spirit injury from Bosnia to Black America. *Columbia Human Rights Law Review, 25*(1), 1–16.

World Health Organization (WHO). (2016, November). *Violence against women: Fact sheet.* WHO: Berne, Switzerland. Retrieved from http://www.who.int/mediacentre/factsheets/fs239/en/

Wronka, J. (2012). Overview of human rights. Chapter in Healy, L. M. & Link, R. J. *Handbook of International Social Work, Human Rights, Development and the Global Profession (pp. 439–446).* New York, NY: Oxford University Press.

# CHAPTER 7

# POVERTY AND HUMAN RIGHTS

> (1) Everyone has the right to work, to free choice of employment, to just and favourable conditions of work and to protection against unemployment. (2) Everyone, without any discrimination, has the right to equal pay for equal work. (3) Everyone who works has the right to just and favourable remuneration ensuring for himself and his family an existence worthy of human dignity, and supplemented, if necessary, by other means of social protection.
>
> Universal Declaration of Human Rights, Article 23, 1948

People in poverty are not necessarily oppressed—the poverty may be shared throughout the society—and people who are oppressed are not necessarily poor. Yet economic oppression is inexplicably linked with social oppression as oppression involves domination over coveted resources. People who are socially oppressed are often poor; persons in poverty are very much inclined to be the objects of discrimination in their everyday lives.

According to US Census data for 2015, the official poverty rate is 13.5% (U.S. Census Bureau, 2016). The poverty rate in 2015 for children under age 18 was 19.7%. The poverty rate for people aged 18 to 64 was 12.4%, while the rate for people aged 65 and older was 8.8%. Many of the working poor are living below the poverty level. Whereas 30 years ago, full-time work at the minimum wage lifted a family out of poverty, today it does not. To make up for the low wages and to compensate for a weakened safety net, more people are working at two jobs and/or longer hours at their primary job.

For people living in the cities where the jobs are, a large percentage of residents cannot afford to pay fair market rent. To make up for the low wages and to compensate for a weakened safety net, more people are working at two jobs and/or longer hours at their primary job.

And yet . . . the nature and extent of poverty in the United States, shameful though it is compared to the countries of northern Europe, pale beside the nature and extent of poverty worldwide. In the poorest nations of the world—for example, countries in sub-Saharan Africa—life expectancy is 25 years less than in the wealthiest nations. According to the Borgen Project (2013), a non-profit organization that collects statistics to address global poverty:

> In our globalized society, access and participation—which are fundamental aspects of human rights—are not truly guaranteed and protected. One in five, or almost 20 percent of the global

> population, face barriers to access to food and are unable to participate in the global economy. Just over 300 million people worldwide have a life expectancy of less than 60 years, partially due to nutrient deficient and incomplete diets as well as the array of maladies and disease that stem from malnutrition and systemic poverty. (4th paragraph)

Poverty in these regions is all-pervasive; every day is a struggle just to survive. This chapter begins with an overview of the problem of poverty as a human rights concern. Core rights relevant to poverty are the right to social security and the right to work with choice of employment. The next section of the paper, "Poverty Worldwide" explores poverty globally and discusses the daily reality of living without adequate food, water, or other essential resources. From a theoretical perspective, we then explore explanations for why poverty is so ubiquitous in society. Before discussing the growing inequalities in the United States and Europe, we consider such topics as economic globalization, and the power of transnational corporations. Finally, because of its impact on the economic structure of society, we examine what is happening to work and to the worker in today's world in the face of new technologies and the heightened demand for productivity.

## POVERTY AS A HUMAN RIGHTS ISSUE

David Androff (2016), in his landmark book, *Practicing Rights: Human Rights-Based Approaches to Social Work Practice*, explores a number of social problems related to human rights but begins with poverty. First, in his reasoning is the centrality of the problem of poverty to the world and to social work practice. A second rationale is that international organizations, such as, Amnesty International and the United Nations, view poverty as a violation of economic human rights. Androff's approach is striking within social work and media reports inasmuch as the priority in the human rights literature and mass media accounts of violations are much more apt to be associated with political and civil rights.

Discrimination against poor and minority groups of people and deprivation of these people from having an adequate standard of living when many others are living well are forms of oppression and therefore, violations of human rights. Such oppression may involve exploitation of the working poor. This process of exploitation may consist of harnessing poor and often foreign workers to do the dirty work of society or, at the macro level, of using workers from poor nations as cheap sources of labor.

A universal component of economic oppression is marginalization. Marginalization occurs when certain classes of persons are denied full participation in the fruits of citizenship. When van Wormer lived in Northern Ireland, for example, Catholics, herded into gerrymandered districts, had limited voting impact, and therefore their political power was severely restricted (hence the slogan of the Irish civil rights movement: "One man, one vote"; following mass protests in the 1960s, the Catholics won their basic rights, and anti-discrimination laws were passed.)

*Structural violence* refers to the various forms of harassment, ridicule or intimidation to which oppressed groups are subjected. Structural or societal violence may be used by dominant social classes, as David Gil (2013) suggests, to defend the established way of life against challenge from dominated and exploited classes. Poverty, as we learned from Gandhi, is a form of violence in itself, "the worst form of violence" (quoted by presidential candidate Bernie Sanders, 2016). There is much overlap, of course, between these categories of poverty and violence. There is fighting by the poor among themselves over scarce resources, for one thing. Then there may be violence against people in certain impoverished and unsafe neighborhoods by forces of law and order. We may say, in short, that the poverty itself is a form of structural violence when it is the society's wealth that is not fairly distributed. We can also take a global perspective and see how poor countries are subject to exploitation by the rich. The sale of land mines by US companies to warring nations, for example, can be considered both violence (consider the numbers of children who have lost legs after stepping on a land mine) and exploitation of the worst sort. By the same token, marketers often dump products that are not acceptable in highly regulated nations onto the poor countries. This includes addictive products such as cigarettes as well.

When marginalized populations are deprived of the right to participate in the decision-making of a society as citizens, this is a violation of their human rights, as Androff suggests. One thinks of the millions of people in the United States who have served time in prison and who now are denied the right to vote as ex-felons. Advocates for these disenfranchised people would do well to use a human rights focus to hold the government accountable for such wrongs.

In the topics to follow, readers will see the links to human rights and to the violation of human rights, whether it be the structural adjustments to welfare programs enforced by the world banks, the exploitation of workers at the lower rungs of the society and in nations of the Global South, in the contrast between welfare policies for the poor and the policies providing welfare benefits for the rich.

As we move on to a deeper examination of poverty, that scourge in this technologically advanced age, keep in mind the three aspects of oppression—exploitation, marginalization, and structural violence. First, we will take a look at poverty on a global scale, then at poverty in the world's richest country—the United States.

To learn of human rights in conjunction with ideals as set forth in international declarations and conventions, see chapter 6.

## POVERTY WORLDWIDE

Poverty kills. In its wake, it brings hunger, disease, high infant mortality, homelessness, and even war. The weight of poverty falls most heavily on vulnerable groups in every society—women, the elderly, minority groups, and children. In poor households on the Indian subcontinent, for example, men and boys usually get more sustenance than do women and girls, while they also invest more in male than female education and health (Sonwalkar, 2016). Amid the wealth of new economic opportunities today, 1.2 billion people still live on less than $1.25 a day (United Nations, 2015). According to the same report, work opportunities have improved for many, but inequalities are substantial. Sustainable work provides benefits beyond material wealth and fosters community bonding, inclusion, and contributes to human progress. As a negative, work entails exploitation of the poor in the form of forced labor, child labor and human trafficking. People's human rights are violated in this way. There are still 168 million child laborers worldwide. Although the poorest of the poor tend to come from rural areas of Asia and Africa, there are also pockets of poverty in the industrialized world. See Figure 7.1.

In rich countries, most discussion of poverty centers on a person's situation in comparison to others' in the society—lack of adequate housing, access to quality education, good jobs, etc. *Relative poverty* is based on such comparison (Barusch, 2015); it is defined by the general

**FIGURE 7.1.** Syrian child laborers picking cotton on the Turkey border. © Shutterstock, photo by Yavuz Sariyildiz/.

standard of living in various societies and by what is culturally defined as deprivation. Thus by the standards of most inhabitants of India, the Mexican villager would be "well off." The Mexican, in turn, would perceive migrant work in the United States as an opportunity to "get ahead" (Macionis, 2014).

In contrast to relative poverty, *absolute poverty,* which readily can be identified in a global context involves a deprivation of resources that is life-threatening. Arguably, there is a degree of absolute poverty even in a rich nation such as the United States where inadequate nutrition, health care, and heating are unfortunate realities. Yet as Macionis reminds us, such immediately life-threatening poverty in a modernized nation strikes only a small proportion of the population. By contrast, over one billion inhabitants in the non-industrialized world are unable to satisfy such basic needs as adequate nutrition, access to safe and sufficient water, clean air to breathe, proper sanitation, and health care including vaccines and family planning. Since 1990 World Bank analysts estimate that the number of people living in extreme poverty globally has been cut in half (Caulderwood, 2015). The number of extremely poor people has fallen in all regions except sub-Saharan Africa, where population growth exceeded the rate of poverty reduction. This region ranks the lowest of all regions on gender equality and environmental sustainability.

## GLOBAL HUNGER

According to the United Nations World Food Programme (WFP) (2016b), there are 795 million hungry people in the world and 98% of them are in the Global South. The large majority of all hungry people live in rural areas, mainly in the villages of Asia and Africa. Overwhelmingly dependent on agriculture for their food, these populations have no alternative source of income or employment. Overdependence on the exportation of cash crops to other nations in exchange for hard currencies has added considerably to the food shortage problems in some of these poor nations.

In sub-Saharan Africa, just under one in every four people, or 23.2% of the population, is estimated to be undernourished (Food and Agriculture Organization [FAO] (2015). This is the highest prevalence of undernourishment for any region.

Another serious problem is drought. Ethiopia is in the grip of its worst drought in recent history (WFP, 2016a). More than ten million people are in need of assistance, according to the government and humanitarian agencies. One 23-year-old mother describes her situation:

> "When the rain stopped raining, our crops failed and our livestock started dying because there was no grass for them to feed on. I had three cows. They all died. Now we are {living on} the assistance from the government." she said. (WFP, 2016a)

The extent of world hunger is staggering. Simply put, poverty has a global face; people are dying every minute of the day from lack of basic nutrition.

As an example of a poor country in this hemisphere, we will consider Guatemala, where the majority of the citizens live in abject poverty. Guatemala has the highest chronic undernutrition rate in Latin America and the Caribbean, and fourth in the world, according to the World Food Programme (2016b). The situation worsens in rural areas where chronic malnutrition reaches 55% and 69% among indigenous populations. In the highlands of the country, seven out of ten children under 5 are chronically undernourished. This is just one example of many vicious cycles facing the poor. Many are caught in a series of vicious spirals: lack of food leads to ill health, which limits their earning ability, leading to still poorer health (Stiglitz, 2013).

Also in the Western hemisphere, squalor reigns supreme in the small, deforested nation of Haiti. An article in the *Wall Street Journal,* McKay (2010) reveals the interconnectedness of malnutrition, lack of sanitation, and disease following a massive earthquake in an already impoverished country. More than 300,000 people are living in 280 "spontaneous settlements," mainly in parks and open spaces. And now five years after the earthquake, with conditions still deplorably bad, volunteers are struck by the graciousness and gratitude of the people even in the midst of persistent squalor.

Macionis (2014) provides a graphic portrait of the face of poverty in Madras (Chennai), India, one of the largest cities in a country which contains one of three of the total number of the world's hungry. In his powerful description, Macionis juxtaposes the western visitor's response of horror with the traditional coping strategies of the survivors: Arriving in Madras, the visitor immediately recoils from the smell of human sewage and contaminated water which is unsafe to drink. Madras, like other cities of India, teems with millions of homeless people; people work, talk, bathe, and sleep in the streets. Macionis suggests, however, that the deadly cruelty of poverty in India is eased by the strength of families, the religious tradition of dharma—the Hindu concept of duty and destiny—and a sense of purpose to life. The absence of danger, illegal drug activity, and anger are striking to the outsider. Compared to North Americans, East Indians have an altogether different experience of poverty, as of life itself. Yet the suffering resonates.

## US POVERTY

Traditionally, the United States has prided itself on being a land of high social mobility, a land of opportunity where hard workers can achieve "the American dream." Given the high educational requirements or level of skills for entry into the professions or trades today, people with a low level of education are closed out. As a result, moving up the social ladder in the United States is not as common as it once was. And even many college educated young people are stuck in the low wage jobs that have become so plentiful (Associated Press, 2014).

Financial worries are a major source of stress in the United States, according to a survey from the American Psychological Association (McNamee, 2015). The survey was done through cooperation with a Harris poll. Survey results showed that 72% of participants reported stressing over money at some point during the past month, with 22% saying their stress level was extreme. Money worries were found to be associated with neglect of health problems and to be related to relationship problems.

Most of the people with money worries are not below the poverty level, which is the level determined by the government, below which people can't get their basic needs met. The worries experienced by working class people stem from the lack of a safety net in American society to shield them from crisis such as job loss or serious illness. Moreover, they are apt to have indebtedness that grows larger each month.

So what does poverty really mean? Poverty, even in a society of plenty, is not merely the absence of wealth; it means people having to live on diets consisting of beans, macaroni and cheese, stale bread, and even dog and cat food. It means lack of security against criminals—high susceptibility to victimization by shooting, robbery, rape, and/or assault. Privation is associated with the urgent social ills of homelessness, substance abuse, and infectious diseases such as tuberculosis and HIV/AIDS.

Being poor is not just one aspect of a person's or family's life, in short; it is a whole way of living. Each deprivation and disability becomes all the more intense because it exists within a web of deprivations and disabilities. Poverty is self-perpetuating. Consider the following examples of how the poor pay more for practically everything:

- To purchase a car with a loan, people often end up paying twice the value of car; if a used car, expenses on car repairs can equal more than payments on a new car would be;
- If the car buyer misses a payment, the car can be repossessed; without a car to drive, the person can miss work;
- Low-income individuals are likely to be hit with bank fees when their balance falls below a certain amount, and significant fees if a check is written on insufficient funds;
- Emergency expenses, such as a plumbing problem or visit to the emergency room, may lead one to exorbitant payday loans which further compounds indebtedness as does credit card debt;
- Poor people are often taken advantage of by rent-to-own furniture stores in which they pay around three times the value of what they are paying on;
- People who lack resources on hand will often shop at high-priced Kwik Stop stores and at the grocery store are unable to buy merchandise in bulk;
- People without cars who must take buses to work can lose a lot of time in transit;
- People who are poor avoid the dentist; eventually they may have to have their teeth pulled and get false teeth at great expense;
- At the bottom of the social structure, homeless people may get arrested for disobeying one of the city's rules to keep homeless people out of sight.

Poverty feeds on itself, increases stress considerably, and even affects one's life expectancy. This is the finding from research published in *The American Journal of Public Health*. Poverty, as shown in the report, results in poor access to health screening, poor access to quality care for those who actually have heart disease, greater vulnerability to stresses associated with heart disease and a greater likelihood of engaging in unhealthy behavior (Galea, Tracy, Hoggatt, DiMaggio, & Karpati, 2011). Smoking, obesity, and diabetes are closely correlated with social class.

Research published by Dickman, Himmelstein, and Woolhandler (2017) in the British medical journal *Lancet*, found that Americans who live in poverty have reduced life spans compared to the rich, that the richest 1% live up to 15 years longer than the poorest 1%. The researchers also found that more than one-third of low-income Americans avoid medical care because of costs (compared to 7% in Canada and 1% in the United Kingdom).

Perhaps the harshest and most unmitigated poverty in the United States is to be found in the agricultural fields. The poverty rate for farm worker families has decreased over the past 15 years, but it is still more than twice that of all wage and salary employees combined, and it's higher than that of any other general occupation. Hired farm work is among the lowest-paid work in the country (Wainer, 2014). The squalor that migrant workers typically live in in run-down migrant camps in Florida can be compared to life in non-industrialized countries. Many of these workers are undocumented and therefore have no legal right to complain about low pay or unsanitary living or working conditions. The fear of deportation forever hangs over them.

## EXPLANATIONS FOR THE EXISTENCE OF POVERTY

International forces shape the economic structures of all nations. These forces are sociological, economic, situational, and cultural. From the international literature, we have filtered out the following explanations germane to an understanding of the persistence of poverty: poverty as functional for the power elites; poverty due to global competition for markets; overpopulation; war and preparation for war; and social welfare provisions. We will look at each one separately.

### FUNCTIONS-OF-POVERTY EXPLANATION

To discover the functionalist explanation for the existence of poverty we have to go back to Gans (1995). Keep in mind that, as Gans, noted, what is functional for affluent groups in the society is not necessarily functional for the society as a whole. Gans' arguments are that poverty is endemic in society in their capacity to:

- Assure that society's "dirty work" is done;
- Subsidize through low wages many activities of the affluent;
- Create jobs for a number of occupations and professions (e.g., correctional officers, the police, and Salvation Army ministers) which serve the poor;
- Provide buyers for goods—such as day-old bread—that no one else wants;
- Maintain the legitimacy of dominant norms by identifying the poor as deviants;
- Allow for a source for charity which enables the givers to feel noble and altruistic;
- Guarantee the status of those in higher classes;

- Act as a source for arousing conservative opposition such as against "welfare chiselers;"
- Provide foot soldiers for wars and land for urban renewal;

A useful exercise is to take the same list and apply it on the global level. What are the functions that poor nations serve for rich ones? A source of cheap labor? Brain drain of the educated elites to more prosperous lands? A place for corporations to dump banned or defective products? Countries that can be controlled politically through the dispensing of financial aid?

The *dysfunctions* from the point of view of poor people and poor countries are of course obvious, more obvious than the functions. They are seen in intense suffering, economic dependency, and high death rates. The dysfunctions to the dominant groups are more subtle: they are manifest in deep divisions between the haves and the have-nots, violence that is an outgrowth of harbored resentment, environmental despoliation and the spread of disease, including epidemics.

In *Color-Blind*, Tim Wise (2010) offers an explanation for poverty in the United States that is related to racial divisions and resentment. When a society is divided along racial lines, dominant political groups can then play one group off against the other. They can even entice lower class and working class members of the majority race to vote against their economic interests and with the power elites. In *Under the Affluence*, Tim Wise (2015) discusses the uniqueness of the class system in the United States and how it evolved. Historically, race and class were intersected and black people relegated to work in the fields from childhood and prevented from obtaining the education or skills that would have enabled them to rise. Progressive government programs during the 1960s and well-paying job opportunities during an economic boom, did help many to pursue the so-called American dream, but, as Wise suggests, many of those jobs have now disappeared, and a "culture of cruelty" or a contempt for the nation's poor prevails (p.21).

## POVERTY DUE TO GLOBAL COMPETITION FOR MARKETS

Survival in a highly competitive global economy affects the modern social welfare state of the industrialized and non-industrialized world. To aid corporations and compete for their services, governments typically lower the companies' tax rates. The loss of tax revenue encouraged by corporate growth exacerbates the staggering levels of government debt, and leads to an eventual deterioration in public services (Karger & Stoesz, 2013). Corporations grow richer and more powerful. The greater the accumulated capital by industry, the greater the investment in technology to manufacture the products.

Multinational corporations grow and expand, marketing their products all across the world. Markets are created through advertising and introducing products to people on a trial basis, for example, soft drinks, cigarettes, and alcohol. Trade imbalances stemming from a combination of declining exports and increasing imports have had an especially devastating impact on nations with already high levels of foreign indebtedness. Free trade agreements between the Global North and Global South can result in the sale of cheap farm products such as corn to poor nations, thus undermining local farmers whose products are more expensive. Trade barriers deliberately inhibit certain imports that especially hurt farmers from poor regions of the world (Stiglitz, 2013). The poorest countries whose inhabitants are on the brink of starvation end up exporting their own scarce food grains as cash crops to generate the foreign exchange required to pay their foreign debts.

## POPULATION GROWTH

The highest population growth rates are being registered in the world's poorest countries, giving support to the notion that poverty fuels population growth. This is especially true in Africa. Meanwhile, falling fertility rates in countries ranging from Japan to Korea to Germany to the countries of the former Soviet Union, have serious implications for the economies of those nations. In Western Europe, France, Norway, and Sweden have the highest fertility rates at about two children. South Korea, in contrast, whose economy is more developed than many others in Asia and with a fertility rate of only 1.2, is trying to reduce the expenses associated with raising children, including looking for ways to expand child care and to curb the cost of education (Hookway, 2014).Chile's government last year announced plans for a "baby bonus" for parents who have a third child, following the lead of countries such as France and Australia, which already have incentives for parents to have more children. Singapore, in a desperate move to increase the supply of babies, rewards couples who have children with thousands of dollars and housing supports for each child they have (*The Economist*, 2015a.)

Literacy for women is highly correlated with low birth rates. In the nation of India, for example, in southern states such as Kerala, where the literacy rate for girls and women is quite high (estimates range from 85-100%) despite a relatively high poverty rate, birth rates have fallen in contrast with most of the rest of India where family planning efforts have been less effective (Sinha, 2012).

The connection between poverty and overpopulation is apparent in the pressure that conditions of poverty put on families to produce more offspring to have additional hands to carry out the work—fetching water, planting, chopping wood, etc. The connection between poverty and overpopulation is apparent, too, in the scarcity of resources and the territorial disputes that ensue when the population exceeds maximum limits. Internal battles and even warfare often result as migrating populations seek new territory and as nations compete with nations for control over arable land, fresh water, and oil. Fighting also forces millions of people to flee their homes, leading to hunger emergencies as the displaced find themselves without the means to feed themselves. The conflict in Syria is a recent example.

## WAR AS A CAUSE OF POVERTY

While economic rivalry of one sort or another can be considered a key factor in war, war and the preparation for war can have dire economic consequences. In war, as the World Food Program (WFP) (2016b) indicates, food itself sometimes becomes a weapon. Enemy soldiers will deliberately destroy crops and livestock in order to starve opponents into submission. Fields are often mined and water wells contaminated, forcing farmers to abandon their land. Ongoing conflict in Somalia and the Democratic Republic of Congo has contributed significantly to the level of hunger in the two countries. By comparison, hunger is on the retreat in more peaceful parts of Africa such as Ghana and Rwanda.

Competition over resources is of course a phenomenon related to greed as well as need. We need only consider the history of conquest and internal fighting in the Middle East.

When massive supplies of arms have been shipped into countries in desperate need of economic aid, both the death toll and the flood of refugees have increased. Prolonged fighting across the globe has destroyed crops and devastated agricultural areas, turning countries into ecological wastelands. At the same time, the crops are not tended to as men are carried away to war or killed. Seasonal workers who ordinarily would arrive for the harvesting do not come as trade routes are cut off due to conflict. Famine may result as in South Sudan, which is torn by tribal warfare. Two years of civil war have left nearly 4 million people—particularly young children—facing severe hunger, according to the United Nations (British Broadcast Company [BBC] News, 2015).

Warfare is predominantly a male activity. Yet the economic costs of war and the preparation of war often fall more heavily on girls and women as they become less valued than boys and men. This inequity is reflected in infanticide, and in reduced health care and nutrition for females. In some regions, and especially in South Asia, men and boys eat first. Girls in impoverished nations are several times as likely to be malnourished as boys (United Nations Development Programme, [UNDP] 2015).

War is self-perpetuating. As groups take up warfare in response to war-like neighbors, the fighting spreads geographically. As losses mount, the seeds are sown for continuous fighting, and the costs of war to the countries and the people are enormous. In North Korea, for example, where children suffer from growth stunting due to malnutrition, the government invests its resources in nuclear weapons development (Food and Agricultural Organization, 2016). The war on terrorism has pushed the war against poverty that afflicts billions of people off the international agenda (Astore, 2015).

### POVERTY STEMMING FROM INADEQUATE SOCIAL WELFARE PROVISIONS

Social welfare provisions are available for disabled, unemployed, and other vulnerable people in the society to shield them from the throes of cruel circumstances. Whether care is formal or informal, the availability of help in times of severe crisis is essential to ensure survival of a population. The lack of such aid compounds the social problems related to poverty.

*Structural adjustments* or requirements imposed upon debtor nations by the world banks necessitate cost cutting in domestic spending to pay off the debt. (Sometimes this process is simply called austerity.) Indebtedness to foreign powers prevails as well; such debt sometimes is connected to borrowing money for military expenditures. Cutbacks in health care and other social services are reflected in maternal and infant mortality rates and the spread of disease. We will now consider the dynamics of globalization in greater depth.

## POVERTY AND GLOBALIZATION

From the richest and most generous social welfare states to the most impoverished nations, globalization affects us all. Constraints of the marketplace and dominance by the rich nations over the poor create a situation of economic oppression on a massive scale. All politics, in this sense is global; the most productive nations can be expected to seek markets for their products and trade arrangements that work to their advantage. As the powerful nations set the rules through their big banks, one expects a climate conducive to increasing privatization and the accumulation of vast sums of capital in the hands of the few.

According to the capitalist growth/trickle-down theory, all nations are seen as developing along a predictable continuum of progress from the traditional societies composed of isolated tribes to modern economies. This is why poor nations are considered to be "developing." The stated expectation is that rapid increases in economic growth will "trickle down" to the masses, and that loans from the world banks will expedite these nations' progress on the path to solvency. In truth, the reality is quite the opposite: The source of much oppression can be found in the economic development model itself--in the neo-liberal (which is really neo-conservative) agenda.

Economic globalization, in short, is not working for many of the world's poor (Stiglitz, 2013). Nor for the environment. Nor for the stability of the global economy. The transition from Communism to a market economy has been so badly managed in some countries, as Stiglitz (winner of the Nobel Prize in economics and author of the national bestseller, *Globalization and Its Discontents*) points out. Poverty has soared as wealth has accumulated in a few hands. The problem as Stiglitz further indicates, is with some of the rules of the game, rules set up by the IMF (International Monetary Fund), World Bank, and the WTO (World Trade Organization). Global trade is highly regulated through these organizations, with the powerful holding sway and the playing field far from level.

Few companies have the scale and financing to compete with the top US and European multinationals on an open market. Free trade, in fact, is not so much free as restrictive for producers in the poor countries; Industrialized nations have held onto their trade barriers in such areas as agriculture, while demanding that less influential nations lower their tariffs.

## WORLD BANKS AND MONETARY POLICIES

The cornerstone for international trade agreements was laid after World War II with the establishment of two international agencies to be accountable to member nations and to address the needs of the post-World War II world. The IMF was established to encourage expansionary policies in nations in need of financial assistance for economic development and to oversee monetary policies (Karger and Stoesz, 2013). In its original conceptualization, as indicated, the IMF's focus was primarily to preserve economic stability (Stiglitz, 2013). A public institution, the IMF reports to ministries of finance and world banking institutions.

In contrast to the IMF, the establishment of the World Bank was specifically for the purpose of providing credits and long-term loans to the poorest nations (Healy,2008). In recent years, under pressure from women's groups, it has embarked on some progressive policies geared to helping poor women in poor countries obtain loans for microenterprise creation. Stiglitz, who served as senior vice president of the World Bank until 2000, has seen change occur at the World Bank; he has seen more working *with* rather than against governments in promoting exports and new enterprises. In this regard, the worldwide anti-globalization protest movement has had a positive impact.

Much of the focus of the global protest demonstrations has been on the world trade organization (WTO). Founded in 1995, the WTO was created to accelerate the emergence of global markets and to produce the equivalent of a global constitution to ensure a healthy business climate for international commerce. The Geneva-based WTO is described in an article in *The Global Exchange* (2011) as representing the interests of corporations rather than the people. In agriculture, for example, the leading principle is that market forces should control agricultural policies rather than a national commitment to guarantee food security and maintain decent family farmer incomes. WTO policies have allowed dumping of heavily subsidized industrially produced food into poor countries, undermining local production and increasing hunger.

Fueled by policies of the IMF, industrializing countries in order to obtain loans, have been forced to cut spending, privatize, lower taxes, reduce labor rights, and eliminate subsidies for basic food items (Hellinger, 2014). Essentially a transfer of resources to foreign banks is the result. In parts of Latin America where governments are often corrupt, privatization as of public utilities, may promote greater efficiency. Results have been uneven, however. Privatization has become deeply unpopular; privatization of a water firm in Bolivia in 2000, for example, was scrapped after riots (Hellinger, 2014). Collectively these privatized policies made nations and regions more attractive to foreign investment. Corporations, in order to remain competitive move across the globe in search of ever cheaper labor and increased tax incentives from governments (McCormack, 2013).

Within nations as well as among nations, the gap between rich and poor has been getting larger. Although exact data from cross-country and within country comparisons are hard to come by, a review of the available evidence on inequality by the UNDP (2016) indicates that worldwide, within-country income inequality has been increasing over the past 30 years. Since 1990, the gross domestic product has increased in most countries and life expectancy in the Global South has risen from 63.2 years to 68.6 years. Yet during this same time period, income inequality in the poor nations increased by 11%. From the perspective of the world as a whole, the richest 8% of the world's population earn half of the world's total income, while the remaining 92% of people are left with the other half. The richest 1% of the world population owns about 40% of the world's assets, while the bottom half owns no more than 1%.

In Mexico, a poor country, there are now 16 billionaires, including one man who for a while was considered the richest man in the world (Woody, 2015). The richest 10% of Mexicans earn 30 1/2 times as much as the poorest 10%, a measure that places Mexico last in economic equality among the Organization of Economic Cooperation and Development's 34 member countries.

Improvements have been seen in a number of countries, however. The UNDP (2013) reports that in Latin America cash transfers targeted to poor households have had a noticeable redistributive effect and can be considered responsible for a part of the decline in inequality in many countries in the region. Mexico, Peru, Bolivia, and Argentina were among the countries singled out. In South Africa, cash grants such as the Child Support Grant and the Old Age Pension helped reduce the level of inequality.

Despite the potential that social protection holds for inequality reduction, social protection coverage is still low in many countries. In sub-Saharan Africa, for instance, only 25% of the population is covered by social assistance or social insurance and the situation is similar in the Arab States and in South Asia.

## FREE TRADE AGREEMENTS IN NORTH AMERICA

The same new political, neoliberal (meaning free-market oriented) ideologies that guide the global economy across continents shape the nature of capitalism closer to home (for residents of North America). Just as in Latin America and Africa, world banks have become the principal movers of social policy, under the North American Free Trade Agreement (NAFTA), the erosion of the people's social and economic interests was a given. Because NAFTA was the first free trade agreement with a low-wage country (Mexico), some critics predicted a negative outcome for the United States (Greeley, 2016). As predicted, in the United States, and Canada, thousands of manufacturing jobs were lost and labor protection legislation repealed. The impact of the replacement of full-time, highly paid manufacturing jobs with part-time, temporary labor coupled with a reduction in social welfare benefits has been especially evident in Canada, while in both Mexico and Canada, small home-grown businesses have folded in competition from major corporations such as Walmart that sell high-quality, low-priced goods imported from Asia. Corn and grain imports from north of the border have driven Mexican farmers into deep crisis (Johnson, 2011). Some two million have been forced to leave their farms since the passage of NAFTA, and many have headed north across the border (Carlsen, 2013).

As for the promise of new and better jobs with trade liberalization, working conditions at the *maquiladoras* (export processing plants) have become notorious for human rights violations against the poorly paid, mostly young female employees who toil 12 hour workdays in these plants, and live in shantytowns near the US border.

There was much controversy in Canada in the 1990s concerning whether or not the nation would join NAFTA with the United States and Mexico. In the end, the right-wing politicians won out, and Canada joined the free trade agreement. Now, in the 21st century, we can survey the results, still preliminary though they are. Canadian author Naomi Klein (2002; 2014) known for her iconoclastic books such as, *No Logo,* and *This Changes Everything: Capitalism vs the Climate* provides documentation that, in many ways, the corporations' profit strategies have backfired and produced a core of activists from Toronto to Buenos Aires who no longer feel they have a stake in the system. Klein (2014) summarizes the three policy pillars of contemporary free trade agreements as: "privatization of the public sphere, deregulation of the corporate sector, and lower corporate taxation paid for with cuts to public spending" (p. 19). The costs of such policies, as she further states, are in the instability of financial markets, excesses of the super-rich, and the desperation of the increasingly disposable poor.

In Canada, the promised growth in jobs in high technology sectors did not materialize. In the name of making Canada more competitive, worker benefits have declined while worker productivity has increased through new labor-saving technology, speedups, and more overtime work (Klein, 2014; Tencer, 2014). Productivity, similarly, is up south of the Canadian border while the total employment rates in high-wage jobs have fallen (Ehrenreich, 2015).

Under NAFTA's investment provisions, foreign investors are allowed to sue governments if domestic environmental regulations are detrimental to business. This is the most controversial aspect of NAFTA and other free trade agreements, as the corporation's financial interests are placed above environmental concerns, for example, in the construction of a pipeline to transport oil or natural gas (Harris & Roach, 2018). A large number of lawsuits have arisen in Canada over this matter.

Let us now consider the implications of economic globalization for poverty in the United States.

## IMPACT IN THE UNITED STATES

At the other end of the equation from Mexico and Canada is the country with presumably the most to gain from global trade—the United States. To gauge the impact, let us turn to the results of a 20-year anniversary report by Public Citizen. The report showed the loss of 1 million net US jobs under NAFTA (Wallach, 2014, p. 1).

For confirmation of the numbers of factories moving production to Mexico, a search on google.com reveals a huge number from virtually every state. You can read on the google search engine of factory closings in places like Galesburg, Illinois and Amana, Iowa, not to mention Detroit. Such closings in rural America, which leave the areas destitute, are casualties of the competition with cheap labor in other parts of the world. The gain is to US manufacturers, to the major, transnational corporations. The loss is to the US worker and to the government in lost tax revenues both from the overseas businesses and from workers who lose their source of income. And the trend is not in manufacturing alone (which workers eventually will lose to automation anyway), but also in the highest paying service industries. Information technology is leading the offshore exodus. As a presidential candidate, Donald Trump focused the nation's attention on problems with free trade and the loss of US jobs to low-wage countries (Bredemeier, 2017).

According to Roberts (2010), outsourcing jobs to foreign countries does not just create job loss to call-center operators, customer service and back-office jobs, but also in the high-paying fields of information technology, accounting, architecture, advanced engineering design, news reporting, stock analysis, and medical and legal services. Today, India, China, Ireland, Israel and the Philippines all are experiencing a boom in exporting computer-based services. The relocation of factories or movement of operations through cyberspace represents a boom to such regions where the cost of living is low and the imported jobs allow for a high standard of living that could not be obtained otherwise. Now, hundreds of thousands of Indian and Chinese technicians, programmers, and software engineers are working for US and British companies from their own computers in Asia. Indian radiologists now analyze CT scans and chest X-rays for American patients; they do their work not far away from where accountants are processing US tax returns.

In 2015, the CEO of Hewlett-Packard announced plans to locate 60% of the company's information technology jobs to low-cost offshore locations like Manila, Philippines; Costa Rica; and Bangalore, India (Bort, 2015). The reason, according to the CEO, is global competition. The construction boom in research and development labs all over Bangalore represents a new wave of investment that is making this region a hub of global research activity. The attraction to computer firms such as Hewlett-Packard and Texas Instruments of India is the high standard of engineering education, command of the English language, and global experience of Indian educated engineers. Another key advantage of reliance on labor on the other side of the globe is the time difference. Work orders sent at the end of the day in the United States are received in the morning in India, then returned for the start of the following day in the United States. A similar state of affairs occurs in Ireland where the educational level is high, English fluency is outstanding, and the time difference a major advantage.

America's loss is China's gain as well. Chinese factories are flooding the world with cheap goods, everything from television sets and DVD players to bicycles and clothes. Yet Mexico today is winning out over China, in automobile manufacturing for a number of reasons—ease of transport to the United States, well-trained workers, and free trade agreements between Mexico and dozens of countries (Priddle & Snavely, 2015). The big loser in all this is the other NAFTA partner, Canada.

In summary, world economics today is highly complex. For the United States, Canada, and Mexico, the free trade agreements are far from the win-win-win situation that the true believers in unfettered capitalism had predicted. The outsourcing trend with manufacturing and white collar jobs to Mexico and Asia continues to expand at the expense of American workers.

## POWER OF THE CORPORATIONS

In conjunction with a grasping of the unique American values discussed in chapter 3—the Puritan-based Protestant ethic, the tendency to blame society's unfortunates—an understanding of the disparities in the distribution of wealth starts with the political system, with the way candidates are elected in a two-party system.

India, similarly, relies on extensive corporate funding of political parties; most European countries, however, place severe limits on such funding. True campaign finance reform, in which the government paid for TV and press coverage rather than the candidate's private resources, would do much to democratize the process. Such finance reform would free politicians from the influence of powerful interest groups such as the gun industry, military-industrial complex, pharmaceutical companies, and for-profit hospitals, to name only a few.

Unearned income, which is income that comes from investments and mainly concerns people with money, is taxed at a lower rate than income that is earned through work. Stock dividends are only taxed at a rate of 15% to benefit stockholders (Solin, 2014). Another tax, which is a payroll tax, relates to the thousands of dollars that workers pay in Social Security taxes and Medicare tax each year. Later, when older people receive their Social Security checks, it is taxed along with personal income. Kentucky Representative Thomas Massie has introduced a bill in Congress to eliminate the double tax (Nelson, 2017).

From a global perspective, we can clearly see the extent to which the world's wealth is concentrated in the coffers of the most highly industrialized nations of the Global North. Among these industrialized nations, the United States leads in the proportion of income going to the wealthiest fifth (Piketty, 2014). Some countries in Latin America, such as Brazil, of course, have far higher disparities. Still, measures of income alone are not the best way to gauge the gap between the rich and the poor. Individuals do work for income, after all, but wealth is inherited as a birthright. So we need to look at overall wealth rather than income. *Class polarization* is the term used by Day and Schiele (2012) for this disparity in the economic gap between the poor and the wealthy which, according to these writers, is one of the most crucial problems facing the American institution of social welfare at the present time. While more of the middle classes are moving into a lower standard of living through unemployment, lower wages, and a rise in the number of single-parent families, people with wealth are consolidating their holdings.

Because of the indirect but very significant impact of the global economy on all of us, including social work clients, Day and Schiele suggest that an internationalist perspective is vital. For many of the same reasons, the poor are growing poorer the world over. Many countries in addition to the United States have made similar adjustments to award high income earners so they could keep a higher percentage of their income. When neo-liberal conservatives come into power in the government, they tend to support policies that favor themselves and their class.

One reason for the plethora of conservative legislation that has been passed in Congress over the past decades is the influence of the lobbyists who represent business interests. When President George W. Bush decided to expand Medicare to provide insurance for medication for older people, the pharmaceutical companies spent over $130 million on lobbying in the year when the law passed (*The Economist*, 2015b). Thanks to their efforts, no attempts were made to control costs and the drug companies were able to reap enormous profits.

Keeping government regulations away from corporations is predictably a goal for which business interests will fight. This includes a fight against restrictions on lobbying. In this section we will look at a Supreme Court decision that opened the flood gates to unrestricted lobbying and at a once-secret organization responsible for the introduction of legislation geared to benefit business interests at the expense of the people.

One reason for the triumph of neoliberal ideology and corporate power was the influence that corporations have in financing elections. At a time when many in the general public and some politicians have favored campaign finance reform, judicial decisions have reinforced this role (Reich, 2015b). In a momentous decision of 2010, the US Supreme Court decided in Citizens United that corporations are people, in the legal sense of the word. Under the First Amendment to the Constitution, therefore, corporations are entitled to freedom of speech. A later decision in 2014 built on Citizens United to allow corporations and individuals the right to make unlimited campaign contributions. Most of the money goes for TV ads and other campaign expenses. Contributions can even be anonymous (Scherer, 2014).

There is always some hope that in the future these decisions will be overturned in the interests of democracy. The connection with poverty is that the likelihood that political leaders will be influenced by their sponsors is great and that big money interests will win out over the "little people." One major force to reckon with, however, is the influence of think tanks, such as the Heritage Foundation that produces platforms for politicians to follow, usually involving mass budget cuts for welfare programs. This is on the intellectual side. On the economic side is a powerful right-wing group financed by American billionaires including the Koch brothers and corporations, the American Legislative Exchange Council or ALEC. The strategy of this organization is to shape legislation in a prepackaged form, templates of which are passed to conservative legislators to be introduced as bills in their state legislators (Scola, 2012). Among bills that were passed were: "stand your ground" laws endorsed by the NRA to give more rights to people to shoot to kill others in threatening circumstances; voter ID laws that keep people without official identification from voting; measures to cut corporation taxes; initiatives to support charter schools at the expense of public schools and their unionized teachers; and other measures supporting privatization of services.

The war weapons industry, according to Reich (2015a) is one of the top lobbyists of members of Congress. Lockheed Martin, the largest contractor, for example, maintains a squadron of Washington lawyers and lobbyists dedicated to keeping and getting even more federal contracts. The firm spent over $14 million lobbying Congress in one recent year. The manufacturers not only produce weapons for the Unite States, but also to sell to foreign countries. Military expenditures by the United States are the highest of any country. (See chapter 8 for a comparison of military versus social welfare spending.)

We now explore in more detail the expanding economic inequality in the United States today.

## GROWING INEQUALITY IN THE UNITED STATES

The top-earning 20% of Americans receive around 60% of all income generated in the United States (Domhoff, 2013). It has only been in recent years that the American public came to resent this disproportionate economic control of society by the top 1%. There are three key factors that have led to such an awareness: The Occupy Wall Street Movement, the publication of economist Piketty's *Capital*, and the Bernie Sanders political campaign.

"We are the 99%" was the catchy slogan that college students and others in the Occupy Wall Street movement chanted and displayed in signs all across the towns and cities in the United States in 2011. Once the media took notice, and with facts spread on the Internet about the encampments that were being set up in public parks and on college campuses, the issue of inequality was front and center in the news. Levitin (2015) credits the grassroots movement with giving America a new language, leading to worker demands for an increased minimum wage, and shaping the political debate to the extent that inequality and the wealth gap became core tenets of the Democratic platform for the 2016 elections. Although the organization was weak, and the momentum gradually faded, the awareness of the concentration of income, wealth, and political power has remained in the public consciousness. The presidential campaign of Bernie Sanders achieved much of its appeal in challenging the power of Wall Street.

A great deal of media attention accompanied the publication (translation from the French) of Thomas Piketty's (2014) *Capital in the 21st Century*. Through the use of a plethora of charts and graphs and a scholarly review of history, Piketty documented the growth of inequality over the last three decades. Unless capitalism is regulated, he argues, the nation's wealth is likely to become even more concentrated in the hands of a few. A nation's economic growth, Piketty further suggests, is impaired when the rate of return on wealth (investments) is greater than the growth of the economic system as a whole.

The impact of the publication of this 700 page piece of scholarship, which surprisingly was on the top of the best-selling lists for months and months, was that it revealed the irrefutable facts about the ascendancy of the rich and superrich and further sparked the global debate on inequality. Commentators such as Krugman (2014) attribute the success of Piketty's book to the way that it successfully demolished the America-as-a-meritocracy myth, the belief held by conservatives that people achieve success on their own merits, and the belief that the system is just.

Keep in mind the significance of wealth when compared to income. Wealth accumulates over generations and is passed down. The inequality level when measured in terms of income shows that the top 1% receive 19% of all income (McCormally, 2016). When you look at the disparity in terms of wealth, you learn that the richest top 1% own 40% of the nation's wealth (Reich, 2016). The bottom 80% own just 7%. Wealth accumulates over generations and is passed down. As former Labor Secretary Robert Reich explains, most Americans have no savings, and live paycheck to paycheck. It takes savings to buy a house or invest in stocks or saving to send a child to college. Wealth generates its own income, so the rich get richer, and the level of inequality rises.

This is why wealth inequality is compounding faster than income inequality. Recent research shows that as the level of inequality in a society rises, such as in the United Kingdom and the United States, economic status is generated through inheritance (*Bloomberg Businessweek*, 2013). A comparison among nations on the basis of the difference in income between the top 1% and the rest of society shows that where differences are relatively small as in Finland, Norway, Canada, and Australia, the levels of social mobility are high.

Given the facts just mentioned, it is little wonder, as revealed in a recent study by the Pew Research Center (2016b), that, across the cities in the United States, the middle class is shrinking. This fact emerged through research data on over 200 cities on income levels for the years 2000 to 2014. Findings were that more families were in a high income bracket than before at the same time that increasing numbers had fallen down to just above the poverty level.

In essence, this rise in inequality is a major threat to the welfare state because it concentrates power in the hands of the very people in whose interest it is to destroy it.

## INEQUALITY AS A HUMAN RIGHTS ISSUE

Economic inequality can trigger financial crises, which in turn can entrench inequalities further. This happens as the tax base declines, a result of powerful forces that reduce the tax burden for the rich while the non-rich lack the income to pay much in the way of taxes. A financial crisis occurs as the national debt increases. As happened in Greece, the austerity measures that governments often adopt in response to financial crises tend to have terrible social impacts, exacerbating inequality and pushing disadvantaged groups below minimum income thresholds (Bohoslavsky, 2016). The economic situation of individuals often translates into unequal access to education, health care or other rights resulting in discriminatory outcomes within societies. This is where, as Bohoslavsky correctly argues, human rights comes into play. Inequality, as he further suggests, can have negative effects on marginalized group's enjoyment of political and civil rights. This is clearly happening in the United States where law enforcement efforts are directed toward the poor and where, as in the title of Reiman and Leighton's (2012) incisive book, "the rich get richer and the poor get prison." As the authors effectively argue, even before the process of arrest, trial, and sentencing, the system is biased against the poor in what it chooses to treat as crime and the penalties provided.

## WAR AGAINST THE POOR

Historically, there were always efforts, according to Piven (2006), to attack welfare recipients and welfare, usually on the same grounds: that welfare causes poverty, laziness, and sexual immorality. These arguments were pronounced in England in the 1830s, and then they resurfaced in the US and UK in the 1980s. The war against the poor is reflected in the lack of a living wage which in the past has made "being on welfare" in many states more remunerative than full time work and in the retrenchment in social welfare benefits. The blaming-the-poor ethos has focused attention on the supposed shortcomings of the poor, and the passing of regulations to force adults, even mothers of young children, into the work force. The blaming-the-poor focus has diverted attention from the more structural problems related to corporate domination of the economy.

This ideology is nothing new. An explanation was provided in less complicated times by Michael Harrington (1962), author of *The Other America:*

> As long as the illusion persists that the poor are merrily freeloading on the public dole, so long will the other America, continue unthreatened. The truth, it must be understood, is the exact opposite. The poor get less out of the welfare state than any group in America.
>
> History and ideology, in short, have caused us to take one attitude toward public or private welfare services for the affluent, another attitude toward subsidy for the upper-middle classes, and still another attitude toward public welfare services for the poor. (p. 172)

Another scenario is displacing the aggression not onto the poor but onto minority groups. In an interview, Senator Elizabeth Warren described her impoverished upbringing and her family's losing their home after her father had a heart attack. Then she said:

> People across America now understand there's a lot that's broken. People feel like I did when I was 12 years old: "I'm about to lose the whole thing." And they feel that way because it's true. Millions

> of people were turned upside-down in the financial crash, and they can't get a foothold. Young people with college debt are starting out 10 yards behind the starting line. And this is the Donald Trump moment. He says, "Blame the immigrants, blame women, blame people who have different religious beliefs than you, blame people who aren't the same color as you." Because if everyone turns on each other. . . . Then the same old system that keeps billionaires on top stays right where it is. (Warren and Tyagi, 2016, p. ST17)

How do people live on 40 hour-a-week minimum wage jobs of seven or so dollars when rents take up most of it, not to mention other expenses such as car repairs and emergency room visits? Rental prices soar, but wages fail to rise. Homelessness is often one paycheck away. In fact, many of today's workers are homeless. In a well-publicized book titled *Evicted*, Harvard sociologist Matthew Desmond (2016) shares the personal stories of families who live in places such as a Milwaukee trailer court who struggle to make ends meet. The biggest problem that Desmond found, in his participant observation study of these families, was that the breadwinners didn't earn enough money through their low-wage earnings to pay their often overdue rent. Evictions were common, and once evicted, it becomes very hard to find another place to rent. Today, most poor renting families are spending more than half of their income on housing, and eviction has become ordinary, especially for single mothers.

If the economy takes a nosedive, people lose their jobs and homes. Some move in with relatives; others especially persons with mental disorders are apt to end up on the streets. The war against the poor is perhaps at its most ferocious in the crackdown directed at the nation's estimated one to three million homeless people (numbers are uncertain). Many cities are passing tough laws against panhandling, loitering, and sleeping in public places.

Although there was general agreement that welfare reform, which was designed to force welfare recipients who were able-bodied to enter the job market, was not successful in reducing poverty, many states continued to move forward with further rules and regulations that make the process of receiving benefits a rough, even humiliating, experience (Samuels, 2016). Arkansas, for example, just became one of a long line of states to require drug testing for all welfare recipients, a costly proposition that nets few abusers. Governors are also adding work requirements for low-income people who are benefiting from the state's Medicaid expansion or food stamps.

The treatment of single parents with children is clearly relevant to classism. Consider the contrast between the admiration by society accorded middle and upper class parents who choose to stay home with their children in the early years to give them a good start in life, while poor mothers, with far fewer resources, are essentially pushed out of the home even with an infant at home. Another fact related to class (and social mobility) to consider is that the states have cut support for four-year education in favor of two-year education or other job-training programs. This effect is especially evident in departments of social work education which earlier had prided themselves on helping welfare recipients move into professional careers.

As we discuss issues related to class and classism, a point worth bearing in mind is that, in the United States, unlike in most European countries, there is a denial of class identity—no working class newspaper, and no labor party to represent the interests of the working class. Let us now see how inequality issues are played out in Europe.

## WELFARE IN THE EUROPEAN UNION

Major accomplishments are the use of a common currency—the Euro—in many of the countries, and a Court of Justice to interpret community law, protect citizens' human rights, and settle disputes between states. A major advantage of EU membership is that workers can move freely among the countries; agreements are currently being reached to recognize professional credentials cross-nationally. Students can attend universities throughout the region as well. Perhaps the most promising dimension of the EU is its attention to social problems, especially those that transcend national boundaries. In anticipation of workers' displacement through global competition, for example, the Commission of the European Union has taken a stand in favor of shortening the work week for everyone. (NAFTA would do well to emulate this position).

In countries in Western Europe, the emphasis is on child allowance, family services, daycare provision, and the overall well-being of the child. Unlike in the US where parental care is not recognized as a form of work for the good of the nation, the social charter of the European Union recognizes the value of work in the home, especially of child care.

On the negative side, the leveling of standards mandated in the agreement is resulting in serious "modifications" in welfare programs in Denmark, Finland, and Sweden. Although these modifications likely have improved provisions in the countries with the least developed social welfare systems, states with generous benefits are required to reduce them (Healy, 2008). Farmers cannot be subsidized as they have been—their produce will have to compete with food grown much more cheaply in southern Europe, and women stand to lose many of their special benefits. Accordingly, much political controversy has ensued throughout Scandinavia over some of the consequences of Europeanization to these welfare states and is referred to within the EU as the "North/South divide." In Sweden, where opposition to EU membership has always been strong, especially among women, membership has been generally regarded as partly responsible for the erosion of the Swedish welfare state (Agius, 2012). To date, as of 2016, Norway and Iceland have resisted joining the EU to preserve their high standards of social welfare (Lakey, 2016). And the United Kingdom, following a much-heated referendum, decided to break away. The move was famously termed Brexit for British exit.

## WORK IN THE GLOBAL ERA

Inasmuch as the economic viability of a nation depends on its having a productive and high-functioning work force, the nature of work becomes a vital human rights consideration. Article 23 of the UN Declaration of Human Rights (1948) is composed of four parts, providing: the right to free choice of employment; to just and favorable conditions; to equal pay for equal work; and sufficient remuneration to ensure an existence worthy of human dignity (See Appendix A). Article 23, is in the second covenant of the Universal Declaration, unfortunately, the part not signed by the United States because the rights granted went beyond those of the US Constitution.

Worker rights are the strongest under conditions of a labor shortage and reduced competition. Solidarity of workers through unions enhances their bargaining position and protects them from an influx of cheap labor. Modern global economics has transformed labor relations rendering workers, except the most highly skilled, dispensable and replaceable. Shrinking paychecks, and eroding health and pension benefits are the new reality for many Americans at the same time that the gap between the chief executives of America's big companies and their average workers has increased. In 1978, the CEOs of large companies were paid 30 times as much as their average worker; now their pay is 300 times as much (Reich, 2015b). No other industrialized nation has such a discrepancy: Norway has the lowest pay differential—big business executives are paid 16 times the average worker (Berglund, 2013), a matter that is always closely monitored by the government.

Perhaps both the cost-cutting at lower levels and pay raises at the highest levels are symptomatic of the global imperatives. Downsizing, outsourcing, wage flexibility, cost-efficiency, accountability, productivity— these are just a few of the buzz words causing workers in many parts of the world to cringe. We can look to almost any company as a case in point, but the prime example is Walmart, the $230-billion-a-year retailer.

Because of the success of Walmart's strategies, this company has drawn the attention of Harvard Business School, which even sells Walmart case studies to business schools around the world (Alcacer, Agrawal, & Vaish, 2013). Its policies, everything from its fight against the unions to its extremely generous funding of charter schools, which are seen as a business enterprise, are highly influential and receive close scrutiny by economists.

One effective strategy of the Walmart business model was to bring their stores into small towns and cities across the country, undersell the local businesses including grocery stores, and then force them to close down. Once there was no competition, Walmart could close their stores and force customers to travel some distance to the nearest Walmart, often in a neighboring town (Bryant, 2016). Such policies are callous but make some business sense. The company does provide a lot of community supports to its Arkansas home community through generous philanthropy to the arts, but through the Walton Family Foundation, it uses its business model. to replace neighborhood public schools with charter schools (Ravitch, 2010). Part of the impetus for this nationwide effort is the Walton's family historic animosity for unions and for teachers' unions.

If unchecked, the destruction of worker rights along with structural shifts in the economy can have devastating consequences for workers and their families. Consider the following headlines from a variety of news sources:

> "Why America's Nurses Are Burning Out," *Everyday Health*, (Gupta, 2016);
>
> "Middle Class Shrinks in Colorado, Across U.S. Incomes Fall," *The Denver Post*, (Rugaber, 2016);
>
> "'He Was Masturbating . . . I Felt Like Crying': What Housekeepers Endure to Clean Hotel Rooms," *Huffington Post*, (Jamieson, 2017);
>
> "Why the Teen Summer Job Is Disappearing," *The Wall Street Journal*, (Moise, 2017);
>
> "Trump Administration Tightens Scrutiny of Skilled Worker Visa Applicants," *Wall Street Journal*, (Meckler, 2017);
>
> "Japan Struggles with 'Karoshi,' or Death by Overwork, after Deaths of 2 Young Women," *USA Today* (Molina, 2017);
>
> Robots Could Take Over 38% of U.S. Jobs Within about 15 Years, Report Says," *Los Angeles Times* (Masunaga, 2017).

The list could go on and on. What we learn from such sources as the above is that competition among companies is reflected in competition among workers. We learn that poultry processors and nursing home aides epitomize the harshness of much of the new low-wage work where workers suffer soaring injury rates and yet frequently lack health benefits. In many high-growth industries, work is faster than ever before and, therefore, the personal stress is greater also. In Iowa, well known for its strong work ethic, to make ends meet, many workers are taking two jobs and some are even relying on methamphetamines to stay alert (van Wormer & Davis, 2018). See Figure 7.2 of Mexicans engaged in lawn work.

For a closer look at the world of work from the vantage point of the lowest paid worker, we turn to two sources, both of them bestsellers—*the McDonaldization of Society* and *Fast Food Nation*. Interchangeable workers, homogenization of the product, standardized work routines, and technologies that take care of most of the "brain" work (such as making change)—these are among the characteristics of the fast-food restaurant singled out by sociologist George Ritzer (2015) in his popular (especially in Britain) *The McDonaldization of Society*. The process by which the principles of the fast-food restaurant "are coming to dominate more and more sections of American society as well as of the rest of the world" (1) is epitomized in the global McDonald's chain, according to Ritzer. Not only characteristic of the restaurant business, the process is also affecting education, travel, organized leisure-time activities, politics, the family, and of course, work itself. Significantly, the term *Mc* has come to symbolize mass-produced services as in *Mc*Dentists, *Mc*Papers, *Mc*Day Care. The McDonald's model has succeeded because it offers the consumer efficiency, predictability, and food at reasonable prices. For the worker, however, the setting is often dehumanizing; the average fast-food worker lasts only three months. Workers can take no pride in their work or creations; the pseudo friendliness with customers can be taxing in its own way.

*Fast Food Nation: The Dark Side of the All-American Meal* by Schlosser (2002; 2012) takes us into the world of the modern food industry, a world that is founded on the premise of cheap

**FIGURE 7.2.** Immigrant day labor: Seattle. Photo by Rupert van Wormer.

food, cheap labor. Many of the facts in this book are widely known due to the popular 2006 film by the same name. The actual cost to life is reflected on food-borne disease, near-global obesity, loss of the family farm, animal abuse, and chopped-off fingers. Learning of the chemicals that are added to food to make it taste like what it is (hamburger flavor, for example) not to mention the chemicals fed the animals for abnormally fast growth, your appetite for this food will wane. Our interest here is in the work angle, in meat-packing which is now the most dangerous job in the United States, and farming and cattle-raising which are now corporate enterprises. In his new afterword, added to the re-issuing of the book, Schlosser (2012) notes that little has changed over the past decade except that people who can afford it, now are buying organic food. And the fast food industry is targeting African Americans, Latinos, and the poor to buy their products. The work conditions remain the same as described in his original text:

> Responding to the demands of the fast food and supermarket chains, the meatpacking giants have cut costs by cutting wages. They have turned one of the nation's best-paying manufacturing jobs into one of the lowest-paying, created a migrant industrial workforce of poor immigrants, tolerated high injury rates, and spawned rural ghettos in the American heartland. (p. 149)

IBP (Iowa Beef Packers), which is now owned by Tyson Foods, has been inundated with lawsuits related to: unsafe working conditions (workers typically are forced to make one knife cut of beef every two or three seconds); pressure not to report injuries; scandals related to the recruitment of undocumented workers; and the fondling of female employees.

To avoid lawsuits and for economic reasons, much of the most dangerous manufacturing work is being relocated abroad where safety standards are lax. According to recent research from the International Labor Organization (ILO) (2016), 2.3 million workers die each year through work-related accidents and diseases. The biggest killer in the workplace is cancer related to work with hazardous material such as asbestos and radiation. Agriculture, logging, fishing, and mining are the most hazardous industries.

## WORKER STRESS IN THE INDUSTRIALIZED SOCIETY

There are two kinds of stress related to the pressures of competition in the global economy. The first is the job stress itself; the second relates to the insecurity of work in an era of rapid change when the worker may become "redundant," to use the British term.

Many of the US service jobs such as at Wendy's announce on their billboards that they are hiring "smiling faces." Hy-Vee of Iowa, the grocery chain, has as its advertising slogan "a smile in every aisle." In a lawsuit from California, thirteen workers filed grievances against Safeway's smile-and-make-eye-contact orders, complaining that such a policy makes them vulnerable to being propositioned by shoppers who mistake the company's imposed friendliness for flirting.

Job related stress is exacerbated in a tight job market. When Barbara Ehrenreich (2002) applied for low wage jobs as a part of her research for the exposé *Nickel and Dimed*, she was shocked at the intrusiveness of the application process. For jobs ranging from store clerk to Walmart greeters, as Ehrenreich discovered, the applicant must submit to invasive drug screenings.

Forced overtime is a growing source of dissatisfaction. As more workers are laid off, the remaining workers are working harder than ever to fill the slack. Due to high cost to companies for health care insurance and other benefits, it is cheaper to pay overtime to the regular staff than to hire more staff. Yet research shows that the long days are increasingly unpopular and harmful to workers and their families. Productivity is even impaired when workers are deprived of sufficient time off the job (Carmichael, 2015). Much recent labor strife such as airline pilots' strikes is related to the desire of workers to spend more time with their families or simply to rest from the pressure at work.

The consequences of overwork are reflected in lack of sleep for the worker and related safety problems on the job (Bukowski, 2014). Today many of the factory jobs are moving to 12-hour, four-days-a-week shifts. The pressure on truck drivers to deliver goods on time has resulted in their spending too many hours on the road. The consequence has been a death toll in highway accidents involving the big trucks (Rhee & Valiente, 2014).

A recent investigation by Oxfam America into work conditions in the poultry industry, where many immigrants work, found that the stress on productivity was such that workers could not take a bathroom break (Ferdman, 2016). Findings were obtained by hundreds of interviews with line workers from major US companies such as Tyson Foods, and Pilgrim's Pride, and Perdue. In some cases, according to the investigators, the reality is so oppressive that workers urinate and defecate while standing on the line. Some wear diapers to work. Other employees say they avoid drinking liquids for long periods and endure considerable pain in order to keep their jobs. From the point of view of the companies, competitive forces are blamed for driving poultry processors to produce as much meat as possible, as fast as possible, leading to inhumane conditions for the workers.

In Canada, as elsewhere high levels of worker stress are evident. Research from the University of Toronto (2013) found that roughly one-third of Canadian workers report that they "often" or "very often" feel overwhelmed by work or that the demands of their job exceed the time to do the work. Four out of 10 workers report having to work on too many tasks at the same time "often" or "very often." In Britain, more than 51% of workers surveyed admit to experiencing rage at work. This outcome related to a feeling of loss of control by the worker has been termed "desk rage" or displaced aggression against work equipment or fellow workers (Subramanian, 2013).

## IMPACT ON THE FAMILY

Grueling work schedules coupled with increasing job insecurity are taking a toll on working class families. When there is a shortage of money, tensions mount, and conflict often develops among individual members. Depressed wages, a frenetic pace set at the workplace, the rapid rise in temporary work, decreased long-term employment, the growing disparity between the haves and have-nots, and the dramatic shrinking of the middle class are placing unprecedented stress on the American work force (Rugaber, 2016). As jobs have been eliminated, and companies are cutting down on the labor force to save costs, the survivors are often doing the tasks of two or three people.

On the subject of crisis, a survey taken by the Federal Reserve Board, which monitors the financial status of Americans, got an astonishing answer to the question, how they would pay for a $400 emergency. Personal illness, funeral expenses, a car breakdown—these are typical examples. Almost half of respondents said they would borrow the money, sell something, or wouldn't be able to pay the bill (Gabler, 2016). To understand how this high-risk financial situation had come about, Gabler did some background research. He found that median net worth has declined steeply in the past generation for people at the middle income level, and that it was down much more so for people at the lowest one-fifth income level.

As hard as Americans work, the Japanese dedicate themselves to their work with a sense of obligation that is difficult for the Westerner to understand. The boundaries between work and after-hours recreation (often at a karaoke bar) are not clearly drawn. Overwork leading to death is common enough to have been given a name—*karoshi*—dropping dead at your desk (Molina, 2017). A recent government report found employees at nearly one in four companies are at risk of dying from working too much.

While the major economic debate in America concerns inequality and the wealth gap, in Japan, the major division is between those with full-time jobs and those engaged in temporary work (Clenfield, 2014). In fact, 40% of Japan's labor force have part-time and temporary work and are paid 38% less per hour than full-time workers. The full-time workers enjoy a guaranteed job for life and have many benefits such as subsidized housing, travel, and lunch. The number of such lifetime jobs, however, has been declining for decades. The majority of the temporary workers are women. This fact is leading to activism by female Japanese women on the basis of discrimination.

Work-related family crisis is occurring not only in North America and East Asia but universally. In India, where poor migrants are brought in to work on construction sites, small children are sometimes literally tied to rocks while the parents work (Amit, 2016). This lack of childcare is a worldwide phenomenon, especially in the Global South.

At the opposite end of the work continuum among industrialized nations is the attitude toward work in Scandinavia. A guide to business customs in Sweden describes business meetings as formal and goal oriented. At the same time, the business person is advised to:

> Arrange the timing of meetings thoughtfully. Offices are often deserted on Friday afternoons, particularly in the summer, and the whole country seems to close down from July to August and during the winter school half-term holiday. Try to fix meetings for early morning. Late afternoon is equally unpopular due to thoughts of going home, as are the few days before a public holiday such as Easter, when executives want to clear their desks. (Hutchings & Hatchwell, 2002, p. 328)

Van Wormer's experience working at a Norwegian alcoholism treatment center was comparable. She found that Norwegians work hard while at work, but their leisure time is highly valued. Social workers expect to work about six hours a day. Workers thought nothing of taking the day off for a dental appointment, and of course a year's (paid) leave for pregnancy was provided. Sick leave for emotional problems related to work stress could last a year as well. The pay they received on sick leave was comparable to what they had earned while working. Sweden, under pressure from the EU, because of the excessive number of sick days workers were taking, has placed some restrictions on such absences. An outside observer would probably conclude that Scandinavians are hard-working, but that much of their industriousness is directed toward activities outside of work—toward building cabins in the mountains or teaching their children (toddlers) to ski, for example. Family ties are close and family life is enhanced thereby.

## THE NEW TECHNOLOGIES AND UNEMPLOYMENT

Public services have changed enormously through the availability of new technologies, as there is less contact between the business personnel and the consumers. Efficiency has increased for the business because there are fewer workers on the payroll. But is it more efficient, as Ritzer (2015) asks, to pump your own gas or use exact change on a bus? Or check yourself in for an air flight? Are prerecorded voices on the telephone more responsive to our needs?

One area where people, at least air force pilots, will be happy to surrender their role to machines involves dangerous bombing missions. In Silicon Valley, in university offices, hospitals, and practically everywhere else, the new technologies are helping employees do more work in less time. For this reason, productivity is up even as firms are getting leaner in terms of job opportunities.

Ultimately, the big threat to jobs, according to economist Jeremy Rifkin (2015), who sounded the alarm as early as the 1990s, is automation, and not outsourcing. His new book, *The Zero Marginal Cost Society*, effectively captures the new economic ethos. Wave after wave of technological innovation not only has affected manufacturing sectors (where robots are replacing people) but the service sector as well (where computers, automated teller machines, and voice-recognition technologies are eliminating the need for human contact). What is happening is clearly revolutionary for the marketplace and capitalism itself. Much that we paid for before is now available for free, or at least without the middleman. Students today take courses for credit via Skype, exchange information on Facebook and Twitter; travelers share homes, bikes, cars, and just about everything else online. Books are published at little cost through self-publishing resources. Energy sources also are being revolutionized through reliance on the sun and wind. Self-driving vehicles could eventually put truck drivers and taxi cab drivers out of work, and already new systems are being developed in restaurants which enable customers to get their food orders in without interacting with a server (Miller, 2014).

But just as important as technology is the society's response to the reduced demand for labor. One approach, which is widely publicized in the media is the falsely optimistic claim that if people just develop more skills the jobs will be there for them. This argument is effectively challenged by Martin Ford (2015) in *Rise of the Robots: Technology and the Threat of a Jobless Future*. From janitors to surgeons, book keepers to lawyers, virtually no job will be immune from the technological revolution. And offshore workers in India are just as vulnerable as their counterparts in the West. The society must prepare for a time when large numbers of workers are obsolete and for the fact that with fewer workers the whole economy will suffer, because who will be able to buy the products? The social consequences could be grave. Ford's answer is to pay every adult a minimum basic income. Another possible solution, which we propose, would be to divide the work around for a shorter work week and more income for all.

In her review of Ford's book, Ehrenreich (2015) discusses the implications for the field of publishing where computers do much of the editing, work that can now be outsourced to India. For the military field as well, the new technologies have been transformative. Drones are taking over much of the combat roles. These killing machines reduce the risks to air force pilots and the numbers of troops needed on the ground, but are a major threat to civilians in the area (de Luce & McLeary, 2016).

Today's work world, in short, is changing, and the old ways are not coming back. The psychological toll from loss of a job can be enormous, especially in a society such as in the United States, where a person's status in society is determined by his or her occupational role and achievement in that role. Widespread unemployment can be devastating not only for the individual, but for the society as a whole. The consequences are reflected in early teenage pregnancy, homelessness, crime statistics, and even mass civil disorder, inasmuch as persons outside of the work economy are divorced from the ordinary social structure.

Researchers find a strong association between unemployment and emotional problems. During a recession, mental hospital admissions increase, as do suicides, divorce rates, and incidences of child abuse (Zastrow, 2013). Even children of the unemployed suffer from mental health problems as well as rejection by peers, developmental delays, and increased depression (Melson, 2014). Joblessness, poverty, reluctance to marry, and family breakup are all highly correlated. Job loss increases marital conflict, ups the risk of divorce, and leads to more ineffective parenting, sometimes too harsh, sometimes too neglectful. Children pay a severe price for the hard economic times their parents endure. These long term effects help explain why African Americans marry at much lower rates than other groups in the United States (Coontz & Fobre, 2003). Substance abuse and job loss are reciprocally related. Zastrow (2013) lists suicide, emotional problems, insomnia, psychosomatic illness, social isolation, and marital unhappiness among the consequences of long-term unemployment.

Young men today increasingly are finding it hard to get a start in a job with good prospects for the future. A recent national survey from the Pew Research Center (2016a) contains information that is striking: For first time in more than 130 years, adults aged 18 to 34 are more likely to be living in their parents' home than they were to be living with a spouse or partner in their own household. For men ages 18 to 34, living at home with their mother and/or father has been the dominant living arrangement since 2009. Part of the reason is the later age of marriage today, but this, in turn, is related to career opportunities for young people.

In light of the changing realities in the workplace in the absence of a cultural shift in sync with the new realities, no longer will parents be able to pin their hopes on the next generation to accomplish what they could not. Workers in a highly competitive society can't count on the generosity of government assistance to help them out with generous job benefits or innovative worker training programs. Reich (2015b) sees the solution in terms of job retraining, but a logical question we might ask is retraining for what? If highly skilled computer experts in Silicon Valley are losing their jobs, perhaps we had better get beyond the platitudes and be more pragmatic in sharing the work around and reducing the hours for all workers.

Nations with high productivity and low labor needs will be in a position to take advantage of the labor-saving technologies to free up time for the people to perform more meaningful, community building functions, providing care for the frail elderly and so on. And could we not find a way to share enormous wealth accruing to the soaring productivity?

## SUMMARY AND CONCLUSION

The dysfunctions of poverty at home and abroad are represented in disease, malnourishment, the daily struggle to survive, chronic indebtedness, and personal resentment. Whether within nations or between nations, disparities in wealth are associated with greed, resentment, and war. Wars, in turn, lead to mass migrations of people. Across the world refugees from conflict migrate from the poor countries into the wealthier ones, joining the already large number of immigrants who cross borders for economic reasons. A significant loss to the poor countries is the brain drain of doctors and scientists who were educated at their governments' expense but whose talents will be utilized elsewhere. We talked in this chapter of the dysfunctions of poverty. A major dysfunction in regard to mass poverty is engendered in the system of rationalization, which arises to justify it and perpetuate it. Just as we dehumanize the enemy during wartime in order to reduce any qualms in battle or guilt feelings later, so we dehumanize poor and homeless people in order to justify our society's treatment of them. In dehumanizing the poor, we are dehumanizing ourselves.

Only by helping people to understand and confront their personal troubles of economic and social hardship within the context of human rights can we hope to find appropriate solutions. Such has been the aim of this chapter in a nutshell—to pinpoint the correlates of poverty in areas as diverse (and interconnected) as war; pressures from the global markets to raise capital at the expense of welfare programs and reduced funding to the states; retrenchment of government support for social services; privatization; the "race to the bottom" associated with one-sided free trade agreements; the elimination of factory jobs by new technologies and, in the immediate present, of labor unions due to industry's ability to relocate. The revolution in industry that got under way at the turn of this century is replicated in agriculture in mass production of cash crops. The revolution is not necessarily bad; the new technology can be regarded as a godsend, freeing people up to use their talents, to develop social capital in the local community instead of industrial products. But the challenge to the global age is to promote cultural values to correspond to the new work realities and provide for greater flexibility and more family time.

As workers become increasingly expendable, their sense of security vanishes. The byproducts of pressure on the job—family violence, employee violence, substance abuse, divorce, and stress-related illness—are on the rise in the United States and elsewhere. Hovering over the whole issue of work are these questions: What is the meaning of work in our lives and our family lives? How can society adapt to a rapidly changing work milieu? And what happens to people who have lost their livelihood? The loss is in human potential.

Nevertheless, there are government programs geared to help meet people's needs, many of which focus on the children and people with disabilities. Because poverty relates to practically every social problem, the majority of the government programs are designed to alleviate poverty in one way or another. We will explore the role of such policies and programs in the next chapter.

## THOUGHT QUESTIONS

1. Consult the Universal Declaration of Human Rights (Appendix A). Which articles pertain to economic human rights? How is poverty in a rich country a violation of human rights?
2. What is the significance of the quote from President Eisenhower concerning military expenses?
3. What does globalization mean? Distinguish between globalization in general and economic global market competition as discussed in this chapter.
4. "Literacy for women is highly correlated with low birth rates." What do you think is the reason for this correlation?
5. Compare working conditions in the United States with those in other countries, more progressive and less progressive. How could having an American labor party affect workers' rights and benefits?

6. How is membership in the EU a move forward to some countries and a move back for others?
7. How has NAFTA benefited or not benefited Mexico? How about the United States?
8. Show how war and poverty are related to each other. How is the relationship reciprocal?
9. Can an argument be made that structural adjustments required by the IMF on the macro level are replicated in welfare reform at the local level?
10. Discuss the growing gap between rich and poor in today's world. How do you think the inequality in the United States could be remedied?
11. What are some of the basic findings in the literature concerning income inequality in the United States compared to other countries? Relate this to social mobility.
12. List three major changes in the nature of work in the global era. What is the human toll of over- and under-employment?
13. What is the significance of the title, The McDonaldization of Society?
14. How are the new technologies affecting employment today? Can you think of any way that this situation could lead to a happier life for workers?
15. What are some of the consequences to families and the society of the scarcity of meaningful jobs?

## REFERENCES


Agius, C. (2012). *The social construction of Swedish neutrality: Challenges to Swedish identity and sovereignty.* Manchester, England: University of Manchester Press.

Alcacer, J., Agrawal, A., & Vaish, H. (2013, October 11). Walmart around the world. *Harvard Business Review*. Retrieved from www.hbr.org

Amit, D. (2016, March 17). On building site, parents tether toddler to rock while they work. *Reuters.* Retrieved from www.reuters.com

Androff, D. (2016). *Practicing rights: Human rights-based approaches to social work practice.* New York, NY: Routledge.

Associated Press. (2014, March 13). Low-wage jobs new reality for many. Waterloo, Iowa: *Waterloo/Cedar Falls Courier*, p. A6.

Astore, W. (2015). Tomgram: William Astore, "Hi, I'm Uncle Sam and I'm a war-oholic." *Tom Dispatch.* Retrieved from www.tomdispatch.com

Barusch, A. (2015). *Foundations of social policy: Social justice in human perspective.* Belmont, CA: Cengage.

Berglund, N. (2013, May 29). Executive pay low in Norway. *News in English.* Retrieved from www.newsinenglish.no

Bloomberg Businessweek. (2013, December 12). How inequality became a household word. *Bloomberg Businessweek*, pp. 16–17.

Bohoslavsky, J. (2016, May 12). The vicious spiral of economic inequality and crises. *Open Democracy.* Retrieved from www.opendemocracy.net

The Borgen Project (2013, December). The impact of poverty on life expectancy. Retrieved from https://borgenproject.org/impact-poverty-life-expectancy/

Bort, J. (2015, September 15). Meg Whitman: HP will offshore 60% of the jobs in its "essential" business unit. *Business Insider*. Retrieved from www.businessinsider.com

Bredemeier, K. (2017, February 23). Trump vows push to bring back jobs lost to other countries. *Voice of America News*. Retrieved from www.voanews.com

British Broadcast Company (BBC) News. (2015, October 22). South Sudan war: 30,000 people face starvation, UN warns. Retrieved from www.bbc.com

Bryant, J. (2016, March 26). How the cutthroat Walmart business model is reshaping American public education. *Truth-Out*. Retrieved from www.truth-out.org

Bukowski, T. (2014, May 23). Sleepy and unsafe. *Safety and Health Magazine*. Retrieved from www.safetyandhealthmagazine.com

Carlsen, L. (2013, November 24). Under NAFTA, Mexico suffered and the United States felt its pain. *New York Times*. Retrieved from www.nytimes.com

Carmichael, S.G. (2015, August 19). The research is clear: Long hours backfire for people and for companies. *Harvard Business Review*. Retrieved from www.hbr.org

Caulderwood, K. (2015, April 14). Sub-Saharan Africa falls behind in fight against extreme poverty: World Bank Report. International Business Times. Retrieved from www.ibtimes.com

Clenfield, J. (2014, June 8). Miho Marui's campaign against wage discrimination shakes up Japan's vast part-time economy. *Bloomberg Businessweek*, pp. 13–15.

Coontz, S., & Folbre, N. (2003, April 26–28). Marriage, poverty, and public policy. Retrieved from www.prospect.org

Day, P., & Schiele, J. (2012). *A new history of social welfare*. Boston. MA: Pearson.

de Luce, D., & McLeary, P. (2016, April 5). Obama's most dangerous drone tactic is here to say. *Foreign Policy Report*. Retrieved from www.foreignpolicy.com

Desmond, M. (2016). *Evicted: Poverty and profit in the American city*. New York, NY: Crown Publishing Group.

Dickman, S., Himmelstein, D., & Woolhandler, S. (2017) Inequality and the health-care system in the USA. *The Lancet, 389*(10077), 1431–1441.

Domhoff, G. W. (2013). *Who rules America? The triumph of the corporate rich*. New York, NY: McGraw Hill.

The Economist. (2015a, July 25). Breaking the baby strike. *The Economist*, p. 47.

The Economist. (2015b, June 13). The unstoppable rise in lobbying by American business is bad for business itself. *The Economist*, p. 66.

Ehrenreich, B. (2002). *Nickel and dimed: On not getting by in America*. New York, NY: Metropolitan Books.

Ehrenreich, B. (2015, May 18). Welcome to your obsolescence. *New York Times Book Review*, pp. 1, 26.

Ferdman, R. (2016, May 11). "I had to wear Pampers": The cruel reality the people who brought your cheap chicken allegedly endure. *Washington Post*. Retrieved from www.washingtonpost.com

Food and Agriculture Organization. (FAO). (2015). *The state of food insecurity in the world*. Rome, Italy: FAO.

Food and Agriculture Organization. (2016, April 27). North Korea's food production falls for first time since 2010 as water scarcity hits agricultural sector. Retrieved from www.fao.org

Ford, M. (2015). *Rise of the robots: Technology and the threat of a jobless future*. New York, NY: Basic Books.

Gabler, N. (2016, May). My secret shame. *The Atlantic*, pp. 52–63.

Galea, S., Tracy, M., Hoggatt, K., DiMaggio, C., & Karpati, A. (2011). Estimated deaths attributable to social factors in the United States. *American Journal of Public Health, 101*(8), 1456–1465.

Gans, H.(1995). *The war against the poor*. New York, NY: Basic Books.

Gil, D. (2013). *Confronting injustice and oppression: Concepts and strategies for social workers*. New York, NY: Columbia University Press.

Greeley, B. (2016, May 22). How do you solve Kevin's problem? *Bloomberg Businessweek*, pp. 35–36.

Gupta, S. (2016, May 6). Why America's nurses are burning out. *Everyday Health*. Retrieved from www.everydayhealth.com

Harrington, M. (1962). *The other America: Poverty in the United States.* Baltimore, MD: Penguin.

Harris, J. M., & Roach, B. (2018). *Environmental and natural resource economics: A contemporary approach.* New York, NY: Routledge.

Healy, L. (2008). *International Social Work.* (2nd ed.). New York: Oxford University Press.

Hellinger, D. (2014). *Comparative politics of Latin America.* New York, NY: Routledge.

Hookway, J. (2014, March 19). Slumping fertility rates in developing countries spark labor worries. *Wall Street Journal.* Retrieved from www.wsj.com

Hutchings, J., & Hatchwell, E. (Eds.) (2002). *Insight guide: Sweden.* Masapath, NY: Langenscheidt Publishers.

Jamieson, D. (2017, November 18). "He was masturbating . . . I felt like crying": What housekeepers endure to clean hotel rooms. *Huffington Post.* Retrieved from www.huffingtonpost.com

Johnson, T. (2011, February 1). Free trade: As U.S. corn flows south, Mexicans stop farming. *McClatchy DC.* Retrieved from www.mcclatchydc.com

Karger, H., & Stoesz, D. (2013). *American social welfare policy: A pluralist approach,* 7th edition. Boston, MA: Pearson.

Lakey, G. (2016). *Viking economics: How the Scandinavians got it right—and we can too.* Brooklyn, NY: Melville House Printing.

Klein, N. (2002). *No logo: No space, no choice, no jobs.* New York, NY: Picador.

Klein, N. (2014). *This changes everything: Capitalism vs the climate.* New York: Simon & Schuster.

Krugman, P. (2014, April 28). The Piketty panic. *New York Times,* p. A19.

Levitin, M. (2015, June 10). The triumph of Occupy Wall Street. *The Atlantic.* Retrieved from www.theatlantic.com

Macionis, J. (2014). *Society: the basics* (13th ed.) New York, NY: Pearson.

Masunaga, S. (2017, March 24). Robots could take over 38% of U.S. jobs within about 15 years, report says. *Los Angeles Times.* Retrieved from www.latimes.com

McCormack, R. A. (2013, July 13). America's biggest companies continue to move factories offshore and eliminate thousands of American jobs. *Manufacturing and Technology News, 20* (10). Retrieved from www.manufacturingnews.com

McCormally, K. (2016, April 23). What's your rank as a taxpayer? *Kiplinger.* Retrieved from www.kiplinger.com

McKay, B. (2010, January 22). Disease, malnutrition risks grow in Haiti. *Wall Street Journal.* Retrieved from www.wsj.com

McNamee, D. (2015, February). Stress levels are down, but money worries continue to trouble Americans. *Medical News Today.* Retrieved from www.medicalnewstoday.com

Meckler, L. (2017, November 19). Trump administration tightens scrutiny of skilled worker visa applications. *Wall Street Journal.* Retrieved from www.wsj.com

Melson, G. F. (2014, January 22). Parents lose jobs and children suffer. *Psychology Today.* Retrieved from www.psychologytoday.com

Miller, C. C. (2014, December16). Rise of robot work force stokes human fears. *New York Times,* p. 1A.

Moise, I. (2017, May 23). Why the teen summer job is disappearing. *Wall Street Journal.* Retrieved from www.wsj.com

Molina, B. (2017, October 6). Japan struggles with 'karoshi,' or death by overwork, after deaths of 2 young women. *USA Today.* Retrieved from www.usatoday.com

Nelson, S. (2017, September 25). Massie wants to eliminate taxes. *Washington Examiner*. Retrieved from www.washingtonexaminer.com

Piven, F. (2006). *Challenging authority: How ordinary people change America*. Plymouth, UK: Rowman & Littlefield Publishers.

Pew Research Center. (2016a, May 24). For first time in modern era, living with parents edges out other living arrangements for 18- to 34-year-olds. Retrieved from www.pewsocialtrends.org

Pew Research Center (2016b, May 12). The shrinking middle class in U.S. metropolitan areas. Retrieved from www.pewresearch.org

Piketty, T. (2014). *Capital in the 21st century*. Cambridge, MA: President and Fellows of Harvard College.

Priddle, A., & Snavely, B. (2015, June 15). More car manufacturing jobs move South—to Mexico. USA Today. Retrieved from www.usatoday.com

Ravitch, D. (2010). *The death and life of the great American school system: How testing and choice are undermining education*. Philadelphia, PA: Basic Books.

Reich, R. (2015a). How to disrupt the military-industrial-congressional complex. *Nation of change*. Retrieved from www.nationofchange.org

Reich, R. (2015b). *Saving capitalism: For the many, not the few*. New York, NY: Knopf Doubleday.

Reich, R. (2016, April 28). Wealth inequality is even more devastating than income inequality. *Salon*. Retrieved from www.salon.com

Rifkin, J. (2015). *The zero marginal cost society: The Internet of things, the collaborative commons, and the eclipse of capitalism*. New York, NY: St. Martin's Press.

Reiman, J., & Leighton, P. (2012). *The rich get richer and the poor get prison*. New York, NY: Routledge.

Rhee, J., & Valiente, A. (2014, September 1). The danger of forcing truck drivers to drive sleep-deprived exposed). *ABC News*. Retrieved from www.abcnews.go.com

Rifkin, J. (2015). *The zero marginal cost society: The Internet of things, the collaborative commons, and the eclipse of capitalism*. New York, NY: St. Martin's Press.

Ritzer, G. (2015). *The McDonaldization of society* (8th ed.) Thousand Oaks, CA: SAGE.

Rugaber, C. (2016, May 12). Middle class shrinks in Colorado, across U.S. as incomes fall. *The Denver Post*. Retrieved from www.denverpost.com

Samuels, A. (2016, April 1). The end of welfare as we know it. *The Atlantic*. Retrieved from www.theatlantic.com

Sanders, B. (2016, March 20). Poverty is the worst form of violence—-Gandhi. Twitter.com.

Scherer, M. (2014, April 14). Money talks: A divided Supreme Court loosens the reins on campaign—again. *Time*, p. 14.

Schlosser, E. (2002). *Fast food nation: The dark side of the all-American meal*. New York, NY: Houghton-Mifflin.

Schlosser, E. (2012). Afterword in reissued edition. *Fast food nation: The dark side of the all-American meal*. New York, NY: Houghton-Mifflin.

Scola, N. (2012, April 14). Exposing ALEC: How conservative-backed state laws are all connected. *The Atlantic*. Retrieved from www.theatlantic.com

Sinha, K. (2012, February 2). Goa, Kerala best states in which to be born in India. *Times of India*. Retrieved from www.indiatimes.com

Solin, D. (2014, February 4). Seven myths about dividends. *U.S. News and World Report*. Retrieved from www.money.usnews.com

Sonwalkar, P. (2016, April 27). Boys in India eat better than girls, Oxford study. London: *Hindustan Times*. Retrieved from www.hindustantimes.com

Stiglitz, J. (2013).*The price of inequality: How today's divided society endangers our future.* New York, NY: W.W. Norton & Company.

Subramanian, C. (2013, August 20). The silent "deck rage" epidemic. *Time.* Retrieved from www.time.com

Tencer, D. (2014, September 4). One in four Canadians fear they'll lose job to technology. *Huffington Post Canada.* Retrieved from www.huffingtonpost.ca

United Nations Development Programme. (UNDP). (2013). Human development report. Retrieved from www.hdr.undp.org

United Nations Development Programme (UNDP). (2015). Humanity divided: Confronting inequality in developing countries. Retrieved from www.hdr.undp.org

United Nations Development Programme (UNDP). (2016). Human development report. Retrieved from www.hdr.undp.org

University of Toronto (2013, February 28). "'Crazy-busy' Canadians under pressure on the job." *Science Daily.* Retrieved from www.sciencedaily.com

U.S. Census Bureau (2016). Income, poverty and health insurance coverage in the U.S., 2015. Washington, DC: U.S. Census. Retrieved from www.census.gov

van Wormer, K., & Davis, D. R. (2018)4th ed. *Addiction treatment: A strengths perspective.* Belmont, CA: Cengage.

Wainer, A. (2014). Immigrants in the U.S. food system. *Hunger Report.* Retrieved from www.hungerreport.org

Wallach, L. (2014, March 8). NAFTA at 20: One million U.S. jobs lost, higher income inequality. *The World Post.* Retrieved from www.huffingtonpost.com

Warren, E. (2016, September 18). Elizabeth Warren and Tracee Ellis Ross on the road to activism. *New York Times.* Warren interviewed by P. Gallenes. *New York Times*, pp. ST1, ST17.

Warren, E., & Tyagi, A.W. (2016). Introduction. In E. Warren & A.W. Tyagi (Eds.), *The two-income trap: Why middle-class mothers and fathers are going broke* (pp. xiii–xxiv). New York, NY: Basic Books.

Wise, T. (2010). *Colorblind: The rise of post-racial politics and the retreat from racial equity.* San Francisco, CA: City Lights Books.

Wise, T. (2015). *Under the affluence: Shaming the poor, praising the rich and sacrificing the future of America.* San Francisco, CA: City Lights Books.

Woody, C. (2015, August 7). One jarring stat reveals just how vast Mexico's wealth gap has become. *Business Insider.* Retrieved from www.businessinsider.com

World Food Programme (WFP). (2016a, February 3). Drought in Ethiopia: 10 million people in need. Retrieved from www.wfp.org

World Food Programme (WFP). (2016b). Who are the hungry? Retrieved from www.wfp.org

Zastrow, C. (2013). *Introduction to social work and social welfare, Empowerment series.* (11th ed.). Belmont, CA: Cengage.

CHAPTER 8

# PUBLIC ASSISTANCE AND OTHER STRATEGIES TO END POVERTY

> Everyone, as a member of society, has the right to social security and is entitled to realization, through national effort and international co-operation and in accordance with the organization and resources of each State, of the economic, social and cultural rights indispensable for his dignity and the free development of his personality.
>
> Universal Declaration of Human Rights, Article 22, 1948

This chapter discusses anti-poverty strategies as administered by the US government. Public assistance or residually based, means-tested programs, are compared with social insurance programs which are available to the general public. Among the public assistance policies discussed are (TANF), Supplemental Nutrition Assistance Program (SNAP), formerly called food stamps, supplemental security income (SSI), Medicaid, the Earned Income Tax Credit, Head Start, and housing assistance. These are the programs for low-income people who meet certain criteria such as being below the federal or state poverty line. Social insurance programs are those that workers typically pay for themselves through making regular contributions, such as Social Security and Medicare. We explore each form of assistance from a historic and contemporary perspective. We also consider the topic of tax structure in terms of special policies and loopholes that favor the rich and the corporations. This discussion of economic policies to prevent poverty concludes with a description of a rights-based approach to poverty and development and some thoughts on how some of the most unsavory aspects of economic globalization can be ameliorated.

## STRATEGIES TO END POVERTY IN THE UNITED STATES: PUBLIC ASSISTANCE

Before the war in Vietnam broke out and monopolized the attention and the funding, it was President Lyndon Johnson's mission to prevent and end poverty. Many of his war on poverty's programs—like Medicaid, Medicare, food stamps, Head Start, Job Corps, and VISTA—are still in place today. Matthews (2014), writing in the *Washington Post*, provides a review of research concerning the effectiveness of such programs between the years 1967 and 2012. His conclusion is that government action is literally the only reason for the decrease in poverty over those years. Without such programs, in fact, the poverty rate would have increased. In 2012, food stamps alone kept 4 million people out of poverty. Largely because people rely on the official poverty rate, which is a horrendously flawed measure, it is commonly believed that the programs have been ineffective. Official measures of the poverty level exclude income received from major anti-poverty programs like food stamps or the Earned Income Tax Credit (EITC). These measures also fail to take into account expenses such as child care and out-of-pocket medical spending.

Some of the programs mentioned above were designed to be universally available—social insurance programs—and others were only intended for poor people—public assistance programs. Social insurance operates much like any other type of insurance in that people pay against future risk.

Sometimes called "welfare" by the general public, public assistance programs are restricted to the income eligible in which applicants must undergo a "means test" are highly stigmatized. Instead of being financed by the employee though his or her job, support for the public assistance comes out of general tax revenues.

Examples of means-tested programs are Temporary Assistance for Needy Families (TANF), Supplemental Nutrition Assistance Program (SNAP), formerly called food stamps, supplemental security income (SSI), Medicaid, the Earned Income Tax Credit, Head Start, and housing assistance. These programs, in contrast to social insurance benefits, are all based on need rather than entitlement. An important fact to note about means-tested programs is that when they are available only to people below a certain income and not available to others, resentment builds up, and the programs are stigmatized (see Seccombe, 2013). Over time they are underfunded. For this reason, a clever strategy is for conservatives to try to get universal programs to be available only to people whose incomes are below a certain level, even a fairly high level. Then ultimately support for the program will decline.

The work ethic (as discussed in chapter 2) figures strongly in the experiments conducted by Congress in the anti-poverty policies that have been passed over the years. In addition, legislators have restructured benefits and tax breaks intended for the poor so that they penalize unmarried parents and people who are not working—the modern-day version of the "undeserving poor" (Edsall, 2014). At the same time, working parents, older adults, and persons with disabilities have been treated with greater respect.

## WELFARE FOR THE RICH

Tax policy helps eradicate poverty by providing funding for social welfare including educational programming and social services; recent changes in the tax code allow tax credit for low income people, an important development in providing relief to the working poor. But the bulk of government assistance is meted out not to the economically disadvantaged—the women and children and older adults or even to the middle classes whose real wage earnings have declined steadily over the past decade—but to the richest 10% of the US population. There is a kind of welfare for the wealthy and for large corporations (such as tax relief for mismanaged savings and loans institutions) not available to the poor (Dolgoff & Feldstein, 2012). In fact, the share of the national wealth going to the richest segment of the population continues to rise.

An article in the *Washington Post* lists 10 ways in which the rich get government handouts not available to others:

- The mortgage interest deduction for big houses and second homes
- The yacht tax deduction on interest
- Rental property that brings big tax deductions
- Business meals that are tax deductible
- The capital gains tax rate, which is substantially lower than that paid by work income
- The estate tax fee, which is only paid on estates worth over $10 million as of 2018
- Gambling loss deductions from one's taxes
- The cap on social security taxes, which are only paid on the first $127,200 as of 2017, so the higher one's income, the lower the percentage paid of the social security payroll tax
- Deduction for tax preparation by an accountant (Badger & Ingraham, 2015; www.washingtonpost.com)

Laws are made by members of Congress. Because of limited restrictions in the United States on media efforts and campaign finance, elected officials typically represent the interests of big spenders. Without a US labor party as mentioned previously, the interests of the working class are apt to be overlooked. And without a Parliamentary system which allows for representation of multiple parties representing a variety of interests, no labor party (or Green party) is apt to gain many votes or to be a viable force in shaping legislation.

In 1964 incomes over $200,000 were taxed at the rate of 70%; this rate was lowered to 50% in 1981. In 2001 the top taxable rate was 38.6% (Tax Policy Center, 2002). In 2003, under President George W. Bush's tax cut that largely favored the wealthy, the tax rate was reduced to 33%. (As of 2016, the rate was raised to 39.6% (Poppick, 2015), and to 37% as of 2018). Bending the tax code in response to lobbying, as Karger and Stoesz (2013) indicate, is a long-standing practice often associated with corporate influence. Corporations are the beneficiaries of huge tax breaks and subsidies at state, local, and federal levels that come at the expense of public services and the individual taxpayer (Reich, 2015). Subsidies to massive agribusiness operations and defense industry are examples of gigantic public relief programs (Stiglitz, 2013).

Subsidies for the rich and the superrich are seen in caps in social security contributions which are only paid up to a certain level of income, tax deductions for one's home mortgage, and a lower rate of taxation on their investments than their salaries. Another fact to keep in mind is that, unlike with income from salaries which is removed for one's paycheck in advance, the government only gets to use this money at the end of the year when taxes are paid. Self-employed persons and business owners have a wide number of deductions at their disposal. Purchase of expensive pieces of artwork for the office, for example, are often acquired in this manner, as a tax dodging scheme. (Remember the priceless paintings that were lost in the collapse of the World Trade Center.)

Still these tax loopholes of self-employed persons are nothing compared to the kind of tax maneuvers available to major companies. One such legal maneuver was actively opposed by Donald Trump in his campaign for the presidency. This is the tax dodge in which companies move their headquarters abroad, hire cheap labor there, and hoard their earnings tax free overseas. The profits aren't taxed unless the companies return to the United States, so they don't (Eichelberger & Gilson, 2015).

How do the major corporations get away with such practices? The best answer is the tremendous investment made by the corporations, tax lawyers, and other lobbyists in political campaigns to enhance their power. (Warren & Tyagi, 2016). Microsoft lobbyists, as one example, when rebuffed by the IRS, took their issues to Congress to rewrite the tax law.

## WELFARE FOR THE POOR

Anti-poverty policy, like all public policy set in the political arena, is determined more by the balance of power than by evidence-based analysis or by humanitarian concerns. Keep this in mind as we examine the history around welfare reform. Temporary Assistance for Needy Families (TANF) is predicated on the belief that recipients should be moved off public welfare and into private employment as quickly as possible (Karger and Stoesz, 2013).

### BACKLASH AGAINST PEOPLE ON THE WELFARE ROLLS

From the 1960s to the 1980s, as we saw in chapter 4, there was much compassion for the poor. The first backlash then happened under President Ronald Reagan, and welfare myths about women on welfare driving Cadillacs were commonly expressed during this period. Prosecutors made great efforts to prosecute welfare recipients for welfare fraud.

A second backlash legislatively took place in the late 1990s under President Bill Clinton when the welfare-to-work legislation was passed. Politicians and journalists alike praised the results for the following accomplishments: reducing the welfare budget, breaking the cycle of dependency for mothers who received welfare, and slashing the nation's welfare rolls in half. Case after case of success stories of former welfare mothers who now were happily employed filled the press and air waves. A rising economic tide around the turn of the present century did ease the transition for single mothers with limited skills into the job market (Ehrenfreund, 2016). But as some critics wondered, what would happen to these people in a recession? (In 2008, the job layoffs and huge medical expenses had devastating results for many.) And how about people who were unemployable or unable to keep a job due to personality factors?

Indeed, Edin and Shaefer (2015) found that many weren't able to maintain a stable earned income, and as a result they could not reap the benefits of a work-based safety net and the earned income tax credit given to low-income workers.

When welfare reform passed in 1996, there were about 636,000 American households living on $2 per person per day or less. As of mid-2013, that figure has more than doubled, to about 1.5 million such households, with about 3 million children living in these circumstances (Edin & Shaefer, 2015). For the poorest of the poor, the poverty rates doubled under welfare reform. There are other factors affecting this upward trend in extreme poverty, including broader economic trends affecting low-wage employment and housing stability. But there's no doubt that removal of the safety net through monthly welfare aid has played a role.

An unintended consequence of welfare reform is that policies that were intended to increase the number of low-skilled, single mothers in the workforce led to a decline of young, low-skilled, single men in the workforce. Groves (2016) notes that less-educated men who do not attend school or have jobs are more likely to commit crimes and less likely to form stable relationships with their partners. For the first quarter of 2017, the unemployment rate for black men aged 20 to 24 years was 16.2%, on average, compared to 9% for Hispanic men, according to the US Department of Labor (2017). The unemployment rate for all men in that age group averaged about 9%—double that of all men 25 years old and older. What these figures indicate is there simply are not enough jobs to go around, and punishing people for not working is only effective when work is available.

And then we need to ponder the question that is looming through all the claims and counterclaims about the effectiveness of welfare reform: -Why is the work of nurturing small children in the home not regarded as work?

Before we explore the basic programs that provide assistance to poor people, let us look at the eligibility criteria. The starting point for this determination is the poverty line.

## THE POVERTY LINE

Median household income in the United States in 2016 was $59,039, which was an increase from the year before (US Census Bureau, 2017). (For blacks, the median income was $39,490 and for white non-Hispanics, it was $65,041.) An improvement was seen in health care coverage, with the percentage without insurance at a historic low of 8.8%%. In 2016, 9.8% of families were in poverty; the poverty level showed a decline from the year before in all groups except for those over age 64.

Around 1 out of 7 Americans lives below the poverty line. When we think of people living in poverty, we often mean that they are below the poverty level. The official US government poverty level is based on the cash income for individuals to satisfy minimum living needs according to comparative expectations. For 2017, a family of 4 is considered to be below the poverty line if their income does not exceed $24,300. For a family of three the cut-off point is $20,160 (Obamacare.Net, 2017). There is no way a family can meet their needs to afford food, housing, child care, health insurance, transportation, and utilities on these incomes. Still, for the families that qualify, the supplements in the way of food stamps, free health care, and child care reimbursement are invaluable aids.

To qualify for the welfare supplements, a single person or family must be below the poverty line, although there is leeway depending on the state. The poverty line is calculated by means of a formula that is over 50 years old. It was first calculated by a federal worker who estimated the cost of a basket of food, multiplied by three, and added estimates of expenses for rent, transportation and other necessities. This is the formula used today to determine how much income a family needs to live on. No heed is taken of regional cost variations, out-of-pocket medical expenses that vary dramatically among age groups or transportation costs. Tying estimated cost of living to housing, rent or mortgage payments, and child care costs, which have gone up over the years far more than food would have a dramatic impact in terms of poverty estimates and help families have enough to live on (Light, 2013). Other calculations would be affected as well by a reformulation: Due to higher medical costs, more older adults, for example, would be considered below the poverty level than are at present. Critics of the system often look to the United Kingdom's system of multifaceted measurement as an alternative model the United States might follow.

## TEMPORARY ASSISTANCE FOR NEEDY FAMILIES (TANF)

TANF is a part of the Personal Responsibility and Work Opportunity Reconciliation Act that was passed by the Clinton administration in 1996. Permitting the states to exempt only 20% of their welfare population, welfare reform put TANF administration into the hands of the states in the form of block grants. This means that states can use the funding for cash benefits or for administering programs intended to increase employment, like childcare or job training (Carroll, 2016). Exempted from lifetime and work requirements were persons with disabilities, older adults, and those who care for a developmentally disabled family member. Many of the working poor were better off as a result of welfare reform which moved them into the job market and rendered them eligible for earned-income tax credits (Edsall, 2014). But for those single parents who did not find work, the results were dire.

Two basic philosophical beliefs underpinned this legislation. First was the impetus to get tough with people who did not work full time or who had children while receiving family assistance. Second was the desire to transfer responsibility for public assistance from the federal government to the states—this is called *devolution* (Zastrow, 2013). The so-called *devolution revolution* was an experiment that was destined to lead states to compete in a "race to the bottom" in trying to reduce their attractiveness to the non-taxpayers. The punitive thrust was certainly evident in the welfare-to-work initiatives. In terms of social justice, the abolition of the notion of welfare aid as a rational entitlement for persons in need is a revolutionary step, a repudiation of the very concept of the social welfare state.

TANF was described in chapter 4 from a historical perspective and also in this chapter's section under welfare reform. The significant fact about this block grant program, which replaced Aid to Families of Dependent Children (AFDC), was the work requirement and the key word "temporary." As before, most recipients are mothers, but unlike the earlier program, the mothers of small children are expected to work or to get training, generally through a two-year community college program to prepare oneself for work in a technical job. This program provides limited support for five years at the most.

Some policymakers have pointed to TANF as a model for reforming other programs, but the facts suggest otherwise, according to the Center on Budget and Policy Priorities (2015). TANF provides a greatly weakened safety net that does far less than AFDC did to alleviate poverty and hardship. The national TANF caseload has declined by over 60% over the last 18 years, even as poverty and deep poverty (i.e., income below half the poverty line) have worsened. The program is seriously underfunded and is only worth one-third as much as it did at the start in 1996.

## SUPPLEMENTAL NUTRITION ASSISTANCE PROGRAM (SNAP)

The current Food Stamp Act was passed in 1964; eligibility depends on family size and income. Until 1977, there were purchase requirements, but these were dropped as many poor people could not afford to buy the stamps. Today, there are stringent work requirements for the able-bodied recipients between 16 and 60 years old. Nationally, due to cutbacks across the states, there was a Supplemental Nutrition Assistance Program (SNAP; food stamps) participation decrease of 1,323,485 persons compared with January 2015. For the rest who still receive the benefit, the children benefit enormously with good nutrition even as the family struggles against problems of underemployment, stagnant wages and natural disasters.

A well-being survey collected by Gallup found that 17% of respondents did not have enough money to feed themselves or their family in the first six months of 2015 (Food Research and Action Center, 2016). That the widespread hunger and food insecurity in America is driven by gaps in federal nutrition programs and low family incomes is a key finding of the report by the Food Research and Action Center (2016).

For those who no longer qualify for food stamps because of changes in eligibility, their plight is serious as they also suffer loss of free medical care, and other forms of public assistance. Some of the workers with the worst and lowest-wage jobs are former recipients of welfare aid, mothers with small children removed from welfare rolls because they have exceeded the new time limit of five years. Because some are physically or emotionally incapable of holding a job if they could even get one, they are apt to join the ranks of the hungry and malnourished.

With extreme poverty rates on the rise and compassion for the poor at a low ebb, the richest nation in the world forces millions of its citizens to rely on private charity for handouts. As the minimum wage has failed to keep up with housing increases, food has become the expendable item in the low wage workers' budget. Food programs for older adults have suffered a steep decline in federal appropriations such as for the once generously funded Meals on Wheels program. In Springfield, Illinois, for example, many poor older adults now have to go to food banks to obtain food for themselves and their families (Olsen, 2015).

## MEDICAID (TITLE 19)

Title XIX of the Social Security Act is a jointly funded cooperative venture between the federal and state governments to assist states in the provision of adequate medical care to the poor. Known as Medicaid, this program became law in 1965. Because each of the state's administers its own program, specific policies vary from state to state.

To be eligible for federal funds, states are required to provide coverage for individuals who receive federally assisted income-maintenance payments such as TANF or SSI. Pregnant women without resources are provided with services also.

The Personal Responsibility and Work Opportunity Reconciliation Act of 1996 (or "welfare reform") made restrictive changes regarding eligibility for SSI coverage that affected the Medicaid program. For example, legal resident aliens and other qualified aliens who now entered the United States were ineligible for Medicaid for five years.

This program helps people below the poverty line (the level for eligibility varies by state), and in states that have their own health care exchanges under the Affordable Care Act, many more people qualify for the Medicaid rolls than in non-participating states. Although the program is stigmatized as a means-tested program, and many doctors refuse to accept Medicaid patients because the reimbursement is so small, having free medical care available is a salvation for many.

## THE EARNED INCOME TAX CREDIT

Some government measures to reduce poverty are commendable. Federal tax policy, as Karger and Stoesz (2013) concede, has shifted from actually exacerbating poverty to alleviating it. Elimination of income tax on very low incomes was a measure that was palatable to the American people in its reinforcement of the work ethic. The earned income tax credit (EITC) which was introduced in 1979, has been expanded in recent years. The increasing popularity of tax credits, particularly those aimed at low income families, suggests that policy change efforts could well be directed here. According to Dolgoff and Feldstein (2012), incentives for TANF families to work is enhanced through EITC because a program subsidizing *earned* income is not stigmatized. The working poor in a moralistic society are considered among the deserving poor. Moreover, this program brings a large benefit to children in the families of the working poor, though benefits are not increased beyond two children: This is one aspect of the program that is criticized. Other drawbacks are that recipients receive payments in one lump sum; many parents are unaware of the program, poor workers without children get only minimal benefits, and what about destitute persons who can't find work?

A significant additional recommendation is that education and training count toward state work participation rates. Also included under work activities should be treatment for mental disorders and substance abuse that impede people's success in living a full life, taking care of their children and so forth.

## HEAD START

Another excellent program to prevent poverty in terms of an investment in young children is Head Start. Originally envisioned as an anti-poverty program within the Department of Health and Human Services, Head Start is the country's oldest and best-known publicly funded preschool program. It tackles the needs of the entire family, annually serving more than almost one million children from primarily low-income families. Because results in the literature concerning the long-term effectiveness of the program has shown mixed results, critics have argued for discontinuation of Head Start. Some research has shown that the initial IQ-boosting benefits of Head Start fade over time, particularly for African-American children (Hechinger Report, 2010). Other analyses of the results, however, have indicated that children who go to Head Start are more likely to graduate from high school and less likely to commit crimes as adults. Since education is the key to success in contemporary society and the early years are considered crucial to child development, it makes sense to invest resources in high quality preschool education. See Figure 8.1 which shows a child who is getting off to a good start with the help of a Head Start program.

## SUPPLEMENTAL SECURITY INCOME (SSI)

The Supplemental Security Income (SSI) is a federal public assistance means-tested program which provides income support to persons aged sixty-five or older, blind or disabled adults, and blind or disabled children (Social Security Administration, 2016). The Federal benefit rate in 2016 was $733 per month for an individual. Often several members in one family are eligible. Individuals who are eligible include the intellectually disabled and mentally impaired, the aged with little or no income, the legally blind, the physically disabled, and drug addicts and alcoholics who enter treatment.

A recent liberal criticism of SSI is the fact that men are more likely to be SSI recipients while women predominate on the TANF rolls. Another liberal argument against SSI states that SSI is a

**FIGURE 8.1.** Social worker at Head Start preschool in Waterloo, Iowa. Photo by Rupert van Wormer.

very insecure source of income since people may be knocked off the rolls in response to public outcry. From the conservative perspective, there has been resentment towards SSI concerning what seemed to be a scandal involving people who were drug addicted using their income for drugs rather than treatment. In addition, there was media-generated outrage at reports of parents who had obtained SSI benefits on behalf of their children whom they reportedly had coached to "act crazy" when evaluated. Under the influence of a Republican-controlled Congress, more restrictions were placed on this benefit to the point that many people who would have qualified earlier were denied coverage. In 1996, under the Clinton administration, legislation was passed to deny eligibility for alcoholism or other drug addiction in the absence of another disabling condition. This dumping of people with severe addictions problems off the rolls had the unintended effect of increasingly the rate of homelessness in America.

## HOUSING ASSISTANCE

The shortage of affordable housing is a major problem in the United States. Only one in four eligible low-income households receives federal housing assistance because of program limitations (Mauer & Smith, 2013). TANF benefits, which have not kept pace with inflation, cover a smaller share of housing costs over time and are leaving many families without permanent housing if not homeless.

Housing and health care are closely linked. Karen Seccombe (2013) in her book on welfare recipients, describes in graphic terms the plight of minimum-wage workers and women on public assistance who can't afford even a modest two-bedroom unit. Often they have to grapple with child care expenses as well. Seccombe describes poor children whose health and safety are at risk due to their substandard housing: This can include exposure to rodents, crowding, and cold due to faulty heating systems. Many children each year are hospitalized because of asthma attacks caused by such exposure to rodents and roaches indoors and air pollution in the neighborhood. There are also safety issues related to living in high-crime neighborhoods and the dangers of children being left unattended for long hours while their parents work.

Enacted in 1937, the US Housing Act was passed to help the poor get adequate housing. Similar to food stamps and Medicaid, housing assistance is an in-kind program to ensure the purchase of services. Several public programs assist in the purchase or rental of housing for low-income families. The Section 8 rental assistance program is currently the best-known housing support for low-income families. Often assistance is provided in the form of public housing, usually government-owned projects. It is evident that such programs are inadequate to meet the needs of the increasing number of homeless people crowding the streets and under bridges everywhere. The home owners are often pleased to rent to people on Section 8 because the rent is guaranteed. In most towns and cities, however, there are long waiting lists to receive this benefit.

## STRATEGIES TO END POVERTY: SOCIAL INSURANCE PROGRAMS

Social insurance programs are government programs to protect citizens from the full consequences of the risks and situations (such as unemployment) to which they are vulnerable. These programs are highly respected because they provide a kind of security for all the people. And workers have paid in to these programs expecting some day to get a return on their money.

### SOCIAL SECURITY

Created as Old Age, Survivors, Disability, and Health Insurance Act (OASDHI) by the Social Security Act of 1935 (see chapter 3), Social Security is the largest income insurance program and is designed to partially replace income when a worker retires or is disabled. Social Security is financed by a payroll tax paid equally by employer and employee. Payments area based on previous earnings and provided at age 66 or 67 (depending on one's birth date). Smaller benefits can be obtained at age 62, and many unemployed people are forced to choose this option. (Chapter 9 discusses the meaning of Social Security to older adults.) The monthly payments received by retired workers through this program effectively keeps large numbers out of poverty.

Box 8.1 provides a synopsis of facts pertaining to the recipients of social security benefits.

## BOX 8.1 Social Security Tax Sheet

Fact Sheet: Social Security

In 2017, over 62 million Americans will receive approximately $955 billion in Social Security benefits.

SNAPSHOT OF A MONTH: DECEMBER 2016 BENEFICIARY DATA

- Retired workers: 41.2 million, $56 billion, $1,360 average monthly benefit; Dependents, 3 million, $2 billion.
- Disabled workers: 8.8 million, $10.3 billion, $1,171 average monthly benefit; Dependents, 1.8 million, $0.65 billion; Survivors, 6.1 million, $6.8 billion

SOCIAL SECURITY IS THE MAJOR SOURCE OF INCOME FOR MOST OF THE ELDERLY.

- Nearly 9 out of 10 individuals age 65 and older receive Social Security benefits.
- Social Security benefits represent about 34% of the income of the elderly.
- Among elderly Social Security beneficiaries, 48% of married couples and 71% of unmarried persons receive 50% or more of their income from Social Security.
- Among elderly Social Security beneficiaries, 21% of married couples and about 43% of unmarried persons rely on Social Security for 90% or more of their income.

Social Security provides more than just retirement benefits.

- Retired workers and their dependents account for 71% of total benefits paid. Disabled workers and their dependents account for 16% of total benefits paid.
- About 90% of workers age 21–64 in covered employment in 2016 and their families have protection in the event of a long-term disability.
- Just over 1 in 4 of today's 20-year-olds will become disabled before reaching age 67; 67% of the private sector workforce has no long-term disability insurance.
- Survivors of deceased workers account for about 13% of total benefits paid.
- About 1 in 8 of today's 20-year-olds will die before reaching age 67.
- About 96% of persons aged 20–49 who worked in covered employment in 2016 have survivors insurance protection for their young children and the surviving spouse caring for the children.

An estimated 171 million workers are covered under Social Security.

- 51% of the workforce in private industry have no private pension coverage; 31% of workers report that they and/or their spouse have no savings set aside specifically for retirement.
- In 1940, the life expectancy of a 65-year-old was almost 14 years; today it is about 20 years.
- By 2035, the number of Americans 65 and older will increase from approximately 48 million today to over 79 million.
- There are currently 2.8 workers for each Social Security beneficiary. By 2035, there will be 2.2 covered workers for each beneficiary.

---

Source: Social Security Administration. Baltimore, MD: Press Office. US Government. Available at https://www.ssa.gov/news/press/factsheets/basicfact-alt.pdf

## MEDICARE

Federal health insurance for the aged, Medicare, was incorporated in law in 1965 and OASDI became OASDHI (Old Age, Survivors, Disability, and Health Insurance). Medicare consists of two separate but coordinated programs: Part A is hospital insurance, and Part B is supplementary medical insurance of which beneficiaries are charged a monthly premium. Part D (prescription drug coverage) is voluntary and the costs are paid for by the monthly premiums of enrollees and Medicare. Unlike Part B, in which you are automatically enrolled and must opt out if you do not want it, with Part D you have to opt in by filling out a form and enrolling in an approved plan (Medicare Interactive, 2017). Unlike social security, Medicare spending does contribute to the national deficit. The reason is that former President George W. Bush added a benefit—the unfunded prescription drug program that gave the pharmaceutical companies free rein to name their prices, because of a prohibition against government negotiation in this regard (Bartlett, 2013).

Under Medicare, hospital insurance helps pay for inpatient hospital care, inpatient care in a skilled nursing facility, home health care, and hospice care. Coverage is limited to ninety days in a hospital and to one-hundred days in a skilled nursing facility.

Having this medical insurance, even though it doesn't cover 100% of costs, is a blessing to Americans who are over age 65. Hillary Clinton, in her campaign for president, talked of lowering the age to 50 or 55 so more people will be able to receive this health care benefit (Meckler, 2016). Her opponent, Bernie Sanders, campaigned on extending Medicare for all.

## UNEMPLOYMENT INSURANCE

Unemployment benefits are provided to workers who are laid off or unemployed through no fault of their own. Created by the 1935 Social Security Act, benefits vary by the state in which one lives and are only paid for up to a year as long as the recipient gives proof of a sincere attempt to apply for work.

This program is available through federal and state cooperation. The weekly benefit amount for which the unemployed are eligible, along with the number of weeks of eligibility for payment (usually for up to 26 weeks), varies from state to state. In most states, the formula is designed to compensate for a fraction of the usual weekly wage, normally about 50%, subject to specified dollar maximums. Extensions are granted during periods of economic recession. Eligibility requirements in most states are that the worker must have worked a certain number of weeks in covered employment, must be able to work, available for work, and be free from disqualifications.

The unemployment benefit program is fraught with difficulties, according to Karger and Stoesz (2013). For one thing, many of the states have steadily tightened eligibility requirements. For another, older workers separated from their jobs, may have little chance of finding new, gainful employment when competing with younger applicants. People who have been fired from their jobs for cause do not qualify. Additionally, restrictions against students receiving benefits hinders recipients in long-term preparation for career change. Due to the very temporary nature of the coverage, when the unemployment rate is high, as it is today, only a fraction of unemployed workers are receiving benefits.

An article in *Bloomberg Business Week* puts these benefits in global perspective. In Norway, where unemployment is a mere 3.3%, laid-off or fired workers keep 72% of their annual pay in combined unemployment pay and state benefits (Scott, 2010). This compares to 28% on average in the United States, and the time frame is far different. Germany pays one-third of the salaries of workers whose hours and wages are slashed by companies and provides job training in a fake supermarket in Hamburg. In Japan, with almost 5% unemployment, the government gives former workers 45% of their work pay the first year and only 3% after that.

### SOCIAL SECURITY DISABILITY INSURANCE (SSDI)

SSI should not be confused with Social Security Disability Insurance (SSDI), which is a federally funded social insurance program granted to a worker who has paid into social security and become blind or disabled and is no longer able to work. The monthly disability benefit amount is based on the Social Security earnings record of the insured worker and the length of time worked. In contrast, the SSI allotment is based on need.

Partly due to changes in workers' compensation laws, large numbers of workers in need of financial support applied for SSDI benefits. Because payments to these former workers comes out of the Social Security budget, the explosive rise in the number of recipients is part of the reason for the dire projections about this social insurance program (Daly, Lucking, & Schwabish, 2013). Population growth explains part of this increase, according to economists Daly et al., but much of the growth is due to workers' disincentives to return to work once they are on this program. When the program's eligibility criteria shifted from a list of specific impairments to a more general consideration of a person's ability to work and medical condition, including pain and other symptoms, workers found it easier to qualify. Additionally, over the past 20 years, the relative value of cash benefits has risen for low-wage workers. Although Daly et al. do not mention working conditions, one would think that given the increasing competition and job pressures in the working world today, the appeal of staying at home or of working part-time at some other job would outweigh the incentive to return to the original full-time position. Much of low-wage work is very high-pressured (Ehrenreich, 2002).

## SOME PROGRESSIVE PROPOSALS

Elizabeth Warren and her daughter, Amelia Tyagi (2016), list a number of suggestions to eliminate poverty and protect the middle and working classes with a true safety net. Among them are to step up investments in public education; rein in the cost of college, including student loans; create universal preschool and affordable child care; upgrade infrastructure—mass transit, energy, and communications; and disability coverage, retirement coverage, and paid sick leave.

Raising the minimum wage level is of course the most obvious way to lift workers out of poverty. The minimum wage is 20% lower than it was 40 years ago, when adjusted for inflation (Schlosser, 2012). To address the problem, dozens of cities and 14 states in January, 2016 raised their minimum wages (National Conference of State Legislatures, 2016). Of those, 12 states increased their rates through legislation passed in the 2014 or 2015 sessions, while two states automatically increased their rates based on the cost of living. More recently, New York and California enacted increases to bring the wages to $15 per hour wages by 2018 and 2022 respectively. The real way to eliminate the "welfare problem," as Seccombe (2013) informs us, is to restructure or enhance jobs in the lowest tiers of our labor market, that, even with its faults, is a logical refuge in times of trouble.

Devoted to the principle that people who work full-time should not live in poverty, the living wage movement is a grassroots effort that is directed at the local level where business groups are less all-powerful than they are in Congress. At several college campuses, students have successfully protested on behalf of campus cleaning crews and other low wage workers that their pay be sufficient to support a small family.

Strategies to provide high-quality and affordable child care for workers are crucial as well. So argues Robert Reich (2015). Other effective strategies are paid parental leaves, tax deductions for child care and elder care, and flexible work times. Minnesota, forever a progressive state, has achieved some success in providing generous transitional help for persons on the welfare rolls to get them in sustainable jobs. Looking to Scandinavia in this context, we find that Sweden, along with Norway, is the prototype of the child caring society (Lakey, 2016). Most Swedish children spend the first year or two at home with their parents because parental leave covers most of the lost income. According to a comprehensive article in *The Guardian* comparing European welfare states, France has the most generous policies for people who are unemployed (Penketh, Connolly et al., 2015). And while Sweden falls short in this area, Sweden still leads Scandinavia, and probably the world, in parental leave and childcare arrangements. Swedish parents are entitled to 480 days (16 months) of parental leave for each child, with most of it on 80% of full pay. On average, fathers take about a quarter of this shared time off to be with the baby. When that ends, all-day, five-days-a-week childcare in well-staffed kindergartens costs as little as $150 a month per child. Swedish economists view these policies as beneficial in terms of increasing the labor force by helping both parents to remain in work. Child development experts point to advantages to the child in being cared for at home during the first year or so of life and to the bonding with both parents (Gillett, 2015). The long 5-week vacations that most European workers get are beneficial for the whole family as well. In the United States, federal law allows men and women to take three months of unpaid leave, but many people simply can't afford to take time off. (Gillett). Without the guarantee of paid leave while caring for a child, many new parents are faced with the choice between economic hardship and returning to work prematurely.

If health care were universal in the United States, the work week could be shortened and vacation time could be extended. Without the added expense of health benefits, employers would be free to employ more workers instead of pushing the present work force into overtime. The end result is that now there would be more jobs to pass around. Japan, facing unaccustomed threats of unemployment due in part to automation, is looking into job sharing as a plausible solution (Toyohashi University of Technology, 2015).

Keep in mind Rifkin's (2015) points about the technological revolution that is only barely under way in an ever more automated global economy—the workerless factories, the association between high productivity, rising stocks and a drastically reduced work force. Then consider the federal mandate to reduce the welfare rolls even while the availability of well-paying jobs is shrinking. Why have fewer workers doing more work at this time? Why are people silent in the face of these assaults? Piven (2006) perceived the necessity of mass protests to effect needed social change:

> Across the Southern Hemisphere people are emerging from the backwaters of traditional economies to occupy land and facilities and block roads in order to influence national and even

> international policies. These are only hints of the forms that disruptive power challenges might take in the future. . . . [A]ll of our past experience argues that mobilization of collective defiance and the disruption it causes have always been essential to the preservation of democracy. (p. 146)

Another area demanding of social work attention is the lopsided spending practices of the US government, which favors military over welfare or educational spending.

## EFFORTS TO REPRIORITIZE RESOURCES

When a nation's tax revenues are concentrated on military deployment, this means that money and other resources are not available to boost the quality of the welfare state. Read what President Eisenhower (1953) famously said in a speech before news editors:

> Every gun that is fired, every warship that is launched, every rocket fired, signifies, in the final sense, a theft from those who hunger and are not fed, those who are cold and are not clothed. The world in arms is not spending money alone. It is spending the sweat of its laborers, the genius of its scientists, the hopes of its children.

Each year the War Resisters League calculates from official government figures the proportion of the federal income tax dollars that go to the military. The league's analysis is based on federal funds, which do not include trust funds—such as Social Security—that are raised separately from income taxes for specific purposes. We can compare the government's statements concerning the percentage of the national spending with the league's to show how statistics can serve to bolster one's argument one way or the other. By the government's calculations 23% went to the military and veterans, and much of the rest to entitlements such as Medicare. The war resister's league (2016), in removing the Medicare and Social Security from the tax budget since the government collects payroll taxes for these expenditures, comes up with 45% for military, past military, and interest on the national debt to pay for the military expenses, 43% for human resources, 8% general government, and 4% physical resources. (Readers can examine the pie charts at https://www.warresisters.org.)

A remarkable feat of activism taking place today in Philadelphia provides a rare example of social work activism framed in human rights language.

## WELFARE RIGHTS AS HUMAN RIGHTS

A multifaceted movement has emerged to challenge not the poverty of the people, but the poverty of the policies that denies them a decent standard of living. This grassroots organization of poor and homeless families, known as the Kensington Welfare Rights Union (KWRU), has been actively building a mass movement to end poverty since 1991. Social workers involved in the movement see themselves not as advocates but as allies, seeking collaboration in all dimensions of the necessary work in organizing to end economic oppression. One of the highlights of KWRU was the "New Freedom Bus Ride" which crossed the country. At each stop along the route, local groups joined members of the radical social work organization SWAA (Social Welfare Action Alliance) for rallies and teach-ins to focus on ways the United States was in violation of the UN Declaration of Human Rights (Bricker-Jenkins, Barbera, Young, & Beemer, 2013). Today, KWRU is one of over 50 groups that have come together in a network called the Poor People's Economic Human Rights Campaign (PPEHRC). Androff (2016) describes the PPEHRC as a human rights-focused organization that aims to end poverty through advancing economic human rights by uniting the poor across racial lines into a broad social movement. Many marches, "freedom ride" bus tours, and staged demonstrations in tent cities have been conducted through this group. In 2006, the PPEHRC held a Truth Commission to publicize poverty as a human right violation. (Truth Commissions are a restorative justice format of reconciling injustice through public testimony of wrong committed; see chapter 6.) Testimony was provided at this event about violations concerning poor housing and lack of sanitation in the community; there were over 500 participants including human rights leaders, social workers, students, and people who lived in poverty (Androff, 2016). This same organization has testified about economic human rights issues before branches of the United Nations.

Bricker-Jenkins et al. (2013) refer to a similar movement for economic rights in Chile, a country in which human rights concepts have been more fully integrated into social work. Social workers in Chile, historically, have seen their role as partners in solidarity with exploited Chileans. Their mission is transformative now that democracy has been restored in the country. Bricker-Jenkins et al. provide a case study of a social worker working with women in jail to help them develop self-esteem and reframe their situations in which they have been blamed so they come to see them in economic human rights terms. Human rights-based practice is viewed as strengths and empowerment in action.

(For information about the campaign see http://www.ppehrc.org) To check out a framework for conducting an anti-oppressive policy analysis of a proposed policy change, see the outline in Appendix B. To learn about lobbying initiatives at the state and national level, consult http://influencingsocialpolicy.org.

The involvement of social workers and students of social work in such mass organizing efforts is consistent with CSWE (2015) educational policy, which stipulates that the purpose of social work "is actualized through its quest for social and economic justice, the prevention of conditions that limit human rights, the elimination of poverty, and the enhancement of the quality of life for all persons, locally and globally" (p. 5). See Figure 8.2 which shows social workers at the Women's March on Washington, 2017. On January 21, 2017, over two million women marched on Washington, in many cities in the United States and all over the world to declare that human rights are women's rights and to protest setbacks under the Trump administration affecting environmental, children's, health care, racial, and immigrant concerns. As stated by social worker Kristin Battista-Frazee (2017):

> As a social worker, I realized our profession would be on the frontlines in fighting for the many people Trump policies would impact. At the Women's March, my goal was to soak in the energy, observe the strength of so many people coming together, as well as understand the depth and fervent nature of what is shaping up to be 'the resistance.' (1st paragraph) Put Figure 8.2 about here. (faces in crowd scene)

From a global perspective, Midgley's (2017) advocacy for an empowerment approach for social change should be heeded. Empowerment is what the welfare rights movement centered

**FIGURE 8.2.** Social workers Rudra Kapila, Sunya Folayan, Karen Zgoda, and Kristin Battista-Frazee, members of #MacroSW, are pictured at the Women's March on Washington, January 2017. Permission by Karen Zgoda.

in Philadelphia is all about. Such an approach attributes women's subjugation not only to patriarchy but to imperialism and neocolonialism. To achieve control over their lives, women must mobilize through coalition building, much aided today by electronic communication and organization such as UNIFEM, a United Nations effort to advance gender issues within regional trade treaties and to strengthen women's economic capacity as entrepreneurs and producers. Such global networking for the dismantling of corporate rule and the construction of an alternative global reality is now well under way (see www.unwomen.org). Until recently, women's needs have been almost entirely overlooked by international development agencies, but today the women themselves are providing important leadership in this movement.

## SUMMARY AND CONCLUSION

This second chapter on poverty was concerned with programs and strategies to address people's needs across the life span. The reader of this chapter will undoubtedly have been aware of most of the programs described in this chapter, programs designed by the US Congress and presidents over the years to maintain a certain level of civilization for the people. Our aim in writing this chapter was to provide a historic and political context for the programs, such as Medicaid and Medicare and to argue for their viability. Collectively, the programs evolved to meet the needs of the people; they all have constituents who depend on the benefits and representatives in Congress who will fight to keep them.

Most of the programs—both public assistant and social insurance—have stood the test of time; some were designed to provide a safety net for people and really work as intended. Others were instituted with mixed, often punitive motives under the guise of helpfulness, and still others were introduced as loopholes for the rich. The tax structure is a case in point. One of the most effective and even surprisingly progressive programs is the Earned Income Tax Credit. Its popularity can be attributed to the aid it gives to low-income working class people; the drawback is it doesn't help those who can't find a job. Because it rewards workers and parents, it is not stigmatized in the way that other welfare benefits are. SNAP or food stamps bring food to the table for many families and are a success in that regard. This program is criticized as being controlling in allowing the spending only on food, but on the whole it is considered to work well in providing nutrition for children in poor families. Head Start shines as another program with huge dividends in giving children a good start in life. All such programs are underfunded. That money spent on the military could better be redirected into the social welfare and public transportation systems are major arguments of this chapter. Social insurance programs such as Social Security and Medicare are highly popular with the general public and cost-effective due to the low administration costs. The risk to these programs comes from free market proponents who wish to destroy them through means-testing or privatization, which will ultimately lead to their demise. Like other universal programs, however, the social insurance programs have strong support across the board, and most likely their beneficiaries can resist all attempts to undermine them. This is an appropriate stopping point as we move into the realm of environmental justice, the theme of chapter 9.

## THOUGHT QUESTIONS

1. What is the significance of the poverty line for people applying for welfare benefits? How is it determined who qualifies?
2. List the major differences between public assistance programs and social insurance benefits.
3. What does the chapter heading "Welfare for the Rich" mean?
4. What is the history of TANF? What is unique about this government program?
5. What are some of the unintended consequences of welfare reform passed under the Bill Clinton administration?
6. How is Medicaid different from Medicare? What impact does being means-tested have on a program?
7. How is SSI different from SSDI?
8. Study Box 8.1. What do the statistics on social security benefits in one month tell you? Do any surprising facts emerge in these data from the government?
9. What did President Eisenhower say about military spending in the United States? State if you agree or disagree with his statement and why.
10. Check out the War Resisters League research on where the tax dollar goes. Compare the league's pie with that of the government's; what can you learn from these charts?

11. What are some alternative strategies for alleviating poverty listed by Senator Elizabeth Warren and her daughter?
12. Discuss roles for social workers in regional movements for poor people's rights. How do the protesters rely on an international document such as the Universal Declaration?
13. Discuss the work of The Kensington Welfare Rights Union. How have social workers been involved in this form of community organizing?

## REFERENCES


Androff, D. (2016). *Practicing rights: Human rights-based approaches to social work practice.* New York, NY: Routledge.

Badger, E., & Ingraham, C. (2015, April 9). The rich get government handouts just like the poor, here are 10 of them. *The Washington Post.* Retrieved from www.washingtonpost.com

Bartlett, B. (2013, November 19). Medicare Part D: Republican budget-busting. *New York Times.* Retrieved from www.nytimes.com

Battista-Frazee, K. (2017). Kristin's story. #MacroSW at #WomensMarch: Kristin's story. Retrieved from https://macrosw.com/2017/01/31/macrosw-at-womensmarch/

Bricker-Jenkins, M., Barbera, R., Young, C., & Beemer, M. (2013). In D. Saleebey (Ed.), *The strengths perspective in social work practice* (6th ed., pp. 255–278). Boston, MA: Pearson.

Carroll, L. (2016, March 2). Sanders: Welfare reform more than doubled "extreme poverty." *PolitiFact.* Retrieved from www.politifact.com

Center on Budget and Policy Priorities. (2015, June 15). Policy basics: An introduction to TANF. Retrieved from www.cbpp.org

Council on Social Work Education (CSWE). (2015). *Educational Policy and Accreditation Standards.* Alexandria, VA: CSWE.

Daly, M. C., Lucking, B., & Schwabish, J. (2013). The future of Social Security Disability Insurance. *Federal Reserve Bank of San Francisco.* Retrieved from www.frbsf.org

Dolgoff, R., & Feldstein, D. (2012). *Understanding social welfare* (9th ed.) Boston, MA: Pearson.

Edin, K., & Shaefer, H. (2015). $2.00 a day: Living on almost nothing in America. New York, NY: Houghton Mifflin Harcourt.

Edsall, T. (2014, June 17). Cutting the poor out of welfare. *New York Times.* Retrieved from www.nytimes.com

Ehrenreich, B. (2002). *Nickel and dimed: On not getting by in America.* New York, NY: Metropolitan Books.

Ehrenfreund, M. (2016, February 27). Bernie Sanders is right: Bill Clinton's welfare law doubled extreme poverty. *Washington Post.* Retrieved from www.washingtonpost.com

Eichelberger, E., & Gilson, D. (2015, February 6). How US companies stack billions overseas—tax free. *Mother Jones.* Retrieved from www.motherjones.com

Eisenhower, D. (1953, April 16). Speech delivered before the America Society of Newspaper Editors, Washington, DC. Quoted at the Eisenhower National Historic Site. Retrieved from https://www.nps.gov/features/eise/jrranger/quotes2.htm

Food Research and Action Center (FRAC). (2016). SNAP/food stamp participation data. Washington, DC: FRAC. Retrieved from frac.org

Gillett, R. (2015, August 5). The science behind why paid parental leave is good for everyone. *Business Insider.* Retrieved from www.businessinsider.com

Groves, L. H. (2016). Welfare reform and labor force exit by young, low-skilled single males. *Demography, 53*. doi: 10.1007/s13524-016-0460-3.

Hechinger Report (2010, March 17). Head Start program targets poorest children. Retrieved from www.hechingerreport.org

Karger, H., & Stoesz, D. (2013). *American social welfare policy: A pluralist approach,* 7th edition. Boston, MA: Pearson.

Lakey, G. (2016). *Viking economics: How the Scandinavians got it right—and we can too.* Brooklyn, NY: Melville House Printing.

Light, J. (2013). Why is the Federal Poverty Line So Far Off? What Matters Today. Moyers & Company. Retrieved from http://billmoyers.com/2013/09/18/why-is-the-federal-poverty-line-so-low/

Matthews D. (2014). Everything you need to know about the war on poverty. *Washington Post.* Retrieved from www.washingtonpost.com

Mauer, F., & Smith, C. M. (2013). *Community/public health nursing practice: Health for families and populations* (5th ed.). St. Louis: Elsevier Saunders.

Maysville, KY: *The Ledger Independent.* Retrieved from www.maysville-online.com

Meckler, L. (2016, May 10). Hillary Clinton says she's weighing Medicare for 50-year-olds. *Wall Street Journal.* Retrieved from www.wsj.com

Medicare Interactive (2017). What does Medicare cover? Medicare Rights Center. Retrieved from http://www.medicareinteractive.org

Midgley, J. (2017). *Social welfare for a global era: International perspectives on policy and practice.* Thousand Oaks, CA: Sage.

National Conference of State Legislatures (NCSL). (2016, April 14). State minimum wages. Washington, D.C.: NCSL. Retrieved from www.ncsl.org

Olsen, D. (2015, October22). Cuts to meal delivery program cause stress for seniors, caregivers. Springfield, IL: *The State Journal-Register.* Retrieved from www.sj-r.com

Penketh, A., Connolly, K., Kirchgaessner, S., McDonald, H., McCurry, J., Crouch, D., et al. (2015, April 15). Which are the best countries in the world to live in if you are unemployed or disabled? *The Guardian.* Retrieved from www.theguardian.com

Piven, F. (2006). *Challenging authority: How ordinary people change America.* Plymouth, England: Rowman & Littlefield Publishers.

Poppick, S. (2015, October 21). Here's how tax rates and brackets will change in 2016. *Time.* Retrieved from www.time.com

Reich, R. (2015). *Saving capitalism: For the many, not the few.* New York, NY: Knopf Doubleday.

Schlosser, E. (2012). *Afterword in reissued edition. Fast food nation: The dark side of the all-American meal.* New York, NY: Houghton-Mifflin.

Scott, M. (2010, May 6). The best countries to be unemployed in. *Bloomberg Business Week.* Retrieved from www.bloomberg.com

Seccombe, K. (2013). *"So you think I drive a Cadillac?": Welfare recipients' perspectives on the system and its reform.* Boston, MA: Pearson.

Social Security Administration (SSA). (2016). Social Security changes. Retrieved from www.ssa.gov

Stiglitz, J. (2013).*The price of inequality: How today's divided society endangers our future.* New York, NY: W.W. Norton & Company.

Tax Policy Center. (2002). Historical individual income tax parameters. Citizens for Tax Justice and the White House. Retrieved from www.ctj.org

Toyohashi University of Technology (2015, May 27). Job sharing with nursing robots. *Science Daily.* Retrieved from www.sciencedaily.com/releases

U.S. Census Bureau (2016). Income, Poverty and Health Insurance Coverage in the United States: 2016. Retrieved from https://www.census.gov/newsroom/press-releases/2017/income-povery.html

U.S. Department of Labor (2017). Labor statistics from the current population survey: unemployment. Washington, DC: Bureau of Labor Statistics. Retrieved from www.bls.gov

War Resister's League (2016). Where your income tax money really goes. Retrieved from https://www.warresisters.org/sites/default/files/FY2016piechart_b%26w-B.pdf)

Warren, E., & Tyagi, A.W. (2016). Introduction. In E. Warren & A.W. Tyagi, *The two-income trap: Why middle-class mothers and fathers are going broke* (pp. xiii–xxiv). New York, NY: Basic Books.

Zastrow, C. (2013). *Introduction to social work and social welfare, Empowerment series.* (11th Ed.). Belmont, CA: Cengage.

# PART II

# SOCIAL WORK ACROSS THE LIFE CYCLE

## INTRODUCTION TO PART II

*With chapter 9, we begin the second of the two parts of this book. Whereas Part I dealt more or less with the structure of social welfare systems, Part II unites policy and practice across the lifespan of human behavior. It is appropriate, therefore, to begin with an introduction into the natural environment as a key component of the person/environmental configuration. The biological aspect of social work's biopsychosocial and spiritual realm of life is also emphasized. The focus on cultural diversity in chapter 5 has as its parallel here the discussion of the importance of biological diversity in plant and animal life.*

*Cognizant of the notion of interactionism, we are dealing with society and self in constant interaction, with the person in the environment and the environment in the person. We are thus dealing with social dynamics even as we explore the biological and psychological dimensions of human existence. Life is fraught with horrendous obstacles as people struggle to meet their basic needs. Insecurity and greed are two common pitfalls that often lead to oppression and, in the extreme form, to war. The late social work theorist, Dennis Saleebey, who was renowned for his strengths-based rhetoric, was prone to see the light in the darkness: "From out of the ashes of oppression and destruction," he said, "we still may witness the flourishing of the human spirit" (2001, p. 7).*

*What are the biological attributes and constraints that make survival possible? How is the message of the global environmental crisis for the world? What kind of environment is amenable to or destructive of psychological growth and development? What is environmental justice? These are among the questions that we will consider in chapter 9. Then we move into the realm of child welfare and consider human rights issues as they pertain to the rearing and education of children (chapter 10). Care for older adults follows in chapter 11. Aging is viewed globally and in terms of the biology, psychology, and social aspects of aging in US society.*

*The final chapters cover health care and mental health care as human rights. Attention to social work roles are discussed in all these chapters in this, the second half of the book. Consistent with the first part of the text, controversial issues are delved into head on and critical thinking questions provided at the conclusion of each chapter. The Epilogue "puts it all together," encapsulating basic themes of social work and of this book. Included in the appendices are relevant websites, is the IFSW code of ethics, the Universal Declaration of Human Rights, a framework for formal policy analysis of US governmental policies in historical and international perspective, and a list of relevant websites.*

## REFERENCE

Saleebey, D. (2001). *Human behavior and social environments: A biopsychosocial approach.* New York, NY: Columbia University Press.

CHAPTER 9

# ENVIRONMENTAL JUSTICE

> 1. Indigenous peoples have the right to the conservation and protection of the environment and the reproductive capacity of their lands or territories and resources....
>
> 2. States shall take effective measures to ensure that no storage or disposal shall take place in the lands or the territories of l-indigenous peoples without their free, prior and informed consent.
>
> *UN Declaration on the Rights of Indigenous Peoples*, 2007, Article 29, p. 31

In 2015, the Council on Social Work Education (CSWE) launched a Committee on Environmental Justice. As stated on the CSWE (2015a) website, the committee will explore the history of "green" social work, current work on environmental social work, and social work practice related to environmental issues. The charge of the committee is to make recommendations to the commissions (one focused on diversity and one focused on global issues) about the ways in which social work education should consider integrating issues of environmental justice into the social work curriculum.

This is an exciting development indeed, as CSWE traditionally has limited its focus to a study of persons within the social environment to the neglect of the natural or physical surroundings. The concept of social justice received much emphasis, but here again the concept was generally limited to discussions of economic and social equality and advocacy to confront discrimination in the society; environmental rights, however, were rarely mentioned. Now CSWE has given us as a third mandate for social work education Competency 3: Advance Human Rights and Social, Economic, and Environmental Justice. According to this competency graduates with so cial work degrees are expected to "apply their understanding of social, economic, and environmental justice to advocate for human rights at the individual and system levels; and engage in practices that advance social, economic, and environmental justice" (CSWE, 2015b, pp. 7–8).

With these standards in mind we explore environmental justice and environmental racism in human rights context. Following a presentation of theoretical models of sustainability and ecosystems concepts, this chapter considers the global environmental crisis with a focus on water, air, and soil as foundations of life. The impact of global warming, risks to human health from pollution and pesticide use, corporate control of farming, and the fate of the world's indigenous populations are among the topics discussed in some depth. Based on our review of the literature we have filtered out a list of recommendations from a social work perspective. The chapter concludes with a discussion of religious teachings on care for the earth and the earth's creatures, and innovative developments in conservation.

## ENVIRONMENTAL JUSTICE AND HUMAN RIGHTS

What is the meaning of environmental justice? Since the term justice refers to fairness or fair play, environmental justice would refer to fairness in a population's access to resources, for example, to a clean water supply or if the supply was limited that it be shared equally with residents of the community. The social work dictionary is remiss in that it does not contain a definition of environmental justice. A search of the literature reveals that this term is most clearly defined in the CSWE (2015b) curriculum standards:

> Environmental justice occurs when all people equally experience high levels of environmental protection and no group or community is excluded from the environmental policy decision-making process, nor is affected by a disproportionate impact from environmental hazards. Environmental justice affirms the ecological unity and the interdependence of all species, respect for cultural and biological diversity, and the right to be free from ecological destruction. This includes responsible use of ecological resources, including the land, water, air, and food. (CSWE, 2015b, p. 20)

In their survey of 373 social work professionals, Nesmith and Smyth (2015) found that environmental justice is a significant practice issue in that client exposure to environmental hazards was common. At the same time, the social workers felt unprepared to address these issues. Now that CSWE mandates coverage of such material, social workers of the future can be expected to be much more knowledgeable about the human impact of exposure to toxic materials in the home or neighborhood and to assess for environmental safety in their client visits or interviews.

In her landmark contribution to the field, *Green Social Work*, Dominelli (2012) extends the notion of environmental justice to a consideration of the earth as a public, not private good, accessible to all people to meet their needs as defined by the Universal Declaration of Human Rights. When Dominelli speaks of the differential impact of human-caused climate change on poor regions of the world, for example, she sees this as an issue of environmental justice. The duty to care for the earth and to be cared by it is also included in Dominelli's conceptualization.

Often a concept related to such ideals as truth, ethics, and justice is defined more in terms of its absence or violation than its presence. We will see this tendency in this chapter which focuses more on the reality of environmental injustice as opposed to the ideal standards for environmental justice. In our discussion of environmental racism, for example, the focus is on situations in which economically disadvantaged racial and ethnic groups have suffered disproportionately due to exposure to chemical contamination and other forms of pollution. The human right of all people to health thus is violated when their surroundings are unhealthful.

Environmental rights, therefore, are human rights. In 2010, the United Nations General Assembly and the UN Human Rights Council recognized access to safe drinking-water and sanitation as a human right. The concept of progressive realization inherent to the rights-based approach ideally means that there will be intensified monitoring to hold governments accountable for meeting their human rights obligations related to access to clean water (World Health Organization, 2017a).

In August, 2015, the UN's 193 member states agreed to an agenda for sustainable development over the next 15 years. The new Sustainable Development Goals include among the aims: to reduce inequality, eradicate hunger, improve water management and energy, and take urgent action to combat climate change (World News, 2015).

The link between environmental and human rights is nowhere better evidenced than in a citizens' tribunal that took place in October, 2016 at The Hague, The Netherlands (Paul, 2016). The charges were that since the early 20th century, Monsanto has marketed toxic products that have been used in warfare for defoliation and in agriculture, products that have contaminated the environment and permanently sickened or killed thousands of people around the world. Each charge is couched in terms of a human rights violation. We discuss the charges in a later section on agriculture.

## SUSTAINABILITY AND RELATED CONCEPTS

*Sustainability* is a term that came into prominent usage with the publication of the Brundtland Report (UN World Commission, 1987). The standard definition of sustainability focuses on the meeting of present needs while preserving resources for future generations. In other words, the focus is on two dimensions of time—the present and the future. We might add that the past enters into play as well in that restoration is essential to repair the damage to the earth done by ourselves and over previous generations. As defined in the *Social Work Dictionary, sustainable development* is:

> The international goal of achieving more permanent economic well-being within the existing physical environment. An economy is sustainable only when it uses but does not deplete its resources or ruin its environment for immediate economic gain. (Barker, 2014, p. 421)

The orientation toward the future is consistent with Erik Erikson's notion of generativity. Erik Erikson's (1963) seventh life stage development crisis is *generativity versus stagnation* and has important implications for human's relationship to the environment and its resources. As enunciated by Erikson, generativity involves what the older generation imparts to the young and what it leaves behind—the legacy of life from generation to generation. Protection of the environment is an active part of this legacy. In its absence, the opposite of generativity—stagnation—prevails. Although the statistics are fairly bleak concerning environmental havoc across the globe, there is hope in a universal awakening to the pending global crisis.

The notion of sustainability is founded on four key values that apply to all institutions: "an increasing value of human life and the lives of all species, fairness and equality or economic and social justice, decision making that involves participation and partnership, and respect for the ecological constraints of the environment" (Mary, 2008, p. 33). Mary applies these four ideas in developing a model of social work that is consistent with the evolution of a sustainable world. Population control and biodiversity are goals that are essential to such sustainability.

Protecting people and the natural environment through sustainable development is arguably the fullest realization of the person/environment perspective. Social work, with its focus on political advocacy, can be an important force in addressing the problem of environmental degradation and pollution, especially in poor neighborhoods (NASW, 2015).

## THE EARTH AS ECOSYSTEM

As discussed in chapter 1, a multidimensional approach of viewing reality brings our attention to the interrelatedness of phenomena in our natural environment. Cause and effect are viewed as intertwined and inseparable. This is the related concept of *interactionism*: the parts of the whole are seen as in constant interaction with other parts. Viewed in its totality, we say, "The whole is more than the sum of its parts." Just as the emotional health of the growing child requires a nurturing environment, so the health of the larger whole is essential to the health of the parts. Because the notion of *ecosystem* is a concept that originated in the science of ecology "pertaining to the physical and biological environment" (Barker, 2014, p. 135), it offers a useful conceptual lens for the discussion of the natural environment as it shapes and is shaped by human behavior.

## ECOFEMINISM

Besthorn and McMillan (2002) define ecofeminism as an environmental philosophy that originated with French feminism as a reaction to the "twin oppressions of women and nature within the dominance structure of patriarchal social conventions" (p. 224). The involvement of women in environmental politics bolstered this movement. Ecofeminism asserts that the dualistic division between humankind and nature is a false one, and that famine and overpopulation are rooted in oppressive power structures.

Ecofeminists view the oppression of women and oppression of nature as inextricably linked. We see this with natural disasters where women bear the brunt of the crisis and challenges. Research has shown that in many parts of the world, women die in higher numbers than men during and after natural disasters (Kingsolver, 2015). As family caregivers, they are last to leave an unsafe home, and fear of sexual assaults makes them reluctant to go to shelters.

An insight offered by the novelist William Faulkner (1964/1936; on the lot of poor women) is "to endure and endure, without rhyme or hope of reward—and then endure" (p. 144). This quote provides us with an apt description of the fate of the world's women as they cope with the torments of drought and flood in their struggle to grow food for their families. The unpredictable weather patterns are jeopardizing subsistence farming and the water supply so vital to the harvesting of crops. In a typical village in central Kenya, for example, the women and girls must get up before dawn to begin the long trek to fetch water (Kingsolver, 2015). With the family's survival at stake due to extreme drought conditions, the girls do not go to school or have the chance to earn money. As the climate changes, in short, women of the world carry a heavy burden.

Besthorn and McMillan's recommendation is for an expanded ecological social work model of social justice; such a model is directed toward ending oppressions in all its forms—sexual, political, economic, and environmental. Hoff and McNutt (2009) concur: social policymaking requires a new paradigm to guide progress toward a building, caring sustainable social development. Such a policy involves restoration and preservation of the natural environment including protection of human and nonhuman life. For humans, the health of the physical surroundings has a strong impact on people's psychological health and on the social and community health. The interconnectedness between nature and spirituality is strong as well.

The Mother Earth conceptualization—the view of earth as our mother and nurturer—is epitomized in the belief systems of poets, Native peoples, as well as of the inhabitants (both indigenous and non-indigenous groups) of Norway. Nature is a source of spirituality. As expressed by Blue and Blue (2001), "The spiritual essence of the First Nation's people comes from the earth, comes from this land" (p. 79).

This organic view of nature is in sharp contrast to the modern worldview which originated in the age of rationalism (1500s–1800s). Influenced by the teachings of rationalism, the older, organic view of nature was replaced by a scientific worldview in which nature was regarded as a commercial resource, as something to be cultivated, exploited.

The European American exploitation of the buffalo for their hides is a case in point. The mass and reckless slaughter of buffalo is realistically portrayed in the 1990 epic drama, *Dances with Wolves*, starring Kevin Costner. Such careless slaughter as shown in this film typifies the new settlers' relationship with nature that they sought to subdue and enjoy for their immediate pleasure. This practice was perceived as a sacrilege to the Native peoples.

Native Americans and Canadians and many other indigenous peoples share a notion of oneness with the universe. Viewing themselves as one with the earth and its creatures, historically Native tribes had no notion of land ownership (Coyhis & Simonelli, 2008). Blue and Blue (2001), articulate this consciousness: "In the First Nations' sense, prayer usually involves the Father Sun, Mother Earth, and the four compass directions as well as the Creator" (p. 69). Central to the Native belief system is reverence for the Plant Order and Animal Order. "The spiritual essence of the First Nations' people comes from the earth, comes from this land" (p. 79). All living creatures are one under the universe.

Ecofeminist Vandana Shiva is at the forefront of a movement in India, where old-growth forests are being replaced with commercial monocultural plantations, to protest the destruction of forests. This is called the Chipko or tree hugging movement. We must move "from thinking of ourselves as consumers to realizing we are Earth citizens and exercising our duties as citizens," Shiva says (2014, p. 36).

To Norwegians, adoration of nature is a vital ingredient in their national identity. Arne Naess, the founder of the deep ecology movement (which combines a love of the earth and earth's creatures with spirituality) spent a great part of his time in a rustic, geographically isolated mountain cabin (Eriksen, 1998). Norwegians, a highly secular people, often turn to nature for solace and mental health. As described by Fred Besthorn, the land and landscapes in Norway, some of the most beautiful in the world, are understood as having deep spiritual/existential meaning and significance (in van Wormer and Besthorn, 2017). Much like indigenous groups around the world, many Norwegians share a wide-ranging belief that the land is a sacred place. Natural environments are a spiritual sanctuary. For this reason, everyone has the right of free and open entry into both public and private lands. Every worker has the right to access to a window with an outside view at his or her work station. Every prison inmate has a similar right not to be shut off from nature, even in confinement.

This notion of oneness with the universe is congruent also with the Darwinian notion of the interrelatedness of species in a "web of life." In this belief system, science and religion are joined in an appreciation for the genius of nature. Mosher (2010) points to an additional linkage of science and spirituality in the teachings of Eastern mystics in their descriptions of reality and by high energy physicists who express a sense of mystery in their descriptions of particles in the nucleus of the atom. Common to both is the sense of awe and mystery.

## BIOPSYCHOSOCIAL-SPIRITUAL MODEL

Just as the ecofeminist view of nature is holistic, so also is the biopsychosocial-spiritual approach of social work. The biopsychosocial framework itself can be viewed as part and parcel of ecosystems theory. It reminds social workers that even in individual micro-level intervention, a holistic, environmental approach will enhance understanding. Each component in the system—whether biological, psychological, or social—is intertwined with every other component.

Our societies and the people who live within them are paying a high price for having followed policies of economic development that operate at the expense of social development and of the protection of nonrenewable resources. The smog of Eastern Europe, eroded hillsides of Nepal, toxic waste sites of Russia, and denuded forests of Brazil and the Pacific West Coast testify to the massive destruction. Yet today, fortified by United Nations summits and much grassroots energy surrounding these international events, a new paradigm may lead to a re-appraisal of the traditional focus on growth, progress, and "modernization" as ends in themselves. The notion of sustainable development is here to stay.

We now turn our attention to the environmental portion of the person/environment configuration.

# THE NATURAL ENVIRONMENT

With publication of *Silent Spring*, Rachel Carson (1962) presented shocking data on the biological impact of chemical pollution that raised the consciousness of the world. Carson's work was so catalytic because it linked conservation of nature to human health (Dorsey & Thormodsgaard, 2003). The title of her painstakingly documented book refers to the silencing of songbirds due to the spraying of insecticides and herbicides.

To consider human behavior in the social environment without consideration of the impact of the physical environment on human behavior, is to omit a vital part of the equation. A full understanding of human functioning requires assessment of the physical and social environment concurrently—the physical environment includes the natural world of animals, plants, and land forms (Besthorn & McMillan, 2002). Yet conventional ecological/system models of social work have done precisely that. Such constructs, as Besthorn and McMillan suggest, have defined the person-in-the-environment only narrowly with little or no recognition of an individual's rootedness in the natural realm. In light of the impact of the increasing environmental degradation on poor people the world over, a person-in-nature focus cannot be separate from social work's conceptualization of social justice. Such a holistic consideration effectively incorporates the macro realm with the micro, and the personal (health and living standards) with the political (corporate power and public calls for governmental regulation).

Central to the study of human behavior is human growth and development. Both globally and locally a toxic environment is associated with reproductive disorders, spontaneous abortions, and malformed limbs. Consider the effect of Agent Orange sprayed by US forces during the Vietnam War to defoliate forests to deny the enemy cover. According to the Red Cross of Vietnam, up to one million people are currently disabled or have health problems due to Agent Orange, 100,000 of which are children (Andan, 2015).

Hardest hit by environmental problems are countries on whose soil wars are fought, poor nations of the world, and women within those nations who work closely on the land. The most common environmental problems include: rural land degradation which push people into overpopulated cities (for example, in Mexico); fertile soils rendered barren by drought (as in Ethiopia) and by monocrop planting; the depletion of water through intensive irrigation (in the US West, for example); and pollution of fresh water resources (extensive in Russia) (Harris & Roach, 2018; Kluger & Dorfman, 2002).

In a strong policy statement on the environment, NASW (2015) urges that citizens of the world embrace a moral code that recognizes the vulnerabilities of the natural environment. The responsibility falls heaviest on the more economically developed countries which have caused much of the world's climate-related problems in the first place. The position of NASW-US is that environmental justice requires that no population, because of policy or economic disempowerment, be forced to bear a disproportionate burden of the negative human health or environmental effects of pollution.

## THE ENVIRONMENTAL CRISIS

Extreme droughts, such as that that plagues California every summer, catastrophic flooding such as that that occurred in West Virginia and Louisiana in the summer of 2016, and storms that sweep in from the oceans in the fall—all are a part of the destabilization of the climate due to greenhouse gases. And we saw in 2017, in close succession three major hurricanes—Harvey in Texas, Irma in Florida, and Maria, which did the most damage, in Puerto Rico.

Air pollution in New Delhi, India has soared to 70 times the safe limit. The pollution was so bad recently that airplanes were unable to land, and thousands of schools had to shut down (Schultz, Kumar, & Gettleman (2017). Worldwide, air pollution is recognized by official agencies and health organizations to be a major public health crisis (Reed, 2016). Around 6.5 million deaths a year worldwide are attributed to contaminated air, With many of its root causes found in the energy industry, around 6.5 million deaths a year are attributed to air toxicity. The International Energy Agency singles out pollution in nations with emerging economies that draw energy from coal-fired power plants and have lax vehicle emission standards for the increase in air pollution in various parts of the world.

As most environmentalists are painfully aware, human activities—burning fossil fuels, emitting pollutants from industry, and clearing forests that are the habitats for plant and animal species—now match or even surpass natural processes as agents of change. The list of deeply troubling ecological disturbances encompasses a long inventory of pressing environmental problems. These include such vital concerns as overpopulation, global warming, depletion of the ozone layer, wetland and coastal estuarial erosion, water pollution, air pollution, species extinction, loss of genetic diversity, overfishing, toxic waste, poisonous effects of chemical-based fertilizers and pesticides, desertification, mass population dislocations due to the collapse of strategic environmental systems, famine, global pandemics, and dozens of less well-publicized but nonetheless troubling environmental issues.

Loss of biodiversity is a major concern of the world's scientists. In the fourth comprehensive study of the issue, the Global Biodiversity Assessment, a UN report, notes that although progress has been made over recent years with much greater awareness for the need for preserving the biodiversity of the forests, seas, and plant life, there still is a lot of work to be done (Secretariat of the Convention on Biological Diversity (2014). Since 1810, nearly three times as many bird and animal species have disappeared as in the previous two centuries. The UN report decries the loss of genes, habitats, and ecosystems. Evidence of the intensifying conflict between the economy and the ecosystem can be seen in the dust bowl emerging in China; the burning rainforests in Indonesia; the collapsing cod fishing industry in the North Sea; falling crop yields in Africa, and the declining water tables in India.

Although global economics and environmental concerns are often depicted as at loggerheads, the health of the natural environment is vital to a healthy economy. As we learn from the Worldwatch Institute (2013), the value of "nature's services" can actually be quantified. The soil-holding capacity of tree roots, and the flood projection offered by coastal swamps and barrier islands, for example, have direct economic benefits, for example, while the consequences of a human-generated pollution of natural resources—loss of top soil, clean air and water—represent severe economic losses. Deforestation, which occurs primarily in tropical forest regions, accounts for an estimated 12–20% of human-caused greenhouse gas emissions, according to the Worldwatch report.

The earth can be conceived as a giant ecosystem—a change in one part of the system reverberates throughout the whole. Consider the impact of climate change, marked by melting of the polar icecap. The warming of the oceans leads to migrations of fish and other species to colder waters. At the polar regions, the expansion of the Arctic Sea leads to the extinction of animal life dependent on ice floes for survival. People dependent on animal life are forced to migrate southward. With more water dumped into the oceans, land is gradually submerged including coastal areas of many countries. Mass human migrations take place as populations are forced to move inland. These are just a few of the possible ramifications of one change—an increase of the earth's temperature and repercussions that ricochet from one effect to another. Environment, plant, animal, and human life, and economy are all intertwined.

In the ecosystem, one can easily see in our economic interconnectedness our ecological interconnectedness as well. The founder of the Worldwatch Institute and author of *Eco-Economy*, Lester Brown (2009) writes of the economic impact of the environmental changes that are under way. He urges a reversal in our thinking, that we regard the economy as a part of the environment rather than vice-versa, that we must restructure the global economy to make it compatible with the earth's ecosystem. Economists see the environment as a subset of the economy; ecologists, see the economy as a subset of the environment. To envision the extent of the destruction in store for us as a world community, we must consider the depletion of much of the earth's capital in the name of economic progress. The good news, according to Brown, is that economists are becoming more ecologically aware, recognizing the inherent dependence of the economy on earth's ecosystem. Clearly, at our present rate of industrialization, economic development is not sustainable development. Instead of living in harmony with nature, our notion of progress is more often played out as war against nature (see Bonneuil & Fressoz, 2016).

Next we look at three of the nature's richest resources—water, air, and soil.

## WATER

As described by Cozzetto, Chief, et al. (2013):

> Native Americans revere water and water is life. It is integral to many Native American practices such as purification and blessing rituals and is used to acknowledge all relations and to establish connection to Mother Earth and Father Sky. . . . Without water, life would not exist as we know it. Water is the one thing we all need, all of us, all of life. As Native Americans, we honor and respect the tradition of water and must protect it always. (p. 570)

The ocean is the world's single largest ecosystem and plays a central role in supporting all life on Earth. The global ocean produces almost half of all the oxygen we breathe and absorbs more than a quarter of the carbon dioxide we emit into the atmosphere (Global Ocean Commission, 2014). The international community has expended a tremendous amount of political capital and diplomatic effort on establishing policy commitments aimed at reversing ocean degradation. Yet a report at the Rio+20 Summit (United Nations, 2012) revealed that little progress had been made toward meeting this target, especially beyond coastal areas. According to the Commission, acidity is building up in the oceans caused by increasing uptake of carbon dioxide; fish depletion has resulted from overfishing of the seas; and depositing of plastics is a major source of pollution on the high seas where billions of tons have accumulated. The algae buildup that results from chemical contamination suffocates ocean life.

A major threat to the future is offshore oil and gas production. Drilling more and deeper increases the threats to the environment and natural resources. The potential impacts of offshore drilling on the environment are numerous. The Global Ocean Commission (2014) lists: "the disturbance of fish stocks and marine mammals during seismic surveys; carbon dioxide and methane emissions through gas flaring and venting; and pollution of the marine environment through the loss and discharge of various substances, drilling fluids, and cuttings in particular" (p. 18). Eighty percent of global fish stocks have been fished to the limit or beyond, and our failure to protect the ocean as a finite resource now threatens the ocean's ability to recover, as the co-chairs of the organization suggest. Restricting industrial activities like fishing, shipping and deep seabed mining in biodiversity hot spots would go a long way toward restoring ocean health, they say.

Coral reefs are natural habitats, rich in biodiversity that contain 25% of the world's marine fish species (Defenders of Wildlife, 2016). A recent report estimated that 75% of remaining coral reefs are currently threatened, and many have already been lost. Although there are many problems facing reefs today, rising seawater temperature as a result of climate change is one of the most serious causes of stress to corals throughout the world. In addition, increasing ocean acidification has emerged as another potentially serious threat to coral reefs.

What is needed is an international body with sanctions that can be enforced for the protection of the ocean as an ecosystem in which so many species, including humans, depend. Happily, the United Nations General Assembly (2015) is in the process of developing such an international legally binding instrument under the UN Convention on the Law of the Sea. International law would then go beyond mere national jurisdiction to more effectively enforce the conservation of marine biological diversity. If consensus is reached from the member nations, the UN biodiversity agreement will finally give scientists the framework they need to set oceans on the path to recovery.

There is a global water crisis of another sort, and this concerns fresh water. Lack of sanitation and clean water are primary concerns of the Global South and, in some instances, of communities in the Global North, though on a much smaller scale. Only 3% of water is fresh, found in glaciers and ice, below ground, and in rivers and lakes, and only a fraction of that is accessible (National Ocean Service, 2015). Global consumption of water is doubling every 20 years, twice the rate of population growth. Worse, as Maude Barlow (2013), author of *Blue Future*, indicates, toxins from cities, factories and farms have polluted more than half of the world's rivers. Rivers, lakes, and wetlands have become repositories for excess agricultural nutrients. According to the Iowa Department of Natural Resources, high nitrate levels in the water plague 60 counties with 13 total violations (Eller, 2015). The nitrates come from fertilizers and sewage and in many places are above the health limits allowed.

Economic mismanagement, global warming, factory farming, fracking, and population growth are at the heart of this crisis. Let us look at the impact on underground water caused by hydraulic fracturing or "fracking."

## FRACKING

Fracking is a process in which large amounts of water, sand and chemicals are injected deep underground to break apart rock and free trapped natural gas. This unconventional drilling method, which is associated with earthquakes in areas where the injection of fracking fluid into wells is common, is a serious risk to our drinking water.

The Environmental Protection Agency (EPA) recently confirmed as much (Banerjee, 2015). Unable to conduct its own research due to a lack of cooperation by the oil and gas companies, this government agency had to rely instead on scientific studies in the existing literature and of cases of fracking-related water pollution investigated by state regulators. The report is significant, nevertheless, and represents a reversal in its acknowledgment of risks to drinking water at every step of the fracking process: from acquiring water to use in mixing the fracking chemicals with the water to constructing wells, to injecting the fracking fluid into the well, and to the handling of fracking waste water that flows back up out of the well.

Though the process has been used for decades, recent technical advances have helped unlock vast stores of previously inaccessible natural gas, resulting in a fracking boom. Proponents of fracking correctly argue that the United States would be facing a serious energy crisis if the entire practice were banned, and that the practice would reduce, or even eliminate our dependence on foreign oil. They claim that less reliance on coal for energy with its concomitant environmental damage would be a secondary benefit. In states such as Wisconsin where fracking is commonly used, some landowners have become extremely rich overnight, while their neighbors must endure heavy traffic, dust, air pollution, light-pollution and blight on the landscape caused by the mining. Environmentalists cite such scientific research as that conducted by hydro geologist Tom Myers (2012) to argue that chemicals introduced far below the earth in connection with fracturing eventually will move upward and affect the aquifers, the source of fresh water drinking supplies.

While there is a great deal of cautionary information available on the Internet, the corporately controlled media have not been at the forefront of environmental education when it comes to extraction of the earth's resources through fracking. National Public Radio (NPR), in fact, which used to be known for its controversial investigative reporting, Today, on NPR, which depends on the major corporations such as the American Natural Gas Alliance, carries sponsored pro-fracking messages, there is evidence that information about the dangers of being suppressed, information about water contamination and environmental research findings, for example. Corporate money, as the writers at Environmental Action (2014) suggest, are controlling the news content that we are getting even on public broadcasts.

## WATER SHORTAGE WORLDWIDE

Several billions of people worldwide, most living in poor countries of the Global South, lack access to safe water. Water scarcity is of special concern for women and children. Every year, 361,000 children under 5 years of age die due to diarrhea. Poor sanitation and lack of indoor toilets are also linked to transmission of diseases such as cholera, dysentery, hepatitis A, and typhoid. Women and girls spend on average up to 30 minutes roundtrip collecting and gathering water, a process they must do numerous times each day (WHO, 2017b). In parts of rural Africa, because of the depletion of the water supply and drought, women must walk further and further for clean water or risk their and their family's health in fetching unsanitary water.

It's hard to believe but in the United States, in some tribal areas, people haul water. Up to 12% of American Indian and Alaskan Native homes lack safe and adequate water supplies and/or waste disposal facilities compared to 1% of the rest of the country (Cozzetto et al., 2013). We need to consider that contamination of the water supply or loss of water through drought is significant beyond its immediate usefulness to the Indian people. Water to Native Americans has a spiritual and cultural meaning; locations such as water falls and springs are held sacred (Cozzetto et al., 2013). An example of the impact of climate change is experienced by the western and Alaskan tribes. The warming in Alaska, for example, is melting the permafrost. This causes the water to seep down to the earth and lakes and rivers to be depleted of water. Some animal species are threatened in the polar regions as the ice platforms on which the polar bears and other animals depend disappear.

Tragically, water is viewed by international banking associations as a human need rather than a human right. The distinction between need and right is crucial, as Barlow (2013) indicates. A human need can be provided (as with health care) through private business. This is what is happening, in fact, as a handful of transnational corporations financed by the World Bank and IMF are reaping enormous profits through their delivery and sales of private water and wastewater services. The bottled water industry, one of the fastest growing and least regulated industries in the world, is depleting aquifers for profit. In allowing the commodification of the world's freshwater supplies, we are losing the capacity to avert the looming water crisis. Hope is found in organized political resistance to water privatization by a coalition of environmentalists, indigenous human peoples' rights, and antipoverty activists (Barlow).

## IMPACT OF GLOBAL WARMING

It is increasingly becoming evident that global warming and problems of overpopulation are linked. This is because of the loss of arable land through floods and droughts. As the glaciers melt and the oceans rise, mass migrations of people can be anticipated. From the Andes region of Peru, where the glaciers are steadily melting, to parts of Africa and Asia, the resources that sustain human life are threatened by natural disasters that are associated with climate change.

The science is clear and unambiguous. The United States Global Change Research Program determined, as so many studies and research efforts have previously concluded, that:

> Evidence for climate change abounds, from the top of the atmosphere to the depths of the oceans. Scientists and engineers from around the world have meticulously collected this evidence, using satellites and networks of weather balloons, thermometers, buoys, and other observing systems. . . . Taken together, this evidence tells an unambiguous story: the planet is warming, and over the last half century, this warming has been driven primarily by human activity. (USGlobal Change Research Program, 2014)

With global warming comes melting of the glaciers and polar ice caps. This, in turn, raises the water level considerably. In a climate impact study conducted at Climate Central, scientists estimated a rise in the sea level by 14 to 32 feet by the next century (Phys.org Science Network, 2015). This means that coastal cities in the United States, such as Miami, New Orleans, and New York City, will be under water. New Orleans is already sinking, according to the report. Across the world, small islands are already going under, and whole nations, such as Bangladesh are at risk in the future (Brown, 2011; Mellino, 2015).

While the science and news reports are mainly about global warming, there is a real chance that some countries in Western Europe will actually get colder. This is because as the glaciers in Greenland melt, the cold non-salt water will rise over the heavier salt water and move southward (Sosnowski, 2015). The impact will be to lessen the effect of the warm Gulf Stream. The climate would then be drastically affected with very cold winters in Ireland, the United Kingdom, and Norway, among others.

The Intergovernmental Panel on Climate Change (2014) has predicted that average global temperature will increase from 2 to 10 degrees Fahrenheit over the next 100 years—and most alarmingly perhaps over the next 40–50 years. Let us see what the health consequences of this increase in temperature along with erratic shifts in weather patterns will be. According to the World Health Organization (WHO; 2015):

> Rising sea levels and increasingly extreme weather events will destroy homes, medical facilities and other essential services. More than half of the world's population lives within 60 km of the sea. People may be forced to move, which in turn heightens the risk of a range of health effects, from mental disorders to communicable diseases.
>
> Increasingly, variable rainfall patterns are likely to affect the supply of fresh water. A lack of safe water can compromise hygiene and increase the risk of diarrheal disease, which kills approximately 760,000 children aged under 5, every year. In extreme cases, water scarcity leads to drought and famine. By the late 21st century, climate change is likely to increase the frequency and intensity of drought at regional and global scale. (quoted from the WHO website at http://www.who.int/mediacentre/factsheets/fs266/en)

As we have seen from an overview of scientific reports, climate change is a reality. The general consensus is that it is caused by human activities that if unchecked, will pose significant risks to all of us. No place on earth is immune from the consequences, not the arid land of eastern Africa, nor the grain exporting regions of Australia, nor the low lying gulf coast areas in the southern United States. Just as the problems are global, so too are the solutions global. International cooperation can be promoted through agreements to restrict the emissions of carbon dioxide and other forms of air pollution from coal-burning power plants and automobiles. This will mean the passing of international laws and setting up mechanisms of enforcement.

## AIR

In satisfying the energy needs of burgeoning human population, humans are likely affecting the climate of the entire planet. The same pollution—primarily from fossil fuels—that causes warming of the atmosphere is also causing respiratory illness (Chiras, 2013). Poor children in urban areas are at special risk from asthma related to poor air quality. Most scientists agree that so-called greenhouse gases such as carbon dioxide and methane are depleting the ozone layer of the atmosphere. The amount of carbon pumped into the air by fossil fuel burning has steadily risen while deforestation added billions of additional tons of carbon into the atmosphere. The emissions released in the atmosphere surpass the rate at which the world's oceans and forests can absorb the chemical (Raven, Hassenzahl, & Berg, 2012). Fishing industries are on the brink of collapse. Trees and other plants counter the carbon dioxide in the atmosphere and replace it with oxygen. Destruction of the earth's vegetation is thus extremely damaging to life on earth, affecting the very air we breathe. As more pollution enters the atmosphere, sun rays become more penetrating. The recent rise in skin cancer rates may be related to this fact (Raven et al.).

Air pollution in Eastern Europe was so shockingly high during the 1980s and 1990s that trees and grass are stained with soot. In some areas of Poland children, are taken down in mines periodically to escape the buildup of gases in the air. The grassroots initiative "Clean up Poland" expanded across the nation and has involved millions in the ongoing campaign to clean up wastes; Polish waterways are still heavily polluted with industrial wastes, however. Mexico City suffers some of the worst air pollution of any city in the world.

According to a recent report from the British journal, *Lancet*, environmental pollution, from air to water, is killing more people every year than all war and violence in the world. One out of every six premature deaths in the world can be attributed to disease from toxic exposure (Watts, Amann, et al., 2017). Worldwide, nine million people died from pollution in 2015.

Recently, attention was turned to China. China has more than 170 million vehicles on its roads, including around 150 million light vehicles. Their total emissions were estimated at 45.3 million tons in 2015, according to the government (Rapoza, 2016). The "Asian brown cloud," which is estimated to be two miles thick may be responsible for almost two million premature deaths in China and 2.5 million in India each year (Vidal, 2014; Watts, Amann, et al., 2017). The toxic air pollution, is mostly from minute particles of diesel soot and gases emitted by cars and trucks, as well as half-burned vegetation from forest burning. Most of the deaths are in east Asia, China, and India. More cities in India than China see extremely high levels of air pollution, both indoors from dung-fueled fires and paraffin stoves and outside. Outdoors, heavy truck traffic operates under conditions of little regulation of toxic vehicle emissions (The Economist, 2015).

There are signs, however, that the situation will improve as economic incentives to improve air quality through mass transit initiatives to reduce car travel are under way. China announced that it was increasing its standards for gasoline and diesel in order to immediately start cutting automobile emissions (Rapoza, 2016). New legislation was introduced that eventually will put a tax on chemical plants, coal fired power plants and other polluters. In the United States, Canada, and Western Europe, a great deal has been done to prevent the kind of "killer smog" that paralyzed cities in the 1950s. Air pollution, however, reaches every place on earth, and one country's neglect is paid for, in one way or another, by the entire world.

There are over five million cars in Beijing, China today, cars that are concentrated in the downtown area (China Daily, 2012). The smog can be overpowering on many days. Such automobile congestion is becoming life threatening in terms not only of air pollution but also to pedestrians and other drivers. In India, one finds a similar situation. "Road Rules Give Way to Rage in New Delhi" is one headline that says a lot (Associated Press, 2010).

Economic growth must be sustainable growth, and economic development is not the same as social development. Many of the above problems could be alleviated through an emphasis on sustainable and social development over economic expansion. If the World Bank is to promote such development, economic success must be judged not by standard financial indicators but must be measured against the depreciation of natural assets such as forests and fisheries and by how the people as a whole are getting their needs met.

The good news is that we can tap into the energy from the air and sun; a switch to use of these natural resources is already happening with wind and solar energy. Such a switch, as Lester Brown (2016) indicates, will come sooner or later because, unlike the extraction of oil or the mining of coal, wind and solar energy don't use water; we can already see the rapid use of these alternative sources of energy across the globe. The great thing about solar and wind energy as a replacement for fossil fuels is that it never runs out. You can't say that about coal and oil.

## SOIL

In the novel, *A Thousand Acres* by Jane Smiley (1991, pp. 131–132), the narrator depicts her love affair with the Iowa wetlands teeming with life—"sunfish, minnows, nothing special, but millions or billions of them: I liked to imagine them because they were the soil, and the soil was the treasure, thicker, richer, more alive with a past and future abundance of life than any soil anywhere" (pp. 131–132).

Poet and environmentalist Wendell Berry (1977), in his classic work on agriculture, *The Unsettling of America*, states that if we regard plants as machines, we wind up with huge monocultures (corn and soybeans) and if the soil is regarded as a machine, then its life, its involvement in living systems and cycles, must perforce be ignored. If, like the strip miners and the "agribusiness" interest groups, we look on all the world as fuel or as extractable energy, we can do nothing but destroy it. And ultimately, what we turn against, turns against us.

Soil is the source of life. Food chains are the living channels which conduct energy upward; death and decay return it to the soil (Leopold, 1966). In his collection of essays called *A Sand Country Almanac* originally published in 1949, Aldo Leopold defined fertility as the ability of the soil to receive, store, and release energy. Agriculture, by overdrafts on the soil, or by too radical a substitution of domestic for native species in the superstructure, explains Leopold, may derange the channels of flow or deplete storage. Soils depleted of their storage or of the organic matter which anchors it, wash away faster than they form. This is erosion.

Wendell Berry (1993) goes further and talks of *land abuse*. Any form of land abuse—a clearcut, a strip mine, an overplowed or overgrazed field—is a dire threat to the earth's ecosystem. Land abuse goes back to early American history. In *Grassland*, Richard Manning (1995) offers a critique of modern agricultural practices that began with procedures done to the rich prairies of early America. European Americans transformed a land that supported 50 million bison into one that supports about 45 million cattle. As for the soil, the cattle ate plants right to the dirt, killing saplings that could have controlled erosion. Whereas bison migrated with the seasons allowing the plant life to be replenished, the cattle stayed permanently on the land. Plowing too took its toll, turning long-evolved plant communities into a system of monocrop farming.

On a global basis, unsustainable land use has led to desertification, deforestation, and environmental contamination. To force some life out of the depleted soil, farmers use an incredible amount of chemicals—many of them highly toxic—which seep into the rural waterways, drinking water, soil, and air. The average size of cropland is shrinking commensurate with population growth. This fact is especially pronounced in Nigeria, where rapid population growth has outrun grain production, and in India, and Bangladesh where land is divided each generation among heirs (Brown, 2011).

A popular myth is the belief that a green revolution through the wonder of fertilizers and pesticides could feed the world. Worldwide, farmers use 10 times more fertilizer and spend 17 times as much on pesticides as in 1950 (Shiva, 2008). The problem is that after a few years of treating (mistreating) the soil in this way, the increased yields taper off and soil erosion and water pollution hinder further food production.

The threat to human health and to the health of other animals, earlier documented so graphically in Rachel Carson's (1962) *Silent Spring*, still persists in the United States today. In Iowa, pesticides are showing up in the state's wells and streams, and at least a million fish have been killed by manure spills over the past few years. The pollution is agricultural fertilizer run-off, firehosed into the rivers by all the channelized creeks, drained former wetlands and tiled fields in the region. It's not just farmers, however, who are responsible (Herring, 2013). Researchers are studying the health consequences in humans and decline in the bee population associated with the use of pesticides. Overuse is especially common among homeowners who are fighting weeds with herbicides. According to state officials, home owners in Iowa in order to get a perfect-lawn look are applying pesticides to the grass with little consideration of the health risks of exposure to these toxic chemicals (Kaufman, 2016). Then there are golf courses which represent the most artificially managed acreage in existence.

## FARMING AND CARE FOR THE SOIL

Without soil, we are without food. Soil loss has a lot to do with unsustainable agricultural practices. Every year from every plowed acre in Kansas, an average of two to eight tons of topsoil wash away. Half of the topsoil on the planet has been lost in the last 150 years. In addition to erosion, soil quality is affected by other aspects of agriculture (World Wildlife Fund, 2016). The transition to agriculture from natural vegetation often cannot hold onto the soil and many of these plants, such as coffee, cotton, palm oil, soybean and wheat, can actually increase soil erosion beyond the soil's ability to maintain itself.

Soil forms the basis for healthy food. Yet because the soil has been under assault due to the use of pesticides and herbicides associated with a loss of minerals and other nutrients, oranges have lost their vitamin C content, and iron and calcium levels are down in vegetables that used to be rich in nutrition (Bewsey & Paul, 2014).

The theory behind organic agriculture lies in creating a healthy environment free from synthetic fertilizers, pesticides, and herbicides and avoidance of mono-cropping. Farmers' markets help the community by providing fresh produce to the local area and supporting the local economy. Thanks to refrigerated trucks and subsidized highways, the average food item travels 1,500 miles from the farms to our tables, 25% farther than in 1980 (Roosevelt, 2003). Fruits and vegetables lose nutrients and flavor along the way. In Iowa, the "buy fresh, buy local" campaign urges people to strengthen regional markets for locally grown foods and to choose food from farmers who avoid or reduce their use of chemicals and antibiotics. The campaign has successfully convinced local restaurants, the university, and grocery stores to purchase locally grown or raised food (Visit www.foodroutes.org to learn how the "Buy Fresh, Buy Local" campaign is reintroducing Americans to knowledge concerning their food and the farmers who produce it.)

At the same time, the marketing of processed food continues. As described in *Fast Food Nation:*

> The typical preschool child now sees about three fast food ads on TV every day, teenagers, five. Obesity rate among preschoolers has doubled, tripled 6–10. Only 4% of US spending is spent on organic food. More than 23 million low-income Americans now live in food deserts lacking supermarkets. Two different food cultures for rich and poor. (Schlosser, 2012, pp. 271–278)

For health-oriented parents and organic farmers, good news has come from an unlikely source: McDonald's. Giving formal recognition that heavy use of growth-stimulating hormones and bacteria-controlling antibiotics is a threat to human health, McDonald's got their meat suppliers (especially of chicken and also what they call "sustainable beef") to phase out unhealthy practices (Katsnelson, 2015). It is generally believed that the change at the demand level will have a major impact on livestock production nationwide. Several other meat producers and restaurant chains are following suit.

So far, however, there has been no reduction in the infection rate of people who fall victim to serious infections such as MRSA, considered one of the superbugs that is resistant to the available antibiotics. The resistance is caused by the widespread prescription of antibiotics by doctors. But nowhere, according to an extensive article in *Consumer Reports* (2016), are the drugs more inappropriately employed than in the meat and poultry industries. These drugs are used along with hormones to make the animals grow faster and to enable them to live in such crowded conditions on factory farms that they hardly can move. Through eating the meat, people are heavily exposed to antibiotics. At least two million Americans suffer from antibiotic-resistant infections every year, and 23,000 die. One of the most serious problems facing hospitals today is the spread of such infection.

Industrialized agriculture puts food on the table, but at a price—both to the farmers and to all the species that depend on the land. Farmers follow what they were taught at the land grant colleges—using artificial fertilizer and irrigation systems. Yet this scenario is typical: beef sells for less than the cost of raising it and there's a glut of wheat. While small farmers go bankrupt, the giant corporations thrive as the major beneficiaries of modern agricultural policies.

## MODERN AGRICULTURE

Not only in the industrial arena is the nature of work undergoing transformation in the industrial arena but in agriculture, too, a high-technology revolution is well under way. Family farms have been replaced by corporate operations that stretch for thousands of acres (Schlosser, 2012). Widespread use of chemical pesticides, fungicides, herbicides, and advanced harvesting equipment associated with this type of land usage promotes high productivity with little land and few farm laborers. Worldwide subsidies and IMF inducements promote the planting of high-yield advanced harvesting equipment monoculture crops, often for international export. Like ranching, farming is not just an occupation but a whole way of life, an expression of values of independence, hard work "sun up to sun down," community bonding, and intergenerational pride in land ownership. So the economic crisis facing the family farmers and ranchers is a threat to more than one's livelihood. The suicide rate among ranchers and farmers in the United States is now about three times higher than the national average (Schlosser, 2012). The farm income crisis has decimated rural communities in the United States and Canada.

The massive displacement and dislocation of farm labor over the past century has deprived millions of people of their chosen livelihood. Through mechanical, biological, and chemical innovations, productivity has risen considerably. Fewer and bigger farms have been the end result. Today in Iowa, John Deere has successfully produced a robot-tractor that will plow the fields by remote control.

In Costa Rica, agricultural intensification has occurred rapidly in one generation. Cultivation of tobacco, a highly profitable crop, makes possible the purchase of modern consumer goods. Through the use of dangerous chemicals, several other crops can be produced on one plot of land. The temptation to risk damage to the ecosystem for short-term gains and to go into debt to invest in expensive equipment to maximize production can lead to ecological and financial disasters in the long-run.

Throughout Latin America, in fact, much of the land is now devoted to pasture for cattle, an export commodity that employs relatively little labor. And peasant agriculturalists have become an underemployed urban poor struggling to survive as shoeshine boys, servants, and street vendors.

## THE CASE AGAINST MONSANTO

Farmers all over the world are also being affected by agricultural corporations of which Monsanto is the best known and the most criticized. This St. Louis-based company has a monopoly of seeds and, according to Katherine Paul (2016) of the Organic Consumers Association, is the poster child for an industry that is the source of greenhouse gas emissions and is largely responsible for the depletion of soil, water and biodiversity.

Popular documentaries such as the 2003 Canadian film *The Corporation* and the 2008 film *Food, Inc.* devote much attention to the strategies of Monsanto, a company, famous for the producing of Agent Orange which destroyed so many lives in Vietnam, and which today plays a dominant role in the genetic engineering of crops. Agent Orange contains dioxin, which was used by the US military during the Vietnam war and continues to be a major cause of birth defects and cancers. Also about the same time Monsanto became a producer of another toxic chemical—PCB—which was sold to insulate electrical transformers (Ratcliff, 2017). The chemical got into the air and the soil and the creek that flowed into a river where poor, mostly African American people fished. In a lawsuit, evidence revealed that Monsanto administrators and chemists knew about the health risks to the people but deliberately kept them in the dark. In the legal settlement that was reached, Monsanto agreed to pay $700 million to the over 20,000 residents of the area near the factory, all with neurological defects and other serious health problems (Robin, 2010). Many others had already died or would die of cancer.

After Monsanto finally discontinued use of PCB, which the government later banned, the company moved into the agricultural realm. Today, Monsanto's bioengineered soybeans command over 90% of the US market, and genetically altered corn is up to 80% of corn. These crops are designed to be unaffected by the weed killer Roundup which is also produced by Monsanto. Roundup, a highly toxic herbicide or weed killer, sprayed on GMO crops including soybeans, corn and rapeseed for animal feed or for the production of biofuels, was recently classified as a probable human carcinogen by the World Health Organization (Paul, 2016). A fact that was suppressed earlier through misleading faux scientific research is that a key ingredient of the herbicide—glyphosate—is linked to cancer in humans. Any attempt to ban this product, which would reduce the effectiveness of Roundup runs against stumbling blocks in Washington where Monsanto has spent almost $60 million on lobbying since 2008 (Waldman, Mulvany, Stecker, & Rosenblatt, 2017).

In addition to health problems, farmers using this product may run into legal problems. Those who buy the genetically modified seeds do so on the promise of higher yields, but they must sign a contract that dictates how and when the crop is grown. Saving seeds is forbidden; in fact, Monsanto has sued farmers for doing so (Karger & Stoesz, 2013).

Given its questionable business and ethical tactics, it is understandable that Monsanto was held to be accountable by a citizens' court of law. The trial of Monsanto took place at The Hague in the Netherlands. Monsanto was charged by the European tribunal of human rights violations (Fulton, 2017). Testimony was offered by people who had been harmed by Monsanto. The decision by the judges was that Monsanto is guilty on two counts: of ecocide, a crime not recognized in law, and of violating the right of people to a safe, clean, and healthy environment. Although not legally binding, the trial held in the Netherlands has gathered important information that can be used by future organizations.

The use of products such as Monsanto provides is associated with monocultural farming which consists of the planting of row and row of one crop year after year. Reliance on biodiversity to replenish the soil seemingly has become a thing of the past.

## LOSS OF BIODIVERSITY

In the Midwest as a whole, perennial plants have now been replaced with annuals. This change has caused a major change in the ecology of the region, making for greater vulnerability to flooding. In addition to the absence of the perennial grasses to soak up water nine months out of the year, other factors increasing the likelihood of flooding are the use of a substance called tiles placed below the plants to aid in drying, a procedure that causes run-off of the water into rivers, and the compression of the soil by tractors which make it less spongy and absorbent, also leading to more water run-off. Iowa and some neighboring states have had two historically severe floods, which caused billions of dollars in property damage in 1993 and 2008.

Growing such monocrops is inefficient in terms of land usage. Only a tiny fraction of pesticides reach their targets, for example, and insects, having developed resistance, are destroying crops at an increasing rate. Loss of biological diversity has become acute. Diversity, such as that found in the Land Institute's (2016) prairie features a diversity of species. Such an ecosystem maintains its own health: some plants thrive in dry years, others in wet; some in sun, others in the shade.

Apart from prairie research centers, a kind of traditional planting persists in scattered plots of land cultivated by the Old Order Amish people. The Amish treat the soil with special care, plant only perennial crops, and rely on work horses to till the land instead of soil-compressing tractors. There is much we can learn from the Amish people.

In Iowa, everywhere you look are cornfields, and soybeans, which are planted if the warm weather comes too late. The industrialization of the farms entails the conversion of family sized farms into milk factories where cows never graze and the manure pollutes the water in the lakes and streams. Paradoxically, the smell of hog farms sends people from the country to city parks to enjoy nature.

## LOSS OF THE FAMILY FARM

Large farms, with more land in production and more crops to sell, are in a position to benefit from subsidies. While they deplete the soil with monocropping, overproduction, and heavy use of chemicals, the large farmers produce at a lower cost, eventually driving traditional farmers out of business. And when the family farm goes, so does the local hardware store, the farm equipment store, the local school, and the café. Food prices are kept artificially low by the government; today US farmers sell their products for low prices in a market glutted with food. They operate an intensified farming system that requires capital that must be borrowed at high interest rates. Families forced off the farm often end up in factory work or domestic labor.

The loss of the family farm has been going on for some time with tragic personal consequences. The 1984 movie, *Country*, movingly depicts the tragedy befalling an Iowa family after the banks foreclose and the father suffers a breakdown. According to an article in *Newsweek*, since the farm crisis in the 1980s, the suicide rate for male farmers has remained high: just under two times that of the general population (Kutner, 2014). Across the globe, the same crisis among farmers is taking place. In India, a combination of severe drought conditions for several years and indebtedness for loans has led to over 3,000 farmers taking their lives in the past year, according to a government report (Biswas, 2016). The suicides mirror the state of India's ailing farms, which account for 14% of India's GDP, but on which more than half of its more than a billion people depend on for an uncertain living. Many farmers are simply not earning enough. After their deaths by suicide, their widows struggle to survive.

During the first seven years of NAFTA, all three participating nations saw commodity prices and farmer incomes plummet (Hansen-Kuhn, 2013). While all of the Central American countries have been devoting substantial effort to industrialization, agriculture has been an important part of their attempts to finance this process. Export agriculture in combination with cheap food policies is an essential part of the southern hemisphere's linkage with the world market. In Mexico, the elimination of tariffs on US produce threatens to wipe out the livelihood of millions of Mexican farmers.

In France, farmers are blocking the roads with their tractors to protest the difficulties of the agricultural industry, as an estimated 600 are killing themselves each year (The Local France, 2016). And in China, farmers are killing themselves to protest the government's seizing of their land for urbanization. There is some speculation that contact with toxic chemicals in pesticides is responsible as these products are known to cause physical symptoms like fatigue and numbness as well as psychological symptoms like anxiety, irritability, and depression. Those maladies are known to be caused by pesticides interfering with an enzyme that breaks down the neurotransmitter that affects mood and stress responses. Another theory is that pressure from banks for loans and competition from the global markets and corporate seed companies coupled with natural disasters has increased the stress to the small farmer (Shiva, 2008).

Across Europe the standardization demanded by modern agricultural methods is diminishing the number of species and varieties grown accompanied by pesticide-born damage and risks for human health (European Environment Agency, 2016). In Asia rural villages are dying as cities become overpopulated due to developing agricultural technology, and rural values and support systems are eroding as well. Overgrazing in China, for example, has created a disastrous dust bowl situation in northern areas while irrigation is depleting the aquifers of much-needed water (Brown, 2011).

Our ways of doing agriculture are not sustainable because of the loss of soil associated with monocultural farming and the contamination of waterways on which the growing of crops is dependent. Severe drought associated with global warming has further reduced the amount of arable land available. We need a national agricultural policy that is based upon proven ecological principles for the growing of life-sustaining and healthy food. Implicit in the quest for sustainability is the need to integrate the economic, social and environmental dimensions of development. Sustainability in any one area will boost sustainability in all.

Global agribusiness threatens the small farmer while the big landowners are in a position to accumulate great sums of wealth. This is one form of environmental injustice; environmental racism is another.

## ENVIRONMENTAL INJUSTICE: ENVIRONMENTAL RACISM

Poverty and the environment are mutually reinforcing; as the world's poor stretch their environmental resources to the maximum for the sake of survival, they have used up their natural capital and are further impoverished thereby. While all humans are affected by environmental degradation, women, people of color, children, and the poor throughout the world experience these harms disproportionately. The communities most affected by environmental pollution are often the same communities where social workers are entrenched in service provision at the individual, family, and community level (Teixeira & Krings, 2015).

The incinerators and toxic-waste dumps, and the contaminated air, drinking water, and rivers are located disproportionately in African American neighborhoods and on Indian reservations. Enforcement of environmental laws, significantly, is far less vigorous in communities of color than in white communities. Most of the companies spewing the toxins that contaminate the communities receive massive tax incentives from state government and deny culpability for the illnesses that result from exposure to the toxins. Because American Indian lands are self-governed, many of the states' waste management laws can be ignored by commercial waste operations. Tribes are offered financial incentives to allow their land to be used as toxic dumping ground (Bienkowski, 2012).

In their collection of essays on environmental racism, sociologist Robert Bullard and Beverly Wright (2012) document the glaring disparities in who pays the price of the nation's extravagant use of energy. Contained in their book, *The Wrong Complexion for Protection*, is the story of Louisiana's "Cancer Alley." Here in the lower Mississippi River valley where more than a quarter of the nation's chemicals are produced, incredibly high cancer rates are found. Activists from NGOs such as Greenpeace organized to expose this fact have revealed to the world the severe health problems of children living near the industrial sites. In Louisiana the pollution is so life threatening that whole communities are fighting for relocation.

Another focal point of environmental concern with racial implications, was the horrendous damage to the African American community of Anniston, Alabama, as described in a previous section. For years residents of the local African American community farmed the contaminated soil and ate the tainted fish. Monsanto continued to dump cancer-causing PCBs into the creek without warning the community of the dangers. Using some of the same evidence that was used in the Anniston case, the city of Spokane, Washington is now suing Monsanto alleging the company sold chemicals—PCBs—that it knew for decades were a danger to people and the environment. Portland plans to join Spokane and five other West Coast cities—Seattle, Berkley, Oakland, San Diego, and San Jose—that have sued the company over toxic pollutants it produced (Templeton, 2016). The Willamette River is still contaminated today from dumping in the 1970s.

Also in recent times, the water contamination in Flint, Michigan is a prime example of environmental injustice. This situation of serious neglect of the welfare of black children was discussed as a case of institutional racism in chapter 4. See Box 9.1 for a closer analysis of the situation by a health expert read Box 9.1.

A new civil rights battle for clean air and water is brewing (Milman, 2017). Activists and some in Congress have started to view the blight of pollution as a vast, largely overlooked civil rights issue that disproportionately affects people of color and low-income communities. On their behalf, environmental groups are taking industries to court based on Title VI of the Civil Rights Act which guarantees equal protection under the law. Built from the grass roots up, the environmental justice movement is an effort with long-term implications for changing national policies. Surveys have shown that Hispanics are more likely than non-Hispanic whites to view global warming as a problem that affects them personally, both due to the fact that they live on the poor side of town and in the work that migrant workers due which exposes them to dangerous chemicals in the fields (Davenport, 2015). Latino researchers also note that Hispanics outside of the united States are particularly concerned about the impact of climate change associated with storms and droughts, the effects of which their governments are not equipped to deal.

In 2010, off the coast of Louisiana, the largest oil spill in US history took place. The BP (Beyond Petroleum) disaster claimed the lives of 11 workers and released more than 4.1 million barrels of crude oil over 87 days into the Gulf, a region that provides one-third of all seafood consumed in the United States (Fisk, 2012). This oil spill killed animal life, made a mess of sand beaches, and accelerated the loss of Louisiana's delicate marshlands, which were already rapidly disappearing before the largest oil spill in US history.

When Hurricane Harvey struck Houston, the impact was disastrous, not only because of the strength of the storm but because of the vulnerability of the city to the damage due to wasteful and high-risk practices (Wehrmann, 2017). For example, Houston was so heavily built up with concrete that there would be no place for the water to go. And the location of industrial waste

## BOX 9.1 Water Contamination in Flint, Michigan

Marta Vides Saade

The human body requires clean water for basic health. According to the UN Millennium Development Goals, reasonable access to safe drinking water is defined as the availability of at least 20 liters, or 5.28 gallons, per person per day from a source within 1 kilometer, or a little over half a mile (.62 miles), of the person's dwelling (Global Education, 2012). Keep this in mind as you read of the scandal that happened in Flint, Michigan.

What had started as a city project to build its own pipeline connecting to the Karegnondi Water Authority (KWA), a new and cost-saving measure, became a nightmare when the current provider, Detroit Water and Sewerage Department (DWSD), terminated its service effective in one year. A temporary switch to the Flint River, through old pipes, began the health crisis for the people of Flint.

In May 2014, the people of Flint became aware that something was wrong with their water. The smell, color, and hardness of the water had changed. By August, *E.coli* and total coliform bacteria were detected in the water. By October, the General Motors plant decided to stop using the water in production for fear the metal in the water would corrode company machines. In January 2015, Flint was found to be in violation of the Safe Drinking Water Act because of the level of total trihalomethanes (TTHM), by-products of interaction between chlorine and organic matter in the water and possible carcinogens for human beings. By February, the community was aware its drinking water was contaminated with lead that had leached into the water supply (Kennedy, 2016).

The city is 57% black, 37% white, 4% Latino, and 4% mixed race. More than 41% of its residents live below the poverty line (Martinez, 2016). This contamination exposed an estimated 30,000 children up to age 19 to lead contamination in tap water at home and school according to a lawsuit filed by residents of Flint requesting special education screening and services for affected children (Knight, 2016a). As of the end of 2016, the tap water in Flint is still not safe to drink (Knight, 2016b) so that the blood-lead level had doubled in the first year from 2.5% to 5% in 2015 (Hanna-Attisha, 2016).

The people are poor. They do not want to pay for tainted water they cannot use. The result is that the water additives that would re-scale the corroded pipes is not reaching the pipes. The people of Flint have no drinkable water despite federal state of emergency funds from FEMA for provision of water, water filters, and other items, and two lawsuits against companies involved and criminal charges against state officials involved (Kennedy, 2016).

Lead has been restricted in plumbing since 1986, although older homes and neighborhoods still contain lead service lines, connections, solder, or other lead-based materials. Blood screening is recommended and routine for high-risk populations and children insured by Medicaid at one and two years old. This protocol was intended to catch exposure to lead from peeling lead-based paint. But lead in water places infants at most risk for the effects of lead on developmental and biological processes, notably intelligence, behavior, and overall life achievement (Hanna-Attisha, LaChance, Sadler, & Schnepp, 2015).

Flint is not alone. A *Reuters* investigation has uncovered nearly 3,000 communities with lead levels higher than those found in Flint, Michigan (Prupis, 2016). All of these had levels at least two times higher than Flint. More than 1,000 had levels four times higher. These communities included older homes in poor communities across the United States. In December 2016, the US Senate approved a $170 million aid package for Flint alone, but that is 10 times the annual budget the Center for Disease and Prevention (CDC) has available for lead poisoning assistance.

REFERENCES

Global Education (2012). Water and sanitation. Retrieved from www.globaleducation.edu.au

Hanna-Attisha, M., LaChance, J., Sadler, R.C., & Schnepp, A.,C., (2016). Elevated blood lead levels in children associated with the Flint drinking water crisis: A spatial analysis of risk and public health response. *American Journal of Public Health, 106*(2), 283–290.

Kennedy, M. (2016, April 20). Lead-laced water in Flint: A step-by-step look at the makings of a crisis. National Public Radio (NPR). Retrieved from www.npr.org

Knight, N. (2016a, October 19). Class-action lawsuit seeks justice for at-risk children of Flint. *Common Dreams*. Retrieved from www.commondreams.org

Knight, N., (2016b, November 28). Still without clean water, Flint demands aid from lame-duck Congress, *Common Dreams*. Retrieved from commondreams.org

Martinez, M. (2016, January 28). Flint, Michigan: Neglected because city is black, poor? *Cable News Network (CNN)*. Retrieved from www.cnn.com

Prupis, N., (2016, December 20). Nearly 3,000 U.S. communities have lead levels higher than Flint. Reuters, *Common Dreams*. Retrieved from www.commondreams.org

Source: Marta Vides Saade, Associate Professor of Law and Society, School of Social Science and Human Services, Ramapo College of New Jersey.

facilities (which were in predominantly minority neighborhoods) left the door open for the disastrous massive leak of chemicals into the flood waters which occurred in the aftermath of the storm.

Hurricane Maria's devastation of Puerto Rico and the Caribbean was of historic proportions. The island had its entire power grid destroyed, and most of the people lacked access to clean drinking water even months after the storm. The poor-rich gap among residents was clearly evident as wealthier residents were sealed up in air conditioned homes with their generators and bottled water or boarded flights to leave while the poor struggled against the elements and to find food and water (Associated Press, 2017).

Turning to Japan, the nuclear explosion at Fukushima in 2011, as described by Dominelli (2012), was a multiple hazard situation that confirmed the fears of many people who already were opposed to this form of energy production. When an earthquake reached a magnitude of point 9 on the Richter Scale, and a subsequent tsunami breached the protective seawall and flooded the area in which the nuclear plant resided, dangerous radiation leakages took place. At least 28,000 people died or went missing, and over 465,000 were displaced. Strikingly, the region that was struck was characterized by economic decline, outmigration, and disproportionate numbers of aging residents.

Much of the environmental destruction, as discussed above, is a casualty of corporate excess, a willingness to inflict the consequences on people at the margins of society, and poor urban planning. Another form of environmental injustice is the wilfull destruction of the earth and of human and non-human life associated with military operations and war.

## WAR AND THE ENVIRONMENT

Unlike the deliberateness of the war on nature where the goal is the taming of nature for human consumption, wars against people may or may not deliberately attack the environment as a part of a military "bring-the-enemy-to-its-knees" campaign. Yet the military has played a major role historically in environmental destruction.

Throughout history, as Bonneuil and Fressoz (2016), historians of science, indicate, the environment has been one of the war's worst casualties: Romans spread salt on the fields of Carthage; Sherman's troops marched through Georgia; the United States defoliated Vietnam's jungles; and Saddam Hussein set fire to the oilfields in Kuwait. Long after the wars are over, major unanticipated effects linger.

Just as war leads to environmental decimation, so does depleting the environment produce ethnic and territorial conflict (Mapp, 2014). Waves of refugees fleeing war zones further ravage environmental resources. During the Gulf War, for example, the white mountain peaks of Iraq's northern mountains turned black, and the burning oil inferno in Kuwait blackened the skies, polluted waterways, and wiped out lower-level animal life for years thereafter. Six to eight million barrels of oil were spilled into the sea by the Iraqis (Tutton, 2010). In Afghanistan, landmines continue to destroy human and other animal life and the uncontrolled use of resources, such as the cutting of forests for firewood, by six million refugees from the bombings has depleted the land of forest cover (Jha, 2014). Bulldozers and tanks used by Israel have wreaked havoc on Palestine and damaged the water system and disposal of sewage.

Preparation for war is often as destructive as war itself. Following World War II, extensive environmental destruction occurred at US bases in the Philippines and Panama (Closmann, 2009). In the Philippines, the US military dumped huge amounts of hazardous waste, and the local groundwater was contaminated by leakage from underground petroleum tanks. Panama was chosen as a testing ground for nerve gas and the defoliant, Agent Orange, produced by Monsanto. Then, in the United States itself, on deserts in the West, over 19,000 sites were contaminated due to testing of weapons and the dumping of hazardous waste material.

The NATO bombs that demolished the bridges of the Danube in the late 1990s did more than close the passageway to road traffic. They filled the river with debris and possibly unexploded bombs that will take years to clear (Jha, 2014). The use of depleted uranium in recent wars can be considered a weapon of mass destruction in terms of life and radioactive contamination (Closmann, 2009). Such toxic weaponry goes on killing for years after a war has ended, killing the victors as well as the defeated. The chemically toxic and radioactive depleted uranium dust which inflicted children in Iraq with leukemia and all sorts of physical deformities later entered the water table and fauna and flora and will still be polluting our earth for endless generations Jha, 2014). Doctors in Iraq have reported a disturbing number of birth defects, information that was covered up for years by international organizations (Ahmed, 2013).

Depleted uranium vaporizes when it hits a target; once released the particles are easily spread by the wind. This product is used by the military because of its high density which enables it to penetrate heavy armor and military vehicles. Depleted uranium, as Closmann (2009) indicates, is strongly suspected as a cause of Gulf War Syndrome, the assortment of health problems that has affected many members of the military who fought in recent wars. (For more information visit the National Gulf War Resource Center at www.nhwrc.org) and the website, Environmentalists Against War (www.envirosagainstwar.org).

## RELEVANT UNITED NATIONS CONVENTIONS

The sustainability movement strives not only for replenishment of natural resources and "saving the earth" but goes beyond that, moving in the direction of a human rights focus—the belief that access to potable water, nutritious food, and arable land is a human right. Sustainability entails an economic and political order that is in harmony with the biological resource base of society.

Such conferences as the Rio de Janeiro Earth Summit in 1992, the World Summit on Sustainable Development in Johannesburg in 2002, and the World Summit for Social Development at Copenhagen in 2009 were inspired by the principle that only through global partnership and careful future planning could sustainable development become a reality and the steady degradation of the earth's environment be reversed. However, the lack of legally binding agreements and firm plans for collective action to end climate change proved problematic (Dominelli, 2012).

In 1994, the International Conference on Population and Development in Cairo put the spotlight on the desperate need to curb overpopulation. Solutions were seen in expanding access to family planning, stress on education for girls, and improving women's and children's health and literacy. Protecting the environment, slowing population growth and preventing poverty were now recognized as inter-linked priorities. The link between sustainability and women's issues has only been recognized in a meaningful way at the end of the last century. This link was articulated for the first time by an international body at the Population Conference and later at the Copenhagen Summit. At these conferences, the terms of the discourse shifted. Not only were women on the agenda, women helped set the agenda (United Nations, 1995; Worldwatch Institute, 2002).

The well-publicized involvement of the world's citizenry at each recent international forum has bolstered the understanding of the human dimension of the environmental crisis. In Rio, for example, twenty thousand concerned citizens and environmental activists from around the world outnumbered official representatives by at least two to one. The same at Cairo and most strikingly at the Women's Conference at Beijing. At these conferences, members of non-governmental organizations (NGOs), rather than official delegates, captured the imagination of the world. Many of the organizations represented, for example, Greenpeace, Amnesty International, International Planned Parenthood, and Friends of the Earth, are themselves international. And the participation of the world scientific community also has been crucial in providing the data to inform the world of the need for renewable energy sources, a very important development to counterbalance the lobbying efforts of oil and coal companies.

The next big meeting was the World Summit on Sustainable Development in Johannesburg, South Africa in 2002, ten years after Rio. The purpose was to address one of the most fundamental issues facing the human race at the dawn of the new century: will the global economy make an adjustment to the contemporary biological imperatives? Significantly, this was the first UN conference in which the phrase "sustainable development" was in the name of the meeting (Harris & Roach, 2018). In the Plan of Implementation that emerged from the meeting, science and business were given main roles. Then, in 2012 the global society met in Rio again for the UN Rio+20 conference on sustainable development. Sustainable economics was the theme, a theme that underscored the importance of including environmental concerns in economic development.

Over the past three or so decades, in short, the world community has responded to the environmental challenge through the signing of numerous treaties protecting the oceans, the land (from desertification), the air (from pollution in Europe and in polar regions), and endangered species of wild flora and fauna (Secretariat of the Convention on Biological Diversity, 2014).

## AGREEMENTS ON CLIMATE CHANGE

In 2015, the Secretary of State, John Kerry, took a leadership role at the Paris climate conference. This agreement, which, has been adopted by 195 countries, can be considered the first-ever universal, legally binding global climate deal to accelerate the global transformation to a low-carbon and climate-resilient society (European Commission, 2016; Harris & Roach, 2018). Individual countries submitted comprehensive national climate action plans to increase renewable energy. These are not yet enough to keep global warming below 2°C (3.6°F), but the agreement, which is due to be enforced in 2020, paves the way to achieving this target. Both the United States and China, which are responsible jointly for 40% of global emissions, agreed to ratify the deal nationally during 2016.

A major setback to progress toward enforcement of this global agreement, was the election of Donald Trump to the US presidency. As a climate-change denier and proponent of America-first economic policies, the new president had little support in the global community. The appointment of Scott Pruitt, the former attorney general of Oklahoma, well known for the lawsuits he had filed against the Environmental Protective Agency (EPA), was consistent with Donald Trump's campaign promise to work toward dismantling the EPA and bolstering the coal industry (Ratcliff, 2017). In his rejection of scientific evidence of climate change and of human activities as its source, the president's decision to withdraw the United States from the Paris Agreement was no surprise. Nor was it any surprise that the EPA has proceeded to peel back dozens of clean air regulations that were seen as stymying economic growth.

Because President Obama had been unable to get his environmentally-friendly proposals through a Republican-controlled Congress, he relied on executive orders to push his agenda through. These victories therefore were vulnerable to being reversed by later administrations. Now the Trump administration has been able to unwind a host of regulations from tightened emissions standards for trucks to elimination of a proposed ban on a pesticide linked to developmental delays in children (Milman, 2017). His repeal of the Clean Power Plan was applauded by the coal industry.

Still, there are positive developments in the United States as well as in the world at large. Legislation in support of clean energy is being passed at the state and local levels in the United States. The governors of California, Oregon, and Washington, along with mayors from five of their leading cities, have committed themselves to continue to invest in clean energy and work toward ambitious targets (Fitzgerald, 2017).

Another encouraging development is the forceful manner in which China and the EU, nations have rallied around the Paris Agreement in the interests of environmental sustainability (Blanchard & Doyle, 2017). China, a nation so vital to progress in slowing of climate change, is now playing an active role toward this end. Already, the state governments in China are closing coal-fired power plants to curb air pollution so that people can breathe, and they have their overpopulation under control (Brown, 2016), although at a high cost (see chapter 11).

One criticism of these conferences on climate change and other environmental issues is that, until recently, the voices of indigenous or aboriginal populations have not been heard; however, there are reasons to suggest this might change.

## UNITED NATIONS DECLARATION ON THE RIGHTS OF INDIGENOUS PEOPLES

There are over 370 million indigenous people in Africa, the Americas, Asia, Europe and the Pacific (International Group for Indigenous Affairs, 2008). These are among the most impoverished, marginalized and frequently victimized people in the world. Their impoverishment comes not from their lack of survival skills or resourcefulness, but rather from encroachment on their ancestral lands and depletion of their natural resources.

Following more than 20 years of discussion about the plight of these people, in 2007, the United Nations General Assembly adopted the Declaration on the Rights of Indigenous Peoples. This universal human rights instrument is celebrated globally as a symbol of triumph and hope. Although it is not legally binding on any state, this 44-page document is a landmark development in human rights history in recognition of the rights of people who have often been trampled on by outside groups who establish settlements over the natives' territory. The United States formally endorsed this agreement in 2010.

Who are these indigenous people? The Declaration does not define indigenous peoples so we turn to *The Social Work Dictionary*, which does. Indigenous peoples are

> Descendants of earlier or original inhabitants of a nation or region, for example, Native Americans in the United States, First Nations Peoples in Canada, Aboriginal Peoples in Australia, Sami (Lapps) in Scandinavia, and Roma (Gypsies) in Eurasia. (Barker, 2014, p. 213)

The modern age has not been kind to the indigenous tribes in Central America. *The Violence of Development* by Martin Mowforth (2014) provides a disturbing account of their suffering. Even though a wide range of rights have been accorded to indigenous populations by Central American governments, the recognition is often only on paper. Battles over natural resources have led to a human rights crisis for the people who live on the land and own it communally. Governments, corporations, loggers, and cattle-ranching companies covet the land and the oil and gas that lie beneath the surface.

The goal of the export agriculture as directed by the world banks, is to enhance foreign exchange on the global market. As a result, poor and indigenous people have been displaced. The increased concentration of land ownership in the hands of a few in Mexico has led to violent uprising and much political unrest among the Chiapas Indians. This situation exists not only in Latin America but also in Russia, Canada, Cambodia, and much of Africa.

Exploitation of tribal lands is an issue in North America as well. In a keynote presentation at the University of Northern Iowa, Erica Littlewolf (2013), a spokesperson on indigenous issues from the Northern Cheyenne tribe of Montana, shared the following facts:

> The Montana reservation is situated on land in which there are rich deposits of coal. Because of this there has been exploitation. We are one of the poorest regions in the U.S. with a very high unemployment rate. The reservation has a high rate of teen pregnancy and also teen suicide—the teens commit suicide in groups of four or five together. The life expectancy on the reservation is only 57.
>
> Resource extraction of the land is a big issue in Canada as in the U.S. today because much of the tar sands from which oil is extracted is in indigenous territory. Along with the mining and building of railways, outsiders have come to the area, and this has placed the Native women in danger of sexual attack by white men. As a child I was raised to stay away from white men.

Recently, the hopes of many of the world's indigenous people were revived when the UN Declaration on the Rights of Indigenous Peoples was reaffirmed (Ford, 2014). This took place at the first UN World Conference on Indigenous Peoples, which was attended by over 1,000 delegates. The purpose of the conference was to focus attention on the poor implementation of the 2007 document, to empower indigenous groups, and to work toward the elimination of violence against these groups, especially in reference to attacks on women. A member of the Sami delegation who is president of the Sami Parliament in Norway called the commitments by the UN representatives "a historic moment."

## RECOMMENDATIONS FROM A SOCIAL WORK PERSPECTIVE

Measures of the gross domestic product (GDP) gauge economic growth in terms of production and sales of merchandise; no accounting is made of loss of resources. Defense spending can make a nation at war look very productive on paper even while the cost to the human habitat is enormous. Hoff and McNutt (2002, 2009) advocate for expanded government funding for research to develop sustainable techniques of production of food, energy, low-impact housing, and transportation. Moreover, they call for a tax policy that provides incentives for the restoration of environmental resources and a strengthening of regulatory agencies. These recommendations are consistent with the core social work value of social justice and with the NASW-US policy statement on environmental justice. We, as citizens of the world and as social workers with a world view, advocate for the following governmental policies:

- *Ratify relevant environmental treaties.*

Endorse the Paris Agreement of 2015 which was signed by President Obama by executive order and rescinded by President Trump. We need to restore the role of the EPA in setting as a major step toward the setting of targets to reduce toxic emissions into the air.

We strongly recommend as well that the United States sign and ratify the Ottawa Landmine Ban Treaty. The treaty calls for the end to the development, stockpiling, transfer and use of land mines. It also requires the signatory nations to clear land mines and assist victims, most of whom are children (Editorial staff, *National Catholic Reporter*, 2014). No US president has been willing to sign this treaty, which became international law in 1999. This unwillingness is attributed to the influence of the Pentagon which wished to keep open the possibility of use of these weapons. Worldwide, the human toll has been enormous—some 25,000 fatalities occurred annually in the early 1990s. As a human rights and environmental issue, land mines have thwarted agricultural development and rendered vast tracts of land uninhabitable. The United States, to its credit, has followed the treaty's requirements, provided medical care and artificial limbs for children who have stepped on a landmine, and contributed the most funding of any nation for clearing the land of these mines. As a result of the treaty, the death and injury toll has been considerably reduced.

- *Support organically grown and diversified farming practices.*

Organic milk is healthy because it comes from cows that aren't treated with antibiotics and synthetic growth hormones. Vandana Shiva of India has set an eco-friendly standard in India through her organization, Navdanya (Nine Seeds) that encourages farmers, who are mostly women, to form their own seed banks to produce hardy varieties of crops that can be grown with natural fertilizer. Trained as a physicist, Shiva is one of the most prominent world leaders in the fight against industrial agriculture. In an interview with Karlin (2016), Shiva describes the advantages of agro-biodiversity, which she has found produces abundant food with a high yield per acre. The food is rich in diverse nutrients since the biodiversity rejuvenates the soil and promotes water retention. Agro-biodiversity also contributes to ecological functions of pest control, weed control, water conservation and soil conservation.

The Land Institute in Salina, Kansas similarly, relies on traditional methods to produce crops with high yields at little cost to the environment. According to a statement on the Land Institute (2016) website:

> We are breeding perennial grains, and discovering the science that will make it possible to grow them in polycultures—mixtures that enjoy the benefits of the complex ecosystems found in the prairie. This promises crops that don't require pesticides to survive or fertilizer to thrive, and can be maintained with minimal energy inputs.(www.landinstitute.org)

Instead of encouraging mass food production by any means, governments could help protect the environment by eliminating pesticide subsidies and tax the use of harmful chemicals instead. France, Denmark, Norway, and Sweden do so at the present time (Bocker & Finger, 2016). Cuba, which lost its main supplier of fertilizers and pesticides when the Soviet Union collapsed, became a nation of organic farmers. At first, the people were hungry as they lost access to farm tools and tractors as well as food imports from the Soviet Union. The Havana city government supported urban food production, and a booming garden movement developed. And the farms in the countryside flourished as well (Goodman, 2015). The results are excellent in terms of producing healthy food and protecting the soil. This country uniquely is independent of the influence of transnational corporations. We can learn from the Cuban experience.

- *Support the growth of urban gardens.*

Madison, Wisconsin provides generous funding through a block grant that supports 75 gardens in the area by providing resources, information, and connecting master gardeners to community gardeners (Becker, 2016). Many of the people who maintain an active garden in a plot at a community garden do so to have their own food source and to raise their children to know about the process of providing the food one eats at the table. Community gardens, according to supporters, create a space to increase the social capital that cities sometimes lack.

In Waverly, Iowa, social work educator Tammy Faux who teaches at Wartburg College and her husband, Rob, raise a variety of wildflowers on their five-plus acre organic farm west of Tripoli, Iowa. They also grow organic vegetables. Here is their story as expressed to reporter Karris Golden (2007):

> We typically start lettuce, radishes, spinach and peas in early April. We don't use any chemical pesticides, fertilizers or herbicides. It's hard work; it means pulling weeds by hand . . . and sometimes we lose some of the crops. Deer are one of our worst enemies! We do a lot of research to find things that will protect the crops naturally.
>
> The method of pest management that is used at Genuine Faux Farms is known as "companion farming." This involves planting potatoes and beans next to each other to repel bean beetles that don't like potatoes and potato beetles that will avoid beans. The mission of the farm is to support the health of the community and work in harmony with nature while supporting the community's need to have access to fresh food and local produce. (pp. 1–2)

- *Promote the use of viable alternative energy sources.*

The average American's car covers nearly 13,500 miles every year (Sui, 2015). With our present reliance on fossil fuels (coal, oil, and natural gas) unable to meet current demands, we must seek alternative sources. For guidance, Lester Brown (2011) suggests that we look to the Danes. Denmark is farther along than any other nation in the shift to the reuse/recycle model, the new "eco-economy." The eco-economy of the future, notes Brown, will be powered by sources of energy that derive from the sun, wind, and by geo-thermal energy from within the earth. Denmark has stabilized population growth, banned the use of coal-fired power plants and of non-refillable beverage containers, promoted fuel efficiency in cars, and is now getting 15% of its electricity from wind. Workers typically ride bicycles to work. Brown also commends South Korea for its successful reforestation program, and Iceland for its plans to shift entirely to the use of renewable energy in the decades ahead.

All countries can tap into wind power to generate electricity. The United States at present leads the world in wind power production but China and Germany are close behind (Brown, 2011). China, Denmark, and Germany are now building off-shore wind farms. Denmark gets 20% of its electricity from wind. The energy future, according to Brown, belongs to wind.

- *Develop environmentally friendly bicycle transportation.* [see sustainable transport at the UNEP website]

Denmark isn't the only country to rely on bicycle transport. The Netherlands, Germany, and China also have a high ratio of cyclists to drivers. More and more local governments are recognizing that bikes reduce pollution and traffic. In the United States and Canada bicycles are rarely used for trips to work. Most bike trails are strictly recreational. Bike lanes on the side of heavy traffic is downright dangerous. Since housing tends to be miles away from work, commuting by car is often the only way to get there anyway.

- *Advocate for light rail.*

The city of Portland, Oregon is a leader among US cities in providing extensive light rail from housing developments to the city center, because it got an early start when federal funding was more generous than it became later. Each weekday, the Portland transit system carries 13,000 people, who can track arriving cars on their smartphones (Associated Press, 2013). In some cities, such as New York City, Boston, and Philadelphia, residents do not need to own cars. Research shows that property values rise considerably near access to trolleys and subways (Stone, 2014). As part of the return to urban living by young professionals, and in the interests of "going green," new projects are sprouting up, and American companies are even making streetcars again for the first time since the 1950s (Associated Press, 2013). See Figure 9.1 of light rail in one of the most transit-friendly cities in the United States.

When alternative transit within cities is provided, motorists can be charged to drive into the city center. To alleviate central city congestion, some cities such as London, Singapore, and

**FIGURE 9.1.** MAX (Metropolitan Area Express) Light rail in Portland, Oregon connects to all the large suburbs and the airport. Photo by Rupert van Wormer.

Trondheim are charging motorists right now. The US federal budget allocations, unfortunately, are biased toward the construction of highways over rail transport.

To understand why the United States went from a nation that in its heyday (in the 1920s) had a network of streetcars and trains that linked neighborhoods in cities and cities to each other, and to nearby parks and beaches, to the far less navigable system we have today, one has to consider the history of policymaking. Basically, as British energy economist Ian Rutledge (2006) explains, the car industry, mainly General Motors, worked out a scheme to invest in interurban electric railways and then replace them with uncomfortable, unpopular city bus operations; from there it was easy to sell more cars. By the mid-1950s, General Motors could lay claim to almost the complete destruction of electric street transportation. This in conjunction with urban sprawl created a huge market for privately owned cars and a bonanza for the automobile industry. From there, the motor industry was in a position to successfully lobby influential politicians for tax dollars to go into highway construction. Once the mass construction got under way many lobbying groups, including highway construction workers, the manufacturers of the equipment involved, the trucking industry, and the airline industry, joined in. See Figure 9.2 which shows truck congestion on the highway.

Today, most projects involve spending millions of dollars to put back something that used to be there, to rebuild a system that the corporations destroyed (Associated Press, 2013). Only

**FIGURE 9.2.** Big trucks use a lot of fuel and emit millions of tons of carbon into the atmosphere. Photo by Robert van Wormer.

a few cities, such as New Orleans and Philadelphia resisted the pressures to purge them of their streetcars, a fact their residents still can enjoy today.

- *Bring back the passenger trains.*

Talk to tourists who have visited Europe or Japan and you will hear of the convenience of high-speed rail travel. The Chunnel train from London to Brussels, for example, travels at 188 mph. In the United States, in contrast, passenger trains were driven out of business and huge, heavily polluting trucks have displaced railroads as carriers of most high value freight. If we were selecting seven wonders of the modern world, notes Lester Brown (2011), Japan's high-speed rail system would be among them. He also has praise for China in its development of the world's fastest trains. In terms of fuel consumption, Amtrak is 31.2% more efficient than automobiles and trucks, and 13.8% more efficient than airplanes on a per passenger mile basis. And the United States saves 4.2 billion gallons of oil each year through the use of public transportation (National Association of Railroad Passengers, 2016). Readily available mass transportation, moreover, alleviates poverty by connecting jobs and homes to transit. And it provides mobility for older people no longer able or willing to drive.

Highway construction companies, trucking companies, the airlines, car manufacturers—all had vested interests in destroying competition from the railroads. Due to lobbying, the politicians have complied, and today vast sums are spent in highway construction over the pittance, in comparison, that goes to the railroads. According to Rutledge (2006), America's addiction to oil stems from this history.

There was much excitement by train enthusiasts in 2009 when the Obama administration earmarked stimulus money for high-speed rail projects through grant money to the states. Several Republican governors rejected the federal dollars, however, most notably in Wisconsin, Florida, Iowa, and Ohio, and Republicans in Congress consistently have fought increased train construction funding (Clayton, 2012). And because General Motors, Ford, and car dealers provide a major source of the revenues to mass media outlets, campaigns to promote passenger rail service have had to rely on the Internet to publicize the cause. Only in the Northeast corridor (from Washington, DC to Boston) and California (from Los Angeles to San Francisco) are plans under way for Amtrak to offer build high-speed trains, and these projects will take years before completion. See Figure 9.3.

## RELIGIOUS TEACHINGS

The Koran is replete with references to nature and the sacredness of the earth's resources. The Prophet Muhammad in his 7th-century teachings provided instructions about water conservation, avoiding the wasteful consumption of resources, proper land use, and stewardship of the land. Today one finds an authentic green Muslim movement within the nations of Islam, including Turkey, Indonesia, Iran, and Malaysia, as well as among Muslims living in the United States (Wihbey, 2012). Since 2007 in Washington, D.C., an organization, Green Muslims, has been actively engaging in a variety of community activities focused on conservation and sustainability.

**FIGURE 9.3.** High-speed train service across the United States would revolutionize travel service. Photo by Robert van Wormer.

Among Jews, there are dozens of organizations set up to address Jewish efforts on the environment, both in the United States and around the world, especially in Israel (Halpert, 2012). The principal philosophical teaching is found in Genesis, where humans are put in the Garden of Eden to be "stewards" of the Earth. And we gain from the Book of Job a sense of nature as teacher and nurturer:

> But ask now the beasts, and they shall teach thee;
> And the fowls of the air, and they shall tell thee;
> Or speak to the earth, and it shall teach thee.—Job 12:7–8

Leaders of the Interfaith Center for Sustainable Development are especially concerned with the need for environmental education throughout the synagogues and the need to respect the earth and its natural resources.

Catholics also have articulated a sustainable environmental position (Catholic Education Resource Center, 2012). Pope Francis, who took his name from St. Francis of Assisi, the patron saint of the environment, has expressed a strong belief that it is the church's mission to protect all creation (Speciale, 2013). In response to the slowness of the world leaders to take drastic action to arrest the global warming, Pope Francis delivered one of the most far reaching and radical papal encyclicals ever issued by the Catholic Church. Pointing to climate change as the most significant moral and spiritual issue of our times, the Pope saw a direct link between unrestrained capitalism and climate change's disproportionate impact on the world's poor (Schiffman, 2015).

The Catholic Worker House movement, which stands for service to the poor, and resistance to war and social injustice, also supports environmental justice and sustainable agriculture. In Des Moines, Iowa, the Catholic Worker House, has protested against Monsanto and the World Food Prize, which gives recognition to businesses involved in ending world hunger, usually through the controversial production of genetically modified food (Curtis, 2012).

Increasingly, all major religious bodies are concerned with issues of environmental injustice. Here are some quick facts provided by the National Council of Churches (2012) Eco-justice website:

- Neighborhoods with the most polluted air are those with the highest percentages of African American, Latino, and Asian American residents.
- African American men are more likely to develop and die from prostate cancer than any other ethnic group, and prostate cancer is linked to pesticides and BPA, which is found in food cans and infant formula cans.
- Puberty age is falling across girls of all racial/ethnic backgrounds, but it is falling most dramatically among African American and Latina girls. Chemicals in pesticides, the air, and consumer goods are linked to falling ages of puberty.

Today, there is much social activism on behalf of environmental causes and organized protests against discriminatory practices, such as locating highly polluting factories in low-income, populated areas. An important ally in the cause of environmental protection is the Evangelical Environmental Network; this group of fundamentalist Protestants cites the Old Testament teachings concerning the need to acknowledge the presence of God in the land and proscriptions against waste. (information is at http://www.creationcare.org/)

## THE SPIRITUAL REALM

When we talk about the sanctity of nature and of life, we are getting beyond the realm of the knowable into the realm of the spiritual. Throughout history, men and women have experienced a dimension of the spirit that seems to transcend the mundane world (Armstrong, 1993). Spirituality is often defined in terms of its opposite—as the opposite of materialism.

The sense of truth in nature and of a Presence in nature is reminiscent of the following lines from the English romantic poet, William Wordsworth (2008/1798):

> One impulse from a vernal wood May teach you more of man, Of social evil and of good, Than all the sages can. ("The Tables Turned," lines 21–24)

A small but growing movement within social work, Deep Ecological Social Work echoes this theme. As eloquently described by Besthorn (2002):

> Deep-Ecological spirituality recognizes that humans share a common destiny with the earth. It celebrates an ongoing cultivation of a deeper identification of self with the whole of the cosmic order. From this vantage point of self-interest becomes identical with the interest of the whole. Humanity and nature cannot be separated—the sacred is in and of both. (p. 4)

A celebration with a close connection to the bounty of the earth and the harvest is the African American Kwanzaa. Such ceremonies and rituals as are represented in the Kwanzaa holiday celebration play an important role in providing meaning and purpose in life, bringing the generations together, enhancing a collective sense of peace and harmony, as well as connections to the sacred (Canda & Furman, 2010). Kwanzaa is a Swahili word that means "first fruits." From December 26 to January 1, the African American Celebration of Kwanzaa occurs. It is a celebration based on African traditions when the ancestors gathered together to celebrate the harvesting of the first crops. In Bowling Green, Kentucky, social workers and church leaders are actively involved in the annual celebration that generally takes place at State Street Baptist Church near downtown (see van Wormer & Besthorn, 2017).

The challenge for social work is to contribute to an alternative vision of the good life, to make common cause together to begin redefining social work's existing ecological awareness to incorporate environmental, spiritual, and political dimensions. Values such as sustainability, Deep Ecology, and spirituality within a social justice framework are social work values.

## INITIATIVES AT THE UNIVERSITY LEVEL

Big things are happening on college campuses, in small ways and large. The following information has been obtained on the various university websites. Beginning in 2011, Central College in Pella, Iowa developed a sustainability minor option. Earlier the college revamped its curriculum to infuse sustainability concepts in the liberal arts as well as the natural sciences coursework. The minor is intended as an "add-on" for students whose primary interest area and career goals lie elsewhere. Central students add the concentration—Global Sustainability—to diverse majors, from political science and education, to communication studies and art.

At Luther College in Decorah, Iowa, sustainability is a guiding concept that is woven within the fabric of campus life. In 2010 Luther College became one of eight recipients of an A on the College Sustainability Report Card awarded by the Sustainable Endowments Institute. Among the areas judged by this institute were: administration, climate change and energy, food and recycling, green building, student involvement, transportation, and investment priorities. The social work major at Luther integrates sustainability concepts into the required curriculum.

Arizona State University went beyond any others and founded a School of Sustainability which, according to their website, is a "new model for state universities." The university offers a bachelor's, master's, and doctoral degree in sustainability; the programs are interdisciplinary.

In North Carolina, the University of North Carolina is working to make the campus environmentally friendly in every area, from recycling and waste management to multimodal transportation, to the reduction of carbon emissions in every way. And further west, Warren Wilson College offers a curriculum that infuses sustainability education across the board. The social work department, according to its website, stresses the relationship between social work and environmental justice.

The social work department at the University of Northern Iowa is housed in the first Leadership in Energy and Environmental (LEED) certified building on the campus. This older building was completely redesigned in 2010 to provide the construction of new walls and doors with recycled or eco-friendly material such as bamboo plywood; a covered atrium Light Lounge that reintroduces natural light to all levels of the building's core to help individuals who experience Seasonal Affective Disorder (SAD) during the winter months; new modular paving to reduce storm water runoff; and upgrades to building entrances. Sustainability education is a major theme of the university.

In Europe as well, innovations are rapidly taking place. Aston University in the United Kingdom, which has been awarded the highest environmental standard for its new Aston Student Village residences project, will spend over $300 million to build a sustainable university community consisting of thousands of new *en suite* bedrooms. Special features include a wind turbine on the roof, wastewater recycling, green roofs, and recycling plants in each block. The residences will be powered by Aston's combined heat and power plant to vastly improve its energy efficiency.

## SUCCESS STORIES WORLDWIDE

Because the global consciousness is raised concerning the impact of climate change and the need for restrictions on wasteful human activities, there is cause for some optimism. Consider these examples as provided by the United Nations Environment Programme (UNEP, 2011) website:

- As many as 30% of the journeys in the cities of Denmark and the Netherlands are by bicycle; Chile has embarked on a natural project and has become a model for sustainable practices through government promotion of this form of transportation.
- Cuba, as mentioned previously, is one place in the world where organic farming is being practiced on a large scale.
- In the Makete District of Tanzania, forest, woodland, and grassland resources are essential to the local economies and are crucial for the protection of vital watersheds for the conservation of the environment for agriculture and livestock production. The use of smallholder woodlot management practices as a strategy for climate change adaptation has been effective.
- China is taking considerable steps to shift to a low-carbon growth strategy based on the development of renewable energy sources. The country's investment in solar and wind power is substantial.

To this list we add the following encouraging facts:

- The 2015 Paris Agreement discussed earlier has become a symbol of hope and commitment for the future, as more than 195 countries, including China, have reached a historic agreement to protect the climate from the most dangerous impacts of climate change.
- Facts from Energy Matters (2016): 19% of Australian households used either rooftop solar panels or solar hot water systems, and around 800,000 homes in the United Kingdom have solar panels. The World Bank Group plans to provide more than $1 billion this year to support India's goal of 100 gigawatts of solar energy by 2022.
- There are more than 500 wind related manufacturing facilities located throughout the United States, and the US wind energy industry currently employs more than 73,000 people (Energy.gov, 2015).
- Women are leading the way in sustainable and organic agriculture. And as consumer demand increases there is a significant market growth of 11% in the United States, the

world's largest organic market (Research Institute of Organic Agriculture, 2016). More farmers cultivate organically, more land is certified organic, and 172 countries report organic farming activities. As in previous years, the countries with the most producers were India, Uganda, and Mexico.

- Dam construction in Kenya and other projects to save the water eventually will reach 4,000 people; the access to water is allowing women to bathe and wash their clothes and given them renewed energy (Kingsolver, 2015).
- In recognition of the wide-ranging social consequences of environmental and natural disasters and the need for social work professionals to be involved at the decision-making as well as crisis intervention levels, social work education is headed toward a paradigm shift linking social and environmental justice (Alston, 2015).

## SUMMARY AND CONCLUSION

Two aspects of the biopsychosocial-spiritual framework of social work—the biological and the spiritual—provided a natural organizational scheme for this chapter. A major argument of this chapter is that the person/environmental conceptualization of social work must include interaction between the physical/spiritual realm as well as social surroundings. Environmental forces directly affect the well-being of social work clients; social workers often have clients who live in communities that bear the impact of atmospheric pollution, contamination of the water, and other environmental toxins.

The biological component of the biopsychosocial-spiritual model encompasses the external physical realm of the world around us, and the inner physiological world. These two worlds are interconnected in that human physical problems often emanate from environmental abuses; among them are birth defects, cancer, respiratory problems, and lead and radiation poisoning. It is imperative that social welfare professionals be guided by sustainable social development principles, what we call a sustainability ethic, to contribute to policy decisions needed in this time of unprecedented global challenge.

A sustainability ethic for social work brings our attention to four major problem areas in need of attention:: the concentration of greenhouse gases leading to climate crisis; the collapse of biodiversity of plant and animal life resulting from industrial agriculture and urbanization; environmental destruction in connection with military operations, and the threat of overpopulation in relation to available resources to sustain life. This chapter has discussed each one in some detail.

Central to all these challenges is the issue of environmental justice. Environmental justice is the ideal—the belief that all people have the right to get their needs met and have access to a clean and bountiful natural habitat. Environmental injustice, as we have seen, is the reality— the distribution of environmental burdens, like the benefits, is decidedly uneven. It is well known that communities of color are disproportionally impacted by the disposal of industrial wastes, and the residents have been unduly affected by health problems such as asthma and cancer. Poor people, indigenous and other minority populations, and the poor countries of the world inevitably experience the greatest harm from ecological practices that are unsustainable. In this way, environmental justice issues become human rights issues.

A healthy atmosphere—clean air and water, and uncontaminated and abundant plant and marine life—is essential to all life. Environmental justice is achieved when everyone enjoys the same protection from environmental health hazards caused by human-inflicted despoliation of the air we breathe, the water we drink, and the food we eat. Environmental justice is also achieved when all people have an equal role in decision-making concerning protection of environmental resources. As a global issue, we can draw encouragement as governments join together through the United Nations to reach international agreements to protect vulnerable populations from the ravages of climate change. And we can find hope in the extent of social activism on behalf of conservation of our natural resources that is attracting followers across the globe. Consider also the reverence shown to nature in healing ceremonies practiced by First Nations Peoples, in the African-inspired Kwanzaa celebration of the harvest, by Norwegians who legislate to protect the planet, and in the sustainability ethic provided by formal religious bodies.

Related to spirituality is the concept of restorative justice, a concept that was described in some depth previously in chapter 6. Restorative justice teaches the power of truth telling about the damage that was done, the importance of restitution or restoring something that was lost, and community healing. The urgency of climate change compels us to take an honest look at the state of the world today, of the impending risks to its people and habitat and in doing so to move toward what Besthorn (2013) terms restoration of the earth—"environmental restoration" (p. 233).

## THOUGHT QUESTIONS

1. What does chapter 9 add to the person/environment configuration of social work theory?
2. How does environmental justice relate to human rights?
3. How is sustainability defined? Relate this concept to Erikson's notion of generativity.
4. What do ecofeminists say about women and the environment?
5. Discuss the most common environmental problems creating a climate crisis today. Which countries contribute the most to pollutions?
6. What is the role of the oceans in preserving human life? Discuss some of the major threats to the health of the ocean.
7. Describe the process known as fracking. Why do some environmentalists object to this means of providing energy?
8. Discuss the importance of water to human life. What is the impact of water contamination?
9. What can we learn from First Nations people concerning respect for our planet?
10. Explain the connection between antibiotics used in farming and hospital infections that don't heal. What can we do about this problem?
11. Describe the ethical issues related to Monsanto's history. How are many farmers dependent on Monsanto's products today?
12. What is the importance of biodiversity? How is it being lost today?
13. What can we learn from the Amish regarding their treatment of the land?
14. How does agribusiness threaten the family farm? What are the consequences to the community?
15. Discuss several ways that wars ravage the environment. What do chemicals such as depleted uranium do to people?

16. Highlight some of the recent UN conventions. What is the significance of the convention pertaining to indigenous people?
17. Discuss the global dependence on fossil fuels; propose ways this can be alleviated.
18. Compare new methods of farming and the economic and environmental impact.
19. Argue the case that environmental racism is a reality. Refer to specific situations.
20. What would be some of the advantages of a well-funded, European style, high-speed train system in the United States today?
21. Discuss promising developments for environmental sustainability. How could investment in mass transportation such as trains and streetcars help?
22. Based on your own research, what is one significant success story in the world today pertaining to environmental sustainability?

## REFERENCES


Alston, M. (2015). Social work, climate change, and global cooperation. *International Social Work, 58* (3), 355–363.

Ahmed, N. (2013, October 13). How the World Health Organization covered up Iraq's nuclear nightmare. *The Guardian*. Retrieved from http://www.theguardian.com

Andan, A. (2015, May 25). Vietnam's horrific legacy: The children of Agent Orange. Australia: News.com.au. Retrieved from www.news.com.au

Armstrong, K. (1993). *A history of God: The 4,000 quest of Judaism, Christianity and Islam*. New York, NY: Random House.

Associated Press. (2010, December 29). Road rules give way to rage in New Delhi. *USA Today*, p. 6A.

Associated Press. (2013). Once nearly extinct, streetcar gets new life in U.S. (2013, November 13). *Waterloo/Cedar Falls Courier*, p. C5.

Associated Press. (2017, November 26). Hurricane Maria recovery puts Puerto Rico's deep rich-poor gap in stark relief. *The Japan Times*. Retrieved from http://www.japantimes.co

Banerjee, N. (2015, June 5). Fracking has contaminated drinking water, EPA now concludes. *Inside Climate News*. Retrieved from www.insideclimate.news

Barker, R. L. (2014). *The social work dictionary.* Washington, DC: NASW Press.

Barlow, M. (2013). *Blue future: Protecting water for people and the planet's future*. Toronto, Canada: House of Anansi Press.

Becker, A. (2016, June 1). Madison, Wisconsin: *Capital Times*, pp. 24–26.

Berry, W. (1977). *The unsettling of America: Culture and agriculture.* San Francisco, CA: Sierra Club Books.

Besthorn, F. H. (2002, February 15). Toward a deep ecological social work: Its environmental, spiritual, and political dimensions. Paper presentation. University of Northern Iowa, Cedar Falls.

Besthorn, F. H. (2013). Speaking earth: Environmental restoration and restorative justice. In K. van Wormer & L. Walker (Eds.), *Restorative justice today: Practical applications* (pp. 233–244. Thousand Oaks, CA: Sage.

Besthorn, F., & McMillan, D. P. (2002). The oppression of women and natives: Ecofeminism as a framework for an expanded social work. *Families in Society, 83*(3), 221–232.

Bewsey, H., & Paul, K. (2014, September 11). How industrial agriculture is making the soil—and us—unhealthy. *Organic Consumers Association*. Retrieved from http://www.organicconsumers.org

Bienkowski, B. (2012, June 12). Pollution, poverty and people of color: A Michigan tribe battles a global corporation. *Scientific American*. Retrieved from www.scientificamerican.com

Biswas, S. (2016, March 21). Why women are worst hit by India's farm crisis. *British Broadcasting Company (BBC)*. Retrieved from www.bbc.com

Blanchard, B., & Doyle, A. (2017, March 29). China, EU reaffirm climate pledges after Trump backs away. *Reuters*. Retrieved from www.reuters.com

Blue, A.W., & Blue, M.A.R. (2001). The case for aboriginal justice and healing: The self-perceived through a broken mirror. In M. L. Hadley (Ed.), *The spiritual roots of restorative justice* (pp. 57–79). Albany, NY: State University of New York Press.

Bocker, T., & Finger, R. (2016). European pesticide tax schemes in comparison: An analysis of experiences and developments. *Sustainability, 8*(378), doi:10.3390/su8040378

Bonneuil, C., & Fressoz, J.-B. (2016). *The shock of Anthropocene: The earth, history and us*. London, England: Verso.

Brown, L. R. (2009). Our economic worldview needs a Copernican shift. *Inside Climate News*. Retrieved from www.insideclimatenews.org

Brown, L. (2011). *World on edge: How to prevent environmental and economic collapse*. New York, NY: Earth Policy Institute.

Brown, L. (2016, January). Rebuilding the world: An interview with Lester Brown. Interviewed by A. Pal. T*he Progressive, 79*(1), 62–64.

Bullard, R., & Wright, B. (2012). *The wrong complexion for protection: How the government response to disasters endangers African American communities*. New York, NY: New York University Press.

Canda, E. R., & Furman, L. (2010).). *Spiritual diversity in social work practice: The heart of helping*. New York, NY: Oxford University Press.

Carson, R. (1962). *Silent spring*. New York, NY: Houghton Mifflin.

Catholic Education Resource Center (2012, March 18). Current issues: Environment. Retrieved from www.catholiceducation.org

China Daily (2012, June 11). Experts explore Beijing's air pollution. Retrieved from www.chinadaily.com.cn

Chiras, D. (2013). *Environmental science*. Burlington, MA: Jones & Bartlett Learning.

Clayton, M. (2012, August 21). Obama plan for high-speed rail, after a hitting a bump, moves forward. *Christian Science Monitor*. Retrieved from csmonitor.com

Closmann, C. (2009). *War and the environment: Military destruction in the modern age*. College Station, TX: Texas A & M University Press

Consumer Reports (2016, January). Making the world safe from superbugs. *Consumer Reports, 81*(1), 40–47.

Council on Social Work Education (CSWE). (2015a). Committee on environmental justice. Center for Diversity and Social and Economic Justice. Alexandria, VA: CSWE.

Council on Social Work Education (CSWE). (2015b). *Educational Policy and Accreditation Standards*. Alexandria, VA: CSWE.

Coyhis, D., & Simonelli, R. (2008). The Native American healing experience. *Substance Use and Misuse, 43*, 1927–1949.

Cozzetto, K., & Chief, K., & Dittmer, K., Brubaker, M., & Gough, R., Souza, K., . . . . Chavan, P. (2013). Climate change impacts on the water resources of American Indians and Alaska Natives. *Climatic Change, 120*, 569–584.

Curtis, P. (2012, June 18). Occupy Iowa speaks out against World Food Prize. *Radio Iowa*. Retrieved from www.radioiowa.com

Davenport, C. (2015, February 10). Climate is big issue for Hispanics, and personal. *New York Times*, p. A1.

Defenders of Wildlife (2016). Threats to coral reefs. Retrieved from www.defenders.org

Dominelli, L. (2012). *Green social work: From environmental crises to environmental justice*. Cambridge, England: Polity Press.

Dorsey, E., & Thormodsgaard, M. (2003, January). Rachel Carson warned us. *MS*, pp. 43–45.

Economist. (2015, February 7). Breathe easy. *The Economist*, p. 38.

Eller, D. (2015, July 7). High nitrate levels plague 60 Iowa counties, data show. *Des Moines Register*. Retrieved from www.desmoinesregister.com

Energy Matters. (2016). Wind and solar power statistics. Retrieved from www.energymatters.com

Energy.gov. (2015, August 10). Top 10 things you didn't know about wind power. U.S. Department of Energy. Retrieved from www.energy.gov

Environmental Action. (2014, April 4). Pumping up the volume at NPR. Retrieved from www.environmental-action.org

Eriksen, T. (1998, March). Norwegians and nature. *The Norseman*, 10–15.

Erikson, E. (1963). *Childhood and society* (2nd ed.). New York, NY: W. W. Norton.

European Commission. (2016, June 10). Climate action: EU prepares the way for a quick ratification of Paris Agreement. Retrieved from www.europa.eu

European Environmental Agency. (2016, June 3). Agriculture. Retrieved from eea.europa.eu

Fisk, L. (2012, February 23). BP spill victims still feel economic impact as trial nears. *Bloomberg Business Week*. Retrieved from www.businessweek.com

Fitzpatrick, J. (2016, April 21). Is Paris climate accord Kyoto 2.0? *Morning Consult*. Retrieved from htts://morningconsult.com

Ford, L. (2014). Indigenous groups give cautious welcome to deal struck at UN. *The Guardian*. Retrieved from http://www.theguardian.com

Fulton, D. (2017, April 18). Tribunal finds Monsanto endangers right to food, health, environment. *Common Dreams*. Retrieved from www.commondreams.org

Global Ocean Commission. (2014). From decline to recovery: A rescue package for the global ocean. Retrieved from www.globaloceancommission.org

Golden, K. (2007). Faux real: Couple plants seeds in classroom, at home. *Wartburg Magazine Online, 23*(3), 1–2. Retrieved from www.wartburg.edu

Goodman, A. (2015, June 3). Organic farming flourishes in Cuba, but can it survive entry of U.S. agribusiness? *Democracy Now!* Retrieved from www.democracynow.org

Halpert, J. (2012, February 29). Judaism and climate change. *The Yale Forum on Climate Change and the Media*. Retrieved from www.yaleclimatemediaforum.org

Hansen-Kuhn, K. (2013, November 22). NAFTA and U.S. farmers—20 years later. Institute for Agriculture and Trade Policy. Retrieved from www.iatp.org

Harris, J., & Roach, H. B. (2018). *Environmental resource economics: A contemporary approach*. New York, NY: Routledge.

Herring, H. (2013, May 21). Iowa's water problem is no myth, it's a warning. *Field and Stream*. Retrieved from www.fieldandstream.com

Hoff, M., & McNutt, J. (2002). Social policy and the physical environment. In J. Midgley, M. B. Tracey, & M. Livermore (Eds.), *The handbook of social policy* (pp. 461–475). Thousand Oaks, CA: Sage.

Hoff, M., & McNutt, J. G. (2009). Social policy and the physical environment. In J. Midgley & M. Livermore (Eds.), *The handbook of social policy* (pp. 296–311). Thousand Oaks, CA: Sage.

Intergovernmental Panel on Climate Change (IPCC). (2014). *Climate change 2014: Impacts, adaptation and vulnerability—Summary for policymakers.* Retrieved from http://www.ipcc.ch

International Work Group for Indigenous Affairs (IWGIA). (2008, October). UN Declaration on the Rights of Indigenous Peoples. Copenhagen, Denmark: IWGIA.

Jha, U. C. (2014). *Armed conflict and environmental damage.* New Delhi, India: Vij Books India.

Karger, H. J., & Stoesz, D. (2013). *American social welfare policy: A pluralist approach* (7th ed.). New York, NY: Pearson.

Karlin, M. (2016, May 29). Women around the world are leading the fight against corporate agriculture. *Truth-out.* Retrieved from www.truth-out.org

Katsnelson, A. (2015, January 13). Will McDonald's "sustainable beef" burgers be any better? *The Guardian.* Retrieved from www.theguardian.com

Kaufman, C. (2016, April 19). Opinion, wake up, homeowners: Lawn chemicals are toxic to Iowa. Around Iowa. from www.aroundiowa.com

Kingslver, B. (2015, winter). The weight of a falling sky. *MS Magazine*, pp. 43–47.

Kluger, J., & Dorfman, A. (2002, August 26). The challenge we face. *Time*, A4–A11.

Kutner, M. (2014, April 10). Death on the farm. *Newsweek.* Retrieved from www.newsweek.com

The Land Institute. (2016). Transforming agriculture, perennially. Salina, Kansas: The Land Institute. Retrieved from www.landinstitute.org

Leopold, A. (1966). *A Sand County almanac.* New York, NY: A Sierra Club/Ballantine Book.

Littlewolf, E. (2013, November 8). Indigenous women's issues. Keynote presentation at the *15th Annual Cedar Valley Conference on Human Rights.* Cedar Falls, IA: University of Northern Iowa.

The Local France (2016, February 28). French farming hit by "600 suicides a year." Retrieved from www.thelocal.fr

Mapp, S. C. (2014). *Human rights and social justice in a global perspective* (2nd ed.). New York, NY: Oxford University Press.

Mary, N. (2008). *Social work in a sustainable world.* Chicago: Lyceum Books.

Mellino, C. (2015, May 22). Which country will be first to go completely underwater due to climate change? *Eco Watch.* Retrieved from www.ecowatch.com

Milman, O. (2017, November 20). A civil rights "emergency": Justice, clean air and water in the age of Trump. *The Guardian.* Retrieved from www.theguardian.com

Mosher, C. (2010). A wholistic paradigm for sustainability: Are social workers experts or partners? *Critical Social Work, 11*(3), 102–121.

Mowforth, M. (2014). *The violence of development: Resource depletion, environmental crisis, and human rights abuses in Central America.* London, England: Pluto Press.

Myers, T. (2012). Potential contaminant pathways from hydraulically fractured shale to aquifers. *Ground Water, 50*(6), 872–882.

National Association of Railroad Passengers (2016). Railroad myths and facts. Retrieved from www.narprail.org

National Association of Social Workers (NASW). (2015). *Environmental policy. In Social work speaks: NASW policy statements 2015–2017* (10th ed., pp. 108–113). Washington, D.C.: NASW Press.

National Catholic Reporter Staff. (2014, July 16). Editorial: Why isn't the U.S. signing a land mine treaty? *National Catholic Reporter.* Retrieved from www.ncronline.org

National Council of Churches. (2012). Unequal exposures: Toxic chemicals in communities of color. Retrieved from http://nccecojustice.org/downloads/health/ejchemicals.pdf

National Ocean Service. (2015, September). *Where is all the earth's water? National Ocean and Atmospheric Administration.* Retrieved from www.noaa.gov

Nesmith, A., & Smyth, N. (2015). Environmental justice and social work education: Social workers' professional perspectives. *Social Work Education, 34*(5), 484–501.

Paul, K. (2016, May 31). Six questions for Monsanto. *Organic Consumers Association.* Retrieved from www.organicconsumers.org

Phys.org Science Network. (2015, October 12). Sea level rise will swallow Miami, New Orleans, study finds. Retrieved from www.phys.org

Rapoza, K. (2016, December 26). China's tougher environmental policies not only good for the locals. *Forbes.* Retrieved from http://www.forbes.com

Ratcliff, K. S. (2017). *The social determinants of health: Looking upstream.* Cambridge, UK: Polity Press.

Raven, P., Hassenzahl, D., & Berg, L. R. (2012). *Environment* (8th ed.). Hoboken, NJ: Wiley & Sons.

Reed, S. (2016, June 27). Study links air pollution to over 6 million deaths. *New York Times,* p. B5.

Research Institute of Organic Agriculture. (2016, February 10). Growth continues: 43.7 million hectares of organic agricultural land worldwide. Forschungs Institut für Biologischen Landbau. Retrieved from www.fibl.org

Robin, M.-M. (2010). *The world according to Monsanto.* New York, NY: The New Press.

Roosevelt, M. (2003, November 3). Fresh off the farm. *Time,* 60–61.

Rutledge, I. (2006). *Addicted to oil: Americans relentless drive for energy security.* London, England: I. B. Tauris.

Schiffman, R. (2015, June 18). Pope Francis sounds the alarm on climate change. *Truth-Out.* Retrieved from http://www.truth-out.org/speakout/item/31444

Schlosser, E. (2012). Afterword. In revised edition of *Fast Food Nation.* New York, NY: Houghton Mifflin]

Schultz, K., Kumar, H., & Gettleman, J. (2017, November 9). India closes 4,000 schools over dirty air. *New York Times,* p.A5.

Secretariat of the Convention on Biological Diversity. (2014). Global biodiversity outlook 4. Montreal, Canada. Retrieved from www.gbo4-en-hr.pdf

Shiva, V. (2008). *Soil not oil: Environmental justice in an age of climate crisis.* Berkeley, CA: North Atlantic Books.

Shiva, V. (2014, June). The Progressive interview: Vandana Shiva. Interviewed by D. Barsamian. *The Progressive, 78*(6), 33–36.

Smiley, J. (1991). *A thousand acres.* New York, NY: Knopf.

Sosnowski, A. (2015, October 15). "Cold blob" in North Atlantic ocean may affect weather in Europe, Eastern U.S. *Accu Weather.* Retrieved from www.accuweather.com

Speciale, A. (2013, May 19). At inaugural mass, Pope Francis calls for defending environment, poor. Religious News Service. Retrieved from www.religionnews.com

Stone, M. (2014, January 30). The US cities with the best transportation systems. *Business Insider.* Retrieved from www.businessinsider.com

Sui, J. (2015, July). How many miles does the average American drive each year? *Auto Guide.* Retrieved from www.autoguide.com

Teixeira, S., & Krings, A. (2015). Sustainable social work: An environmental justice framework for social work education. *Social Work Education, 34*(5), 1–15.

Templeton, A. (2016, March 16). Portland to join suit against Monsanto. *Oregon Public Broadcasting.* Retrieved from www.opb.org

Tutton, M. (2010, June 4). Lessons learned from the largest oil spill in history. Cable News Network (CNN). Retrieved from www.cnn.com

United Nations. (1995). *The world's women 1995.* New York, NY: United Nations Development Programme.

United Nations. (2007). *UN Declaration on the Rights of Indigenous Peoples.* Adopted by the General Assembly of the United Nations. New York, NY: United Nations.

United Nations. (2012). United Nations Conference on Sustainable Development (UNCSD), Rio+20. New York, NY: United Nations. Retrieved from http://sustainabledevelopment.un.org/rio20.html

United Nations Environment Programme (UNEP). (2011). Success stories. Green Economy. Retrieved from www.unep.org

United Nations General Assembly. (2015, June 2). Oceans and the law of the sea. Retrieved fromwww.un.org

United Nations World Commission (1987). *Our common future—Brundtland report.* New York, NY: Oxford University Press.

U.S. Global Change Research Program. (2014). 2014 *National Climate Assessment-Overview Report.* Retrieved from http://nca2014.globalchange.gov/highlights/overview/overview

van Wormer, K., & Besthorn, F. H. (2017). *Social work and the social environment, macro level.* New York, NY: Oxford University Press.

Vidal, J. (2014, March 22). Indonesia's forest fires feed "brown cloud" of pollution choking Asia's cities. *The Guardian.* Retrieved from www.theguardian.com

Waldman, P., Mulvany, L., Stecker, T., & Rosenblatt, J. (2017, July 17). Roundup: The usual suspect. *Bloomberg Business Week*, pp. 42–47.

Watts, N., Amann, M., Ayeb-Karlson, S., Belesova, K., Bouley, T, Boykoff, M., . . . Costello, A. (2017). Lancet countdown: Tracking progress on health and climate change. *The Lancet.* Retrieved from http://www.lancetcountdown.org/

Wehrmann, K. (2017, November). Environmental justice challenge awaits. *NASW News*, p. 3.

Wihbey, J. (2012, April 11). "Green Muslims," eco-Islam and evolving climate change consciousness. *The Yale Forum on Climate Change and the Media.* Retrieved from www.yaleclimatemediaforum.org

Wordsworth, W. (2008/1798). The tables turned. In *William Wordsworth: The major works.* Oxford, England: Oxford University Press.

World Health Organization (WHO). (2015). Climate change and health. Geneva, Switzerland: WHO. Retrieved from www.who.int

World Health Organization (WHO). (2017a, July). Drinking water, fact sheet. Geneva, Switzerland: WHO. Retrieved from www.who.int

World Health Organization (WHO). (2017b). 2.1 billion people lack safe drinking water at home, more than twice as many lack safe sanitation. Geneva, Switzerland: WHO. Retrieved from www.who.int

World News. (2015, August 3). UN states agree post-2015 sustainable development agenda. Retrieved from http://www.news24.com/WorldNews.

World Wildlife Fund (WWF). (2016). Soil erosion and degradation. Washington, D.C.: WWF. Retrieved from www.worldwildlife.org

Worldwatch Institute. (2002). *State of the world 2002. Worldwatch Institute.* New York, NY: Norton.

Worldwatch Institute. (2013). Valuing nature's services today is an investment in the future. Retrieved from www.worldwatch.org

## CHAPTER 10

# CHILD WELFARE

> The Convention on the Rights of the Child is the most rapidly and widely ratified international human rights treaty in history. . . . The Convention changed the way children are viewed and treated—i.e., as human beings with a distinct set of rights instead of as passive objects of care and charity.
>
> United Nations Children's Fund (UNICEF), 2016 (www.unicef.org)

> Children cannot tie their shoes but can fire guns.
>
> Bill Sternberg, *USA Today*, Wednesday, May 18, 2016, p. 7A.

The term *child welfare* is used here not in the narrow sense of a specialized field of social work practice, but also in its literal meaning of children's welfare or the general well-being of children. Well-being in this context refers to the care and protection that families give their children and also how the society supports families in providing this care. The basic needs of children are a place in which to live safely, having shelter and enough to eat, and receiving the love and encouragement of parents and the surrounding community. In the United States, which has one of the highest rates of child abuse and neglect in western societies and one of the highest rates of child poverty (UNICEF, 2014), the child's level of well-being is impaired.

Basic assumptions of the chapter are, first, that children are the most powerless members of the human community, and second, that the primary source of help and nurturance for children is the family. Many families, however, cannot do the job they were meant to do, so some form of help or even substitutive care has to be provided. This is where social work comes in.

In the United States, there is no current social security for children as there is for other groups—older adults, persons with disabilities, or veterans. And there is no guaranteed family allowance to provide child support for all parents as exists in many nations. In fact, the opposite is true in that, since 1997 Temporary Assistance for Needy Families (TANF) has inflicted penalties on families, usually single parents, who do not work. Also poor, minority children who get into trouble at school all too hastily are sometimes criminalized and set on the path for the school-to-prison pipeline.

In this context, as advocates for children's welfare, social workers have the frustration of living in a society that is reluctant to put children's needs first. But they also have the opportunity to look out for the best interests of children in their charge. Children are our future and the future of the world. When we do not provide for children's well-being at the front end, we pay a larger price later in intergenerational ignorance, poverty, and crime.

This chapter, as others in the book, adopts a human rights perspective. This brings us into the global realm. In many countries, what we find is that under life-threatening conditions such as war, plague, drought, and overpopulation, childhood as we think of it does not exist. Consider these images that we frequently see in the media:

- Row after row of tents in refugee camps in Jordan for families displaced by war
- Child refugees being rescued from stormy seas off the coast of Greece
- Children on the streets of Chicago at risk of being shot by stray bullets
- Escapees from gang violence in Central America on a hopeless journey to the US border
- Rubbish heaps in Nicaragua where children search for food and useable items
- Whole families confined in immigrant detention centers in Texas
- Girls attending school in Afghanistan in defiance of the Taliban

The roles of child welfare professionals often come into play in the midst of such hardship or tragedy, situations with causes rooted in the global economy and social structure over which social workers have little control. An overview of this complex field of work—child welfare—is presented by this chapter in the following sections:

- **UN Convention on the Rights of the Child.** Using the United Nations (UN) Convention on the Rights of the Child (CRC) as a framework, we consider the definition of a child as well as children's rights to protection. The reader can also refer to chapter 6 on human rights for a background in the language of conventions and rights.
- **Social work roles in child welfare.** How do social workers support families in order to protect children including their physical, environmental and financial needs? What are the needs and expectations of families and what are the challenges? When families come apart through loss, poverty, crime or other separation, who stands in for parents, who supports the emotional development of the child? The foster and adoption services of a country are now regulated through international policies and laws and this international approach will be illustrated through a discussion of transnational adoption and children crossing borders.
- **Meeting children's personal and physical needs.** Child abuse and neglect in the family raise important issues for social workers and for the society as a whole. The dilemma that is considered in this section is at what point should child protective services intervene and what should the nature of that intervention be—child removal or family therapy to teach proper methods of child management?
- **Children's education and cognitive development.** We discuss this psychological aspect of child welfare in relation to resources and disparities across states. There are states in the US with high rates of achievement across cultural groupings, while in other states such as Iowa and Mississippi, children of color for example, are over-represented in those not completing high school and their GED.

- **Barriers to the physical and mental health of children.** When children are in stable, well-nourished families with adequate housing, safe sleeping space and warmth, they usually thrive. Sometimes they are born with conditions that hamper their development (for example hearing impairment; blindness; cleft palate) and require specialist services. Most significant in terms of numbers affected is when children are in environments that are life-threatening and have no choice but to try to escape. This can range from the extremes of fleeing war and forced migration at the international level, to living in health damaging environments at the local level, such as a damp basement, with high levels of lead or cadmium in the water, or alcohol and drugs in the home.
- **Meeting the social needs of children.** How does a community set about making children's opportunities for socializing outside the home safe and accessible? The final section of our chapter on child welfare describes the values of child-friendly cities or other places for children to live and feel safe. Safety from being killed, such as by gun violence is one of the topics discussed, a situation that is fraught with political and legal connotations in the United States and a high death toll for children.

## UN CONVENTION ON THE RIGHTS OF THE CHILD

When planning a career in child welfare it may be useful to start by asking, What is the definition of a child? In social work, we refer to the United Nations (UN) definition set down in the Convention on the Rights of the Child (CRC). To learn more about this worldwide organization that the United States participates in, see chapter 6 for the history and current wide range of work of the UN, including designing policies for vulnerable populations, such as children.

The CRC was the first international policy to define childhood. The CRC was established in 1989, and countries across the globe have been signing on and then ratifying—which means agreeing to its definitions and expectations, framed as rights—ever since. Now most countries are part of the reporting process and accountable for the expectations laid out in the convention. This accountability in the form of regular reporting and audits by people called "rapporteurs" affects and can support or critique the work of people in child welfare.

In Box 10.1 you will see a summary of the CRC, and the implications for children. First, the definition: a child is a person under the age of 18, unless a country law specifically states otherwise. Why is this definition important? For lots of reasons in terms of how children are held accountable and how our expectations change when they become "adults." An adult 18 years and over can enlist in the military; can marry; can make independent decisions about his/her/hir life. Why use the pronoun hir? The reason is that young people in many countries are claiming their right to gender identity. We discuss gender identity in the section, Meeting the Social Needs of Children. The key point here is that some people may be transgender; some may choose not to identify by gender. A person 18 and over may choose.

Following the definition of child, the CRC provides guiding principles for the well-being of a child as summarized in Box 10.1.

The serious impact of the definition of a child is evident in relation to incarceration. Prior to the CRC, children were held in adult prisons all over the world. Until quite recently, the US retained the "right" to imprison children to serve life sentences without parole for extremely violent crimes, such as murder. People were also executed for crimes they had committed as

**BOX 10.1. The Seven Clusters of the Convention on the Rights of the Child: 54 articles grouped in seven clusters**

- Definitions of the child
- Guiding principles, including promoting best interests of the child, non-discrimination, and standards for institutional care
- Civil rights—the right to access to information and the right not to be subjected to cruel or inhuman treatment
- Family environment and care—protection of the child from all forms of violence
- Health and welfare—the right to an adequate standard of treatment and the right of children with disabilities to appropriate care
- Education, leisure, culture—the right to free primary education and access to education at higher levels, the right for indigenous children to culturally sensitive education
- Special protection—protection for refugee children and those in armed conflict, in the juvenile justice system; protection from labor exploitation, sex trafficking, and use as child soldiers

juveniles. These practices have been challenged as cruel and unusual and in 2005, the Supreme Court took this step:

> Bowing in part to world opinion, the U.S. Supreme Court abolished the juvenile death penalty in a ruling that immediately sparked controversy over whether the justices should listen to the views of foreign countries when interpreting the U.S. Constitution (Waldmeir, 2005, p. 10).

The tension continues amongst those who support the worldwide commitment to the well-being of children brought about by the work of the United Nations and those who think the US should stick to its own legal system, but this 2005 decision has had far reaching impact. Shortly after the Supreme Court decision children were taken off death row. Legal battles followed concerning children on the brink of adulthood and many continued to go to adult prison after being sentenced as an adult.

The decade since 2005 has seen major changes. In July, 2016, for example, after 28 years in prison for murder, Yvette Louisell was among a group of child offenders to be moved out of prison into a work release program. According the report:

> [This ended] years of legal wrangling that overturned an earlier sentence of life without parole . . . she is one of the first Iowa inmates convicted as a teenager to be granted conditional parole after it was declared that life without parole sentences are unconstitutional treatment for those who committed their crimes before turning 18 . . . Louisell had a turbulent childhood growing up in a family scarred by divorce and her mother's mental illness. (Rodgers, 2016)

In his powerful research into the lives of children committing violent crimes, the social worker James Garbarino discovered that the majority had violence inflicted upon them and were frequently caught up in domestic abuse in their families (see Garbarino & Haslam, 2005). The accumulation of risks and absence of opportunities was the key. This does not excuse the violent behavior of the child, but the research gives social workers indicators of the causes of violence and the triggers for children who have not had role models in recognizing non-verbal cues of tension, de-escalating anger and managing aggressive impulses (Fraser, 1996).

Before we leave this section, consider the following news headlines that relate to human rights:

- A Black Teen Died Following an Encounter with Police Near Dallas (Mettler, 2017, *Washington Post*)
- Local Social Worker Speaks Out against Spanking on International No Spank Day (Canadian Broadcast Company [CBC], 2017)
- Why Are Black Children So Much More Likely to Die of Asthma? (National Public Radio [NPR], 2017)
- Young Boy and Loaded Handgun Found in Car; Dad Arrested. (Novak, 2017, *Wisconsin State Journal*)
- The Foster Care Crisis: The Shortage of Foster Parents in America (De Garmo, 2017, *Huffington Post*)
- Growing Number of City's Students Live in Homeless Shelters (Harris, 2017, *New York Times*)

All these situations have important implications for social workers who might very well be involved in these and other similar situations.

## SOCIAL WORK ROLES IN CHILD WELFARE

Child welfare services in the United States evolved from voluntary "child saving" efforts in the 19th century. One program was the orphan train movement that lasted from 1853 to the early 1900s when poor children from the slums and streets of New York City were sent by train to farm areas in the Midwest to be adopted by farm families. They were lined up at the train station at pre-scheduled times and selected right there on the spot and taken home by people. Altogether almost 250,000 children found homes in this manner (Herman, 2012). Under the direction of the Children's Aid Society, this historic intervention marked the beginning of an organized system of largely government-funded programs to protect children from abuse and neglect and to find them permanent homes (Courtney, 2013).

Services to families evolved from casework and child removal, to family intervention in cases of abuse and neglect to teach parents better child-rearing methods. The focus was on permanency planning through preserving biological families. This changed during the 1990s when family preservation was found by a number of researches to be less effective than claimed. The focus of work shifted by 1995-2000, when child safety was emphasized and where deemed necessary, children were removed to foster care. This change of direction is seen in the Adoptions and Safe Family Act of 1997 (Courtney, 2013; Lindsey, 2004).

Today, the usual practice is for the court to require the child welfare agency to make reasonable efforts to preserve the child's family of origin, in most cases by providing services intended to help reunite the child with the family (Courtney). Some social workers were concerned that the new act required faster decision making for children in foster care so that they could be adopted; fast being a complex idea where children's lives and sense of family are concerned. There is a need for speed where children are in danger; for those who languish in foster care, accountability and planning needs to be evident, but the tide is again turning as prevention and concern for cultural ties to family origin are recognized as key to a child's future sense of identity and well-being.

The debates continue in the second decade of the 21st century as to the most effective way to support the healthy development of children. In some ways the debate is answered by reduced funding for child welfare leading to a narrower focus on child protective services as the main domain of child welfare in terms of public service. A welcome development has been the thrust toward the offering of services from an individualized and family strengths-based approach as endorsed by the Children's Bureau (2008; see also Saleebey, 2013). There is much still to be accomplished for those entering the field of child welfare—which in many ways means a career that is exciting and full of promise to leave services in a better state than found.

When thinking about child welfare we can approach children's well-being and security through several levels of service. At the individual level, the social worker may respond to a call from the family for help or to a call from outside the family reporting abuse or neglect. Many social workers are employed by a system such as a school or hospital that involves work with children. A third level may be employment by a non-governmental organization (NGO) such as the Children's Defense Fund (CDF). The CDF works on advocacy, as does a number of agencies that offer services to families, such as the Red Cross or Salvation Army.

Advocacy on behalf of children's rights is an area in which social workers are active; such advocacy may be through a professional organization, such as the National Association of Social Workers (NASW-US) which lobbies politicians for improved policies. At the international level, social workers who are employed in the field of adoption may become involved with children and families across borders and become knowledgeable about international laws and policies. Finally, social workers pursue global interests through membership in an organization such as the International Federation of Social Workers (IFSW) and attend global conferences. Here are the basic levels of child welfare work:

- Micro: children's day-to-day lives including with their families; natural or interrupted development of their potential according to their socioeconomic-health status
- Mezzo: cultural and community surroundings that reinforce identity and safety, for examples through school
- Macro: larger national and international forces affecting children: trafficking, migration, disaster, poverty, war, health
- Gaia: global interdependence can be both positive (World Health Organization) and negative (human trafficking).

Another way to think about child welfare is to ask, are these services available to all children (universal services) or are they only available to those determined to be in need (residual services)? We differentiated universal and residual approaches to social welfare services in chapter 2.

**FIGURE 10.1.** Children who attend a well-run preschool have a head start when they start grade school. © Shutterstock, photo by Monkey Business Images.

*Universal policies* refer to those that all children receive, such as children's allowances and preschool in Italy, and the child savings project in the UK. *Residual policies* govern most of those laws affecting children in the US and are geared to those in need; they are often means-tested, as described in chapter 8. Exceptions are K–12 education, which is universally available, and more recently, the expanded access to health care through the "Affordable Care Act," sometimes referred to as "Obamacare." Some social workers argue that the United States, in comparison to Norway, Finland or France has too few universal policies and that residual policies partly contribute to the high rates of poverty amongst American children (Lindsey, 2009). In any case, there is much we and policy makers can learn in going beyond national boundaries to discover what is working in other countries that might be adopted here. See Figure 10.1 to see preschool children happily engaged in learning activities.

## EMPLOYMENT IN CHILD WELFARE

Child welfare, the broad term used to refer to all services that support and nurture the lives of children, is a key area of social work practice. One of the largest employers of social workers in the United States is the school system. Many schools across the US have school social workers who liaise with local Departments of Human Service and Child Protection. Similarly, hospitals employ social workers to work with children and their families. These large organizations are *public* services, funded by state and federal government.

There is also a wide array of *nonprofit* services funded by grants and donations, such as the Southside Family Nurturing Center (www.SSFNC.org) in Minneapolis. SSFNC offers preschool services, nutrition and parenting programs. Similarly, in Des Moines, Iowa, the Youth Emergency Services (YES) offers housing where children feel safe, and crisis counseling to young people who are homeless or without adult caregivers. Box 10.2 lists some of the jobs in child welfare and the qualifications that are needed for a social worker to be employed.

When we think about the well-being of children, we also think about their social interaction and opportunities for meeting other children, families, neighbors, school mates and local community. When children are deprived of these social interactions, their development suffers. Parents may home school their children to protect them from unwanted influence in the wider community, but in order to live sustainable adult lives, socializing is a key aspect of development. Many authors have researched the social and cognitive development of children and this too will be a focus of the chapter (Center on the Developing Child, 2014; Garbarino & Haslam, 2005; Kozol, 2008).

Perhaps the two central aspects of a child's life are family and school. Education is something all children need in order to succeed in their future career and to sustain themselves later as adults. As part of the "well-being" of children this chapter will examine some of the disparities in access to education and to educational resources, using the examples of Iowa and Mississippi as states that have struggled to fulfill the needs of their children.

### BOX 10.2 Employers of Social Workers in Child Welfare

A search in the local press and online will reveal the wide variety of employment opportunities in this field. Among typical avenues of work in this field are

1. Kinship care for children where families are struggling; aides and care workers in children's residential homes where they may be staying for protection or due to homelessness (degree: Associate of Arts).
2. Non-profit agency assistant, family support worker, day care worker, advocacy such as LGBT youth, teenage parent support (degree: BA in human service or social work).
3. Public financial aid and income support, food stamp, assistance center welfare officer, financial assistance workers (BA: Social work or Human Services).
4. Social worker in public service, such as child protection services or school social work (BA in Social Work; more often Master of Social Work (MSW) and in some states, license to be named and employed as a "social worker").
5. Social worker in the court and corrections system, also known as a probation officer or child welfare officer (MSW).
6. Community College or University educator of social workers, policy analyst, advocate, and researcher (PhD).

## MEETING CHILDREN'S PERSONAL AND PHYSICAL NEEDS

How do social workers protect children, including their physical, environmental, and financial needs; what are their roles; what are the needs and expectations of families and what are the challenges?

When families come apart through loss, poverty, crime or other separation, who stands in for parents? Who supports the emotional development of the child so that their development and experiences are not impeded by feelings of loss, separation and abandonment? Most frequently the response comes from child welfare social workers in public service sometimes supported by non-profit agencies. The foster and adoption services of a country are regulated through international policies and laws and this international approach means that there is now greater collaboration between social workers in different countries when children are crossing borders (Healy & Link, 2012).

Rotabi (2012) in her presentation of research into international adoptions demonstrates that often adoption has been the result of political crisis (such as in Romania), economic distress, conflict and natural disaster (such as South Korea and Central America). Certainly, some countries have had patterns of international adoption that reflect their economic and social development. In the United States, however, adoption is closely supervised and regulated.

Another wide area of service is child protection and this corresponds to those Articles of the CRC that relate to their best interests and their family standards of care. It is in the best interests of a child to be part of a family or substitute family. The majority of research agrees that institutional care does not lead to positive outcomes for children (Garbarino, 1999; Tough, 2016). Also, recent research indicates that high levels of stress in children's early years can hinder their cognitive development (Tough, 2016). Stress comes from many sources, including homelessness. In a report on New York's homeless children, it was discovered that there are many obstacles for children who are homeless and that getting to school is one of them. Harris (2016) summarizes:

> The report, which draws largely on data from 2013–14 school year, vividly maps out just how difficult it is for students who live in shelters to get an education. It is a crisis that has grown: roughly one out of every 13 children in the New York City school system is now homeless. . . . Many of the programs intended to help them are either insufficient or poorly executed, while a surge in family homelessness in recent years has strained the system to its breaking point, or perhaps beyond it. The key issue is getting to school . . . due to the location of the shelter in relation to their original school. (Harris, 2016, p. A19)

One solution is to provide affordable housing. This recommendation is unlikely to receive the financial resources needed unless there is greater awareness of the problem in the wider community. Otherwise many children who have already faced the emotional and social disruption of losing their home have their problems compounded by missing out on school and dropping out of sight. See our section on child homelessness toward the end of this chapter.

Another key area of healthy growth and reinforcing positive cognitive development for children (and adults) is adequate nutrition. In 2008 the Supplemental Nutrition Assistance Program (SNAP) replaced the food stamp program, with a focus on nutrition and benefit increases. Michelle Obama has made child nutrition a key theme in her role as First Lady in the Obama

Administration, and has had great success role modeling play, exercise, gardening and growing your own food as ways for children to thrive. This program is a direct result of data indicating the extent that individual states struggle to ensure children have enough to eat. For example, Cory Berkenes, Director of the Iowa Food Bank Association, reported in October 2015, that 1 in 8 people in Iowa are food insecure and 1 in 5 children are food insecure (Berkenes, 2015). We know hunger among children exists in the richest nation on earth, and social workers are involved in organizing and providing resources, but often this is collaborative work across for profit and non-profit agencies and organizations (www.iowahungersummit.org).

## CHILD PROTECTION FROM ABUSE AND NEGLECT

Clearly, child protection and some of the related challenges is a wide area of inquiry and social work. Child welfare authorities receive complaints, often from teachers or members of the public, when it is brought to their attention that a child is abused or neglected. Social workers and teachers are mandatory reporters, which means they must report instances of abuse and neglect that are brought to their attention. See Table 10.1 for statistics on reports of child abuse and neglect in the United States.

Statistics on childhood victimization are presented in the fact sheet from the US Department of Health and Human Services in Box 10.3. Data are drawn from reports by state child

### Table 10.1 Child Maltreatment: Summary of Key Findings

This fact sheet presents excerpts from Child Maltreatment 2014, a report based on data submissions by State child protective services (CPS) agencies for Federal fiscal year (FFY) 2014.

WHO REPORTED CHILD MALTREATMENT?

For FFY 2014, three-fifths (62.7%) of all reports of alleged child abuse or neglect were made by professionals. . . . The most common report sources were law enforcement personnel (18.1%), education personnel (17.7%), social services staff (11%), and medical personnel (9%).

WHO WERE THE CHILD VICTIMS?

In 2014, an estimated 702,000 children were victims of abuse and neglect nation wide. Among the children confirmed as victims by CPS agencies in 2014:

- Children in the age group of birth to 1 year had the highest rate of victimization at 24.4 per 1,000 children of the same age group in the national population.
- Slightly more than one-half (50.6%) of the child victims were girls, and 48.9% were boys. The gender was unknown for less than 1% of victims.
- Three races or ethnicities comprised nearly 88% of victims: African American (21.4%), Hispanic (22.7%), and White (44.0%).

WHAT WERE THE MOST COMMON TYPES OF MALTREATMENT?

As in prior years, neglect was the most common form of child maltreatment. CPS investigations determined the following:

- 75% of victims suffered neglect.
- 17% of the victims suffered physical abuse.
- 8.3 of the victims suffered sexual abuse.
- 6% of the victims suffered psychological maltreatment.

HOW MANY CHILDREN DIED FROM ABUSE OR NEGLECT?

Child fatalities are the most tragic consequence of maltreatment. During FFY 2014:

- An estimated 1,580 children died due to abuse and neglect.
- The overall rate of child fatalities was 2.13 deaths per 100,000 children in the national population.
- Nearly three quarters (72.3%) of child fatalities were attributed to neglect only, and 44.1% died exclusively from physical abuse or from physical abuse in combination with another maltreatment type.
- Nearly three-quarters (70.7%) of the children who died due to child abuse and neglect were younger than 3 years old.
- Boys had a higher child fatality rate than girls at 2.48 boys per 100,000 boys in the population compared to 1.82 girls per 100,000 girls in the population.

WHO ABUSED AND NEGLECTED CHILDREN?

In 2014, states reported a total unique count of 522,945 perpetrators (each perpetrator counted once, regardless of the number of children or reports involved).

- The great majority of perpetrators were parents—one or both parents maltreated 91.6% of victims. Of the percentage of perpetrators who were parents, 78.1% were biological parents.
- A perpetrator who was not the child's parent maltreated 12.6% of victims, sometimes alone and sometimes with other perpetrators.
- Women comprised a larger percentage of all perpetrators than men: 54.1% compared to 44.8% (unique count).
- Four-fifths of all perpetrators were between the ages of 18 and 44 years.

WHO RECEIVED SERVICES, AND WHAT DID THEY INCLUDE?

As a result of an investigation or alternative response, CPS agencies provide services to children and their families, both in the home and in foster care. For the 2014 duplicate count of children:

- Approximately two-thirds (63.7%) of victims and one-third (32%) of nonvictims received post-response services.
- Among the states reporting a breakdown of service type, almost one-fourth (23%) of victims who received services and 3.4% of nonvictims who received services were removed from their homes and received foster care services.
- The remaining almost two-thirds (63.7%) of victims and 32% of nonvictims who received services received in-home services only.

Source: Child Welfare Information Gateway (2016). Child maltreatment 2014: Summary of key findings. Washington, DC: US Department of Health and Human Services, Children's Bureau.

protection agencies. Keep in mind that, as Finkelhor et al. (2009) indicate, although victimization has enormous consequences for children, often affecting personality development, many of the most harmful forms of attacks on children are discounted in the data and by agencies. The physical abuse of children, although technically criminal, is not frequently prosecuted; peer assaults and many forms of family violence—for example, physical punishment—are generally ignored by the criminal justice system. Such acts would clearly be crimes if committed by one adult against another adult. Note the high rate of fatalities revealed in the report; an analysis of the data by the report from the Every Child Matters Education Fund (2009) puts these figures on the fatalities in international perspective. The US death rate for children is more than double the rate in France, Canada, Japan, Germany, Great Britain, and Italy, countries that have less teen pregnancy, violent crime, and poverty, according to the report. One in five children in the United States, as we have seen, is now living below the poverty line, a factor that is highly correlated with child abuse and neglect. To learn the specifics of mistreatment of children in the United States, refer back to data from the US Department of Health and Human Services as shown in Table 10.1, which presents data from the US Department of Health and Human Services: Children's Bureau:

## PHYSICAL PUNISHMENT OF CHILDREN

Closely related to child maltreatment is the practice of physical punishment. One thinks of such punishment as a form of discipline that many condone. In the United States there is a cultural ambivalence about how to discipline children and also a strong resistance to the state's interference in the life of a family and the methods of social control used with children.

Social workers understand that parents are in charge of their children, and that most families are nurturing and focused on the safe and fulfilling development of children physically, emotionally, socially, psychologically, and cognitively. When we refer to cultural ambivalence we are identifying that some parents disagree with any legal interference in how they raise their children. You might hear it said, "I was given the belt when I was a child and it didn't do me any harm." Now, in 2017, it is not illegal to physically punish and risk harming a child psychologically. This is one of the reasons, no doubt, that the United States has failed to ratify the Convention on the Rights of a Child, because the Convention makes clear such violence against a child is not acceptable.

According to the Convention on the Rights of the Child:

> States Parties shall take all appropriate legislative, administrative, social and educational measures to protect the child from all forms of physical or mental violence, injury or abuse, neglect or negligent treatment, maltreatment or exploitation, including sexual abuse, while in the care of parent(s), legal guardian(s) or any other person who has the care of the child. (Article 19, p. 5)

In most western European countries, it is against the law to physically strike a child. It is illegal in the United States to hit another adult human on the street or in an argument indoors; and children, are, after all, human beings (van Wormer & Link, 2016 p. 221). Apart from legal considerations, there are psychological consequences of using physical forms of discipline with children (as there would be with adults).

In their research into corporal punishment (CP), Taylor, Manganello, Lee, and Rice (2010) examined the connection between a parent using corporal punishment, such as spanking, on a young child and the child's future behavior, including aggression. The results of their research included the following:

> Frequent use of CP (i.e., mother's use of spanking more than twice in the previous month) when the child was 3 years of age was associated with increased risk for higher levels of child aggression when the child was 5 years of age. . . . Despite the American Academy of Pediatrics recommendations to the contrary, most parents in the United States approve of and have used CP as a form of child discipline. (Taylor et al., 2010, online).

The opportunity for social workers is to work alongside parents, and rather than judging to give parents a sense of support and instead of criticizing parenting styles, to offer alternatives to physical punishment. This is the task of nonprofits such as the Southside Family Nurturing Center in Minneapolis, or the Fulford Family Center in Bristol, England (www.ssfnc.org). In doing such work at the micro level, with one family in trouble, it is necessary to recognize the structural forces at work, in such cases, of the interplay between parent frustration and tension at home with the physical circumstances and financial resources of the family. Tough's research (2016) refers to the statistics that demonstrate the challenges for children and their parents from homes in which there are few resources and severe economic stress.

## SOCIAL WELFARE SUPPORTS FOR CHILDREN

Since the efforts to cut back the costs of social welfare expenditures in the Reagan presidency, there has been a "transformation of child welfare into protective services that has not been the result of scientific breakthrough (Lindsey, 2004)." Unlike some changes in medical interventions resulting from research, child welfare is much more subject to generalized views about the morality of families (Bray & Schommer-Atkins, 2016; Link & Bibus, 2000). By morality we mean judgments made for example that families receiving welfare aid are likely taking advantage of the system, that single mothers are immoral if they have children out of wedlock, or that people shouldn't have children if they can't afford to take care of them. Single women with children are more likely to be in poverty than their male counterparts. The Children's Defense Fund is a lobbying group for children and they have identified that of Americans struggling in poverty, children are the largest group (www.childrensdefensefund.org).

How does a wealthy society like the United States come to have so many children in poverty? We can shed light on this question if we continue to contrast the situation of children with older people. Aging which happens to everyone, is not questioned in terms of legitimate need, especially for people who have worked their whole lives. It was therefore easier to argue from the New Deal policies of 1935 onwards to introduce the universal policies of Social Security based on individual or spousal earnings (see chapter 3). These policies for seniors combine individual saving through social security tax on income and government contribution for a basic income to be guaranteed. For children, there is a much more complicated debate. For one thing, to ensure that children have their needs met means caring for the whole family. It may be believed that the parents, for various reasons, do not deserve help or would be unwilling to work if they were not forced to do so. Policy dialog is therefore often connected to moral prejudgments about single parents, poverty and race, even though the children have no choice in the economic circumstances that they are born into.

From a more generous period in the years after the Civil Rights decades of the 1960s and 1970s to the 2000s there was a shift from fairly adequate benefits to families with children, called Aid to Families with Dependent Children (AFDC) to a reduction in aid. During the 1980s and 1990s writers and social commentators (rather than researchers) convinced the public that benefits that were too high caused dependence on the government and undermined the impetus to work. Libertarian economist Charles Murray's (1984) manifesto, *Losing Ground*, for example, became the veritable bible of the Reaganite assault on welfare and thereafter of the Bush presidency (Myers-Lipton & Lemert, 2015). In this book and others to follow, Murray argued that welfare was the cause of poverty. His claims concerning race and IQ were even more controversial and made him a pariah on the college speaking circuit and even have been the cause of student riots (Savidge, 2017).

The Charles Murray debates resulted eventually in a clamor in Congress for change to a saving of taxpayer's money by introducing in 1996 welfare reform known as the Personal Responsibility and Work Opportunity Reconciliation Act (PRWORA), which introduced new rules, lifetime limits on benefits, and the concept of temporary assistance for needy families (see chapters 4 and 8). Unfortunately, this change in policy reduced support to children and according to Lindsey (2009), ended the historic social contract between the federal government and poor children. This is important background for social workers to understand because there are other policies in other countries that represent the choice to provide universal financial support to children and families. Such an approach presents a model that could be perhaps adopted at some future time (Moore, 2015).

Child protective services are the main avenue whereby poverty amongst children becomes evident. It comes as no surprise as documented by Block (2017) in his empirically based analysis that fatal child abuse and neglect fatalities are found to be closely correlated with the stress of poverty. Accordingly, social workers employed by child protection services are apt to see many clients living in poverty.

The current focus of child protection is to respond to reports of abuse by intervention, surveillance and data gathering. The family may receive supportive visits and planning but if uncooperative, proceedings may begin to take the child into foster care. Unfortunately, research does not indicate that children do better when separated from their families (Lindsey, 2009). Also, there is much debate about the effectiveness of child protection services since many of the children who die at the hands of their parents or boyfriends of mothers are already known to social workers. This is a very difficult part of the function of social workers—how best to intervene with a family who are caught up in cycles of poverty and abuse. A key intervention would be financial support and in other countries that is a universal approach. In the United States, there has been concern about creating "dependency" on the state that might interfere with a parent seeking work. This is an ongoing debate. The trouble is that the majority of people suffering from poverty are children.

Generally, the two favored interventions in the United States include maintaining surveillance of the families or taking the child away. There are additional interventions, for example, whole family foster care through crisis as explained by the British writer, Archard (2004), in *Children Rights and Childhood*, and the family center movement in Europe. As mentioned, social workers may be employed by public child protection services or by non-profit or for-profit agencies. In the United States, family centers are usually non-profit agencies, so their provision of services varies widely.

## CHILDREN'S EDUCATION AND COGNITIVE DEVELOPMENT

Education and cognitive development is a category of child welfare that is closely intertwined with the social values of a society and its racial and class divisions. There are major differences in racial disparities within the United States. While some states have high rates of achievement across cultural groupings, in other states, children of color, for example, are overrepresented in those not completing high school and their GED. In the state of Iowa a 2016 report, "Black Iowa, Still Unequal," has identified racial disparities in educational achievement and the criminal justice system:

> Whether it's preschool accessibility, wealth or incarceration, essentially nothing is equal between races in this state. While 3% of residents are African-American, 23% of state prison inmates are black, 49% of black students read at grade level by third grade while 81% of white students read at grade level by third grade. (*Des Moines Register*, 2016, p. 1OP)

The increased public knowledge of this research and data are key steps in changing the environment, but for professionals such as social workers, teachers and police officers, it also takes training and understanding of the components of prejudice and racism. Ramanathan refers to "cultural efficacy" in his summary of steps needed in order to work with sufficient cultural understanding and appreciation of difference (in Link & Ramanathan, 2011).

Box 10.3 provides a personal narrative of social work within the field of education based on the author's experiences as an education welfare officer and school social worker. The vignettes

### BOX 10.3 School Social Work, England

by Rosemary Link

#### A PERSONAL NOTE ON MY EXPERIENCE IN SCHOOL SOCIAL WORK PRACTICE AND HOW IT CONNECTS TO HUMAN RIGHTS

Knowledge of Children's Rights took me out of a time of feeling overwhelmed by the needs and losses of children on my "patch" in North London as a school social worker in the early 1980s. Before I moved to the United States, I worked with schools in Camden and Kentish Town just North of the huge train terminals at Kings Cross, Paddington, Euston, and St. Pancras. At these terminals unattached youth and isolated children arrive as runaways or members of displaced families. This is a locality where people work hard for minimum wage and where many housing estates (projects) and high-rise buildings went up in response to the acute housing shortage following the bombing of the Second World War. These buildings are lacking in adequate play space, surrounded by urban "blight" in terms of wastelands, railways, underpasses smelling of urine, and alleys where drug deals were completed.

Sometimes, I was working with families who had lived in London for generations but had fallen on hard times. "Tony" will be vivid to me all my life; he taught me so much when I was a young social worker. As the eldest of 4 siblings, at age 12 he was helping his father keep the family together following the death of his mother. His father was drinking heavily and the family was in dire circumstances. The school authorities had a clothing voucher scheme and the state schools had a uniform policy. Those who qualified could receive clothing vouchers from certain suppliers at the beginning of each term. Tony came in to see me for his vouchers. I already knew him due to a spell of truanting when it turned out he was working on a market stall to make some money for food. Picture him: bright eyed, mischievous, poorly dressed, thin but full of creativity, also very proud of his siblings and protective of them. So I gave out full sets of vouchers for the family.

Fast forward: Juvenile Bureau police call me to say they have arrested Tony for selling new clothing items on a market stall they suspect are stolen even though he says he got some of it from me. A lot of detail unfolded, conferences, and meetings with police and school. Tony was discharged "with a warning." But in Tony's words: "Mrs. Link, I just wanted to make a bit on the side to keep us right at home." Eventually we managed to raise a grant to bring his grandmother from Ireland to help with the family. I always believed in Tony's basic goodness; I perhaps trusted him too much but I will never regret supporting him through this period in his life. My supervisor had a different perspective and warned me not to be so trusting. I think finding the balance as a social worker, to trust first, is a lifelong challenge.

Picture Diana: mother drinking too much after father left. Diana was suspended from school for truanting; she was feeling depressed and unable to see her way forward. The school educational psychologist was called in to make a full assessment, and asked me for the social enquiry report. Dr. P and I worked to get Diana back to school after a long break; only to have her shouted at by the Assistant Head (Principal) for wearing ear-rings and being "insolent," so that she left and told me "it's for good this time." We lurched from crisis to crisis, but my main role became to advocate for her when she tried to get back to school, to create some space, and to find teachers (and there were some) who saw her strengths. Unfortunately, once a label is pinned to a child, it is hard for the adults in their life to take it off and reframe their view when small improvements are made.

Picture this: Peter W; school phobic was the assessment we referred to in the psychologist's report, although now we would recognize complexity in terms of bullying a timid, frail child and gender identity. At that time (1980s) we were not yet discussing fluid gender identity; we were still selling boys and girls toys and checking gender boxes in just about every document. I worked with Peter and his mother trying to set up tutorials and encourage him back to school. His absences mounted up so that the authority insisted I either find a doctor to support intervention or take his mother to juvenile court. We referred Peter to the Tavistock Institute for family relations and they worked wonders, listening to him and his mother, sculpting family dynamics and helping Peter explain his fears. A few years later I came to my office full of worries about children not in school, to find a bright bunch of flowers on my desk and a note: Peter graduated, thank you.

Chris was a student who sat for prolonged periods in his father's chair following the father's sudden death in a traffic accident. It was quite inexplicable to a 10-year-old child and probably to the adults surrounding him: acute loss on a rainy Wednesday afternoon. Chris stopped going to school and would not leave that chair for days. His grief was complex and deeply affecting, as though he carried it for everyone in the family. The younger siblings demanded his mother's attention and she struggled with the practical realities of a much more insecure future. After a few weeks of missing school, Chris developed anxiety about even going outside. Fortunately, the school social work team had developed a useful Friday case conference time together with the school psychologists and we brainstormed ways to help this lonely child. The ironic insight for me was the way Chris's mother was unwittingly allowing this prolonged social isolation by bringing to the chair Chris's food and drink and allowing television and passivity. We developed a support plan that included me bringing school work home so that he did not have such a huge gap; we talked with his teachers so that he would not be embarrassed by questions he could not answer, and a plan for re-entry eventually proved successful, with many of us involved.

Why are these vignettes important? They speak to the journey that we were on then and still are, to find better ways of respecting children's needs, be they ways to meet their economic needs through their families, their relational and social needs to feel attached to adults who could care for them, to understand their gender identity and cultural realities, or their educational needs to be in an environment that fosters inclusion. At that time it was still possible for a baby to be given a letter for a name: no longer is this allowed, due to the lobbying and progress of human rights activists. In the 1980s we had a lack of research on gender issues. This is no longer the reality with expanding research; retailers are dropping gender markers in stores (such as for boys' and girls' toys or clothing), and we find that children are getting to express themselves in all sorts of forums to get their voices heard (including the UN Assembly). For a long time we were sending juveniles to adult court and jail without question—today, the "raise-the-age" movement has been effectively moving most juveniles except those committing violent felonies, back to family court, a change due in part due to the work of youth advocates like James Garbarino, and to large international organizations such as UNICEF (www.unicef.org) and American Civil Liberties Union (ACLU).

Human rights legislation and conversation make this range of work feasible and accessible. The devoted practitioners who have helped generate information and case studies that reflect the CRC are helping to "pass it on"—passing on the knowledge that takes years to generate, can be destroyed with poisonous rhetoric, and is most likely in the United States to survive through the interest and commitment of those of you reading this text. Thank you.

cover the "micro" level interventions and needs of children ranging from issues of poverty, to loss, fear, and abuse. School social work also brings system levels of opportunity for intervention, including grouping issues for action, such as keeping pregnant teens in school and supporting their babies (MICE—maternal infant care in Minneapolis Schools).

## BARRIERS TO THE PHYSICAL AND MENTAL HEALTH OF CHILDREN

Children's health is closely connected to all aspects of development—when children are in stable, well-nourished families with adequate housing, safe sleeping space and warmth, they usually thrive. Individual physical, psychological and mental health services are an integral part of child welfare and wellbeing, services that provide a wide array of social work employment. This section on physical, psychological and mental health services will identify a spectrum of services from those that are more of a mental health/illness approach for children with critical needs for intervention, to services that are more preventive and strengths oriented for children who have less supports in their lives and need additional recognition and encouragement.

This section identifies some of the greater challenges to children's ongoing health, including the gravest challenge at the international level of forced migration to local needs for shelter. Current research establishes a strong connection between a young child's early experiences and the developing of his or her brain structure. The experiences of both poverty and homelessness in infancy and toddlerhood are associated with poor academic achievement and engagement in elementary school (Department of Health and Human Services [HHS], 2016). Let us look at the statistics.

### CHILD POVERTY IN THE UNITED STATES

As mentioned earlier, one area of relative success in recent decades is the reduction of poverty amongst seniors. Universal policies of access to health services, known as Medicare and policies of financial support, known as Social Security have improved the circumstances of all seniors. Perhaps the work of social workers in the coming decades will tackle child poverty in similar universal ways, but it is not just up to the social work profession. The whole society needs to commit to changing the distribution of wealth, and demonstrate commitment to the welfare of children through new financial policies, such as child allowances for example, and universal child care for children under six (Lindsey, 2009). Child poverty in the United States makes no sense given the wealth and resources, research and innovation of the country in just about any field, for example in medicine, technology, and energy. Table 10.2 shows the current state of poverty among children by race/ethnicity in the United States. Note differences between levels in 1973 for all children, which was 14.2% and the rise to 1 in 5 by 2014.

When we look beyond US borders we find a variety of approaches to child well-being. Instead of a crisis-oriented approach, with limited options of child support through family surveillance or child removal, in Norway the focus is universal economic support and social service to the whole family; the focus is preventive and based on risk reduction (Skivenes & Skramstad, 2013). Children's allowances (monthly government payments to all families for child support) continue to be key in Scandinavia; France has experimented with cutting allowances to families where children are truant from school, and the UK has worked to set up children's savings accounts from birth (Lindsey, 2009).

In Norway, social workers have a variety of resources for families, including children's allowances, pre-school and nursery state funded and an expectation that families can thrive when they have the necessary community, economic and kinship supports. Similarly, in the United Kingdom,

**Table 10.2 Persons Below Poverty Level, by Selected Characteristics, Race, and Hispanic Origin: United States, Selected Years 1973–2014 (Data are based on household interviews of the civilian noninstitutionalized population.)**

| Selected characteristic, race, and Hispanic origin, in 1973 compared to 2014 | 2014 | 1973 |
|---|---|---|
| White only | 8.4 | 12.7 |
| Black or African American only | 31.4 | 26.2 |
| Asian only | — | 12.0 |
| Hispanic or Latino | 21.9 | 23.6 |
| **Related children under age 18 in families below poverty level** | | |
| Total, all groups | 14.2 | 20.7 |
| White only | 9.7 | 17.4 |
| Black or African American only | 40.6 | 37.1 |
| Asian only | — | 13.4 |
| Hispanic or Latino | 27.8 | 31.3 |

Source: Centers for Disease Control and Prevention (CDC; 2015). Table 2, Persons below poverty level, by selected characteristics, race, and Hispanic origin: United States, selected years 1973–2014. Retrieved from www.cdc.gov

family centers have received a mix of public and private funding which has resulted in community efforts to support families, especially through structural economic change.

This discussion has focused on individual children and their families and *individual* assessment of circumstances, but there is a wider perspective. *Structural* economic change refers to changes that are affecting more than one family, in fact whole groups of families. For example, when a coal mine closes and people are out of work, or a company moves to a new location, from Minnesota to Mexico for the production of Tonka toys, often society blames the individual family (and indirectly the child) for their plight of unemployment and poverty. The concept of structural, community wide effects (for example, the lead contamination in water in Flint, Michigan) has gained ground in recent years.

When reviewing the table of comparisons in child poverty rates across countries (see Lindsey, 2009), it is clear that a country can have more successful policies that affect children and sometimes pass laws with one goal in mind that end up having a negative impact on children. In 1996 when the Personal Responsibility and Work Opportunity Reconciliation Act was passed, the intent was to encourage parents to work rather than take benefits which were considered too costly to the federal budget. The idea at that time was to address long-term unemployment amongst some families that had been linked to increasing poverty. The expectation was that with incentives to work, with penalties for not seeking work, and with time limits, parents would improve the economic situation of their families.

Unfortunately, there was insufficient realization that the reasons for not working are complex (Link & Bibus, 2000). For a young parent under 25 years, with his or her GED and one child the opportunity to find work and to develop skills was indeed more likely. For a parent over 35 years of age, with no GED and few work skills and more than two children, the likelihood of returning to the workforce is less. Also, work in the home is not recognized as work; we pay for childcare in the home, but not for mothers who provide it. Other countries recognize the expense of child care for preschoolers and provide nurseries and services. In the United States, this is a slow process. For many families, a significant chunk of household spending goes toward child care. In some states, such as Mississippi and West Virginia, child care costs account for 40 to 45% of total household income (Pao, 2016). After making car payments, rent or house payments, parents find they often don't have enough to cover child care. Another complexity is the underpayment of child support. Many fathers are behind on child support payments, as they have lost income, are unemployed, or unwilling to pay (Pao, 2015). The worst possible outcome of loss of family income is homelessness.

## CHILD HOMELESSNESS

- Just under 6 million children under 6 years old or 1 in 18 lived below Federal Poverty Level in 2013.
- Children under age 6 experiencing homelessness in the United States: 1 in 18.
- About 4.7% of children served in Head Start and Early Head Start are children who were experiencing homelessness.
- Looking at the early childhood data available in the profiles, states with the highest percentage of young children under age 6 experiencing homelessness were Kentucky,10.6%; New York, 9.6%; California, 9.1%. (HHS, 2016, pp. 2–3)

Unfortunately to be homeless means a sea of troubles follows, with higher rates of illness, hunger, anxiety, and missed school:

> Up to 25% of homeless pre-school children have mental health problems requiring clinical evaluation . . . the impacts of homelessness on the children, especially young children, may lead to changes in brain architecture that can interfere with learning, emotional self-regulation, cognitive skills, and social relationships." (National Center on Family Homelessness Report, 2014, p. 2)

The role of social workers who work with homeless families varies according to their employer. If they work for a nonprofit agency they may be advocates for housing, they may help a parent with basic resources such as bedding or health care access or access to financial assistance. If they are employed by the state and are called due to a report of neglect, they may find that the child is at risk, and even though the neglect may occur primarily for economic reasons and the lack of low income housing, they may take action to remove the child to foster care.

It could be argued that having a home and a dry bed to sleep in is a key contributor to a child's mental and physical health. When basic needs are met, many other challenges that are part of children's lives can be coped with. One such challenge for parents is having a child with a physical or mental disability.

## CHILDREN WITH DISABILITIES

Sometimes children are born with conditions that hamper their development (for example, hearing loss; blindness; cleft palate) and require specialist services. It is especially challenging for children whether healthy or born with a disability, when they live in under-resourced circumstances, such as a damp basement, or are exposed to lead poisoning and cadmium in water, or to alcohol and drugs. In these circumstances the child's health is doubly affected: by their environment and their particular family situations.

When children are born with physical or developmental challenges, social workers work beside parents as advocates and supporters. In a remarkable piece of research from a number of years ago by Fraiberg (1968) on an intervention program for parents who had given birth to infants who were blind, Fraiberg showed how the social workers advocacy role was vital. For this writer (Rosemary Link), reading this research for the first time as a young social worker was like turning a mental light on.

Fraiberg's work is remarkable and enduring because it challenged social norms. It is a longitudinal study of blind infants, as described by the researcher:

> The research began out of our deep concern for the very large number of children blind from birth who show gross abnormalities in ego development which are closely related to autism. If we separate from this group the children with known brain damage, there remains a very large group of blind children who are condemned to something like a sensory void for the rest of their lives. A very small percentage develop normally. . . .

The research demonstrates how at that time parents grieved the loss of sight in their infant and did not know how to respond with the joy and energy that accompanies a normal birth. Many of the children had bald patches on the back of their heads, indicating a lack of movement and stimulation and less picking up by the adults around them:

> Nearly all of the young parents were depleted of their own emotional resources, without hope, without expectations . . . even grandparents and relatives were caught up in a conspiracy of silence . . . no one said the baby was adorable, or cute, or any other things that are uttered upon seeing a new baby . . . apart from anything else we did in our work with the families, we were often the first people who entered these mourning households who could say such things as "he's a fine baby; she's a beautiful baby, look how strong she is . . . we were reclaiming his and her human rights for the family. (Fraiberg, 1968, p. 385)

Where a parent may only focus on the loss of sight, the social worker can value the attributes of the infant. While complex in the details of the children's development and the research knowledge that has unfolded since this research, one aspect that stands out as an enduring skill, to this day, is that of re-framing the loss of sight by focusing on the ways to nurture, hold, speak, sing to the infant where a smile could not be seen and the touch or vibration became crucial reassurance and connection to the world. What is taken for granted in the development of sighted infants, for example crawling after a ball or toy they can see, "were typical developmental road blocks which could not be clearly seen as impediments due to blindness itself; a few parents found the adaptive routes, most could not without help" (Fraiberg). Adaptive routes included toys with bells or extra sensory qualities for example. Research since the work of Fraiberg has taken parents to new understanding of multiple capacities for bonding and perception.

The loss that is experienced when a child is born without sight or other challenges does not lessen, but the potential for healthy development and adaptive learning and loving exists. Often it is a social worker who walks with the parents to this discovery of pride and joy in their child.

In contrast to the child born with great challenge, is the irony of society putting great challenge in the way of the child. One immense challenge is that of adult migration and the effects on children of crossing national borders under dire, life-threatening circumstances with or without their parents.

## CHILD MIGRANTS AND REFUGEES

In the United States, there has been growing concern at the number of children crossing from Mexico into the United States, both accompanied and unaccompanied and the impact of being detained. In their study of detention centers, Zayas and Miller (2015) identify the negative effects of such detention on children:

> Within a few weeks of being detained at the South Texas Residential Facility in Dilley, Daniela's 9-year-old, daughter (names changed to protect privacy) started having difficulties with incontinence at night and began crying herself to sleep. She had little to no appetite and became agitated and emotionally volatile. Despite seeing the psychologist stationed at the family detention facility, her emotional state continued to deteriorate. . . . In response to a recent court ruling that should effectively end family detention, the Obama administration has claimed that family detention centers are being transformed into "processing centers," with the goal of cycling women and their children through in a few weeks. But in the case of Daniela and her children—as in the case of hundreds of mothers and children—even a few weeks in detention can do long-lasting damage to the mental and emotional well-being of a child. . . . As clinical social workers, we have been to the Dilley and Karnes family detention facilities to document the horrific traumas that many of these mothers and their children endured in their home countries experiencing and witnessing systematic rape, murder, death threats. . . . These mothers and their children arrived in the United States only to face a new kind of horror found in these facilities. (Zayas & Miller, 2015)

In this example, two social workers, Zayas and Miller are applying their social work research knowledge to provide a report that highlights and advocates for children detained through no fault of their own, in circumstances that lead to secondary trauma and mental stress. The data on the vulnerability of child migrants and their journeys are alarming; the role of social workers is crucial, in bringing forward the awareness and concern that has led to Congressional hearings and efforts to reduce the length of time families are held by the Department of Homeland Security (Zayas, 2015).

The challenge and opportunity of migration is worldwide. Migration has been positive historically in that it is a way to build countries such as the United States and share labor for example across the continent of India or the European Union. But when migration is forced as a result of war and conflict it creates acutely negative consequences for children's well-being and is seen by some researchers as a "catastrophe" (Murphey, 2016). Murphey's report, "Uprooted: The Growing Crisis for Refugee and Migrant Children," which is written for the research organization, Child Trends, presents for the first time, comprehensive, global data on children who arriving in the United States as refugees and migrants. According to the report:

> As of 2015, the number worldwide who are considered refugees was 21.3 million—an all-time high. Children make up a majority of refugees (51 percent, as of 2015. The focus in this report is on children, fleeing war and other forms of violence, who arrive in the United States from abroad (who, we estimate, will number more than 127,000 in 2016).
>
> An estimated 37,500 children arriving in 2016 will be officially designated as refugees or asylees, statuses which grant them eligibility for health care and social services immediately upon arrival, and eligibility for citizenship after 5 years. . . . In contrast, nearly 3 times as many children (about 90,000) will arrive without legal status, first apprehended by the Border Patrol, then subject to a chain of administrative procedures that offers few protections and may include detention for prolonged periods; this presents a great many hazards to their well-being—including re-traumatization.
>
> Beginning in 2013, there has been a surge in the number of children, either accompanied by a parent or unaccompanied, who are apprehended in the United States after fleeing the countries in the Northern Triangle of Central America: El Salvador, Guatemala, and Honduras. Many children in these countries are under siege by organized crime and gang violence, including homicide and rape.
>
> Available data show that unaccompanied refugee children have an elevated risk for mental illness and difficulties with concentration and regulation of emotions, and often take on, at an early age, what are commonly seen as adult roles. Unaccompanied children are particularly at risk for psychological disorders. Post-traumatic stress disorder is common. When it comes to mental health, in particular, the following factors have been identified as frequently protective for this group of children: living with both parents, good parental mental health, perceived safety and sense of connection at school, social support (especially emotional and instrumental—or help getting things done), and caring relationships in child care settings. (Murphey, 2016, pp. 2, 3, 8, 14)

It is difficult to envision ways to replace lost childhoods due to the extent of this trauma in young lives. This is the challenge of resettlement agencies—federal agencies such as the Office of Refugee Resettlement, non-profits such as Lutheran Social Service and a wide array of family services and centers. Social workers are often at the center of these services. As advocates for child well-being, social workers are at the center of community dialog at a time when there is discrimination and intimidation of newcomers to the United States at unprecedented levels, in part due to the extremely negative statements about immigrants made during the presidential race of 2016. In response, there are cities in the United States such as Denver, Colorado addressing such prejudices and working to establish the elusive goal of being "Child Friendly" as documented in section iii.

The lost childhoods and mass trauma are especially apparent worldwide, in war zones such as Iraq, Afghanistan, and Syria, where the death toll of child civilians is incredibly high. There are also many child refugees, who are the living casualties of war. See Figure 10.2 of beaming Syrian girls at school. Some of these refugees have escaped unconscionable horrors, having been captured or recruited as child soldiers. This is the topic to which we now turn.

**FIGURE 10.2.** Syrian children attending school at a Turkey refugee camp. © Shutterstock, photo by Tolga Sezgin.

See Figure 10.2 which shows a happy moment for these schoolgirls at a United Nations refugee camp in Jordan.

## CHILD SOLDIERS

Thousands of children are serving as soldiers in armed conflicts around the world (Human Rights Watch, 2016). Boys as young as eight years-old serve in government forces and armed opposition groups. They may fight on the front lines, participate in suicide missions, and act as spies, messengers, or lookouts. Girls may be forced into sexual slavery.

Children are especially likely to get caught up in warfare under conditions of impoverishment, inequality, discrimination and human rights abuses, that are known to contribute to the risk that children will be recruited by armed groups. In recent years, large numbers of children have been reported to have been used in hostilities in 14 countries including Afghanistan, Chad, the Democratic Republic of Congo, Somalia, Sudan and Uganda. In Myanmar (Burma), boys below the age of 18 continue to be forcibly recruited into the army in large numbers and are used in active combat as well as other roles. The long-term financial and political support needed to successfully reintegrate former child soldiers has not been forthcoming except for small-scale pilot studies.

Theresa Betancourt has conducted empirically based research throughout the war-torn world following the cessation of fighting. Betancourt and her team of mental health workers have conducted mental health interventions among former child soldiers in Sierra Leone,

Uganda, Rwanda and other countries affected by war (see Betancourt & Williams, 2008; Betancourt, 2011). The adolescents the team worked with were suffering from persistent mental health problems including nightmares, intense sadness, intrusive thoughts, and recurring violent images. Yet they were amenable to treatment. Betancourt and her team have documented through their applied research demonstration that effective treatments are feasible in poor, rural, illiterate, war-torn communities.

The treatment model developed by Betancourt's team, The Youth Readiness Program, was directed toward work in three areas: restoring community ties that had been broken, reducing trauma-related distress, and the setting of future goals. Meetings were held weekly for two months. Therapists helped the adolescent girls in their struggle with feelings of guilt and shame to recognize that what happened to them was not their fault. Attention was paid to helping the youths curb high-risk behavior and substance use and reintegrating them into their communities. Because family support is a key factor in resilience and necessary to for their future care, the program focuses on reuniting these children with their families.

## MEETING THE SOCIAL NEEDS OF CHILDREN

How does a community set about making children's opportunities for socializing outside the home or school safe and accessible? This section will review the work of those cities identified by the United Nations as "Child Friendly Cities." What are the criteria to be deemed child friendly? Why are so few cities as yet in this category, and what stands in the way? The "gun culture" is one obstacle to a child friendly environment and will also be discussed in this section. And one everyone is familiar with: discrimination. The United States is a country that grew its population through immigration, and yet there is widespread racism and discrimination. People are judged by the color of their skin or the sound of their name, or their religious affiliation rather than their character and contribution to society (Presidential candidate Donald Trump caused an uproar over his characterization of an American born Judge as Mexican because of his name, when the judge was born in the United States.) We start with a discussion of gender identity and the right of the transgender child, like any child, to feel safe.

### GENDER IDENTITY ISSUES

In many countries of the world there is a broad acceptance and honoring of people who are transgender or "third" gender. In a discussion of the fashion industry the life of a 17-year-old boy named Apichet Atilattana, who grew up in Thailand, has been recognized for his success in visual art and fashion by drawing on natural, everyday objects such as grass or wire, to design clothes. Apichet Atilattana, with the pseudonym Madaew is described in the following way by the journalist Charlie Campbell:

> Madaew grew up in Thailand's impoverished northeastern region of Isaan, the country's rice-growing heartland. He knew as a young child that he identified as a kathoey, a transgender female sometimes referred to as a "third sex" in Thailand. His parents never tried to change who he was, letting him play dress up without feeling ashamed." (Campbell, 2016, p. 42)

Acceptance of the third sex is also common in India and other parts of Asia, but slower in acceptance in the United States until recently, when changing attitudes to gender identity have come to the notice of the media due to questions about use of public bathrooms. Still, the issue has come to a head in some states, such as North Carolina in its refusal to allow trans children to use the school bathroom of the gender with which they identify. On May 9th, 2016, Attorney General Loretta E. Lynch and Principal Deputy Assistant Attorney General Vanita Gupta, head of the Civil Rights Division, announced:

> Law enforcement action against the state of North Carolina over a state law that dictates that transgender people must use public bathrooms, showers . . . that correspond to the gender on their birth certificate. . . . " The complaint we file today speaks to public employees who feel afraid and stigmatized on the job; it speaks to students who feel like their campus treats them differently because of who they are. . . . Here are the facts. Transgender men are men—they live, work and study as men. Transgender women are women—they live, work and study as women." (Vanita Gupta, 2016, p. A3).

Trump's election led to the withdrawal of this decision, however, and the US Supreme Court seems unwilling to take up any challenges to discriminatory state laws at the present time. A child-friendly school or city would not discriminate, would prevent bullying, and help all children to feel wanted and safe.

## CHILD FRIENDLY CITIES

The Child Friendly Cities project is an empowering one and for some people may seem overly optimistic (UNICEF, 2014). However, for the cities participating in the goal, it is inspiring. The concept was first introduced to the author (Link) while watching a film about the city of Pistoia, north of Firenze (Florence), Italy. The video shows streets that are car free; jugglers and clowns mingle with shoppers and enchant the children present, creating an air of safety and fun for everyone. The United Nations describes this initiative in the following way:

> The CFC website provides information on how to build a Child Friendly City or Community. Here you will find data on good practices and interventions, relevant publications, and updates on current research and initiatives . . . the framework translates the process needed to implement the UN Convention on the Rights of the Child by national governments into a local government process. (UNICEF, 2014)

The Child Friendly cities project is unfolding in a variety of cities across the world, including Brighton, United Kingdom; Denver, United States; Firenze, Italy; San Salvador, El Salvador. Adults are invited to think through the most inviting characteristics in an urban area and cultivate them for children. For countries with strong gun control, such as Finland and Norway, it is easier to imagine than for New York or Chicago– but just imagine. Social workers are just one set of professionals to be involved; personnel at every level of the government and city life are part of the successful projects' planning.

Where a city has pedestrian walkways rather than freeway interchanges, it is easier to begin when they present flights of steps and cobblestone pathways, there is invitation to children to enjoy the nooks and courtyards of ancient city life. Child Friendly Cities emphasize community policing, adults who walk the streets, volunteers and an atmosphere that has become free of the fear of abduction. Voluntary workers, classrooms on the street, language nests (a place for celebration of first language, for example, Gaelic language in Wales, United Kingdom), art festivals, and in Denver a "city passport" for all children that gives them access (depending on age, they have to be accompanied) to all attractions, swimming pools, zoo and parks.

## SAFETY NEEDS: PROTECTION FROM HANDGUNS

In contrast to this idea of "child friendly cities," many cities in the United States continue to struggle with a rash of gun deaths by handgun, including of children. In the article: "Kids can't tie their shoes, but they can fire guns," Bill Sternberg (2016) reports:

> Roughly five times a week in America, children accidentally shoot themselves or someone else. Just this past Saturday in Baton Rouge, for example, a 6-year old boy was playing with a gun when he shot his 3-year-old sister. She survived, but the 5-year-old Detroit girl who found her grandmother's gun under a pillow last week and shot herself in the neck did not. Nor did the 3-year-old in Dallas, Ga, who found his dad's .380 caliber semiautomatic pistol on April 26 and shot himself in the chest. Patrice Price was killed by her 2-year-old son in Milwaukee . . . this toll is a national scandal in a country that has as many guns as people and the world's highest rate of firearm homicides. (p. 7A)

For social workers who are often those picking up the pieces when families are torn apart by gun violence, the question is, how to fully understand the opposition to stricter gun safety laws and how to visualize and learn about the impact of policies in other countries in order to join advocacy efforts. What is it that other countries such as Finland, Germany, Canada, Singapore, are doing to keep their rates of homicide and death by guns below 100 a year? Fewer than 50 people died in gun violence in the United Kingdom in 2015 and more than that die every day in the United States (Onyanga-Omara, 2016). For US child welfare professionals, who have not visited countries free of weapons on the street, it is difficult to imagine what a secure environment can feel like. For children, it is the opportunity to develop without trauma and loss of family members.

Safety regulations in the United States are strictly enforced to protect children. All states, for example, require child safety seats for infants and children fitting specific criteria, and requirements vary based on age, weight, and height. There are no comparable safety regulations for children and guns. Yet according to the Children's Defense Fund (2015), each year over 2,500 children are killed by guns. Here are the facts:

> The US has more guns than people. . . . A gun in the home makes the likelihood of homicide three times higher, suicide three to five times higher, and accidental death four times higher. For each time a gun in the home injures or kills in self-defense, there are 11 completed and attempted gun suicides, seven criminal assaults and homicides with a gun, and four unintentional shooting deaths or injuries. (Children's Defense Fund, 2015, p. 2)

In the aftermath of a shocking assassination of a Member of Parliament in the United Kingdom in June 2016, it was reported that gun violence is rare in England, Scotland, Wales and therefore more of a jolt to the culture. Jane Onyanga-Omara (2016) reported that

> The gun homicide rate in England and Wales is about one for every 1 million people, according to the Geneva Declaration of Armed Violence and Development, a multinational research organization based in Switzerland. In a population of 56 million, that adds up to about 50 or 60 gun killings annually. In the USA, by contrast, there are about 160 times as many gun homicides in a country that is roughly six times larger in population. There were 8,134 gun homicides in 2014, according to the latest FBI figures. (p. 1A)

Recall from chapter 6 that the number of gun-inflicted suicides well exceeds the number of homicides that involve firearms. Male teens, bent on suicide, are especially likely to use a gun. For social workers, the key learning point is the power of legislation to build the scaffolding for healthy social development for children. In those countries that are embracing the United Nations concept of building "Child Friendly Cities" there is a drive to intentionally build environments that put children first. Where there are carefree walking precincts, such as the center of Ljubljana in Slovenia, the center of Bath in the UK, the center of Postoia, Italy, children can explore city life safely. Where there are strict gun ownership laws, deaths by handgun are rare. For the US with far more permissive attitudes and lack of legislation restricting the ownership of guns the rate of child death by gun continues to climb and is a key challenge for establishing safe social environments. Everyone can take a children's rights temperature of their community to see how closely they match to a "child friendly city."

## SUMMARY AND CONCLUSION

This chapter began with a description of the rights accorded to the child in The Convention on the Rights of the Child. This UN document, which has reformed laws affecting children throughout the world, spells out protection of children from all forms of violence, from discrimination, and gives special protection for children in war zones and as refugees. Although the United States did not ratify this document, it carries a moral weight and has inspired more than one US Supreme Court decision with references to international law.

This chapter also focused on situations where the welfare of children is threatened: in the home in the form of abuse, neglect, gun violence, and physical forms of punishment. The impacts of homelessness, immigration, refugee status, and war on children's physical and psychological health were also discussed. As demonstrated in this chapter, child welfare is a wide and sometimes controversial field of services, from the formal social work roles in schools, hospitals, corrections and child protection offices of local city administrations to the wide variety of non-profit direct service organizations and advocacy programs supporting child well-being.

Social workers operate at a variety of system levels—moving between the face-to-face work with children and families, to advocacy in the wider community to involvement in international situations and organizations in order to provide services. In the U.S. there are challenges ahead.

Too many children live in poverty and the goal for social workers in the 21st century is to generate a level of financial support and service that provides "social security" to all children. This would mean that they have enough to eat, a safe bed, access to immunizations and health care, and family support systems so that they can grow in "child friendly" cities and find their careers, engage in their communities, eventually build their own families and achieve well-being that benefits society as a whole.

## THOUGHT QUESTIONS

1. Study the United Nations Convention on the Rights of the Child at http://www.ohchr.org/en/professionalinterest/pages/crc.aspx. Which Article do you think is especially important for the well-being of children?
2. What does the Convention on the Rights of the Child mean for children's lives?
3. Identify four areas of work with children that social workers may follow as a career. Which one, in your opinion, would be the most challenging to work in?
4. Study the statistics provided by the US Department of Health and Human Services on child abuse and neglect. What do you learn from Table 10.1 about child deaths? Which facts are the most significant for social workers to know?
5. Study Table 10.2 What does it say about poverty from the 1970s and today? What does the racial/ethnic background tell you?
6. Why is it controversial in the United States to say that "children should not be disciplined by physical punishment such as hitting?" Compare discipline in how you were brought up with how you will discipline your children.
7. Explain the areas of child welfare work that you might be interested in pursuing. What are the reasons for your choice?
8. What are some of the concerns about the impact of detention centers for children migrating to the United States?
9. Identify the arguments for and against the sale of handguns (this question does not refer to rifles and guns used in hunting and sport). What can we learn from other countries?
10. If the last century was a time of drafting international legislation that supports the lives of children, what do we mean when we say that the 21st century is the time for implementation and action?
11. Go to the UNICEF website at www.unicef.org. How does UNICEF serve children? Identify one policy that it is currently involved in aiding child development.
12. What would your city be like if it were identified as "Child Friendly?"
13. Discuss a recent war in the news involving a child refugee crisis. What is the fate of those children? What are non-governmental agencies such as UNICEF doing to help the children?
14. Which country in the world do you think would be the best country for a child to grow up in? Which one do you think would be the worst from the standpoint of children's rights? State reasons for your opinion.

# REFERENCES


Archard, D. (2004). *Children rights and childhood.* Hove, England: Psychology Press.

Berkenes, C. (2015, October). Food insecurity. Keynote to the *Hunger Summit,* Des Moines, IA.

Betancourt, T. S. (2011). Developmental perspectives on moral agency in former child soldiers [Commentary]. *Human Development, 54,* 307–312.

Betancourt, T. S., & Williams, T. P. (2008). Building an evidence base on mental health interventions for children affected by armed conflict. *Intervention: International Journal of Mental Health, Psychosocial Work and Counseling in Areas of Armed Conflict, 6*(1), 39–56.

Block, R. W. (2017). No surprise: The rate of fatal child abuse and neglect fatalities is related to poverty. *Pediatrics, 137*(5). Published online. doi:10.1542/peds.2017-0357

Bray, S. S., & Schommer-Atkins, M. (2016). Health professions students' ways of knowing and social orientation in relationship to poverty beliefs. *Psychological Research, 6*(10), 579–587.

Campbell, C. (2016). Madaew Thai a la Mode. *Time,* October 17, 2016, pp. 42–42.

Canadian Broadcast Company (CBC). (2017, April 30). Local social worker speaks out against spanking on International No Spank Day. CBC. Retrieved from www.cbc.ca/news

Center on the Developing Child. (2014). *A decade of science informing policy. National Scientific Council on the Developing Child.* Cambridge, MA: Harvard University.

Children's Bureau. (2008, March). An individualized, strengths-based approach in public child welfare driven systems of care. Washington, DC: U.S. Department of Health and Human Services. Retrieved from www.childwelfare.gov

Children's Defense Fund (2015). Protect children not guns factsheet 2014: Child gun deaths. Washington, D.C. Retrieved from www.childrensdefense.org

Courtney, M. (2013, July). Child welfare history and policy framework. In C. Franklin (Ed.), *Encyclopedia of social work* (21st ed.). New York, NY: Oxford University Press. Retrieved from www.socialwork.oxfordre.com

De Garmo, J. (2017, May 1). The foster care crisis: The shortage of foster parents in America. *Huffington Post.* Retrieved from www.huffingtonpost.com

Department of Health and Human Services (HHS). (2016, January). Early childhood homelessness in the United States: 50-state profile. Administration for Children and Families. Retrieved from www.acfhhs.gov

Des Moines Register. (2016, June 19). Editorial, Iowa can do more to address racial disparities. *Des Moines Register,* p. 1OP.

Every Child Matters Education Fund. (2009). We can do better: Child abuse and neglect deaths in America. Washington, DC. Retrieved from http://www.everychildmatters.org/images/stories/pdf/wcdb_report.pdf

Finkelhor, D., Turner, H., Ormrod, R., Hamby, S., & Kracke, K. (2009, October). National survey of children' s exposure to violence. National Criminal Justice Reference Statistics. Retrieved from http://www.ncjrs.gov/pdffiles1/ojjdp/227744.pdf

Fraiberg, S. (1968). *Parallel and divergent patterns in blind and sighted infants.* The Psychoanalytic Study of the Child, *23,* 264–300.

Fraser, M. W. (1996). Cognitive Problem Solving and Aggressive Behavior among Children. *Families in Society, 77*(1), 19–31.

Garbarino, J. (1999). *Lost boys: Why our sons turn violent and how we can save them.* New York, NY: Free Press.

Garbarino, J., & Haslam, K. (2005). Lost boys: Why our sons turn violent and how we can save them. *Paediatrics and Child Health, 10*(8), 447–450.

Gupta, V. (2016, May 20). Law reversed for transgender people. *India Abroad*, p. A3.

Harris, E. A. (2016, October 11). For New York's homeless children, getting to school is the hard part. *New York Times*, p. A19.

Harris, E. A. (2017, April 25). Growing number of city students live in homeless shelters. *New York Times*, p. A1.

Healy, L. M., & Link, R. J. (2012). *Handbook of International Social Work, Human Rights, Development, and the Global Profession*. New York, NY: Oxford University Press.

Herman, E. (2012). The adoption history project orphan trains. Eugene, Oregon: University of Oregon. Retrieved from www.darkwing.uoregon.edu

Human Rights Watch. (2016). Child soldiers. New York: Human Rights Watch. Retrieved from https://www.hrw.org/topic/childrens-rights/child-soldiers.

Kozol, J. (2008). Children's rights to be heard. Keynote to the *Annual Program Meeting, Council on Social Work Education*, Philadelphia, PA. March.

Lindsey, D. (2004). *The welfare of children*. New York, NY: Oxford University Press.

Lindsey, D. (2009). *Child poverty and inequality: Securing a better future for America's children*. New York, NY: Oxford University Press.

Link, R. J., & Bibus, A. (2000). *When children pay*. London, England: Child Poverty Action Group.

Link, R. J., & Ramanathan, C. (2011). *Human Behavior in a Just World*. New York: Rowman & Littlefield, p. 122.

Mettler, K. (2017, May 2). A black teen died following an encounter with police near Dallas. *Washington Post*. Retrieved from www.washingpost.com

Moore, M. (2015). *Where to invade next*. Video, Dog Eat Dog Films.

Murphey, D. (2016, September). Moving beyond trauma: Child migrants and refugees in the United States. *Child Trends*. Retrieved from http://www.childtrends.org/

Murray. C. (1984). *Losing ground: American Social Policy*. New York, NY: Basic Books.

Myers-Lipton, S., & Lemert, C. (2015). *Social solutions to poverty: America's struggle to build a just society*. New York, NY: Routledge.

National Center on Family Homelessness (2014). A staggering 2.5 million children are now homeless each year in America. American Institutes for Research. Retrieved from http://www.air.org/center/national-center-family-homelessness

National Public Radio (2017, July 7). Why are black children so much more likely to die of asthma? National Public Radio (NPR). Retrieved from www.npr.org

Novak, B. (2017, May 2). Young boy and loaded handgun found in car; dad arrested. *Wisconsin State Journal*. Retrieved from wwwhostmadison.com

Onyanga-Omara, J. (2016). Gun homicide rates report. *USA Today*, p. 1A, June.

Pao, M. (2015, November 19). How America's child support system failed to keep up with the times. National Public Radio (NPR). Retrieved from www.npr.org

Pao, M. (2016, October 22). US parents are sweating and hustling to pay for child care. National Public Radio (NPR). Retrieved from www.npr.org

Rodgers, G. (2016, July 9). Killer at 17 granted freedom via work release. *The Des Moines Register*, pp. 1A, 11A.

Rotabi, K. (2012). International adoption. In L. M. Healy, & R. J. Link (Eds.), *Handbook of international social work, human rights, development, and the global profession* (ch. 11, pp. 81–91). New York, NY: Oxford University Press.

Saleebey. D. (Ed.). (2013). *The strengths perspective in social work practice.* New York, NY: Pearson.

Savidge, N. (2017, May 2). Controversial political scientist Charles Murray to speak at UW-Madison groups' event. *Wisconsin State Journal.* Retrieved from www.host.madison.com

Skivenes, M., & Skramstad, H. (2013). The emotional dimension in risk assessment: A cross-country study of the perceptions of child welfare workers in England, Norway and California. *British Journal of Social Work, 45*(3): 809–824.

Sternberg, B. (2016, May 18). Kids can't tie their shoes, but they can fire guns. *USA Today,* p. 7A.

Taylor, C. A., Manganello, J. A., Lee, S. J., & Rice, J. (2010). Mothers' spanking of 3-year-old children and subsequent risk of children's aggressive behavior. *Pediatrics, 125,* e1057–e1065.

Tough, P. (2016, June). How kids really succeed. *The Atlantic,* pp. 56–62.

United Nations Children's Fund (UNICEF). (2014). *Hidden in plain sight. A statistical analysis of violence against children.* New York, NY: United Nations.

van Wormer, K., & Link, R. J (2016). College students offer their views about corporal punishment. Boxed reading in van Wormer, K., & Link, R. J., *Social welfare policy for a sustainable future: The U.S. in global Context* (p. 221). New York, NY: sage.

Waldmeir, P. (2005, May 2). Top court abolished US death penalty for juveniles. Financial Times. Retrieved from https://business.highteam.com

Zayas, L. H., & Miller, A. (2015). Immigrant detention centers harm children's mental health. www.mystatesman.com. Posted 12 am. Thursday, August 13, 2015.

Zayas, L. H. (2015). *Forgotten citizens: Deportation, children and the making of American exiles and orphans.* New York, NY: Oxford University Press.

CHAPTER 11

# CARE AT THE END OF THE LIFE CYCLE

Article 16
The family is the natural and fundamental group unit of society and is entitled to protection by society and the State.

Article 12
No one shall be subjected to arbitrary interference with his privacy, family, home or correspondence, nor to attacks upon his honour and reputation. Everyone has the right to the protection of the law against such interference or attacks.

*Universal Declaration of Human Rights*, United Nations, 1948

Across the lifespan, we are all aging, constantly changing over time. Aging occurs from the moment of conception until death. How old a person looks, in fact, is one of the primary characteristics we notice about a person. Sometimes there are age restrictions for certain privileges as evidenced in the statements, "Let me see your ID card" (asked of youths to buy an alcoholic beverage) or "Do you qualify for a senior discount?" at the other end of the age spectrum.

Erik Erikson (1963) saw life development as a series of tasks to be mastered at various stages. In the final stage, the challenge is to achieve integrity rather than despair. Retirement, widowhood, and the accumulation of losses can lead to loneliness and depression. Ideally, at the final stage of life, one comes to accept his or her life as having been meaningful and worthwhile. In this vein, renowned neurologist and storyteller Oliver Sacks (2015), expressed his thoughts. Writing shortly after receiving a surprise terminal diagnosis, he said:

> I cannot pretend I am without fear. But my predominant feeling is one of gratitude. I have loved and been loved; I have been given much and I have given something in return; I have read and traveled and thought and written. I have had an intercourse with the world, the special intercourse of writers and readers.

> Above all, I have been a sentient being, a thinking animal, on this beautiful planet, and that in itself has been an enormous privilege and adventure. (p. A25)

Sacks died six months later. Maya Angelou, similarly, expressed gratitude for the life she had lived and for her mother and grandmother. Author of the classic autobiography, *I Know Why the Caged Bird Sings*, which chronicles the story growing up black in segregated Arkansas. Angelou (2013) covered some of the same ground in her final work, *Mom and Me and Mom*. Maya Angelou's book, as she states in the introduction, was written "to examine some of the ways love heals and helps a person to climb impossible heights and rise from immeasurable depths" (p. 1). Of her mother, she says, "You were a terrible mother of small children, but there has never been anyone greater than you as a mother of a young adult" (p. 197). Angelou died at age 86, one year after her book was published.

## DEMOGRAPHIC FACTS

The dramatic growth of the population age 65 and older is referred to as a demographic imperative because it affects all social institutions—families, the workplace, educational settings, health and mental health care delivery systems, and the leisure industry (Hooyman, 2013). Androff (2016) refers to this increase as "the demographic tsunami in global aging" (p. 88). This increasing disparity in population age already is altering every aspect of human existence, from the jobs we hold, to housing architecture, to the products we buy, to the medical care we receive. Major changes in the advertisements on TV and in magazines tell the story: Many are now beamed at the caregivers of an older population who might be in the market for mood-altering medications for Alzheimer's, walk-in bathtubs, and/or safety alarm systems. For the baby boom age group, ads for ocean cruises are commonly seen.

In all practice areas, including child welfare, addictions, corrections, family services, mental health, and work with the homeless, social workers work with older adults, in many cases as sources of stability to help other family members.

Today, about one in every seven, or 14.5%, of the population is an older American—over age 65 (Administration on Aging [AoA] 2015). This represents a population increase of 28% in just the past 10 years. In 2014, 22% of persons 65 or over were members of racial or ethnic minority populations—9% were African-Americans; 8% were Hispanic; 4% were Asian or Pacific Islander; and 0.5% were Native American.

There are now over 10 times as many people aged 65 and older as there were 100 years ago. The proportion of older people in the population is rising because there are fewer births occurring. Because of the shorter lifespan of men, generally, women will continue to outnumber men in this age group by a wide margin, with over twice as many women as men in the over 85 age group (AoA, 2015). The reason for the bulge in older Americans is the baby boom that took place after the second world war when the soldiers returned home.

In 2014, an estimated 78% of the older population were non-Hispanic white. This population will be much more diverse in the future, however, with the older Hispanic populations significantly outnumbering the non-Hispanic black population in the next 20 years (Older Americans, 2012).

Never before will so many people live as long. A child born in 2014 could expect to live 78.8 years, about 30 years longer than a child born in 1900 (AoA, 2015). Much of this increase occurred because of reduced death rates for children and young adults.

The graying of America, where 1 in 10 Americans will be over age 80 early into the 21st century, is a trend found virtually everywhere in the industrialized world. The graying of the world is bound to change the way we live and the way we view aging. This demographic revolution, depending on the viewpoint, is both a triumph and a problem, a triumph in terms of longevity and a problem in terms of medical costs. As our nation ages, how will we respond to the population shift? How will we handle the health care demands? Who will care for the frail older population? And what lessons can we learn from other nations concerning attitudes toward aging and care of persons who can no longer care for themselves? These are among the questions that will be addressed in this chapter.

The demographic shift has major implications for social welfare policy and social work practice. Policy challenges, as indicated by Hokenstad and Choi (2012), include how to pay for increased health care costs, long-term care, and financial support. Creative strategies are needed to promote well-being in older persons and to help expand their support systems.

The biopsychosocial-spiritual model provides a ready framework for the study of the aging process. Following a global overview of aging with a focus on Europe and Asia, we discuss society's treatment of older adults as a human rights issue. Then we view the physiological, psychological, social, and spiritual dimensions of advanced age. The remaining portion of this chapter explores government services, empowering practice approaches to aged clients, and ways of confronting ageism in the society. That there is much we can learn from other nations, other cultures, is an underlying theme of this discussion.

## AGING AND HUMAN RIGHTS

All human rights articles of the Universal Declaration of Human Rights (United Nations, 1948) refer to older members of the society as they do to all age groups, and there is one specific mention to old age in Article 25. This Article spells out the right to an adequate standard of living, which includes the right to security in old age. As quotations for the start of this chapter, we chose Article 16: "The family is the natural and fundamental group unit of society and is entitled to protection by society and the State." We can conclude from these Articles that it is the state's duty to protect the rights of vulnerable older citizens to adequate housing, food, and security.

Androff (2016) views gender equality as a human right as affirmed in the Convention on the Elimination of All Forms of Discrimination against Women. Although older women are not singled out in this document, the rights to which all women are entitled apply to all age groups. However, in 2010, the Committee on the Elimination of All Forms of Discrimination against Women did clarify that the document pertained to older women and that ageism was one of the forms of discrimination covered. In some parts of the world, women cannot inherit property. The state should protect women from this form of discrimination and from financial as well as physical abuse. More is needed, however, to protect all older people from discrimination. Androff (2016) suggests that a Convention on the Rights of Older Persons be passed by the United Nations. Such a convention would provide imperatives for states to enforce the human rights of their older citizens; the nations that ratified this treaty would be required to submit reports on their progress. In what might be considered a first step to having such a convention, the member states of the Organization of American States (OAS) approved the Inter-American Convention on Protecting the Human Rights of Older Persons which was signed by the governments of Argentina, Brazil, Chile, Costa Rica, and Uruguay at OAS headquarters in Washington, DC (Organization of American States, 2015).

## CONCEPT OF AGING WORLDWIDE

The same global economy that is having a demonstrable impact on the most industrialized of nations also is promoting individualism and materialism elsewhere. Increasing materialism has been at the expense of the traditional family values of respect and care for older relatives and familial interdependence. Worldwide, the communications revolution promoting modern and Western commercialism has continued to undermine the traditional foundations of family roles and function. But let us start with a view of aging closer to home.

### HISTORICAL VIEW

A self-proclaimed member of the baby boom generation, psychologist Mary Pipher (2000) describes the landscape of old age as "another country." Aging in America, she says, is harder than it needs to be. The distance between parents and their adult children in a highly mobile society is part of the problem. Ignorance about the needs of the older generation due to physical separation is another part. Whereas historically humans of all generations spent time together, people today tend to be grouped by age: Three-year-olds are together, pre-teens together, and many retired people live in segregated communities.

During the Colonial period, older individuals generally were looked on with respect (Popple & Leighninger, 2010). Older relatives played active roles in the family, on the farm, and in helping with the young. At the end of their lives, they could be expected to be cared for by their grown children, of which there were many. Attitudes toward old age began to shift by the mid-1800s, however, in part, related to industrialization, and in part, to the new philosophy of social Darwinism which stressed survival of the fittest and efficiency. Rapid advances of science and technology and access to books tended to limit the value of elders' knowledge (Zastrow, 2013). (In the computer age of today, the knowledge gap between the old and the young is probably far more striking.) As the older generation lost its central function, old age came to be associated with uselessness and decay.

Consistent with the economic demands of modern industrialization and urbanization, is the gradual decline in the extended kinship system (Barusch, 2014). Interestingly, today, although the situation is not what it was on the farm in the 19th and early 20th centuries, the rate of three-generational families has increased in recent years. Many grandparents are raising grandchildren, and many families are doubling up for economic reasons. According to a special report by the US Census Bureau (2014), 10% of grandparents live with a grandchild. Most of these grandparents are grandmothers and these families are disproportionately poor. In one-third of these intergenerational households, there is no parent present.

The policies of today are linked to the orientations and solutions of yesterday. Two developments from the eighteenth and nineteenth centuries are germane to our treatment of the older adults at the present time—a lack of coordination in a federally operated system that developed in an ad hoc fashion, and a tendency to favor the young for their future potential. In European countries, in contrast, operations under one government are less complex and less fraught with power imbalances and irregularities in providing services.

In mainstream America, the first retirement programs inadvertently reinforced the idea that older people were incapable of useful work (Popple & Leighninger, 2010). By 1910, poorhouses had been transformed into old-age homes. Meanwhile, the numbers of the aged in the population continued to rise. Only after the social turmoil associated with the Great Depression did the idea of Social Security catch on as a means of providing social insurance for workers and their families—insurance against loss of a parent, disabilities, and old age. Today, there is concern because of the gap between the baby boom bulge in the population now aging at a time when fewer younger workers are in the population to pay into the system.

## NATIONS COPING WITH POPULATION IMBALANCE

In Europe, Italy and Germany have extremely low birthrates of 1.4, while Greece has 1.3 (*The Economist*, 2015). In these countries, the numbers of sons and daughters to take care of their aging parents are dwindling. For point of comparison, American women each have about two children on average. Northern Europe has done better than countries southward because of lower unemployment, adequate child care provisions, and strong economic incentives for childbearing. In fact, according to *The Economist*, subsidized child care and nurseries for children is the best strategy a country can use to boost the fertility. Then women can both have a career and mothers, more than one child. That would be good for women and good for productivity as well.

The ratio of taxpaying worker to retired person has important implications for governments and businesses concerning the labor force, taxation, education, housing, production and consumption, retirement, pensions and health services. Today, according to the calculations of Yale University demographers, the world ratio of worker to person over age 65 has declined from 12 to 1 to 8 to 1, and by the year 2050 it is projected to decline to 4 workers for every older person (Chamie, 2015). Keep in mind, these figures include nations with very young populations, such as those in sub-Saharan Africa and India as well as countries with low birth rates. Japan, for example, has two workers for every older person at the present time. In Japan, Italy, and Germany following decades of low fertility rates closer to one child rather than two children per woman and increasing longevity, the proportions of older people in those countries exceed 20%. In response to concerns about having too few taxpayers to support older generations, some governments, such as Australia, Canada and Germany, have increased immigration levels to maintain the size of their labor force. Other countries, such as Denmark, encourage people to stay in the workforce longer and/or to have more children by providing economic incentives and affordable day care.

In light of the challenges posed by the world's rapid aging and to promote the rights of older adults globally, The Madrid International Plan of Action on Ageing was adopted by the United Nations in 2002 to promote the rights of older adults globally in health care and supportive living arrangements (Brownell & Kelly, 2013). Protection from abuse was also emphasized. The

Madrid Plan was significant because it embodied the hope for broad social change in making the world a better place in which to grow old.

While the challenge of caring for progressively larger numbers of vulnerable older persons is the same the world over, the way in which this challenge is met varies greatly from country to country. Nations with collectivist approaches assume that frailty among the aged is a social problem engendering social solutions. Sweden, Finland, Israel, and France, for example, provide services universally and with dignity for those in need of aid. In Scandinavia, pensions and housing allowances are viewed as essential components of elder care. Britain and Canada, in contrast, despite an entitlement approach to health care which provides a great deal of aid, place the responsibility on the family to provide long-term care. The promotion of greater privatization in both countries is threatening to create a greater gap between the "haves" and the "have-nots." In the United States, the continued emphasis on individualism and self-reliance fosters a tradition of privately provided support including support by family members.

## GROWING OLD IN ASIA

In the emerging economies, economic progress has created work incentives for women and disincentives to have large families. As young adults migrate to the cities, their older relatives are left behind. The Asian countries are aging at a rapid rate at the same time that the fertility rate declines (Hokenstad & Choi, 2012).

The situation facing Japan is somewhat unique. An extremely low birth-rate is connected to women's liberation and reluctance to marry in a nation in which the wife-mother traditionally stays home to tutor children and care for her and her spouse's parents (The Economist, 2015). Because of the stigma of out-of-wedlock pregnancy, the abortion rate is high. Compounding the problem, the Japanese do not welcome foreigners, much less immigrants, into their homogenous society. An influx of young immigrant workers as exists in the United States and Canada would help correct the age imbalance though at the risk of overpopulation. Japan also is feeling the effects of the custom of underpaying young workers as part of a seniority system which guarantees job security and much higher salaries for long-time employees.

The Tokyo government is doubling the number of senior apartments and other specialized facilities. In workaholic Japan, retired persons, especially men, have much difficulty with leisure time so the government is organizing activities at neighborhood centers.

In Hong Kong, the birthrate is only 1.1 (The Economist, 2015). In Japan, one quarter of the population is 65 or older; women live to age 86.4 on average, and tens of thousands are over age 100 (Spitzer, 2015). The older population is said to be much healthier than earlier generations of the same age, and they are increasingly willing to stay in the workforce. And India, where care is provided through the extended family, is unprepared for the explosion of old people as it still struggles to feed the young.

China has the fastest ageing population in human history, and the worry is who will care for all the older people (Hatton, 2015). Traditionally, every generation of a Chinese family lived under the same roof. Increasingly, the pattern of fierce loyalty to older members seems to be breaking down under the influence of capitalism, world trade, and the results of the one-child-only policy. Most of the older parents no longer live with their children. China's government, meanwhile, is promising support to its citizens in their old age and building retirement homes at a rapid pace, but is nowhere near meeting the need. To protect the older people from emotional neglect, the Chinese government even passed a law requiring that grown children visit their parents on a regular basis (Wong, 2013). (Singapore has a similar law).

Throughout the world, care of a frail, older parent is often regarded by the children as an unwanted burden. Generally, in media reports in the industrialized world, the situation of having responsibility to one's parents while still raising children is depicted in negative terms. The doomsayers, as the author of *The Upside of Aging*, notes, use phrases such as "gray dawn" to describe older societies (Irving, 2014). And we hear on talk shows and in economic forecasts that the older citizens will break the economy, destroy health care and the social security system, create intergenerational strife, hurt the job market, and remove support from children. (Wacker & Roberto, 2011).

## OVERLOOKED POSITIVES OF POPULATION IMBALANCE

The reader undoubtedly will have noticed, as we did, that the literature on global aging cited is decidedly negative. The information from UN reports and academic research alike is replete with dire forebodings of falling productivity rates, low-consumption of goods, and a financial burden on our social welfare, health, retirement, and family systems.

And yet there are positive aspects to the longevity phenomenon that are almost entirely overlooked. Older citizens, for example, provide a vital resource; both collectively and as individuals, their potential contribution to society is enormous. A challenge for nongovernmental groups (NGOs) advocating for the needs of the older men and women is to convince countries, particularly countries struggling to be economically competitive, that most seniors can be viewed not as a liability but as a resource. Their wisdom and experience can be utilized by providing them with opportunities for decision making in their respective communities. In a positive vein, the United Nations (1999) developed a set of principles essential to the situation of older persons. The UN Principles for Older Persons is a foundational document that delineates human rights for older citizens. As Brownell and Kelly (2013) indicate, a paradigm shift was evident at the time from a focus on the infirmities of old age and need of care to more holistic notions of people moving into old age with vigor, health, and a desire to remain productive in the workplace. The following are the UN's five principles that were to become a blueprint for the International Year for Older Persons:

- *Independence* including the opportunity to work and earn income
- *Participation* in the life of the community
- *Care* in the home and community as needed
- *Self-fulfillment* in the cultural life of the community
- *Dignity* to be preserved regardless of one's economic circumstances

Regarding the need for independence, some sort of mass transportation is essential so that people who no longer can drive can get where they need to go without having to depend on others. Quite apart from (and in contradiction to) the literature on the pending age imbalance, we have drawn up my own list of positives. Keep in mind, in any case, that the dreaded population imbalance that has received such negative media coverage is related to the baby boom population bulge, and therefore this imbalance is strictly temporary. Here is our list of positives:

- A low crime rate in society in which there are proportionately fewer youths
- A reduced rate of illicit substance use and alcohol problems in the older population (many of the hardened drug users and alcoholics never reach old age)
- More jobs available for the young, a crucial factor as technologies continue to replace workers
- A pool of retired persons available for caregiving and volunteer work
- An older generation to provide a sense of connectedness with the cultural past
- An older generation to be a source of love and guidance to the young
- The chance for grown children to return the care that was once given to them

Because of later marriage and childbirth today, parents may be in their 50s with teenage children and grandparents in their 80s. In contrast to the negativism associated with this term in media reports, Suppes and Wells (2012) cite a study commissioned by the American Association of Retired Persons (AARP) that found that 70% of the middle aged caregivers of the "sandwich generation" felt comfortable in their roles rather than burdened by them.

In the next several sections of this chapter, we consider biological, psychological, and social aspects of aging.

## BIOLOGICAL FACTORS IN AGING

Shakespeare (1958/1600) summed up the physiological changes—ravages—very old age as a time characterized by losses:

> (The) last scene of all
> That ends this strange eventful history
> Is second childishness, and mere oblivion
> Sans teeth, sans eyes, sans taste, sans everything.
>
> —Shakespeare, *As You Like It*, Act II, Scene 7

The pace of biological aging differs among individuals, but its course is inevitable over time. The morbid side of growing old—illness, infirmity, and looming death—often is underplayed in the literature which is filled with optimism. TV ads, on the other hand, in the interests of promoting sales, play up the negatives. The process of aging does involve a certain deterioration; health and vitality decrease, and vulnerability increases. The process of aging is not uniform, however, but occurs in spurts (Zastrow, 2013).

Aldous Huxley's *Brave New World* (1969; orig. 1932) depicted a future that contained death but not aging. Through the miracle of chemistry, the old did not physically age and therefore died young. In the real world, however, only through death can we stave off the effects of the ravages of time. The inevitability of growing old is accompanied by an obvious physical decline. Four out of five people over age 65 can count on having at least one chronic condition; among the most common are arthritis, hearing impairments, various forms of cardiovascular diseases, and cancer. Heart disease and cancer pose their greatest risks as people age, as do other chronic diseases and conditions, such as stroke, chronic lower respiratory diseases, Alzheimer's disease, and diabetes (Centers for Disease Control and Prevention [CDC], 2013) The exact relationship between chronological age and the decrease in capabilities, however, has yet to satisfactorily be determined.

Many of the health problems faced by older people result from a general decline in the circulatory system (Zastrow, 2013). Reduced blood supply impairs mental sharpness, and other body organs are affected as well. Adjusting to changes in external temperature becomes increasingly difficult. Bones become more brittle; sensory capacities decline as well. Because it affects all of one's dealings with people, hearing impairment is crucial in its consequences. Other age-related changes—in vision, muscular strength, and reaction time—lead to a sense of vulnerability and fear in strange and unusual surroundings.

Physical limitations coupled with lack of adequate transportation limit older persons in their ability to shop, obtain legal counsel, or get needed medical care. About 35% of people over age 65 have disabilities of some sort ("A Profile of Older Americans" [AoA], 2016).). With the rapid increase in the number of people over age 85, Alzheimer's disease and other forms of dementia are much more frequent occurrences than in the past. Around 3% of those 65 and older and 9% of persons over age 85 are living in a nursing home, but many more reside in nursing homes for shorter periods. Half of all nursing home residents suffer from Alzheimer's or a related form of dementia. Because an individual with Alzheimer's disease lives an average of eight years beyond the onset of symptoms, the demands of care can be formidable (Holland, 2013).

"Every age," notes Grossman (2003), "has its own way of dying. The 19th century had consumption; the 20th century had the heart attack, and the 21st century will be the age of Alzheimer's disease" (p. 65). Medical science is frantically searching for a cure for this dread disease; some medications have recently been developed in hopes of arresting its progress. The Allen Institute for Brain Science (2014) in Seattle is a privately funded institute with the goal of mapping every gene's role in the human brain so that medical researchers can find new drugs and treatments for disorders such as Alzheimer's and schizophrenia.

*Still Alice* is a 2015 film starring Julianne Moore as a linguistics professor at the height of her academic career. Moore won the best actress award for her portrayal of a woman facing a diagnosis of early stage Alzheimer's. Celebrating her 50th birthday, there are already subtle signs that her memory and judgment are beginning to fail her. This film realistically shows the impact on Alice and her family of the tragedy of a disease that takes so much that is meaningful in life away.

Cancer is of course another important target area of medical research. Over a half a million Americans die of cancer each year. In his State of the Union address, President Obama announced a new $1 billion initiative directed toward this work (The White House Office, 2016). Through studies of gene instability (one of the major hallmarks of malignancy), it is hoped that the secrets of how the life span operates its own clock might be uncovered; recent advances have led to the ability to activate the immune system against cancer cells. Such research is crucial inasmuch as after reaching late-middle age, men face a 50% chance of developing cancer, and women have a 35% chance.

As the population ages, we can expect that the increasing medical attention to treatments for older adults will continue. Consider the plethora of TV ads for drugs for arthritis, impotence, depression, and the like. Historically, medical care was instituted to treat the young, to deal with war wounds, industrial accidents, childbirth, and children's diseases. Consequently, physician-oriented, and cure-based nature of health care is unsuited to the needs of older persons who typically have chronic conditions with social dimensions. The use of advanced technologies on the aged who may finish out their lives on a respirator in intensive care results in unnecessary pain for such patients, guilty feelings for family members, and great expense for the society. This process further creates a convenient scapegoat—the older people themselves—for a society facing rising health care costs.

Although people 65 years of age and older comprise only 13% of the population, they account for almost 30% of all medications prescribed in the United States (SAMHSA, 2013). Because an estimated one in four older adults has symptoms of mental illness, many are prescribed psychotropic medication. Drug interactions are common with the result that, according to SAMHSA, more than 80% of emergency room department visits made by older adults result from adverse drug reactions. Death due to the synergistic effect of drug interactions is higher among the older population than among any other group, including adolescents. Excessive drinking can trigger a dangerous synergistic effect with the prescription drugs taken.

## THE PSYCHOLOGY OF AGING

*Psychological* aging is related to biological aging in the same way that the mind is very closely linked to the body. The psychological dimension refers to changes in personality or ways of processing information accompanying the aging process. Factors of health, idleness, loss of contemporaries, reduced income, and many other social variables shape the psychological reality experienced by older adults. The 2002 Hollywood movie *About Schmidt* poignantly yet humorously takes us on a journey with Warren Schmidt (convincingly played by Jack Nicholson) as he attempts to find meaning in his seemingly meaningless life following his retirement party and death of his wife. With the vastness of the future no longer before him and the typical emptiness of the present, the past assumes an ever-increasing importance to him as to many older persons.

Sometimes suicide becomes a tragic solution to a host of problems, including loneliness and depression. In the United States, older white men have a high rate of suicide, often through use of firearms (Kaplan, Huguet, McFarland, & Mandle, 2012). Veteran status and rural residence increased the chances of firearm use in this age group. In Western Europe where firearms are not commonly found in the home and where older people receive better care, the suicide rate of older people is less than in the United States. Drug-related suicide attempts among older women have increased significantly; the drugs used in these attempts were often those used to treat anxiety and insomnia, along with pain relieving narcotics (SAMHSA, 2011). More recently, startling facts concerning a heightened death rate for late middle-aged men and women have come to light. Misuse of prescription drugs, drinking problems, and suicide are identified as probable causes (Bernstein & Achenbach, 2015).

Individual experiences of aging are very different. During the seventh stage of our lives, Erik Erikson (1963) taught that we can achieve a state of well-being through a feeling that our lives have been meaningful, and that we have made and are making a contribution to future generations. He called this notion generativity. Generativity, as Robbins, Chatterjee, and Canda (2011) note, has two faces—charity and *agape* from the Greek word for love. This notion is expressed in following poem by an 81-year-old woman who was inspired by the following exchange with an irascible old man. "Why don't you plant some flowers?" she had asked. "What's the point?" he asked. "I probably won't live long enough to see them bloom." That's when she (Elise Talmage) sat down to write this poem which is found in Box 11.1. (This story was shared in private conversation with van Wormer in May, 2012.)

The work of the final stage of life, as defined by Erikson, is geared toward the achievement of integrity. In this last scenario, the older person may want to feel that his or her life has been meaningful and worthwhile (Popple & Leighninger, 2010). Advanced age is a time of reflection on one's life and on the life choices that one has made at various turning points along the way. Allie Walton (1981) who described herself as "a freelance Quaker do-gooder and peacemaker," once wrote a piece on aging that was widely read in Quaker circles. Here it is in part:

> Long ago, when I was still quite young, I discovered George Bernard Shaw's witty remark—Youth is such a wonderful thing; it's too bad it is wasted on the young."
>
> And now—I'm 70, and it's been awhile since I dared to climb a tree, and I take the stairs one at a time. I still chuckle over Shaw's wit, but it seems a dated joke. By now, I realize life is not divided into "youth" and "middle age" and "old age." It all runs together. It is all part of a piece, constantly moving and growing and intertwining. Physical activity is a joy, your grandchildren are a treasure, and work keeps body and soul together, but at 70 I am chuckling over new discoveries. How relaxing to be past the time of constant attention to the many details of family needs. How nice to know it doesn't matter whether or not you are a wall-flower (p. 8).

This is generativity in a nutshell.

### BOX 11.1 But Someone Surely Will

ELISE TALMAGE

Let's rake leaves in little piles
So hurry while the wind is still.
I may not see the spring time grass
But someone surely will.
Let's dig holes for tulip bulbs
And spread on rich black dirt to fill.
I may not be here in the spring
But someone surely will.
Let's plant yellow poplar trees
all along the left hand hill.
I may not see them really grow
But someone surely will.
I feel very spry today
not ready for the shelf.
I bet I'll fool the hour glass
and see the spring myself.

Source: Unpublished poem by Elise Talmage who died at the age of 91 in Bowling Green, KY.

# THE SOCIAL SIDE OF AGING

In a youth-oriented, fast-paced industrialized society, the process of aging begins to acquire a negative meaning as we move past early adulthood.

The *social* side of aging refers to the cultural expectations for people at various stages of their lives. Socially constructed definitions are important because they ultimately are translated into public policies. To the extent that older parents and grandparents are expected to continue making an active contribution to their families and to society, or conversely, to disengage from responsibility in deference to the younger generation, this has profound—and perhaps unsettling—implications for one's social adjustment to growing old.

With the aging of the baby boomers, who may live a third of their lives in a healthier and more financially secure retirement than previous cohorts, increasing attention is given to concepts of productive aging and civic engagement (Hooyman, 2013).

Race, ethnicity, and social class status are significant determinants of an individual's experience with aging. Minorities, only around 16% of the population of people over age 65, are projected to represent about one fourth of the total by 2030 (Delgado, 2015). Membership in an extended family is a primary buffer against the losses associated with advancing age. More older men than women are married and live with their spouses. About two and a half times as many African American, Latina, and Asian women live in extended family situations as do European Americans ("Older Americans 2012"). The group with the smallest percentage of persons living alone are the Asian and Pacific Islander populations.

Social worker Lydia Pérez Roberts presents a Latina perspective on caring for older family members. Just as her family has joyfully provided care for her *abuelita* (great-grandmother), so Roberts looks forward to sharing a household with her mother one day. Lydia Roberts, in an email communication, describes how she was struck by the contrasting attitudes between the two Latina social work students in class and their Iowa classmates. By way of explaining to the class how mainstream Anglo-Saxon culture tends to shut problems away, Roberts stated:

> I then gave examples, like the mentally ill who society shuts out, the criminals in jails, the pregnant teens in alternative schools, the runaways in shelters, and the elderly in nursing homes. . . I explained that in Mexican culture, to put people away because they are an inconvenience is almost unheard of. . . I told them how we even joke about it in our family (sending our parents off to nursing homes when they're old). . . . This is kind of how the Dia de los Muertos celebration is too. Mexicans have a fun celebration of the day of the dead because it is their way of honoring the dead but at the same time laughing in the face of death. Not letting it get the best of them. (quoted in van Wormer, 2017, p. 262.)

Extended family ties are strong among many North American Indian groups as well. Most tribes assign to elders meaningful roles as transmitters of traditional culture, values, and education. Among upper-upper class Anglos, similarly, older persons occupy a position of honor due to their link to an illustrious and perhaps more prosperous past. Across the lifespan people with higher incomes report their health as being much better than that of those with lower incomes (Popple & Leighninger, 2010). Regardless of ethnic background or social class, nevertheless, health and loss of functioning are constant concerns, while ageism in the society at large can lead to feelings of worthlessness. This is especially true for workers over age 50 who lose their jobs and have to compete in a competitive job market.

Sadly, because of society's prejudice against older workers who are considered slow to learn new things, people are dying their hair and altering their résumés to shorten long work histories and remove graduation dates of out of desperation. The sense of worthlessness may result, not from the aging process itself, but from the perception of themselves as embarking on a downward spiral, as being "over the hill" Tugend, 2013). Such a perception may set in as early as the late thirties. Social workers who work with older unemployed men can help them, while they job search, to define themselves in other ways than through their jobs, for example, as parents or grandparents or active church workers.

## AGEISM

A society that equates beauty with youth, denies aging and death, and lacks valued rituals for passages through all the stages of life, is a society that practices ageism. Ageism refers to discrimination against older people and stereotyping about people on the basis of their ages (Barker, 2014). Examples of ageism are: devaluing older workers because they are regarded as slow and having skills that are outmoded; using the word old in an intolerant and pejorative way; avoiding dining in restaurants frequented by older diners; using the word burden in reference to care for older adults but not for care for the young; derogatory mass media portrayals of older persons such as comedy routines making fun of aging bodies; having upper age limits for car rentals as in parts of Europe and North Africa; and politically attacking social welfare programs that make life tolerable for the older population (prevalent in the United States and Canada). If you visit a nursing home, note the tone of voice sometimes used by staff, a condescending tone that is usually reserved for use with small children. See Figure 11.1 for a similar display of ageism that permeates US culture without even being recognized.

Before the passage of the Affordable Care Act, notes Gullette (2017), the high death rate suffered by people over age 55 who were too young for Medicare was a scandal. But still, today, the ageism infused in the health care system can be life-threatening. An empirically based longitudinal study of over 6,000 people with a median age of 67 found that ageism in health care is widespread (Rogers et al., 2015). One out of five adults surveyed reported experiences of discrimination in healthcare settings. One in 17 experiences frequent healthcare discrimination, and this is associated with new or worsened disability four years later. Fortunately, health systems should have a strong economic incentive to reduce the perception of discrimination in healthcare settings, as Medicare payments under the Affordable Care Act, if they survive the right wing opposition, will be tied to patient satisfaction and quality of care delivered to older patients.

To the extent that Western culture venerates maturity, respect is reserved for older people who seem young, those who don't look or act their age. The critical observer will note that ageism is particularly pronounced in the conversations of people in their late middle years, often as they perceive signs of aging in themselves. Such ageism often takes the form of self-deprecating remarks such as, "this dates me" or "I'm showing my age" or "this person has been around the block a few times" or was "over the hill." Students often belittle older professors as "a relic from the 60s," or "an old" this or that. So infused in the system is ageism that it is rarely named and even less examined in the field of gerontology (Gullette, 2017). Recently at a conference

**FIGURE 11.1.** One of the authors came across this life-size doll seated in her bank. Note the many stereotypical features of this doll. Photo by Rupert van Wormer.

on gerontology (attended by van Wormer), a participant in self-introductions said, "I certainly hope I don't seem to be a member of the group we came to discuss." Several years ago, at the 50th birthday party of one university dean (also attended by van Wormer), the entire event took the form of gallows humor related to the aging process. Each joke present that the dean received was more tasteless than the next. Apparently such "over the hill" birthday parties are a tradition in our society, a way of using humor to cope with our fears about aging. Pipher (2000) concurs. Such jokes, she says, reflect our anxieties about aging in a youth-oriented culture. Checking out the birthday cards at her local drugstore, Pipher found the following examples:

> "Have you picked out your bench at the mall yet?" There are jokes about hearing loss, incontinence, and losing sexual abilities and interest. There are cards on saggy behinds, gray hair, and wrinkles, and cards about preferring chocolate or sleep to sex. (p. 40).

Instead of celebrating age, in short, we seek to escape by one means or another, whether through games of denial, self-depredating humor, or cosmetic cover-ups. Cosmetic surgery to hide the signs of age is a booming industry. Almost as many dermatologists today perform Botox and similar procedures as treat skin cancer (Stein, 2015). But most of the $13 billion Americans spend on cosmetic procedures is for surgery, including liposuction and breast enhancements as well as facelifts.

Internalized ageism is inevitable in an atmosphere of so much negativism. No wonder so many of the members of the older generation come to devalue themselves as worthless, useless, ugly, and inferior to the young. They well remember how they felt about older people, "way back then." Paradoxically, the category of old age is a rarity among minority groups toward which we both are prejudiced against and end up joining.

Much of the literature and mass media today are decidedly unsympathetic to the needs of the aged. Often older adults' needs are pitted against the needs of the very young who, it is said, lack voting power unlike their elders and are therefore neglected (Irving, 2014). According to some public officials, the demands of older citizens are consuming a disproportionate share of the national budget. These sentiments expressed in the media plus the influence of special interest groups on politicians have created a climate ripe for a retrenchment of the popular and smooth-functioning Medicare program and continuous attacks on Social Security. In her pioneering and iconoclastic book—*Ending Ageism, or How Not to Shoot Old People*, Gulette (2017) notes the bombardment of anti-old age sentiment in modern society. A certain panic has set in about the aging boom generation. "The system behind the ugly 'Graying Nations' charges," she writes, "is *decline* ideology, stating pointblank the people normally aging are ruining nations" (p. xvii).

An increasing number of people are seeking or remaining in employment beyond the traditional retirement age of 65 due to financial necessities such as reduction in expected retirement benefits, need to support younger dependents, love of the job or of the status derived therefrom, or a combination of factors. And yet these older workers are apt to experience ageism at work. Sometimes it is just in the form of questions like, "Are you thinking of retirement?" At other times, the older workers are given increased workloads or inconvenient schedules compared to newly hired workers.

Freedom from discrimination on the basis of age is every bit as much a human rights issue as is discrimination on the basis of race and gender. Federal legislation protects people over the age of 40 from employment discrimination, and employees have the right to sue under the Equal Employment Occupational Act, and increasing numbers do so (Jackson, 2014). Most of the discrimination, however, is a matter of attitude; its manifestation is subtle and difficult to verify. Negative ageist stereotypes commonly held by employers include beliefs that older workers are inferior to younger workers in ability to learn new things, productivity, ambition, mental health, flexibility, and commonly, proficient in computer skills. Although research shows that most older adults maintain high levels of functioning, performance, and resilience when well supported with environmental demands in their life, health, sociocultural, and employment contexts (Jackson), in situations of economic distress, the level of functioning is altered.

## OLD-OLD AGE

Before delving into issues during the last stage of life, such as death and dying, we need to make a distinction between two segments of the older population—the young-old (age 65 to 75) and the old-old (age 75 and up). Newly retired people, compared to other age groups in the United States, are doing quite well. Their health is good; marriages and relationships boost their income and reduce expenses; and their retirement benefits have not yet been eaten up by inflation. After age 75, the numbers of the living are diminished, and after age 85, the losses escalate.

The final line in the final episode of the 2016 Public Broadcasting Service's (PBS) of the British series, *Downton Abbey*, caught many viewers by surprise. The scene is the New Year's celebration, and the family members in this elegant household are making toasts. "What else could we drink to?" asks Mrs. Crawley. "We're going forward to the future, not back into the past." Violet, the Dowager, (played by Maggie Smith) gets the last word. "If only we had the choice," she replies.

The lack of choice to which the Downton Abbey character refers shows a feeling of regret that many of the old-old have facing the end of life. Whether rich or poor, we all experience loss of loved ones and face death. The developmental period of old age is about major physical and social disruptions and psychological stresses. As with all age groups, there is a close link between a person's physical health and his or her state of mind. One of the greatest challenges of old age is learning to accept vulnerability and to ask for help. The old-old (those over age 75), as Pipher (2000) explains, lead lives filled with the loss of friends and family, of habits and pleasures, and of autonomy. "One of the cruel ironies of old-old age is that often when people suffer losses, they must search for new homes" (Pipher, p. 30). Moving away, in turn, makes life more difficult through loss of familiar places and lifelong routines.

Despite their forgetfulness, older people often have a rich storehouse of memories. Some of the memories involve buried parts of the past such as war memories that return in later years. Like other victims of trauma, the old-old can become obsessed with deeply disturbing events of the past and be inclined to tell the same story over and over. Sadly, the younger listeners are apt to complain bitterly about the repetition.

In a cruel twist of fate, people who had survived unimagined horrors earlier in life against all odds and who had refused to dwell on such memories, often end up returning in old age to those long-ago horrors. The Baycrest Centre for Geriatric Care in Toronto provided residential services for around a thousand Holocaust survivors, most of whom have now died. Baycrest (2008) published a manual to share what social workers and other staff members who worked at the Jewish-centered home for the aged had learned. Called *Caring for Holocaust Survivors*, the book describes the phenomenon of dementia-related return to long-repressed memories from the past. With the onset of age-related conditions such as Alzheimer's, people can no longer separate the past from the present; short-term memories begin to disintegrate, while earlier memories may remain sharply in focus. In the Holocaust survivors, hoarding of food, refusal to board a bus, the sight of security's uniforms, arrangements to take a shower—all were triggers that could lead to reactions of hysteria.

## THE ELDERIZATION OF POVERTY

"You can be young without money, but you can't be old without it." These words of wisdom were spoken by Maggie in the Tennessee Williams (1954) play, *Cat on a Hot Tin Roof* (p. 54). In fact, the rich even have longer life expectancies than the poor. Analysis of data from the University of Michigan's Health and Management Study reveals that 55-year-old men have on average 34.9 years to live if they are in the richest 10% bracket but only 22.6 to live in the poorest 10% bracket (Zumbrun, 2014). And it's a gap that is widening over time, particularly among women.

Paralleling the *feminization of poverty* which refers to the social and economic structures and processes that increasingly lock women in poverty (Barker, 2014), we are introducing the term the *elderization of poverty* or alternatively, the *povertization of older citizens* to refer to a trend that goes beyond the census data statistics. This trend relates to the quality of life that awaits a large percentage of the rapidly growing group of older people who can expect to live in poverty, many in abject poverty.

The oldest-old (85 years and over) experience a higher poverty rate than do their younger counterparts. An investigation by *Time* magazine on the crisis in elder care discusses a system that Edwards (2017) suggests is riddled with exploitation at every level. She faults the forced arbitration agreements that leave patients and their families no access to lawsuits in the case of malpractice, and the rapid growth of for-profit hospice centers that provide inadequate services to the terminally ill. As well, most private nursing homes don't have to keep residents once the cash runs out. Then the family must locate a less expensive facility at a time when more specialized care is needed. Only people with vast accumulations of wealth, therefore, are invulnerable to financial problems as they get past a certain age.

Research shows a sharp contrast in values between Americans and Europeans. When it comes to who should be primarily responsible for people's financial well-being in their old age, Italians and Germans point to the government, while Americans say families should take care of their own financially (Zoroya, 2015). When it comes to personal care, however, Americans fall behind (Pew Research Center, 2015). In all three countries, more financial aid by middle aged people goes to their grown children than to their aging parents, but more assistance goes to one's parents.

The median income for males over age 65 in 2015 was $31,372 and $18,250 for females. The overall poverty rate for the over-65 age group was 8.8%. (AoA, 2016), a number that is deceptively low because it lumps together all persons over age 65 and fails to take into account high expenses related to advanced aging—living alone, costs of medication, and the need to hire help for physical tasks that one or one's spouse could previously perform. For greater accuracy, the US Census Bureau released a new Supplemental Poverty Measure (SPM). The SPM methodology shows a significantly higher number of older persons living in poverty than is shown by the official poverty measure (AoA, 2016). This higher figure takes into account expenses such as medications and housing as well as government benefits such as SNAP (food stamps) and earned income tax credits. This more realistic measure is not used officially at this time.

When ethnic and racial characteristics are factored in, the situation becomes ever more dismal. The following statistics come from "A Profile of Older Americans" (AoA, 2016). The poverty rate of non-Hispanic whites over age 65 is 6.6% compared to 11.8% of older Asians, 17.5% of older Latinos, and 18.4% of older African-Americans. Older women had a higher poverty rate (10.3%) than older men (7%) in 2014. Older persons living alone were much more likely to be poor (15.4%) than were older persons living with families (5.7%). The highest poverty rates were experienced among older Hispanic women (40%) who lived alone.

Women's high poverty rate seems to be the case for the following reasons: the fact that so much of women's work has been unpaid and thus without retirement benefits (even the majority of working women are not covered by private pension plans); the likelihood that women will take care of their spouses and then be left alone (only 46% of women over age 65 live with a spouse compared with 72% of men); and because so many women live to advanced age. Throughout the rest of the world, older women are much more likely to be below the poverty level than older men. From these statistics, we might conclude that women's greatest blessing—longevity–turns into their greatest woe, and the feminization of poverty and the elderization of poverty become one.

Social work professor Melvin Delgado (2015), author of *Baby Boomers of Color*, provides a number of reasons why racial and ethnic groups suffer economic hardships as they reach old age. Around half of this group, as Delgado indicates, will be relying primarily on Social Security for their support; these payments are low for retired people who had worked at low-paying jobs. African Americans and Latinos rarely have jobs that offer pension plans; if they did have retirement plans such as a 401K, chances are they had to withdraw money early to pay for other expenses. For example, in the recession of 2008, many home owners who lost their jobs, could not make the mortgage payments so withdrawal of retirement funds was common. Most are not home owners, however. In contrast to middle class white collar workers who often can physically hold onto their jobs well into their sixties and seventies, laborers are not in a physical condition to do so. Poor blacks and Latinos are especially vulnerable to taking out high-interest predatory loans as they lack other sources to borrow money. Due to poor credit or lack of trust, many in these older minority groups, do not have bank accounts in the first place.

Globally, we can look for data on living standards for older adults in the Global Age Watch Index which provides a ranking of the best and worst countries in which to grow old (Gladstone, 2015). Switzerland, Norway, Germany, Canada, and the Netherlands emerged as the best places for older people to live, and Afghanistan, Malawi, Mozambique, and the Palestinian territories received the lowest rankings. Norway is rated by The Global Watch Index as the best place to grow old, followed closely by Sweden. The pension system in those countries enables people to live at home with health aides or in a senior living facility (Lakey, 2016).

A frail older woman, typically, may have to find a way to obtain long-term health care for an ailing spouse when she no longer can physically provide the care herself. But with expenses for institutionalized health care skyrocketing, even the most scrupulous handling of finances over decades of retirement cannot protect a formerly middle income family from eventual ruination. From a global perspective, we can consider the extent of older-woman hardships in such places as: sub-Sahara Africa where nearly half the adult relatives are caring for children orphaned by AIDS are grandmothers; in China where the grown children have moved to the cities leaving many older people to fend for themselves; and in many of the African countries where widows become destitute due to inheritance laws that don't allow them to inherit from their husbands. Millions of older women worldwide, live on the margins of their societies, in short, face daily economic pressures, and receive negligible health care and support services.

The fate of many poor older people was brought to the public consciousness during two extreme heat waves—one in the US and one in France. Sociologist Eric Klinenberg (2015), author of *Heat Wave*, provides the facts. Tragically, in Chicago during the heat wave of 1995, over 700 people died of the heat; the majority were older people who lived alone. Their burglar-proof homes prevented adequate ventilation, pushing indoor temperatures to dangerously high levels. When pronouncements are made about how well older Americans are doing, it is important to be aware of the stark realities. Heat waves in the United States kill more people during a typical year than all other natural disasters combined, and it is the older people who die. The same thing happened in Europe. In 2003, over 3,000 died in Paris when the temperature soared to a record breaking 104 degrees. Social isolation again was as much a cause as the temperatures.

Interestingly, in his statistical analysis, Klinenberg found that the death toll consisted of older whites and African Americans in poor urban areas, but that the death toll for older Latinos was extremely low. Cultural factors clearly come into play here, factors that probably help to explain why Latinos in the United States have a life expectancy that is higher than that of other ethnic groups (Delgado, 2015).

Because of the social isolation today of so many persons of advanced age, there is an increasing need for government-supported services. We will now see what kinds of social services are available.

## US GOVERNMENT PROGRAMS

Most older Americans rely on Social Security benefits. Much is made of the fact that, due to social security and Supplemental Security Income (SSI), poverty has been reduced in the overall oldest population to nearly the average for the population as a whole. In fact, however, in the belief that they need less income, the Census Bureau applies a different poverty standard to elders than to those below age 65 assuming that they eat less than younger people (Suppes and Wells, 2012). So estimates of the poverty level in this age group can be considered an underestimate.

The Social Security Act of 1935, described in chapter 4, is the cornerstone of legislation for older people. Never intended to be the main source of income for people in old age, but rather as a supplement to assets, the social security system has become the sole support for many individuals (Zastrow, 2013). About 90% of seniors receive social security benefits; the more they paid in to this program in their working years, the more they receive. Married persons can receive benefits based on the spouse's contributions. Unlike most private pension plans, Social Security is indexed to inflation.

In the 1960s, before a reorganization of government programs, one-third of all older people had incomes below the poverty line. Due to improvements in the standard of living and the social security and pension benefits, the poverty rate was cut in half between 1966 and 1974 (Desilver, 2014). Social security is considered an entitlement program in that recipients have a legal right to its benefits. Supplemental Security Income (SSI) was initiated in 1972 as an extra supplement for very low income persons with disabilities and those over age 65 (Suppes & Wells, 2012). Food stamps are also available to poor older adults.

To finance such programs, four out of five American workers pay more in payroll taxes than they do in income taxes (Gleckman, 2015). As discussed in chapter 8, this tax is paid only up to a threshold of around $127,000 of income. So the very rich, pay only a fraction of what others do, percentage-wise. In the years ahead when social security no longer generates a surplus due to the aging baby boomers, the solution is obvious, to eliminate the threshold, not to reduce the benefits to older Americans.

To review from chapter 4, Medicare and Medicaid were signed into law by President Johnson in the 1960s. Medicare provides health care to people 65 and over and to persons who are disabled, but typically it does not cover long-term care. Medicaid, a means-tested program, provides health care to poor and older Americans as well as long-term care to individuals of all ages. The greatest single outlay of Medicaid funds goes to older adults for nursing home care (Karger & Stoesz, 2013).

Although Medicare has clearly been a blessing and eased the cost of aging for older Americans, still, nearly one-in-five (19%) Americans ages 65 and older say they had a medical problem but did not visit a doctor, skipped a medical test or a treatment recommended by a doctor, did not fill a prescription or skipped doses of their medicine because of cost constraints (Stokes, 2014). By comparison, a far smaller share of older Canadians (9%), British (5%) and French (3%)—all of whom have government-funded health insurance programs—reported cost-related constraints on their access to health care.

The expense of Medicare is tied to inflated drug prices. The Medicare drug prescription program, passed by Congress under the George W. Bush administration and under the guise of reform, has been described as more a windfall for the pharmaceutical and insurance companies than a program to protect seniors. The legislation forbids the following: negotiating bulk discounts on drug prices as other nations do, the purchase of supplemental insurance for drugs unacknowledged by Medicare, and importing less expensive drugs from Canada (Lapham, 2004; Silverman, 2015). Medicaid, in contrast does negotiate prices (Silverman, 2015).

Many of the expenses of institutionalized care could be avoided if home health care provisions were sufficient. Access to choices such as assisted living facilities are restricted to those with independent resources.

We can predict with some certainty that the cohort known as the baby boom generation of "boomers" who did so much to change the meaning of education, marriage, and the family will not stand idly by when it comes to public policies pertaining to people in their age group. The political clout of people over age 65 likely will grow as their numbers double in the years ahead. But in the meantime, services for older Americans are under great strain. As the government relinquishes control over all forms of health care, private providers are rapidly moving in to claim the territory.

The Older Americans Act, enacted in 1965, provides for an array of human and social services for older adults. This federal program provides funding to the states for community programs and informational services for those over age 60. The Older Americans Act created the AoA, which through grants provided to states establishes supportive services, senior centers, home-delivered meals, training and research, supportive employment, protective services, and funding for older Native Americans (Morrow-Howell & Hasche, 2013).

Following five years of advocacy by NASW-US and other organizations, President Obama reauthorized the Act in 2016. The renewed Act provides family caregiver support, wellness protection, transportation, and programs to prevent elder abuse (Pace, 2016b). Other community social service organizations provide health counseling services including Area Agencies on Aging, health care facilities, community action programs, and senior citizen centers.

Case management services which are most often provided by licensed social workers or nurses are often based in public agencies, Medicaid waiver programs, hospitals, and managed care organizations. The assessment and care arrangements ensure the continuity of care between acute care and residential, in-home, community, and informal care systems (Morrow-Howell & Hasche, 2013). Often the case manager helps the family and older individual in need of care understand financial arrangements necessary for home health care or nursing home care. Entitlements counseling, where the worker helps the older person and the family members understand which social service programs, benefits, and services they may be eligible for, is offered as well. Because of the emotional nature of such planning, social workers need to prepare themselves for the psychological challenges associated with the decisions that must be made.

For poor older adults, government assistance is provided in the form of SNAP (food stamps) and other welfare benefits such as housing assistance. Eligibility is determined by national federal poverty level guidelines that determine how much it takes for a person to live on. A recent study by the UCLA Center for Health Policy Research (2015) that shows that in California income must be more than twice the federal poverty level estimated income level for an older person to pay rent and buy other necessities in California. The research center has produced an Elder Index to account for geographical differences in costs for housing, food, and medical care. It is hoped that this index could be used nationally; the recommendation is to raise the eligibility level to 200% of the federal poverty level from 100% and expanding food benefits (Sundaram, 2015).

## FAMILY CAREGIVING

What is the role of the immediate family in caring for frail older members? Generally, throughout the world, informal caregiving is in the women's domain.

Survey research from the Population Studies Center at the University of Pennsylvania found that in the United States., family members are actively involved in care for older relatives (Zoroya, 2015). In fact, more are involved in such care today than ever before because of today's increasing longevity. In the survey, three out of four respondents said that it was their duty to provide financial help if needed to their older parents, and three out of 10 Americans with an older parent said they did so. Almost 60% said they assisted with personal care or daily tasks. Americans, Italians, and Germans alike actively help their older relatives by making home repairs and running errands but not dressing or bathing the older adult. Italians provide more personal care, however, than Germans or Americans.

NASW-US staff have formed an association geared to the training of elder care coordinators through the setting up of pilot programs (Pace, 2016a). Elder care coordinators are receiving training in five pilot programs. The Association for Conflict Resolution Task Force on Eldercaring Coordination is a resource that can help resolve disputes for family members and others who are under court order to do so. The task force urges social workers who work with caregiving families to reach out to local judges to see about setting up a pilot site.

In China, as part of the Confucian concept of filial piety, the obligation for parental care fell to the daughters-in-law. This was a major reason that Chinese parents, under the one-child policy favored having sons. Because of the significant increase in life expectancy, and migration to the cities, this tradition is unsustainable (*The Economist*, 2016b).

In Japan, over 60% of people age 65 and over and nearly 80% of those aged 80 and over, live with their adult children. Relatives are still the main caregivers; family members even quit work and use their savings to take care of their parents with dementia (The Economist, 2016a). Policy and spending lag behind the need. Cases of older people committing suicide are common; recently, 10,000 dementia sufferers went missing; some walked into paths of trains. In one such case, the railway company charged the family for neglect of responsibility to provide proper care. However, attitudes are changing; the Supreme Court ruled that the family did not have to pay.

In all of these countries, when personal and physical care requirements become too great, families often turn to nursing home care.

## NURSING HOME CARE

By way of introduction to some of the jarring facts concerning present day nursing home care, let us trek back to the world of Jane Addams. Following her visit to older women confined in the Cook County Infirmary, Addams (1910) commented:

> To take away from an old woman whose life has been spent in household cares all the foolish little belongings to which her affections cling and to which her very fingers have become

> accustomed, is to take away her last incentive to activity, almost to life itself. To give an old woman only a chair and a bed, to leave her no cupboard in which her treasures may be stowed, not only that she may take them out when she desires occupation, but that her mind may dwell upon them in moments of reverie, is to reduce living almost beyond the limit of human endurance. (p. 156)

Similarly, today a forced move from home to a nursing facility can be traumatic. And as surprising as it is, even older prison inmates can find this transition severely disturbing. This fact is revealed in the popular 1994 Hollywood film, *The Shawshank Redemption* in which Morgan Freeman's character loses his place in the world upon his release. This movie echoed a similar theme in a 1979 satirical movie, *Going in Style* (remade in 2017). In that film, George Burns' played one of three very old men who decided to rob a bank. "What have we got to lose?" asks Burns. In prison, in the grand finale, the unrepentant hero remarks that his life on the outside was a prison anyway. Actually his life could have been much worse; he could have ended up in a nursing home.

Nearly one in three of persons aged 85 and over will find their way to these eventually, although most will stay only for a limited time. Created as an alternative to expensive hospital care, nursing homes, for the most part, are supported by the federal government through Medicaid and Medicare (Zastrow, 2013). A billion-dollar industry, nursing homes now contain more filled beds than do hospitals. These institutions, moreover, have become the repositories for older mentally ill people, released prisoners, and even some formerly homeless people. To account for America's reliance on institutional care, I-Jen Poo (interviewed by Ervin, 2016), a domestic workers advocate, states that Medicaid pays so well for nursing home care but not for home health care because of the powerful lobby; nursing home administrators and employees have vested interests in removing competition from the system they helped create. Poo mentions that Hawaii, however, plans to create a fund through taxes to cover long-term in-home needs of state residents.

A report from New York City states that under the constraints of managed care and pressures from state-implemented federal programs, aimed at reducing health care costs, patients who don't require skilled nursing care often are discharged from nursing homes to homeless shelters (Runyeon, 2016). As hospitals close or drastically shorten the length of stays as a part of government-enforced cost containment measures, nursing homes themselves are under pressure.

Due to poor working conditions and better options for nurses and social workers elsewhere, turnover rates of professional nursing home staff are quite high. At small facilities, social workers tend to feel isolated from others of their profession and devoid of peer support. Stevenson (2015) lists several other factors related to social worker burnout in this field—relatively low salaries, excessive paperwork requirements, unpaid overtime work, continual government cutbacks, and increasingly large workloads. At larger facilities, however, programs may be more diversified, and there is a team of social workers for personal and professional support. Nursing home practice does have one key advantage over acute-care hospital practice—long-term involvement with the patient and his or her family which brings its own special reward. While federal inspectors focus on medical protocol, it is often the relationship element that is more essential to patient well-being. Social workers hold family meetings and intercede with staff members in situations of difficulty. Greene (2012) urged schools of social work to offer courses in gerontology due to the increasing need for social workers in this expanding field.

Personal care facilities range enormously in price, quality, size, and services offered. For self-paying patients, costs average thousands of dollars per month. Nationwide, just over 15,500 nursing homes are certified to provide care to Medicare or Medicaid beneficiaries (Boccuti, Casillas, & Neuman, 2015). The vast majority (92%) are certified for both programs. Among these nursing homes, most (70%) are for-profit, about a quarter (24%) are non-profit and a very small share are government-owned (6%). Because Medicaid payments are actually below the cost of nursing home care, the Medicare reimbursements are vital to keep the nursing homes financially solvent.

All nursing homes in the United States with more than 120 beds are required to employ at least one full-time social worker (Bern-Klug & Sabri, 2012). Social workers are required, according to NASW-US standards, to demonstrate a recognition of basic human rights and resident rights. Federal standards for nursing care only requiring care by a registered nurse (RN) to be on duty for at least at least eight consecutive hours per day. Many states have somewhat higher standards (Boccuti et al., 2015).

A danger of nursing home care is the potential abuse and neglect of the residents by staff members. In a survey of 4,451 nurse aides in which researchers asked about elder abuse over a 3-month period, 36% reported observing staff members engaging in argumentative behavior with clients, 28% reported witnessing staff members intimidating clients, and 10% heard staff threaten to cease caring for a client (Castle, 2012). Zastrow (2013) describes scandals related to patients found lying in their own feces or urine, being overly sedated, given unappetizing food high in carbohydrates, and living under conditions with poor sanitation standards and serious safety hazards.

Overmedication is a major problem in nursing homes as drugs are used to sedate highly active nursing home residents and those who have sleeping problems and are inclined to get out of the bed when few staff are on duty. The use of antipsychotic medications for residents with dementia is another problem. Almost 300,000 nursing home residents are currently receiving antipsychotic drugs, usually to suppress the anxiety or aggression that can go with Alzheimer's disease and other dementia, according to a report on National Public Radio (NPR; Jaffe & Benincasa, 2014).

One helpful initiative from the federal government is the publishing of inspection reports of all licensed nursing homes. The Centers for Medicare and Medicaid Services (CMS) provides a star rating system based on the absence of deficiencies that cause immediate jeopardy to resident health or safety (Boccuti et al., 2015). Measurements are provided on such matters as the percentage of patients with bedsores, pain, and weight loss. Non-profit nursing homes, which comprise about a quarter of all Medicare-and Medicaid-certified nursing homes, tend to have higher overall star ratings. One-third of the nursing homes received very low scores for their failure to provide adequate care. The ratings are done on a comparative basis within each state; the results are available online and easily accessible.

## INSTITUTIONALIZED CARE WORLDWIDE

Americans are often criticized for sending their older family members to nursing homes. Yet countries in the Global North have similar institutionalization rates, usually around 5% as in the United States, but with a low of 2% in Japan (Rodrigues, Huber, & Lamura, 2012). The situation in the United Kingdom as in the United States is characterized by understaffing, high staff turnover, abuse of patients, and excessive use of medication. During the 1990s, long-stay National Health Service (NHS) hospital beds were available; now the choice for the frail elderly often is premature discharge from the hospital to home or receiving inadequate care in a nursing home (Triggle, 2016).

The situation in Canada is somewhat better. In response to complaints of extensive waiting times for home care services in Ontario, the Ontario government is increasing spending to keep people out of nursing homes and hospitals for less expensive care (Ferguson, 2016). The government already allots $3 billion a year for home care services. The additional money will pay for another 350,000 hours of nursing care, extensive respite care, and 1.3 million more hours of personal support for services like dressing, bathing, grooming and homemaking. Representatives from professional agencies applaud the improvements, particularly in respite care given that surveys show caregiver burnout rates have doubled in the past few years.

Nursing homes in many of the countries studied by Rodrigues et al. (2012), however, provide normal, homelike atmospheres as opposed to medical environments. There is also a trend in Israel and elsewhere toward funding for home and community-based care. Service apartments in Scandinavia provide a wide range of supportive services including prepared meals.

Although Germany is seeking options to institutionalized care, for those who require intensive care, to save expenses, family members in need of care are being transported out of the country, to Poland, where expenses are far less (Kresge, 2015). The move is subsidized by the German government. The nurses speak German, and residents are served classic German food.

In examining care-related policies in the Western European welfare states, we see that care is as much a feature of a society's value system as it is of the circumstances of rapidly aging societies. The concept of social citizenship in the Scandinavian countries guarantees care of dependents at every stage of the life spectrum. In southern Europe in contrast, the notion that care of older people should in the first instance be provided by the family prevails (Rodrigues et al., 2012). Home, however, is not always the best place for the aged.

## ELDER ABUSE

Elder abuse occurs most often when the parents live with their children or are dependent on them. Tensions can mount. Under the category of elder abuse, Suppes and Wells (2012) include physical mistreatment, emotional abuse, material or financial abuse, violation of rights, and life-threatening neglect. Although exact statistics are not available due to the strong reluctance of older family members to report their children or spouses for abuse, it is generally estimated that 3 to 6% of older adults suffer some form of abuse or neglect. Elder abuse can take place even when the older person isn't frail or helpless, with results that are psychologically devastating. Such abuse can occur in the workplace as well as in the home (Brownell & Powell, 2013). What we know from sources such as the National Center for Elder Abuse is this: women especially over age 80, are most likely to be abused or neglected; the alleged abuser is often a family member such as the spouse; and most mistreatment occurs in the home.

A poignant portrait of emotional mistreatment is presented in *The Trip to Bountiful* by playwright Horton Foote (1954). In the play, Mrs. Watts, a woman in her 80s who is constantly badgered and taunted by her daughter-in-law Jessie Mae, is highly opinionated yet delightfully headstrong. The main sources of contention between the women are the older woman's hymn singing and the whereabouts of her social security check. In a climactic scene, Mrs. Watts slips away to once again visit her home town of Bountiful, Texas for one last look. While on the Greyhound bus, she tells her life story to a young fellow traveler, and the two connect beautifully across generations.

Elder abuse is a problem worldwide. Changing patterns, mass migrations, shortages of food and water—all are creating stress and influencing violence and neglect of older relatives. Among the risk factors are a weakening of bonds between generations; social isolation; and the societal depiction of older people as weak and dependent (Hokenstad & Roberts, 2012). Personal characteristics also come into play, for example, substance use and mental health problems. Caregiver stress and the erosion of family support structures are major risks in the home (Hokenstad & Choi, 2012). In many countries, family violence is regarded as a private matter. In South Korea, according to Hokenstad and Roberts, spouse abuse is the most common form of elder abuse; in India adult children are the likely perpetrators, and in Japan, the daughters-in-law, who customarily provide the care, are the most likely to abuse older adults.

Maschi, Leibowitz, & Mizus (2015) bring our attention to an often overlooked form of elder abuse, that of older inmates. Behind prison walls, especially in men's prisons, the most vulnerable are apt to be taken advantage of economically and attacked physically. Chronic victimization and treatment neglect are human rights violations that are especially pronounced in prison. The failure of the state to protect prison inmates and to provide adequate medical care compound the violations.

How about situations in which the older person is or was the abuser? We are referring to a reversal of elder abuse, to the configuration in which family members are providing care for elderly persons who abused them, usually in their childhoods. This is a rarely addressed, but not unheard of, problem. When an incest survivor faces the prospect of having to care for his or her offender, complex emotions, understandably, are aroused. Other family members, such as a stepmother, are often unaware of the survivor's state of mind. The survivor who refuses to care for the now frail victimizer is often misunderstood.

Two Hollywood movies deal realistically with this happenstance. The 2007 film, *Savages*, starring Philip Seymour Hoffman and Laura Linney are two siblings who have spent their adult years trying to recover from the abuse of their abusive father. Now they are faced with the prospect that he has dementia and is in desperate need of care. Jane Smiley's (1991) Pulitzer prize-winning novel, *A Thousand Acres*, brought to the screen in 1997 with memorable performances by Michelle Pfeiffer and Jessica Lange, fictionalizes a similar situation. A modernized version of Shakespeare's King Lear, the story is told from the neglectful daughter's standpoint. In both renditions, the older father is treated mercilessly by two of his daughters. But in the modern version, as we learn through flashbacks, the reason for the rejection lies in dark secrets from their past.

Social workers are the best equipped to address elder abuse because as professionals they work with families in so many different capacities and in a variety of agency settings. Brownell (2002) offers a social work assessment protocol. Information obtained in this format is pertinent to the intervention strategy. For example, abuse perpetuated by a spouse in the secondary stage of Alzheimer's disease would suggest a different strategy than abuse inflicted by a substance-abusing grandchild. By remaining alert to the possibility of abuse, social workers, as Brownell suggests, can improve the safety and well-being of the clients they serve.

## LATE-IN-LIFE ADDICTION PROBLEMS

Surveys of various age groups suggest that older adults consume less alcohol and have fewer alcohol-related problems than younger persons. But the great concern with this population is prescription drug misuse. Such drug misuse is estimated to affect almost 4% of older adults in the 50–59 age range and a significantly smaller percentage of those over 60 (Reardon, 2012). Addiction to benzodiazepines, such as diazepam (Valium) and alprazolam (Xanax), is quite common in this age group.

The rate of smoking is 9.1% by older men and women, with a somewhat lower rate for women than for men (SAMHSA, 2011). Around 42% % of those over age 65 are regular consumers of alcohol, about half as many as among those in the younger age group (SAMHSA, 2014). Whites are more likely to drink than are members of minority groups. Unlike young adults, who seek out drugs for recreational use, older adults may be seeking a therapeutic effect, such as pain relief. Patterns of binge drinking are reported by 9.1% of adults over age 65, with heavy drinking reported by 2.1% of the binge drinkers (SAMHSA, 2014).

Visitors to local casinos will notice the presence of older women, often playing the slot machines. Baby boomers and older adults constitute 60% of all active gamblers, 10% of whom are persons of color (Delgado, 2015). Around 40% of casino patrons are over age 65. To attract these older gamblers, casinos offer bus transportation to and from the casinos and billboard advertising geared to their interests (van Wormer & Davis, 2018). Because of the social isolation of many older women, casino life can be a huge attraction. Money spent in this manner can come at the expense of purchase of medications or food. People who have suffered significant loss or trauma are highly susceptible to gambling addiction or some other form of addictive behavior.

Nursing homes and assisted living centers increasingly are seeing addictions problems in the residents. One survey on alcohol misuse conducted by University of Pittsburgh researchers, found that 20% of assisted living residents had health problems related to drinking (Span, 2012). The survey was done on over 800 nursing aides who worked with the residents. The risk to these older heavy drinkers is that many of them are taking other medications, even addictive medications, at the same time. With these facts in mind and to caution older adults about the risks associated with pain medication, SAMHSA and the Food and Drug Administration (FDA) have launched an information campaign for older adults called "Do the Right Dose."

The isolation and withdrawal associated with substance misuse reduce one's inclination to socialize and lead an active life. Family members may avoid or reject heavy-drinking individuals out of embarrassment and/or accumulated anger over previous episodes. In the belief that older family members are unlikely to change, relatives rarely bring them in or commit them to treatment. Older clients often come to substance abuse treatment because of arrests for drinking and driving. Others are referred to gambling-disorder treatment related to indebtedness. Happily, once in treatment, the recovery prospects of older clients are good to excellent (Farkas, 2014).

## COMMUNITY CARE OPTIONS

Much can be done to help families keep their older, disabled members at home, such as providing tax breaks for informal caretakers or better yet, paying them for their care. Homemaker services, visiting nurse services, "meals on wheels," adult foster care, day care, and group home care are among the offerings that can prevent the need for nursing home care. An innovative program in Wisconsin offers a host of alternative services such as homemaker services, home-delivered meals, adult foster care, and group home care. The program is cost-effective and preferred by clients over institutionalized care (Zastrow, 2013). It is only for the indigent, however; social workers and nurses assess patients for eligibility.

Adult foster care programs offer care in private homes at about half the cost of nursing home care. Most of the programs are for veterans with disabilities. Through the Medical Foster Home program run by Veterans Affairs (VA), veterans who can no longer live safely on their own can apply to be taken care of in a private home close to their community (Botek, 2016). Care in the family-like setting is overseen by a VA-regulated group of physicians, nurses, social workers, mental health professionals, pharmacists, and rehabilitation therapists, as well as the actual caregivers themselves. The plan is to expand such facilities to cover non-veterans as well in a private capacity.

Services to help older adults remain in their homes are vital, services such as homemaker care and help bathing and dressing and visits by home health aides to change bandages and give injections. Yet public recognition of the contribution of professional caregivers to both individual and family well-being is largely absent (Ervin, 2016). Formal caregivers often work for agencies and are paid very little for their work at the same time that the families are overcharged. Moreover, Medicare and Medicaid reimbursement for such services is problematic due to complicated eligibility requirements for active medical care of a serious nature to exist (Suppes & Wells, 2012). For effective care of frail older people, a continuum of care is required; this would include a health care component as a part of the funded package. Home care is the happiest solution. See Figure 11.2.

**FIGURE 11.2.** This older woman is able to live at home with the help of a paid caregiver. © Shutterstock, Photo by Alexander Raths.

Some communities offer social health maintenance organization (HMO) initiatives for people, many of whom would be otherwise institutionalized. Social HMOs offer social services that are Medicare funded on an experimental basis; the purpose is to prevent hospitalization. Tremendous cost savings accrue to Medicare with such arrangements due to the focus on prevention rather than treatment (Suppes & Wells).

One outstanding program that has come to our attention is found in Denmark, where care of older people is seen as a state responsibility (Thorsteinsson et al., 2016). Denmark provides generous provisions to all persons over the retirement age of 67. Offerings include access to recreational centers, cafeterias, sheltered living with alarm systems and home help services as needed. For those in need of it, the Danish legislation includes care services in the form of home care, which can be given as practical help, such as help with groceries, cleaning or laundry or as personal assistance with medications, and bathing. All residents of Denmark are eligible for these services. The legislation includes care in nursing homes following a thorough multidimensional needs assessment. All residents in Denmark above the age of 75 years are offered preventive home visits two times a year to ensure that those in need of care receive the help they require. An offer of placement in a nursing home or apartment may be made; acceptance is entirely up to the recipient. Although expensive, such a program would be well received in the United States, and bring a sense of security to every family that is forced to deal with difficult issues related to elder care.

All workers in the Netherlands pay taxes which covers "cradle to grave" care. For those who develop dementia, one option is to live in a place known locally as "Dementia Village" and to us as Hogewey. In this village, residents can live a seemingly normal life, but in reality are being watched all the time (Tinker, 2013). Caregivers staff the restaurant, grocery store, hair salon and theater, generally without the residents knowing it. Although it is criticized as being a fantasy world, the residents are happy and loneliness is unknown.

## FACING DEATH

The late Oliver Sacks (2013), a neurologist whose research on bizarre behavior related to brain damage and rare gifts, shared his thoughts on turning 80 in a *New York Times* essay. The essay begins with an expression of regrets: that the author is still as agonizingly shy at 80 as he was at 20, that he can only speak his mother tongue, and that he is not widely traveled. Still, he counted his blessings:

> At 80, one can take a long view and have a vivid, lived sense of history not possible at an earlier age. I can imagine, feel in my bones, what a century is like, which I could not do when I was 40 or 60. I do not think of old age as an ever grimmer time that one must somehow endure and make the best of, but as a time of leisure and freedom, freed from the factitious urgencies of earlier days, free to explore whatever I wish, and to bind the thoughts and feelings of a lifetime together. (p. SR12)

To learn about happiness across the life span, George Vaillant (2002), a psychiatrist and expert on human development, examined the extensive data from an earlier longitudinal study in which data were collected on three cohorts of men and women of various social classes who were born in 1910, 1920, and 1930. What Vaillant found was that the goals so prominent early in life, such as high achievement, are less prominent late in life. Successful aging, he found, was associated not with achievements but with close relationships and with generativity.

As we live in the present and invest in the future, old age and death are commonly denied. The painful paradox of death in the midst of life is addressed with rare eloquence in Becker's classic, *The Denial of Death* (1973):

> We saw that there really was no way to overcome the *real* dilemma of existence, the one of the mortal animal who at the same time is conscious of his mortality. A person spends years coming into his own, developing his discriminations about the world, broadening and sharpening his appetite, learning to bear the disappointments of life, becoming mature, seasoned—finally a unique creature in nature, standing with some dignity and nobility and transcending the animal condition, no longer a complete reflex, not stamped out of any mold. And then the real tragedy, as André Malraux wrote in *The Human Condition*: that it takes sixty years of incredible suffering and effort to make such an individual, and then he is good only for dying. (p. 268)

Elisabeth Kübler-Ross (1969), taught the medical community and the world to deal with death honestly and humanely. The co-founder of the hospice movement, she was also the author of the groundbreaking book, *On Death and Dying*. The significance of her legacy is revealed in empirically based research that shows the effectiveness of hospice as compared to a control group in controlling persistent pain and facilitating healthy grief responses for surviving family members (Morrow-Howell & Hasche, 2013). Her legacy is also evidenced in the many excellent hospice-connected programs which provide quality of life to the terminal patient who is diagnosed to have six months or less to live, to assist the patient at home or in a home-like setting. Pain relief is encouraged to keep the person as comfortable as possible (Zastrow, 2013). The Medicare hospice program provides extensive services—home health aides, short-term inpatient care, medical supplies, and occupational therapy, to terminally ill persons (Wacker & Roberto, 2011). Hospice workers, often social workers, also assist families throughout the bereavement process. Knowledge and understanding of the dynamics of dealing with the loss of a patient or loved one is essential to effective social work with individuals who are at the end of their lives.

## ASSISTED SUICIDE

Increasingly, Americans and some Europeans are seeking ways to exert some measure of control over where and how they die. The topic of death with dignity or (physician-assisted suicide) is highly controversial, and frightening both in society's acceptance and in society's rejection. The former opens up the possibility of people being coaxed to die; the latter presents images of the horrible pain and indignity of life prolonged artificially by machines.

According to survey data cited by McInnis-Dittrich (2013), two-thirds of the public and a majority of physicians in the United States support physician-assisted suicide as a legitimate right in cases of incurable and debilitating disease. The US Supreme Court has ruled that the decision to allow physician-assisted suicide should be decided by the states. Oregon, first among the states, legalized this process under strictly controlled conditions. Oregon's Death with Dignity Act allows doctors to prescribe (but not administer) a lethal dosage of drugs at the request of terminally ill patients with less than six months to live (Zastrow, 2013). As of 2016, almost 20 years since the Oregon law was passed, there have been just over 900 cases of assisted suicide (Oregon Health Authority, 2016), so the system has not been abused as opponents had feared. The vast majority who chose this route were people in the late stages of cancer under hospice care. The three most frequently mentioned end-of-life concerns as revealed in the medical records were: decreasing ability to participate in activities that made life enjoyable (96.2%), loss of autonomy (92.4%), and loss of dignity (75.4%). Other states permitting physician assisted suicide to dying patients are California, Vermont, Washington, and Montana (ProCon, 2016). At the present time, only in the Netherlands, Belgium, Finland, Canada, Luxembourg, and Germany are physicians permitted to give dying patients who qualify a lethal dose of drugs. Columbia allows death with dignity to occur but only outside of the presence of a doctor. The advantage of the voluntary death-with-dignity option for elders is in empowering them to exert some control over the manner of their death and its timing.

## AVENUES TO EMPOWERMENT

Social workers are well positioned to promote active aging and well-being for all older adults, and the need for social workers in the field of gerontology far exceeds the supply (Hooyman, 2013). The opportunity and challenge for social work, with its social justice mission, is to address both increased longevity along with life course inequities for women, persons of color, and gay, lesbian, and transgender individuals.

Recognition of the importance of autonomy and patient participation in community-based long-term care and other social service agencies has increased over the past several decades. Empowering social workers help older clients and their families draw on their own resources to make difficult decisions and to gain access to the desired services to maintain an optimum level of self-sufficiency (Hooyman, 2013). As a primary provider of mental health services, social workers are also central to addressing growing rates of depression, harmful substance use, and mistreatment of elders. From a strengths-based approach, relevant questions to ask older clients are

- Are there people in your life who you care for?
- Are there people you can depend in if you're in need?
- As a child, did you develop special skills or talents? Can you use those today?
- What has worked well for you in the past?
- What is your greatest joy in life?
- Do you have a religious or spiritual connection?

Instead of leading the client to view old age as a period of decline from youth, in short, social workers help older clients forge creative adaptations to the challenges of later life. Many older women, for example, form "families of choice" that may consist of friends and neighbors. However, they accomplish it, older people need to be productive, to feel that they continue to make a contribution to society and to other people's lives. Some older persons are resuming work roles on a part-time basis; others are engaging in volunteer activities through organizations such as the Retired Senior Volunteer Program (RSVP). RSVP places volunteers in hospitals, schools, and libraries, for example.

## SPIRITUALITY

Attending to the spiritual realm of human life is central to a strengths perspective. In the lives of elders, the role of both organized religious institutions and more holistic spiritual engagement provides a sense of meaning and fulfillment.

The postmodern emphasis of the social work profession on spirituality is particularly relevant to social work practice with elders. McInnis-Dittrich (2013) draws our attention to the aesthetic and social functions of religion to older African Americans and Latinos—the enlivening music, the energizing sermons, the deep sense of communal worship, and catharsis of emotional expression.

Edward Canda (2006), a social work educator at the University of Kansas, writes of resilience in the lives of people coping with chronic illness. Spiritual beliefs, he found, provide resources for managing suffering, persevering in health care, appreciating life and loved ones, and looking into and beyond the physical aspects of mortality. Through his research and his own personal growth, Canda became appreciative of the diversity in spiritual styles and language as he recognized themes of commonality in transcending the self and personal limitations to grasp a higher meaning and interconnectedness.

## ADVOCACY AND POLITICAL EMPOWERMENT

In a social climate of federal budget cuts and increasing competition among various interest groups for scarce resources, advocacy on behalf of the needs of older people or by the older people themselves is a must. The social work profession plays an important role in this regard. Located in Washington, DC, NASW-US lobbies politicians on behalf of geriatric programming and social justice issues.

Using more confrontational tactics, the Gray Panthers, seeks to end ageism and to effect social change through organizing older people to vote as a bloc on behalf of their special interests (Zastrow, 2013). Founded in 1970, and inspired by the Civil Rights era to fight discrimination based on age, the activism of the Gray Panthers was instrumental in promoting enforcement of the Age Discrimination in Employment Act in 1967. This act provides some protection against blatant age bias in the workplace, but cannot protect people from discrimination in its subtler forms. The Gray Panthers are credited with banning mandatory retirement laws which has made a difference for many workers.

Another form of militancy is provided by a left-wing protest group—the Raging Grannies—who dress up in funny hats and use sarcastic humor and songs to promote peace and environmental protection. See their website,www.raginggrannies.org (Raging Grannies International, 2016.) Figure 11.3 shows a direct-action event by this group in Seattle.

According to their mission statement:

> Grannies are best equipped to make public, corrupt things that have been hidden (often for profit). Local toxic waste sites that no-one seems prepared to tackle, asbestos sites employing young people desperate for work, nuclear waste products being dumped outside an uninformed small town, laws that affect an entire community, passed quickly with no opportunity for study. The list goes on. (www.raginggrannies.org)

**FIGURE 11.3.** This organization—Raging Grannies—uses humor to protest social injustices and war. Photo by Rupert van Wormer.

In mainstream America, one of the most powerful political organizations in the United States is the AARP (originally standing for the American Association of Retired Persons. Membership is open to anyone over 50; for a minimum fee, members receive subscriptions to *Modern Maturity* and *The AARP Bulletin* as well as discounts on goods and services (especially hotel fees). "To serve, not to be served" is the motto (see www.aarp.org).

Continued or renewed militancy by older adults and their allies will go a long way to confront political issues and address ageism and its manifestations. Perhaps advocacy for exemplary programs like the following will someday bring about favorable results:

- Pay to family members for caregiving (available in northern Europe and Nova Scotia, Canada)
- State hiring of retired persons to clean for and care for the frail elderly in their own homes (available in a few areas of the United States and Norway)
- Passage of a long-term care act providing the right to nursing care for all older people in need of such care (as legislated in Israel)
- Extensive home help services, day care centers, and communal-owned old people's homes (as offered in Finland)
- Guaranteed income whether one was a wage-earner or not and service apartments for semi-independent living (as in Sweden)
- Subsidized medication

### MULTIGENERATIONAL COMMUNITIES

The Green House project was the brainchild of Bill Thomas, who never forgot his experience working part-time in the sterile, medicalized atmosphere of a nursing home (Brody, 2014). The first Green House was built in Tupelo, Mississippi. Living in cottages, people who were moved in from nursing homes came to life again; people who were in wheelchairs started walking again; people who were uncommunicative started talking, and people who had been fed started feeding themselves. Today, there are hundreds of Green House homes all across America where residents live in cheerful surroundings; they are treated as residents rather than as patients.

Appealing to the baby boom generation are options that reflect the modern belief that older Americans should stay active in mind and body, build new relationships, and choose what kind of living arrangements they want. "Boomers," according to the *AARP Bulletin* "are helping to shape the future of housing" (Abrahms, 2011, p. 10). Two innovative options are described in this article: These are niche communities and cohousing.

Niche communities are living arrangements for people with common interests such as writing, acting, painting, or playing golf. University-based retirement centers and retirement homes for gays, lesbians, and transgender persons are expected to multiply. Cohousing developments are generally intergenerational communities with separate units but some shared common space. The model for cohousing comes from Denmark; there are presently over 100 of these communities in the United States, mostly in large cities. The group may buy the property and design it, make the rules by consensus and manage it independently. Residents eat some meals together and engage in recreational activities in small groups with common interests.

The daughter of one of the authors is a resident of the Arboretum cohousing community in Madison, Wisconsin where she lives with her two small children. "Arbco" consists of 38 units built to be environmentally sustainable. Among the residents of all ages are nurses, retired lawyers and professors, persons with disabilities and their caretakers, and families with small children. Members of the cohousing group tend to be politically active and to organize for progressive issues such as human and labor rights. Decisions, such as, cohousing purchases and other projects, are made through consensus.

Other multigenerational community models are increasingly being developed. Designed for people with special needs, one such arrangement has foster families and wounded veterans living side-by-side with adults in their 50s and 60s. The children get the closeness and stability they need from the surrogate grandparents in a neighborhood where the residents are actively involved in each other's lives (Jones, 2014). Models of such communities are now found in cities across the United States, such as Portland, Oregon, Washington, D.C., New Orleans, and Tampa, Florida. In Germany, similarly, shared living arrangements are common for people over age 80. In Berlin, 2,000 senior residents live in multigenerational homes that combine assisted living apartments with nursery schools (Lupieri, 2013).

## SUMMARY AND CONCLUSION

This chapter in conjunction with chapter 10, child welfare, addressed social welfare needs across the lifespan when dependency needs were the greatest. Taken together, one theme that emerges is demographic: Mass aging coupled with a huge drop in the birthrates is a phenomenon worldwide. A major challenge in the Global North and large parts of the Global South thus becomes, Who will care for older adults in the late stages of life?

Given the demographic realities, social workers, whatever the professional setting of their encounter, must be knowledgeable about the biological changes that accompany aging and the concomitant psychological, social, and spiritual dimensions. This chapter was designed to summarize such knowledge organized from a lifespan perspective. Accordingly, attention was devoted to some of the most prominent physiological changes that take place at the end of the life cycle, and the psychological means of coping with changes in bodily functioning and with the inevitability of ultimate debilitation and death. The social side of aging constituted most of the space of this chapter, starting with the introduction of the concept, the *elderization of poverty*, a term introduced to depict a reality that transcends the statistics. This recognition of economic factors in aging is a major theme of this chapter. The reality is that those who are born poor are apt to die poor. This fact is true within the United States and cross-culturally. Children at risk for poverty, ill health, and maltreatment enter the world with a tremendous vulnerability both educationally and socially. Lack of access to the essential preventive health care, nutrition and housing, compounds any existing problems and may lead to loss of health or homelessness.

The plight of older people who finish their lives in overcrowded, understaffed nursing homes is the plight of those who so often have outlived their health, their husbands, wives, and siblings, and who face exhausting their savings as well. In order to qualify for services in the United States, people generally have to pay for the care themselves until they qualify under a means-tested welfare system for expensive long-term care.

The retrenchment of federal funding for housing, health care, and financial aid pits the interests of children against the interests of senior citizens. What is needed is not an array of piecemeal policies providing benefits to one group at the expense of another, but a unified agenda ensuring economic security, health care, and adequate housing across the lifespan.

Ethnic and racial diversity are further variables in the sociology of aging. In parts of American society and of the world, the older generation continues to function in multigenerational contexts until the time of death. Elsewhere, in the context of chronic underfunding of government services for elders and the increasing unavailability of women to play caretaking roles, a decline in the quality of care for older persons is inevitable. Consider what happened during the record breaking heat waves in Chicago and France. The horrendous death toll of the very old, left alone while their relatives vacationed, brings into sharp relief the world's desperate need to provide preventive care and somehow maintain the interconnectedness of the generations. Only when all ages are integrated into the mainstream of life can our culture maintain its communal and spiritual health.

From the literature on aging, policy recommendations as reviewed in this chapter are the assurance of minimal income levels to protect the many who are without adequate pensions to the provision of universal health care covering prescription drugs, effective housing and transportation assistance, comprehensive homemaker and home health care programs, mass transit, and the availability of home-like nursing homes for persons in need of round-the-clock assistance. The best prevention of the *elderization of poverty*, in short, is a social welfare system guaranteeing the right to health, housing, and quality of life across the life span. In this way, the child who learns to trust (as Erikson's first stage) can achieve integrity (as in Erikson's final stage). In the wise words of Erikson (1963) "Children will not fear life if their elders have integrity enough not to fear death" (p. 269).

## THOUGHT QUESTIONS

1. Consider some autobiographical accounts in which the older person becomes reconciled to his or her past. How do you explain the changes in outlook that people have as they grow older?
2. What is the image of old age in the United States? How has old age been viewed historically?
3. Think of treatment of older people historically? What was family life like then and how has it changed?
4. What does it mean to describe old age as "another country?"
5. Discuss the demographic changes across the world pertaining to aging. What are the challenges and positives?
6. Review the UN's five principles for treatment older people. How well does the United States abide by these principles?
7. What is the Japanese experience of aging? How is the situation in sub-Saharan Africa unique?
8. What are some of the challenges in China today related to the economy and an aging society? What is the government's response?
9. Discuss the contributions of older persons to society from a strengths perspective. Relate to the poem introduced in Box 11.1, "But Someone Surely Will."
10. Discuss the concept of generativity. What are some ways this can be achieved?
11. What are some of the joys and challenges in providing care to frail older people who live at home?
12. How is Germany dealing with its aging population? How will the present situation of refugee immigration affect the situation?
13. Describe the service apartments in Scandinavia and the types of services they provide. How do collectivist approaches differ from individualist approaches?
14. Distinguish between young-old and the old-old in terms of health care needs.
15. What are some chronic conditions that older people in your family are wrestling with.
16. Analyze the prescription drug ads on TV involving older actors. What do these ads say about our society? How are these older people being portrayed?
17. What did you learn in the chapter about trauma in one's life and how it comes back later to haunt a person?
18. Explain how aid to one group—children—is played off in media arguments against another group—older adults.
19. How can ageism be confronted? What has social activism achieved to date?
20. What can we learn about Mexican-American care for older relatives?
21. There is a controversy concerning whether or not many of the older people in the United States can be considered poor. What is your understanding of this issue?
22. What is the significance of the Older Americans Act?
23. Describe how the average citizen finances nursing home care. What situations do you know personally of families that have difficult choices to make?
24. Discuss some options to nursing home care. How is Denmark handling care for its older citizens? How about the Netherlands?

25. What are the facts concerning elder abuse? Contrast domestic and institutional elder abuse.
26. Discuss some addiction problems concerning older people. Why do so many get addicted to gambling?
27. Discuss assisted suicide and how it is being administered. What are the positives and negatives of having this option?
28. Discuss advocacy and political organizing as avenues of empowerment. How can social workers advocate for relevant changes in the system?
29. What do you think of multigenerational communities? How does this concept work?

## REFERENCES

Abrahms, S. (2011, April). Happy together: Reinventing home. *AARP Bulletin*, pp. 10–14.

Addams, J. (1910). *Twenty years at Hull-House.* New York, NY: Macmillan.

Administration on Aging (AoA). (2016). A profile of Americans 2016. Washington, DC: U.S. Department of Health and Human Services.

Allen Institute for Brain Science. (2014, June 4). A new approach to Alzheimer's disease research. Seattle, WA. Retrieved from www.alleninstitute.org

Androff, D. (2016). *Practicing rights: Human rights-based approaches to social work practice.* New York, NY: Routledge.

Angelou, M. (2013). *Mom and me and Mom.* New York, NY: Random House.

Barker, R. (2014). *Dictionary of social work* (6th ed.). Washington, DC: NASW Press.

Barusch, A. (2014). *Foundations of social policy: Social justice in human perspective* (11th ed.). Belmont, CA: Cengage.

Baycrest. (2008). *Caring for Holocaust survivors: A practice manual.* Toronto, Canada: Baycrest Centre Toronto Holocaust.

Becker, E. (1973). *The denial of death.* New York, NY: Free Press.

Bern-Klug, M., & Sabri, B. (2012). Nursing home social services directors and elder abuse staff training. *Journal of Gerontological Social Work, 55*(1), 5–20.

Bernstein, L., & Achenbach, J. (2015, November 2). A group of middle-aged whites in the U.S. is dying at a startling rate. *Washington Post.* Retrieved from www.washingtonpost.com

Boccuti, C., Casillas, G., & Neuman, T. (2015, May 14). Reading the stars: Nursing home quality star ratings, nationally and by state. The Henry Kaiser Foundation. Retrieved from www.kff.org

Botek, A.-M. (2016). Unique care option may keep elderly vets out of nursing homes. *Aging Care.* Retrieved from www.agingcare.com

Brody, J. E. (2014, December 16). Growing old without a nursing home. *New York Times*, p. D8.

Brownell, P. (2002). Elder abuse. In A. Roberts & G. Greene (Eds.), *Social workers' desk reference* (pp. 723–727). New York, NY: Oxford University Press.

Brownell, P., & J. Kelly (2013). Looking ahead. In P. Brownell & J. Kelly (Eds.), *Ageism and mistreatment of older workers: Current reality, future solutions* (pp. 181–184). New York, NY: Springer.

Brownell, P., & Powell, M. (2013). Definitions and theoretical models for understanding ageism and abuse in the workplace. In P. Brownell & J. J. Kelly (Eds.), *Ageism and mistreatment of older workers: Current reality, future solutions* (pp. 17–28). New York, NY: Springer.

Canda, E. R. (2006). The significance of spirituality for resilient response to chronic illness: A qualitative study of adults with cystic fibrosis. In D. Saleebey (Ed.), *The strengths perspective in social work practice* (4th ed., pp. 61–76). Boston, MA: Allyn & Bacon.

Castle, N. (2012). Nurse aides' reports of resident abuse in nursing homes. *Journal of Applied Gerontology, 31*(3), 402–422.

Centers for Disease Control and Prevention (CDC). (2013). *The state of aging and health in America 2013*. Atlanta, GA: Centers for Disease Control and Prevention, US Department of Health and Human Services

Chamie, J. (2015, December 22). Number of workers per retiree declines worldwide. Yale Global online. Retrieved from www.yaleglobal.yale.edu

Delgado, M. (2015). *Baby boomers of color: Implications for social work policy*. New York, NY: Columbia University Press.

Desilver, D. (2014, January 13). Who's poor in America? 50 years into the 'War on Poverty,' a data portrait. Pew Research Center. Retrieved from www.pewresearch.org

The Economist. (2015, July 25). Baby love. *The Economist*, p. 10.

The Economist. (2016a, April 9). Grey zone. *The Economist*, p. 39.

The Economist. (2016b, February 20). State of minds: Dementia. *The Economist*, p. 36.

Edwards, H. S. (2017, November 27). Dignity, death and America's crisis in elder care. *Time*, pp. 48–59.

Erikson, E. (1963). *Childhood and society*. New York, NY: W. W. Norton.

Ervin, M. (2016, April). Expanding the realm of what's possible. *The Progressive*, pp. 35–38.

Farkas, K. J. (2014). Assessment and treatment of older adults with substance use disorders. In S. L. Straussner (Ed.), *Clinical work with substance abusing clients* (3rd ed., pp. 421–441). New York, NY: Guilford Press.

Ferguson, R. (2016, July 19). Home care gets $100 million boost from province. Toronto, Canada: *Toronto Star*. Retrieved from www.thestar.com

Foote, H. (1954). *The trip to bountiful*. New York, NY: Dramatists Play Service.

Gladstone, R. (2015, September 9). Older people are invisible in key data, U.N. warns. *New York Times*, p. A4.

Gleckman, H. (2015, April 2). For most households, it's about the payroll tax, not the income tax. Tax Policy Center. Retrieved from www.taxpolicycenter.org

Greene, R. R. (2012). Geriatric social work: A field of practice. In C. N. Dulmus & K. M. Sowers (Eds.), *Social work fields of practice: Historical trends, professional issues, and future opportunities* (pp. 183–206). Hoboken, NJ: Wiley.

Grossman, L. (2003, March 24). Laughter and forgetting. *Time*, 65.

Gullette, M. (2017). *Ending ageism, or how not to shoot old people*. New Brunswick, NJ: Rutgers University Press.

Hatton, C. (2015, December 21). Who will take care of China's elderly people? British Broadcasting Corporation (BBC). Retrieved from www.bbc.com

Hokenstad, T., & Choi, M. (2012). Global aging. In L. Healy & R. J. Link (Eds.), *Handbook of International Social Work: Human Rights, Development, and the Global Profession* (pp. 138–141). New York, NY: Oxford University Press.

Hokenstad, T., & Roberts, A. R. (2012). Older persons and social work: A global perspective. In K. Lyons, T. Hokenstad, M. Pawar, N. Huegler, & N. Hall (Eds.), *The SAGE handbook of social work* (pp. 372–387). Thousand Oaks, CA: Sage.

Holland, K. (2013, December 6). The facts about Alzheimer's life expectancy and long-term outlook. *Health Line*. Retrieved from www.healthline.com

Hooyman, N. (2013, December 2). Aging: Overview. In C. Franklin (Ed.), *Encyclopedia of Social Work* (20th ed.). New York, NY: Oxford University Press. Online edition.

Huxley, A. (1969; orig. 1932). *Brave new world*. New York, NY: Harper and Row.

Irving, P. (2014). *The upside of aging: How long life is changing the world of health, work, innovation, policy, and purpose*. Hoboken, NJ: Wiley.

Jackson, M. (2014). Counseling older adult victims of ageism for the workplace. In C. Franklin (Ed.), *Encyclopedia of Social Work* (20th ed.). New York, NY: Oxford University Press. Online edition.

Jaffe, I., & Benincasa, R. (2014, December 8). Old and overmedicated: The real drug problem in nursing homes. National Public Radio (NPR). Retrieved from www.npr.org

Jones, A. (2014, September). The age-old old age problem, Newsweek. Retrieved from http://www.newsweek.com

Kaplan, M. S., Huguet, N., McFarland, B. H., & Mandle, J. A. (2012). Factors associated with suicide by firearm among U.S. older adult men. *Psychology of Men and Masculinity, 13*(1), 65–74.

Karger, H., & Stoesz, D. (2013). *Social welfare policy: A pluralist approach*, 7th ed. Boston, MA: Pearson.

Klinenberg, E. (2015). *Heat wave: A social autopsy of disaster in Chicago*. Chicago, IL: University of Chicago Press.

Kresge, N. (2015, September 15). Germany exporting its grandmas. *Bloomsberg Businessweek*, pp. 20–22.

Kübler-Ross, E. (1969). *On death and dying: What the dying have to teach doctors, nurses, clergy, and their own families*. London, England: Macmillan.

Lakey, G. (2016). *Viking economics: How the Scandinavians got it right—and how we can, too*. Brooklyn, NY: Melville House Printing.

Lapham, L. H. (2004, February). Notebook: Bad medicine. *Harpers*, pp. 9–11.

Lupieri, S. (2013, June 19). Aging gracefully: Germans grow gray together. Cable News Network (CNN). Retrieved from www.cnn.com

Maschi, T., Liebowitz, G., & Mizus, L. (2015). Best practices for assessing and treating older adult victims and offenders. In K. Corcoran and A. R. Roberts (Eds.), *Social workers' desk reference* (3rd ed.). New York, NY: Oxford University Press.

McInnis-Dittrich (2013). *Social work with older adults* (4th ed.). Boston, MA: Pearson.

Morrow-Howell, N., & Hasche, L. (2013, September 3). Aging services. In C. Franklin (Ed.), *Encyclopedia of Social Work* (20th ed.). New York, NY: Oxford University Press. Online edition.

Older Americans 2012: Key indicators of well-being. Washington, D.C: Federal Interagency on Aging. Retrieved from www.agingstats.gov

Oregon Health Authority. (2016). Oregon Death with Dignity Act: Data summary. Public Health Oregon. Retrieved from www.publichealth.oregon.gov

Organization of American States (OAS). (2015, June 15). The Americas becomes first region in the world to have an instrument for the promotion and protection of the rights of older persons. Retrieved from www.oas.org

Pace, P. R. (2016a, July). Eldercaring social workers receive training in five pilot programs. National Association of Social Workers (NASW). *NASW News, 61*(7), 5.

Pace, P. R. (2016b, June). NASW highlights work in aging during conference. *NASW News, 61*(6), 4.

Pew Research Center. (2015, May 21). Family support in graying societies. Washington, DC: Pew Research Center. Retrieved from www.pewsocialtrends.org

Pipher, M. (2000). *Another country: Navigating the emotional terrain of our elders*. New York, NY: Riverhead Books.

Popple, P., & Leighninger, L. (2010). *Social work, social welfare, and American society* (8th ed.) Boston, MA: Pearson.

ProCon (2016, July 20). Euthanasia and physician-assisted suicide around the world. Retrieved from www.euthanasia.procon.org

Raging Grannies International. (2016). Welcome to the International Grannies website. Retrieved from www.raginggrannies.org

Reardon, C. (2012, January/February). The changing face of older adult substance abuse. *Social Work Today, 12*(1), 8–11.

Robbins, S., Chatterjee, P., & Canda, E. (2011). *Contemporary behavior theory: A critical perspective for social work* (3rd ed.). Boston, MA: Pearson.

Rodrigues, R., Huber, M., & Lamura, G. (2012). *Facts and figures on healthy ageing and long-term care.* Vienna, Austria: European Centre for Social Welfare Policy and Research.

Rogers, S. E., Thrasher, A., Miao, Y., Boscardin, W., & Smith, A. (2015). Discrimination in healthcare settings is associated with disability in older adults: Health and retirement study, 2008–2012. *Journal of General Internal Medicine, 30*(10), 1413–1420.

Runyeon, F. (2016, April 4). New York City nursing homes forcing residents into homeless shelters. *City and State.* Retrieved from www.cityandstateny.com

Sacks, O. (2015, February 19). My own life: Oliver Sacks on learning he has terminal cancer. *New York Times*, p. 25.

Shakespeare, W. (1600). *As You Like It* II, VII: 139.

Silverman, E. (2015, July 23). U.S. could save up to $16 billion if Medicare Part D prices are negotiated. *Wall Street Journal.* Retrieved from www.blogs.wsj.com

Smiley, J. (1991). *A thousand acres.* New York, NY: Knopf.

Span, P. (2012, February 7). Drinking in assisted living. *New York Times.* Retrieved from www.nytimes.com

Spitzer, K. (2015, March 5). World's oldest person has lots of company. *USA Today*, p. 5a.

Stein, J. (2015, June 29). Nip, tuck, or else: Why you're getting cosmetic procedures even if you don't really want to. *Time*, pp. 38–48.

Stevenson, S. (2015, November 18). Social worker secrets to reducing stress. *A Place for Mom.* Retrieved from www.aplaceformom.com

Stokes, B. (2014, December 3). Health Affairs: Among 11 nations, American seniors struggle more with health costs. *Pew Research Center.* Retrieved from pewresearch.org

Substance Abuse and Mental Health Services Administration (SAMHSA). (2011). Results from the 2010 National Survey on Drug Use and Health: Volume I. Summary of National Findings. Rockville, MD: Office of Applied Studies.

Substance Abuse and Mental Health Services Administration (SAMHSA). (2013). Get connected: Linking older Americans with medication, alcohol, and mental health resources. HHS Publication No. (SMA) 03-3824. Rockville, MD: SAMHSA.

Substance Abuse and Mental Health Services Administration (SAMHSA). (2014). Results from the 2013 National Survey on Drug Use and Health: Summary of National Findings, NSDVH, Series H-48, HHS Publication Number 14-4863. Rockville, MD: SAMHSA.

Sundaram, V. (2015, September 6). Households headed by single elder African American and Latinos have highest proportion of hidden poverty. New America Media. Retrieved from http://newamericamedia.org

Suppes, M., & Wells, C. (2012). *The social work experience: An introduction to social work and social welfare* (6th Ed.). Boston, MA: Pearson.

Thorsteinsson, K., Andreasen, J., Mortensen, R., Kragholm, K., Torp-Pedersen, C., Gislason, G., et al. (2016). Longevity and admission to nursing home according to age after isolated coronary artery bypass surgery: A nationwide cohort study. *Interactive Cardiovascular and Thorack Surgery, 22*(6), 792–798.

Tinker, B. (2013, December 27). "Dementia village" inspires new care. Cable News Network (CNN). Retrieved from www.cnn.com

Triggle, N. (2016, February 1). Care homes and the NHS: The silent scandal? British Broadcasting Corporation (BBC). Retrieved from www.bbc.com

Tugend, A. (2013, July 27). Unemployed and older, and facing a jobless future. *New York Times*, p. B4.

UCLA Center for Health Policy Research. (2015, August). The hidden poor by age group. University of California-Los Angeles: Health Policy. Retrieved from www.healthpolicy.ucla.edu

United Nations. (1948). *Universal declaration of human rights.* New York, NY: United Nations.

United Nations (1999). *Principles for the older person.* Retrieved from www.un.org

Vaillant, G. (2002). *Aging well: Surprising guideposts to a happier life.* Boston: Little Brown.

van Wormer, K. (2017). *Human behavior and the social environment, micro level: Individuals and families.* New York, NY: Oxford University Press.

van Wormer, K., & Davis, D. R. (2018). *Addiction treatment: A strengths perspective* (4th ed.). Belmont, CA: Cengage.

Wacker, R. R., & Roberto, K. (2011). *Aging social policies: An international perspective.* Thousand Oaks, CA: Sage.

Walton, A. (1981, Spring). Youth is such a wonderful thing. *The Friendly Woman,5*(2), 8.

The White House Office (2016, February 1). Fact sheet: Investing in the National Cancer Moonshot. Washington, DC: The White House. Retrieved from www.whitehouse.gov

Williams, T. (1954). Cat on a hot tin roof. In T. Williams (Ed.), *The theatre of Tennessee Williams,* Vol. 3. New York, NY: New Directions.

Wong, E. (2013, July 3). A Chinese virtue is now the law. *New York Times,* p. A4.

Zastrow, C. (2013) *Introduction to social work and social welfare: Empowering people* (11th ed.). Belmont, CA: Brooks/Cole.

Zoroya, G. (2015, May22). People fulfill duty to parents. *USA Today*, p. 5A.

Zumbrun, J. (2014, August 18). The richer you are the older you'll get. *Wall Street Journal.* Retrieved from www.blogs.wsj.com

CHAPTER 12

# HEALTH CARE AS A HUMAN RIGHT

**MARTA VIDES SAADE**

> Everyone has the right to a standard of living adequate for the health and well-being of himself and of his family, including food, clothing, housing, and medical care and necessary social services, and the right to security in the event of unemployment, sickness, disability, widowhood, old age or other lack of livelihood in circumstances beyond his control.
>
> United Nations Universal Declaration of Human Rights, Article 25

> *El sol, el agua y el ejercicio conservan perfectamente la salud a las personas que gozan de una salud perfecta.*
>
> Translation: The sun, water, and exercise preserve the health of persons who enjoy perfect health.
>
> Noel Clarasó (Spanish Author)

This chapter considers health and access to health care not as a privilege but as a human right. The United Nations (UN) Declarations and Conventions, and other international and global provisions provide the theoretical framework for our discussion. Headlines from around the world provide an overview of contemporary issues. Challenges such as the Zika virus and mosquito borne illnesses, the effect of water sanitation on health, and the World Health Organization (WHO) concerns about antimicrobial resistance of a range of bacteria caused infections are highlighted. While we celebrate the victories of global collaboration in the eradication of health conditions affecting the quality of life for so many around the world such as the end of the guinea worm scourge, as well as alleviating unnecessary suffering, we also focus on the continuing global health needs, personal and political violence as a public health concern, and the threat to basic necessities, such as the lack of water. The impact of the Affordable Care Act (ACA) on caring for an ill parent is highlighted by a boxed reading that bridges personal with policy issues. Throughout the chapter, attention is paid to systemic health inequities, including disparities based on age, class, race, gender, sexual orientation and gender identity. Mental health care needs are addressed in the following chapter.

## HEALTH CARE AS A HUMAN RIGHT

The right to health as a human right was first recognized globally in the constitution of WHO that came into force on April 7, 1948, the anniversary now celebrated as World Health Day. In 1945, diplomats from around the world met to form the United Nations and one idea discussed was establishing a global health organization. From this idea WHO was formed. According to its Constitution, WHO (2017a) is established "for the purpose of cooperation among themselves and with others to promote and protect the health of all peoples" (1st paragraph). The agency was established under Article 57 of the Charter of the United Nations (WHO, Constitution, Preamble). Health is broadly defined as "the opportunity to live a healthy life." In addition to combatting infectious and noncommunicable diseases, WHO seeks to "ensure the safety of the air people breathe, the food they eat, the water they drink—and the medicines and vaccines they need" (WHO, 2017a, 2nd paragraph). It is now governed by The World Health Assembly headed by its Director-General. Among the current leadership priorities as defined by WHO are to: advance universal health coverage and end health care disparities, address challenges related to environmental factors, and respond to acute public health threats including from violence.

Although WHO, a United Nations organization is recognized as a policy-making body, it has little authority to require compliance, and its heavy dependence on funding from private sources, such as the Bill and Melinda Gates Foundation renders it susceptible to influence by outside donors in setting priorities (Harmer, 2012; WHO, 2015b). Nevertheless, WHO plays a vital role in improving the health of the world's people and in spreading knowledge based on the collection of data and the dissemination of research. With a medical staff of more than 7,000 people working in 150 country offices, WHO has its headquarters in Geneva, Switzerland and continues to promote the human right to health care (2017a; 2017b).

## THE UNIVERSAL DECLARATION OF HUMAN RIGHTS AND HEALTH CARE

Following the Second World War, the United Nations General Assembly adopted 30 articles as a global expression of the rights to which all human persons are entitled (see chapters 1 and 6). In some ways, the document was an extension of the "Four Freedoms" adopted by the Allies: freedom of speech, freedom of religion, freedom from fear, and freedom from want (United Nations Charter, 1945, Preamble and Article 55). Article 25 of the Universal Declaration of Human Rights (UDHR), as shown in the opening quote to this chapter, provides for the right to a standard of living adequate for health as well as the right to housing and medical care. In the United States, most of those standards relevant to physical and mental health are not legal entitlements, and although laws may protect certain populations, existing laws may also exclude persons as long as it's not done on the basis of race.

In 1990, following a long-standing criticism by various Muslim countries that the UDHR ignored the cultural and religious context of non-Western countries, the Cairo Declaration of Human Rights in Islam was adopted. This document provided for the right of all people "to live in a clean environment, away from vice and moral corruption" (Article 17, reprinted by Forced Migration, 2017).

In many economically developing countries, scarcity as well as the aftermath of war and internal conflict in which the basic infrastructure of a functioning society is destroyed or severely compromised, or where persons flee as refugees or are internally displaced, morbidity and mortality are caused by failure to meet basic human needs such as safe drinking water, sanitation, and food distribution. The result is malnutrition and the spread of infectious disease (Ruth & Sisco, 2015). Even in economically advanced countries there is sometimes scarcity and food insecurity as well.

At the International Federation of Social Workers (IFSW, 2016) General Meeting of 2016, the IFSW adopted a policy paper, "The Universal Right to Social Protection," including health concerns as part of social protection, recognizing that unexpected medical expenses plays a role in creating personal insecurity—such as the risk of loss of job, livelihood, habitation, and living. The IFSW cited WHO estimates that nearly 100 million persons fall into poverty every year due to unaffordable health care. Of particular concern to the IFSW are underprivileged and vulnerable groups. The IFSW views its recommendations, such as to promote wellbeing for all ages and to offer universal health care coverage, as consistent with United Nations Sustainable Development Goals.

Let us now consider global disease prevalence, needs, and priorities in health care, beginning with a listing of recent news headlines from around the world.

## GLOBAL DISEASE PREVALENCE AND HEALTH CARE NEEDS

Headlines from national and international services, and social media, call our attention to the world's health crises and the need for prioritizing economic investment in primary health services, education, and training of professionals to provide local solutions for global priorities such as prevention and early-state disease care:

- Drug-resistant TB rates in west Africa higher than previously thought (Boseley, 2016, *The Guardian*).
- There are now 234 pregnant women in the US with confirmed Zika virus (Hrala, 2016, *Science Alert*).
- The U.S. legacy in the malaria fight (Blumenfeld, 2016, *Malaria No More*).
- Why the Return of Polio to Nigeria is Such Bad News (Samuelson, 2016, Time magazine).
- Muslim world in denial about HIV spread: Expert (Ilyas, 2016, *Dawn*).
- American obesity in 2030: Most U.S. residents will be obese within two decades (Gates, 2012, *Huffington Post*).

The deadly communicable diseases in contemporary times are hepatitis, tuberculosis, malaria, and neglected tropical diseases that are often mosquito-borne. Half of those living with HIV are unaware of their infection and therefore do not receive necessary treatment and continue to spread the disease. Tuberculosis (TB) has felled 9.6 million people, and 1.5 million died of the illness (WHO, 2016a). Every year over 400,000 African children die of malaria. Viral hepatitis kills more than 1.4 million people each year. One billion people are infected with one or more tropical diseases. One in five children does not receive immunizations.

World attention has shifted now away from a focus on malaria eradication and to the deaths caused by Ebola to the Zika virus. This mosquito-borne virus was first detected in Africa in the 1940s and unknown in the Americas until May 2015 when it created widespread anxiety regarding the 2016 Summer Olympic Games to be held in Rio de Janeiro, Brazil. Case after case of mothers who had contracted the virus and given birth to infants with microcephaly was presented in graphic news reports. WHO estimates as many as 4 million people could have been infected (Coghlan, 2016).

The impact of the Zika virus is yet unknown, but what is certain is that 23 countries in the Americas have active virus transmission. A vaccine is not yet available, and the latest evidence is that in addition to a particular type of mosquito, the virus may be spread by blood and sexual contact. The lesson learned from the migration of the virus is that global health concerns are interconnected (Singer, 2016).

Global progress in control and eradication of these communicable diseases is largely a result of crisis response. Such a crisis response was directed toward the spread of HIV/AIDS in previous years with some success. The Centers for Disease Control and Prevention (CDC; 2014b) brings our attention to the following results of well-coordinated efforts: Over 15 million people living with HIV/AIDS are on lifesaving antiretroviral therapy, and since 2000, over 43 million lives have been saved with TB treatment. Regarding malaria, half the people at risk in Africa now sleep under an insecticide-treated bed net, and Hepatitis B vaccination has reached more than 80% of children worldwide.

Health crises that inspire rapid responses are those pandemics that give rise to the fear and horror of the catastrophic Black Death of 1348 which wiped out one-third of the population of Europe. Medical and scientific responses greatly reduce the effects of widespread death. Since the beginning of the AIDS pandemic in the 1980s, 78 million people have contracted HIV and 35 million, or .5% of the world's population, have died of AIDS-related causes. East and Southern Africa account for 46% of the global total of new infections. While the individual and regional impact is devastating, the reality is that as of 2015, 17 million people living with HIV, that is 46%, had access to antiretroviral medication (American Foundation for AIDS Research [AMFAR], 2016). AIDS, takes its greatest toll among young adults, the population least likely to be linked with medical care. In the United States, 1 in 5 new HIV diagnoses were of youth aged 13 to 24. For young gay and bisexual males, the rate of diagnosis is exceptionally high, and many do not know they are HIV positive. People aged 50 and over have the same risk factors as younger people, but may be unaware of their risk factors, and more likely to be diagnosed later in the course of the disease (CDC, 2015a).

More recently, Ebola, a similar virus, also transmitted through blood and bodily fluids, with high mortality rates and emerging from Africa raised fears of "the next AIDS." The difference between the diseases is the latency period, or incubation period during which people may spread the disease, through sexual activity or sharing of hypodermic needles, or blood transfusions, before symptoms emerge (Rettner, 2014). The symptoms of the hemorrhaging and fever are extreme and coincide with contagiousness.

Globally, a system of health care that includes preventive and elective health care is rare. Health concerns such as the rise of diabetes and obesity, the lack of access to essential medicines and education regarding diet, alcohol use and tobacco use, are more elusive to systemic resolution. For most people in the world, well-care is available to the wealthy, while the poor manage health crises through emergency care once the illness has become life threatening.

Take a look at vitamin deficiency, for example. According to WHO, vitamin A deficiency is the leading cause of preventable blindness in children, and also increases the risk of disease and death due to compromised immune systems. For pregnant women, vitamin A deficiency causes night blindness and increases the risk of maternal death (McCauley, van den Broek, Dou, & Othman, 2015). Attention to such preventable yet devastating risks has resulted in the near elimination of iodine deficiency once the world's most prevalent and preventable cause of brain damage (WHO, 2017c). Public attention is focused on communicable diseases such as HIV, Ebola, and Zika, and yet millions of children and adolescents live with or are affected by non-communicable diseases (NCDs), which are non-infectious diseases that cannot be spread person-to-person, such as cancer, cardiovascular disease, diabetes, mental disorders, and chronic respiratory diseases, such as asthma. Half of adult NCDs begin in childhood or adolescence. For children in low and middle-income countries inadequate access to medical care for diagnosis and treatment often results in long-term disabilities due to chronic conditions, or even premature death in adulthood. Prenatal care for the mothers often boosts disease prevention in the child as well (Global Health Council, 2016).

## WOMEN'S SPECIAL HEALTH ISSUES

The "weaponization" of HIV in armed conflicts throughout the globe raises serious human security or social protection issues in post-conflict societies. This phenomenon that includes sexual violence in the rape of women and young girls is global. It is as true of the Rwandan conflict during which an estimated 250,000 to 500,000 women and girls were raped, as in the ongoing conflicts in the Democratic Republic of the Congo and surrounding region, in the Liberian civil war of 1999 to 2003 when approximately 49% of women and girls experienced at least one military-related act of sexual violence, and in Sierra Leone where 64,000 women experienced war-related sexual violence. History and region does not limit this violence, such as in the Balkan conflicts of the 1990s, in Europe and Asia during WWII involving the German and Japanese army, respectively. The difference is the contemporary emergence of "willful" transmission of HIV to the victims, based on outcome as well as victim accounts. This has led to the "securitization" of HIV/AIDS by the United Nations Development Programme as of 1994, and ongoing attempts to gather statistics and build the needed post-conflict public health infrastructure needed (United Nations University, 2012).

In July 2010, the United Nations General Assembly created UN Women. UN Women is the United Nations for Gender Equality and the Empowerment of Women. Its formation was part of the UN reform agenda and demonstrated a commitment by member states to accelerate the UN goals for women's equality and empowerment through a coordination of resources and mandates that had previously been located in different offices and regions. UN Women works to develop a comprehensive plan to end early child and forced marriage, toward implementation of a ban against genital mutilation, as well as supporting service providers in shelters for women and girls who survive sex trafficking. In a speech at the Royal College of Nursing International Centenary Conference, Phumzile Mlambo-Ngcuka, UN Under-Secretary-General, and Executive Director of UN Women, emphasized the role of UN Women as a champion for women's rights and highlighted the role of women health professionals in responding to the Ebola pandemic (UN Women, 2016).

Globally, the risk of a child dying before completing the first year of life was highest in the WHO African Region: 55 deaths per 1,000 live births. In the WHO European Region that ratio was five times lower: 10 deaths per 1,000 births (WHO, 2016b). Maternal mortality is defined as the death of a woman during pregnancy, childbirth, or within 6 weeks after birth. Maternal deaths around the world dropped from 532,000 in 1990 to an estimated 303,000 in 2015. This constitutes a current ratio of maternal deaths per 100,000 live births of 216 to 100,000 compared to 385 to 100,000 in 1990 (WHO, 2015a).

This brings us to the subject of deaths due to unsafe abortions. Of the 21.6 million women who experience an unsafe abortion worldwide each year, 18.5 million of these occur in poor countries. Although the number of unsafe abortions has increased from 19.7 million in 2003, the rate remains at about 14 unsafe abortions per 1,000 women aged 15–44 years, primarily because the population of women of reproductive age has increased correspondingly. Worldwide, 47,000 women die from complications of unsafe abortion annually. These constitute 13% of all maternal deaths (WHO, 2008).

Because of the impact that contributions from the United States have on global health initiatives, its policies impact the quality of life for women around the world. The "Global Gag Rule" is an example of fluctuating policy that has such an impact. On and off since 1984, this policy applies to foreign aid organizations that provided abortion services preventing them from using US funds, or separately obtained non-US funds to inform the public or educate their government on the need to make safe abortion available, provide legal abortion services or provide advice on where to get an abortion (Center for Health and Gender Equality [CHANGE], 2016; Sherwood, 2015). First imposed by Reagan administrations, and sometimes called the "Mexico City policy" because it was announced at the UN International Conference on Population in that city, it was rescinded by President Clinton in 1993, then reinstated by President George W. Bush in 2001, and once again rescinded by President Obama in 2009 only to be revived again on the third day of the Trump Presidential administration (Sengupta, 2017). This time, Melinda Gates, as co-chair of the Bill & Melinda Gates Foundation stepped in to prioritize private foundation funding for contraceptives, and family planning worldwide as an anti-poverty strategy.

The challenge for a sustainable health care system is the need to provide careful planning that avoids unintended consequences, an approach that puts people ahead of profits, and adequate funding. Before we continue with the specifics of health care offerings, we explore various approaches to health.

## WAYS OF THINKING ABOUT HEALTH

The CDC (2014b) defines health as a "state of complete physical, mental, and social well-being and not just the absence of sickness or frailty." The CDC takes an integrative approach to health in that it considers prevention a health strategy that includes priorities such as tobacco free living, healthy eating, and reproductive and sexual health (CDC, 2014a). This approach is consistent with emerging trends in the United States to focus on health disparities, that is, the quality of health across racial, ethnic and socioeconomic groups, with emphases on health care across age transitions (Harris, 2010).

Individual approaches to health vary as do individual needs. Some persons prefer to manage their health in such a way that medical intervention is used to manage acute symptoms, or sometimes as a last resort. This could mean that instead of visiting a medical office first, a person experiencing some symptoms of disease would seek out a holistic healer. Holistic medicine, sometimes referred to as alternative medicine, considers the whole person: body, mind, spirit, emotions. The goal is to restore balance to maximize the natural healing capacity of the body, including the immune system. For example, if a person were experiencing migraine headaches, a holistic doctor might prescribe medication to alleviate symptoms that interfered with the patient's day-to-day activities, but would also consider other factors such as diet, sleep habits, stress, and personal problems, in order to develop a treatment plan that would include lifestyle modifications to help prevent recurrence of the headaches, as well as the medication to stop the immediate problem (Holistic Medicine, 2015a). A positive development in recent years related to diet is the growth of urban gardens and farmers' markets. See Figure 12.1 which shows an active farmers market in Iowa.

A well-care visit is defined as a medical visit for preventive care for a person with no disease or physical symptoms of immediate concern. It includes a review of a person's current health and medical history; counseling about ways to improve health; a physician examination tailored to a person's age and gender; includes necessary screening tests and immunizations. Medical visits may also include a consultation for specific medical conditions including disease care

**FIGURE 12.1.** When local farmers sell their produce directly to the people, they benefit as do people seeking a healthy diet with food straight from the farm. Photo by Robert van Wormer.

and management, as well as consultations regarding elective medical treatment (MedicineNet.com, 2016).

## VARIETIES OF HEALTH CARE OFFERINGS

Rehabilitative care is available when illness or injury leave a person unable to perform their usual skills and functions. For example, illness such as a stroke might require assistance for a patient to be able to walk or speak clearly, an injury to muscle or bone might require physical therapy to restore full movement, or an acute mental health need might require focused attention. Rehabilitative care, or "rehab" can be "short-term" or "long-term." Short-term rehabilitation is available on an out-patient basis that allows the patient to remain at home and either visit a rehabilitation center, or be visited by skilled therapists. Short-term rehabilitation, for a duration of about one month, is also available in-residence at the same places where long-term care is offered, such as, nursing homes, rehabilitation facilities, inpatient behavioral health facilities, and long-term chronic care hospitals (MedicineNet.com, 2016).

Long-term care is usually part of the range of services needed for elder care, sometimes referred to as senior care, because of cognitive impairment, or loss of muscular strength or control due to aging. It may be provided at home, in community service settings, or in facilities such as assisted living facilities, or nursing homes. Elder care includes rehabilitation services to help older people adjust to or overcome limitations that come with aging. Palliative care is a particular kind of medical care that focuses on quality of life treatment of persons living with chronic illness such as cancer, Parkinson's disease, or heart failure. This medical care deals with ameliorating of symptoms caused by treatment of the underlying disease, such as pain, nausea, loss of appetite, depression, or fatigue. Palliative care addresses the needs of the patient as well as the family and caretakers. Hospice care is palliative care offered to those with chronic illness who may have less than six months to live. Palliative care is considered a holistic approach (WebMD, 2015b).

## THE FINANCIAL SIDE OF MEDICAL CARE

Managing health care costs is complex both for individuals seeking health care, and the medical providers. For the patient, this contributes to the stress of any health care concern. Reform of health care is one of the major economic and political issues of the 21st century. Medical advances have increased the life expectancy of persons from 68 years for those born in 1950 to 78 years for those born in 2014 to the point the number of non-working older persons who need medical care is growing steadily. A person age 65 in 2014 has a life expectancy of 18 years—to age 83 years (CDC, 2016a). Doctors and hospitals struggle to find ways to close the gap between the cost of the business of health care and the ability of patients to pay. The unregulated cost of medications is causing an ethical crisis.

In the United States, 13% of the population, 40.3 million Americans are age 65 and older. That number is expected to double by 2050 to comprise 20% of the population. This reflects a similar increase globally. The corresponding decrease in a younger population has implications for the funding of government health care programs for the most vulnerable populations that in the United States depend on personal income tax funding (Demographics of Aging, 2016). Medical needs will shift accordingly. For example, in 2010, Alzheimer's-related death comprised 32% of all older adult deaths, or 600,000 persons. In 2050, this number is projected to be 43% of all older adult deaths, or 1.6 million persons (Weuve, 2014).

Here are six things we know for sure about the health care issues challenging the United States:

1. Nearly half the people who want medical insurance cannot obtain it due to its cost.
2. A rapidly aging population and a predicted increase in the need for Alzheimer's care must be addressed.
3. Depression is a growing and prevalent mental disorder in the United States and worldwide.
4. An unmet need exists for custodial care living arrangements for the aged, the disabled, and mentally ill.
5. Accidental drug overdoses due to opioid use problems are contributing to a lower life expectancy in the United States.
6. In 2015, he United States spent 16.9% of its Gross Domestic Product (GDP) on health care (Organization for Economic Cooperation and Development [OECD], 2017).The inefficiency is staggering when you consider that real per capita expenditures for health care grew 4.4% per year between 1950 and 2011, while the real GDP grew at an average of 2.4% per year. A gap of this magnitude is not sustainable going forward (Fuchs, 2013).

The rising cost of health care has created an urgent need for medical providers to find ways to provide health care access at an accessible cost. The United States leads the world in the percentage of Gross Domestic Product (GDP) spent on health care with 16% of GDP dollars spent yet this high cost does not correspond to better outcomes. The GDP is a measurement of a country's overall economic activity calculated by a formula that includes private consumption and government spending and a country's investment multiplied by its exports. In 2015, the United States is estimated to rank 30th in life expectancy of 79.3 years. Most developing countries spend less than 8% of their GDP on health, and many less than 5% (WHO 2016b). Switzerland, Japan, Germany Sweden, and France ranked second, third, fourth and fifth, and sixth, in the world in terms of percentage of GDP dollars spent on health care, at 11%, and had better health outcomes than that of the US (Organization for Economic Cooperation and Development [OECD], 2017). Let us look at how health care in the United States is financed.

In the 1990s, desperate to control costs, employers and their insurers worked to move people into health maintenance organizations (HMOs; Rosenthal, 2017). The idea was to provide services accessible to all those in the system at minimal cost yet providing a profit to both insurers and the HMOs. HMOs often received a fixed payment per patient per month. The result is a managed care system in which options for the individual consumers are limited by insurance companies, and selected by employers, which use in-house medical professionals to monitor delivery of health care services for cost-benefit to the companies. Managed care decisions often override physician recommendations either through approval or denial of costs for certain services, or a reduced level of reimbursement to physicians. Effects can include shortening hospital stays while depriving patients of certain treatments, denying referrals to specialists, and so on. Too short hospital stays, in the end, lead to multiple re-admittance for emergency treatment.

Only those patients with sufficient financial resources have full discretion regarding their health care decisions.

While the emphasis of managed care systems is preventive, most health care dollars are spent on five conditions: heart disease, cancer, mental disorders, trauma-related disorders, and chronic obstructive pulmonary disease (COPD)/asthma. The 10% sickest portion of the population accounts for 65% of health care costs (Agency for Healthcare Research and Quality, 2012). Critics of the current system have documented the consequences of an unnecessarily complex health care delivery system as including costly inefficiencies, an inability to manage deepening clinical knowledge, and the lack of a focus on clear patient needs (Institute of Medicine, 2013).

## THE ROLE OF PHARMACEUTICAL COMPANIES

According to industry advocates, advertising of available medications directly to patients is of value to patients and clinicians in making informed choices about available prescription medication for use in emerging clinical options. Advocates work with the Food and Drug Administration (FDA) to tailor regulations in order to be able to provide innovative medication. Nevertheless, marketing strategies can have unfortunate medical consequences resulting in overmedication of patients, pressures on physicians to prescribe inappropriate or useless medications that patients learned about on TV ads, and inflated costs of pharmaceutical products to pay for the advertisements (Rosenthal, 2017).

Because of the time delay between results of clinical trials and implementation of recommended protocols in clinical practice, Americans receive only half of the preventive, acute and chronic care recommended by clinical guidelines, and only 60% of recommended pharmaceutical treatments (Institute of Medicine, 2013). In addition to obstacles of availability due to lack of medical awareness, the high cost of prescription medication may present other problems. Managed care does not impose price controls or guidelines on pharmaceutical products. The price of medication, including emergency or life-sustaining medication, is subject to free market conditions. Companies hold ownership interest either directly through the patent itself, or through exclusive rights to license sale of the medicines. Accordingly, when Valeant Pharmaceuticals acquired the patents on two heart medications, Isuprel and Nitropress, in 2015, the company was able to immediately raise the price of Isuprel more than 500%, and Nitropress by 200%. The end result of such high charges is a steady increase in the cost of patient medical insurance premiums. Also in 2015, Turing Pharmaceuticals acquired the rights to Daraprim, a 62-year-old drug for a life-threatening parasitic infection, toxoplasmosis, used to treat patients with compromised immune systems due to AIDS, cancer, organ transplants, or pregnancy, and raised the price fiftyfold from $13.50 to $750 per pill (Pollack & Huetteman, 2016; Almendraia, 2015). In 2016, a group of high school students in Australia reproduced the drug for $20 per dose, yet sales rights belong to Turing (Hoffer, 2016). Around 2,000 Americans have the rare condition that this company is exploiting. And the same unethical practices—putting profits over people—such as those described here apply in situations affecting much larger segments of the population.

In 2016, Mylan Institute of Nevada increased the price of the allergy EpiPen, a life-saving dose of epinephrine prescribed to an estimated 3.6 million Americans per year to treat anaphylactic shock experienced as a result of allergic reactions, by 400%. Mylan CEO, Heather Bresch, is the daughter of Senator Joe Manchin, III, Democratic Senator for West Virginia, which gave the pharmaceutical company a great deal of political clout (Rockoff, 2016; Edney & House, 2016). The price increase came just as the drug's only competitor was taken off the market. A backlash ensued and the company was forced to back down (Egan, 2016).

## GOVERNMENT PROGRAMS

The federal government provides three major programs that make health care accessible to people for whom private managed health care is unavailable or prohibitively expensive: Medicaid, Medicare, and the Affordable Care Act (ACA). Medicaid, as was pointed out in chapter 8, is a public assistance program unlike Medicare, and one that is underfunded and stigmatized, but still a crucial program for people who could not otherwise afford health care and for nursing home residents who have exhausted their savings.

### MEDICAID

In 1965 the Social Security Act was amended to add the Medicaid program in Title 19, to establish federal financing to assist the states in providing health care to their low-income adult residents. The structure and financing of Medicaid has been adjusted over the years. Currently, the federal government provides matching funds to states through a state-federal partnership for administration Medicaid and its Children's Health Insurance Program (CHIP) which was established in 1997. The purpose of the CHIP program is to provide medical coverage for children from families who cannot afford private coverage but whose income is too high to qualify for Medicaid. The program, which is credited with helping to bring the rate of uninsured children to a record low of 4.5 percent, was placed in serious risk when the Republican-controlled Congress was slow to reauthorize the popular program (Itkowitz & Somashekhar, 2017).

Medicaid, which covers 64 million people, provides health coverage eligible low-income adults, children, pregnant women, older adults, and people with disabilities. When Medicaid and Medicare were first established in 1965, Medicaid was intended to provide health care for low income families and children, while Medicare was intended to provide health care for adults over age 65. However, due to the increase in this portion of the US population, and additional costs to each state for care, Medicaid funding has also been used to cover costs for assisted-living facilities and nursing-home care, as well as other costs not covered for elder care. Due in large part to the Deficit Reduction Act of 2005 as a legacy of the Bush administration, adult benefits were limited, coverage for children became subject to cost sharing, and care for living facilities for older adults became fraught with problems related to delays in payment and coverage. Instead of cost-savings to states and the federal government, low-income adults and children saw their preventive care reduced by nearly half when co-payments were required, thereby increasing the need for emergency and hospital and critical care and the corresponding funding of expenses for that care (Ambrosino et al., 2016). See Figure 12.2 which gives some idea of the expensive equipment used today in hospital treatment.

In 2016, mandatory Medicaid benefits that states are required to provide under federal law include inpatient and outpatient hospital services; early and periodic screening; diagnostic and

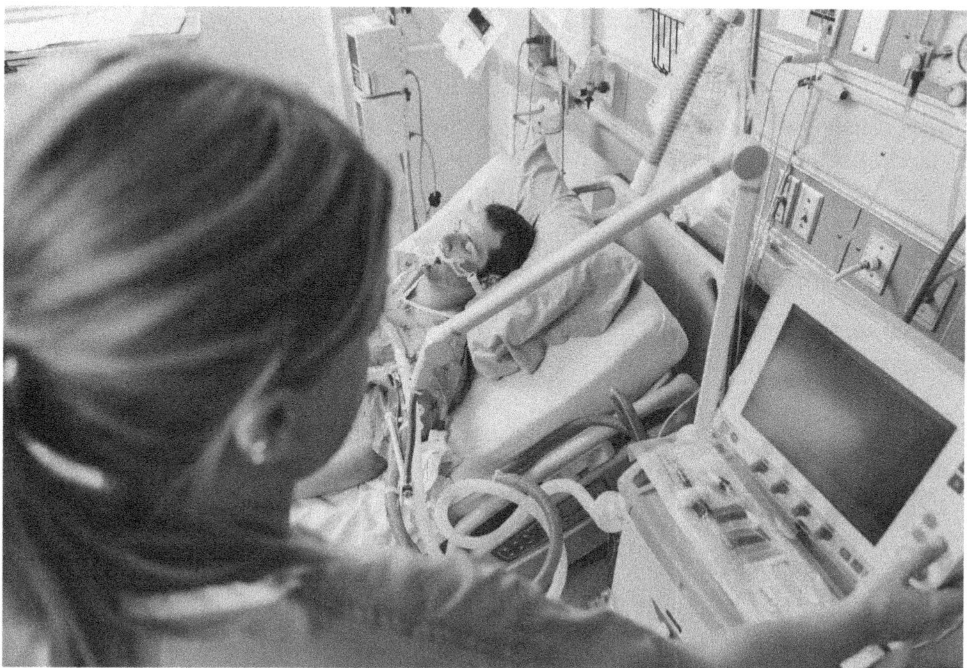

**FIGURE 12.2.** Nurse presses the monitor to check on patient: Consider all the technologies used in intensive care to keep this patient stable. © Shutterstock, Photo by Tyler Olson.

treatment services (EPSDT); nursing facility service; home health services; physician services; rural health clinic services; federally qualified health center services; laboratory and x-ray services; family planning services; nurse and midwife services; certified pediatric and family nurse practitioner services; freestanding birth center state licensed/recognized services; transportation to medical care; and tobacco cessation counseling for pregnant women.

## MEDICARE

In 1965 the Social Security Act was also amended to add the Medicare program in Title 20, to provide health insurance to people age 65 and older, regardless of income, or medical history, and who have worked for at least 10 years, and who have paid into the Social Security system, usually through wage deductions (see chapters 8 and 11). Medicare coverage for certain tests and procedures varies from place to place. However, there are a range of tests and procedures that are covered wherever a person lives, such as preventive services like yearly physical exams, yearly eye exams and eyeglasses or contact lenses, dental services, hearing exams, emergency services, EKG (electrocardiogram), shingles and other vaccines, flu shots, cardiac care, sleep apnea, obesity screening, mammograms, cervical and vaginal cancer screenings, prostate cancer screenings, surgery and second surgical opinions as well as diabetes screenings, depression screenings, and colorectal cancer screenings, and so on. Most treatment for diagnoses from such screenings is covered, such as chemotherapy, kidney dialysis and dialysis for children, diabetes management, kidney transplants for adults and children, mental health care, hospice and respite care, home health services, and more. Then there are some less conventional, almost holistic or alternative medicine, services covered such as nutrition therapy services, acupuncture, massage therapy, gym membership and fitness programs, religious non-medical health care institution (RNHCI) items and services, sleep study, and clinical research studies (Medicare.gov, 2016b). By now the overlap between Medicaid and Medicare coverage should be clear. People who require medical care accessible to them only through these government benefits must learn to navigate a maze of procedures. Medicare arranges its coverage in different parts: Part A Hospital Insurance, Part B Medical Insurance, Part C Medical Advantage Plans (MA) that are offered by private companies approved by Medicare to provide the same services as Medicare, and sometimes more, for which the private plan receives a fixed amount from Medicare and a premium payment from the customer, and a Part D Prescription Plan.

For people covered by Medicare, the biggest concern is the incomplete coverage. For example, considering long term care, if a person needs skilled nursing care, such as changing sterile dressings, that is covered whether in a hospital, long-term care facility or skilled nursing facility. But if a person needs assistance with activities of daily living, like bathing or dressing as part of recovery from illness or because of aging that counts as custodial care, and is not covered (Medicare.gov, 2016a).

## THE PASSAGE OF THE AFFORDABLE CARE ACT (ACA)

Enacted in 2010, the Patient Protection and Affordable Care Act (PPACA), is abbreviated to the Affordable Care Act (ACA) and informally referred to, sometimes pejoratively, as Obamacare in reference to President Barack Obama, under whose administration it was implemented. The ACA is the most recent comprehensive federal government health care reform that has been enacted in the United States.

Various models of health care reform have been discussed over the last two decades. Public health care programs that began in the early 20th century as a response to epidemics such as cholera, malaria and typhoid fever, or economic crises such as the Great Depression were expanded in the 1960s under President Lyndon Baines Johnson's "Great Society" programs of which Medicaid and Medicare are a legacy (van Wormer & Link, 2016). With the economic crises of the 21st century, came an urgent need for providing health care to people who had previously relied on their employment, or savings to cover health care costs. According to *The American Journal* of Medicine, research based on US census data, revealed that a total of 1.7 million Americans in 2009 were living in households at risk of bankruptcy (Himmelsteen, Thorne, Warren, & Woolhandler, 2009). A conservative estimate is that 57% of those bankruptcies could be attributed to medical debt (LaMontagne, 2014). These desperate times renewed efforts for a national health insurance program that protected those who needed medical care and were left jobless, or under-employed, and depleting savings for medical needs. Some advocates proposed a universal-access, single-payer system with national standards to eliminate the reliance on employment and to provide health care to people with prior existing medical conditions. The Medicare-for-all plan would have been far simpler since the mechanisms already existed and insurance companies played no role except in the optional coverage for prescription medication under Part D (Zhou & Mamula, 2017). But passage of a single-payer plan did not seem feasible at the time.

When President Obama introduced his initiative for health care reform, it was to include eight basic principles:

- Reduce long-term growth of health care costs for businesses and government.
- Protect families from bankruptcy or debt because of health care costs.
- Guarantee choice of doctors and health plans.
- Invest in prevention and wellness.
- Improve patient safety and quality care.
- Ensure affordable, high-quality health coverage for all Americans.
- Maintain coverage when you change or lose your job.
- End barriers to coverage for people with preexisting medical conditions.

(Ambrosino et al., 2016, p. 223)

Comment 14 of the International Covenant on Economic, Social and Cultural Rights (ICESR) provides specific implementation guidelines for the "right of everyone to the enjoyment of the highest attainable standard of physical and mental health" set forth in the ICESR. Specifically, Comment 14 sets forth the right to health care as having four essential elements: availability, accessibility, acceptability, and quality (McGill & McNaughton, 2016).

Although the ICESR was not ratified by the US, the guiding principles of the ACA coincide with the ICESR's key elements. The mission was for a national health insurance program to ensure affordable, high-quality health coverage for all Americans, and to do so "American Style" providing choice of doctors, plans and even the freedom to take employment without constraint as to whether medical insurance was provided.

The distinct features of the ACA that are most obvious to patient-consumers include choice of plans providing different cost and coverage options, a transparent "Health Insurance Marketplace" where persons are able to shop and compare plans, a provision allowing children up to age 26 to remain on a family plan under the ACA, coverage for children whose parents did not have available medical insurance either through employer, private or Medicaid, and coverage for all persons regardless of pre-existing conditions (Healthcare.gov, 2016). The requirement for all persons not otherwise insured to obtain health insurance through the ACA by 2014, or pay a fine, referred to as the individual mandate, was phased in. The penalty was challenged as an unconstitutional tax, although a sharply divided US Supreme Court rejected the merit of that challenge and upheld the individual mandate (*National Federation of Independent Business v. Sebelius*, 2012). Success retaining the individual mandate was crucial for the survival of the program as a method of keeping healthy people paying into the system. Realizing this fact, President Trump has made several attempts to remove the insurance mandate, a move that would have ripple effects on the ACA. At the same time, the ending of cost-sharing payments to the insurance companies to pay for premiums and deductibles has led to a major rise in insurance premiums (Alonso-Zaldivar, 2017). People eligible for coverage under the ACA plans include those who have no employer provided health insurance, and who do not otherwise qualify for Medicaid or Medicare. For persons already receiving coverage through Medicaid or Medicare, the advantages of the ACA are built in to the care already being received. For example, regarding Medicaid minimum eligibility was made standard nationally; the ACA benefits package became the benchmark for newly eligible Medicaid recipients; and some states expanded Medicaid coverage; technology systems were streamlined, and, states received 100% matching funds for increase in payments

(Medicaid.gov, 2016a). Medicare is not part of the Health Insurance Marketplace of the ACA, however, the ACA did add preventive services such as mammograms and colonoscopies for no Part B or deductible charges, plus a free "wellness" visit. Prescription discounts for brand-name medication were instituted. Finally, the Medicare Trust Fund is extended to at least 2029 based on cost savings, including those due to fraud and inefficiency (Medicare. gov, 2016a).

The plans available in the Health Insurance Marketplace are arranged by how cost is apportioned between the plan and the patient. In selecting a plan, the consumer must have a sense of how much they can pay for health care, as well as how much coverage they need based on individual and/or family needs. These categories are: Bronze, Silver, Gold, Platinum and Catastrophic. Certain benefits are required to be covered by all insurance plans listed in the marketplace. All categories include free preventive care. The required benefits include: ambulatory or outpatient services; emergency services; hospitalization; pregnancy-maternity-newborn care as well as birth control coverage and breastfeeding coverage; mental health and substance abuse disorder services—including counseling and psychotherapy; prescription drugs; rehabilitative and habilitative services and devices to assist people with injuries, disabilities or chronic conditions gain or recover mental and physical skills; laboratory services; preventive and wellness services including chronic disease management, and vision care for children. All the "metal levels" and catastrophic plans cover these health needs (Healthcare. gov, 2016).

The plan categories are sorted in order of highest contribution for cost of care paid by the consumer. For example, estimated as typical, the Plan/Consumer percentage split is as follows: Bronze 60/40, Silver 70/30, Gold 80/20, and Platinum 90/10. Under the least costly Bronze level plan, for example, with low premiums but high deductibles, insurance companies are required to cover 60 percent of individual's healthcare costs. Cost to the patient who is the consumer of the insurance plans comes in three basic forms: the monthly premium to be paid for coverage; plan deductibles which are the amount of medical costs the patient must pay before the insurance plan begins to pay; as well as co-payments which are a fixed payment coming out of the patient's pocket once the deductible has been reached, or coinsurance, which is a percentage amount after deductible is reached. Each state provides information about available insurance providers in that state. While all providers must be approved by the ACA administrator, some are listed in the federal marketplace exchange and often available across states. Others are listed on state-run exchanges for provider information. The health plan categories serve as a guide to thinking about how to shop. The silver category is the required pick for consumers who qualify for "extra savings" based on income and household size according to the standard set by the consumer state of residence. The gold plan is advisable for patients who require extensive medical care because although the premium is high, the deductibles are low, so the cost of care when the patient needs it is low. The Platinum plan premiums are higher than gold plans, as are the deductibles, but most all other costs are covered. Finally, the catastrophic plan is available only for people under 30 or those with a hardship exemption. It features a high deductible and only certain preventive care is covered. The patients pay for most routine care themselves. The 2016 deductible is $6,850. The premium tax credit is not available for this plan. Health and income influence much of the selection.

In addition to the distinctive provisions of the ACA, its notable impact on Medicaid, sometimes called the socialist part of the plan, provided an option for each state to expand Medicaid benefits to a new eligibility category. As originally drafted, the ACA would have required all states to expand Medicaid coverage to cover this uninsured group. However, a legal challenge allowed states to opt out and states with Republican governors often did so (*National Federation of Independent Business v. Sebelius*, 2012). At the start of 2016, 32 states and the District of Columbia had expanded Medicaid coverage resulting in a net savings of medical costs in hospital and emergency care due to the regular medical care available to the new population of insureds (Families USA, 2016). The ACA also permanently reauthorized the Indian Health Care Improvement Act which funds the Indian Health Service (IHS), and expanded health insurance for Native Americans through Medicaid and marketplace coverage. Data one year after the ACA indicates Medicaid is being used to supplement the cost of health care provision by IHS, not replacing it (Frean et al., 2016).

Each state responds differently to the public's need for affordable health care. According to a 2014 study, the states with the best return on investment for dollars spent on health are Minnesota, Utah, and Kansas, with Hawaii and Iowa tied for fourth (WalletHub, 2014). When comprehensive indicators are considered, Minnesota, Vermont, Hawaii, Massachusetts, Connecticut, New Hampshire and Rhode Island, are the top ranked health care states for quality of health care in both 2014 and 2015. Comprehensive factors include: access and affordability, prevention and treatment, avoidable hospital use and cost, healthy lives, and equity (Commonwealth Fund, 2015). Let's take a closer look at two states that are ranked in the top quartile--Minnesota and Hawaii.

The Minnesota Care program extends insurance to low-income residents, charging on a sliding-fee basis. Dental care and prescriptions are included. The program is funded by a tax on Minnesota hospitals and health care providers as well as state funding and participant premiums and cost sharing (Minnesota Department of Human Services, 2016). In 2015, Minnesota was the top ranked state in health care for healthy lives, measuring factors that affect people's ability to live long and healthy lives such as rates of smoking, premature death and obesity. If all states performed as well, there would be approximately 84,000 fewer premature deaths before age 75 for conditions that can be detected early and effectively treated with good follow-up care, and remarkably there would be nearly 8 million fewer adults, aged 18 to 64, who would lose six or more teeth to decay, infection, or gum disease (Commonwealth Fund, 2015). Significant factors contributing to edentulism include limited access to dental insurance, affordable dental services, community water fluoridation, and programs that support oral health prevention and education for older Americans are (Oral Health America, 2013).

Turning to Hawaii, where the right to health care uniquely is contained in the state constitution, Article IX, Section 1 provides for "the protection and promotion of public health." Article IX includes the power to implement care and social well-being of the vulnerable populations such as persons with special needs and frail older adults. It also includes living environment factors such as rehabilitation of substandard housing areas, and protects against burden on the environment (Hawaii Legislative Reference Bureau, 2016). In 2015, Hawaii was the top ranked state in health care for avoidable hospital use and costs of care. If all states performed as well, older adults who are Medicare beneficiaries would have over 1.4 million fewer emergency room visits for care that could be provided outside the emergency room, and children between 2 and 17 years of age would suffer about 85,000 fewer asthma-related hospital admissions.

Where you live matters. According to 2015 rankings, the best state to live for overall health is Minnesota, while the worst place to live is Mississippi (Commonwealth Fund, 2015). To appreciate the difficulty that individual states have in offering progressive health care programming, we need to recognize the impact of the fiscal crisis that continues to roil through state legislatures. When it comes to health care dollars, "blue states" do better than "red states" meaning when compared to 2012 Presidential election results, those states voting Democratic party do better than states voting Republican party (WalletHub, 2014). And while in a recent study California, and its newly recovering economy, ranked 25 overall, or in the second quartile, it is predicted to flourish with an ambitious health care system that insures more than 12 million poor Californians in partnership with Medicaid, due in part to California's high income taxes on wealthy residents, tough environmental regulations and high wages including a $10/hour 2016 minimum wage compared to the $7.25/hour federal minimum (Reich, 2016).

## CONTEMPORARY CHALLENGES

The contemporary challenge is the uncertainty of funding sources. As the Obama administration drew to a close, there were still many aspects of the ACA that needed to be ironed out. President Obama (2016) himself pointed to problems with the premium hikes by insurers in the marketplace and the effect on consumers, the need for additional state expansion of Medicaid to protect vulnerable populations, accountability regarding payment systems, and needed additional protections for those persons who still cannot afford insurance at the ACA rates. In addition, there was the need to increase the number of competitive providers in places where consumers had no choices. Finally, the issue of prescription drug costs remained to be addressed, including transparency of drug manufacturing production and development costs.

Despite the need for improvements, research shows that the passage of the ACA was a success in many ways. Since ACA Marketplace plans became available for enrollment in 2014, preliminary research of self-reports indicates gains in health coverage and access for low-income adults, particularly in states that expanded their Medicaid programs under the ACA. The number of people who reported they were unable to afford care fell by 5.5%. People who reported they were in fair or poor health dropped by 3.4% (Sommers et al., 2015). Uncertainty for the future of the ACA abounded in early 2017 as President Trump entered his term of office with plans to overhaul ACA and with the support of both houses of Congress controlled by conservatives, including many with extremist viewpoints. Holders of such right-wing conservative views promote free market economics and deregulation, privatization and a reduction in the size of any government-sponsored welfare programming. These views are not supportive of long-held, traditional economic safety net of which Medicaid, Medicare, Social Security, and the ACA are a part. In a report on the impact on hospitals of a repeal of the current ACA system, the American Hospital Administration and Federation of American Hospitals warned of dangerous and systemic disruptions that would occur if the suggested rapid changes were to occur. Insurers echoed the same warnings (Benen, 2016). A repeal of the ACA could see the return of lifetime caps on health insurance that was common in employer-provided health insurance.

A *Washington Post* article titled "Donald Trump Is about to Face a Rude Awakening Over Obamacare" argued that without the mandate to get the young and healthy into the system,

Trump's plan to retain the under-age 26 portion of the ACA and the requirement that insurance companies accept people with preexisting health conditions without restrictions cannot work. A good analogy is to imagine what would happen to car insurance if there was no mandate to pay into policies, and only persons in need of reimbursement, such as after a car crash, would enroll at that time (Pearlstein, 2016). Car insurance policies work because everyone is required to pay in, and the money collected helps pay the few who develop problems. The function of the individual mandate in regards to health care, in short, is to balance costs to insurers; if too few healthy people fail to pay in, the system will fail without strong government backing.

A *New York Times* article proclaims the accomplishments of President Obama in relation to health care which go beyond the personal level of adding of 20 million people to the health care rolls and toward a transformation of the system as a whole. This transformation, in fact, as Goodenough and Pear (2017) indicate, has a momentum that could prove impossible to stop. Under the ACA, health care started moving away from fee-for-service medicine toward preventive care, which now includes a focus on the health of patients in the community. And, in the words of Goodenough and Pear, "Social work has become a larger part of the medical mission" as collaboration among all health care professionals has become accepted as the best way to prevent reoccurrence of the illness.

The most successful accomplishment of the ACA was the liberal aspect, which expanded Medicaid as a government-centered program. When the Trump administration, under the leadership of Paul Ryan, Speaker of the House, tried to rush through the American Health Care Act of 2017 for House approval, which was designed to remove the Medicaid expansion in three years and impose surcharges based on age rather than income, he was forced to withdraw the bill due to a lack of votes (Pear, Kaplan, & Haberman, 2017).

When big social legislation gets passed and improves lives, as Leonhardt (2017) suggests, it becomes even harder to undo than it was to create. People who benefit by the program have a vested interest in seeing the program continue. Accordingly, as Leonhardt correctly indicates, the minimum wage, Social Security and Medicare aren't going away. And now Americans, for the first time, are beginning to see health care as more of a right than a privilege. Americans now think government should help guarantee coverage for just about everyone. A recent trend is that Democrats and some Republicans are beginning to look toward a cost-savings single payer system to provide health care directly from the government, and to cut out the insurance companies as middlemen.

Under the negativism of the Trump administration, bent on destroying the very part of the program that is consistent with neoliberal values and dependent on support from the insurance companies, the future of the ACA is problematic. Since 2016, several large commercial insurance companies ceased to offer insurance in the markets while other carriers scaled back on the number of counties they served. These counties, typically were in rural areas where the medical services were weak (Sanger-Katz, 2017). Without voluntary participation by the insurance companies, and without bailouts from the Trump administration, this part of the ACA, the privatized part, is likely to fail.

To grasp the personal significance of having access to affordable health insurance, read Box 12.1. The author today is a social worker and substance abuse specialist at People's Clinic in Waterloo, Iowa.

## BOX 12.1 What the Affordable Care Act Means to Me

Cynthia Kress, MSW

In 2013, I had a minimally invasive procedure done at Allen Hospital in Waterloo, Iowa. Though simple, it was expensive. I have United Health Care medical insurance, and like every other medical bill I have turned in to UHC, they paid it without dispute. My insurance is great. One week after my procedure, I received a thank you card from the doctor, staff, and hospital. While the card was very nice and professional, it made me angry as I compared the way that I was revered by the health care professionals at Allen Hospital to the way that my mother had been treated by the university hospital 2 years earlier.

My mother became ill with pancreatitis in 2011. At that time she had just opted to take an early retirement from her job as a licensed practical nurse, and she had no insurance. She was only 63 years old, and that is not old enough to qualify for Medicare or Medicaid. The staff at Allen Hospital were initially unable to care for my mother, as she was near death, so they sent her to the state university hospital in Iowa City. Mother was brought from the brink of death by a wonderful pancreatic specialist at Iowa City, but the road to recovery from pancreatitis is slow and extremely painful. Many relapses and readmissions ensued in the year after her initial hospitalization, each one terrifying and stressful for the entire family. My sister and I completed durable power of attorney papers regarding advanced directives for our mother and began to prepare ourselves for the worst. It was only after her doctor was confident that the treatment was working and that she was going to survive that he told us she had only been given about a 33% chance of living through it all. This was the event of my mother's lifetime. It was the most horrific and frightening thing she had ever experienced.

Despite our diligent efforts, my sisters and I were unable to sign mother up for Medicare or Medicaid to pay for her illness. She slipped through every crack in the system. She was approved for a program called Iowa Cares, which is sponsored by the university hospital in Iowa City. Iowa Cares is medical coverage for indigent persons in Iowa who are ill, and local hospitals do not accept it. This brought mother to Iowa City, 70 miles away from home, every time she was to be hospitalized with her chronic condition. We all took turns on our days off from school and work, driving the 70 miles to sit with our mother and oversee her care.

Our mother went from 140 pounds to a stark 97 pounds in a matter of months, due to the constant vomiting and diarrhea that pancreatitis caused. She had to be fed through a feeding tube through her nose. The university hospital repeatedly discharged my mother, stating that she would be vomiting no matter where she was, so she might as well be at home. Every time they discharged her to my care, I would end up bringing her back, because I lack the skills required to care for a person on a feeding tube when complications arise. Each time she would return, the staff would become more irritated with her, and one resident doctor even accused her of removing her feeding tube on purpose so she could return to the hospital to be professionally cared for (the tube had been pulled out while she was sleeping, as it was tangled in her arms). It was a constant battle to get her the care that she needed. At one point, while arguing with a doctor about releasing our mother before she was well, my sister said that she was going to talk to a lawyer about their refusal to care for our mother. They reluctantly provided her the care that she needed after that, but she was always afraid that the doctors were going to "kick her out" again, and she wanted one of her family members to be with her all of the time to fight for her. She did not have the energy to fight for herself.

In March of 2014, I applied to be my mother's consumer directed attendant care provider, through a program called Elderly Waiver. After our battle with the health care system, I was unwilling to trust any institution to care for my mother, so instead of a nursing home, my mother moved in with me. The application process was simple, and the Affordable Care Act made the program more expansive to include people like my mother who fall through the cracks of our country's health care system. The response was immediate, and she was instantly approved for full Medicaid benefits that paid for a wheelchair, diapers, a life alert system in our home, all of her medical bills, and a decent rate of pay for the at home care. It was like I was dreaming; nothing was difficult anymore, and everything was as it should be. I no longer worry about what is going to happen if my mother becomes ill again. I no longer worry about how I will take care of my mother when she needs more intense nursing than I am able to perform. I feel secure and I know that there will be no more fighting for proper medical attention for my mother. She is never turned away from local hospitals or referred to the Iowa cares program. My mother always receives prompt and professional care now for everything from eyeglasses, to the nebulizer that she had gone without for several months, because we could not afford to pay for it. I am confident that our medical system is being improved by the Affordable Care Act.

The Affordable Care Act helps people like my mother who desperately need medical care but have no insurance. People all over the United States have been fighting for proper medical attention for years, some of them going without, and even dying from lack of medical intervention. This is an inexcusable social injustice that most Americans are unaware of. I was unaware of it until it happened to my mother. Yes, there are some glitches, and I have read the stories about people actually losing their insurance because of the Affordable Care Act, and that is definitely inconvenient. However, I have witnessed the shambles that our nation's health care system was in before the Affordable Care Act was initiated, and it is without a doubt helping the people who it was designed to help, at this point.

*Source:* Published with permission of Cynthia Kress.

## WHEN PEOPLE LACK HEALTH INSURANCE

Even with the ACA, some vulnerable populations remain uninsured: undocumented immigrants—who are eligible for emergency services, Medicaid eligible persons not enrolled in Medicaid, people who pay the annual penalty instead of obtaining insurance—usually younger and single, persons who live in state that opt out of Medicaid expansion and earn an income too high to qualify for Medicaid yet too low to purchase insurance. Still, 46% of those not insured say they tried to get insurance but could not afford it (Kaiser Family Foundation, 2016).

For indigent adults, those too poor to pay for medical insurance yet not qualifying for Medicaid or Medicare, the Hill-Burton Act of 1946, as restructured in 1964, provides statewide and area-wide hospital planning to provide patient services to the poor. The Hill-Burton Act includes a provision that any hospital receiving funding through the Act cannot refuse to serve clients who are unable to pay for services. Due to the high demand created by lack of preventive services and adequate medical insurance for people just above the federal poverty level used for eligibility, hospitals have become overwhelmed with the demand leading to the notorious incidents of "patient-dumping." For this reason, later legislation allowed hospitals, referred to as "disproportionate-share hospitals," that were receiving more than their fair share of indigent patients, to be granted additional funds from Medicaid and Medicare to cover their costs (Ambrosino et al., 2016).

Despite this legislation, many hospitals have closed, especially in rural areas and especially in states such as Georgia and Mississippi that have failed to expand Medicaid. Accordingly, a geographical disparity exists regarding one's ability to access health care in emergency situations. Hospitals closures clearly have a life-or-death impact on patients. The situation has been described as a "perfect storm" when hospitals in rural areas are underfunded and then closed down (Families USA, 2016). Consider the situation in Stewart County in Georgia, a state that did not institute a Medicaid expansion, yet where most patients served are indigent and care must be provided by law. For patients who have suffered a heart attack, when treatment is urgently needed to prevent loss of heart muscle and brain tissue, access to the needed medical care was not possible. The emergency rooms had closed for economic reasons due to the large numbers of indigent patients they served. Two ambulances were the only access to the average 90-mile round trip to the nearest hospital (O'Donnell & Ungar, 2014). In another rural county in Georgia, a sick person became so violently ill during the long drive to a hospital that he had two strokes hours later. Another died of a heart attack as his family waited 15 minutes, while his wife and daughter performed CPR, for an ambulance to take him to a hospital 22 miles away. He lived 9 miles from the closed hospital.

## HEALTH CARE DISPARITIES

There are vast differences in the quality of health care treatment that patients receive based on characteristics related to race, ethnicity, geographical location, socio-economic status, lack of insurance, and even the physical trait of obesity. Research has shown, for example, that African Americans and Latinos are less likely than non-Hispanic whites to receive pain relief even when under a doctor's care. Latinos with broken limbs, for example, are twice as likely to go without pain medication during emergency room visits, and black cancer patients in nursing homes were 64% more likely than whites not to get such medication (Malveaux, 2003). This lack of professional awareness requires patients to be more vigilant. In 2008, Dr. Carmen Green, an anesthesiologist was still discussing the findings of her 2003 study stating that "There is nothing like pain to put people into poverty" (interviewed by Field, 2008). Her emphasis was that those with manual or labor intensive jobs are at higher risk for developing chronic pain problems yet their pain complaints get less attention. This ongoing disparity remains true over a decade since that study. In a study of emergency room patients from 2006–2010, results revealed that ethnic minority patients were likely to receive less pain medication for abdominal pain than white patients, and had longer stays in the emergency room due to longer wait times, and less likelihood to be admitted to the hospital for treatment (Shah et al., 2015). After accounting for differences in patient and hospital characteristics, findings were that overall white patients were 57% most likely to receive narcotic analgesic medication, compared to 53% for Hispanic patients, 51% for black patients, and 47% for those of other racial groups despite similar rates of severe pain reported.

We saw in our headlines in a previous section that in the United States, obesity is increasingly more common. Just as what some medical professionals see first, and perhaps overriding all other considerations, is race or ethnicity, some see obesity first, to the exclusion of other health considerations. Weight stigma undermines the opportunity for obese patients to receive effective medical care. The bias seems to be particularly cruel towards women, affecting both gynecological treatment and maternity care (Mulherin et al., 2013). This is due to negative stereotypes adopted by professionals such as the view that obese patients are lazy, lacking in self-discipline, dishonest, unintelligent, annoying, and noncompliant with treatment. Research shows that health care providers spend less appointment time and provide less health education with obese patients. And, patients report feeling disrespected, that their medical issues are not taken seriously because their weight is blamed for all their problems. The result is that obese patients seek less preventive care to avoid these experiences, and experience the psychological stress similar to that of minority patients who experience bias, including the physical cardiovascular stress that accompanies it. This treatment bias ignores research indicating that a considerable percentage of overweight and obese persons are metabolically healthy, and that non-overweight people can exhibit metabolic and cardiovascular risk factors. All weight conditions are heterogeneous (Puhl & Heuer, 2010). The health care industry has responded with a movement called Health at Every Size (HAES) that sets forth principles for inclusive treatment intended to eliminate bias that pathologizes weight (Association for Size Diversity and Health, 2016).

Shocking results on the impact of a nation's wealth inequality on health care, published by the British medical journal, *The Lancet*, found that wealthy Americans live up to 15 years longer than poor people (Dickman, Himmelstein, & Woolhandler, 2017). As the inequality gap in the United States has widened since 1970, so has the life expectancy gap between rich and poor. The medical researchers calculated that at the present time, the poorest women live 10.1 fewer years on average, while the poorest men live 14.6 fewer years. These findings are reminiscent of those from earlier research by Rowlingson (2011), which showed that countries with low income inequality such as Japan, Sweden, Norway, and Finland scored better than countries with unequal distribution such as the United States, Portugal and the United Kingdom. Income inequality, rather than the wealth of a nation was found to be correlated with indices of health such as life expectancy, infant mortality, obesity, mental illness, and addiction among other factors.

The belief that Americans needing treatment are helped regardless of ability to pay is a myth or that poor people without insurance still receive the lifesaving care they need. As former President George W. Bush once declared, "I mean, people have access to health care in America . . . after all, you just go to an emergency room" (Krugman, 2008). And we know from research conducted at Harvard Medical School and Cambridge Health Alliance, that uninsured working Americans have a 40% higher risk of death than privately insured working Americans (Cecere, 2009). Taking into account such factors as education, income and lifestyle factors such as smoking, drinking and obesity, the excess number of deaths attributed to lack of health insurance was 44,789. Researchers estimated that one American died every 12 minutes from lack of health insurance. This was the situation that existed before the ACA was passed.

## THE IMPACT OF RACE

Environmental racism is a term discussed in chapter 9 that is used to describe the situation in which marginalized racial and ethnic groups experience toxic chemical exposure that is beyond their control. Communities that have more political clout are not subject to the same toxic dumping or the presence of waste sites associated with a decline in air, water, and-or soil quality. African Americans and American Indians are the most affected in this regard. In 2014, black males and Native American males are the most disadvantaged, the former with a life expectancy of only 72 years the life expectancy for the former and 71 years for the latter (Indian Health Service, 2015). In contrast, a Latino male can be expected to reach 79.2 years, higher than White males at 76.5 years or Black males at 72 years. For women, the breakdown was similar: 84 years for Latina females, 81.1 years for White females, and 78.1 years for black females (CDC, 2016).

The health disparities between the American Indian and non-Indian population is pronounced. Death rates are significantly higher in many areas for Indians compared to the United States general population, including chronic liver disease and cirrhosis, diabetes mellitus, unintentional injuries, assault/homicide, intentional self-harm/suicide, and chronic lower respiratory disease (Indian Health Service, 2015). In fact, the gap between the indigenous peoples and non-indigenous groups in Australia (Aborigines) and New Zealand (Maori) is likewise revealed in life expectancy differentials. The gap between mainstream and Aboriginal peoples in Australia is 17 years, and among comparable groups in New Zealand it is 7–8 years (Pockett & Beddoe, 2017). Early in life as well, the risk of infant and child mortality is far higher in these marginalized populations than in the non-Native populations. This is true in the United States as well as in Australia and New Zealand.

The effect of exposure to health burdens is measured by the disability life-adjusted year (DALY) which measures both early death and the impact of pollution-related disease. In a study of industrial toxic exposure in the Global South, persons exposed to any of the 10 worst pollution chemicals, lost a DALY of 12.7 years—meaning 6.7 years with a serious disease, as well as dying six years earlier than without the environmental risk. Among those top ten toxic chemicals are lead and pesticides (Biello, 2011). In the United States, urban toxic waste sites are more often located in low income zip codes. Since 1965, hazardous waste facilities have been located in neighborhoods that were disproportionately minority at the time the facilities were sited (Bulalrd et al., 2011). All toxic waste sites are tracked by the US Department of Health and Human Services to determine the health effects of harmful exposures and diseases related to toxic substances (Agency for Toxic Substances and Disease Registry, 2016). From 1975 to 2000, incidence of cancer in children under 15 years increased by 31.7% nationwide, 29% in children under 20 years, an increase scientists attribute to environmental factors during a time of increased use, and ultimate dumping, of a wide range of industrial chemicals such as lead, chromium, arsenic, mercury, and polychlorinated biphenyls (PCBs) in residential areas that include homes and schools that have contaminated the soil, water, and air in poor communities. Exposure to such chemicals can result in neurobehavioral disorders and learning disabilities.

Access to sanitary water is a key component of good health. Worldwide, the death toll is high due to water-related illness. As revealed by the Water Project (2012), in poor countries in the world, about 80% of illnesses are linked to poor water and sanitation conditions. One out of every five deaths under the age of five worldwide is due to a water-related disease.

The problem of lead contamination in the drinking water and the health consequences to the children of Flint, Michigan was discussed in some depth in chapter 9. Lead is not the only danger to drinking water. On the Navajo Nation Reservation in Arizona, Utah, and New Mexico, a now bankrupt uranium mining company, Tronox Inc., has contaminated the drinking water throughout the Navajo Nation land because of abandoned mines. Radiation has seeped into the water, mud, and rocks used as building material. Research is clear that uranium contamination increases the risk of lung and bone cancers, as well as kidney damage. The company has been ordered to pay the US government and Navajo Nation $14.5 million dollars to address the clean-up. Water contamination from petrochemical exposure such as oil spills, pipeline burst, and fracking leaves a range of skin rashes and sores in children, a rise in cancer various types of cancer, as well as the psychological issues that come from economic collapse of a region (Gay et al., 2010).

Having clean air to breathe is equally important to one's health as having clean water to drink. And as is the case with water, children are especially vulnerable to exposure to toxicity. Asthma, which has reached epidemic proportions is especially prevalent among poor children in urban areas in the US. Its prevalence increased from 7.3% in 2001 to 8.4% in 2010. For the period 2008–2010, asthma prevalence was higher among children than adults and higher among multiple-race, black, and American Indian or Alaskan Native persons than white persons (CDC, 2015b). The asthmatic lung swelling and obstruction is a reaction to certain exposures including occupational chemicals, indoor irritants, and pesticides. Conditions commonly occurring in crowded living conditions such as infestations of cockroaches and their droppings together with the pesticides used indiscriminately in multiple-apartment dwellings to eliminate pests can trigger asthma attacks. Dust mites, mold, and pets are other indoor triggers (CDC, 2012). Air pollution such as tobacco smoke and vehicle exhaust are airborne triggers (Massey, 2004). Prevention means changing the living conditions for those who suffer from this condition.

## INADEQUACIES IN HEALTH INSURANCE COVERAGE

As brought out in Michael Moore's satirical 2007 documentary *Sicko,* having insurance coverage does not always guarantee receiving necessary treatment. Examples of denial of coverage included the case of one woman refused coverage for her emergency ambulance ride to the hospital for not clearing the expense in advance. *Sicko* compares the profit-driven health care system in the United States with government-run programs in France and Canada.

Even the US government–insured health care is no panacea because it does not provide complete coverage. A rapidly aging population is making the limitations clear. If persons 65 years or older living with Alzheimer's dementia have a life expectancy of 18 years, limitations in coverage for care will impact a greater number of individuals and families. Currently three levels of care, and the housing associated with it, are most often required for persons with Alzheimer's dementia: custodial care, intermediate care, and skilled care (AARP, 2016). Recall that custodial care is not covered by Medicare, leaving families to cope with the stress and financial burden of caregiving unless intermediate health services are required such as monitoring of blood pressure or blood sugar levels, or 24-hour skilled nursing care. Despite policy emphasis on prevention, coverage is more available for the less healthy—treatment wins out over prevention.

Likewise, people living with kidney failure as a result of other chronic health issues such as diabetes or hypertension face dramatic life choices. Consider, for example, the case of a

60-year old dialysis patient who was able to obtain a kidney transplant. She was completely happy until one day when she learned that after three years Medicare would no longer pay for her expensive medication necessary to sustain the transplant. As a result of this policy, patients often begin cutting back on their doses of medication that costs $15,000 per year, to extend their coverage, resulting in kidney rejection and a return to dialysis which is more costly at $90,000 per year. Some of the dilemma stems from an insurance company strategy classifying these drugs as "specialty drugs" and requiring higher co-pays. Another cause is lack of patient awareness that non-profits foundations are available to cover costs of these drugs for free (Harris, 2016).

## GRASSROOTS ADVOCACY

Efforts by communities to avoid these adverse health effects of petrochemical contamination, and to preserve their communities can be seen in the advocacy filmmaking of Josh Fox in *Gasland* I and II, about the extraction of natural gas from the Marcellus Shale in the Delaware River Basin through the use of hydraulic fracturing drilling (fracking) by Halliburton Corporations (Fox, 2013). Although the Environmental Protection Agency (EPA), finally, in late 2016, based on irrefutable evidence, declared that the process of injecting chemicals underground through fracking contributes to drinking water contamination, the anti-fracking activists face major challenges under the Trump administration, which has pledged to curb the authority of the EPA (Davenport, 2016). According to former EPA head, Christine Whitman (2017), President Trump's reduction in the EPA staff and funding proposals will reduce regulations protecting the air, soil, and water from pollution and endanger human lives. In response to the administration's attack on environmental protection and scientific research, in general, thousands of scientists, teachers, and their supporters participated in a March for Science was held in Washington, DC on Earth Day, 2017. Their call to stand up for science was echoed by protesters in hundreds of cities across the United States, Europe, and Asia (St. Fleur, 2017).

As described in chapter 9, one well-publicized grassroots action was the months-long campout resistance by the Standing Rock Sioux Nation against the construction of the Dakota pipeline. The construction will run through ancestral land including burial sites, and under Lake Oahe jeopardizing drinking water. The resistance movement rapidly gained broad support by indigenous people from all over the world, as well as from non-native people including a group of US armed forces veterans. The protesters, who called themselves, Water Protectors, based their claim to protect their ancestral lands on two human rights agreement—the UN Declaration of the Rights of Indigenous Peoples—and treaty rights to consultation with the federal government concerning ancestral land use. The nonviolent resistance, consisting primarily of prayer, was met with force by state police from various states after the Governor of North Dakota declared a state of emergency. Water protectors emphasized the risk of a pipe leak to the land and water. In response, in December, 2016, the Army Corps of Engineers halted construction until an environmental impact report could be completed (D'Angelo, 2016). One day later, a pipeline spilled 176,000 gallons of crude oil just 150 miles from the site of the Water Protectors (Ramirez, 2016). Water Protectors remained on the land through the harsh winter of 2016–2017 only to be forcibly removed under orders from the Trump administration as plans to restart the pipeline construction were under way (Eilperin & Dennis, 2017).

## IMPLICATIONS FOR SOCIAL WORK

Social workers play an important role in the delivery of health care. Their role is interdisciplinary and involves team work with medical staff as shown in Figure 12.3. Professional training including person-in-environment orientation, strengths-based, and empowerment perspectives provide an understanding of how social, emotional, economic and physical environments affect health. Social workers learn about life span development and are then able to work with all ages. Social workers work in places as diverse as community-based organizations and clinics, hospitals, schools, behavioral health programs, home health agencies, and day care for children and adult day health centers for adults (California Social Work Education Center [CALSWEC], 2011). Relevant to the call for social workers to draw on their social work imaginations, Pockett and Beddoe (2017) stress the importance for social workers in the health care field to develop a "health equality imagination." This involves thinking about health in terms of social impact and identity (for example, the changes in self-identity that accompany chronic disease and disability). Such a clinical approach derives from empathy in grasping the personal side of illness. A strengths perspective is invaluable in helping clients adjust to disability and illness.

Pockett and Beddoe further urge that medical social workers frame their practice within a holistic approach and recognize the impact of health inequalities on the lives of individuals,

**FIGURE 12.3.** To keep informed on the progress a hospital patient is making, the social worker will review the chart and consult with medical staff. Photo by Rupert van Wormer.

groups, and communities, and that they see health care as a domain for action, locally and nationally. This approach is consistent with the social work values of social justice and human rights.

According to the United States' NASW (2016) Standards for Social Work Practice in Health Care Settings, there are both challenges and opportunities facing social workers in medical settings today. The challenges come from the prevalence of supervision by persons from diverse disciplines who are under increasing pressure to reduce the costs of treatment, even at the expense of patient care. The opportunities come from the anticipated improvements from the ACA. According to the NASW-US, "To succeed, these models will rely on social workers skilled and competent in health care navigation, behavioral and mental health integration, chronic care management, and care coordination, among other skills" (p. 7). Time will tell if, under the Trump administration, these improvements will continue to be implemented.

## SUMMARY AND CONCLUSION

James Midgley's (2016) contrast between a market-centered or distorted approach to national development and a social development approach offers a conceptualization that is helpful in uniting many themes of this chapter. Societies that favor a social development approach direct economic policy efforts toward needy and vulnerable groups. Western European countries, for example, all offer universal health care as well as generous welfare programs and protections for persons with disabilities. Throughout the world, however, as we have seen in this chapter and chapter 5, distorted development is widespread, with one segment of the population increasing their access to the resources at the expense of the others.

The universal dilemma is whether the government should play a strong role, part benevolent and part coercive, in ensuring health care and housing for all, or whether nations would do better in focusing on economic investment and technological advancement in the belief that the market forces will ultimately take care of the needs of the people.

Drawing from data collected by WHO and the US Centers for Disease Control and Prevention (CDC) this chapter presented facts on global public health efforts to eradicate disease, data on epidemics and life expectancy rates internationally. From data provided by UN Women we considered the high death rates of women related to lack of reproductive and maternity care.

The United States has a long history of attempts to provide government-based, universal health care, matched by political forces favoring health care provisions through the private sector. Corporate interests have predominated, most strikingly through the influence of the pharmaceutical industry in controlling the drug market. This chapter showed how the Affordable Care Act (ACA) both represented the interests of corporate stakeholders in augmenting the role of insurance companies and of liberal forces in promoting the expansion of Medicaid in the states. The flaws in the system in comparison with much more cost-effective systems found in Western Europe and parts of Asia have become increasingly apparent.

From a human rights perspective, this chapter presented the case that health care is a right, not a privilege, a viewpoint that increasingly is gaining resonance among national leaders and the general populace. Inasmuch as out of crisis comes change it may be that unsuccessful efforts to fix the market-based health care that we have in the US will lead to more flexible ways of thinking. We see this trend in mental health and substance abuse treatment today. To this topic we now turn in the book's closing chapter.

## THOUGHT QUESTIONS

1. What are some of the basic health care priorities as listed by the World Health Organization? To what extent are these consistent with standards from the Universal Declaration of Human Rights?
2. Based on the assortment of headlines presented at the beginning of the chapter, analyze the state of global health. What are the major challenges?
3. What are some appropriate public health remedies to the Zika pandemic or other epidemics of which you are aware?
4. What does the unconscionable high rate of maternal mortality say about women's roles generally?
5. What is meant by the weaponization of AIDS? What does it say about health care needs of women?
6. Account for the political clout of the pharmaceutical companies. What can be done to control them?
7. Differentiate Medicaid from Medicare. Discuss the importance of the Medicaid expansion to states that adopted this program.
8. Discuss the possibility of extending Medicare (as a single-payer program) to all age groups. Which groups in the United States are most likely to resist such a development?
9. What is the history of the Affordable Care Act (ACA)? Discuss the basic levels of benefits that participants in the program can choose?
10. Describe the basic criticisms of the ACA. From media sources describe the Republicans' attempts to repeal and replace this initiative.
11. Describe a successful health care program adopted by Minnesota or Hawaii. To which factors do you attribute the program's success?
12. Using outside sources, relate the ascendancy of the extreme right Republican Party policies, sometimes referred to euphemistically as "Alt-Right" to universal health care.
13. Draw on facts and statistics to argue that there are health care disparities by race, ethnicity, and class. How best can these disparities be alleviated?
14. Can the United States be considered to have the best health care in the world? Why or why not?
15. What is the role of HMOs? Discuss the facts pertaining to various lobbying groups.
16. Consider some of the states' Medicaid expansion initiatives. What gaps remain?
17. How do race, class, and gender relate to the state of one's health? What do the statistics tell us?
18. Delineate the needs a social worker could fill for persons with disabilities.
19. Research health care offerings in a country with universal health care. What can the US learn from that country?

# REFERENCES

AARP. (2016, December 8). Care and housing options for people with dementia, AARP Medicare Plans. Retrieved from https://member.aarpmedicareplans.com/

Agency for Healthcare Research and Quality. (2012, November). Trends in healthcare costs and the concentration of medical expenditures, Slide 13. Retrieved from http://www.ahrq.gov

Agency for Toxic Substances and Disease Registry (ATSDR). (2016, July 25). Public health assessments & health consultation, Retrieved from https://www.atsdr.cdc.gov

Almendraia, A. (2015, September 23). What the daraprim price hike actually does to health care: A bracing reminder that jacking up drug prices is perfectly legal. *The Huffington Post.* Retrieved from http://www.huffingtonpost.com

Ambrosino, R., Ambrosino, R., & Heffernan J., & Shuttlesworth, G. (2016). *Introduction to social work and social welfare* (8th ed.). Belmont, CA: Brooks/Cole Empowerment Series.

American Foundation for AIDS Research (AMFAR). 2016. Statistics worldwide. http://www.amfar.org/worldwide-aids-stats/

Association for Size Diversity and Health (ASDAH). (2016). HAES principles, ASDAH, 2016. Retrieved from: https://sizediversityandhealth.org

Benen, S. (2016, December 7). Hospitals: GOP may create an 'unprecedented public health crisis.' *The Rachel Maddow Show/The Maddow Blog,* Retrieved from http://www.msnbc.com

Biello, D., (2011). World's 10 worst toxic pollution problems [slide show]. *Scientific American,* November 10, 2011. Retrieved from https://www.scientificamerican.com

Blumenfeld, J. (2016, July 25). The US legacy in the malaria fight. *Malaria No More.* Retrieved from https://www.malarianomore.org

Boseley, S. (2016, November 2). Drug-resistant TB rates in west Africa higher than previously thought. *The Guardian.* Retrieved from https://www.theguardian.com

California Social Work Education Center (CALSWEC). (2011). Social work's role in health care reform, summary. Retrieved from http://calswec.berkeley.edu

Cecere, D. (2009, September 17) New study finds 45,000 deaths annually linked to lack of health coverage. *Harvard Gazette.* Retrieved from http://news.harvard.edu

Center for Health and Gender Equity (CHANGE). (2016), Global gag rule. Retrieved from: http://www.genderhealth.org

Centers for Disease Control and Prevention (CDC). (2012, August 20). Common asthma triggers. Retrieved from: https://www.cdc.gov/asthma/triggers.html

Centers for Disease Control and Prevention (CDC). (2014a, January 17). National prevention strategy. America's plan for better health and wellness. Retrieved from https://www.cdc.gov/Features/PreventionStrategy

Centers for Disease Control and Prevention (CDC). (2014b, March 21). NCHHSTP social determinants of health. National Center for HIV/AIDS, Viral Hepatitis, STD, and TB. Retrieved from http://www.cdc.gov/nchhstp/socialdeterminants/definitions.html

Centers for Disease Control and Prevention (CDC). (2015a, April 15). HIV/AIDS—risk by age group. Retrieved from http://www.cdc.gov/hiv/group/age/index.html

Centers for Disease Control and Prevention (CDC). (2015b). Trends in asthma prevalence, health care use, and mortality in the United States, 2001–2010. Retrieved from: https://www.cdc.gov/nchs/data/databriefs/db94.htm

Centers for Disease Control and Prevention (CDC). (2016a). Health, United States, 2015, In brief, National Center for Health Statistics. Retrieved from: https://www.cdc.gov/nchs/data/hus/hus15_inbrief.pdf

Centers for Disease Control and Prevention (CDC). (2016b, June 13). Health, United States 2015. With special feature on racial and ethnic health disparities, National Center for Health Statistics. Retrieved from https://www.cdc.gov/nchs/hus/special.htm

Coghlan, A. (2016). 4 million at risk of Zika infection as El Niño increases spread. *New Scientist*. Retrieved from www.newscientist.com

Commonwealth Fund. (2015). Aiming higher: Results from a scorecard on state health system performance, 2015 Edition. Retrieved from http://www.commonwealthfund.org

D'Angelo, C., (2016, December 4). Army halts construction of Dakota Access Pipeline. *Huffington Post*. Retrieved from: http://www.huffingtonpost.com

Davenport, C. (2016, December 14). EPA shifts on fracking, citing harm to water. *NewYork Times*, p. A19.

Demographics of aging, Transgenerational.org (2016). Retrieved from: http://transgenerational.org/aging/demographics.htm

Dickman S. L., Himmelstein, D. U, & Woolhandler, S. (2017, April 8). Inequality and the health-care system in the United States. Series: America: equity and equality in health 1. *The Lancet, 389*, 1431–1441. Retrieved from http://www.thelancet.com/us-health

Edney A., & House, B., (2016, Aug 24). The senator's daughter who raised prices on the Epipen, Bloomberg Politics. Retrieved from https://www.bloomberg.com

Egan, M. (2016, Aug 29). How the Epipen came to symbolize corporate greed. *CNN Money, The Buzz*. Retrieved from: http://money.cnn.com

Eilperin, J., & Dennis, B. (2017, February 7). Trump administration to approve final permit for Dakota Access pipeline. *The Washington Post*.

Families USA. (2016, February). The voice for health care consumers. A 50-state look at Medicaid expansion. Retrieved from http://familiesusa.org/product/50-state-look-medicaid-expansion

Field, D. (2008). Disparities in pain management: An expert interview with Carmen R. Green, M.D. *Medscape*. Retrieved from: http://www.medscape.org/viewarticle/581003

Forced Migration. (2017). Full text of the Cairo Declaration of Human Rights in Islam. University of Oxford. Retrieved from www.fmreview.org

Fox, J. (Director) & Adlesic, T. (Producer). (2010). *Gasland: Can you light your water on fire?* United States: Home Box Office, An International Wow Company Production.

Fox, J. (Director) & Adlesic, T. (Producer). (2013). *Gasland Part II: The issues have reached new depths*. United States: Home Box Office, An International Wow Company Production.

Frean, M., Shelder, S., Rosenthal, M.B., Sequist, T.D., & Sommers, B.D. (2016). Health care reform and coverage changes among Native Americans. *Journal of the American Medicine. Internal Medicine, 176*(6), 858–860.

Fuchs, V. R. (2013). The gross domestic product and health care spending. *The New England Journal of Medicine, 369*,107–119.

Gates, S. (2012, September 18). American obesity in 2030: Most U.S. residents will be obese within two decades. *Huffington Post*. Retrieved from http://www.huffingtonpost.com

Gay, J., Shepherd, O., Thyden, M., & Whitman, M. (2010, Dec 15). The health effects of oil contamination: A compilation of research. Worcester Polytechnic Institute. Retrieved from https://web.wpi.edu

Global Health Council (GHA), (2016, June 23). GHC WHA statement on agenda item 12.4: Prevention and control of noncomunicable diseases. Retrieved from http://globalhealth.org

Goodenough, A., & Pear, R. (2017, January 3). After Obama, some health reforms may prove lasting. *New York Times*, p. A1.

Harmer, A. (2012, June 5). Global Health Policy.net, Who's funding WHO? Retrieved from http://www.globalhealthpolicy.net/?p=826

Harris, K. M. (2010). An integrative approach to health, *Demography, 47*(1), 1–22.

Harris, R. (2016, December 22). Medicare pays for a kidney transplant, but not the drugs to keep it viable. National Public Radio, Morning Edition. Retrieved from: http://www.npr.org

Hawaii Legislative Reference Bureau (2016, May 5). Bills passed by the Hawaii State Legislature of 2016. Honolulu: State Capitol. Retrieved from http://lrbhawaii.org/reports/legrpts/lrb/2016/passed16.pdf

Healthcare.gov. (2016). All topics. Retrieved from https://www.healthcare.gov/topics/

Himmelstein, D. U., Thorne, D., Warren, E., Woolhandler, S. (2009). Medical bankruptcy in the United States. Results of a national study. *The American Journal of Medicine, 122*(8), 741–746.

Hoffer, S. (2016, December 1).Some Teenagers Recreated Martin Shkreli's Crazy-Expensive Drug For $20. *Huffington Post.* Retrieved from http://www.huffingpost.com

Hrala, J. (2016, June 17). There are now 234 pregnant women in the US with confirmed Zika virus. *Science Alert.* Retrieved from: http://www.sciencealert.com

Ilyas, F. (2016, November 11). Muslim world in denial about HIV spreadExpert. Pakistan: Dawn. Retrieved from https://www.dawn.com/news/1295539

Karachi, Pakistan: *Dawn.* Retrieved from http://www.dawn.com/news

Indian Health Service. (2015, January). Fact sheets. Rockville, MD: US Department of Health and Human Services. Retrieved from https://www.ihs.gov/newsroom/factsheets/quicklook/

Institute of Medicine. (2013). Best care at lower cost: The path to continuously learning *Health care in America*, Washington DC: The National Academies Press. Retrieved from: http://www.nationalacademies.org

International Federation of Social Workers (IFSW). (2016, October 3), The role of social work in social protection systems: The universal right to social protection Adopted at IFSW General Meeting, Seoul, Korea. Retrieved from: http://ifsw.org

Itkowitz, C., & Somashekhar, S. (2017, November 23). States prepare to shut down children's health programs if Congress doesn't act. Washington Post. Retrieved from www.washingtonpost.com

Kaiser Family Foundation (KFF). (2016, September 29). Key facts about the uninsured population. Kaiser Family Foundation. Retrieved from http://kff.org

Krugman, P. (2008, April 11). Health care horror stories. *The New York Times*, Opinion Pages. Retrieved from http://www.nytimes.com

LaMontagne, C. (2014, October 8). Health finds medical bankruptcy accounts for majority of personal bankruptcies. NerdWallet.com. Retrieved from: https://www.nerdwallet.com

Leonhardt, D. (2017, March 28). Republicans for single-payer health care. *New York Times*, p. A27.

Malveaux, J. (2003, Oct 3). Racism holds painful legacy. *USA Today*, p. 20A.

Massey, R. (2004). Environmental justice: Income, race, and health. Global and Environment Institute, Tufts University. Retrieved from: http://www.ase.tufts.edu/gdae/education_materials/modules.html

McCauley, M. E., van den Broek, N., Dou, L., Othman, M. (2015). Vitamin A supplementation during pregnancy for maternal and newborn outcomes. *Cochrane Database of Systematic Reviews, 10.* Art. No.: CD008666. DOI: 10.1002/14651858.CD008666.pub3.

McGill, M., & MacNaughton, G. (2016). The struggle to achieve the human right to health care in the United States. *Southern California Interdisciplinary Law Journal, 25*, 625–685.

Medicaid.gov. (2016a, February 29). Availability of HITECH administrative matching funds to help professionals and hospitals eligible for Medicaid EHR incentive payments connect to other Medicaid providers. Retrieved from https://www.medicaid.gov

Medicaid.gov. (2016b). Medicaid and CHIP eligibility levels. Retrieved from: https://www.medicaid.gov

Medicaid.gov. (2016c) State Medicaid & CHIP Profiles, 2016. Retrieved from https://www.medicaid.gov

Medicare.gov. (2016a). The Affordable Care Act and Medicare. Retrieved at https://www.medicare.gov/about-us/affordable-care-act/affordable-care-act.html

Medicare.gov. (2016b). What Medicare covers. Retrieved from https://www.medicare.gov/what-medicare-covers/index.html

MedicineNet.com. 2016. Medical terms dictionary. Retrieved from http://www.medicinenet.com/medterms-medical-dictionary/article.htm

Midgley, J. (2016). Social welfare for a global era: International perspectives on policy and practice. Thousand Oaks, CA: Sage.

Minnesota Department of Human Services. (2016). *MinnesotaCare*. Retrieved from http://mn.gov

Mulherin, K., Miller, Y. D., Barlow, F. K., Diedrichs, P. C., & Thompson, R., (2013). Weight stigma in maternity care: Women's experiences and care providers' attitudes. *Biomedical Central (BMC) Pregnancy and Childbirth, 13*(19), 1471–2393.

National Association of Social Workers. (NASW). (2016). *NASW standards for social work practice in health care settings*. Washington, DC: NASW.

*National Federation of Independent Business v. Sebelius*. (2012). 567 US. ___ (2012), 132 S.Ct. 2566, 183 L. Ed. 2d 450.

Obama, B. (2016, July 11). United States health care reform progress to date and next Steps. *Journal of the American Medical Association*. Special Communication, Clinical Review and Education. Retrieved from http://jamanetwork.com

O'Donnell, J., & Ungar, L. (2014, November 12). Rural hospitals in critical condition: Rural hospitals serve many of society's most vulnerable. *USA Today*. Retrieved from http://www.usatoday.com

Oral Health America. (2013). State of decay: Are older Americans coming of age without oral healthcare? *Oral Health America*. Retrieved from http://www.dentistryiq.com

Organization for Economic Cooperation and Development (OECD). (2017). OECD. Stat Health expenditure and financing. Retrieved from http://stats.oecd.org/Index.aspx?DataSetCode=SHA

Pear R., Kaplan, T., & Haberman M. (2017, March 25). In major defeat for Trump push to repeal health law fails. *New York Times*, p. A1.

Pearlstein, S. (2016, November 12). Donald Trump is about to face a rude awakening over Obamacare. *Washington Post*. Retrieved from https://www.washingtonpost.com

Pockett, R., & Beddoe, L. (2017). Social work in health care: An international perspective. *International Social Work, 60*(1), 126–139.

Pollack, A., & Huetteman, E. (2016 February 4). Martin Shkreli invokes the Fifth Amendment during grilling by Congress. *New York Times*. Retrieved from: http://www.nytimes.com

Puhl, R., Heuer, C. A., (2010, June). Obesity stigma: Important considerations for public Health. *American Journal of Public Health, 100*(6), 1019–1028.

Ramirez, P. (2016, December 12). Standing Rock: Oil pipeline spills 176,000 gallons of crude oil 150 miles from protest site. *Inquisitor*. Retrieved from http://www.inquisitr.com

Reich R. (2016, November 23). Here is why Robert Reich thinks California will become a nation within a nation. *RawStory*. Retrieved from http://www.rawstory.com

Rettner, R. (2014). Could Ebola really be the 'Next AIDS'? *LiveScience*. http://www.livescience.com

Rockoff, J. D. (2016, August 24). Mylan faces scrutiny over Epipen price increases. *Wall Street Journal*. Retrieved from: http://www.wsj.com

Rosenthal, E. (2017). *An American sickness: How healthcare became big business and how you can take it back*. New York, NY: Penguin.

Rowlingson, K. (2011, September 22). Does income inequality cause health and social problems? York, England: Joseph Rowntree Foundation. Retrieved from https://www.jrf.org.uk

Ruth, B. J., & Sisco, S. (2015). The context of public health and human rights. In C. Franklin (Ed.), *Encyclopedia of social work*. New York, NY: OxfordUniversity Press. Retrieved from http://socialwork.oxfordre.com.

Samuelson, K. (2016, August 12). Why the return of polio to Nigeria is such bad news. *Time*. Retrieved from http://time.com/4450308/nigeria-polio-africa-who-vaccines/

Sanger-Katz, M. (2017, March 13). Obamacare choices could go from one to zero in some areas. *New York Times*. Retrieved from www.nytimes.com

Sengupta, S. (2017, January 24). Trump revives ban on foreign aid to groups that give abortion counseling. *New York Times*, p. A13.

Shah, A., Zogg, C. K., Zafar, S. N., Schneider, E. B., Cooper, L. A., Chapital, A. B., Peterson, S. M., . . . Haider, A. (2015). Analgesic access for acute abdominal pain in the emergency department among racial/ethnic minority patients: A nationwide examination. *Medical Care, 53*(12), 1000–1009.

Sherwood, J. (2015, January 19). Déjà rule: The health damaging consequences of reinstating the global gag rule in 2015. *Huffington Post*. Retrieved from www.huffingtonpost.com

Singer, T. (2016, February 17). What Ebola and HIV/AIDS can teach us about the Zika virus pandemic. Research. Retrieved from http://www.northeastern.edu/news

Sommers, B. D., Gunja, M. Z., & Finegold, K. (2015) Changes in self-reported insurance coverage, access to care, and health under the Affordable Care Act. *Journal of the American Medical Association, 314*(4), 366–374.

St. Fleur, N. (2017, April 22). Scientists, feeling under siege, march against Trump policies. *New York Times*. Retrieved from www.nytimes.com

United Nations University. (2012). Rape and HIV as weapons of war. Retrieved from http://unu.edu/publications/articles/rape-and-hiv-as-weapons-of-war.html

UN Women. (2016, June 23). Phumzile Mlambo-Ngcuka. Through the power of collaboration with health professionals we can make a life or death difference. Retrieved from: http://www.unwomen.org

van Wormer, K. S., & Link, R. J., (2016). *Social welfare policy for a sustainable future: The U.S. in global context*. Thousand Oaks, CA: Sage.

WalletHub. (2014, July 30). 2014's States with the best and worst health. *WalletHub*, Retrieved from: https://wallethub.com/edu/states-with-the-best-worst-health-roi/5247/

The Water Project. (2012). Improving health in Africa begins with water. Concord, New Hampshire. Retrieved from http://thewaterproject.org/health.asp

WebMD. (2015a, May 1). What is holistic medicine? May 1, 2015. Retrieved from: http://www.webmd.com

WebMD. (2015b, August 14). When is palliative care appropriate? Retrieved from http://www.webmd.com/palliative-care/when-is-palliative-care-appropriate

Weuve, J., Herbert, L. E., Scherr, P. A., & Evans, D. A.,(2014). Deaths in the United States among persons with Alzheimer's disease (2010–2050). *Journal of the Alzheimer's Association 10*(2), e40–e46.

Whitman, C. (2017, March 31). I ran George W. Bush's EPA—And Trump's cuts to the agency would endanger lives. *The Atlantic*. Retrieved from www.theatlantic.com

World Health Organization (WHO). (2008). Preventing unsafe abortion. Human Reproduction Programme, Sexual and Reproductive Health. Retrieved from http://www.who.int/reproductivehealth/topics/unsafe_abortion/magnitude/en/

World Health Organization. (2015a, November 12). Maternal deaths fell 44% since 1990—UN, Media Centre. Retrieved from http://www.who.int/mediacentre/news/releases/2015/maternal-mortality/en/

World Health Organization (WHO). (2015b). *Programme budget 2016–2017.* Retrieved from http://www.who.int/about/finances-acountability/budget

World Health Organization. (2016a).). Global health observatory (GHO) data (2016). Retrieved from: http://www.who.int/gho/en/

World Health Organization (WHO). (2016b). World Health Statistics 2016: Monitoring health for the SDGs Annex B: Tables of health statistics by country, WHO region and globally. Retrieved from http://www.who.int

World Health Organization (WHO). (2017a). About WHO. Refer to subsections: who we are, what we do; leadership priorities; constitution. Retrieved from http://www.who.int/about/en/

World Health Organization (WHO). (2017b) Human rights. Retrieved from http://www.who.int/topics/human_rights/en/

World Health Organization (WHO). (2017c). Iodine status worldwide. Retrieved from http://www.who.int/vmnis/iodine/status/en/

Zhou, A., & Mamula, K. (2017, November 23). Single-payer health care gains traction, local physician advocates. Pittsburgh, PA: Pittsburgh Post-Gazette. Retrieved from www.post-gazette.com

CHAPTER 13

# CARE FOR PERSONS WITH MENTAL AND PHYSICAL DISABILITIES

MARTA VIDES SAADE

> The purpose of the present Convention is to promote, protect and ensure the full and equal enjoyment of all human rights and fundamental freedoms by all persons with disabilities, and to promote respect for their inherent dignity.
>
> Persons with disabilities include those who have long-term physical, mental, intellectual or sensory impairments which in interaction with various barriers may hinder their full and effective participation in society on an equal basis with others.
>
> United Nations Convention on the Rights of Persons with Disabilities, Article 1

Physical and mental health care needs are addressed in this chapter in the context of current policy issues and human rights considerations. Unique to this chapter is a focus on treatment strategies from an empowerment perspective. Initial topics discussed are: the definition of disability provided by international conventions, use of non-pejorative terminology, and the impact of the Americans with Disabilities Act. Disability rights are discussed in terms of national developments in the U.S. culminating in the passage of the Americans with Disabilities Act.

The focus of the second portion of this chapter is on mental health care. Covered under this rubric is institutionalization in jails and prisons, homelessness, the availability of mental health care and addiction treatment. Next we turn to harm reduction strategies directed toward the opioid epidemic. An emphasis is placed on new technologies to save lives in the event of overdose and treatment based on trauma-informed care. As in other chapters of this book, a human rights theme provides a backdrop for the discussion. The chapter concludes with a view of how health care programs globally can inform future strategies for meeting challenges of health care in the United States. The boxed readings on disability care for children in Ecuador and substance abuse treatment needs of African Americans illustrate the impact that effective community outreach can have on individuals who receive the services.

## THE CONVENTION ON THE RIGHTS OF PERSONS WITH DISABILITIES

An ad hoc committee of the UN General Assembly established the United Nations Convention on the Rights of Persons with Disabilities and an Optional Protocol, which took effect on May 3, 2008. The intention was to establish a convention "to promote and protect the rights and dignity of persons with disabilities based on a holistic approach that integrated work in the fields of social development, human rights, and non-discrimination." (UN Office of Legal Affairs, 2016, first paragraph). The passage of the Convention by the United Nations followed decades of work by the United Nations to change attitudes and approaches to persons with disabilities. The basic protections provided to persons with disabilities include a range of contexts: health, education, employment, access to justice, personal security, independent living, and access to information. The Convention on disability rights is grounded in the Universal Declaration of Human Rights (UDHR), the Declaration on the Rights of Disabled Persons by the United Nations Office of the High Commissioner formulated in 1975, as well as in subsequent international agreements (UN, Declaration on the Rights of Persons with Disabilities, Preamble). The General Principles of the Convention on Disability Rights are contained in Article 3:

- Respect for inherent dignity, individual autonomy including the freedom to make one's own choices, and independence of persons
- Non-discrimination
- Full and effective participation and inclusion in society
- Respect for difference and acceptance of persons with disabilities as part of human diversity and humanity
- Equality of opportunity
- Accessibility
- Equality between men and women
- Respect for the evolving capacities of children with disabilities and respect for the right of children with disabilities to preserve their identities

The general obligations in Article 4 require the parties to the Convention on Disability Rights to adopt all appropriate legislative, administrative and other measures to implement that Convention, and to repeal or modify all existing laws and practices that discriminate against persons with disabilities. The obligations also include positive steps such as undertaking research, facilitating access to information, and training professional staff to protect these rights.

The United States signed but did not ratify this document. In 2012, the United States Senate fell six votes short of the two-thirds majority required for ratification (United Nations, Office of the High Commissioner, 2016). This is surprising since the United States is a leader in the implementation of laws requiring that public buildings be handicapped accessible as well as the passage of non-discrimination acts to protect the rights of persons with disabilities. See Figure 13.1 to appreciate the importance of accessible public events.

The 2009 United Nations Convention on the Rights of Persons with Disabilities does not explicitly define the term "disability" although its preamble recognizes disability as an "evolving concept" that takes place "between persons with impairments and attitudinal and environmental barriers" and hinders their full and equal participation in society. Additionally, Article 1 states that "(p)ersons with disabilities include those who have long-term physical, mental, intellectual or sensory impairments which in interaction with various barriers may hinder their full and effective participation in society on an equal basis with others" (UN, Division for Social Policy and Development, Disability, 2016). This definition is sometimes called a social definition of disability. Recall from our earlier discussion that the U.S. has not ratified this Convention.

Due to wars, birth defects, and poor health care, aging and an increase in chronic health conditions, disability is an ongoing problem worldwide. The International Classification of Functioning, Disability and Health (ICF) defines disability as an umbrella term of impairments, activity limitations and participation restrictions. Disability is the interaction between individuals with a health condition, such as cerebral palsy, Down syndrome, depression, and personal and environmental factors such as negative attitudes, in accessible transportation and public buildings, and limited social supports. Over a billion people, comprising 15% of the world's population have some form of disability. Article 25 of the UN Convention on the Rights

**FIGURE 13.1.** Once public places became accessible, people using wheelchairs could go many more places than before. Photo by Rupert van Wormer.

of Persons with Disabilities emphasizes the right of persons with disabilities to attain the highest standard of health care without discrimination.

## US NATIONAL LEGISLATION

In the United States, spurred by the Civil Rights movement in the 1950s and 1960s, a consciousness of injustice awakened persons with physical and mental disabilities. Such persons and their families began speaking out against and seeking legal action to end job discrimination, limited educational opportunities, and architectural barriers. Because of the body beautiful cult in the United States and the documented preference in hiring for those who are tall, slim, and physically fit, persons with disabilities have found it necessary to lobby for protection against job discrimination. In 1973, Congress passed the Vocational Rehabilitation Act, one section of which includes an affirmative action policy wherein employers who receive federal funds must demonstrate efforts to hire persons with disability. The Education for all Handicapped Children Act, enacted in 1975, mandated that education be open to all children. In other words, children with various mental and physical impairments were to be included in the schools, either in the mainstream, or accommodated.

In 1990, Congress passed the Americans with Disabilities Act (ADA). The act was intended as a comprehensive statute protecting disabled persons from discrimination in education, employment, and housing and applies to all public entities, as well as those private entities receiving public funds. In addition to the civil rights protection against discrimination, the ADA imposes an obligation for reasonable accommodations at school, work and in public places. When the ADA was first passed, its definition of what constituted a disability under the ADA was open-ended. Over time and case law interpretation, the definition was settled as including "those individuals with mental or physical impairments that substantially limit one or more major life activities." Until 2008, court decisions and amendments narrowly construed the meaning of mental or physical impairment to include conditions such as blindness—but not correctable sight problems, hearing impairment, mobility impairment, HIV infection, alcoholism, drug addiction, chronic fatigue, learning and intellectual disability, head injury and mental illness. At that time, the ADA Amendments Act (ADAAA) of 2008, encouraged a more inclusive definition to add previously excluded categories such as cancer, epilepsy, attention deficit hyperactivity disorder (ADHD) and other learning disabilities to protections required in public places and school. In October, 2016, the ADAAA expanded definition was added to employment protections. Major life activity includes seeing, hearing, walking, breathing, performance of minor tasks, caring for one's self, learning, speaking, or working—but not tasks related to the specific job-related requirements of a specialized job (Department of Justice [DOJ], 2016).

The legal definitions do not reflect the diversity with which the community protected by the ADAAA views itself. Professional definitions do provide a partial view of how society regards people with disabilities over time. For example, until 1961 people with mental disabilities were referred to medically and psychiatrically as feeble-minded, imbeciles, idiots, and mentally subnormal. In 1961, these terms were deemed pejorative, and the American Association on Mental Retardation adopted the term mental retardation in various subcategories to describe in its *Diagnostic and Statistical Manual for Mental Disorders* (DSM). That professional association changed its name to the American Association on Intellectual and Developmental Disabilities.

In 2013, in response to the activism by the parents of a child, Rosa Marcellino, an 8-year-old with Down Syndrome, who was taunted with the pejorative term "retard" until the bullying became too much, the term "intellectual disability" replaced "mental retardation" with the passing of Rosa's Law in 2010. The term became part of the DSM in 2013, as well as the WHO International Classification of Diseases, used by psychologists to categorize mental disorders (Harris., 2013).

Disability rights advocates do not view persons with physical or mental disabilities as in any way inferior to able-bodied persons. Terms such as differently abled, and temporarily able-bodied for the majority of us (in recognition of the fact that most of us will face disability at some point in our lives) are sometimes used in describing physical distinctions. Terms such as mentally challenged or intellectually disabled—which may be used to refer to autism and cerebral palsy, are preferred by some. Even these terms are sometimes considered demeaning because they privilege the non-disabled as the norm (Brown, 2013). The reference to the "person first" is a recommendation from the American Psychological Association (APA) style guide, to reduce bias in writing and referencing, that uses the name or pronoun of the person first, and the disability is identified but does not modify the person, for example, "Rosa, a person with Down Syndrome" (APA, 2009).

## CONFRONTING DISCRIMINATION

Negativism toward persons with physical blemishes harks way back to ancient history when infants seen as imperfect were eliminated one way or the other. Much later, "defective persons" were thrown in concentration camps in Nazi Germany for experimentation and extermination. In the present day, people, and especially children, with mental and physical disabilities or those who are obese are the butt of endless jokes and ridicule. Persons with disabilities, in short, still face discrimination, restrictions, and resentment. Parents of children with intellectual and developmental disabilities experience stress that affects the health of parents such as cardiovascular problems, immune deficiencies, and gastrointestinal problems (Midraq & Hodapp, 2010). Parents with disabilities are at heightened risk of losing custody of their children, often are denied the possibility of adopting, and women with disabilities may be denied fertility treatments (National Public Radio [NPR], 2012).

Before you read Box 13.1, consider the psychological pain and stigma experienced by children who look different because of physical deformity or injury. Consider also the remarkable changes that reparative surgery can bring to their lives. For a photo taken in Ecuador, see Figure 13.2.

Within the disability movement, a paradigm shift is evident. This shift is from a medical diagnostic perspective with a focus on limitations toward a more holistic approach. In *Rethinking Disability: Principles for Professional and Social Change*, DePoy and Gilson (2004) paved the way for social work to recognize persons with disabilities under the diversity rubric, to consider what they have to offer the world. Social workers with disabilities, have a great deal to offer themselves as role models and through conscious use of self. This fact is exemplified in the life and teachings of Augustina Naami. See Figure 13.1.

Augustina Naami (2015), a Ghanaian social worker, and a survivor of polio, describes the resilience of Ghanaian women with disabilities. From her own experience, she chronicles the logistical challenges of traveling in Ghana, the support of her family as an equal person worthy

## BOX 13.1 Cosmetic Surgery for Children with Disfigurement in Ecuador

by Maria Romero

My first trip to Ecuador was quite by chance. I was working in my job at a University Medical Center as a Trauma and Emergency Surgery Nurse Practitioner. One of my managers had been involved with an International Medical Organization, now called ReSurge. This organization provides cleft lip and palate repair and burn and hand reconstructive surgery for underserved areas in Ecuador as well as many other countries in South and Central America and Southeast Asia. The global surgery work of ReSurge, which is funded by private foundations, helps achieve the 2015 UN Sustainable Developmental Goals.

When one of the nurses cancelled her trip at the last minute due to a family emergency, I saw this as an opportunity of a lifetime. One of the things I had wanted to do after I completed my Nurse Practitioner program was to help provide medical care to underserved populations. I hoped to do this in the United States but now I had the opportunity to use my Spanish and serve a population that had so much less. I could secure the time off my job and luckily had a current passport. I had no idea what this adventure would be like and how it would change my life forever.

I arrived in Ecuador with a team of an anesthesiologist, two maxillofacial physicians, myself, a registered nurse, and an outreach coordinator who interacted with the sponsoring organization, Rostros Felices, and helped coordinate the flow of patients and their families, made sure the equipment arrived and passed through customs, and in this case also served as an interpreter. She was a liaison between families, physicians, hospital staff, and volunteers to assure everything went as seamlessly as possible. She was the social worker for our team.

The logistics involved were complicated. We brought some equipment that had to go through customs, and we had long wait times and heavy boxes to take to the hospital. Some of these would remain as donations to the local organization, Rostros Felices (happy smiles), which ReSurge works closely with. The founder of this organization is Dr. Jorge Palacios, a plastic surgeon who comes from a very humble background in one of the very same small towns they work in today.

The population of Ecuador is close to 16 million people. It is considered one of the most inequitable countries in Latin America when it comes to medical care. The incidence of burn injuries and cleft palate deformities is high. Many people live in such remote rural areas that they travel hundreds of miles to see the doctor or have an opportunity to be evaluated for surgery. In the United States, an adult needing cleft lip/palate surgery is unheard of, but in Ecuador I remember seeing adults that had never had this opportunity.

I remember speaking to a mother who walked many miles and traveled by bus just so her daughter would not grow up disfigured and ostracized by people. These children are not accepted in society and are often kept isolated for their whole lives.

We traveled more than 6 hours in "La Ponderosa," a small bus that Dr. Palacios acquired to transport his staff and all the surgical equipment we would need on our trip. The hospital we worked out of essentially closed their operating room to all elective surgeries for the three days we took over the rooms. The volunteers from the local Rotary Club were invaluable, as they would help with the paperwork, organize the patients, and provide food for all of us through the long, 10-hour days. They had also acquired donations of acetaminophen, ibuprofen, antibiotics, and vitamins that we would distribute to the patients and their families post-operatively. The shortage of equipment and lack of even a sink nearby to wash our hands was so foreign to me. Yet the gratitude displayed by families and patients was overwhelming. No matter how long these people would wait, they were always kind and grateful. The tears in their eyes when they would see the physical change on their baby's face was indescribable. The cleft palate surgery is done in stages so for some of these children their families would have to make another trek in the next year.

The burn patients would at times see immediate results. In Ecuador propane power is very common, along with open fires for cooking and heat, and burns are not uncommon in children and some adults. Unfortunately, the care they receive may be minimal, and although the burns heal, the contractures from scars are severe and may even limit the use of limbs or facial muscles. Yet I witnessed children who had been unable to use their arm or hand for almost their whole life who smiled so brightly, even in pain post–operatively, to know they would be like other children now.

This trip opened my eyes to many things. It reaffirmed my belief in human kindness and goodwill. Dr. Palacios and his staff gave so much of their time to this project. It was his passion and dedication that allowed this program to succeed. It also showed me that this passion was contagious, and by witnessing this act, people were motivated to be better, caring human beings. This program has continued to grow and the new generation of physicians in Ecuador working and learning side by side with Dr. Palacios are the future of better health care in their little part of the world. This reinforces the belief in me that if I can help make a difference in my environment, it can lead to a bigger change in the universe.

Source: Maria Romero, nurse practitioner, University of California-Davis.

of dignity and respect, in conjunction with the attitudinal challenges she encountered due to negative perceptions of others. Well aware of the cultural stigma of being a woman who was perceived of as incapable of fulfilling even the traditional woman's role as mother, wife, and sexual partner, as well as being disabled, Naami drew strength from her religious faith as well as from personal and professional support systems. In her MSW (masters of social work) program at the University of Chicago, Naami experienced the loneliness of life in a foreign country away from her home. But she overcame the obstacles she experienced and continued her earlier work in Ghana as part of non-profit group Action on Disability and Development (ADD) where she assisted women with disabilities through internationally funded entrepreneurial ventures and small businesses from seed money provided by ADD. Their pride in becoming economically independent and their roles as community leaders became the source of Naami's doctoral investigative work. See Naami's photograph at Figure 13.2.

**FIGURE 13.2.** During her teaching career at the University of Northern Iowa, Augustina (Tina) Naami shared her expertise on disability human rights with students and faculty. Photo of Augustina Naami. Permission of Augustina (Tina) Naami.

**FIGURE 13.3.** Ecuadoran mother and child born with a cleft palate. The child went to the clinic to receive corrective surgery. Photo permission by Dr. Jorge Palacios.

## OTHER PROMISING DEVELOPMENTS

Independent living is important in allowing persons with disabilities to live the life they choose. One promising piece of legislation was the New Freedom Initiative signed into law under the Bush administration in 2001 as a response to the decision of the United States Supreme Court in *Olmstead v. L.C* requiring state, local and federal governments to increase opportunities for persons with significant disabilities to live where they choose (Olmstead Rights, 2015). Under this law, funding is provided by the Department of Health and Human Services to assist local states and localities to implement alternatives for community living, educational programs, affordable housing, and personal assistance services in the home.

In the United States, the lack of affordable housing is a problem for persons with disabilities as well as for all low-income people. A 2014 study of housing affordability problems experienced by people with disabilities, found that approximately 4.9 million non-institutionalized Americans with disabilities who rely on federal monthly Supplemental Security Income (SSI) have average annual incomes of $8,995. Yet in 2014, the average rent for a one-bedroom apartment nationwide was $780 per month, equivalent to 104% of the average SSI income. Financial assistance for supportive housing through the U.S. Department of Housing and Urban Development (HUD) through Section 811 for low-income people with significant disabilities in which housing is typically integrated into larger affordable apartment buildings linked with voluntary supports and services.

Medicare, not only provides health care for persons over age 65, but also provides health insurance to eligible younger persons with disabilities as determined by Social Security, people with end stage renal disease (ESRD), and persons with amyotrophic lateral sclerosis (MLS) also known as Lou Gehrig's Disease (Medicare.gov, 2016). Many other diseases, however, are not covered by Medicare for persons under age 65.

Another social welfare option is HUD Section 8 housing available to low-income families, those over age 65, and people with disabilities, which allow persons to live in housing of their choice. Limited funding and high need, however, make the availability competitive and subject to long waiting lists. Over 850,000 people with intellectual or developmental disabilities live with an aging caregiver, age 60 or older, usually a parent or relative. Recall that Medicaid does not cover the expense for mere custodial care. As these caregivers continue to age and pass on, many of these adult children are at risk of institutionalization or homelessness due to the shortage of affordable housing and support services (The Arc, 2016). People with severe mental health disorders are especially vulnerable to homelessness as we discuss below.

## MENTAL HEALTH CARE

Mental health and mental illness exist along a continuum as do most human behaviors and states of being. As defined by WHO (2014), mental health is a state of well-being in which a person realizes his or her own abilities, and copes with the normal stresses of life, works productively and fruitfully, and is able to make a contribution to their community. It includes emotional, psychological, and social well-being. In the United States, only about 17% of adults are considered to be in a state of optimal mental health. The emerging research indicates that positive mental health is associated with improved physical health.

The US Department of Health and Human Services, defines mental illness as referring to all diagnosable mental disorders or health conditions characterized by alterations in thinking, mood, or behavior—or some combination of those, and associated with distress and/or impaired functioning. The most commonly occurring mental disorders are: anxiety disorders, autism, bipolar disorder, depression, dissociative disorders, psychosis, eating disorders, obsessive-compulsive disorder, posttraumatic stress disorder, schizoaffective disorder, and schizophrenia (National Alliance on Mental Illness [NAMI], 2016). Depression is the most common type of mental illness in the United States, affecting 26% of the adult population. By the year 2020, estimates are that depression will be the second leading cause of disability throughout the world, trailing only ischemic heart disease (Centers for Disease Control and Prevention [CDC], 2013).

Negative attitudes and beliefs about people with mental illness persist, especially among some minority groups. For example, a one study comparing Asian and European American attitudes about mental illness found that Asian Americans showed stronger negative attitudes about mental illness (Gaba, 2014) Asian Americans also explicitly expressed a greater desire for social distance from people who were mentally ill. And historical stereotypes that may be adaptive in some contexts, such as the strong black woman characterized by unflagging toughness, strength, self-reliance, and denial of self-needs, serve as a barrier to seeking mental health treatment. Racial discrimination like any form of discrimination is a source of pain and has general health consequences associated with stress. The additional burden of having to live with a mental disorder has been referred to as a double stigma.

Some of the effects of such stigma have been mitigated by the outspoken public figures and celebrities such as Chiara de Blasio, the daughter of New York Mayor Bill de Blasio, who spoke openly of her mood disorder (Friedman, 2014) or the late actress, Carrie Fisher, who openly discussed her bipolar disorder and substance use problems (Kennedy, 2010). The struggles of the late Senator Ted Kennedy's family with addiction and mental illness are described in compelling detail by the son, Patrick J. Kennedy (2015), himself a top national leader in mental health advocacy. Taken together, such candid and moving stories allow persons with mental illness to feel less isolated and misunderstood.

Mental illness affects one in five adults in America. A disproportionately high burden from mental disorders exists in communities of color. Some of this unmet need is the result of access to mental health care and/or the lack of availability of culturally or linguistically appropriate services.

Advances in psychotropic medicine have made it easier in many ways for social workers and other professionals to help clients with mental illness by referring them to psychiatrists and by monitoring their use of the prescribed medication. Worldwide, it is not always feasible to prescribe medication, however, and the World Health Organization (WHO) (2016b) recommends an alternative form of holistic treatment that can be applied where the need is most pronounced. Called Problem Management Plus (PM+), this behavioral intervention is designed for treating depression, anxiety, and post-traumatic stress in global conflict-afflicted areas. The initial project in Pakistan used a master trainer who worked first with local mental health specialists who in turn trained lay workers to deal with persons suffering disabling psychological stress and after three months the intervention group showed less anxiety and depression than a control group.

Sometimes organic problems related to mental and physical health stem from stressful life situations, loneliness, and/or a sense of meaninglessness. The death rate, accordingly, may be high in such populations. We can consider, for example, the shocking statistics that approximately 20 veterans commit suicide each day (Shane & Kime, 2016). Then there are the "deaths of despair" as documented in a new report from the Brookings Papers on Economic Activity (Case & Deaton, 2017, p. 3). A combination of unemployment, drug overdose, suicide, and alcohol misuse is taking the lives of white working class Americans in unprecedented numbers even as Medicare offerings for this population have improved. This brings us to a closer look at treatment issues related to substance use disorders or addiction.

Box 13.2 describes mental health issues of special relevance to the African American population. This narrative also shows the importance of empathy when working with persons with mental disorders.

## BOX 13.2 Mental Health Disorders in the African American Community

by Dave Avery

I am an African American male, living in Boston, Massachusetts. As a Licensed Mental Health Counselor and current CEO of a Mental Health/Substance Abuse Clinic which provides services predominantly to people of color, I am acutely aware of the impact that mental illness and substance abuse is having on the African American community.

Mental illness is not new to the African American Community, whose roots precede slavery. However, mental illness was most likely exacerbated by the brutality of slavery, resulting in what we know today as post-traumatic stress disorder (PTSD). Currently, there is a similar brutality imposed on communities of color resulting from police brutality, black on black crime, and socioeconomic disparities.

Inclusive of PTSD, persons who originate from the African Diaspora are impacted by a multitude of mental health issues that are disproportionately different than their white counterparts. According to the US Health & Human Services Office of Minority Health (2017):

- Adult Black/African Americans are 20% more likely to report serious psychological distress than adult whites.
- Adult Black/African Americans living below poverty are three times more likely to report serious psychological distress than those living above poverty.
- Adult Black/African Americans are more likely to have feelings of sadness, hopelessness, and worthlessness than are adult whites.
- And while Black/African Americans are less likely than white people to die from suicide as teenagers, Black/African Americans teenagers are more likely to attempt suicide than are white teenagers (8.3% vs. 6.2%).

Being aware of these differences leads us to client empathy. Being empathic is extremely important if one plans to work with communities of color. One of the main reasons I pursued a career in mental health counseling was the result of an experience that I had involving a complete lack of empathy, which I witnessed while working as a housekeeper at Boston State Hospital. At the time, Boston State Hospital was one of two inpatient mental health/substance abuse treatment facilities located in the City of Boston.

Late one evening while I was cleaning out an office in the main lobby I heard a loud banging on the main glass door. The banging was so loud that the glass seemed like it was going to shatter. The psychologist on duty hid in his office. In fact he did not walk to his office he ran. When I went to the door there stood an older black female crying incessantly for help. She was obviously in emotional pain and in need of services, but the psychologist was so scared he never came out of his office. I felt this women's pain and I consoled her until she stopped crying. When she was stable she thanked me with a sincerity that pierced my heart. She later left the hospital and returned back to her home. Eventually, after the women left, the psychologist came out of his office and scampered to his car, which was parked nearby.

I never forgot this incident! As a result, I decided I was going to make a career choice where I could make a difference in the lives of others, particularly those individuals who were going through difficult times. I wanted to be there to let them know that someone cared!

REFERENCE

US Health & Human Services Office of Minority Health. (2017, February.) *Mental Health & African Americans*. Retrieved from https://minorityhealth.hhs.gov/omh/browse.aspx?lvl=4&lvlid=24

Source: Dave Avery, licensed mental health counselor, Boston, MA.

## MEETING TREATMENT NEEDS

The disparity between countries of the Global South where between 35% and 50% of people with mental disorders received treatment compared to between 76% and 85% in nations of the Global North makes the point that, once again, where you live matters (WHO, 2016a). And yet, treatment needs in nations such as the United States still often go unmet. The fragmented managed care system has been less adequate for mental health care than for general health care.

The ACA Marketplace Plans were required to cover mental health and substance abuse services as essential health benefits. Like general health coverage, these plans were to provide coverage regardless of pre-existing mental health conditions or substance abuse disorders without a lifetime dollar limit on coverage of what are considered essential health benefits. In addition, while plans were required to provide "parity" between coverage of medical and surgical benefits as compared to mental health and substance abuse coverage. What this means is that limits applied to mental health and substance abuse services cannot be more restrictive than limits applied to medical and surgical services. This applies to financial limits such as deductibles, copayments, coinsurance and out-of-pocket limits as well as treatment limits as to number of days or visits covered, or care management such as authorization required for treatment (HealthCare.gov, 2016). The ACA expansion has implications for employer plans as well requiring that most individual as well as large and small employer health insurance plans, cover mental health and substance use disorder services, as well as rehabilitative and habilitative services that help support persons with behavioral challenges. Because of the 2008 Mental Health Parity and Addiction Equity Act, expanding mental health and substance use disorder benefits, an estimated 62 million Americans are entitled to such coverage. Parity with general health also means most health plans must now cover preventive services such as depression screening for adults, and behavioral assessments for children on the same terms as general health preventive services. Finally, Medicaid and Medicare coverage has also been expanded to cover mental health treatment (mentalhealth.gov, 2014).

For persons with co-occurring disorders (addiction plus severe mental illness), lack of access to treatment can be a cause of homelessness as a person's mental state decompensates. Homelessness, in turn, can exacerbate the mental disorder as well as substance use and can also make access to treatment challenging. Now we take a closer look at the problem of homelessness among people with serious mental disorders.

## HOMELESSNESS AMONG PERSONS WITH SEVERE MENTAL HEALTH DISORDERS

Health care and housing can be construed, in short, as two interlocked forms of social welfare. People without shelter are unhealthy people, physically and mentally—health problems, such as foot infections, pneumonia, tuberculosis, and hepatitis C are common (Schiff, 2015). And many of those who live on the streets resort to substance use to cope with the stress, and they join other persons whose mental health and addictive disorders have led them to lose their homes. Housing provides protection against the elements, from communicable disease, injuries, and exposure to external violence and theft of one's goods, thereby reducing psychological and social stresses to a minimum. Just as health and adequate housing are inextricably linked, so also is safe and sanitary housing essential to one's emotional well-being.

As stated in the previous section, the right to adequate housing is one of the basic rights as enshrined in international law (see Article 25 of the Universal Declaration of Human Rights). For persons with mental health disorders, who are among the nation's more marginalized and vulnerable adults, having a safe place to live is primary. And yet, for an individual with a severe mental health disorder, homelessness is a high risk.

A recent survey of 22 cities found that 29% of homeless adults were severely mentally disabled and 22% were physically disabled. For unaccompanied adults, mental illness was cited as one of the top three causes of homelessness by 40% of the cities. For families with children, mental illness was cited as among the top three causes of homelessness by 20% of the cities. Mental illness was cited as a primary cause by 10% of the cities surveyed (U.S. Conference of Mayors, 2015). This disparity between single persons and families is likely the result of efforts over the past decade to ameliorate the effects of homelessness on families.

In 2008 survey by the United States Conference of Mayor, 20% of cities listed better coordination with mental health service providers as one of the top three items needed to combat homelessness. While most people with severe mental illness are willing to accept treatment and services, outreach efforts are more successful when workers establish a trusting relationship through continued contact with the people they are helping (National Coalition for the

Homeless, 2012). For people with mental disorders who are unemployed and lacking family care, supportive services are a necessity. Access to financial and medical help can be obtained through such services, limited though they are by inadequate funding at the national and local levels.

Transitional clinics that have replaced hospitals, as well as hospital emergency rooms, already are strained financially and become the dumping ground for these persons (Szabo, 2016). Three-quarters of emergency physicians report they see at least one patient per shift who requires hospitalization for psychiatric treatment. And, 21% say they have patients waiting two to five days for in-patient beds who were essentially "boarded" in the emergency room. Only 16.9% reported having a psychiatrist on call to respond to psychiatric emergencies (American College of Emergency Physicians, 2016).

Comprehensive treatment is not available in overcrowded emergency rooms with the end result that the psychologically acting-out individual is likely to end up in jail. People having a mental health crisis, in fact, are more likely to encounter police than health care workers. This is where the criminalization of mental illness begins. In local jails, across the nation, 75% of incarcerated women and 63% of incarcerated men have diagnosable mental disorders. In state prisons, where people are incarcerated for terms longer than one year, 73% of the women and 55% of the men were similarly diagnosed (James & Glaze, 2006). The largest mental health center in the United States is Cook County Jail in Chicago, Illinois, where on a single day, up to 60% of the jail population can be persons with mental illness. Cook County Sheriff Dart says he has no choice but to accept persons with schizophrenia, bipolar disorders, and depressive and psychotic symptoms who are delivered there by local police. Although some persons who are mentally ill commit serious crimes, the majority are arrested for crimes that flow from their mental illness (Kristof, 2014). Jails and prisons use restrictive housing to isolate persons until they can be appropriately assessed and classified for housing, or isolate those who need protection from other persons in the facility, or have violated facilities' rules. Restrictive housing generally means no contact with other inmates and little face to face contact with guards, and less time outside a cell. Among incarcerated persons with mental illness or with symptoms of psychological distress, 29% of those in prison, and 22% of those in jail had spent time in restriction as shown in a survey by the US Department of Justice (DOJ). Compare this to the restrictive housing of persons with no symptoms at the rate of 15% in both prisons and jails. Add to this disparity the fact that extended time in restrictive housing has been demonstrated to trigger symptoms of psychological distress (DOJ, 2015). The Federal Bureau of Prisons houses approximately 120,000 persons, including those in private contract facilities it supervises. Given the potential for a negative psychological outcome of solitary confinement, the Bureau recommended that seriously ill inmates be moved to alternative units (Office of the Inspector General, 2015).

The decades of reduced access to mental health care—from deinstitutionalization of the 1970s to Reagan's omnibus legislation of 1981 which shifted responsibility to the states and therefore to managed care—have contributed to the treatment crisis of today. The original plan to provide adequate public funding for well-integrated community mental health services for the newly deinstitutionalized persons never materialized (Suppes & Wells, 2012). The end result is that jails and prisons have now become the new mental asylums. And many of the jail and prison inmates have been convicted of problems related to crimes related to substance misuse.

## THE PLAGUE OF SUBSTANCE USE DISORDERS

Substance use disorder is included as a particular kind of mental disorder in the diagnosis contained in the *Diagnostic and Statistical Manual of Mental Disorders* (DSM) of the American Psychiatric Association (APA, 2013). The DSM no longer uses the terms substance abuse or substance dependence, but rather refers to substance use disorders in terms of mild, moderate, or severe. The older terminology still appears in the ACA, insurance literature, and treatment centers, however, and in popular usage. Substance use disorders are viewed today not in either/or terms but as existing along a continuum. A substance use disorder is characterized as the recurrent use of alcohol and/or drugs associated with significant impairment, such as health problems, disability, and failure to meet major responsibilities at work, school, or home. Diagnosis is based on evidence of impaired control, social impairment, risky use, and pharmacological criteria. The most common substance use disorders in the United States are related to use of alcohol, tobacco, prescription opioids, cannabis, stimulant prescription drugs such as amphetamines, methamphetamine and cocaine, hallucinogens, and overuse of pain medication (Substance Abuse and Mental Health Services Administration [SAMHSA], 2015). All these substances have legal restrictions on their use whether it is age restrictions of alcohol and tobacco, federal legal restriction as to prescription and nonprescription use under the Controlled Substances Act, or through law enforcement.

While a punitive approach is still taken toward illicit drug use, one encouraging trend is the decriminalization of marijuana and even legalization of the drug in a number of states, both for medical and recreational use. Even when decriminalized by a state, certain state legal use restrictions apply. The federal government has been inconsistent in the enforcement of the federal Controlled Substance Act which classifies cannabis as a Schedule 1 drug, not legal for any use.

The drug epidemic that has the nation most concerned is the epidemic of opioid misuse that is sweeping across middle class, suburban neighborhoods. While American doctors have been able to prescribe morphine and other generic opioid painkillers since the early 20th century, the aggressive marketing by companies such as Purdue Pharma, which patented OxyContin in the mid-1990s, is something new. This marketing of the drug to doctors and patients has generated $35 billion revenue, and contributed to opioid addiction first among patients who began use of the drug for legitimate pain management, and then among young persons who began using and selling the drug (Levitz, 2016).

In 2016 over 64,000 people died of drug overdoses, the large majority involving prescription medication—opioids—while a high percentage are also attributed to heroin overdoses, as people who are addicted turn to the streets for a cheaper and more accessible supply (American Society of Addiction Medicine [ASAM], 2016; National Institute on Drug Abuse [NIDA] (2017). The sharpest increase has occurred among deaths related to fentanyl—the most powerful form of opioids, responsible for over 20,000 overdose deaths. To put the death toll in perspective, consider that more Americans now die every year from drug overdoses than they do in motor vehicle crashes (Botticelli, 2016). In fact, the death toll from opioid overdoses is sufficiently high to affect the life expectancy rate in the United States which actually declined for the first time in decades (Bernstein, 2016). President Trump declared the opioid crisis a health emergency (Davis, 2017). Among the questions left unanswered by the president's announcement was whether special funding would be provided and whether the Department of Health and Human Services will use its authority under the public health declaration to negotiate lower prices for naloxone, a drug that immediately counteracts the effects of opioid overdoses. The complicity of giant pharmaceutical companies, wholesalers and pharmacists makes the need to regulate these corporations essential in controlling prescription drug misuse. Consider that in West Virginia where the demand was great, drug firms poured 780 million painkillers into the area despite the publicized rise in overdose deaths. In one West Virginia town of only 392 people, out-of-state drug companies had shipped nearly 9 million hydrocodone pills to a single pharmacy, and no once seemed to notice (Eyre, 2016).

## MENTAL HEALTH COURTS AND DRUG COURTS

A promising innovation, that began as a grass-roots legal movement, is the development of mental health and drug courts. Mental health courts are set up to handle misdemeanor offenses committed by persons with severe mental disorders. Each client appearing before such a court must have a case manager involved in conjunction with judicial oversight. The government's goal is to reduce the incarceration rate and recidivism rate among offenders, by providing persons who are out of touch with reality and/or in need of anti-psychotic medication and perhaps a supervised housing arrangement with the help they need.

Presently, there are over 300 mental health courts nationwide from the original four courts in 1997. Mental health courts receive training and technical assistance from the Council of State Governments (Justice Center, 2016). Since social work is the leading profession providing mental health treatment, clinical social workers play an active role in the administration and provision of services. Drug courts are similarly based on a comprehensive model set up to deal with criminal offenders, juvenile offenders, and parents with pending child welfare cases who have alcohol or other substance use problems affecting the resolution of their cases.

There are currently over 3,000 drug courts nationwide. The courts provide a setting for deciding whether the person who is otherwise facing punitive measures may be diverted to a program for treatment and rehabilitation instead. The courtroom atmosphere is non-adversarial and includes judges, prosecutors, defense attorneys, community corrections, social workers and treatment professionals. Community support is encouraged, and individual successes are celebrated by the court and its workers as well as by all the other persons who are participating in the program (National Institute of Justice [NIJ], 2016). Both innovations owe much of their acceptance and success to the growing movement of restorative justice and therapeutic justice principles applied to the legal system to make it more inclusive of all stakeholders and a more healing, less punitive process.

## HARM REDUCTION STRATEGIES

The opioid epidemic has been addressed in two ways by public officials. The first approach was to urge a cut-back in medical prescriptions for the addictive drug along with the keeping of records on persons prescribed oxycodone and other opioid medications. The second was the promotion of the wide availability of the antidote drug Narcan (naloxone) which is used to revive people who are in an unconscious state from an overdose (Associated Press, 2017). Many lives are now being saved through this harm reduction practice.

Although we applaud these recent developments in harm reduction policies to save lives, we can't overlook the sharp contrast between the present-day approaches to this drug crisis and the government's earlier response to the crack cocaine epidemic. When the nation's long-standing "war on drugs" was focused on poor, predominantly black urban areas, the legal response was zero tolerance criminalization. Now that young and older whites are dying, suburban and rural families seek an approach that would treat use as a disease not a crime (Seeyle, 2015).

"Never clean the water until you get the pigs out of the creek." This traditional Iowa saying describes the philosophy of harm reduction in a nutshell. Harm reduction, is a pragmatic, public health approach to control the risks of unhealthy practices by teaching safer forms of behavior. Harm reduction is to substance use what preventive medicine is to health care. Typical examples are: immunization efforts to halt the spread of disease, sex education in the school system, and birth control clinics to prevent unwanted pregnancy. Such public health approaches are widely accepted practices. At the educational level, Head Start for pre-school age children, and at the nutritional level, food stamps and the Special Supplemental Food Program for Women, Infants, and Children (WIC) are other harm reduction initiatives.

Harm reduction exemplifies the social work value base and our professional commitment to social justice and human rights (Abbott, 2010; Watson, 2015). As advocated by Cayce Watson (2015), this approach is built around social work's values of respect for human dignity, social justice, and client self-determination. Additionally, she notes the parallel between social work practice and harm reduction in collaboration with clients in working toward treatment goals and seeking strengths-based options amid adversity. Watson cites the NASW-US *Standards for Social Work Practice with Clients with Substance Use Disorders* which maintains, "The harm reduction approach is consistent with the social work value of self-determination and 'meeting the client where the client is'" (NASW, 2013, pp. 7–8).

Harm reduction strategies are based on knowledge from research concerning treatment effectiveness of an approach geared to the client's level of motivation for change. The harm reduction model is commonly contrasted with the traditional, confrontational approach to chemical dependency treatment.

Although social work and the harm reduction approach are more highly integrated in Canada and Europe than in the United States, we have seen some promising developments in recent years. NASW (2015), for instance, in its policy statement handbook, endorses a comprehensive public health approach for the prevention of alcohol, tobacco, and other drug problems. It also endorses "harm reduction approaches and alternatives to incarceration" for persons affected by such problems (p. 297).

Ann Abbott (2010) urges a best practices approach to intervention. Harm reduction, as Abbott indicates, exemplifies the underlying social work value base and our professional commitment to social justice and human rights. Harm reduction and its treatment intervention counterpart, motivational interviewing (a person-centered approach), strives to meet the client where the client is and take it from there. When mental illness or drug addiction is manifested, social workers want to ensure that clients receive the least restrictive treatment available. The NASW (2015) policy statement on alcohol, tobacco, and other drugs makes a strong case that substance use is a public health problem and therefore that the focus should be on prevention in addition to treatment.

In 2016, the city of San Francisco launched the Department of Homelessness and Supportive Housing with the goal of bringing 8,000 people out of homelessness over the next four years. One of the innovative ideas being considered is the use of stackable or modular housing units to house individuals and families, but the city is waiting to secure funding before it can partner with Panoramic Interests, which is proposing similar projects throughout the San Francisco Bay Area. In Los Angeles, California, a nonprofit American Family Housing built an apartment building out of recycled shipping containers to house 15 homeless veterans (Larson, 2016).

Methadone maintenance is another popular harm reduction program. Under this program, qualified physicians at methadone clinics provide doses of a synthetic replacement drug for heroin to heroin addicts as a way to prevent illicit drug use. Europe, consistent with a philosophy of pragmatism, has established a more comprehensive harm reduction programming in the effort to monitor drug use. Age limits on alcohol consumption are far less restrictive than are those in the United States as well.

Because of America's punitive approach toward substance abuse and recent cutbacks in treatment options, many persons with substance use disorders do not receive the professional help they need. The Portuguese drug policy's emphasis is on the health aspect of drug use. Officials believe that by removing fears of prosecution, the policy has encouraged people who desire it to enter treatment. Statistics on persons requesting treatment bear this out. Research that has examined Vancouver, Canada's, safe injection site similarly shows that a harm reduction approach reduces behaviors that lead to deadly infections such as HIV and hepatitis C (Picard, 2011). In light of the huge toll that opioid use is taking in the United States, city officials in San Francisco and Seattle are working on legislation to set up sites for supervised injection of opiate drugs to take place safely (Fracassa, 2017). The biggest stumbling block is the opposition by neighborhoods that do not want to attract active drug users to their area. Decriminalization and harm reduction are clearly pragmatic approaches.

## HOUSING FIRST PROGRAMS

With regard to persons in the throes of chemical addiction, often accompanied by a mental disorder as well, harm reduction strategies are considered controversial in some circles. Housing first initiatives, for example, provide housing with no strings attached to active alcoholics and drug users, many of whom have severe mental health disorders as well. This is in contrast to traditional housing programs which require total abstinence for continued stays. Housing-first models, which impose no preconditions such as abstaining from substance use, have been shown to be effective in reducing substance use and in providing general well-being to the participants (Delany-Brumsey, 2016). The cost savings to the cities in which such programs are provided (e.g., Seattle, Portland, Oregon, New York City, Minneapolis) are considerable. The cost savings are measured in terms of reductions in emergency room visits, temporary shelter expenses, arrests for disorderly behavior, and incarceration. A major source of funding for housing first options is through the McKenny-Vento Homeless Assistance Grant through the Department of Housing and Urban Development (HUD) (National Alliance to End Homelessness, 2006). The idea is to get the person into stable housing from which all other issues can be addressed. Largely due to housing first, the total number of chronically homeless people in the United States has fallen 30% from 2007 to 2015 (Sanburn, 2016). Versions of this model have also been used in Australia since 2011, Canada since 2013, Finland since 2007, and France since 2010.

Once people with addiction problems and mental disorders obtain housing, counseling and medical supervision are available. It is important that mental health professionals recognize the history of trauma exposure to which a large majority of the residents have been subjected, both early in life and in their recent experiences of living on the streets. This is where trauma-informed care comes into play. Human service organizations, such as those who work with homeless people, must provide systems of care that are trauma informed.

## PRINCIPLES OF TRAUMA-INFORMED CARE

Trauma-informed care operates at both the organizational and individual levels to reduce the stress and strain on people who have survived extreme hardship and trauma. In such a situation, the risks of retraumatizing clients who have unresolved issues from the past is real. An invaluable source on the principles of trauma-informed care is Substance Abuse and Mental Health Services Administration (SAMHSA's) (2014) *Treatment Improvement Protocol (TIP) 57, Trauma-Informed Care in Behavioral Health Services*. There is much useful information also at the National Center for Trauma-Informed Care (2014) which operates under the auspices of SAMHSA. So, what is the basis of trauma-informed care? As described by the National Center for Trauma-Informed Care (2014), a program or system that is trauma-informed:

- Realizes the widespread impact of trauma and understands potential paths for recovery
- Recognizes the signs and symptoms of trauma in clients, families, staff, and others involved with the system
- Responds by fully integrating knowledge about trauma into policies, procedures, and practices
- Seeks to actively resist re-traumatization (National Center for Trauma-Informed Care, 2014, opening page of website)

The starting point for staff training is to educate all staff members to recognize the centrality of trauma in the mental health/substance abuse treatment field and to introduce appropriate screening and assessment as they relate to trauma. In their guidelines to practice from a trauma-informed perspective, the Council on Social Work Education (CSWE) (2012) states that the rationale for prominent attention to trauma in social work education can be found in the many studies that document the widespread prevalence of trauma exposure and its lasting impact across the life course. Therefore, knowledge about the impact of working with trauma survivors on the worker and on the human service organizations that serve them is critical to trauma informed practice.

Once social workers begin to view their clients' behaviors as adaptive, as a legacy of a past fraught with danger, the counselors can shift from a pathology mindset with a focus on diagnosis to one focused on resilience. In this way, the counselor will come to view traumatic stress reactions as normal reactions to abnormal situations. Consistent with social work practice ideology, trauma-informed care can be conceived as a strengths-based approach that is applied at the personal level with an emphasis on the impact of trauma. Such an ideology is built on empathy and patience. As eloquently stated by SAMHSA (2014):

> Knowledge of a client's strengths can help you understand, redefine, and reframe the client's presenting problems and challenges. By focusing and building on an individual's strengths, counselors and other behavioral health professionals can shift the focus from, "What is wrong with you?" to, "What has worked for you?" (p. 18)

This form of care is not only relevant and meaningful to work with homeless populations but also for work in many of the diverse situations described in this and previous chapters in this book: with oppressed minority groups, indigenous populations who have experienced historical trauma, refugees and child soldiers who have escaped from war zones, and victims of environmental disasters, among others.

At the organizational level, agencies that are trauma informed provide a sense of safety to clients. In their landmark book, *Restoring Sanctuary: A New Operating System for Trauma-Informed Systems of Care,* health management experts Bloom and Farragher (2013) note that the sense of openness and trust must permeate the entire organization, and staff must be trained to adopt an outlook that is informed by the recognition of the impact of a client's history on his or her present behavior. (For more information see SAMHSA's complete guide to trauma-informed care at http://store.samhsa.gov/product/TIP-57).

## WHAT WE CAN LEARN FROM OTHER COUNTRIES

There is much to be learned both from negative and positive examples of health care provision in other countries. Consider Norway, Canada, and the Netherlands through the objective scaling system of their Human Development Index (HDI) which ranks nations on levels of well-being. These are the nations chosen for special attention to their health care policies here. Norway is first in the world on the HDI; the Netherlands is number seven, and Canada ranks at number 10. The United States ties with Canada as number 10 as well, despite a lower life expectancy and significantly higher homicide rate (UNDP, 2017). The per capita income is higher in the United States, however, which boosts its rating. The United Nations Development Programme (UNDP) established the HDI on the idea that a country should be assessed on the people and their capabilities, not economic growth alone. The health dimension is assessed by life expectancy at birth as it relates to the possibility of a long and healthy life. The education dimension is measured by the capability-of-being-knowledgeable measure in years of schooling for adults aged 25 years and more, and expected schooling for children of school entering age. The standard of living dimension refers to the capability of having a decent standard of living as measured by gross national income (UNDP, 2017).

### FROM NORWAY

Norway is a country in which the income equality is considerably high. Its health care system is a universal, tax-funded, single-payer system, under which the government runs and administers health insurance, and likely one of the most centralized of the universal, single-payer systems. It is built on the principle of equal access for all persons regardless of socioeconomic status, ethnicity, and area of residence. It is funded by general tax revenues. In 2014, Norway spent 9.4% of its GDP on health care. Hospital and nonhospital physicians are generally paid on a salaried basis, although some specialists are permitted to charge on a fee-for-service basis or receive an annual government grant. And, residents may opt out of the government system and pay out-of-pocket which often happens when waits are long for a particular medical procedure. About 8% of the population has some kind of private insurance usually through their employer. Under this system a person selects his or her general practitioner who acts as a gatekeeper for specialist services. There are safety nets such as a cap for out-of-pocket expenditures, after which all expenses are paid. This is helpful because Norway does not produce pharmaceuticals, so most patients must pay high market prices. Mental health care for acute conditions is provided in wards of public hospitals, and treatment for rehabilitative treatment of eating disorders or substance use, for example, is provided in smaller, private hospitals. Long-term care is provided in municipalities. Only 3% of nursing homes in Norway are private, and the percentage is lower for home care. The national strategy is focused on efficacy, safety, efficiency, patient-centered care, care coordination, and continuity and equality in access. The system is transparent, and doctors and hospitals communicate through a national registry regarding any adverse medical events (Mossialos et al., 2015). The system is so patient-centered that when a patient is suffering from skin issues such as psoriasis, depression, or asthma due to Norway's cold climate, the coverage will include a trip out of the country to a spa for recovery.

Substance abuse treatment is provided at no charge by the state. Treatment can last up to two years of residential care, and it might include active involvement by family members. To learn of a 12-Step program inspired by the Minnesota model but going far beyond it in terms of client care, see van Wormer and Davis (2018).

## FROM CANADA

The Canadian system is administered by the provinces and territories, and care of local residents is financed by the provinces and territories. Some have established regional systems for delivery of services. The federal government does regulate safety and efficacy of medical devices, pharmaceuticals and natural health products, as well as administer the health care of certain groups such as First Nation peoples and federal penitentiary inmates. In 2014, its expenditures were estimated to be 8.3% of its GDP (UNDP, 2017). Cost-sharing and copayment exemptions vary among the provinces and there is no cap on out-of-pocket expenses. In 2014, about half the physicians were general practitioners and half specialists. The general practitioners act as gatekeepers for specialists. Most physicians are private practitioners and paid fee-for-service, although there is a growing movement toward group practices. Some of these group practices require an annual fee for patients participating. Mental health care is covered although not integrated into primary care. Long-term care and end-of-life care are not considered insured expenses under the Canada Health Act. The Canadian system is highly decentralized (Mossialos et al., 2015). One key role of the federal government is to negotiate pharmaceutical prices. Price controls are based on a price review to order a price reduction whenever the price of a drug exceeds the median of the prices in six European countries plus the United States. This system pushes Big Pharma to engage in price discrimination charging higher prices to some countries, including the United States, to recover the costs of selling for less to Canada. Even with its relatively fragmented delivery system, when compared to other universal, single-payer health care models and gaps in coverage of long-term care, Canadians are pleased with their system. Reasons offered include a rejection of the US competitive market system and a preference for expansion of the public health care options versus privatization (McBane, 2009), and that it represents their values and the belief that no one should be denied health care simply because they do not have money (Low, 2006).

### FROM THE NETHERLANDS

The Dutch system is a publicly financed system. The national government sets health care priorities, introduces legislation, monitors the quality and costs. It also partly funds a basic benefit package of health insurance through a system of taxation and payroll levies. And, remarkably it funds a compulsory insurance for long-term care. In 2015, the system was reformed to give local municipalities responsibility and discretion in delivery of most outpatient long-term care and all youth care. In 2013, the Netherlands spent 12% of its GDP on health care. Most of the population purchases a mixture of complementary voluntary insurance to cover benefits such as dental care, alternative medicine, physiotherapy, prescription eyewear, contraceptives and the full cost of copayments. People may conscientiously object to insurance and opt out (Mossialos et al., 2015). Addressing the challenge of an aging population and the looming specter of an Alzheimer's dementia epidemic, the Netherlands has established dementia villages for people with Alzheimer's and other forms of dementia characterized by memory loss, difficulty thinking, or problem solving (see chapter 11). A dementia village is a small town dedicated to the patients who live there. Other people in the village, like the barber or the restaurant chef, are trained in specialized health care. The goal is to ensure the safety of the inhabitants, preserve their dignity and to offer humane treatment. The idea was inspired by two nurses who did not want to place their parents in extended care (DeCourcey, 2016).

## SUMMARY AND CONCLUSION

A quote included in this chapter reminds us of the need to get the pigs out of the creek first, then clean the water. Get to the root of the problem, in other words, concentrate resources on prevention rather than treatment in the interests of public health. In maternal health terms, the capacity to plan, postpone, or prevent pregnancy, is the best guarantee of reproductive health. Harm reduction proponents, moreover, would favor birth control over abortion, and accessible legal abortion over the back-alley variety or requiring women to leave their state or country to obtain the health care they need.

The tug-of-war between prevention and tertiary care is resolved in modern society in favor of tertiary, or after-the-fact care. This tension is as true in housing as it is in health care. Once people are living on the streets or are terminally ill, all the emergency services in the world cannot undo the damage. Programs that for decades have been the bedrock of what used to be our social welfare infrastructure are being dismantled. People who are already disadvantaged by a myriad of factors bear the most visible cost of the transformation of American social welfare and of American cities through urban renewal and downtown revitalization. What our society fails to grasp is that applying the logic of the market place to human service is fraught with peril.

Compared to the universal programs in other countries discussed in this chapter and chapter 12, the American health care system is generally regarded as a failure, even in terms of the very market economy that influenced its development in the first place. The huge investment in dollars is not providing a good return on the resources invested.

Administrative costs in the United States are staggering, caused in part by the multiplicity of third party payers. Every insurance company has different forms, regulations, and policies. Despite or because of all the efforts at cost containment, the costs cannot be contained. There is much that can be learned from countries such as Canada with universal health care under a single payer system and its negotiation with pharmaceutical companies, as well as from Cuba with its community prevention approach. And when countries universalize health care offerings, addiction treatment options have a ready funding source, as, for example, in Norway.

Whether we were looking at medical care, mental health care, or substance abuse treatment, one theme that has emerged again and again in these pages is to what extent the various politically generated cost-cutting measures are expensive in the long run. Because of the abandonment of a commitment to provide affordable housing, for example, city streets are lined with people who are homeless; and cutbacks in health services including substance abuse treatment make for more serious problems later. When people cannot afford medication, similarly, far more expensive remedies may be required. When society fails, social workers often inherit the task of trying to help their clients pick up the pieces.

The boxed reading included in these final chapters introduced us to issues faced by children across the globe who lack access to life-changing surgery, by ethnic groups who live with the stress of violence and health effects of discrimination, the impact of the ACA on caring for an ill parent, and by the outreach necessary to provide communities with needed mental health care. Because of their work within the system and as advocates for patients in need of medical services, social workers, and persons such as those who contributed their personal narratives for this and the preceding chapter are joining policymakers in the call for change. In order for such transformation to become a reality, some or all of the following steps need to occur:

- Campaign finance reform to reduce the undue influence of special interest groups, and reduce the unsustainable costs required for private profit, including pharmaceutical, and insurance companies
- Concentration on efforts for innovative solutions on a state by state basis.
- An end to the hegemony of the pharmaceutical companies to ensure that the price of drugs can be closer to their actual production cost
- The conducting of informational campaigns in the media and elsewhere to tout the cost-effectiveness of home health care versus institutional care
- A societal paradigm shift from a cure-treatment model to a harm reduction-prevention model to reduce the spread of disease and provide for a better health outcome
- The support for a simplified and transparent system of universal health care using the best features of Medicaid and Medicare as government-funded programs to eventually serve all age groups so that the care for some would be the care for all

## THOUGHT QUESTIONS

1. Discuss the importance of the UN Convention on the Rights of Persons with Disabilities to the world at large.
2. Recount the history of the passage of the 1990 Americans with Disabilities Act. What kind of changes did the Act require, for example, of a university to be in compliance?
3. Consider the importance of terminology. Related to people with disabilities, how have the terms used for their disabilities changed over time?

4. What does the boxed reading on volunteer medical surgery in Ecuador tell us about the importance of a normal appearance to children?
5. Research transportation services in your local community. What kind of accommodations are provided to persons with mobility disabilities. Are there any limitations to the services?
6. Discuss mental health problems in the general population. How are minorities uniquely affected by mental disorders? Refer to the boxed reading.
7. Recall the history of mental health treatment in the United States. What does the statement, "jails and prisons are the mental health institutions of the 21st century" mean?
8. What is the situation facing homeless people in your community? Discuss the various ways these people are stigmatized and the social controls that are used to keep them out of other people's way.
9. What are some basic harm reduction strategies? In what way are these controversial?
10. What does the metaphor about "first getting the pigs out of the creek" have to do with health care?
11. Discuss the concept of harm reduction for various areas of health care.
12. Think of a treatment center or agency serving people in need of help. To what extent does this agency abide by principles such as those described as trauma-informed care?
13. What can we learn from other countries in dealing with the health care and mental health care challenges facing the United States?

# REFERENCES


Abbott, A. (2010). *Alcohol, tobacco, and other drugs: Challenging myths, assessing theories, individualizing interventions* (2nd ed.). Washington, DC: NASW Press.

American College of Emergency Physicians (2016, October 17). Waits for care and hospital beds growing dramatically for psychiatric emergency patients. Retrieved from www.newsroom.acep,org

American Psychological Association (APA). (2009). *Publication manual of the American Psychological Association* (6th ed.). Washington, DC: American Psychological Association.

American Psychiatric Association (APA). (2013). *Diagnostic and statistical manual of mental disorders* (DSM) (5th ed.). Washington, DC: APA.

American Society of Addiction Medicine (ASAM). (2016). Opioid addiction—2016 facts & figures, 2016. Retrieved from http://www.asam.org

The Arc. (2016). The Arc, public policy and legal advocacy, housing issues for people with disabilities, 2016. Retrieved from http://www.thearc.org

Associated Press. (2017). Drug shoot-up rooms get serious look. Waterloo-Cedar Falls, Iowa, *The Courier*, p. A3.

Bernstein, L. (2016, December 8). U.S. life expectancy declines for the first time since 1993. *The Washington Post*. Retrieved from https://www.washingtonpost.com

Bloom, S. L., & Farragher, B. (2013). *Restoring sanctuary: A new operating system for trauma-informed systems of care*. New York, NY: Oxford University Press.

Botticelli, M. (2016, February 2). Addressing the epidemic of prescription opioid abuse and heroin use. Washington, DC: The White House. Retrieved from https://www.whitehouse.gov

Brown, L. X. Z. (2013). How "differently abled" marginalizes disabled people, Autistic Hoya, August 29, 2013. Retrieved from http://www.autistichoya.com

Case, A., & Deaton, A. (2017, March 23–24). Mortality and morbidity in the 21st century. *Brookings Papers on Economic Activity*. Princeton, NJ: Princeton University.

Centers for Disease Control and Prevention (CDC). (2013, October 4). Mental health basics, Retrieved from: https://www.cdc.gov/mentalhealth/basics.htm

Council on Social Work Education (CSWE). (2012). *Advanced social work practice in trauma*. Alexandria, VA: CSWE.

Chuck, E., & Edwards, E. (2016, November 17). 78 people die a day from opioid overdose, Surgeon General says in landmark report. National Broadcasting Company (NBC). Retrieved from http://www.nbcnews.com

DeCourcey, D. (2016, December 10). Here's how America should actually be treating people with dementia. Retrieved from: http://www.attn.com

Delany-Brumsey, A., & Davis, C. (2016, May 9). Drug addiction cannot be decoupled from mental illness. *New York Times*. Retrieved from http://www.nytimes.com/

Department of Justice (DOJ). (2015, October). Special report: Use of restrictive housing in prisons and jails, 2011–2012. *Bureau of Justice Statistics*. Retrieved from: https://www.bjs.gov

Department of Justice (DOJ). (2016). Civil rights division, disability rights section. https://www.justice.gov/crt/disability-rights-section

DePoy, E., & Gilson, S. F. (2004). *Rethinking disability: Principles for professional and social change*. Belmont, CA: Cengage.

Eyre, E. (2016, December 17). *Drug firms poured 780M painkillers into WV amid rise of overdoses*. Charleston, WV: The Gazette-Mail. Retrieved from http://www.gazettemail.com

Fracassa, D. (2017). The mental health parity and addiction equity act. Centers for Medicare and Medicaid. Retrieved from www.cms.gov

Gaba, A. (2014, May 20). The culture of mental health stigma in communities of color. Robert Wood Johnson Foundation, Culture of Health. Retrieved from http://www.rwjf.org

Harris, J. C. (2013). New terminology for mental retardation in DSM-5 and ICD-11, *Current Opinion in Psychiatry, 26*(3), 260–262.

Healthcare.gov. (2016). Mental health and substance abuse coverage, 2016. Retrieved from https://www.healthcare.gov

James, D. J., & Glaze, L. E. (2006, December 14). Mental health problems of prison and jail inmates, Bureau of Justice Statistics: Special Report. Retrieved from https://bjs.gov/content/pub/pdf/mhppji.pdf

Justice Center. (2016). Mental health courts, Justice Center, the Council of State Governments. Retrieved from: https://csgjusticecenter.org/mental-health-court-Project

Friedman, M. (2014, May 13). The stigma of mental illness is making us sicker: Why mental illness should be a public health priority. *Psychology Today*. Retrieved from: https://www.psychologytoday.com

Kennedy, L. P. (2010, November 30). 20 Questions for Carrie Fisher: The prolific performer talks about her experiences with bipolar disorder and addiction—plus what it's like to reach a happier middle age. *WebMD Magazine*. Substance Abuse and Addiction Health Center. Retrieved from http://www.webmd.com

Kennedy. P. J. (2015). *A common struggle: A personal journal through the past and future of mental illness and addiction*. New York, NY: Penguin.

Kristof, N. (2014, February 8). Inside a mental hospital called jail. *New York Times*. Sunday Review. Retrieved from https://www.nytimes.com

Larson S. (2016, December 5). Stackable pods could help house the homeless, CNN Tech, Upstarts. Retrieved from http://money.cnn.com

Levitz, E. (2016, December 21). The opioid epidemic is a symptom of toxic greed. *New York Magazine.* Retrieved from: http://nymag.com

Low, M. D. (2006, October 19). Oh, Canada, ABC News—Opinion. Retrieved from http://abcnews.go.com

McBane, M. (2009, August 13). Canadians love their health care, reject US-style competition. Corrente. Retrieved from: http://www.correntewire.com

Medicare.gov. (2016). What Medicare covers. Retrieved from https://www.medicare.gov/what-medicare-covers/index.html

Mental Health.gov. (2014). Health insurance and mental health services, U.S. Department of Health and Human Service. Retrieved from https://www.hhs.gov

Midraq, N., & Hodapp, R. M. (2010). Chronic stress and health among parents of children with intellectual and developmental disabilities. *Current Opinion in Psychiatry, 23*(5), 407–411.

Mossialos, E., & Wenzl, M. (2015, January 15). International profiles of health care systems. The Commonwealth Fund. Retrieved from http://www.commonwealthfund.org

Naami, A. (2015). 25 years post-ADA: A social worker's experience and reflections about environmental barriers. *Reflections: Narrations of Professional Helping, 20*(1), 36–41.

National Alliance on Mental Illness (NAMI). (2016). Mental health conditions, 2016. Retrieved from http://www.nami.org/Learn-More/Mental-Health-Conditions

National Alliance to End Homelessness (2006, November 27). What is housing first? National Alliance to End Homelessness. Retrieved from http://www.endhomelessness.org

National Coalition for the Homeless (2012, February 21). Mental illness and homelessness, page last modified February 21, 2012. Retrieved from: http://www.nationalhomeless.org/factsheets/Mental_Illness.html

NASW. (2013). *Standards for social work practice with clients with substance use disorders.* Washington, DC: NASW.

National Association of Social Workers (NASW). (2015). Substance use disorder treatment. *Social work speaks: NASW policy statements 2015–2017* (10th ed., pp. 296–297). Washington, DC: NASW Press.

National Public Radio (NPR) (2012). Parents with disabilities and family law. Retrieved from http://www.npr.org

Office of the Inspector General (OIG). (2015, November 10). Top management and performance challenges facing the department of justice. Office of the Inspector General, Department of Justice. Retrieved from https://oig.justice.gov/challenges/2015.pdf

Olmstead Rights (2015). Olmstead v. LC: History and currents status. Retrieved from https://www.olmsteadrights.org/about-olmstead/

Picard, A. (2011, April 17). Vancouvers safe injection site cuts overdose deaths. *Globe and Mail.* Retrieved from http://www.theglobeandmail.com

Sanburn, J. (2016, March 14). The radically simple solution to homelessness. *Time*, pp. 19–20.

Schiff, J. W. (2015). *Working with homeless and vulnerable people: Basic skills and practice.* Chicago, IL: Lyceum.

Seeyle, K. Q. (2015, October 30). In heroin crisis, white families seek gentler war on durgs. *New York Times.* Retrieved from http://www.nytimes.com

Shane, L., & Kime, P. (2016, July 7). New VA study finds 20 veterans commit suicide every day. *Military Times.* Retrieved from: www.militarytimes.com

Substance Abuse and Mental Health Services Administration (SAMHSA). (2014). *Trauma-informed care in behavioral health services: Treatment Improvement Protocol (TIP) 57*. Rockville, MD: SAMHSA.

Substance Abuse and Mental Health Services Administration (SAMHSA). (2015, October 27). Substance use disorders. SAMHSA. Retrieved from: https://www.samhsa.gov/tribal-ttac/resources/substance-use-disorders

Suppes, M., & Wells, C. (2012). *The social work experience: An introduction to social work and social welfare* (6th ed.). Boston, MA: Pearson.

Szabo, L. (2016, November 22). Clinics help keep people with serious mental illness out of ER, Kaiser Health New. Retrieved from: http://khn.org/news/clinics-help-keep-people-with-serious-mental-illness-out-of-er/

United Nations Convention on the Rights of Persons with Disabilities (2008, May 3). Retrieved from https://www.un.org

United Nations Development Programme (UNDP). (2017). Human development report 2016: Work for human development, Human Development Reports, Human Development Index (HDI), 2016. Retrieved from http://hdr.undp.org

United Nations Division for Social Policy and Development, Disability. (2016). Frequently asked questions regarding the Convention on the Rights of Persons with Disabilities. Retrieved from https://www.un.org

United Nations, Office of the High Commissioner. (2016). Human rights by country. Retrieved from http://www.ohchr.org/EN/Countries/Pages/HumanRightsintheWorld.aspx

United Nations, Office of Legal Affairs (2016). Audiovisual library of international law. Retrieved from: http://legal.un.org/avl/ha/crpd/crpd.html

U.S. Conference of Mayors (2015, December). Hunger and homelessness survey: A status report on Hunger and homelessness in Americas cities—a 22 city survey. Retrieved from: https://www.usmayors.org

van Wormer, K. S. & Davis, D. R. (2018). *Addiction treatment: A strengths perspective* (4th ed.). Belmont, CA: Cengage.

Watson, C. (2015, March 24). When "just say no" is not enough: Teaching harm reduction. *The New Social Worker*. Retrieved from www.socialworker.com

World Health Organization (WHO). (2014). Mental health: A state of well-being. Retrieved from http://www.who.int/features/factfiles/mental_health/en

World Health Organization (WHO). (2016a). The global guardian of public health. Retrieved from http://www.who.int/about/what-we-do/global-guardian-public-health/en/

World Health Organization (WHO). (2016b). *Problem management plus (PM+)*. Geneva, Switzerland: WHO. Retrieved from www.who.int

# EPILOGUE

> Don't get discouraged. Hope is like a road in the country. In places where there never was a road before, when many people walk the same path, a road comes into existence.
>
> Romanian saying, contributed by Stela Slapac, MSW

In closing, we welcome you to social work. Key professional knowledge, practice innovations, and ideas have been introduced inviting further research and your reading to inform future practice. This textbook is written in a time of much political uncertainty and divisiveness following the now historic election of 2016. There is a sense of vulnerability to all people who are marginalized—those who are poor, indigenous, and immigrants, among others. There is fear for the future of cherished social welfare programs. The challenges to the social work profession are immense. What we know in our hearts and minds and from history is that social work will not only find a way through, but will emerge even stronger in a spirit of solidarity. Our long-standing focus on human rights will come to the forefront of our social work values and practice.

As the book demonstrates, the social work profession is both complex in its reach into all aspects of individual and community life and clear in its core values:

- Service
- Social justice
- To honor human dignity and the worth of the person
- To support human relationships and self-determination
- Integrity
- Competence (NASW, 2017)

To these core values we add commitment to inclusion, and commitment to human rights and global relationships as they strengthen 21st-century social work. In adding human rights as a core value, we are reflecting the commitment to the inclusion and dignity of all people (chapters 2 and 5). As explained in chapter 1, human rights are inextricably linked with every aspect of our well-being. The language of human rights policies, also known as conventions, has enriched and reinforced practice—as demonstrated in the discussion of children in chapter 10, their right to a name, a voice, safe environments, separate incarceration from adults, health care, and family life.

From this emphasis on human rights it follows that to see "the social work profession in global perspective" has been the mission of the book. This means understanding the structural nature of personal problems at home and abroad, wherever we live. Global developments such as those examined throughout this volume have profound implications for the needs of a nation's people and for the social workers who strive to help people get those needs met. An international perspective is invaluable in revealing not just problems, but also solutions that have been tried elsewhere and found to be successful (see chapters 10 and 11). Many countries of the world are faced with similar challenges. Such challenges include the boundaries for social care between the family and the state, coping with a rapidly aging population and end-of-life decision making in the face of technology that has outstripped our imaginations, and taking responsibility for marginalized groups, including refugees, minorities, and indigenous populations (chapters 5 and 6). We face the same universal paradox of how to achieve a balance between people's welfare entitlements and the conflicting demands of the global market. The paradox of social welfare in the global economy (chapter 3) can be considered the central tension of this book and indeed of social work practice.

Throughout this volume, we have drawn upon international examples and encourage social workers to find resources and evidence of good practice in a variety of countries, not just the United States or their local domain. The first heart transplant happened in South Africa, the technology that resulted in men landing on the moon was generated in the United States, the first women's shelter was established in England, the first UNICEF-sponsored "Child Friendly City" in Italy, closely followed by El Salvador. The work of the United Nations has brought us standards for practice, such as ending the death penalty for children, more transparency in international adoptions, an end to child slave labor, and a collaboration across borders to resist human trafficking. Similarly, looking to other countries to resolve problems, such as the prevalence of handguns in families in the United States and children dying from accidents with guns, can reveal very different ways of organizing and controlling weapons.

The United Nations has set up conventions, for example, for children and women's rights that expect us to institutionalize human well-being: "The Convention on the Rights of the Child changed the way children are viewed and treated—i.e., as human beings with a distinct set of rights instead of as passive objects of care and charity" (United Children's Fund [UNICEF], 2016, www.unicef.org). Similarly, for women, instead of the stigma that has in the past been associated with domestic violence, the Convention on the Elimination of All Forms of Discrimination against Women makes it clear that violence in the home is a crime. Whereas 50 years ago, police did not step over the hearth, it is a vast step forward in nations of the Global North for all women that partners may no longer mistreat or dominate through force of law or custom carried over from biblical times. In the discussion in chapter 5 we hear that these steps to address such violence are still up against great challenges: according to the United Nations physical and sexual abuse affects millions of girls and women worldwide. The key here is that social workers, human rights workers, and NGOs are all pulling together in ways that bring more coordinated strength to the voices and actions for change.

As the discussion of restorative justice demonstrates in chapter 6, we have also made progress in terms of the expectations of incarceration and the goal to rehabilitate rather than simply "punish." It is part of social work that the profession has offered a mirror to society in advocating for policies and services that support human dignity.

Another of the great challenges for the 2020s is the increase in migration and refugees due to war and to illnesses such as Ebola and Zika that know no boundaries. These challenges require countries to communicate with one another, for example through the World Health Organization (WHO), and service personnel to collaborate across borders. Opportunities for social workers to operate in international context are expanding, and this development does not just relate to international adoptions or working with refugees. There is permanent representation by social workers to the United Nations. The profession contributes to new policies, and staff are active in organizations such as the Red Cross/Red Crescent; the International Rescue Committee, providing post-conflict assistance to families; United Nations agencies such as UNICEF; Overseas Aid Programs of several countries; Christian Peacemakers; the Center for Victims of Torture; and International Social Service (ISS), which provides assistance to people caught in conflict, without citizenship, or displaced by war or natural disaster. The list could be much longer and reflects a degree of international collaboration among human service and social workers that did not exist 100 years ago.

In the Preface to this book, a human rights perspective was joined with the expectations of local accrediting organizations. These organizations include the Council on Social Work Education (CSWE) in the United States, the International Association of Schools of Social Work (IASSW), and the professional body, the International Federation of Social Workers (IFSW). Fulfilling these expectations is one hoped-for outcome for this book, which has provided the following:

- The information and research evidence to take pride in the profession of social work
- The history of social work and social welfare that undergirds commitment to practice
- Description of the impact of globalization and the growth of international social policy, particularly demonstrated by the work of the United Nations and the specific conventions that contribute guidelines for practice
- Details of social policies that continue to be refined and worked on in order to provide blueprints for action
- Information and named skills relating to cultural diversity and culturally competent practice
- Ways to work together across borders to strengthen our core value and principle for work: promoting human well-being

The social work profession will always face the harshest circumstances that human beings have to deal with in the knowledge that we have the capacity, and seek to find the collective will, to establish human rights that guarantee child-friendly cities for everyone in the future. As citizens of the world, our mission is to promote peace and justice through working to eradicate racism, poverty, sexism, injustice, and other forms of oppression worldwide. We refer to the social work imagination when we realize the progress made since the work of our founding mothers and fathers, from destitution to social security, from death row for children to restorative justice, from slavery to valued labor. Our book aims to capture the imaginations of new social workers and encourage the next generation of social workers to continue this commitment to human rights and well-being.

## REFERENCES

United Nations Children's Fund (UNICEF) (2016). Convention on the rights of the child. Retrieved from www.unicef.org

National Association of Social Workers (NASW). (2017). *Code of ethics*. Washington, DC: NASW.

# APPENDIX A

## *Universal Declaration of Human Rights*

*Adopted and proclaimed by General Assembly resolution 217 A (III) of 10 December 1948*

On December 10, 1948 the General Assembly of the United Nations adopted and proclaimed the Universal Declaration of Human Rights the full text of which appears in the following pages. Following this historic act the Assembly called upon all Member countries to publicize the text of the Declaration and "to cause it to be disseminated, displayed, read and expounded principally in schools and other educational institutions, without distinction based on the political status of countries or territories."

## PREAMBLE

Whereas recognition of the inherent dignity and of the equal and inalienable rights of all members of the human family is the foundation of freedom, justice and peace in the world,

Whereas disregard and contempt for human rights have resulted in barbarous acts which have outraged the conscience of mankind, and the advent of a world in which human beings shall enjoy freedom of speech and belief and freedom from fear and want has been proclaimed as the highest aspiration of the common people,

Whereas it is essential, if man is not to be compelled to have recourse, as a last resort, to rebellion against tyranny and oppression, that human rights should be protected by the rule of law,

Whereas it is essential to promote the development of friendly relations between nations,

Whereas the peoples of the United Nations have in the Charter reaffirmed their faith in fundamental human rights, in the dignity and worth of the human person and in the equal rights of men and women and have determined to promote social progress and better standards of life in larger freedom,

Whereas Member States have pledged themselves to achieve, in co-operation with the United Nations, the promotion of universal respect for and observance of human rights and fundamental freedoms,

Whereas a common understanding of these rights and freedoms is of the greatest importance for the full realization of this pledge,

**Now, Therefore THE GENERAL ASSEMBLY proclaims THIS UNIVERSAL DECLARATION OF HUMAN RIGHTS** as a common standard of achievement for all peoples and all nations, to the end that every individual and every organ of society, keeping this Declaration constantly in mind, shall strive by teaching and education to promote respect for these rights and freedoms and by progressive measures, national and international, to secure their universal and effective recognition and observance, both among the peoples of Member States themselves and among the peoples of territories under their jurisdiction.

***Article 1.***
All human beings are born free and equal in dignity and rights. They are endowed with reason and conscience and should act towards one another in a spirit of brotherhood.

***Article 2.***
Everyone is entitled to all the rights and freedoms set forth in this Declaration, without distinction of any kind, such as race, colour, sex, language, religion, political or other opinion, national or social origin, property, birth or other status. Furthermore, no distinction shall be made on the basis of the political, jurisdictional or international status of the country or territory to which a person belongs, whether it be independent, trust, non-self-governing or under any other limitation of sovereignty.

***Article 3.***
Everyone has the right to life, liberty and security of person.

***Article 4.***
No one shall be held in slavery or servitude; slavery and the slave trade shall be prohibited in all their forms.

***Article 5.***
No one shall be subjected to torture or to cruel, inhuman or degrading treatment or punishment.

***Article 6.***
Everyone has the right to recognition everywhere as a person before the law.

***Article 7.***
All are equal before the law and are entitled without any discrimination to equal protection of the law. All are entitled to equal protection against any discrimination in violation of this Declaration and against any incitement to such discrimination.

***Article 8.***
Everyone has the right to an effective remedy by the competent national tribunals for acts violating the fundamental rights granted him by the constitution or by law.

***Article 9.***
No one shall be subjected to arbitrary arrest, detention or exile.

*Article 10.*
Everyone is entitled in full equality to a fair and public hearing by an independent and impartial tribunal, in the determination of his rights and obligations and of any criminal charge against him.

*Article 11.*
(1) Everyone charged with a penal offence has the right to be presumed innocent until proved guilty according to law in a public trial at which he has had all the guarantees necessary for his defence.
(2) No one shall be held guilty of any penal offence on account of any act or omission which did not constitute a penal offence, under national or international law, at the time when it was committed. Nor shall a heavier penalty be imposed than the one that was applicable at the time the penal offence was committed.

*Article 12.*
No one shall be subjected to arbitrary interference with his privacy, family, home or correspondence, nor to attacks upon his honour and reputation. Everyone has the right to the protection of the law against such interference or attacks.

*Article 13.*
(1) Everyone has the right to freedom of movement and residence within the borders of each state.
(2) Everyone has the right to leave any country, including his own, and to return to his country.

*Article 14.*
(1) Everyone has the right to seek and to enjoy in other countries asylum from persecution.
(2) This right may not be invoked in the case of prosecutions genuinely arising from non-political crimes or from acts contrary to the purposes and principles of the United Nations.

*Article 15.*
(1) Everyone has the right to a nationality.
(2) No one shall be arbitrarily deprived of his nationality nor denied the right to change his nationality.

*Article 16.*
(1) Men and women of full age, without any limitation due to race, nationality or religion, have the right to marry and to found a family. They are entitled to equal rights as to marriage, during marriage and at its dissolution.
(2) Marriage shall be entered into only with the free and full consent of the intending spouses.
(3) The family is the natural and fundamental group unit of society and is entitled to protection by society and the State.

*Article 17.*
(1) Everyone has the right to own property alone as well as in association with others.
(2) No one shall be arbitrarily deprived of his property.

*Article 18.*
Everyone has the right to freedom of thought, conscience and religion; this right includes freedom to change his religion or belief, and freedom, either alone or in community with others

and in public or private, to manifest his religion or belief in teaching, practice, worship and observance.

*Article 19.*
Everyone has the right to freedom of opinion and expression; this right includes freedom to hold opinions without interference and to seek, receive and impart information and ideas through any media and regardless of frontiers.

*Article 20.*
(1) Everyone has the right to freedom of peaceful assembly and association.
(2) No one may be compelled to belong to an association.

*Article 21.*
(1) Everyone has the right to take part in the government of his country, directly or through freely chosen representatives.
(2) Everyone has the right of equal access to public service in his country.
(3) The will of the people shall be the basis of the authority of government; this will shall be expressed in periodic and genuine elections which shall be by universal and equal suffrage and shall be held by secret vote or by equivalent free voting procedures.

*Article 22.*
Everyone, as a member of society, has the right to social security and is entitled to realization, through national effort and international co-operation and in accordance with the organization and resources of each State, of the economic, social and cultural rights indispensable for his dignity and the free development of his personality.

*Article 23.*
(1) Everyone has the right to work, to free choice of employment, to just and favourable conditions of work and to protection against unemployment.
(2) Everyone, without any discrimination, has the right to equal pay for equal work.
(3) Everyone who works has the right to just and favourable remuneration ensuring for himself and his family an existence worthy of human dignity, and supplemented, if necessary, by other means of social protection.
(4) Everyone has the right to form and to join trade unions for the protection of his interests.

*Article 24.*
Everyone has the right to rest and leisure, including reasonable limitation of working hours and periodic holidays with pay.

*Article 25.*
(1) Everyone has the right to a standard of living adequate for the health and well-being of himself and of his family, including food, clothing, housing and medical care and necessary social services, and the right to security in the event of unemployment, sickness, disability, widowhood, old age or other lack of livelihood in circumstances beyond his control.
(2) Motherhood and childhood are entitled to special care and assistance. All children, whether born in or out of wedlock, shall enjoy the same social protection.

*Article 26.*
(1) Everyone has the right to education. Education shall be free, at least in the elementary and fundamental stages. Elementary education shall be compulsory. Technical and professional

education shall be made generally available and higher education shall be equally accessible to all on the basis of merit.

(2) Education shall be directed to the full development of the human personality and to the strengthening of respect for human rights and fundamental freedoms. It shall promote understanding, tolerance and friendship among all nations, racial or religious groups, and shall further the activities of the United Nations for the maintenance of peace.

(3) Parents have a prior right to choose the kind of education that shall be given to their children.

*Article 27.*

(1) Everyone has the right freely to participate in the cultural life of the community, to enjoy the arts and to share in scientific advancement and its benefits.

(2) Everyone has the right to the protection of the moral and material interests resulting from any scientific, literary or artistic production of which he is the author.

*Article 28.*

Everyone is entitled to a social and international order in which the rights and freedoms set forth in this Declaration can be fully realized.

*Article 29.*

(1) Everyone has duties to the community in which alone the free and full development of his personality is possible.

(2) In the exercise of his rights and freedoms, everyone shall be subject only to such limitations as are determined by law solely for the purpose of securing due recognition and respect for the rights and freedoms of others and of meeting the just requirements of morality, public order and the general welfare in a democratic society.

(3) These rights and freedoms may in no case be exercised contrary to the purposes and principles of the United Nations.

*Article 30.*

Nothing in this Declaration may be interpreted as implying for any State, group or person any right to engage in any activity or to perform any act aimed at the destruction of any of the rights and freedoms set forth herein.

**Source: United Nations, Resolution 217A (111). Passed by General Assembly, December 1948.**

# APPENDIX B

# *Guidelines*

I. Description of the Social Condition/Problem
   A. What is the social condition that is oppressive and therefore is in need of change?
   B. What is the nature of dissatisfaction with the present condition?
   C. What are the facts (from official and unofficial reports) concerning the social condition?
      1. What does documentation through review of the literature show?
      2. What do we know from official data, agency records, surveys, or interviews with key experts?
      3. What are forecasts for future problems and expenses related to the problem?
   D. To what extent is the social condition perceived by constituents as a social problem?
      1. How is the problem defined by various factions in the society?
         a. What value biases are implicit?
         b. To what source is the problem attributed?
      2. For whom is the situation in question a problem?

II. Historical Analysis
   A. What were the relevant social or environmental conditions like in the past?
   B. How did the social condition (e.g., pollution of a local creek, need for affordable child care services, homelessness) come to be defined as a problem?
      1. How was the definition of the problem affected by changing social values?
      2. How was the problem dealt with historically?
   C. Which influential groups were involved in supporting and opposing proposed remedies? Are the groups the same today?
   D. What are the precedents for the ideas and values being used to correct the situation?
   E. To what extent were the approaches to the problem effective or ineffective?

F. How did the manifest goals differ from the unstated or latent goals of potential solutions?
G. Comment on the lessons of history relevant to the present issue.

III. Policy Formulation Overview
A. What are the goals (manifest and latent) of the proposed policy change?
B. Listen to the voices of the people: What can we learn from people's (clients') narratives about the need to strengthen resources?
C. What are the pros and cons of various ways of dealing with the problem?
1. How does each of these competing policies meet the criteria of self- determination, empowerment, adequacy, feasibility, and efficiency?
2. How is this proposal superior to other remedies?
D. To what extent can public opinion be mobilized in support of your proposed policy?
E. In general what do the research findings tell us about the problem?
F. What are anticipated barriers to policy change?

IV. The Global Context
A. What can we learn from other countries about similar policies or approaches to meet the same need?
B. Discuss international differences in funding sources and levels of support.
C. How is your proposed policy integrated within the cultural values of one or more other countries?
D. Could we advocate a similar policy for the United States given US traditional values?
E. Relate the policy under consideration to the relevant section of the Universal Declaration of Human Rights.

V. Economic Analysis
A. How much will the proposed initiative cost?
1. How does this expense compare with present or other proposed offerings?
2. How will the proposed program be funded?
B. What will be the projected cost-savings (the benefits) to the state, county, or agency?
C. Which groups benefit financially from the social problem (e.g., landlords from housing shortages)?
D. Discuss the initiative in terms of its bearing on economic oppression.
E. If relevant, measure the economic benefits in terms of the impact on the physical environment.
1. Is the policy consistent with environmental sustainability?
2. If present conditions continue, what will be the impact on the livelihood of future generations?
F. If the initiative entails an economic benefit, is the benefit means tested?

VI. Political Analysis
A. Who are the major players involved in the policy innovation or policy to be changed (politicians, professionals, populations at risk)?
B. Who are the major stakeholders who have vested interests in making/ resisting the proposed change?
1. Assess the extent of opponents' political backing, clout, and media access.
2. Assess the extent of the supporters' political backing, clout, and media access.

C. What is the political context within which the policy initiative has been conceived? Is political/racial/gender oppression an issue of public concern?
D. What are the major political arguments used by opponents against the proposal? Draw on research data to refute or acknowledge the truth of these arguments.
E. What are the NASW Code of Ethics standards (2017) and NASW policy statements (see NASW, 2015, *Social Work Speaks*) relevant to the policy?
F. Describe any lobbying efforts, if any, and any relevant legislative bills introduced.
G. Which profession (lawyers, psychologists, managed-care bureaucrats, etc.), if any, controls the territory? How does this influence affect the policy's acceptability?
H. Gauge the likelihood of having the policy implemented and anticipate possible unintended (positive and negative) consequences of the initiative's enactment.

# APPENDIX C

# *Websites*

## INTERNATIONAL RESOURCES

**Information for Practice from Around the World:**
http://blogs.nyu.edu/ socialwork/ip/
**International Forum on Globalization:**
www.ifg.org
**United Nations Children's Fund:**
www.unicef.org
**United Nations Division for Social Policy and Development/Disabilities**
https://www.un.org/development/desa/disabilities/
**United Nations Development Programme:**
www.undp.org

## PROFESSIONAL LINKS

**Council on Social Work Education:**
www.cswe.org
**Help Starts Here (by NASW):**
www.helpstartshere.org
**Information for Practice:**
http://ifp.nyu.edu/
**International Association of Schools of Social Work:**
www.iassw.aiets.org

**International Federation of Social Workers:**
www.ifsw.org
**National Association of Social Workers:**
www.naswdc.org
**Social Care Online:**
www.scie-socialcareonline.org.uk/
**Trauma Informed Approach and Specific Interventions:**
https://www.samhsa.gov/nctic/trauma-interventions

## PROFESSIONAL ADVOCACY

**Ability, Disabilities Advocacy:**
www.ability.org.uk
**Addiction Treatment Forum:**
www.atforum.com
**Downtown Emergency Service Center (supportive housing):**
www.desc.org/index.html
**Forum on Child and Family Statistics:**
www.childstats.gov
**National Council on Aging:**
www.ncoa.org
**Parents, Families and Friends for Lesbians and Gays:**
www.community.pflag.org

## SOCIAL POLICY

**Affordable Care Act:**
www.healthcare.gov
**Brady Campaign to Prevent Gun Violence:**
Bradycampaign.org
**Center for Restorative Justice Peacemaking:**
www.ched.uma.edu/ssw/rjp
**Centre for Justice and Reconciliation:**
restorativejustice.org
**Child Welfare League:**
www.cwla.org
**The Corporation:**
www.thecorporation.org
**Disabled People's Association:**
www.dpa.org
**Families Against Mandatory Minimums:**
www.famm.org
**Family Violence Prevention Fund:**
http://endabuse.org

**Global Rescue Relief/End Human Trafficking:**
globalrescuerelief.org
**Hull House Museum (University of Illinois-Chicago):**
www.uic.edu/jaddams/hull
**Influencing State Policy:**
www.statepolicy.org
**Information on Labor and Inequality:**
www.robertreich.org
**Institute for Women's Policy Research:**
www.iwpr.org
**Moratorium Campaign Against the Death Penalty:**
www.MoratoriumCampaign.org
**National Coalition Against Domestic Violence:**
www.ncadv.org
**The Rape, Abuse and Incest National Network:**
www.rainn.org
**Social Welfare Action Alliance:**
https://socialwelfareactionalliance.org/
**Violence Policy Center (gun control):**
www.vpc.org
**War Resisters League:**
www.warresisters.org
**World Health Organization:**
www.who.org

## HUMAN RIGHTS

**American Civil Liberties Union:**
www.aclu.org
**Amnesty International:**
www.amnesty.org
**Black Lives Matter:**
blacklivesmatter.com
**Campaign for Equity-Restorative Justice:**
www.cerj.org
**Child Welfare Information Gateway:**
www.childwelfare.gov/can/
**Disability Information:**
www.disabilityinfor.gov
**Disabled People's International:**
www.dpi.org
**Drug Policy Alliance Action Center:**
www.drugpolicy.org
**Earth Policy Institute:**
www.earth-policy.org

**Gay, Lesbian and Straight Education Network:**
www.glsen.org
**Harm Reduction Coalition:**
harmreduction.org
**Human Rights Watch:**
www.hrw.org
**Minority Rights Group International:**
www.minorityrights.org
**National Alliance to End Homelessness:**
www.endhomelessness.org
**National Alliance on Mental Illness:**
www.nami.org
**National Coalition Against Domestic Violence:**
www.ncadv.org
**National Council of La Raza:**
www.nclr.org/
**National Gay and Lesbian Internet Task Force:**
www.ngltf.org
**National Organization for Women:**
http://now.org
**Office of Violence Against Women:**
www.ovw.usdoj.gov
**Restorative Justice:**
www.restorativejustice.org
**Restorative Justice Consortium:**
www.restorativejustice.org/uk
**Smithsonian National History Museum of African American History and Culture:**
https://nmaahc.si.edu/
**Women's Human Rights:**
www.whrnet.org

## THE ENVIRONMENT

**Alliance of Religions and Conservation:**
www.arcworld.org
**Ecofeminism:**
www.ecofem.org
**Ecological Social Work:**
www.ecosocialwork.org
**Environmental Justice:**
www.epa.gov
**Evangelical Environmental Movement:**
www.creationcare.org

**Global Alliance for a Deep Ecology:**
www.ecosocialwork.org/index.html
**Greenpeace:**
www.greenpeace.org
**Indigenous Environmental Network:**
www.ienearth.org/
**Midwest High Speed Rail Association:**
www.midwesthsr.org
**Sierra Club:**
www.sierraclub.org/
**Sustainable Communities Online:**
www.sustainable.org
**Union of Concerned Scientists:**
www.ucsusa.org/global_warming
**United Nations Environmental Programme:**
www.unep.org/greeneconomy
**United States Environmental Protection Agency:**
www.epa.gov/environmentaljustice
**United States High Speed Rail:**
www.ushsr.com
**World Health Organization:**
www.who.int/en/
**Worldwatch Institute: Vision for a Sustainable World:**
www.worldwatch.org/
**World Wildlife Fund:**
www.worldwildlife.org/

# INDEX